Anarchism & Sexuality

Anarchism & Sexuality aims to bring the rich and diverse traditions of anarchist thought and practice into contact with contemporary questions about the politics and lived experience of sexuality.

Both in style and in content, it is conceived as a book that aims to question, subvert and overflow authoritarian divisions between the personal and political; between sexual desires categorised as heterosexual or homosexual; between seemingly mutually exclusive activism and scholarship; between forms of expression such as poetry and prose; and between disciplinary categories of knowledge.

Anarchism & Sexuality seeks to achieve this by suggesting connections between ethics, relationships and power, three themes that run throughout the book. The key objectives of the volume are: to bring fresh anarchist perspectives to debates around sexuality; to make a queer and feminist intervention within the most recent wave of anarchist scholarship; and to make a queerly anarchist contribution to social justice literature, policy and practice. By mingling prose and poetry, theory and autobiography, it constitutes a gathering place to explore the interplay between sexual and social transformation.

This book will be of use to those interested in anarchist movements, cultural studies, critical legal theory, gender studies, and queer and sexuality studies.

Jamie Heckert holds a PhD from the University of Edinburgh and is a founding member of the Anarchist Studies Network. His writings on ethics, erotics and ecology appear in a variety of activist and scholarly publications.

Richard Cleminson is Reader in the History of Sexuality at the University of Leeds and Associate Editor of *Anarchist Studies*. His research centres on the history of sexuality in Spain and he has published on anarchism and sexuality, the history of male homosexuality and hermaphroditism.

Social Justice
Series editors: Kate Bedford and Davina Cooper
University of Kent at Canterbury, UK

Social Justice is a new, theoretically engaged, interdisciplinary series exploring the changing values, politics and institutional forms through which claims for equality, democracy and liberation are expressed, manifested and fought over in the contemporary world. The series addresses a range of contexts from transnational political fora, to nation-state and regional controversies, to small-scale social experiments. At its heart is a concern, and inter-disciplinary engagement, with the present and future politics of power, as constituted through territory, gender, sexuality, ethnicity, economics, ecology and culture. Forgoing struggle, imagined alternatives and the embedding of new norms, *Social Justice* critically explores how change is wrought through law, governance and institutionalism, everyday social and bodily practices, dissident knowledges, and movements for citizenship, belonging and reinvented community.

Other titles in this series:

Intersectionality and Beyond
Law, Power and the Politics of Location
Emily Grabam, Davina Cooper, Jane Krishnadas and Didi Herman (eds), 2009

Regulating Sexuality
Legal Consciousness in Lesbian and Gay Lives
Rosie Harding, 2010

Rights of Passage
Sidewalks and the Regulation of Public Flow
Nicholas Blomley, 2010

Forthcoming:

Power, Politics and the Emotions
Impossible Governance?
Shona Hunter, 2012

Anarchism & Sexuality

Ethics, Relationships and Power

Edited by
Jamie Heckert and Richard Cleminson

Routledge
Taylor & Francis Group
a GlassHouse book

First published 2011
by Routledge
2 Park Square, Milton Park, Abingdon, Oxon OX14 4RN

Simultaneously published in the USA and Canada
by Routledge
711 Third Avenue, New York, NY 10017

A GlassHouse book

Routledge is an imprint of the Taylor & Francis Group, an informa business

British Library Cataloguing in Publication Data
A catalogue record for this book is available from the British Library

Library of Congress Cataloguing in Publication Data
Anarchism & sexuality : ethics, relationships and power / edited by Jamie Heckert & Richard Cleminson. p. cm. Includes bibliographical references.
1. Anarchism–Philosophy. 2. Sexual freedom. 3. Politics and culture. I. Heckert, Jamie. II. Cleminson, Richard. III. Title: Anarchism and sexuality.
HX833.A5685 2011
306.7–dc22
2010039814

ISBN13: 978-0-415-59989-4 (hbk)
ISBN13: 978-0-203-82844-1 (ebk)

Typeset in Sabon
by Taylor & Francis Books

Printed and bound in Great Britain by
CPI Antony Rowe, Chippenham, Wiltshire

This book is dedicated, with loving memories,
to Sam 'Tumbleweed' Roberts
7 January 1986 – 6 May 2007

Contents

Notes on contributors

Jenny Alexander wrote her PhD on nineteenth-century anarchist autobiography. She has lived and worked in co-operatives and belongs to a queer autonomous community. She previously lectured in the Department of Media and Film at the University of Sussex, where she helped set up the interdisciplinary Gender Studies programmes. Currently she is researching green marketing, writing a science fiction novel and studying tantra. She is a Lecturer in Media and Advertising at the University of Bournemouth.

Gavin Brown currently works in the Geography department at the University of Leicester. He was a late developer and spent many years shuffling paper in offices before deciding he wanted to teach and research. Gavin has had many activist-adventures down the years, some of which he discusses in his chapter. He is currently excited by dreaming and theorising other ways of living in cities.

Judith Butler is Maxine Elliot Professor in the Departments of Rhetoric and Comparative Literature and the Co-director of the Program of Critical Theory at the University of California, Berkeley. She is the author of numerous books on gender, sexuality, politics and violence.

Lewis Call is Assistant Professor of History at California Polytechnic State University, San Luis Obispo. He is the author of *Postmodern Anarchism* (Lexington Books, 2002). He has written extensively about postanarchist science fiction and fantasy, exploring postanarchist themes in the novels of Ursula K. Le Guin, the film *V for Vendetta*, and the television shows *Battlestar Galactica* and *Buffy the Vampire Slayer*. He is an Associate Editor for the journal *Anarchist Studies*.

Richard Cleminson is Reader in the History of Sexuality at the University of Leeds and Associate Editor of *Anarchist Studies*. His research centres on the history of sexuality in Spain and he has published on anarchism and sexuality, the history of male homosexuality and hermaphroditism. His latest books include *Anarquismo y sexualidad (España, 1900–1939)* (University of Cadiz, 2008) and *Hermaphroditism, Medical Science and Sexual Identity in Spain, 1850–1960* (University of Wales Press, 2009, with F. Vázquez García).

Laurence Davis is Lecturer in Politics at the National University of Ireland, Maynooth. His recent publications include *Anarchism and Utopianism* (Manchester University Press, 2009, co-edited with Ruth Kinna), *The New Utopian Politics of Ursula K. Le Guin's* The Dispossessed (Lexington Books, 2005, co-edited with Peter Stillman), and numerous articles and book chapters on anarchist and utopian political thought, countercultural and revolutionary politics, and the politics of art, work and love.

Lena Eckert lives and works in Berlin. She is a researcher and teacher currently at Bauhaus University in Weimar, Germany. She received her doctoral degree at Utrecht University (NL) for a dissertation on 'Intervening in Intersexualisation'. Lena Eckert is co-editor of the online journal *Liminalis* and the collection *Bound and Unbound: Interdisciplinary Approaches to Genders and Sexualities* (CSP, 2008). She has published various essays and has given talks on gender and intersexualisation, queer and postcolonial theory both in academic and non-academic spaces.

J. Fergus Evans is a shit-kicking, boy-kissing activist-in-training and art-maker. He is a founding member of Atlanta's No More Productions/Twinhead Theatre, and has worked with a number of political and artists' collectives, including Get Bent and Kaffequeeria. Fergus' work focuses on restaging spoken word using video, soundscaping and sculpture.

Judy Greenway has been engaged in, and writing about, anarchism, feminism and sexual politics since the 1960s. She is on the editorial board of *Anarchist Studies*, and is a Visiting Research Fellow in Cultural Studies at the University of East London. Many of her articles on anarchism and sexuality are available at www.judygreenway.org.uk.

Jamie Heckert listens, writes and organises, inviting the impossible. An interdependent scholar and founding member of the Anarchist Studies Network, his writings are scattered through edited collections and movement publications. Jamie currently lives in Poole, England, where he practices integral yoga, permaculture and other subtle arts of love and revolution.

Marta Kolářová is a sociologist researching on social movements, globalisation and gender. She has published on the Czech anarchist movement and has been active in the local alter-globalisation and feminist movements.

Tom Leonard was born in Glasgow in 1944. His *Outside the Narrative: Poems 1965–2009* is published by Etruscan Books/WordPower. He retired last year from a professorship of Creative Writing at Glasgow University, and is currently working on a new translation of Brecht's *Mother Courage and her Children* commissioned by Birds of Paradise Theatre Company. It is scheduled to tour in Scotland in February and March 2011.

Helen Moore is an ecopoet and author based in Frome. She publishes poetry in anthologies and journals, including *Resurgence Magazine*, for which she has been guest poetry editor. Regularly performing her poetry around the UK, Helen also works as a Forest Schools practitioner. Her books include: *Changing Nature* (GreenSeer Books, 2006) and, for children, the Hope stories on climate change (Lollypop Publishing, 2008 and 2009). Her ecopoetry is available on a CD. For further information, visit www.natures-words.co.uk.

Stevphen Shukaitis is an editor at Autonomedia and lecturer at the University of Essex. He is the author of *Imaginal Machines: Autonomy & Self-Organization in the Revolutions of Everyday Day* (Autonomedia, 2009) and editor (with Erika Biddle and David Graeber) of *Constituent Imagination: Militant Investigations//Collective Theorization* (AK Press, 2007). His research focuses on the emergence of collective imagination in social movements and the changing compositions of cultural and artistic labour.

Passionately interdisciplinary, **Kristina N. Weaver** holds degrees in Anthropology, History of Science, Creative Writing, and a doctorate jointly supervised in Geography and English Literature. Her work on political violence and the occult in Nigeria is at the experimental edge of literary ethnography. For the past decade, Kristina has practised within social movements resisting neoliberalism in the USA, UK and Nigeria. She currently works as an editor, grant writer and community organiser in Central Virginia.

Acknowledgements

We both want to acknowledge, first and foremost, the contributors to this volume. They have stuck with us through the long process of finding and negotiating the publication of this book. For their trust, we are grateful. We also deeply appreciate their efforts to meet often challenging deadlines and to engage with thought and care our comments and suggestions on their writings. The editorial–authorial dance has been, while challenging at times, a joy. As essayists, poets and interviewees, they have all inspired us. Next, Kate Bedford and Davina Cooper, as series editors and as colleagues, have been wonderfully supportive of our efforts to bring the book to light. Thank you both. For their patience with our numerous queries and for all their work, we are indebted to Colin Perrin, Holly Davis, Melanie Fortmann-Brown, Michelle Whittaker and David Armstrong at Routledge. Likewise, we are deeply grateful to Lisa Williams for the careful copy-editing of the manuscript. We are more appreciative now than ever of funding from the University of Leeds and the Anarchist Studies Network for the conference which made this book even imaginable. While funding can be very helpful in many ways, it was the participants at the conference who made the event into a beautiful anarchy beyond our dreams. Thank you all!

We also acknowledge the following permissions:

'Remembrance Day' © Tom Leonard from *outside the narrative: Poems 1965–2009* Etruscan Books/WordPower Press 2009. Thank you, Tom, for allowing us to reprint this stunning poem.

An earlier version of Stevphen Shukaitis' chapter appeared as 'Questions for Affective Resistance' in his (2009) book *Imaginal Machines: Autonomy & Self-Organization in the Revolutions of Everyday Life*, New York/London: Autonomedia/Minor Compositions. Thank you to Autonomedia for permission to reprint.

An earlier version of Lewis Call's chapter appeared as 'Structures of Desire: Erotic Power in the Speculative Fiction of Octavia Butler and Samuel Delany' in *Rethinking History* Vol. 9, No. 2/3, June/September 2005, pp. 275–296. We thank Taylor & Francis for permission to reprint.

Additionally, Jamie Heckert would like to thank fellow anarchist(ic) scholars, too many to name, for mutual appreciation, support and inspiration. My yoga teachers and the beautiful fauna and flora living in and around my house, especially Paul Stevens, have helped keep me well through the editing process and beyond. And finally, Richard, you've been a delight to work with! Thank you for your much-needed reassurance in times of doubt and your steadfast commitment to our editorial partnership and, more importantly, our friendship.

Preface

Sexual anarchy, anarchophobia and dangerous desires

Anarchism & Sexuality: Ethics, Relationships and Power is a timely intervention into current debates on sexual politics. There is a new excitement about anarchism, and about the relationship between anarchism and sexuality: a sense of creativity and potential, as new connections are made and old ones rediscovered. The Anarchism and Sexuality conference which was the initial inspiration for this book is just one example, providing a space where a diverse and passionately engaged group of participants could come together and discuss research, personal experience and political practice.[1] Meanwhile, sexual anarchy, alias 'western decadence', is blamed for everything from natural disasters to 9/11, and misogyny and homophobia are playing a significant part in the resurgence of the political and religious right. Simultaneously, in the latest twist in an old story, warmongers and political opportunists appropriate the language of feminism and gay rights to assert the superiority of 'western civilisation': part of a long history of using claims about the relative status of women, and attitudes towards sexuality, to valorise one group over another. Such 'us and them' accounts erase differences and commonalities within and between communities, and obscure past and present struggles for change. If there is one thing that unites fundamentalists and bigots of all persuasions, it is their attachment to the so-called 'natural order' of sex and gender hierarchy, and their horror of those who threaten it. In this world view, sexual liberation is a variation on anarchism: an attack on the foundations of society, a form of terrorism – anarchy as chaos.

The interplay between sexual authoritarianism and anarchophobia is nothing new. Coming out as an anarchist has some similarities with coming out as gay, and meets with a similar range of responses, from tolerant amusement, to contempt, to hatred and violence. Like 'deviant' sexuality, anarchism may be denounced as an immature phase to be grown out of, as dangerously seductive to the young and/or as an intrinsically violent threat to the status quo, attitudes that mix together fear, fascination and fantasy in a toxic stew.

But important though it is to address prejudice based on ignorance, the truth is that anarchism and sexual nonconformity do indeed threaten existing power relationships. For this reason, refusing to call oneself an anarchist, or gay, or queer – whether from a theoretical rejection of identity politics, a wish to escape damaging stereotypes or a desire to transcend labelling – provides only a temporary breathing space. It could be argued that to avoid the labels perpetuates stigmatisation and erasure, that sense of a politics-which-must-not-be-named. Ultimately, whatever words we do or do not use, expressing dangerous desires will meet with resistance from those whose power and authority depend on maintaining the status quo.

The association between sexual and political dangerousness began long before anarchy acquired its 'ism'. By the late nineteenth century, growing numbers of people in the USA and Europe were speaking out and organising as anarchists. The commentators who responded to the rise of anarchism with dire predictions of social chaos also railed against the sexual anarchy exemplified by the New Women of the period, who dared to speak of sex and gender and question patriarchal power, and by those men who were beginning to formulate new sexual identities and question or refashion masculinity. The challenge for sexual and political dissidents was to reverse the discourse and develop positive identities while critiquing the very notion of 'civilised' society. Some anarchists, feminists and sex radicals who met through friendship networks, or encountered one another's ideas in campaigns around such issues as free speech, marriage law and reproductive rights, began to develop a politics which intertwined their different perspectives.

But not all anarchists, then or since, have seen sex and gender issues as important – another reason why a book such as this is not just welcome, but necessary. Reading it, I was reminded of my own early involvement with anarchist, feminist and lesbian and gay liberation groups in the 1960s and 1970s. We soon discovered that we were not the first to link sexuality with politics: Emma Goldman and Edward Carpenter were hailed as pioneers, their writings reprinted, their names adopted by a variety of groups and organisations. Those of us in anarchist groups tried to reinvigorate them with some of our new ideas and rediscoveries while confronting their sexism and heterosexism, but with limited success; all too often the response was that of course anarchists are in favour of women's and sexual liberation, so what's to discuss? This attitude of 'Do what you want to do but don't make a fuss or expect *us* to talk about it or change our ways' has a long history in anarchism, and has been repeatedly challenged from a variety of standpoints. Revising what is thought of as 'anarchist tradition' is one way of doing this, as is critiquing anarchist practice in the present.

The latter is what I attempted to do in my first ever piece on anarchism and sexuality, in an anarchist newspaper in 1975. In part an excited report of a Women's Liberation conference on sexuality, the article argued against the glib deployment of a rhetoric of sexual liberation which allowed anarchists and left libertarians to evade the problems and contradictions in their own lives: 'It is easier to theorise and to talk about what we would like to be than to talk about what we are' (Greenway 1975: 6). I wanted to encourage readers to take on board not just new ideas about sexuality, but new ways to discuss it. I recall this long-forgotten piece now, because the excitement of that conference, that electric sensation as personal and political suddenly connected in our own lives, not just as rhetoric or theory, was buzzing around again at the 2006 Anarchism and Sexuality conference – and it is such feelings, recaptured in some of the pieces in this book, which help make change seem possible.

In different times and places, the struggle for sexual and gender liberation takes on different shapes and emphases. In the USA and Western Europe, the anarchists, feminists and sexual radicals of the late nineteenth century and early twentieth century needed to establish ways of discussing sexuality in the face of censorship and social disapproval. In the early 1970s, when talking publicly about sex was more acceptable, the focus was on the sexism and heterosexism not just of what was then called 'straight society', but also of the 1960s' 'sexual revolution' and the radical left. Experimentation with alternative lifestyles played an important part in the sexual politics of both periods. Today, the idea of 'sexual freedom' seems to be trapped in a hall of mirrors, reflected in the grotesque shapes produced by a multimillion-pound pornography industry and globalised sex trade, and by sex-obsessed religious conservatives predicting Armageddon, but also in the smooth and glossy surfaces of a progressive liberalism which is far more limited and restrictive than it appears to be. The question now is, how to expose the exploitation and oppression that lie behind the mirrors, and to find ways to rethink what sexual freedom could mean.

A recurring theme in all these different contexts has been the need to create spaces in which to explore new ideas and solidarities, practise new ways of relating to one another and begin the processes of change. In the early days of the 1970s' Women's and Gay Liberation Movements, process was all-important. To meet to talk about sexuality meant also to think about the conditions that made such a meeting possible. Meetings, conferences and workshops were organised non-hierarchically, with an emphasis on sharing and listening. The aim was to be inclusive; most events were free or as cheap as possible, with childcare provided by groups such as Men Against Sexism. And the conduct of such meetings, though it did not always live up to our ideals, often felt far more anarchistic (in the positive sense) than anything I had experienced in an anarchist group.

Our ideas were inspired by the sharing of personal experiences, but some of these were easier to talk about than others, and often it was a group discussion of a pamphlet or article which made it possible to begin the difficult and exhilarating process of linking theory and practice. In London, we read articles on sexual politics from Italy, Germany and France as well as from the USA and the UK; they were produced and reproduced, translated and retranslated, often hand-typed and duplicated, given away or sold at cost price.

Since then, desktop publishing and the internet have transformed the possibilities of communication. Today, in very different social and political circumstances, the debates continue in new forms, only now some of them are going on inside as well as outside the scholarly academy – a shift of context that has raised new questions about theory, structures and the relationships between academic and activist work. Insofar as Women's Studies, Lesbian and Gay Studies, Queer Studies and now Anarchist Studies have a toehold in academia, it is because they have been fought for by staff and students who wanted the opportunity to integrate scholarship and political commitment, to challenge the educational status quo, and to contribute to the development of new ways of understanding and changing the world.

These gains have brought new anxieties, quite apart from the struggle to hold on to hard-won courses in times of financial cutbacks and political paranoia. There is the not unjustifiable fear of stigmatisation, or at least of not being taken seriously as a scholar. Years ago, one of my students had her thesis proposal for a critique of scientific theories of homosexuality rejected by a homophobic committee, on the grounds that it was intrinsically biased (that is, that she was a lesbian and not a scientist) and that there was no scholarly basis for such a study. Anarchist scholars have encountered similar institutional prejudice. What helped me to get that decision reversed was being able to cite as a precedent the (then tiny number of) relevant academic publications.[2] The more scholarly work is published in these fields, the more it increases the possibilities for others – another reason this book will be so welcome.

Another problem for those who work as academics is how to do research and writing in a way that reaches out to a variety of audiences, and bridges the perceived gaps between theory and activism. This is not just a question of the accessibility of ideas and language, but of where to publish or speak, when only certain publications and venues are academically acceptable. Moreover, many academics feel under pressure to produce theory with a capital 'T'. For those who feel that one advantage of anarchism is that it neither has nor needs a theoretical Big Daddy, the drive towards theory is politically counterproductive, although others have been creatively inspired by it to take old ideas in new directions. Meanwhile, some activists hold theory, history, academic work of all kinds, in contempt, as though ideas can only be credible or effective when seen to emerge from 'real life struggle' as they define it. It can feel as though, rather than integrating different parts of our lives, we have just multiplied the occasions for feeling defensive and hopelessly compromised.

But we need to sidestep the polarisation of 'activism' and 'academia', theory and practice. History, theory, reading and writing can all be forms of resistance and activism. A more constructive response is to find ways of bringing together different perspectives, analyses, ways of doing things: not answers, but questions; not a single, smooth, impenetrable surface, but rough edges which can spark off one another, provide new points of access. Standard methods of propagating ideas – meetings, conferences, books and articles – can be subverted in form and content to become spaces where past, present and future are reimagined and new ways of thinking become possible. A book like this, mingling prose and poetry, theory and autobiography, is just such a space, a gathering place to explore with serious pleasure the interplay between sexual and social transformation.

Judy Greenway

Notes

1 Anarchism & Sexuality: Ethics, Relationships and Power, University of Leeds, 4 November 2006.

2 The most important of these in making the case was Jeffrey Weeks' pioneering work *Coming Out* (Weeks, 1977).

References

Greenway, J. (1975) 'Questioning our Desires', *Wildcat* 6(6), London: Wildcat. Online. Available HTTP: http://www.judygreenway.org.uk/questioning/questioning.html (accessed 22 June 2010).

Weeks, J. (1977) *Coming Out: Homosexual Politics in Britain from the Nineteenth Century to the Present*, London: Quartet.

Chapter 1

Ethics, relationships and power

An introduction

Jamie Heckert and Richard Cleminson

> All of us have to learn how to invent our lives, make them up, imagine them. We need to be taught these skills; we need guides to show us how. If we don't, our lives get made up for us by other people.
>
> —Ursula K. Le Guin, *The Wave in the Mind*

> Like masturbation, anarchism is something we have been brought up to fear, irrationally and unquestioningly, because not to fear it might lead us to probe it, learn it and like it.
>
> —Cathy Levine, *The Tyranny of Tyranny*

Introduction

With this book, we bring the rich and diverse traditions of anarchist thought and practice into contact with contemporary questions about the politics and lived experiences of sexuality. We've attempted to craft a queer book, both in style and in content: a book that aims to question, subvert and overflow authoritarian divisions between the personal and political, between desires categorised as heterosexual or homosexual, between activism and scholarship, between poetry and prose, and between disciplinary categories of knowledge. In doing so, we attempt to enact what Judy Greenway has called a 'methodological anarchism that relinquishes control, challenges boundaries and hierarchies, and provides a space for new ideas to emerge' (Greenway 2008: 324). Bringing this book into the world, we have a number of intentions: first, to make fresh anarchist perspectives available to contemporary debates around sexuality; second, to make a queer and feminist intervention within the most recent waves of anarchist scholarship; and, third, to make a queerly anarchist contribution to social justice literature, policy and practice. But before that, before this book has even been published, we have already been transformed through the process of engaging with each other and each of the contributors and their contributions. Lest we slip into a fetishisation of the future, of ends disconnected from means, of products separated from production, we note that the long slow birth of this book is already making interventions and contributions. The book is not unusual in that respect; all processes, all relationships, have multiple effects. What is unusual, in the goal-oriented 'phallicised whiteness' of capitalism (Winnubst 2006: 6), is to appreciate processes and relationships for themselves. This appreciation is one of many inheritances from anarchist, feminist and indigenous traditions for which we are deeply grateful.

The book's methodology, running through each piece in this collection, concentrates on raising historical, present and practical questions concerning sex and sexuality, love, desire and intimacy, with a specific focus on a triad of interconnected fields: ethics, relationships and power. By means of its consciously interdisciplinary approach, this book attempts to bring contemporary and historical anarchist interpretations into the pressing spheres of current social, political, ethical and legal debate. In doing so, *Anarchism & Sexuality* bridges a supposed gap between theory and activism, between ideas and 'real life struggle'. By drawing inspiration from the rise of the global movement of movements, and the corresponding waves of anarchist activism and scholarship, this book provides much-needed sources of inspiration for putting anarchistic ethics into practice, focusing on issues such as race, class and gender equality, sexual liberation and sexual violence, the experience of one's own body and the interface between these matters and social mores, psychological patterns, laws and other aspects of 'societies of control' (Deleuze 1992).

Before articulating these messages and their relevance to living our lives, first of all we want to say a few words about how anarchism may be understood. For some, anarchism is very easily defined: either it is a symbol and incarnation of chaos or it is an outmoded revolutionary political ideology originating in social movements of nineteenth-century Europe. Despite its evident trajectory, anarchism is dismissed as an ideology that failed historically to create and sustain a revolutionary society, an ideology and practice that is locked into an essentialist concept of human nature as primarily generous and good, and that is bound by prioritising class struggle and workplace issues over and above transforming other social relationships. Thus, anarchism is all too often viewed as having little to offer contemporary questions and strategies for undermining seemingly entrenched hierarchies and violent exploitative social relationships. In this second reading, anarchism is more or less confined to the writings of 'anarchist luminaries' such as Pierre-Joseph Proudhon, Mikhail Bakunin and Piotr Kropotkin, experiencing an upsurge in the late nineteenth century and petering out, save in some isolated spots in the periphery of Europe and Latin America, by the end of World War Two. For others, however, anarchism did not die with the Spanish Civil War. Anarchism has since developed through ongoing practical experiments in non-hierarchical organisation and has broadened and deepened its theoretical foundations to offer a striking relevance nowadays. However, while anarchism remains opposed to capitalism and to the state (whether the state-centred politics of liberal democracy or the centralised vertical structures of authoritarian socialism), its relevance to sexuality is perhaps not all that apparent. This definition of anarchism certainly doesn't *sound* sexy (except, perhaps, to those of us with a fetish for revolutionary theory).

Rather than seeing anarchism as an ideology, anarchist historian Rudolf Rocker suggests that it should be understood as a 'definite trend in the historic development of mankind [sic]' to strive for freedom (cited in Chomsky 2005: 118). Commenting on this, Noam Chomsky argues that there is no need to pin down anarchism as a singular object because

> there will be no doctrine of social change fixed for the present and future, nor even, necessarily, a specific and unchanging concept of the goals towards which social change should tend. Surely our understanding of the nature of man [sic] or of the range of viable social forms is so rudimentary that any far-reaching doctrine must be treated with great skepticism, just as skepticism is in order when we hear that 'human nature' or 'the demands of efficiency' or 'the complexity of modern life' requires this or that form of oppression and autocratic rule.
>
> (Chomsky 2005: 119)

As a trend striving for freedom, for liberation, the significance of anarchism for an examination and living out of sexuality might become more obvious. However, many have understandably become critical of notions of sexual liberation after poststructuralist critiques of 'liberation' and in a time where freedom has individualistic connotations. What might sexual anarchy mean, if not the total lack of order and morality that some might imagine? What characterises this anarchist trend besides dismantling authority?

In order to answer these questions, we believe that it can be helpful to think of this 'trend in history' called anarchism as a kind of ethics of relationships, as advocating and practising very different relations of power than those involved in the state, capitalism, white supremacy and patriarchy (Heckert 2010a, 2010b). Three 'guiding principles' drive the endeavour in this book to bring anarchist ethics to (sexual) relationships. First, anarchism is not viewed as a 'one-size-fits-all' solution to social problems, but rather as a commitment to diversity as an ethical stance in itself, in sharp contrast to the standardisation and regulation of state and bureaucratic rationales. The contributions in this volume reflect this diversity because situations are different, because life itself is diverse; there are, nevertheless, some commonly shared ethics: agreements to respect a diversity of tactics, support for cultural and ecological diversity in the face of neoliberal imperialism, and resistance to any orthodoxy. Second, anarchism has a radical commitment to equality; anarchy means no one gets to claim the unquestionable status of being on top (*an* = no; *archy* = top, from the Greek *anarkhos*).[1] Instead, relationships are always open to renegotiation. Unlike an individualistic notion of freedom, where one person is to be 'free' (that is, *privileged*) at the expense of others, anarchism's idea of freedom is relational: one person's freedom is inseparable from another's freedom. Thus, anarchist organisation practises horizontality, or perhaps a fluidity of power where no one is in any position of leadership for an extended period and where leadership involves following rather than commanding. Likewise, a radical commitment to equality involves an ongoing process of empowerment so that everyone is better able to contribute to change. This ethic of freedom, in resistance to everyday forms of governmentality and normalisation, subtle or more overt, is addressed in different ways and draws on different analytical tools in each of the essays and short pieces contained in these pages. Third, anarchism, as a daily practice, engages in an ethic of care rather than an ethic of control (including control disguised as care). This book explores how love and solidarity can be articulated in the sphere of sexuality and beyond within societies that may seem ever more disconnected, atomised and authoritarian. Thus, rather than supporting charity, anarchism favours solidarity where all practices of freedom are recognised as interconnected.

Finally, anarchist ethics place emphasis on listening to others rather than speaking for them or on their behalf. In addressing the sensitive issues of intimacy, love and desire, the essays and poems in this book both argue for and demonstrate this ethic of listening as an alternative to statist patterns of representation and discipline. In the Zapatistas' *Other Campaign*, this inspired approach is demonstrated through a focus on listening to the struggles of others and supporting their capacity for autonomy rather than electoral campaigns to become their representatives (Marcos and the Zapatistas 2006). In anarcha-feminism and radical psychologies, learning to listen to oneself, to acknowledge one's own emotions and desires, is crucial to unlearning patriarchal hierarchies of the rational over the emotional, of mind over body. For, as Saul Newman put it, 'if the problem of voluntary servitude – so often neglected in radical political theory – is to be countered, the revolution against power and authority must involve a micro-political revolution which takes place at the level of the subject's desire' (Newman 2010: 6). In listening to our own bodies, our own desires, as well as to others (human and non-human), perhaps we can all come to imagine our own lives.

Part of imagining our own lives – and practising them, too – for many of us is related to how we live our sexuality. For some, this is a fundamental part of their life experience; for others, it is one of a wide range of activities to which limited time is devoted. But today, as some commentators have noted (e.g. Weeks 1985), sexuality has accrued the status of being somehow special, different from other social relationships. Of course, what goes on in sexual relationships is in numerous ways different from what takes place in the relationship amongst workers in the workplace or the interactions between citizens and authorities. But many of the same hierarchies, obligations and behavioural patterns coincide in different relationships, whether we label them intimate, economic or political. The special status of sexuality stems, in part, from a patriarchal separation of the personal from the political, the private from the public. Supposedly natural constructions of masculinity and femininity, double standards across these divisions, whereby it is socially sanctioned that men have many partners and women should be 'chaste', are themselves naturalised. Sexuality has become the truth of the self in a way that other aspects of 'private' life have not; such an incitement to 'be sexual' and to consume the wares of sexuality fits with present exhortations to construct our own lifestyles and identities through avid and repetitive consumption. In other words, who you have sex with (or want to have sex with) is assumed to be a fixed characteristic, an answer to the question of what sort of person you are or an essential part of personhood by which you are valued or denied value; sexual performance also becomes an integral and necessary part of the self. Similar assumptions are rarely made about expressions of desire for golfing, swimming or walking on the beach. The result is that sexuality has become emphasised as a special location for liberation, *the* place where desires can be met.

Making sex special like this causes all sorts of problems, as some branches of feminism and later poststructuralism have argued. For starters, profit-oriented media sell this notion of individualistic sexual liberation, saying not only that people can have the great sex lives they want, but that they *should* have them. How is this supposed to happen? Most people spend all day at rigidly differentiated and hierarchised workplaces, are told to suppress their feelings in order to obey the rules, and find it difficult to come home and become capable of expressing their feelings and desires and listening to those of another. And if (or when) people fail to express their feelings and desires, they are told it is their own fault. However, those faults can be fixed, those problems can be solved by spending money on individual solutions: 'beauty' products and cosmetic surgery, self-help books and psychological magazines that disinter one's 'true' desires and self.

As the realm of sex and relationships becomes ever more privatised, the subject of surveillance and the plaything of psychological expertise, the collective and race/gender/class-inflected elements of sexuality fall from view. Faced with the commodification of sexuality, its privatisation and mediation by capitalism as part of what Foucault termed 'governmentality' – basically the setting into motion of refined techniques that ensure one's inner self and actions are governed (and governed by oneself) to a degree that one is unaware of or assumes as natural – what can anarchism offer?

Anarchism and sexuality in history and in the present

Opposition to the acceptability of coercive social relationships, domination and rigid hierarchies and the advocacy of the construction of living alternatives is not something new to anarchist thought. In the late nineteenth and early twentieth centuries the activist and theorist Piotr Kropotkin argued that anarchistic expressions of mutual aid, cooperation and opposition to hierarchical power could be traced back to at least mediaeval European society and that these characteristics continued to prevail in his day. More recently, Colin Ward argued against a simple collapsing of the past and the present by writing that 'an anarchist society, a society which organises itself without authority, is always in existence, like a seed beneath the snow, buried under the weight of the state and its bureaucracy, capitalism and its wastes' (Ward 1982: 14). The very fabric of social life, with its constantly evolving networks of alternatives to hierarchies and its ability to create new forms of social organisation in which control is articulated horizontally, continues to inform day-to-day existence in a way that is easy to overlook, underestimate or forget.

In a fast-changing world we should not forget the historical legacy of past movements which, working with conditions that were in many ways different from those pertaining today, created stories that have a great deal to offer. By looking to the past, we can see how the anarchist critique of the relations of dominance that rely on strictly differentiated gender roles and the organisation of sexuality in accordance with religious or state prerogatives has enjoyed a solid presence in anarchist thought and practice from the late nineteenth century onwards. Examples include early attempts to organise women in revolutionary trade unions in France (Maitron 1983), efforts to promote women's reproductive and sexual freedom as articulated by Emma Goldman (Goldman 1969; Haaland 1993) and others (Passet 2003) in the United States and by small groups of anarchists in Spain, where contraception was demanded and supplied (Nash 1984, 1995). Sexual freedom was, in turn, closely linked to discussions around gender, marriage, the family and free love taking place around the world (Bowen Raddeker 2001; Cohn, 2010; Greenway 2009). Anarchists responded to a diversity of social ills by reconfiguring ways of relating and being in a capitalist world, forging new attitudes towards the body such as nudism (Cleminson 2004), interconnecting the social, political and the literary, as suggested by Oscar Wilde, Edward Carpenter and Daniel Guérin, and making links between sexual freedom and libertarian socialism, as evidenced in anarchist involvement in the early homosexual rights campaigns from the 1920s onwards (Kissack 2008; Lucien 2006). Female anarchists' critiques of male domination within the early twentieth-century Spanish anarchist movement provided a reflexive critique not only of the inequalities of the broader society but of the prejudices and failings still alive in the anarchist movement itself (Ackelsberg 2000, 2005; Espigado Tocino 2002; Nash 1975). More recent historic contributions range from involvement in feminist politics (Brown 1996; Dark Star Collective 2002) and gay liberation (Mecca 2009; Ording 2009) through to Alex Comfort's anarchist-inspired *The Joy of Sex*.

Anarchist histories are a rich resource for engaging with the question of how we live our lives. As Utah Phillips put it, 'the past didn't go anywhere' (in Phillips and DiFranco 1997). At the same time, part of the attraction and enduring relevance of anarchism is precisely its organic ability to adapt and evolve, incorporating new strategies and new fields of action. Such a revitalised anarchism has benefited from the emergence of two recent transformations of the geo-political landscape. Both have roots in anarchistic practice (as well as in anti-state Marxism, radical feminism and movements protagonised by indigenous demands for autonomy and control of land) and have rekindled interest in anarchism as a set of theoretical and practical resources to move towards a freer society. These two new currents are, first, poststructuralist thought and, second, the rise of global anti-capitalist movements.

Inspired at least in part by their participation in the anti-state, anti-capitalist uprisings of May 1968, the writing of figures such as Foucault, Deleuze and Guattari are becoming read as critical contributions to Western anarchist traditions (ASN 2010a; Rousselle and Evren 2011). While these readings are controversial, both because they have, at times, run the risk of setting up a straw figure of a simplistic 'classical anarchism' to be knocked down by a new and improved postanarchism (Cohn 2002; Cohn and Wilbur 2011) and because of the highly theoretical nature of these writings, controversy has been part of the energetic renewal brought about through anarchist engagement with post-structuralist theories. From our perspectives, this wave of radical French theory complements rather than replaces lesser known anarchist theorists who have also had sophisticated and nuanced thoughts on the nature of power, subjectivity and revolution. Nonetheless, this minor revolution in anarchism is powerful, particularly because it is echoed and amplified through similar revolutions taking place in feminist, postcolonial and queer theories.

These theoretical developments have also been of particular value in inspiring and explaining the rise of directly democratic, horizontal networks of protest, community building and resistance to hierarchy variously referred to as the global justice movement, the movement of movements and the alterglobalisation movement. Inspired by a long history of direct action, including the Zapatista struggle for indigenous autonomy and the queer tactics of ACT-UP (Shepard 2002), the mass protests against the World Trade Organisation in Seattle in 1999 were the first globally visible manifestation of this movement; suddenly both scholars and popular commentators were asking how such a huge and powerful protest movement could be organised without a clearly defined leadership. While the existence of these movements cannot be conflated directly with anarchist thought and practice in any simple way, they do seek to construct organisations and activities outside of the formal parameters offered by neo-colonial, Western or liberal notions of democracy. In doing so, these movements are learning to undermine the forms of gendered, racialised and sexualised violence intertwined with individualistic, hierarchical structures of democracy (e.g. Chen *et al*. 2011; Smith 2005) and to create, instead, autonomous spaces.

The critique offered by anarchism of party politics, of the inherent power relationship entailed by the representation of one group's supposed interests by another, unaccountable group, of the desire to homogenise rather than diversify – except within the context of pay-as-you-go fixed sexual and consumer identities – has garnered an analysis of sexuality and gender politics that has much in common with a third strand of contemporary theory and activism: queer. While anarchism traditionally has challenged borders based on nationality and hierarchies of class, the emerging queer theory of the early 1990s critiqued apparently stable orders of gendered and sexualised identity and strict borders of the body, sex and sexuality. Queer theory, radically reappraising the fixity of these discourses, has interrogated, in its feminist aspects, seemingly natural differences and hierarchies around sex. The practice of constant revision of the 'given', of comfortable notions of sex and body, and their political inherence articulated by queer theory and activism, has much in common with anarchism, with its critique of borders, hierarchies and naturalised differences. Further, if queer theory has developed out of the anti-statist thought of figures such as Michel Foucault, Giles Deleuze and the anti-identarianism of Judith Butler, and also out of the direct action politics of ACT-UP and other radical queer groups, and feminist critiques of gendered, racialised and classed hierarchies, then anarchist readings of, and contributions to, queer theory are clearly invaluable. In particular, the transnational (or anti-national) and anti-racist aspects of anarchism may help us address the pressing challenges of 'homonationalism' (Puar 2006) and 'silences in queerness/raciality' (Kuntsman and Miyake 2008) in these times of racialised war and the (white) resentment which fuels both war and other forms of disconnection and violence (see, e.g., APOC 2010; Lamble 2008; Veneuse 2009).

Based on an analysis of the ways in which power constructs discourses on sexuality and the possibility of their material expression, queer theory and anarchist thought provide a resetting of the equation of knowledge/power that aims to use reverse discourses and interstitial practices as possibilities to open up modes of life not based on hierarchical values. They are opportunities to develop, as Foucault suggested, 'non-fascist' ways of life (Foucault 2004), to develop a *chresis* or ethical practice of living whereby our lives are given meaning through the advocacy of democratic socialist principles lived in today's world. This is an active undertaking and, although we are constantly forced to choose, what we choose remains to some degree open. As two authors taking up Foucault's suggestion forcefully argue:

> Whether we like it or not, we are obliged to choose, and every time we choose we give our lives meaning, since it depends on us to create the conditions whereby democratic socialism can be born with strength and vitality. Otherwise, we contribute with our passivity, with our submissive acceptance, or with means more direct, to the triumph of the fundamentalism of the market which will lead humanity once more to the frontiers of barbarism.
>
> (Álvarez-Uría and Varela 1999: 25; our translation)

Such an invitation to live a non-fascist way of life does not mean that sexuality becomes once more the 'secret' to be explored, the physical need to be experienced or the core feature of a liberated self, but a mobile surface from which to play with established identities, the limits of the body and the constraints of exclusionary identities such as 'gay', 'bi' and 'hetero'. It is, succinctly, a matter of 'which ways of understanding ourselves make it possible to act with some chance of bringing about positive changes' (Greenway 1997: 180). The radical decentring of the way in which people can live their lives recognises that freedom cannot come through sex alone; rather it entails a critique that runs through all social relationships and attempts to reconstruct them in non-hierarchical terms.

Sexual anarchy?

Given the commonalities among certain historical and current strands of anarchism, and between anarchism, feminism and queer activism, it would appear that the time is ripe for an engaging intersection between these movements. It might be surprising, therefore, that there have been remarkably few publications that have paid attention to the overlaps and differences in these movements, outside a number of historical studies on anarchism and its links to women's movements or sex-reform programmes and scattered essays through movement literature.[2] While queer and feminist writing often has a strong critique of hierarchy and the state, if not an outright anti-state stance, anarchist sources have rarely been included (e.g. Alexander 2005; Anzaldúa 1987; Brown 1995; Butler and Spivak 2007; Cooper 1994; Mohanty 2003; Seidman 1997; Winnubst 2006; for recent and notable exceptions, see Fahs 2010; Jeppesen 2010; Kissack 2008; Portwood-Stacer 2010; Roseneil 2000; Rowbotham 2008; Shannon and Willis 2010; Shepard 2010; Wilkinson 2009; Windpassinger 2010; and, to a lesser extent, Monro 2005). Of course, inspiration for a libertarian politics can easily be found outside anarchist traditions. In other cases, anarchist sources may be difficult to acknowledge in academic writing (see hooks 1994 for a discussion of the politics of citation). For example, during a lecture in London, Judith Butler acknowledged the inspiration she took from anarchist and syndicalist movements and her desire for their growth, referring, with a mischievous grin, to her appreciation of anarchism as 'a confession' (Butler 2007). Similarly, a number of recent books on contemporary anarchism which we find deeply inspiring in other ways contain little or no reference to topics of sexuality (Amster *et al.* 2009; Franks 2006; Gordon 2008; Kinna 2005). Perhaps these silences are due, in part, to the intense emotional responses that sex and anarchy can trigger, sometimes with violent consequences. What makes the intersections of anarchism and sexuality potentially *exciting* also makes them *dangerous*. Challenging established identities, questioning notions of family and society and even the very idea of what constitutes 'sex' (as both an activity and with respect to what are considered to be biological truths of male and female) can dramatically undercut the foundations of established ways of relating to ourselves, each other and the world. Some will experience this as profoundly liberating, others as deeply disturbing. Most of us will perhaps have a powerful mixture of feelings.

It is in facing the challenges of engaging with the emotionally charged topic of anarchism and sexuality that we find an understanding of anarchism as an ethics of relationships most inspiring. How might those of us advocating sexual anarchy empathise with the anger and fear of others (as well as with our own)? Can anarchist(ic) practices of restorative justice (e.g. Amster 2004; Gaarder 2009; Sullivan and Tifft 2001; Tifft and Sullivan 1980) and violence prevention (e.g. Tifft 1993) respond to understandable desires for order and security in societies where (sexual) violence is all too common? Can an ethic of care in practices of mutual aid create unexpected solidarities? Might even sexual and religious minorities form coalitions based on their shared experiences of state violence (Butler 2004, 2008; INCITE! 2006)? How can difficult questions about power and sexuality in everyday life be opened up for discussion in ways that nurture freedom, equality and community? How might a focus on sexuality, passion and desire help us rethink our way around 'other' issues such as economics (Bedford and Jakobsen 2009; Perelman 2000), ecology (Heller 1999; Mortimer-Sandilands 2005) and power (Foucault 1990; Lorde 1993)? In what ways might sexual anarchy be practised? In other words, how might freedom be queered (Winnubst 2006)?

Out of our desire to create space to open up some of these questions about the intersections between anarchism and sexuality, we organised a conference in Leeds, England, in November 2006. Most of the contributions to this volume derive from this event, having been presented there or having been penned as reflections on the conference at a later date.[3] The rhizomic nature of the conference – with its introduction, multiple sessions, discussion circles, social events, Quaker-style closing plenary, trips to the Common Place social centre and delicious experiences of sharing food – is reflected in this rhizome of a book; the pieces it contains connect with each other in innumerable ways, all exploring ethics, relationships and power. Within the loose structure we created at the Leeds conference, we witnessed participants putting into practice anarchism as an ethics of relationship. Part of this involved an open-mindedness to recasting and even demolishing the supposed divide between academia and activism. Beset with prejudices or at least *partis pris* on both sides (some time after the Leeds event we witnessed at a similar conference the admission of one activist who had begun writing his PhD that now he was in academia, activism was ruled out), after some initial scepticism lodged between the 'usual passive absorption typical of academic conferences' and 'at worst an encounter with the kinds of social policing so common in queer spaces' (Chapter 11, p. 224), one conference participant, Kristina N. Weaver, who reflects on her experience in this book, was captivated by 'the truths expressed, the stories witnessed, the theories spun' (p. 224). Drawing on a variety of participation techniques, such as small group discussions including 'the fish bowl' technique, for Weaver now 'a treasured tool in my kit of anarchist praxis' (p. 226), paper sessions blended academic presentations with anarchist commitments to listening, difference and equality. Kristina was referring to the 'Queer autonomous zones' session, in which Serena Bassi, Mike Upton and Gavin Brown presented papers. Gavin also reflects on that session in his contribution (Chapter 10), acknowledging the fear of presenting a theoretical account of activist events to an audience including activists. He then goes on to refer to the discussion that followed the papers, in the form of the fish bowl, as 'by far the most engaged and inclusive discussion I have experienced at an academic conference in the last decade' (p. 200). We share this appreciation of the Leeds conference and its form less to boost our own egos (always a risk) and more to invite further experimentation, gentleness and playfulness in the organisation of conferences and other shared spaces.

This book, too, is a shared space. We've attempted to be gentle and playful in its organisation. Offering a shift in register between the more or less traditional scholarly prose of chapters, a scattering of poems dance between chapters. An anonymous haiku poses a startling question about identity (p. 23). Eco-feminist erotics in the poetry of Helen Moore invite us to reconsider our relationships with food and nature, bodies and pleasures (p. 67–8, 182–3). J. Fergus Evans' poetic manifesto playfully and seriously questions gay identity and the connections between sex and revolution (p. 181–2). And Tom Leonard offers a powerful reminder that the violence of war is the rule, rather than the exception, in a male-dominated society (p. 101–2).

Also addressing these themes, the first substantive chapter of the book (Chapter 2) returns to anarchism's historical past in order to reassess the prison writings of Russian–American anarchist Alexander Berkman, the companion of the better known anarchist firebrand Emma Goldman. Jenny Alexander highlights not only how Goldman has eclipsed activist and scholarly attention on Berkman (except for the reasons he was sent to prison in the first place, as a result of an assassination attempt on factory owner Frick) but also how the issues that Goldman campaigned on – female emancipation, birth control and the equality of the sexes – have also obscured Berkman's radical appraisal of same-sex desire as depicted in his *Prison Memoirs of an Anarchist* (1912). Using the history of 'first wave' anarchism as a resource to comment on past debates on homosexuality and current assessments of masculinity, desire and queer sexuality, Alexander disinters the significance of Berkman's prison experience, placing it in the context of the time and bringing to light not just the gripping narrative provided in Berkman's *Memoirs*. Alexander also shows, through a careful analysis of the text, how Berkman came to the realisation that society's prejudices against male–male love were unjust and also how his own preconceptions on the matter were dissolved as he experienced such love as part of prison life. Berkman is as taken aback about this as his contemporary readers would have been. The 'openly tender' relationship that emerges between Berkman and a fellow inmate he calls 'kiddie' (the prison slang 'kid' meaning 'catamite') reveals how love can flower even in the harshest of environments. The fact that no sex acts are depicted in the *Memoirs*, that no clear 'gay' identity is formed in his writing, has contributed to the neglect of Berkman's work in anarchist and queer circles. But, from a queer perspective, as part of a continuum of desire, neither fixed nor necessarily completely free-ranging, Berkman's words are inspiring for their potentiality for change and for moving beyond divides between hetero- and homosexual desire and identity. In an age which has been qualified as one of 'liquid love' by Zygmunt Bauman, we need to reconsider how desires, intimacies and sex might relate to one another without imposing a hierarchy of values that forces subjects to assume these as fixed or as more or less consequential. Berkman, nearly one hundred years ago, provides us with some routes towards such a reconsideration.

A reconsideration or re-evaluation of what intimacy could mean within the context of necessary solidarities, especially within current feminist and queer struggles such as wages for housework, is presented by Stevphen Shukaitis (in Chapter 3) as a reconfiguration of how effectiveness in struggle should not take place at the expense of 'affect', or a feeling of commonality and affection towards participants in any particular movement. It is not, Stevphen argues, a question of how effective – that is, how efficient, organised or streamlined – any action or movement should be, but rather how 'affective' it can be in terms of generating resistance to relations of power and building new types of relationship between those who resist. But the author's critique goes further: affectiveness is a crucial element in these struggles, not least in order to make the struggle more effective, but as a means of reconfiguring social relationships in the here and now. This characteristic of anarchism, present in historical movements too in the form of anarchist affinity groups, aims to provide a critique of the social and political relationship as instrumentalist, impersonal and utilitarian. As Shukaitis states: 'Affective resistance starts from the realization that one can ultimately never separate questions of the *effectiveness* of political organizing from concerns about its *affectiveness*' (p. 46). In order to explore this in more detail, Shukaitis takes the example of the anti-capitalist women's organisation *Precarias a la Deriva* as an example of how precariousness and subordination in the socio-economic field *and* within movements for change can be partially arrested by attending to the affectiveness of the participants in the struggle. Thus, a focus by social movements on the traditional subject, the male industrial worker, on the traditional workplace and on traditional issues, is displaced by multiple socio-economic identities that arise from a convergence of social, political and sexual resistances that affectiveness is crucial to. Such a realisation gave rise in the *Precarias*' thought to the concept of 'bio-syndicalism', a strategy that posits a 'caring strike' that would pay attention to the specific realities and subject positions in which people find themselves in terms of the labour they provide, and which would allow for caring for different workers' needs according to their own gendered and sexualised positions.

Tracing other currents of autonomous feminism, Lena Eckert (in Chapter 4), by means of a focus on the 'micro-political' psychological level, the level of subjectivity and the symbolic, articulates an analysis of how power becomes entrenched in every microcosm of daily life, including our notions of sex, the body and sexuality. She argues, by assessing the usability of Lacan's work on the symbolism of the phallus, Foucault's understanding of the 'technologies' of the self and postanarchism's anti-foundational critique, that since symbolic or psychological 'powers' are diffuse and operate everywhere, they require a form of resistance that is equally 'everywhere'. Eckert thus calls into question the symbolic function of the phallus and its role in the theorisation of subjectivity and the conceptualisation of gender, the body and sex/ual difference, and posits, following the work of Beatriz Preciado, Judith Butler and Donna Haraway, an eroticisation of the body in all its parts, a decentring of the symbolism of the phallus, and a reconsideration of the hierarchies of pleasure. By drawing further on some of Max Stirner's, Saul Newman's and Gilles Deleuze's work, the anarchistic project with respect to sexuality and desire would be one of 'the constant process of becoming *not* oneself' (p. 73) as a way of radically revising what is understood as sexuality, notions of male and female and hetero/homosexuality. Such fluidity chimes with postanarchist understandings of a lack of fixed identities, and queer studies' opposition to fixed sexual desires and normativities.

Questions of gender, sexuality and power are further explored in an interview with Judith Butler (Chapter 5). Here she contrasts a Western gay libertarianism with various forms of queer anarchism. Whereas the former is recruited by and affiliated with the state in order to secure positions of privilege without regard to racialised state violence, the latter seek to undermine all hierarchies. She also plays with binaries and resists the temptation to draw a clear line between being inside or outside the state, for or against the law. Rather, she points to the fragility of any given legal code or regime and its possible subversion or even dissolution in favour of popular sovereignty. Linking Benjamin and Althusser with Anarchists Against the Wall, and the Zapatista encuentros (global gatherings of activists against neoliberalism) with everyday questions of dignity and survival, this interview demonstrates the possibility and value of queering the border between activist and scholar. Alongside the other contributions in this volume it might also, we hope, stimulate a greater engagement between contemporary feminist theory and (post)anarchism.

Highlighting the arbitrary nature of given regimes of race, gender, sexuality and law, and their impacts on human beings and other lifeforms constitutes a major element of political science fiction and fantasy literature. Ursula Le Guin, for one, performs a radical revisioning of what many a reader may have originally found static or unquestionable. By means of her poetry and prose she moves us to places that can be both inspiring and uncomfortable. Laurence Davis (in Chapter 6) demonstrates how Le Guin can help us imagine our lives and make them up as a defence against authoritarian constraints and in order to avoid 'our lives get[ting] made up for us by other people' (Le Guin 2004: 208). Davis explores how love and revolution are intertwined and connected in Le Guin's almost entirely neglected science fiction 'story suite' *Four Ways to Forgiveness* (1995), and argues, following Bookchin and others, that if anarchism is worth anything it implies a revolution of and in everyday life. In contrast to many traditional Marxist or socialist movements, part of this revolution for anarchism has to do with the way love and sexual relationships are lived out on a day-to-day basis. Over four interconnected stories, this book explores betrayal, forgiveness, political form, social revolution and love. Love and sexuality – of whatever stripe – are represented in Le Guin's work not as an 'add-on' or something tangential to her novelistic work but as something integral, urgent and fundamental. Le Guin explores how jealousy, deceit, rigidly bound notions of the natural and gender expectations can be transformed by an uncompromising commitment to the interplay and mutual determinacy between the form of revolutionary expression or action and romantic love. Power is seen as something not to be seized by a violent revolutionary movement, but dissolved, nullified, as Davis notes, as part of 'a patient, constructive, organic and open-ended form of revolutionary practice ultimately rooted in a transformation of the individual spirit' (p. 114).

Lewis Call's chapter (Chapter 7) continues the theme of reading science fiction, this time by African–American authors Octavia Butler and Samuel Delaney, to explore topics both uncomfortable and inspirational in order to imagine our lives differently. Unlike Le Guin, neither Butler nor Delaney has associated themselves with anarchism. Nonetheless, their efforts to subvert hierarchies of race, class, gender, sexuality and even genre show a clear affinity with her work and other anarchist intersectional analyses of power. Like *Four Ways to Forgiveness*, slavery is a central theme in Octavia Butler's *Patternist* and Samuel Delany's *Nevèrÿon* books. However, in Lewis' reading, the tales of Butler and Delaney are not describing a dissolution of power but rather a playing with power. They contrast consensual, desired and erotic forms of playing with power (i.e. BDSM) with the unethical, non-erotic, non-consensual, undesired and unplayful practices of power that characterise both slavery as historic institution and its descendant – the modern political economy of state capitalism. Bringing together Foucauldian theory with contemporary writing on sadomasochism to read the shifting play of power in these novels, Lewis refers to this particular strategy for healing the psychic wounds of slavery as an example of what he calls 'postanarchist kink' (p. 132). Like Lena's, Lewis' postanarchist approach is less interested in the immediate abolition of dominant relations and discourses and more interested in their ongoing *subversion*. And, like Jenny Alexander's discussion of sexual borderlands and Gavin Brown's linking of queer with a permaculturist's appreciation of ecological edges, Lewis' chapter emphasises the value of working from the margins. He is also careful to recognise that the marginal position of erotic sadomasochism, as a line of flight, does not necessarily lead to freedom. It, too, can be caught in another 'structure of desire': that of liberal individualism and a minority identity politics dependent on the very power structures it claims to reject. Neither is his analysis limited to the sexual play of power. In our efforts to enact anarchist forms of a potentially hierarchical relationship, that of author and editor, we, too, have found ourselves playing with power.

Both anarchism and queer studies have paid attention to questions of youth and to troubling the relationship between sexuality and youth. Anarchism, historically, has viewed young people not only as a logical and fertile constituency for its ideas of emancipation (see, for example, Kropotkin's 'An Appeal to the Young', in Baldwin 1970: 260–82, originally published in 1880; or Paul Goodman's 1956 classic *Growing up Absurd*), but has also placed great store on attempting to revolutionise youth sexuality by means of a struggle for access to accurate 'scientific' sexual knowledge, as a site where relations between men and women can be transformed and for ready usage of simple materials such as birth control devices. However, anarchism historically has tended to reify categories of maleness and femaleness and has rarely considered homosexuality as a legitimate form of expression alongside heterosexuality. Intertwining these concerns with the power of storytelling demonstrated by Laurence Davis and Lewis Call, Jamie Heckert (Chapter 8) explores questions of educating youth about sex and sexuality while engaging with feminist theory and (post)anarchism. Telling his own 'sexual stories', relating domestic violence and growing up 'different' in an apparently sexually monochrome world, Jamie opens up a path for listening to himself and others as part of the realisation of erotic and anarchic desires. Intensely personal and deeply political, the form of storytelling developed here queers scholarship. Interweaving snippets of autobiography with poetry and political theory, his chapter engages with very practical questions about teaching sex education, doing scholarship and being a political activist while at the same time exploring questions of identity, temporality, embodiment, ethics and emotion. More importantly, it is written from the heart. Working from the insight that hierarchy depends on (a fantasy of) separation, Jamie highlights the centrality of connection, of love, for anarchism, for sex education with young people and for all other relationships. This, he notes, need not be postponed until after the revolution. Love occurs only in the present; the experience of presence is part of the always becoming-revolution.

While the other contributors have based most of their accounts on the capitalist West and long-industrialised countries, part of the remit of the Leeds conference was to explore anarchist discourse and practice in other regions, not least the former 'communist' bloc. Cut off from their own anarchist histories of the early twentieth century, current Eastern European anarchist movements have had to engage in a process of historical and self-discovery to recuperate and (re)construct their organisations along new lines. The Czech anarchist movement re-emerged in the 1980s under the banner of several organisations, some national, some local. Marta Kolářová (in Chapter 9) analyses the reception of debates on sexuality in the Czech anarchist movement and finds not only that the subject area has been under-theorised but that it has generally been neglected. In contrast to some other movements traced in these pages, not least sections of the early twentieth-century North American movement discussed by Jenny Alexander, and some of the newer anarchisms outlined in Stevphen Shukaitis' chapter, the Czech movement appears to have favoured concentration on economic issues and industrial organisation and has only very recently broached issues such as feminism and gay rights. Despite this concentration, Marta identifies numerous strands within the anarchist movement, particulary anarcho-feminist currents, that have taken on board the interconnections between economic, social and sexual exploitation and oppression. While such dimensions have not necessarily come smoothly to other parts of the movement, a discourse and practice responding to what we might call intersectionality has slowly made headway in the Czech movement. Such a convergence has, in part, been due to external factors rather than the ideological realisation that sexuality is an issue that deserves attention. As a result of increased fascist activity, anarchists have been the target of violence. In addition, anarcho-feminists and LGBTQs have suffered violence, individually or during Queer Parades, at the hands of fascists. Such violence has resulted in an increasing cooperation between anarchists and queers, with anarchists on one occasion acting as security (in the absence of the state police) on a gay parade. While this has been largely one-way, according to Kolářová, it can but strengthen the anarchist movement in the Czech Republic and it presages an ongoing engagement with intersectional approaches that can enrich anarchism and the social movements it comes into contact with.

Returning to Anglophone contexts, Gavin Brown's contribution (Chapter 10) links a series of case studies in queer autonomous geography to the theme of amateurism and DIY politics. The anarchist tradition has long acknowledged the entwining of knowledge/power attributed to Foucault. Thus, the questioning of authority claims is not limited to the 'political' but includes all forms of expertise. Bakunin wrote:

> In the matter of boots I refer to the authority of the bootmakers; concerning houses, canals or railroads I consult that of the architect or engineer. For such or such special knowledge I apply to such or such a savant. But I allow neither the bootmaker nor the architect nor the savant to impose his [sic] authority upon me. I accept them freely and with all the respect merited by their intelligence, their character, their knowledge, reserving always my incontestable right of criticism and censure.
>
> (Bakunin, cited in Kinna 2005: 70)

And Bakunin himself is treated similarly. As Juliet Paredes of Mujeres Creando, a Bolivian anarcha-feminist group, said, 'I've said it and I'll say it again that we're not anarchists by Bakunin or the CNT [Confederación Nacional del Trabajo (National Confederation of Labour)], but rather by our grandmothers, and that's a beautiful school of anarchism' (Paredes 2002: 112). Likewise, several of the examples Gavin draws upon might also be considered beautiful schools of anarchism with no links to Bakunin or the expertise of 'activists', whereas others take only what they need from contemporary anarchism's 'hybrid genealogy' (Gordon 2005: 9). From Queer Pagan Camp to a cruisy urban public toilet to nightclubs and Queeruptions, Brown takes us on a whirlwind tour of experiments in autonomous social relations. In doing so, he not only highlights possible queer futures but also the other-than-state, other-than-capitalist spaces which always exist outside official discourses of reality and the possible. He also reminds us that drawing a border between autonomous and non-autonomous spaces is always a fiction. Hierarchies are never spaces of perfect control; autonomous or anarchist spaces are always works in progress, continually learning to let go of hierarchy, continually learning to relate to each other as equals. More important than any anarcho-perfection are the complex, messy and often joyful experiences of learning through doing, directly, together. For Gavin Brown, '[q]ueer is an ethical process' (p. 203) and one which creates very different possibilities to the binaries and hierarchies of official intimacies, genders, sexualities and political economies. It is also one which may undermine the stories of 'not good enough' that one of our (Jamie's) pieces (Chapter 8) reminds us are all too common in academic, activist and other spaces. Finally, the chapter highlights the power of ritual in knitting together community. Whether explicitly labelled as such, by the queer pagans, or as implicitly shared understanding, ritual can offer a particular focus for experiencing together the joys and pains of being alive.

The book concludes with Kristina N. Weaver (Chapter 11) sharing her experiences of an experimental 'structure of desire' utilised in the conference. Like Gavin, she reminds us that this conference, too, was a queer autonomous space and one with wide-reaching consequences for her. While telling her own story, Kristina draws our attention to the reality that every event we organise, every relationship we have, creates ripples of fresh possibilities.

Notes

1 For a more detailed analysis of the etymology and actual uses of the word '*anarkhia*' in ancient Greece, see Gordon 2006. Here he suggests that Antigone, That 'long-standing inspiration to feminists' is also 'the first-ever anarchist' (Gordon 2006: 88).
2 For an extensive bibliography, see ASN 2010b.
3 Lewis Call was invited to contribute his chapter at a later date. One of us (Jamie) contributed a chapter following an anarchist sex education workshop during the conference. Likewise, the poems and the interview with Judith Butler were later additions.

References

Ackelsberg, M. A. (2000) 'Mujeres Libres: Identity, Community, Sexuality, and Power', *Anarchist Studies* 8(2): 99–117.
——(2005 [1991]) *Free Women of Spain: Anarchism and the Struggle for the Emancipation of Women*, Oakland, CA/Edinburgh: AK Press.

Alexander, M. J. (2005) *Pedagogies of Crossing: Meditations on Feminism, Sexual Politics, Memory, and the Sacred*, Durham, NC/London: Duke University Press.

Álvarez-Uría, F. and Varela, J. (1999) 'Introducción a un modo de vida no fascista', in Michel Foucault, *Estrategias de poder. Obras esenciales*, vol. II, Barcelona: Paidós.

Amster, R. (2004) 'Breaking the Law: Anti-authoritarian Visions of Crime and Justice', *New Formulations* 2(2). Online. Available HTTP: http://www.newformulation.org/4Amster.htm (accessed 24 January 2011).

Amster, R., DeLeon, A., Fernandez, L. Nocella, A. and Shannon, D. (eds) (2009) *Contemporary Anarchist Studies: An Introductory Anthology of Anarchy in the Academy*, London: Routledge.

Anzaldúa, G. (1987) *Borderlands/La Frontera*, San Francisco: Spinsters/Aunt Lute.

APOC (2010) 'Join the Movement'. Online. Available HTTP: http://illvox.org/join/ (accessed 6 September 2010).

ASN (2010a) 'Anarchism & Poststructuralism'. Online. Available HTTP: http//anarchist-studies-network.org.uk/ReadingLists_Poststructuralism (accessed 28 July 2010).

——(2010b) 'Anarchism & Sexuality: Texts from and about the Anarchist Tradition'. Online. Available HTTP: http://www.anarchist-studies-network.org.uk/ReadingLists_Sexuality (accessed 28 July 2010).

Baldwin, R. N. (ed.) (1970 [1927]) *Kropotkin's Revolutionary Pamphlets: A Collection of Writings by Peter Kropotkin*, New York: Dover.

Bedford, K. and Jakobsen, J. (2009) *Towards a Vision of Sexual and Economic Justice*, New York: Barnard Center for Research on Women. Online. Available HTTP: http://www.barnard.edu/bcrw/newfeministsolutions/reports/NFS4-Sexual_Economic_Justice.pdf (accessed 6 September 2010).

Bowen Raddeker, H. (2001) 'Anarcho-Feminist Discourse in Prewar Japan: Itô Noe's Autobiographical Social Criticism', *Anarchist Studies* 9(2): 97–125.

Brown, L. S. (1996) 'Beyond Feminism: Anarchism and Human Freedom', in Howard J. Ehrlich (ed.), *Reinventing Anarchy, Again*, Edinburgh/San Francisco: AK Press.

Brown, W. (1995) *States of Injury: Power and Freedom in Late Modernity*, Princeton, NJ: Princeton University Press.

Butler, J. (2004) 'Violence, Mourning, Politics', in *Precarious Life: The Powers of Mourning and Violence*, London/New York: Verso.

——(2007) 'Sexual Politics: The Limits of Secularism, the Time of Coalition', *British Journal of Sociology* 2007 public lecture, London School of Economics, 30 October.

——(2008) 'Sexual Politics, Torture, and Secular Time', *British Journal of Sociology* 59(1): 1–23.

Butler, J. and Spivak, G. C. (2007) *Who Sings the Nation-State? Language, Politics, Belonging*, London/New York/Calcutta: Seagull Books.

Chen, C., Dulani, J. and Piepzna-Samarasinha, L. (2011) *The Revolution Starts at Home: Confronting Intimate Violence within Activist Communities*, Boston, MA: South End Press.

Chomsky, N. (2005) *Chomsky on Anarchism*, Edinburgh/Oakland, CA: AK Press.

Cleminson, R. (2004) 'Making Sense of the Body: Anarchism, Nudism and Subjective Experience', *Bulletin of Spanish Studies* 81(6): 697–716.

Cohn, J. (2002) 'What is Postanarchism "Post"?', Review of: Saul Newman, *From Bakunin to Lacan: Anti-Authoritarianism and the Dislocation of Power*, Lanham,

MD: Lexington, 2001, *Postmodern Culture* 13(1). Online. Available HTTP: http://muse.jhu.edu/journals/postmodern_culture/v013/13.1cohn.html (accessed 24 January 2011).

——(2010) 'Sex and the Anarchist Unconscious: A Brief History', *Sexualities* 13(4): 413–31.

Cohn, J. and Wilbur, S. (2011) 'What's Wrong with Postanarchism?', in D. Rousselle and S. Evren (eds), *Post-anarchism: A Reader*, Ann Arbor, MI/London: Pluto Press. Online. Available HTTP: http://www.anarchist-studies.org/article/articleview/26/1/1 (accessed 22 May 2010).

Colson, D. (2001) *Petit Lexique philosophique de l'anarchisme. De Proudhon à Deleuze*, Paris: Livre de Poche.

Cooper, D. (1994) *Sexing the City: Lesbian and Gay Politics within the Activist State*, London: Rivers Oram Press.

Dark Star Collective (2002) *Quiet Rumours: An Anarcha-Feminist Reader*, Edinburgh/San Francisco: AK Press/Dark Star.

Deleuze, G. (1992) 'Postscript on the Societies of Control', *OCTOBER* 59: 3–7.

Espigado Tocino, G. (2002) 'Las mujeres en el anarquismo español (1869–1939)', *Ayer* 45(1): 39–72.

Fahs, B. (2010) 'Radical Refusals: On the Anarchist Politics of Women Choosing Asexuality', *Sexualities* 13(4): 445–61.

Foucault, M. (1990) *The History of Sexuality*, vol. 1: *An Introduction* (trans. Robert Hurley), New York: Vintage.

——(2004) 'Introduction', in Gilles Deleuze and Félix Guattari, *Anti-Oedipus*, London: Continuum.

Franks, B. (2006) *Rebel Alliances: The Means and Ends of Contemporary British Anarchisms*, Edinburgh/Oakland, CA: AK Press/Dark Star.

Gaarder, E. (2009) 'Addressing Violence against Women: Alternatives to State-based Law and Punishment', in R. Amster, A. Deleon, L. Fernandez A. Nocella and D. Shannon (eds), *Contemporary Anarchist Studies: An Introductory Anthology of Anarchy in the Academy*, London: Routledge.

Goldman, E. (1969 [1917]) 'The Tragedy of Woman's Emancipation', in *Anarchism and Other Essays*, New York: Dover.

Gordon, U. (2005) 'Anarchism and Political Theory: Contemporary Problems', unpublished DPhil thesis, University of Oxford. Online. Available HTTP: http://zinelibrary.info/files/anarchismpoliticaltheory.pdf (accessed 28 April 2010).

——(2006) 'Research Note: *Αναρχία* – What Did the Greeks Actually Say?', *Anarchist Studies* 14(1): 84–91.

——(2008) *Anarchy Alive! Anti-Authoritarian Politics from Practice to Theory*, London/Ann Arbor, MI: Pluto Press.

Greenway, J. (1997) 'Twenty-First Century Sex', in Jon Purkis and James Bowen (eds), *Twenty-First Century Anarchism: Unorthodox Ideas for a New Millennium*, London: Cassell.

——(2008) 'Desire, Delight, Regret: Discovering Elizabeth Gibson', *Qualitative Research* 8(3): 317–24. Online. Available HTTP: http://www.judygreenway.org.uk/ddr/ddr.html (accessed 24 January 2011).

——(2009) 'Speaking Desire: Anarchism and Free Love as Utopian Performance in Fin de Siècle Britain', in L. Davis and R. Kinna (eds), *Anarchism and Utopianism*, Manchester: Manchester University Press.

Haaland, B. (1993) *Emma Goldman: Sexuality and the Impurity of the State*, Montreal/New York/London: Black Rose Books.

Heckert, J. (2010a) 'Relating Differently', *Sexualities* 13(4): 403–11.

——(2010b) 'Listening, Caring, Becoming: Anarchism as an Ethics of Direct Relationships', in B. Franks and M. Wilson (eds), *Anarchism and Moral Philosophy*, Basingstoke: Palgrave Macmillan.

Heller, C. (1999) *Ecology of Everyday Life: Rethinking the Desire for Nature*, Montreal/New York/London: Black Rose Books.

hooks, b. (1994) *Teaching to Transgress: Education as the Practice of Freedom*, London: Routledge.

INCITE! Women of Color Against Violence (2006) *Color of Violence: The INCITE! Anthology*, Boston, MA: South End Press.

Jeppesen, S. (2010) 'Queer Anarchist Autonomous Zones and Publics: Direct Action Vomiting against Homonormative Consumerism', *Sexualities* 13(4): 463–78.

Kinna, R. (2005) *Anarchism: A Beginner's Guide*, Oxford: Oneworld.

Kissack, T. (2008) *Free Comrades: Anarchism and Homosexuality in the United States*, Oakland, CA/Edinburgh: AK Press.

Kuntsman, A. and Miyake, E. (eds) (2008) *Out of Place: Interrogating Silences in Queerness/Raciality*, York: Raw Nerve Books.

Lamble, S. (2008) 'Retelling Racialized Violence, Remaking White Innocence: The Politics of Interlocking Oppressions in Transgender Day of Remembrance', *Sexuality Research & Social Policy* 5(1): 24–42.

Le Guin, U. K. (2004) 'The Operating Instructions', in *The Wave in the Mind: Talks and Essays on the Writer, the Reader, and the Imagination*, Boston, MA: Shambhala.

Lorde, A. (1993 [1978]) 'The Uses of the Erotic: The Erotic as Power', in Henry Abelove, Michèle Aina Barale and David M. Halperin (eds), *The Lesbian and Gay Studies Reader*, New York: Routledge.

Lucien, M. (ed.) (2006) *Inversions 1924–1925 L'Amitié 1925: Deux Revues homosexuelles françaises*, Lille: GayKitschCamp.

Maitron, J. (1983) *Le Mouvement anarchiste en France*, vol. I: *Des Origines à 1914*, Paris: François Maspero.

Marcos, Subcomandante and the Zapatistas (2006) *The Other Campaign*, San Francisco: Open Media Series/City Lights.

Mecca, T. A. (ed.) (2009) *Smash the Church, Smash the State! The Early Years of Gay Liberation*, San Francisco: City Lights Books.

Mohanty, C. T. (2003) *Feminism without Borders: Decolonising Theory, Practicing Solidarity*, Durham, NC/London: Duke University Press.

Monro, S. (2005) *Gender Politics: Citizenship, Activism and Sexual Diversity*, London/Ann Arbor, MI: Pluto Press.

Mortimer-Sandilands, C. (2005) 'Unnatural Passions? Notes Toward a Queer Ecology', *Invisible Culture: An Electronic Journal for a Visible Culture* 9. Online. Available HTTP: http://www.rochester.edu/in_visible_culture/Issue_9/sandilands.html (accessed 24 January 2011).

Nash, M. (1975) *Mujeres Libres, España 1936–1939*, Barcelona: Tusquets.

——(1984) 'El neomalthusianismo anarquista y los conocimientos populares sobre el control de natalidad en España', in M. Nash (ed.), *Presencia y protagonismo. Aspectos de la historia de la mujer*, Barcelona: Ediciones del Serbal.

——(1995) *Defying Male Civilization: Women in the Spanish Civil War*, Denver, Co: Arden Press.

Newman, S. (2010) *The Politics of Postanarchism*, Edinburgh: Edinburgh University Press.

Ording, D. (2009) 'Intimate Fellows: Utopia and Chaos in the Early Post-Stonewall Gay Liberation Manifestos', in L. Davis and R. Kinna (eds), *Anarchism and Utopianism*, Manchester: Manchester University Press.

Paredes, J. (2002) 'An Interview with Mujeres Creando', in Dark Star Collective (ed.), *Quiet Rumours: An Anarcha-Feminist Reader*, Edinburgh/Oakland, CA: AK Press/ Dark Star.

Passet, J. E. (2003) *Sex Radicals and the Quest for Women's Equality*, Urbana, IL: University of Illinois Press.

Perelman, M. (2000) *Transcending the Economy: On the Potential of Passionate Labor and the Wastes of the Market*, London: Macmillan.

Phillips, U. and DiFranco, A. (1997) *The Past Didn't Go Anywhere* (CD), Buffalo, NY: Righteous Babe Records.

Portwood-Stacer, L. (2010) 'Constructing Anarchist Sexuality: Queer Identity, Culture, and Politics in the Anarchist Movement', *Sexualities* 13(4): 479–93.

Puar, J. (2006) *Terrorist Assemblages: Homonationalism in Queer Times*, Durham, NC/London: Duke University Press.

Roseneil, S. (2000) *Common Women, Uncommon Practices: The Queer Feminisms of Greenham*, London: Cassell.

Rousselle, D. and Evren, S. (eds) (2011) *Post-anarchism: A Reader*, Ann Arbor, MI/ London: Pluto Press.

Rowbotham, S. (2008) *Edward Carpenter, A Life of Liberty and Love*, London: Verso.

Seidman, S. (1997) *Difference Troubles: Querying Social Theory and Sexual Politics*, Cambridge: Cambridge University Press.

Shannon, D. and Willis, A. (2010) 'Theoretical Polyamory: Some Thoughts on Loving, Thinking, and Queering Anarchism', *Sexualities* 13(4): 433–43.

Shepard, B. (2002) *From ACT UP to the WTO: Urban Protest and Community Building in the Era of Globalization*, London: Verso.

——(2010) 'Bridging the Divide between Queer Theory and Anarchism', *Sexualities* 13 (4): 511–27.

Smith, A. (2005) *Conquest: Sexual Violence and American Indian Genocide*, Cambridge, MA: South End Press.

Stenstad, G. (1992) 'Anarchic Thinking: Breaking the Hold of Monotheistic Ideology on Feminist Philosophy', in Ann Garry and Marilyn Pearsall (eds), *Women, Knowledge, and Reality: Explorations in Feminist Philosophy*, New York/London: Routledge.

Sullivan, D. and Tifft, L. (2001) *Restorative Justice: Healing the Foundations of Our Everyday Lives*, Monsey, NY: Willow Tree Press.

Tifft, L. (1993) *Battering of Women: The Failure of Intervention and the Case for Prevention*, New York: Perseus Books Group.

Tifft, L. and Sullivan, D. (1980) *The Struggle to Be Human: Crime, Criminology, and Anarchism*, Orkney, UK: Cienfuegos Press.

Veneuse, M.J. (2009) 'To Be Condemned to a Clinic: The Birth of the Anarca-Islamic Clinic', in A. Christoyannopoulos (ed.), *Religious Anarchism: New Perspectives*, Newcastle: Cambridge Scholars Publishing.

Ward, C. (1982) *Anarchy in Action*, London: Freedom Press.

Weeks, J. (1985) *Sexuality and its Discontents: Meanings, Myths and Modern Sexualities*, London: Routledge.

Wilkinson, E. (2009) 'The Emotions Least Relevant to Politics? Queering Autonomous Activism', *Emotion, Space and Society* 2: 36–43.

Windpassinger, G. (2010) 'Queering Anarchism in Post-2001 Buenos Aires', *Sexualities* 13(4): 495–509.

Winnubst, S. (2006) *Queering Freedom*, Bloomington/Indianapolis, IN: Indiana University Press.

Poetic interlude I

To define ourselves
we all create the 'other'.
What's another way?
—Anonymous

Chapter 2

Alexander Berkman

Sexual dissidence in the first wave anarchist movement and its subsequent narratives

Jenny Alexander

> Once upon a time, people who knew the way were subtle, spiritual, mysterious, penetrating, unfathomable.
>
> —Lao Tzu, *Tao Te Ching* (p. 23)

This chapter looks at the autobiography of Alexander Berkman, *Prison Memoirs of an Anarchist* (1912), which covers his prison experience from 1892 to 1906 in Allegheny Penitentiary, Pennsylvania. I want to explore the present-day discourses surrounding this autobiography, alongside those surrounding the autobiography of his rather more famous anarchist comrade, Emma Goldman, *Living My Life* (1931). I am interested in how these texts continue to be interpreted and utilised by anarchists and scholars, specifically in relation to questions of sexuality. I also want to suggest my own particular contribution to re-reading Alexander Berkman in the service of a dynamic anarcho-affective praxis.

Berkman, long-term political comrade of Emma Goldman, was a Russian/Lithuanian/Jewish immigrant to the United States. He was an impassioned political idealist, who, in his early twenties, planned the murder of the strike-breaking steel magnate Henry Clay Frick as an *attentat* (a politically motivated murder for propaganda purposes), hoping that it would inspire the steel workers then under siege at Homestead to rise up and act as the spark that would ignite the social revolution. He shot and wounded Frick, who survived, and his autobiography covers the fourteen years of incarceration served for that act. Emma Goldman, who was a party to the plot (hatched in their Worcester, Massachusetts, ice-cream parlour), publicly defended his attempt. *Prison Memoirs of an Anarchist* was begun by Berkman some three years after his release. 'Back issues' of the underground newspaper *Prison Blossoms*, which he had managed to produce clandestinely whilst inside and copies of which were kept for him by Goldman, assisted the ordering in his memory of times and incidents.[1]

'The anarchist literature of the past weighs heavily on the present and makes it hard for us to produce new literature for the future', says Steve Millett in a review of the academic journal *Anarchist Studies* in *Democracy and Nature* (Millett 1997). It is worth engaging with his point. 'Historical memory is a theatre of autonomous struggles'[2] and so historical understanding should be a crucial component of grassroots activisms. Nevertheless, one might ask, do we need to return again and yet again to the writings of 'first wave' anarchists?

Emma Goldman and Alexander Berkman are richly documented as anarchist figures of note. Their footprints mark the highways and byways of hundreds of related sites on the web today, from the scholarly, such as *The Emma Goldman Papers*, curated at Berkeley under Dr Candace Falk, to the scholar-activist, such as *The Anarchy Archives* set up by Dana Ward, Professor of Political Studies at Pitzer College, in 1995. You can even watch a clip of Emma interviewed on an old Paramount newsreel of the 1930s (at the time of writing this seems to have been removed from YouTube but is archived via Video-surf).[3] This exhaustive documentation and re-remembrance of the lives and work of Goldman and Berkman online, mostly disseminated from the United States, could be said to contribute to 'the construction of anarchism as Western', and to a 'eurocentrism that has permeated the writings of many second and third wave [anarchist] theorists and writers', as Jason Adams suggests in his paper 'Non-Western Anarchisms' (Adams 2002). This problem of Western-centrism pervades the internet with respect to all knowledge forms, access being unevenly distributed, as we know, according to global economic inequalities. Acknowledging that, my chapter *is* nevertheless consciously situated in relation to the encounter between anarchisms and sexualities specifically within Western late capitalism.

I want to look at the ways in which anarchist and scholarly communities have read and continue to read Emma Goldman's and Alexander Berkman's autobiographical writings since the 1960s and 1970s, with particular reference to questions of sexuality. I want to ask how it is that these readings continue to contribute significantly to discourses within and around anarchism and sexuality, particularly because Berkman and Goldman have been treated rather differently in relation to this subject.

Oz Frankel has written a nuanced account of the 'iconisation' of Emma Goldman since the 1930s, of her adoption as a heroic figure by multiple constituencies, particularly in the USA but also internationally, from libertarian liberals to radical feminists. In an article called 'Whatever Happened to "Red Emma"?' (Frankel 1996), he explores the many faces in circulation of a celebretised Goldman. Indeed, her life and writings continue in the twenty-first century to be widely re-circulated in anarchist and scholarly material on- and offline, *particularly* in connection with feminism and sexuality – a legacy of her adoption by the second wave of feminism.

Today Goldman is also referenced significantly on anarcha-activist sites specifically concerned with gender and sexuality. For example Toronto-based anarcho-queer group Limpfist's website names just two anarchist theorists in their 'Links' section – Noam Chomsky and Emma Goldman. Anarcha.org, an online collection of resources on anarcha-feminism, contains contemporary writings by the likes of Wendy O'Matik and Jamie Heckert in their 'Sex and Sexuality' section (under 'Health and Healing'). It also posts links to two of Emma Goldman's essays, 'Anarchy and the Sex Question' (1896) and 'Marriage and Love' (1911).

Of all her writings, Goldman's autobiography *Living My Life* has in particular been addressed within the academy and the mainstream, autobiography and biography being historically bourgeois forms. Many academic studies of Goldman engage extensively with the autobiography and related private correspondence (e.g. Falk 1990 [1984] and Wexler 1986). But it does also appear in activist and teaching resources online too. For example, sections are reproduced on John Simkin's left-leaning UK-based resource Spartacus Educational (2010) and also indeed on Wikiquote. It is linked on infoshop.org (2010), the anarchist Alternative Media Project based in Kansas, and reproduced in entirety on the Anarchy Archives.

The relationship between Goldman's personal life and her politics is frequently highlighted, by both activist and scholarly writing about her. For example, Lori Jo Marso, writing in the academic journal *Feminist Theory*, argues that

> it is not solely Goldman's political life that makes her important for us to study today. Rather, it is the intersection of her life with her thought, specifically her intimate and sexual life as studied in conjunction with her essays on marriage, sex, love, women's emancipation and femininity.
>
> (Marso 2003: 305–6)

Another article, by Anna Propos of Irvington High School California's Anarchist Student Union, 'To the Daring Belongs the Future: The Anarcha Feminist Movement' (Propos n.d.) specifically approaches Goldman's political position on homosexuality with reference to her friendships with the lesbian editor of *The Little Review*, Margaret Anderson, and with fellow activist (also a lesbian) Almeda Sperry, Goldman's sometime passionate correspondent.

Unlike his long-term political comrade, Alexander Berkman is not commonly linked to questions of anarchism and sexuality. He is known and his life and work continue to be memorialised and disseminated today in anarchist and scholarly resources on- and offline, for his *ABC of Anarchism*, for his opposition to the suppression of the Krondstadt revolt, for his assassination attempt on Henry Clay Frick, and finally for his relationship with Goldman. Left US historian Howard Zinn, in the forward to the latest edition of *Life of an Anarchist: The Alexander Berkman Reader* (Fellner 2005), which reproduces the autobiography, calls Berkman a 'lost hero' of American radicalism but does not mention sexuality. Spartacus Educational mentions his autobiography but not its content. Wikipedia has an entry for *Prison Memoirs of an Anarchist* but again no mention of sexuality. The anarchist zine *A Practical Guide to Prisoner Support*, by Kirsten Anderberg (2001), cited on a number of US anarcho-activist sites, recommends several books to prisoners, including *All Things Censored* (1998) by Mumia Abu-Jamal and Berkman's *Prison Memoirs* (reviewed on Phoenix Anarchist Coalition website by Sallydarity), but without any discussion of Berkman's treatment of same-sex love and desire. The International Institute of Social History in Amsterdam, which holds the Alexander Berkman papers, has a more specific reference to Berkman's chapter 'On Homosexuality in Prison' in the 'Introduction' section on their website, but even this is only in passing.

These examples of activist and scholarly interpretation are exemplary of the different ways in which Emma Goldman and Alexander Berkman tend to be discussed in relation to anarchism and sexuality. What Alexander Berkman had to say about sexuality is given the occasional very brief acknowledgement, whilst Goldman's entire political oeuvre is frequently shoehorned into a gender/sexuality boot (and very much linked to her personal life). It is not difficult to see why this is problematic. Questions of gender and sexuality in these re-circulated readings remain and return as the concerns of women/feminisms and LGBTQ agendas linked to/coming out of feminisms, whilst questions of 'general anarchism' remain and return as the concerns of a 'mainstream' (read straight and masculine) anarchist movement. Meanwhile, Berkman's writing on matters of same-sex attachment is given concentrated attention in Jonathan Katz's *Gay American History* (1978), which reproduces extensive excerpts from *Prison Memoirs of An Anarchist*, but Katz does not comment on them in the context of anarchist politics.

What *did* Alexander Berkman have to say about sexuality? Unlike Emma Goldman, who lectured and wrote widely on the subject, sexuality was not a driving political theme of his outside his autobiography. Nevertheless, he devotes significant attention to same-sex intimacy in *Prison Memoirs of an Anarchist*, and without doubt this is a consciously political text, as would be expected from a lifelong political activist. In the late nineteenth century in Britain and the United States, access for the chattering classes to the brutality of prison life (for those not involved in reform work) was likely to be through works of fiction, such as Dickens' novels or Dostoevsky's fictionalised autobiography *Memoirs from the House of the Dead* (1861–2). However, first-hand accounts from British and American gaols, such as Michael Davitt's *Leaves from a Prison Diary* (1885), were beginning to emerge, impacting on calls for prison reform. Anarchist autobiographical accounts of prison (notably Berkman's, Goldman's and Kropotkin's) were among the first texts in the West to call for prison *abolition* – a position adopted by anarchists ever since.

Unsurprisingly, as an anarchist, Berkman challenged the authority of the prison. He documents his attempts to alert the outside world to prison conditions, to stand up for fellow inmates and to communicate with the anarchist press. These were severely punished, and he details time spent in solitary on starvation rations, and even confined to a straitjacket. The text (re-)creates for us a struggle in the terrain of power and the body; between a dis-identified 'bad subject' (Althusser 2006 [1970]) and the repressive apparatus of the state. Berkman's decision to write about desire and passionate affection between men in his autobiography, therefore, was certainly also a consciously political decision.

Berkman was an anarchist committed (until much later in his life) to violent terrorism as a revolutionary strategy. He was also someone with a painfully strong conscience and a stubborn will. The book is narrated in the present tense, but the political self which the text depicts is not static. The book takes the reader through the mental development of fourteen years. This literary device is ideologically powerful. The reader is enjoined/seduced/required to identify with the protagonist, following the intellectual and emotional adjustments that unfold, as if at first hand. Thus the reader is rendered susceptible (as a conscious political device) to adopting or mirroring these adjustments as they progress through the book, in other words to being what Althusser, in his famous essay 'Ideology and Ideological State Apparatuses' (2006 [1970]), called 'ideologically interpellated'.

The young Berkman portrayed at the start of *Prison Memoirs* is idealistic, new to America and steeped in the Russian tradition of revolutionary action. He consciously models himself on Rakhmetov, the Nihilist hero of Nikolai Chernyshevsky's political novel *What Is to Be Done?* (1863), an individual who moulds his life to fit his ideals with stern ideological purity. Berkman depicts himself as emotionally distanced from the working classes whom he idealises. The interior monologue that the autobiographer attributes to his younger self begins 'I am a revolutionist first, man afterwards' (Berkman 1970 [1912]: 10) and continues: 'A being who has neither personal desires nor interests above the Cause! I am simply a revolutionist, a terrorist by conviction, an instrument of furthering the cause of humanity' (ibid.: 12).

The autobiography takes the reader through a series of mental states (again all written in the present tense) that depict the psychological struggle of Berkman-the-protagonist, at sea within his own terms of reference. A gradual transmogrification, from anarchist puritanism to a solidarity that extends beyond anarchist comrades and ideational representations of the 'honest' working classes, and finally embraces his flawed but human fellow inmates, is spelled out for the reader by an autobiographer using himself as an object lesson in social perspective:

> I recall with sadness the first years of my imprisonment and my coldly impersonal valuation of social victims. There is Evans, the aged burglar, smiling at me from the line … With the severe intellectuality of the revolutionary tradition, I thought of him and his kind as inevitable fungus growths, the rotten fruit of a decaying society … But the threads of comradeship have slowly been woven by common misery. The touch of sympathy has discovered the man beneath the criminal … Not entirely in vain are the years of suffering that have wakened my kinship with the

> humanity of *les misérables*, whom social stupidity has cast into the valley of death.
>
> (Berkman 1970 [1912]: 409)

As well as a consciousness shift regarding the constitution of criminality, a move towards solidarity with fellow inmates, and the emotional and physical drama of an ideologically driven (traumatic and unbending) resistance to state power, Berkman takes the reader through another major thought revision, the one which most concerns us here, regarding homosexuality. Homosexuality at this time, of course, was considered in popular and dominant discourses to be another form of criminality and degeneracy. Pre-1930s, *Prison Memoirs of an Anarchist* was unique in its frankness concerning sex practices in prison in the United States and Britain – an area of prison life still often invisible today in official discourses and policies surrounding incarceration. The book was published by Goldman's Mother Earth press because, as she records, she could not find a publisher who would take it unexpurgated; some wanted to 'leave out the anarchist part', whilst others insisted on 'eliminating the chapters relating to homosexuality in prison' (Goldman 1988 [1931]: 483–4). At the nineteenth-century *fin de siècle* there was no public debate whatsoever about sex between prison inmates, although there was some coverage in specialist legal and medical texts. Internally, the rampant fact of these relations was sometimes dealt with by attempts to segregate known homosexuals from other prisoners. Joseph F. Fishman records that, at the turn of the century,

> in the Federal Penitentiary of Levenworth, the barbarous practice of putting a large yellow 'D' (to indicated degenerate) on the backs of prisoners actually discovered in an act of homosexuality was pursued in an effort to stamp out the practice. It was of course unsuccessful.
>
> (Fishman 1935: 99)

Berkman's account of prison homosexuality is delivered to the reader as a road to Damascus experience. Berkman offers us himself at twenty-one, a raw recruit to prison life, completely ignorant of the possibility of sexual intimacy between same-sex individuals. He describes his bewilderment when 'Boston Red', professional thief and man of the road, offers him, in the prison workshops, the chance to become his 'kid'. 'How can you love a boy?' the young Berkman gawps, and Boston Red replies (the authorial Berkman fully conscious of the twinkle that must have been present in the older lag's eye), 'Ever read Billy Shakespeare?' (Berkman 1970 [1912]: 180).

The young Berkman, the older Berkman records, is astounded: 'You actually confess to such terrible practices? You're disgusting. But I don't really believe it Red' (ibid.: 183). Four years later, the text recounts, in a chapter titled 'Love's Dungeon Flower', Berkman finds himself locked in one of the underground punishment cells for attempting to alert prison investigators to conditions at

Allegheny. Johnny Davis, a young prisoner, is in the cell next to him. Another prisoner, 'Dutch' Adams, had been boasting that Davis was his sexual property, and Davis had stabbed him. Over the days, Berkman and Davis exchange whispered histories. They begin to call each other by intimate 'other' names – 'Sashenka' for Berkman and 'Filipe' for Johnny. Berkman re-creates his state of mind autobiographically (as always, in the present tense): 'The springs of affection well up within me, as I lie huddled on the stone floor, cold and hungry. With closed eyes, I picture the boy before me, with his delicate face, and sensitive girlish lips' (ibid.: 336).

The two become 'openly tender and affectionate', and Berkman records that he refers to Davis somewhat ambiguously as 'kiddie' in conversation ('kid' being the prison term for catamite). For his part 'Filipe' confesses how much, if it were possible, he would like to kiss 'Sashenka' and Berkman writes of an 'unaccountable sense of joy' (ibid.: 337). No further intimacy is recorded until Berkman describes his immense sorrow at 'Filipe's' death, when he was found hanging in his cell some three months later.

There was another young man, later during the prison years, with whom, Berkman writes, he formed an intense protective friendship – one Russell Schroger. He also died, given a lethal spinal injection by accident in the infirmary. When Berkman heard news of the accident he smashed his hand in his cell door to gain access to the hospital and his dying friend.

Berkman-the-autobiographer wants us to know that Alexander Berkman changed in prison, from a young man shocked and disgusted by homosexual acts to an older man loving and losing two young men to death. He makes a point of recording that change, setting down a re-creation of a conversation he had near the end of his prison term, with fellow inmate 'Doctor George'. First, they discuss Oscar Wilde, 'the brilliant English [sic] man-of-letters, whom the world of cant and stupidity has driven to prison and to death because his sex life did not conform to accepted standards' (ibid.: 451). Then Doctor George tells Berkman how he fell in love with, and eventually made love to, a young man during a previous prison sentence. He asks Berkman if his feelings for the boy were 'viciousness or what?' (ibid.: 457). Berkman writes himself as replying:

> George, I think it a very beautiful emotion. Just as beautiful as love for a woman. I had a friend here, his name was Russell, perhaps you remember him. I felt no physical passion towards him, but I think I loved him with all my heart. His death was a most terrible shock to me. It almost drove me insane.
>
> (Berkman 1970 [1912]: 453)

Berkman, along with Goldman, was, through his autobiography, one of the first well-known political figures in America to endorse sexual love between same-sex individuals. His treatment of sexuality was noted by at least one contemporary hostile review:[4]

> To relieve the lack of a genuine ring in the narration of events, occasioned by the ponderosity of an overwheening self-esteem and the neurasthenia of lachrymose appeals, the author introduces for the benefit of disordered sexual appetites an abundant series of tickling sensations … he grows eloquent to the degree of a revivalist at a prayer-meeting, as though he were in the business to make converts, as soon as he approaches the subject of sexual perversity.
>
> (Thaumazo 1912)

Why, then, does Berkman's discussion of sexuality go largely unmarked in his re-circulations in anarchist and scholarship-of-anarchism contexts from the 1960s to now, even in those spaces created specifically for the discussion of anarchism and sexuality? His autobiography itself is certainly not forgotten. Why have second and third wave anarchism remembered Emma Goldman's personal/political praxis in the field of sexuality but not Alexander Berkman's? Political machismo and homophobia may be responsible in some quarters, but I think that remains only part of the answer.

For me, this failure to productively remember what Alexander Berkman had to say about sexuality hinges around questions of identity and indeterminacy. *Prison Memoirs of an Anarchist* depicts a nebulous nexus of interpersonal connection, one that dismantles demarcation. On the 'outside', so far as we know, Berkman's romantic and sexual companions were women, yet he writes about passionate attachments to two young men and indeed commits to print his daydream of kissing one of them. He tells his readers that these feelings were not actualised in a desiring or a physical sense, yet through them he came to an empathetic place regarding homosexuality. In other words, Berkman writes from a place of fluidity – from the sexual/emotional borderland.

Scholars of the last forty years concerned with the history of sexuality have produced much insightful work on how the social comprehension and expression of sexual behaviour are culturally and historically situated, from pioneering texts such as Alan Bray's *Homosexuality in Renaissance England* (1982) onwards. Alexander Berkman, writing in the early twentieth century, certainly bridges an epochal shift in the conception of sexuality and identity. The personal intimacies he describes, which changed his political perspective on homosexuality, were neither 'gay' nor 'not-gay', neither physically sexual nor platonic. They do not fit the categories by which we in the twenty-first century are generally given to understand passion, sexual desire and intimacy. They take place just as, according the widely disseminated hypotheses of Michel Foucault, Jeffrey Weeks and others, 'the homosexual' as a type of person was being moulded and manifested in a variety of cultural discourses, principally medical and juridical, gradually replacing earlier conceptions of 'sodomy' as a moveable sin pertaining, potentially, to any body (Foucault 1978 [1976]; Weeks 1989 [1981]).

Whilst the general framing of Berkman today by scholars and activists remains silent on the subject of his writing on sexuality, there is one recent notable exception: Terrence Kissack's book *Free Comrades: Anarchism and Homosexuality in the United States 1895–1917* (2008) contains a chapter specifically on Berkman's autobiography. Kissack recognises the significance of the book, referring to it as 'one of the most important political texts dealing with homosexuality to have been written by an American before the 1950s' (Kissack 2008: 102). Unlike Jonathan Katz, Kissack makes explicit the connection between Berkman's defence of homosexuality and his anarchism, appreciating the way in which Berkman's evolution into a champion of socially taboo desire was born from the crucible of his political incarceration. Kissack is right to suggest that Berkman 'presents love between inmates as a form of resistance to the spirit crushing environment of prison' (ibid.: 102), because Berkman never stopped resisting throughout his fourteen-year sentence, and his attachments to Davis and Schroger, his 'inside' experiences of love, were key sources of nourishment which helped him survive.

In discussing the intimacy which *Prison Memoirs of an Anarchist* describes with young Johnny Davis, Kissack confesses that 'Berkman's relationship with Davis is difficult to evaluate as it falls somewhere along the spectrum of friendship and erotic relations'. That 'difficulty' is not Berkman's however, but ours, a symptom of the evaluative category constraints to which anarchists, as subjects-in-time, are also subject. The 'difficulty' Kissack speaks of is, in my view, the reason Berkman's autobiographical and political writing on sexuality has been passed over by most other anarchist scholars and activists. It is because Berkman's same-sex relationships are 'difficult' to categorise that enquirers have not 'seen' them, or known how to name, recognise or give value to them.

Kissack's book situates Berkman where he indeed belongs, within the crucible of twentieth-century anarchism's developing commitments to sexual liberation, because Berkman spoke up for Oscar Wilde and men like him, deliberatively, politically, at a time when to do so was profoundly socially transgressive. But, nevertheless, to recuperate Berkman into a radical history of homosexuality, on its century-long march, or into a history of anarchist sexual politics, is insufficient. How might we productively engage with Berkman in the field of the sexual today, not only as historians, but as activists?

One might choose to read the personal same-sex prison intimacies Berkman describes as 'queer', in the sense that Eve Kosovsky Sedgwick used the term back in 1994:

> one of the things that 'queer' can refer to [is]: the open mesh of possibilities, gaps, overlaps, dissonances and resonances, lapses and excesses of meaning when the constituent elements of anyone's gender, of anyone's sexuality aren't made (or *can't be* made) to signify monolithically.
>
> (Sedgwick 1994: 8)

Yet queer in the West in the first two decades of the twenty-first century has effectively come to signify, in mainstream culture at least, gay, white and middle class (as in the television makeover programme 'Queer Eye for the Straight Guy'), as Cathy J. Cohen and others have argued (Cohen 1997). Whilst, in a sub-cultural sense, one could argue that queer now denotes the performance of radical sexual acts, as part of a radical sexual identity, marked by certain dress codes etc., Joe Rollins and H. N. Hirsch, for example, conclude, following their survey of sexual identities in the contemporary USA, that 'queer, once a theoretical marker of anti-identity [is] becoming an identity category of its own, one that marks further sexual marginalisation and liberationist political possibilities' (Rollins and Hirsch 2003: 309). The *ideal* of an opposition to all stable sexual identities that can be categorised, part of the original queer political project, is often very different from the practice of an emotionally desired anarcho-queer tribalism, where sexual performance is strongly emphasised.

My observations on current (early twenty-first-century) etymological and practical circulations of queer should not be taken to mean my necessary abandonment of queer as a political project. Central to that project, according to Judith Butler, the philosopher who has become most synonymous with it, is, or rather, should be, a continual collective self-reflection, in order to make good the *praxis* of an anti-identitarian identity politics:

> the critique of the queer subject is crucial to the continuing *democratization* of queer politics. As much as identity terms must be used, as much as 'outness' is to be affirmed, these same notions must become subject to a critique of the exclusionary operations of their own production … the genealogical critique of the queer subject will be central to queer politics.
> (Butler 1993: 227)

It is in this spirit, of radicalising approaches to sexuality within culture as an always-becoming project, that I make my remarks. We might indeed read Berkman productively as 'queer' in its broadest sense. Yet none of the anarcho-queer websites I have come across mentions, memorialises or utilises Berkman's writing on sexuality. Amongst contemporary anarcho-scholarly and activist writings on sexuality, Alexander Berkman is not claimed politically (of course anachronistically) as anarcho-queer, although he writes as an anarchist about same-sex desire, including his own. Oscar Wilde is sometimes so claimed, Edward Carpenter likewise, but not Berkman (see, for example, the Wikipedia entry on 'Socialism and LGBT Rights'). The reason for this silence, I suggest, is that what constitutes anarcho-queer and/or is seen as being of political/sexual interest has become, in the late twentieth and early twenty-first centuries, focussed on *sex acts* as constitutive of identity.

In concert with Peter Lamborne Wilson (otherwise known as Hakim Bey), who calls for 'an explosive reaffirmation of the polymorphic eros' (Bey 1991

[1985]: 63), contemporary anarchist activist writings on sexuality frequently emphasise sexual *performance* as liberatory. 'Don't get mad, get even, lube it up and burn the straight world down!' sloganise the creatively named anarcho-queer 'Anti-capitalist Ass Pirates' of Montreal on their website. Whilst Andy 'Sunfrog' Smith, writing in the anarcho-primitivist paper *Fifth Estate*, produced out of Detroit, argues for a 'principled promiscuity' encompassing 'erotic affinity groups, orgies or safer sex play parties, one-night stands, flings, affairs, and festive flirtations' (Smith 2000/1). He also, incidentally, quotes Emma Goldman's essay 'Marriage and Love' in the service of his twenty-first-century take on 'free love'.

Critiques of the commodification of gay culture notwithstanding, anarcho-queer concern with celebrating the pan-sexual orgiastic does risk sharing an unintentional complicity with the hyper-sexualised spectacle of the market. Western late capitalism enjoins us to be sexual, to be pneumatic high-performance 'fuckers' continuously enacting the work of a sexualised imperative to consume and to market ourselves as sexual commodities. We know this. Our commodity-based economy sells us anti-wrinkle cream, books on multiple orgasms, Viagra, speed-dating, pole-dancing-as-female-empowerment, cosmetic surgery (for both sexes), Belle du Jour and ubiquitous porn. The commodification of the sexual has been commented upon many times since the Situationists and Second Wave Feminism. Anarcho-queer elevations of polymorphous and polyamorous sexual activity to the status of a necessary continuous performance of the revolution risk becoming an extension of what Virginia Blum calls 'consumer-object relations' (Blum 2002).

A text produced by a working group coming out of Queeruption Berlin, 'Queer Is Hip, Queer Is Cool – Dogma in the Queer Scene', invites comment on some of the issues surrounding this hyper-sexualisation of anarcho-queer cultures:

> Queeruption and other queer spaces are characterised by an excessive sexual atmosphere and close bodily contact. People who don't fit in are either excluded or, worse, forced to participate against their will. It seems that the subject of physical boundaries is discussed only superficially. People have been pestered, or subjected to physical contact against their will. There has been sexual harassment, people have been groped, in order to find out what they have in the way of genitals, and other similar assaults have occurred.
>
> (Queeruption Berlin 2003)

In light of these questions, I propose that we rethink our readings of Alexander Berkman's *Prison Memoirs of an Anarchist* for the twenty-first century. This consciously political piece of writing on sexuality and intimacy from the anarchist 'first wave' has been neglected as such by subsequent waves of activism because of its indeterminacy. There are no autobiographical sex acts. There is no definable queer identity, if we judge queer by its contemporaneous, internally hegemonic tendency towards sexual performance. Let us now, therefore, reconsider the political significance of indeterminacy. Can this historical anarchist text assist a contemporary anarchist politics to respond to the challenge not to simply, albeit with alternative window dressing, reproduce the hyper-sexualisation of the market?

Consensual sexual practices which challenge ruling categories and structures of control, sex-positive anarcho-queer performances like the work of Ron Athey and anarcho-sexual spaces such as Club Wotever can, I believe, have continuing radical potential. But so, perhaps even more urgently at this juncture in the West, does the re-remembrance and revaluation of intimacies without definitive sexual aims or definitions – passionate friendships, affectionate touch between those who are neither family nor lovers, acts divorced from erotic conclusions. These traces in history are *not* simply embryonic forms of queer sex before gay liberation (although to strategically read them as such has had political value). They are part of the complexity and the potential of networked human interactions. Not grounded in fucking but in feeling, such intimacies cross the boundary between straight and queer.

Some earlier feminist scholars of same-sex desire emphasised the significance of emotional intimacy in a spectrum of same-sex relations across history. Lillian Faderman's book *Surpassing the Love of Men* (1980) remains one of the most famous texts in this vein, not to mention the poet Adrienne Rich's concept of the *lesbian continuum* which she envisaged as 'includ[ing] a range – through each woman's life and throughout history – of woman-identified experience; not simply the fact that a woman has had or consciously desired genital sexual experience with another woman ... [but also] ... the sharing of a rich inner life ... the giving and receiving of practical and political support ... etc.' (Rich 1980). These approaches were subjected to critique during the decade of the so-called 'Feminist (Lesbian) Sex Wars' that took place in Britain and the United States during the 1980s. Rich and others were called to account both for their trans-historicism and their (stereotyped) association of female sexuality with cuddles rather than the clitoris (see Ferguson 1981, for example). It is well known that the heated political and theoretical disagreements between 'anti-porn' feminists such as Andrea Dworkin and Catherine McKinnon and 'pro-sex' feminists such as Carole Vance and Pat(rick) Califia led to Gayle Rubin's foundational call, in her essay *Thinking Sex*, for 'a radical theory of sex' (Rubin 1993 [1984]: 9) divorced from feminism – for 'an autonomous theory and politics specific to sexuality' (ibid.: 34). That essay contributed to the momentum in the academy that led to the development of queer theory. In the 1990s, in Britain and the United States, queer theory and queer politics achieved a high profile, upholding a rainbow coalition of 'non-normative' sex practices and identifications, grounded initially, and importantly, in anti-essentialism and AIDS activism. Queer raised the profile of sex-positivity in an era of backlash fuelled by virulent HIV-related homophobia. It recognised and promoted solidarity with transgendered and bisexual communities, creating the banner 'LGBT', under which most non-straight sexual minority-related public organisations now function, from student union groups to the Metropolitan Police.

However, the decades of the sex wars and of AIDS as 'gay plague' are now behind us. This, in the West, is a decade of increasing 'integration' in which same-sex sex is becoming almost as publicly commodified as straight sex, from gay weddings to lesbian sex toys. We need to ask how useful, in this new century, contemporary anarcho-queer strategies are, as significant revolutionary cultural forces (outside, that is, their own sub-cultural frames of reference) for thinking about liberation and intimacy. Critiques of monogamy, assimilation and a pink pound-fuelled gay-oriented consumer culture are certainly pertinent. But 'radical sex' and temporary autonomous zones are not, I think, sufficient answers. Without doubt someone like the now deceased BDSM activist and cystic fibrosis sufferer Bob Flannigan was, in performing his ethical, bodily erotic practices as living 'teach-in' art, a revolutionary. And such 'life's work' at the margins of culture, as Jonathan Dollimore and others have so convincingly argued, does significantly affect the centre (Dollimore 1991). But, as the centre moves, to stay challenging so too must the margins.

Secular Western subjects are increasingly sold a narrative that they are 'free' to have sex how, when, where and with whom they choose. But as sex and sexual attractiveness are profoundly commodified, and therefore profitable, so it takes personalised commercial 'work' to perform them. They become the only conduit through which, as adults, we are permitted to experience non-familial passionate intimacy (with the boundaried exception of the arena of sport). This injunction to express passion only through sex leads, arguably, to an impoverished range of affect. Conservatism may lament the profligate promiscuity of our era, but it is above all, as Jean Baudrillard taught us, a promiscuity of the image. Most ten-year-olds in Britain today receive initiation into sexuality by learning what sex is via online porn and Bluetooth – pneumatic, fantastic, plastic, (male) orgasm-oriented commercial sex as signifying of intimate relations for the next generation. A critique of such a state of affairs should not be left to 'family values' traditionalists. If pornography is not an evil to be suppressed (supposing even that this were practicable), neither is it a cultural terrain to be abandoned to *laissez faire* capitalism. It continues to encode powerful messages about gender, the body, sexuality, sexual relations and intimacy. Our present level of saturation means that sexual liberation, as a surfeit of 'sex-positive' sexual signs and practices, quite simply is no longer a radical message.

In tandem with what Brian McNair has called the 'pornocratisation' of culture (McNair 1996), whereby the sexual increasingly permeates the entire media sphere, from late evening 'sexed-up' versions of popular television soaps to mobile phone downloads, an accompanying new social conservatism in the public sphere is, one could argue, likewise attempting to process all non-kin intimacies through the field of the sexual. Lesbian and gay assimilationist agendas, understandably seeking acceptance, have joined these forces in promoting sexually pair-bonded monogamy as *the* form of intimate expression that should receive powerful social sanction over and above all others. And so, monogamous partnership (gay or straight) as the expected culmination-for-living, together with an anatomical smorgasbord of always on-tap variegated sexual imagery, constitutes a powerful contemporary erotogenic regulation of intimacy. This has resulted in a society where sex is everywhere and nowhere. One must be extravagantly, openly, endlessly and skilfully sexual, and yet ultimately seek to preserve and perform this within a closed duality. Late capitalism enjoins the perpetual commodity-spectacle of sex. The public sphere purports to sanction this erotic treadmill if it occurs (by adulthood) decorously in economically interdependent units of two. Such units, as Engels taught us long ago, are designed to reproduce the labour force, and, one might add, to minimise the time necessary for 'personal life', both of which serve the interests of capital (Engels 2010 [1884]). Each trajectory, towards a pneumatic sex consumer machine, but one ultimately coupled, produces an erotic landscape wherein all non-kin love, all touch which falls outside these permitted expressive arenas, becomes subjected to intense scrutiny, constraint and speculation – both internally within each subject and externally. Witness the longstanding media speculation around Oprah Winfrey's intimate friendship with Gayle King, a connection that seems to both threaten and fascinate, as it appears impossible to categorise within permitted terms of reference. The two of them have spoken of their connection as love, but have said they are not in a sexual relationship. 'BFFs' ('best friends forever') are not supposed to want to choose to live with one another over and above their menfolk, unless they are 'actually' lesbians, and so the column inches continue in their quest to 'nail' Oprah and Gayle.

In such a climate, the celebration of polyamorous polymorphously perverse fucking, although not strategically defunct, cannot stand alone as radical critique. In many ways it mirrors, and is implicated in, the contemporary festival of sexual consumption and display that places sexual activity at the centre of personhood today and frequently shames those who are not sexually active (for whatever reason) into silence as *less self-actualised*. Montreal's *Les Panthères Roses* write, in 'The Pink Panthers Agenda' (2002), that their mission is 'bolstering the radical movement by adding a more visible and less inhibited queer element. We've got to be just as multi-sexual as we are multilingual'. Liz Highleyman, San Francisco anarcha-feminist, says something similar in her essay 'Radical Queers or Queer Radicals' (2002): 'Radical queers have succeeded in harnessing erotic/sexual energy to enliven their activism in a unique way.' As a solidarity-building mechanism for political activist queers, such spaces and sentiments can be powerful. But are we failing to notice that anarcho-queer identity, foundationally grounded in sexual activity, is, in some ways, a mirror of a mainstream in which sexual performance and consumption become the 'truth' of identity?

Ask yourself, is it easier for most ordinary Britons in their thirties to pick up a stranger in a bar, gay or straight, or to hold a friend's hand (any gender combination) and walk down the street? Which one breaks the boundary taboo? Friend handholding, without that gesture of intimacy signifying a sexual 'move' (or a perceived threat of one by sexual partners) or, to onlookers, a sexual identity or a sexual relationship, seems constrained and evokes internal discomfort, at least in British and North American culture (the situation is quite different in other parts of the world). Of course, the need to take gender and sexuality into account in any analysis remains; same-sex adult handholding carries the added anxiety of attracting potential homophobia. But, in queer and anarcho-queer sub-cultural spaces, have handholding taboos really been unmade? Who is holding hands with whom may be more varied, but the spectre of the sex imperative (who is, and who ought to be, 'doing it' with whom) haunts, as Queeruption Berlin's communiqué identified, the gestural liberation of intimacy.

I propose that it is now time to return, within Western queer, anarcho-queer and anarchist political and scholarly contexts, to considerations of intimacy. I am not advocating anything like a simplistic 'return to the lesbian continuum'. Rather, I am concerned with all (consensual) non-blood-kin passionate intimacies between people, historically and contemporaneously, which do not fit into categories defined by sex acts. Is flirting not a form of experience and communication in its own right? Why should emotionally significant deep attachments where those concerned choose not share bodily fluids be deemed less socially significant than fluid-bonded states? Certainly there is a need for historicity in this re-examination of intimacy. The grey zone between friendship, passion, sex and sexual love can and does metamorphose across time, space and *habitus*. Neither is such a call to 'consider intimacy' intended to (re-) invisibilise sex, particularly sex which has a history of denial and taboo. There are still laws against homosexuality, carrying in many cases penalties of imprisonment or death, on the statute books of over seventy countries worldwide. The recent sentencing of Malawians Steven Monjeza and Tiwonge Chimbalanga to fourteen years in prison for taking part in a commitment ceremony attests to that.[5] And even in nation-states where this is not the case, explicit representations of same-sex sex are undoubtedly still contested. Witness the fact that the groundbreaking UK/US drama *Queer as Folk* (1999–2005) has not been purchased or permitted screen time in a number of European countries for 'moral' reasons, for example in Poland and Greece, where the show was pulled from the Star Channel after the screening of season one of the US version invited significant protest. Moreover, let us not forget that the expression of autonomous female sexuality as a part of public culture and discourse remains, in many parts of the world, unthinkable.

This important global picture notwithstanding, in our Western marketised hyper-sexualised culture, in which, according to Zygmunt Bauman, a transitory 'liquid love' assumes a consumer sensibility (Bauman 2003), the re-reading of uncategorisable intimacy can, I suggest, reinspire us to practise a liberation of human relations which does not confine all closeness to concupiscence. Sleeping beside someone which does not assume sex, running your fingers over the arm of a person you have just met without having to categorise that erotic gesture as 'only foreplay' with an expectation of 'progression', sitting with your arms around someone non-familial which does not mean seduction; acts of tenderness, gestures that cross and recross, belonging simply neither to friendship nor to orgasmic desire, at once possible between intimates and between strangers. How many of us wish for these intimacies and fear to have them, because they breach current cultural codes that mark all such interactions with the seal of the performatively erotic? In this world of the everyday everywhere sexual spectacle, are we not in danger of being constrained by the imperative to *be* sexual, as surely as pre-1960s' generations were by the imperative to be sexually continent?

Struggles for sexual liberation are by no means over, neither in the West nor in the Majority World, on many fronts. But because the market now so aggressively sells to us in the West sexual liberation as individualised non-stop self-gratification, perhaps we need to refocus on the terrain of the intimate – to re-create space for the indeterminate, for forms of passionate and affectionate connection that do not necessarily translate into sexualities or sex acts. History can help us do that; by reading the past in context, with its many different sex/friendship/intimacy codes, its otherness of borders and boundaries, we may be inspired to challenge the sex/capital machine which in our own time seeks to turn a profit by sexualising all physicality, all passion. This does not, and should not, signal a retreat from struggles for sex-positivity, rather a recognition that streaming sex acts on broadband and MTV by no means necessarily equates with sex-positivity. Quantity is not quality. Many LGBT activists and narrators have conceptualised the borderland between intimacy and desire as a terrain to be liberated, the frontier between the closet and a state of 'out-ness', between physical longing and its actualisation.[6] However, to see the borderland *only* in such terms impoverishes our understandings of intimacy.

It is true that one can find recent spaces where the boundaries of non-sexual intimacy have been extended without sex-negativity; 1990s 'rave culture' was one such space, briefly revolutionary, where strangers and friends would massage one another's shoulders or heads whilst 'rushing' and hugging ecstatically, lost in touch and connection. But it was an escapist space fuelled by drugs (specifically MDMA), and there was no accompanying articulated *politics* of intimacy. We should be speaking about reinventing intimacy in the world out there, not simply in the anarchist ghetto, because intimacy *connects* people to one another, it forges networks, and in a sea of image-sex we are an increasingly lonely culture. A lonely society is a more controllable society. Networks of people are better than units of people at resisting and creating.

So, to return to the anarchist who was the subject of our first pages, Alexander Berkman was not interested in speaking only to anarchists. Indeed, for him, as for Goldman, the very idea of anarchism not being a revolutionary force with something to say to ordinary people was anathema. Challenging sexualised commodity culture in ways that neither simply end up mirroring it nor return to the puritanical (encompassing the particular control of women and LGBTQI people) is a broad and urgent social issue. Sexual bullying in schools has increased dramatically in the past twenty years, and so have fundamentalist forms of religion (and there is a lot to say on the need for a renewed gender politics here). We are a culture caught between sex–violence–spectacle, for example the murder of prostitutes in *Grand Theft Auto* for points in the game, and the resurgence of religious narratives of continence – witness Stephanie Meyer's wildly popular *Twilight* series, with its 'erotics of abstinence'[7] before monogamous marriage. We need another way.

Let us now re-remember Alexander Berkman, as an anarchist who had something important to say about intimacy and sexuality. Let us remobilise Berkman's contribution. He was an anarchist who championed same-sex intimacy through the experience of his own passion. Yet he did not accord sex a significance over and above other physical and emotional expressions as the *only* 'truth' of passion. He made a political commitment whilst inhabiting the borderland. In resisting the current totalising commodification of sex, and its perpetual, impossibly perfectible, cash-cow copulating machinery, let us, in re-remembering what Alexander Berkman had to say about desire, rediscover the borderland.

Notes

1 Berkman and Goldman's relationship, first as youthful lovers experimenting with 'free love', then as lifelong friends and political soulmates, is a fascinating one, well documented in Goldman's autobiography.
2 To adapt somewhat the Kate Sharpley Anarchist Library's (1999) 'The Fight for History: A Manifesto', which says that 'historical memory is a theatre of the class struggle'.
3 See http://vids.myspace.com/index.cfm?fuseaction=vids.individual&videoid=5485027 (accessed 30 June 2010).
4 In fact in a pamphlet, Thaumazo, a critic of left politics, wrote a short treatise devoted to excoriating Berkman's autobiography.
5 The pair have now been pardoned thanks to an international outcry, but are not able to live a life together without fear of lynching. Interestingly, the website www.questioningtransphobia.wordpress.com reports that Tiwonge identifies as 'a woman inside' but notes that the pair have been discussed almost exclusively within a Western framing as a 'gay couple'.
6 For example the 'coming out' film, which depicts young intense same-sex friendship as a step on the journey towards an adult out gay identity, e.g. Marco Kreuzpainter's *Summer Storm* (2004) and Hettie MacDonald's *Beautiful Thing* (1996).
7 See Grossman Lev, 'Stephanie Meyer: A New J. K. Rowling', *Time Magazine*, 24 April 2008.

References

Adams, J. (2002) 'Non-Western Anarchisms: Rethinking the Global'. Online. Available HTTP: context.http://www.infoshop.org/texts/nonwestern.pdf (accessed 27 October 2006).

Althusser, L. (2006 [1970]) 'Ideology and Ideological State Apparatuses', John Storey (ed.), *Cultural Theory and Popular Culture: A Reader*, 3rd edn, Edinburgh: Pearson Education Ltd.

Anarcha.org (2006) The 'Sex and Sexuality' pages. Online. Available HTTP: http://www.anarcha.org/sallydarity/health.php (accessed 1 June 2010).

Anderberg, K. (2001) 'Zine Review: A Practical Guide to Prisoner Support'. Online. Available HTTP: http://www.phoenixanarchist.org/modules.php?op=modload&name=News&file=article&sid=411 (accessed 15 October 2008).

Bauman, Z. (2003) *Liquid Love: On the Frailty of Human Bonds*, Cambridge: Polity Press.

Berkman, A. (1970 [1912]) *Prison Memoirs of an Anarchist*, Pittsburg: Frontier Press.

——(1995) *The ABC of Anarchism*, London: Freedom Press.

Bey, H. (1991 [1985]) *TAZ: The Temporary Autonomous Zone, Ontological Anarchy, Poetic Terrorism*, New York: Autonomedia.

Blum, V. (2002) 'The Liberation of Intimacy: Consumer–Object Relations and [Hetero] Patriarchy', *Antipode* 34(5): 845–63.

Bray, A. (1982) *Homosexuality in Renaissance England*, London: Gay Men's Press.

Butler, J. (1993) *Bodies that Matter: On the Discursive Limits of 'Sex'*, London/New York: Routledge.

Cohen, C. J. (2001) 'Punks, Bulldaggers and Welfare Queens – The Radical Potential of Queer Politics?', in Mark Blasius (ed.), *Sexual Identities: Queer Politics*, Princeton, NJ: Princeton University Press.

Davitt, M. (1885) *Leaves from a Prison Diary*, London: Chapman & Hall.

Dollimore, J. (1991) *Sexual Dissidence: Augustine to Wilde, Freud to Foucault*, Oxford: Oxford Press.

Engels, F. (2010 [1884]) *The Origin of the Family, Private Property and the State*, London: Penguin Classics.

Faderman, L. (1980) *Surpassing the Love of Men: Romantic Love and Friendship between Women from the Renaissance to the Present*, London: Junction Books.

Falk, C. (1990 [1984]) *Love, Anarchy and Emma Goldman*, rev. edn, New Brunswick, NJ: Rutgers University Press.

——(curator) (2010) *The Emma Goldman Papers*. Online. Available HTTP: http://sunsite.berkeley.edu/Goldman/ (accessed 1 June 2010).

Fellner, J. (ed.) (2005) *Life of an Anarchist: The Alexander Berkman Reader*, New York/London: Seven Stories Press.

Ferguson, A. (1981) 'Patriarchy, Sexual Identity and the Sexual Revolution', *Signs: Journal of Women in Culture and Society* 7(1): 158–72.

Fishman, J. F. (1935) *Sex in Prison*, London: John Lane.

Foucault, M. (1978 [1976]) *The History of Sexuality*, vol. I: *An Introduction*, London: Penguin Books.

Frankel, O. (1996) 'Whatever Happened to "Red Emma"? Emma Goldman, from Alien Rebel to American Icon', *Journal of American History* 83(3): 903–42.

Goldman, E. (1988 [1931]) *Living My Life*, vols I and II, London: Pluto Press. Online. Available HTTP: http://dwardmac.pitzer.edu/Anarchist_Archives/goldman/living/livingtoc.html (accessed 28 July 2010).

Highleyman, L. (2002) 'Radical Queers or Queer Radicals? Queer Activism and the Global Justice Movement'. Online. Available HTTP: http://www.lespantheresroses.org/textes/radical_queers_or_queer_radicals.html (accessed 1 June 2010).

infoshop.org (2010) 'Alexander Berkman'. Online. Available HTTP: http://wiki.infoshop.org/Alexander_Berkman (accessed 30 June 2010).

Kate Sharpley Library (1999) 'The Fight for History: A Manifesto', *KSL: Bulletin of the Kate Sharpley Library* 20, October. Online. Available HTTP: http://www.katesharpleylibrary.net/wm38sh (accessed 28 July 2010).

Katz, J. N. (1978) *Gay American History: A Documentary; Lesbians and Gay Men in the U.S.A.*, New York: Avon.

Kissack, T. (2008) *Free Comrades: Anarchism and Sexuality in the United States 1895–1917*, Edinburgh: AK Press.

Lao Tzu (1997) *Tao Te Ching: A Book about the Way and the Power of the Way* (trans. U. K. Le Guin with J. P. Seaton), Boston, MA: Shambhala.

Limpfist (n.d.) 'Toronto'. Online. Available HTTP: http://www.tao.ca/~limpfist/ (accessed 1 June 2010).

McNair, B. (1996) *Mediated Sex: Pornography and Postmodern Culture*, London and New York: Arnold.

Marso, L. J. (2003) 'A Feminist Search for Love: Emma Goldman on the Politics of Marriage, Love, Sexuality and the Feminine', *Feminist Studies* 4(3): 305–20.

Millett, S. (1997) 'Review of *Anarchist Studies* 2.2 and 3.1', *Democracy & Nature* 4(1). Online. Available HTTP: http://www.democracynature.org/dn/vol4/millett_anarchist.htm (accessed 26 October 2006).

Les Panthères Roses Montreal Chapter (2002) 'The Pink Panthers Agenda'. Online. Available HTTP: http://www.lespantheresroses.org/textes/pinkpanthers_manifesto.htm (accessed 1 June 2010).

Propos, A. (n.d.) 'To the Daring Belongs the Future: The Anarcha Feminist Movement'. Online. Available HTTP: http://a4a.mahost.org/anna.html (accessed 31 January 2006).

Queeruption (2010). Online. Available HTTP: www.queeruption.org (accessed 1 June 2010).

Queeruption Berlin (2003) 'Queer Is Hip, Queer Is Cool – Dogmas in the Queer Scene'. Online. Available HTTP: http://www.queeruption.org/queeriship.htm (accessed 2 July 2007).

Rich, A. (1980) 'Compulsory Heterosexuality and Lesbian Existence'. Online. Available HTTP: http://www.terry.uga.edu/~dawndba/4500compulsoryhet.htm (accessed 01 July 2007).

Rollins, J. and Hirsch, H. N. (2003) 'Sexual Identities and Political Engagements: A Queer Survey', *Social Politics* 10(3): 290–313.

Rubin, G. (1993 [1984]) 'Thinking Sex: Notes for a Radical Theory of the Politics of Sexuality', in H. Abelove, M. A. Barale and D. M. Halperin (eds), *The Lesbian and Gay Studies Reader*, London/New York: Routledge.

Sedgwick, E. K. (1994) *Tendencies*, London: Routledge.

Smith, A. ('Sunfrog') (2000/1) 'Group Sex: Communal Ethics of Eroticism, Free Love and the Extended Family', *Fifth Estate* 35(2); reproduced in *Alternative Press Review* (2001) 6(1). Online. Available HTTP: http://www.altpr.org/apr14/group_sex.html (accessed 31 October 2006).

Spartacus Educational (2010) Online. Available HTTP: http://www.spartacus.schoolnet.co.uk/USAberkman.htm (accessed 30 June 2010).

Thaumazo, F. (1912) *The Martyrdom of Berkman*, unknown binding. Online. Available HTTP: http://dwardmac.pitzer.edu/Anarchist_Archives/bright/berkman/martyrdom/martyrdom.html (accessed 1 February 2007).

Ward, D. (curator) (2010) *The Anarchy Archives*. Online. Available HTTP: http://dwardmac.pitzer.edu/Anarchist_Archives/aboutus.html (accessed 1 June 2010).
Weeks, J. (1989 [1981]) *Sex, Politics and Society*, 2nd edn, Edinburgh: Addison, Wesley, Longman Ltd.
Wexler, A. (1986) *Emma Goldman in America*, Boston, MA: Beacon Press.

Chapter 3

Nobody knows what an insurgent body can do

Questions for affective resistance

Stevphen Shukaitis

> From a multitude of revolts, miniscule or general, intrinsic to all that exists, through a passionate struggle, an inexpiable affective combat in which one risks death, libertarian action attempts first of all to select and liberate new forces within situations and beings and in the interstices of the existing order. It attempts to create a common and emancipatory plane of existence, able to traverse the totality of present worlds and realities, and to recompose the totality of that which exists.
>
> (Colson 2001: 241)

Baruch Spinoza once said that no one knew what a body could do, what it was capable of, when not determined by the mind. In saying this he was rejecting the idea that the body and mind, reason and emotion, are separate. For Spinoza, far from their being separate, it was only by understanding the nature of bodies and motions, bodies and their emotions, that one could understand the potential created when they interacted. Unfortunately, this unified approach to understanding emotions and creative potential was lost and forgotten for much of the past several hundred years, to be rediscovered in the most recent forty years by thinkers such as Antonio Negri, Gilles Deleuze, Genevieve Lloyd, Etienne Balibar, Daniel Colson, as well as many others. What can anarchist politics and theorizing learn from these developments. What is it that an insurgent body can do?

To foreground questions of our individual and collective capacities to affect and be affected by the world around us means that questions and concerns about personal relations and caring for each other are not insignificant concerns that can be brushed aside to tackle whatever is the pressing demand of the day. As famously observed by Gustav Landauer, 'the State is a condition, a certain relationship between human beings, a mode of human behaviour; we destroy it by contracting other relationships, by behaving differently' (Landauer 1973: 226). Politics is not external to the relationships and interactions we have – it grows out of, is intensified by, and ties them together. Affect, developed through interaction and care, exists as expansive and creative powers: 'it is a power of freedom, ontological opening, and omnilateral diffusion ... [that]

constructs value from below' and transforms according to the rhythm of what is common (Negri 1999: 86).

Surely the path to creating a better, joyous, freer, more loving world is not one that is premised upon a constant struggle that leaves one tired and run down. The question is one of creating communities of resistance that provide support and strength, a density of relations and affections, through all aspects of our lives, so that we can carry on and support each other in our work rather than having to withdraw from that which we love to do in order to sustain the capacity to do those very things. This is to create a sustainable culture of resistance, a flowering of what I am calling affective resistance – that is, a sustainable basis for ongoing and continuing political organizing, a plateau of vibrating intensities, premised upon refusing to separate questions of the effectiveness of any tactic, idea or campaign, from its affectiveness.

The simple gestures, even sometimes ones that seem insignificant, are often the ones that mean the most in creating affective community. Not that they are glorious tasks by any means – asking how someone is doing, taking an extra five minutes to work out what's bothering someone or why they're preoccupied – but because of this it is easy to overlook how important they really are. They form the basis underlying our ongoing interactions, lodged within the workings of our affective memory. Immersed within the constant and ever-renewing nourishment contained within the gift economies of language, motions and affections, all too often we fail to appreciate the ongoing work of social reproduction and maintaining community that these acts entail.

Creating a vibrant political culture, one that exists 'beyond duty and joy', to borrow the phrasing of the Curious George Brigade (2003: 33–40), is not an easy task. Indeed, as our very joys, subjectivities, experiences and desires are brought further and further into the heart of the production process, creating autonomous spaces based upon their realization becomes all the more tricky. Fortunately some people have begun to explore and find ways to cope with and overcome the traumatic stress and tensions that can build up as a part of organizing. But what about the less spectacular or obvious forms, the damage of the everyday? What happens as all the constantly mounting and renewing demands on our very being, our capacity to exist and continue to participate in radical politics, build up? We find ourselves in ever more cramped positions, unsure of how to work from the conditions we find ourselves in. Do we carry on as we can, slowly burning out and finally withdrawing from ongoing struggles, perhaps consigning them to some part of our former youth that had to be left behind to deal with other things? Might there not be other options and paths to take?

Affective resistance starts from the realization that one can ultimately never separate questions of the *effectiveness* of political organizing from concerns about its *affectiveness*. They are inherently and inevitably intertwined. The social relations we create every day prefigure the world to come, not just in a metaphorical sense, but also quite literally: they truly are the emergence of that other world embodied in the constant motion and interaction of bodies – the becoming-tomorrow of the already-here and now. And thus the collective practices of relating, of composing communities and collectives, exists where 'the interplay of the care of the self ... blends into pre-existing relations, giving them a new coloration and greater warmth. The care of the self – or the attention that one devotes to the care that others should take of themselves – appears then as an intensification of social relations' (Foucault 1984: 53). And so it is from considering the varying affective compositions and dynamics that affective resistance begins. It is the unfolding map that locates what Precarias a la Deriva have described as affective virtuosity, where

> what escapes the code situates us in that which is not yet said, opens the terrain of the thinkable and livable, it is that which creates relationships. We have to necessarily take into account this affective component in order to unravel the politically radical character of care, because we know – this time without a doubt – that the affective is the effective.
>
> (Precarias a la Deriva 2006: 40)

Autonomous feminism and affective revolt

> Strike or unemployment, a woman's work is never done.
>
> (Dalla Costa and James 1972: 30)

To find inspiration and some kernels of wisdom for teasing out a basis to expand the concept of affective resistance, perhaps one could turn to the experiences and knowledges in the history of autonomous feminism,[1] from the writings of figures such as Mariarosa Dalla Costa and Silvia Federici to campaigns like Wages for Housework and the more recent organizing of groups like Precarias a la Deriva. Their efforts come from experiences where the very basis of their being, the capacity of their bodies to care and relate are directly involved in necessary functions for the reproduction and continued existence of capitalism; involved in necessary social reproduction, but in ways that for a long time have been unacknowledged by large segments of the so-called progressive and revolutionary political milieu. From this necessary but unacknowledged position one can learn from their insights into organizing to find routes and passages toward more affective forms of resistance.

Despite the importance that autonomist feminism has played in the development of autonomous politics and struggles it is commonly relegated to little more than a glorious footnote of figures emerging out of autonomist thought (Katsiaficas 2001). Strangely enough, because housework, caring labour and many other forms of social labour were not directly waged, it was often assumed that they simply took place outside the workings of capitalism, as if they existed in some sort of pre-capitalist status that had mysteriously managed to persist into the present. Organizing around gender, affective labour and issues of reproduction posed numerous important questions to forms of class struggle that focused exclusively on the figure of the waged industrial worker (Hardt 1999). The revolts of housewives, students, the unwaged and farm workers led to a rethinking of notions of labour, the boundaries of the workplace and effective strategies for class struggles: they enacted a critical transformation in the social imaginary of labour organizing and struggle. Because the labour of social reproduction and unwaged work was not considered work, was not considered to produce surplus value or to be of relevance for capitalism, it was often ignored and overlooked as an arena of social struggle. Relegated to an adjunct status compared to what was held as a/the real focus of power, economic power and class struggle, it was assumed that these sorts of concerns would be worked out after capitalism had been overthrown. But, as argued by Alisa Del Re (1996), there is a great importance in learning from and taking seriously the concerns put forth by autonomous feminism, precisely because attempting to refuse and reduce forms of imposed labour and exploitation without addressing the realms of social reproduction and housework amounts to building a notion of utopia upon the continued exploitation of female work.

Autonomous feminism, by exhorting that this simply was not going to stand any more – that it was ridiculous to be expected to constantly care for and attend to the tasks of social reproduction, from childcare to caring for parents to housework, all the while being told that what one was engaged in was *not work at all*[2] – shattered the ossified and rigid structures of the narrowly and dogmatically class-oriented radical imagination. As observed by Elisabetta Rasy, feminism is not external to politics, neither is it necessarily part of class struggle in an already determined manner; rather it is a movement within these various groupings, a movement creating conditions for the emergence of other subjects and experience to finally be acknowledged and learned from:

> feminism opens up a magnetic crack in the categoric universe of the male-Marxist vision of the world, painfully exhibiting a history of ghosts behind the slippery façade of facts and certainties. The absolute materiality of the ghosts who embody need and desire stand in contrast and opposition to the phobic philologies of the existent and the existed.
>
> (Rasy 1991 [1978]: 78)

Organizing around issues such as legalizing and creating access to abortion, divorce, contraception, sexuality, violence against women, while not reducible or contained within the framework of class struggle, embodies a challenge to forms of class-based social domination as it exists through the ability to control and restrict possibilities for social reproduction.

This shattering of the previously hermetically sealed dead-end of the radical imagination opened up a long-needed avenue for contesting and confronting forms of domination in all aspects of capitalist society (Shukaitis 2009). As argued by Leopoldina Fortunati, while it may have appeared that the processes of production and reproduction operated as separate spheres governed by different laws and principles, almost as if their relation was a 'mirror image, a back-to-front photograph of production', their difference was not a question about whether value was produced, but rather one of how the production of value in social reproduction '*is* the creation of value but *appears otherwise*' (Fortunati 1995 [1981]: 8). This is directly contrary to claims that housework and forms of domestic labour produced use values and thus were not involved in the production of value for capitalism.[3] In other words, by only focusing only certain forms of social labour and the exploitation involved in them (which was considered the basis for an antagonistic political subjectivity capable of overthrowing capitalism), this analysis overlooked myriad forms of social power and exploitation that operated within fields of social production and reproduction that, because of their unwaged status, did not appear as such. And perhaps even more importantly, this blindness, a situation created by the obfuscation of the theoretical baggage, also blinded radicals to the possibilities for political action emanating from these positions. But, as long as housewives, or the unwaged, or the peasants, or other populations were excluded from the narrowly defined Marxist framework of analysis and politics, 'the class struggle at every moment and any point is impeded, frustrated, and unable to find full scope for its action' (Dalla Costa and James 1972: 35).

Wages for/against housework

> We want to call work what is work so that eventually we might rediscover what is love and create what will be our sexuality which we have never known.
>
> (Federici 1980: 258)

> Slavery to an assembly line is not a liberation from slavery to a kitchen sink.
>
> (Dalla Costa and James 1972: 35)

There has long existed a relation between the nature of social reproduction and women's forms of political self-organization.[4] But this relation is not specifically between women and the form of political organization as much as it is the influence of the resources and possibilities available for supporting social reproduction. Rather, because of their location within specific articulations of social roles and relations, it is more often women that are affected with a greater intensity by various forms of political domination and power that attack the basis of social reproduction. Just as the destruction of the commons was accompanied by the enclosure of the female body (Federici 2004) (which largely came to replace the role formerly played by the commons through countless hours of unacknowledged labour), neoliberal assaults from the 1970s until the present have targeted collective ownership as well as the meagre gains congealed in the form of welfare state programmes and the gains won by feminism.

Given the often-harsher effects that capitalism and the whole array of forms of social domination have on women, it really should not be of any great surprise that they would play important roles in struggling against these forms of domination. From the mothers' demand for 'bread and herring' that started the Russian revolution (Sorokin 1950), to the role of women in struggling against the International Monetary Fund and World Bank imposed structural adjustment programmes and austerity measures that accompany the disciplinary devices of international loan slavery, the importance of and roles played by women all too often get ignored or passed over because they do not fit into the form of what is generally recognized as political action. This makes the reluctance of much of the Left, from Marxist theoreticians to union organizers, to see the relevance of feminist organizing as a class issue all the more exasperating. It's one thing to be exploited constantly and seemingly throughout all moments of the day and spaces of one's life, but then it's another, even worse, condition to find that one's allies and comrades don't consider one's struggle against these conditions to be part of a common endeavour. In other words, women found themselves trapped in conditions not only with a 'double shift' of work in both the formal waged sense and in tasks of social reproduction, but also during what Ursula Huws has referred to as their 'third shift'. This is the third shift of labour that is necessary for the social reproduction of political organizing, whether union organizing or otherwise. Many such movements were replete with people who did not understand these multiple layers of labour or their difficulties, and treated organizing around them as 'reactionary' and 'divisive' (Huws 2003: 112). Or, as quipped by Silvia Federici, 'We are seen as nagging bitches, not workers in struggle' (Federici 1980: 255). Given that, feminist separatism is clearly a totally sensible response to 'comrades' that are often little more than condescending and patronizing allies.

Autonomous feminism is thus not just important in itself, but also in that it works as an important reopening of a sedimented imaginary of struggle. It is a cracking apart of an imaginary blinded by its own categories and presuppositions. By demanding that housework and caring work be recognized *as work*, that labour takes place not just in the physically bounded workplace but also exists all throughout the tasks of social reproduction and community life, autonomous feminism opened, and continues to open, a space for a reconsideration of many of the concepts and tactical baggage that had been held on to. 'Once we see the community as a productive centre and thus a centre of subversion, *the whole perspective for generalized struggle and revolutionary organization is re-opened*' (Dalla Costa and James 1972: 17). In other words, the personal is political, but it is also economic, as well as social and cultural. Struggles around issues of care and housework, of the tasks of the everyday, are not just individual concerns unrelated to broader political and economic questions – they are the quotidian manifestations of these larger processes. Recognition of their connections, as well as the connections against questionable power dynamics in the home, school, office, hospital and all spaces of social life, is an important step in socializing and connecting minor moments of rupture and rebellion into connected networks of struggle (Shukaitis 2008). As Dalla Costa and James argue, there is great importance in understanding the relation of domestic labour and its exploitation to struggles diffused throughout society precisely because '[e]very place of struggle outside the home, precisely because *every sphere of capitalist organization presupposes the home*, offers a chance for attack by women' (Dalla Costa and James 1972: 38). Organizing around domestic labour acted as a key point in the development of autonomous struggles because of its locations within intersecting dynamics of gender, race and class (Van Raaphorst 1988);[5] learning from these struggles is all the more important precisely because of the multiple constraints and difficulties women faced, and ways that they found to contest multiple forms of social power and domination.

One of the ways these demands would become embodied was in the various Wages for Housework campaigns. Originating initially in Italy and the UK, these campaigns, based on demanding recognition of the countless hours of unpaid work involved in typically female labour, quickly spread to many locations across the globe. Originating from struggles of women of the classical working class (such as demands around equal pay in the workplace), student groups, the New Left and various feminist organizations, the campaign used many of the concepts and framing of Marxist categories while at the same time attempting to move past the limitations of and assumptions about the 'true' revolutionary subject that often accompanied them. Admittedly the campaign and demand for remuneration for housework were controversial and received much criticism from both the right and the left.[6] In particular, it was argued that the campaign could have the effect of further consigning and limiting women to a domestic sphere, this time in a way that had been argued for through a feminist lens. Anna Ciaperoni makes this argument:

> It is insidious to try to re-establish – even through filters from feminist experience – a theoretical value for the age long confinement of women to domestic activities, though unconstrained, because how many women actually choose housework? In this way one risks erasing ten years of feminist struggle and practice, for the destruction of the ideological basis of female subordination.
>
> (Ciaperoni 1991 [1982]: 270)

Alternatively it was argued that the demand for wages represented a further commodification of yet another aspect of life and was harmful in that way. But what is most inspiring here, and most useful for rebuilding movements of affective resistance, is how these women found ways to formulate new demands from the ambivalent positions in which they found themselves. Working from within these constraints they formulated new modalities for political antagonism, finding ways to socialize and connect struggles based around the ways their capacities and very existence were exploited. This could be understood as Wages for Housework's function as a pole of class recomposition and route for the increasing of collective political capacity of struggle. In the words of Mariarosa Dalla Costa:

> The question is, therefore, to develop forms of struggle which do not leave the housewife peacefully at home, at most ready to take part in occasional demonstrations through the streets ... *The starting point is not how to do housework more efficiently, but how to find a place as protagonist in the struggle: that is, not a higher productivity of domestic labour but a higher subversiveness in the struggle.*
>
> (Dalla Costa and James 1972: 36)

The various Wages for Housework attempted to do just that: to find positions of higher subversiveness in struggle from which it was possible to organize against the isolation and misery that accompanied the miserable conditions of capitalist patriarchy.

In that sense the ultimate goal of such campaigns could be seen not as the demand of wages themselves, but rather as using the demand for wages to ferment and spread antagonisms against the structural systems of patriarchy and capitalist control that have long instituted and relied upon the unwaged and unacknowledged burden of women's labour. This was the source of much of the antipathy towards the campaigns, based on confusing the demand of wages for housework as object (from which it could be seen to keep women in the home, the commodification of caring labour, etc.) rather than as a perspective and catalyst of struggle and change. This confusion, argues Silvia Federici, separates a moment and temporary goal of the struggle from the dynamics of composition and the formation of collective capacities, and thus overlooks 'its significance in demystifying and subverting the role to which women have been confined in capitalist society' (Federici 1980: 253). The demand for wages for housework is not then an embracing of and struggle for waged status, but it is a moment in finding effective methods to struggle against the imposition of work and the dynamics of class power that exist under capitalism. That is, Wages for Housework is precisely the construction of a composition of social forces that makes it possible to struggle against the forms of housework, social roles and dynamics of exploitation that underpin them: 'To say that we want money for housework is the first step towards refusing to do it, because the demand for a wage makes work visible, which is the most indispensable condition to begin to struggle against it' (Federici 1980: 253). In other words, Wages for Housework is a moment in the struggle of wages *against* housework: a strategy of composing class power from the position that women have found themselves in, but precisely to escape from that position. In the words of Roberta Hunter-Hendersen,

> The essential task was to re-appropriate our own energy, intellectual, social and emotional, and it meant working together with patience as we unfolded our constricted limbs, began to stretch our oppressed kinds, and learnt again to interact with each other.
>
> (Hunter-Hendersen 1973: 41)

We've drifted a long way (or have you?)

> The oppression of women, after all, did not begin with capitalism. What began with capitalism was the more intense exploitation of women as women and the possibility at last of their liberation.
>
> (Dalla Costa and James 1972: 23)

Despite the amazing feminist upsurge that entered public visibility and consciousness during the 1960s and 1970s, many of the issues that inspired it continue to exist, even if there have been vast improvements in addressing some of them. Disparities in wages, gender discrimination, differences in power and violence against women continue to be major issues for almost the entire world to a greater or lesser degree. The neoliberal onslaught of the 1980s and ongoing dismantling of the welfare state in much of the industrialized west have also created difficult questions for many women. And, perhaps most depressing in some ways, large sections of the left, and even the 'radical left', continue to largely ignore issues around gendered labour and forms of organizing around them.

It is from this realization that Precarias a la Deriva, a feminist research and organizing collective which in many ways is one of the most notable inheritors of this strand of feminist politics, began. Precarias a la Deriva formed in Spain in 2002, starting out of a feminist social centre, La Eskalera Karakola, initially as a response to a call for a general strike. The problem is that a strike did not address the forms of labour that many of the women were involved in, namely forms of care work, invisibilized jobs and precarious work. For those involved in these forms of work, participation in the strike would be unlikely to have any positive effect on their circumstances and could very easily end with them losing their jobs altogether. In fact, a majority of people who were increasingly involved in such forms of work, which have come to be discussed under the concept of precarity, were not even that affected by the proposed changes in labour legislation that inspired the call for a strike because their social position was already so unstable.

The members of Precarias a la Deriva thus set out to find methods to investigate and understand the changing nature of work and social relations and to develop methods of generating conflict that would suit this changing terrain. The method they initially chose to work with was that of the dérive, which is drawn from the Situationists, who employed forms of wandering through the city while allowing themselves to be attracted to and repulsed by its features and thus hopefully to open up new spaces and experiences that would otherwise and usually be ignored or overlooked (Debord 1958). Precarias a la Deriva modified the concept of the dérive, which they argue in many ways was particularly marked by the social position of the bourgeois male subject who had nothing better to do. Instead they sought to update the dérive to drift through the circuits and spaces of feminized labour that constituted their everyday lives.[7] The drift was thus converted into a mobile interview, a wandering picket that sought out women who were involved in the many forms of precarious and caring labour, to find out how the conditions affected them, and how they might work from them. They decided to investigate five overall sectors and interconnected spaces: (1) domestic; (2) telemarketing; (3) manipulators of codes (translators, language teachers); (4) food service (bars, restaurants); (5) health care. Using this method, the mobile interview/picket was used

> to take the quotidian as a dimension of the political and as a source of resistances, privileging experience as an epistemological category. Experience, in this sense, is not a preanalytic category but a central notion in understanding the warp of daily events, and, what is more, the ways in which we give meaning to our localized and incarnated quotidian.
>
> (Precarias a la Deriva 2003b)

Precarias used this practice of drifting as a means to explore the 'intimate and paradoxical nature of feminized work', to wander through the different connections between the spaces of feminized labour, and to find ways to turn mobility and uncertainty into strategic points of intervention:

> to appropriate the communicative channels in order to talk about other things (and not just anything), modify semiotic production in strategic moments, make care and the invisible networks of mutual support into a lever for subverting dependence, practice 'the job well done' as something illicit and contrary to productivity.
>
> (Precarias a la Deriva 2003b)

They aim to use these forms of intervention to construct what they describe as points of aggregation which, borrowing from the Buenos Aires militant research group Colectivo Situaciones (with whom they have corresponded a great deal), will be constructed based not a notion of aggregation capacity (the construction of mass forms of organization) but rather on consistency capacity, or the ability to form intense and dense networks of relations (Colectivo Situaciones 2005).

The practice of the *dérive*, the drift, as wandering interview and as a form of militant research, was thus an important starting point (and continues to be an important practice) for Precarias because it operates, in their words, as a form of 'contagion and reflection' whose potentiality is not easily exhausted; it is '[a]n infinite method, given the intrinsic singularity of each route and its capacity to open and defamiliarize places' (Precarias a la Deriva 2003a). The shifting and transformation of everyday social relations and realities does not cease during the first phase of engaged research and intervention into a social space. Hence the need to continue to ask questions about how those spaces, and those living within them, are formed. As methods for visible political intervention transform the composition of a particular space, the relations within it also change. While militant research is often employed briefly to get a sense of the situation in which intervention will take place, after the initial inquiry the projects cease, and organizers continue to rely on their knowledge of the composition of social relations and realities without taking into account how they have changed. Precarias, by utilizing the openness and fluidity of the drift, of its capacity to defamiliarize one in an environment, emphasized the need to keep the inquiry open. The aim is to keep circulating and exchanging knowledges, often through the forms of workshops, gatherings, *encuentros* and publications, which are then fed back into other projects.

For Precarias in many ways find themselves, though they have drifted quite far to discover new methods of intervention, having to confront many of the same questions that faced feminist organizers in the 1970s, particularly those involved in campaigns such as Wages for Housework. While Precarias argue that 'care is not a domestic question but rather a public matter and generator of conflict', they are also quite aware of the difficulty in this task, for, as they observe, there is 'the question of how to generate conflict in environments which are invisible, fragile, private' (Precarias a la Deriva 2003a). This division between the political and the personal, the public and the private, has long been one of the dividing lines that feminists have confronted as a barrier to the raising of their concerns and demands without having them merely dismissed as *their* concerns and demands. One can see this dynamic, for instance, in the ways in which concerns about retreat from public life, the spectre of bowling alone, overlook the invisible networks of civic engagement embodied through forms of care which are at the same time forms of political involvement (Herd and Meyer 2002). This is the process whereby discussions around gender become understood as 'women's issues', rather than the construction of gender and social roles more broadly. Or the ways in which domestic labour and care, even in discussion of them within radical political circles, can become assigned and narrated as a feminist issue alone, rather than seeing the ways in which these forms of labour and interaction relate to and are enmeshed within the larger frameworks of power being contested. Critically involved in primary socialization, they are, perhaps, the primary tasks in keeping together a society.

Precarias' answer to this encompasses multiple parts of their overall project and centres to a large degree around questions of affect. Rather than treating issues of domestic labour, the role of empathy and the creation of relations, interaction, sexuality and forms of care as separate issues and concerns, they describe them as the communicative continuum sex–attention–care. This continuum connects the diverse sectors and areas of their investigations, along which they point out that sex, care and attention are not pre-existing objects but socially narrated and constructed ones. They are by no means naturally formed in a specified arrangement (although they are often *naturalized* as if this were the case), but rather are 'historically determined social stratifications of affect, traditionally assigned to women' (Precarias a la Deriva 2006). It is along this continuum that Precarias see the role of affect as being key, existing at the centre of the chain that

> connects places, circuits, families, populations, etc. These chains are producing phenomena and strategies as diverse as virtually arranged marriages, sex tourism, marriage as a means of passing along rights, the ethnification of sex and of care, the formation of multiple and transnational households.
> (Precarias a la Deriva 2003a)

This perspective of looking at the interconnections between forms of activity that have often been constructed as feminine is extremely important, especially in a period where the forms of activity described as such have become much more enmeshed and widespread across the functioning of the economy, from the 'service with a smile' or 'phone smile' of the McDonald's employee and telephone operator to the hypervisibility of the (female) body in media and advertising as a way to excite libidinal desires for the glories of consumption. And it has been argued that those involved in caring labour, who constitute an estimated 20 per cent of the workforce, tend to be more highly class conscious regardless of the gender of those involved (although notably there are higher percentages of women employed in such positions) (Jones 2001). Thus the question of affective resistance, attention to the dynamic of affective labour, becomes all the more pressing because those involved in such work contain a potentiality for rebuilding an inclusive revolutionary class politics at a moment when it may appear to have vanished from the realm of existing possibilities.

Arguably, the increasing rise of forms of human resource management, particularly those stressing the appreciation of diversity and cultural difference, as well as attention to issues of gender, are also part of the growing presence and importance of skills of communication and interaction extended through the social fabric as directly productive activities and abilities. But this 'becoming woman of labour' (Negri 2004; Corsani 2007; Osterweil 2007), which as an ambivalent process has highlighted the potentiality found within forms of affective labour and relations, has also continued to be marked by forms of social division and domination in which gender relations are historically embedded: 'a tremendously irregular topography, reinforcing, reproducing and modifying the social hierarchies already existent within the patriarchy and the racial order inherited from colonialism ... [upon which] the global restructuring of cities and the performances and rhetorics of gender are imprinted' (Precarias a la Deriva 2003b).

Precarias a la Deriva thus propose a typology for considering forms of feminized and precarious labour, based not upon overall transformations in social and economic structure (although such is clearly related), but rather on the nature of the work and the possibilities it opens up or forecloses for insurgencies against it. Typologies based on specific forms of economic transformations in labour markets (for instance distinguishing between chainworkers and brainworkers) lack coherence, they argue, and tend to overlook the many ways in which similar dynamics overlap and affect multiple positions (as well as tending to homogenize various positions and particularities). Developing this typology based on unrest and rebellion, they propose three general types of labour:

1. jobs with a repetitive content (telemarketing, cleaning, textile production) which have little subjective value or investment for those involved – tendency for conflicts based upon refusal of the work, absenteeism, sabotage
2. vocational/professional work (anything from nursing to informatics, social work, research, etc.) where there is a higher subjective component and investment – conflict tends to be expressed as critique of the organization of labour, how it is articulated, and the forms it takes
3. jobs where the content is directly invisibilized and/or stigmatized (cleaning work, domestic labour, forms of sex work) – conflict tends to manifest itself as a demand for dignity and recognition of the social value of the work.

(Precarias a la Deriva 2005a)

The question for Precarias, as already observed, is finding points for commonality and alliances, lines of aggregation where intense forms of relations and communities can emerge and are strengthened. Precarias have also been involved the creation of various social centres and feminist spaces where such can occur and have been involved in the EuroMayDay Networks and parades, which have acted as key points of visibility for those contesting existing conditions.

Thus the central problem, and one that has become much more pressing in recent years, is around the issue of security. The military and neoliberal logic of security,[8] involving anything from increased border controls and migration regulation to the proliferation of private security firms and non-governmental, has risen during the past twenty to thirty years, during the same period that the decline of the welfare state and apparatuses of social security and welfare measures have been taken apart. This overall shift in the macropolitical situation is articulated in what Precarias describe as a 'micropolitics of fear' that is directly related to the regulation of the labour market (and the configuration of state–labour–business) and to increasing forms of instability and precarization of life that extend over the whole of society as regimes of discipline. The increasing importance, or perhaps overwhelming nature, of the logic of security is such that Precarias have argued that it is 'the principal form of taking charge of bodies and organizing them around fear, contention, control, and management of unease' (Precarias a la Deriva 2005b). At the same time as regimes of security, visibility and exploitation come together in a particular kind of state form, parts of the state devoted social welfare are dismantled. Precarias see this as a moment where it is necessary to put forth a logic of care as the counterpoint to the logic of security which has become the hegemonic dispositif of politics in many locations, because, as they argue, '[c]are, with its ecological logic, opposes the securitary logic reigning in the precaritzed world' (Precarias a la Deriva 2006: 39).

This involves four key elements: affective virtuosity, interdependence, transversality and everydayness (Precarias a la Deriva 2006). These four elements are used to address questions of the sustainability of life, of the ability to continue in the everyday tasks of life, labour and communication in which we are constantly immersed. Thus it becomes possible to create cracks in these forms of articulation (Sharp 2005), and by doing so to focus on the role that forms of care, affects and relations have in the continual process of social reproduction. Or, as Precarias describe it, to develop 'a critique of the current organization of sex, attention, and care and a practice that, starting from those as elements inside a continuum, recombines them in order to produce new more liberatory and cooperative forms of affect' (Precarias a la Deriva 2006: 41).

Precarias have pursued this through two related proposals, arguing for what they have described as 'biosyndicalism' and the proposal of a 'caring strike'. Biosyndicalism, which as the name itself implies, is a drawing together of life and syndicalist traditions of labour struggle while stripping them of their more narrowly economistic elements. This is not to propose that life has 'become productive' or that it has 'been put to work', as starting from a feminist analysis of affects, caring labour and social reproduction makes it quite clear that affects have always been productive, productive of life itself, even that forms of life existed for many years that were not enmeshed in capitalist relations because they did not yet exist. Rather than claiming that life has now become productive, the argument here is that there are changing compositions of capitalism, modulated as eruptions of social resistance are reintegrated into its workings. In these transformed arrangements affective labour is more directly exploited, occupying a more central position. Similarly, it is not that conditions of instability and a precarious existence are a new phenomenon (as they have been perhaps more the rule than the exception for the vast majority of the history of capitalism); rather this process of precarization comes to currently encompass a much broader swath of the population than it has in recent times. Biosyndicalism for Precarias does not mean that labour struggles are no longer important. Rather it indicates that as processes affecting the composition of labour are not restricted to a clearly definable sphere of 'work', conflicts over them likewise cannot be easily marked in one area or sphere. Thus it becomes all the more important to learn from these struggles and their successes (as well as their failures) in order to 'invent forms of alliance, of organization, and everyday struggle in the passage between labour and non-labour, which is the passage that we inhabit' (Precarias a la Deriva 2005a).

Thus they propose what they call a 'caring strike', a strike carried out at the same time by all those involved in forms of work all along the sex–care–attention continuum, from those involved in domestic labour to those involved in sex work, from telecommunications workers to teachers, and so forth. While this in many ways is close to the idea of the general strike so cherished (and fetishized) within the syndicalist tradition, the difference is that this is a combined strike by those involved in related forms of labour involving the dynamics of care. It is these dynamics, that are increasingly productive and important to the workings of the economy, that are the most often invisibilized, stigmatized, and underappreciated. While campaigns like Wages for Housework were built upon bringing visibility to forms of struggle and care within the home, Precarias are for expanding this notion to include the same dynamics and processes involved in the home that are spread across the economy, and bringing visibility to them, to organize around them, and to consciously withdraw their productivity, that which holds together the whole arrangement. In their words,

> because the strike is always interruption and visibilization and care is the continuous and invisible line whose interruption would be devastating ... the caring strike would be nothing other than the interruption of the order that is ineluctably produced in the moment in which we place the truth of care in the centre and politicize it.
>
> (Precarias a la Deriva 2006: 42)

It is not that Precarias magically solve all the most pressing questions of revolutionary politics for today. Indeed, there are difficulties contained in what they propose; what about forms of caring labour that are difficult (and perhaps sometimes even impossible) to refuse? For instance for those involved in critically intense forms of health care, of caring for relatives and children, and so forth? The rhetorical weight and power of such a proposition might very well lie in the reality that it is nearly impossible for those engaged in these forms of 'affectively necessary labour' (and perhaps more varying forms of socialized labour) to go on strike at all (Spivak 1985). Precarias' proposal of the caring strike and their concept of biosyndicalism do not solve these difficulties *per se*, but rather productively reopen these questions in much the same way that campaigns like Wages for Housework opened the question of feminist organizing and class. In this manner Precarias bring the focus back to aspects of gendered labour and feminist organizing in ways that should not be forgotten. With the proposal of the caring strike, Precarias take part in an ongoing process of bringing visibility to underappreciated aspects of social reproduction (including for this discussion the social reproduction involved in maintaining the lives of communities of resistance) and by doing so raise the question of what it would mean to withdraw them. While there is great potential for social rupture and upheaval to be '*dérived*' from the sometimes manic movement of the radical imagination, it is likewise important to never forget the conditions and processes that underlie the possibility of its emergence and continuation.

A thousand affective plateau: anticapitalism and schizophrenia

> I think Utopia is possible, I see Utopia in humanity. We can reconsider our existence as completely utopian. Bringing a baby to life or simply the act of walking or dancing are examples of utopist action. Utopia should be in our streets.
>
> (Anita Liberti, quoted in Kendra and Lauren 2003: 23)

> The problem that confronts us today, and which the nearest future is to solve, is how to be one's self and yet in oneness with others, to deeply feel with all human beings and still retain one's characteristic qualities.
>
> (Goldman 1998: 158)

It's 3 a.m. ... and several months after I initially began writing this. And I must admit that in some ways things don't seem a whole lot clearer than when I began. There are still too many things to do (the pile in a different order than several months ago is about the same height) and I'm still tired. Have things ended up right back where they started, with the circle unbroken, by and by, but with no pie in the sky when I die? Joe Hill already told me that was a lie. And perhaps that is the point after all: that any sort of politics which promises all the glories of heaven/revolution to come some day after one spent all one's time and effort in devotion/organizing is deeply troubled. And perhaps most troubled in the sense that without attention to the ongoing forms of care, interaction and relations that constitute a community, especially a community in resistance, it is very unlikely to hold together for very long.

It is in this space that a focus on care, on affective relations, reveals its true importance: when framed as the question of affective resistance. For, as Precarias argue, care acts as the 'passage to the other and to the many, as a point between the personal and the collective' (Precarias a la Deriva 2005a). Affective resistance, the creation of new forms of community and collectivity, involves the creation of subjectivities, which in turn are produced in the formation of these emerging communities. So it is never possible to clearly differentiate between the formation of subjective positions and the formation of collective relations, as they emerge at the same time and through the same process. But by focusing on this process of co-articulation and emergence, not as a means to stated political goals, but as political goals in themselves which are related to a whole host of other emerging communities, concerns and articulations, the care of self in relation to the community in resistance is clearly understood as necessary and important.

This is, perhaps not very surprisingly, quite close to arguments that are made and have been made within strains of radical political thought for some time, from arguments about the importance of pre-figurative politics (the refusal to separate the means of organizing from their ends leading to creating forms of organization which prefigure the kind of social arrangements to which struggles are organized) and the more recent emphasis on creating open spaces, networks and forums (Nunes 2005). The difference here is that one cannot overlook the very real forms of labour, effort and intensity that are required for the ongoing self-constitution of communities of resistance. To do so all too often is to reproduce patterns of behaviour that communities in resistance are working to undermine. Sexism, racism, homophobia, heteronormativity, classism reappear as people fall back on structures of thought and assumptions that have become normalized through their daily lives, or are assumed to have been dealt with.

Affective resistance does not proceed by making a giant leap through which all existing dynamics that one could wish to do away with are magically dispersed forever more. Indeed, if it were possible to radically change all the structures of thought, mental schemas and shortcuts and forms of socialization that construct our lifeworlds at once, it would be very difficult to do so without getting dangerously near insanity. Schizophrenia even. Rather, it is, to borrow a phrase from Italian feminist theorist Luisa Muraro, about creating 'relations of entrustment', an attention to the composition of relations as a necessary basis for revolutionary politics (Muraro 1991). It is to understand the composition of relations and affections as an important pole for a process of political recomposition, one that underlies and is necessary for such a compositional process. To prevent the radical imagination from ever settling into a notion that politics occurs 'over there' or at certain moments, rather than as something that grows out of the very relations and ethical interactions that constitute the fabric of everyday social life.

There are cracks in the structure of the everyday, uprisings, where it is possible to create new forms of relations and sociabilities: moments of excess. But it is also very difficult to maintain them for any length of time (Free Association 2006). Perhaps it might make more sense to wander towards creating a thousand plateaux of affective intensities, vibrating locations where forms of energy, community and intensity can be sustained and build links among other plateaux as they emerge. Thus affective resistance is not something that needs to be built from scratch, or something that only concerns relations within movements themselves. Rather it is a focus on intensifying and deepening both the relations and connections that exist within movements, as well as finding ways to politicize connections and relations throughout everyday life. Gestures of kindness and care, random acts of beautiful anticapitalism, exist and support life in many more places than just where black flags are flown and revolutionary statements issued. Rather then considering interpersonal and ethical concerns as an adjunct and supplement to radical politics, affective resistance is about working from these intensities of care and connection.

Notes

1 The category I'm employing here, autonomous feminism, is admittedly a bit clunky. While in this particular piece I'm drawing mainly from currents of thought coming out of autonomous Marxism (unorthodox Italian radical politics coming out of the 1960s and 1970s), this category is not meant to be a delimiting one. It is definitely not intended to be a historically or geographically closed category. Autonomous feminism can thus be understood as any feminist current focusing on the autonomous capacities of people to create self-determining forms of community without forms of hierarchy of political mediation and direction.

2 One should also note that the recognition of forms of gendered labour as work doesn't necessarily mean that struggles around them start from a better position. As Angela Davis notes, black women were paid wages for housework for many years in the USA before the advent of the Wages for Housework campaign, but that didn't mean they were in a better position in their struggles around such work. This should make clear that the potentiality for political recomposition found within a strategy such as Wages for Housework is always dependent on the particular social situations it is deployed within. See Davis (1981: ch. 13).

3 Mariarosa Dalla Costa and Selma James emphasized the point this way: 'We have to make clear that, within the wage, domestic work produces not merely use values, but is essential to the production of surplus value' (Dalla Costa and James 1972: 33). It was on this point, the domestic labour produced value, surplus value in the Marxist sense, that provoked a great deal of controversy, particularly from those who held to their sense of Marxist categories regarding the dividing lines between productive and unproductive labour. It was often argued that women produced use values, not surplus value for capitalist production, and therefore were in a position more akin to feudalism or pre-capitalist relations. Alternatively, it was argued by people like Carla Consemi that, regardless of whether women were producing surplus value or not, the complex and multilayered nature of circuits of production and social reproduction makes this very difficult to directly perceive: '[Housework] does not produce "goods," it will not be transferred into money – unless it is in a very indirect, incalculable way (which is still to be examined)' (Consemi 1991 [1982]: 268). In some ways the question of whether domestic labour does or does not *really* produce surplus value might seem a bit silly from the outside of it. But to appreciate the significance of this it is important to remember that in the debate carried on in the terrain of Marxist thought to argue that such forms of labour did not produce value was an important part of marginalizing and arguing against their importance. Thus one can see how making the argument that domestic labour does produce surplus value expands the spaces where labour struggle occurs precisely because it is organizing around the production of value necessary for the functioning of capitalism. As argued by James and Dalla Costa, 'The possibility of social struggle arises out of the *socially productive character* of women's work in the home' (Dalla Costa

and James 1972: 37). It might be possible to argue that domestic labour either does not produce value or does so in a way that is indirect, subtle and ephemeral, while still affirming the importance of feminist struggles around domestic labour. This was not an argument commonly made, and would be somewhat strange, and difficult to continue to make, within a Marxist framework centred on issues of exploitation in value production.

4 See on this Balser (1987) and Brenner and Laslett (1991), as well as the work of Aiwa Ong, who argues that the widening gap between current analytical constructs and workers' actual experiences comes from a limited theoretical grasp of both capitalist operations and workers' response to them (Ong 1991; 1987).

5 Two examples of organizing around domestic issues are the Household Technicians of America, which functioned perhaps more like a guild than a union, and the National Committee on Household Employment, which was formed in 1964 by the joint efforts of the National Urban League and National Council of Negro Women. Particular articulations of power relations through gender and class are obviously enmeshed within dynamics of slavery, colonialism and imperial conquest, and how their effects continue to live on and shape social relations. In the USA, for example, organizing around domestic labour was very important for African American women still living within a social context shaped by the lingering effects of slavery, particularly in their struggle to clearly define their roles as independent employees (rather than servants of household masters). For more about this relation of race and the organizing of domestic labour, see Rio (2005), Kousha (1994) and Palmer (1984).

6 For information on some of these controversies, as well as useful background information and history, see Malos (1980). It is also worth noting that there is some divergence and disagreement about whether the analysis put forth by Mariarosa Dalla Costa, which would be the inspiration for the wages for housework approach, supports this strategy. The main text of *The Power of Women and the Subversion of Community* seems to imply that this demand would not be a suitable basis for organizing, while the footnotes appended afterwards in subsequent editions printed by the Wages for Housework Campaign, not surprisingly, claim that it is. There also seem to be some contested questions about which parts were jointly written and which were not. For more information on this apparent lack of sisterhood in struggle, see Laura Sullivan (2005). For a more recent overview and reinterpretation of these issues from multiple theoretical perspectives, see Caffentizis (1999).

7 Arguably there could be seen to be some tension in this kind of updating. Notably, if the purpose of the *dérive* were to open up unforeseen possibilities and connections through the drift's openness, stipulating an already understood framework and space for drifting then could foreclose possibilities for connection that might exist outside that framework. Alternately one could argue that the Situationist notion of the *dérive* already had an understood framework and space of its operation (provided by the subjective positioning of those involved and the understood spaces of the city) that was not quite as open as they would have liked to believe. The alternations of Precarias have thus not limited the possibilities *per se*, but have thus made more explicit about their framework and positioning compared to that which was assumed in the SI version.

8 Precarias a la Deriva's translators have often used the phrase 'securitary logic' to indicate the difference between more onerous forms of security (military, border, etc.) and security as a more positive value (sense of personal safety, freedom from assault). While such seems a useful distinction to make, I find 'securitary logic' quite awkward and thus have avoided using it. This should be taken to be a dismissal of attempts to found a politics based upon other notions of security, such as the True

Security action during the protests against the Republican National Convention in 2004 (which tried to put forward a notion of security appropriate to the building of self-determining communities as opposed to a military logic of security). See also Wendy Brown (1995).

References

Balser, D. (1987) *Sisterhood and Solidarity: Feminism and Labor in Modern Times*, Cambridge: South End Press.

Brenner, J. and Laslett, B. (1991) 'Gender, Social Reproduction, and Women's Self-Organization', *Gender & Society* 5(3): 311–33.

Brown, W. (1995) *States of Injury*, Princeton, NJ: Princeton University Press.

Caffentizis, G. (1999) 'On the Notion of a Crisis of Social Reproduction: A Theoretical Review', in M. Dalla Costa and G. Dalla Costa (eds), *Women, Development and Labor of Reproduction*, Trenton, NJ: Africa World Press.

Ciaperoni, A. (1991 [1982]) 'What If There Were Only Thorns?', in P. Bono and S. Kemp (eds), *Italian Feminist Thought: A Reader*, Oxford: Blackwell.

Colectivo Situaciones (2005) 'Something More on Research Militancy: Footnotes on Procedures and (In)Decisions', *ephemera* 5(4): 602–14.

Colson, D. (2001) *Petit Lexique philosophique de l'anarchisme de Proudhon à Deleuze*, Paris: Livre de Poche.

Consemi, C. (1991 [1982]) 'Without Polemics: Reasons for a Debate', in P. Bono and S. Kemp (eds), *Italian Feminist Thought: A Reader*, Oxford: Blackwell.

Corsani, A. (2007) 'Beyond the Myth of Woman: The Becoming-Transfeminist of (Post) Marxism', *SubStance* 36(1): 107–38.

Curious George Brigade (2003) *Anarchy in the Age of Dinosaurs*, New York: CrimethInc Ex-Workers Collective.

Dalla Costa, M. and Dalla Costa, G. (eds) (1995) *Paying the Price: Women and the Politics of International Economic Development*, London: Zed Books.

Dalla Costa, M. and James, S. (1972) *The Power of Women and the Subversion of Community*, Bristol: Falling Wall Press.

Davis, A. (1981) *Women, Race, and Class*, New York: Vintage.

Debord, G. (1958) 'Theory of the Dérive'. Online. Available HTTP http://www.bopsecrets.org/SI/2.derive.htm (accessed 30 July 2010).

Del Re, A. (1996) 'Women and Welfare: Where is Jocasta?', in M. Hardt and P. Virno (eds), *Radical Thought in Italy: A Potential Politics*, Minneapolis: University of Minnesota Press.

Federici, S. (1980) 'Wages Against Housework', in E. Malos (ed.), *The Politics of Housework*, London: Allison & Busby.

——(2004) *Caliban and the Witch: Women, the Body, and Primitive Accumulation*, Brooklyn: Autonomedia.

Federici, S. and Caffentzis, G. (2001) 'A Brief History of Resistance to Structural Adjustment', in K. Danaher (ed.), *Democratizing the Global Economy*, New York: Common Courage Press.

Fortunati, L. (1995 [1981]) *The Arcane of Reproduction: House, Prostitution, Labor and Capital*, Brooklyn, NY: Autonomedia.

Foucault, M. (1984) *The Care of the Self*, vol. 3: *The History of Sexuality*, London: Penguin Press.

Free Association (2006) 'What Is a Life?', Leeds: self-published. Available at www.nadir.org.uk.
Goldman, Emma (1998) 'The Tragedy of Women's Emancipation', *Red Emma Speaks: An Emma Goldman Reader*, 3rd edn, ed. Alice Kats Shulman, Amherst, MA: Humanity Books.
Hardt, M. (1999) 'Affective Labor', *boundary 2* 26(2): 89–100.
Herd, P. and Meyer, M. H. (2002) 'Care Work: Invisible Civic Engagement', *Gender & Society* 16(5): 665–88.
Hunter-Hendersen, R. (1973) 'A Sense of Liberation', *Papers from the Women's Liberation and Socialism Conference 22/23*, London: 41–5.
Huws, U. (2003) *The Making of a Cyberteriat: Virtual Work in a Real World*, New York: Monthly Review Press.
Jones, A. W. (2001) 'Caring Labor and Class Consciousness: Dynamics of Gendered Work', *Sociological Forum* 16(2): 281–99.
Katsiaficas, G. (2001) *The Subversion of Politics: European Autonomous Movements and the Decolonization of Everyday Life*, Atlantic Highlands, NJ: Humanities Press.
Kendra and Lauren (2003) *Beyond Gallery Walls and Dead White Men*, New York: self-published.
Kousha, M. (1994) 'African American Private Households and "Control" of the Labor Process in Domestic Service', *Sociological Focus* 27(3): 211–26.
Landauer, G. (1973) *Prophet of Community: The Romantic Socialism of Gustav Landauer*, Berkeley: University of California Press.
Malos, E. (1980) 'Introduction', in E. Malos (ed.), *The Politics of Housework*, London: Allison & Busby.
Muraro, Luisa (1991 [1985]) 'Bonding and Freedom', in Paola Bono and Sandra Kemp (eds), *Italian Feminist Thought: A Reader*, Oxford: Blackwell, pp. 123–9.
Negri, A. (1999) 'Value and Affect', *boundary 2* 26(2): 77–88.
——(2004) 'Back to the Future', *MakeWorlds*. Online. Available HTTP: www.makeworlds.org/node/140 (accessed 24 January 2011).
Nunes, Rodrigo (2005) 'Nothing Is What Democracy Looks Like', in *Shut Them Down! The G8, Gleneagles 2005, and the Movement of Movements*, Brooklyn, NY: Autonomedia.
Ong, A. (1987) *Spirits of Resistance and Capitalist Discipline: Factory Women in Malaysia*, Albany, NY: SUNY Press.
——(1991) 'The Gender and Labor Politics of Postmodernity', *Annual Review of Anthropology* 20: 279–309.
Osterweil, M. (2007) '"Becoming Woman?" 'In Theory or in Practice?', *Turbulence: Ideas for Movement* 1. Online. Available HTTP: http://turbulence.org.uk/turbulence-1/becoming-woman (accessed 24 January 2011).
Palmer, P. (1984) 'Housework and Domestic Labor: Racial and Technological Change', in K. B. Sacks and D. Remy (eds), *My Troubles Are Going to Have Trouble With Me: Everyday Trials and Triumphs of Women Workers*, New Brunswick, NJ: Rutgers University Press.
Precarias a la Deriva (2003a) 'Close encounters in the Second Phase: The Communication Continuum: Care-Sex-Attention'. Online. Available HTTP: www.sindominio.net/karakola/antigua_casa/precarias.htm (accessed 20 June 2009).
——(2003b) 'First Stutterings of Precarias a la Deriva'. Online. Available HTTP: www.sindominio.net/karakola/antigua_casa/precarias.htm (accessed 20 June 2009).

——(2005a) 'Precarious Lexicon'. Online. Available HTTP: www.sindominio.net/karakola/antigua_casa/precarias.htm (accessed 20 June 2009).
——(2005b) 'Bodies, Lies, and Videotape: Between the Logic of Security and the Logic of Care'. Online. Available HTTP: www.sindominio.net/karakola/antigua_casa/precarias.htm (accessed 20 June 2009).
——(2006) 'A Very Careful Strike – Four Hypotheses', *the commoner* 11: 33–45.
Rasy, E. (1991 [1978]) 'An Interpretation: Marching in the Night', in P. Bono and S. Kemp (eds), *Italian Feminist Thought: A Reader*, Oxford: Blackwell.
Raunig, G. (2007) *Art and Revolution: Transversal Activism in the Long Twentieth Century*, New York: Semiotext(e).
Rio, C. (2005) '"On the Move": African American Women's Paid Domestic Labor and the Class Transition to Independent Commodity Production', *Rethinking Marxism* 17(4): 489–510.
Sharp, H. (2005) 'Why Spinoza Today? Or, "A Strategy of Anti-Fear"', *Rethinking Marxism* 17(4): 591–608.
Shukaitis, S. (2008) 'Dancing Amidst the Flames: Imagination and Self-Organization in a Minor Key', *Organization* 15(5): 743–64.
——(2009) *Imaginal Machines: Autonomy & Self-Organization in the Revolutions of Everyday Life*, Brooklyn, NY: Autonomedia.
Sorokin, P. (1950) *Leaves from a Russian Diary*, Boston, MA: Beacon Press.
Spinoza, B. (1949) *Ethics*, New York: Hafner Publishing.
Spivak, G. C. (1985) 'Scattered Speculations on the Question of Value', *Diacritics* 15(4): 73–93.
Sullivan, L. (2005) 'Wages for Anyone Is Bad Business', *Mute Magazine* 29. Online Available HTTP: http://www.metamute.org/en/Wages-for-Anyone-Is-Bad-for-Business (accessed 24 January 2011).
Van Raaphorst, D. L. (1988) *Union Maids Not Wanted: Organizing Domestic Workers 1870–1940*, New York: Praeger Publishers.

Poetic interlude 2

RED, OR THE THINGS I LEFT UNSAID

Helen Moore

Red is becoming, I said.
No, they said, *red is not at all becoming—*
that colour of dissembling, it lies
in the bed
of our daughter's undoing …

Oh, yes (I'd liked to have said,
sparing my blushes),
red has been all my undoing,
and my becoming—

free to throw off the dishonesty
of clothes, to stampede through
damp, crimsoned leaves,
fall flat on my face laughing.

You've made your bed and you can
lie in it, they said. And so with sheets
to hoist a harlot, walls daubed
with rich Moroccan clay,

pleasure shipped me through the ebb
and flow of pain to the waters of the Lethe,
where I washed away their fear—

that deep red of my undoing,
that becoming one
with the coursing energies of love,

the pulse of early dawn,
the stars, the damask of plants,

being wholly woman—
not their little girl.

CUNT MAGIC

Helen Moore

This gap in the hedge
is neither absence nor lack

but a green Moon – the frame
around the young Wheat beyond,

a heavenly gateway
that beckons us to quit the path,

its stiles and bridleways,
the blue willow-patterns of our thought,

and pass through this cunicle,
this cunning – finger its tender flowers,

its pitted stems, feel frissons
of what we once knew as holy.

Thereafter trust that the bird *not*
in the hand is worth a cunctipotence

in the bush, and reawaken the desire
for Life's wild fecundity.

Chapter 4

Post(-)anarchism and the *contrasexual* practices of *cyborgs* in *dildotopia*

Or 'The War on the Phallus'[1]

Lena Eckert

> Utopia has been a subversive form: that is perhaps the first point to make in 'mapping' utopia. The very uncertainty over the intention of the author – is this satire? is it wish-fulfilment? is it a call to action?
>
> —Krishnan Kumar, *Utopianism* (p. 87)

The criticism which has been aired towards utopia is apparently well founded since one meaning of the word is 'no place' – so how can it exist? Yet, utopianism can also be viewed as 'perpetually exploring new ways to perfect an imperfect reality' (Niman 1997: 302) or as a 'condition of permanent revolution, a continuing rebellion against our own tendencies toward entrenchment and domination' (Amster 2001: 31). In that sense, anarchism has a lot in common with utopianism. As much as utopia is always comprised of both 'critical' and 'constructive' aspects (Kumar 1991: 97), the anarchist formation of denial or rejection always carries with it constructive potentialities, although it often positions itself as negating the *status quo*. Utopia is critique in itself because it proves that envisioning something different is possible. The possibility of envisioning something holds the prospect of it becoming a viable project. To put it simply: we can't do what we can't think, so why not think what we could do?

Krishan Kumar states that the value of utopia is not in its relation to present practice; its value is rather in its relation to a 'possible future' (ibid.: 3). He argues that utopia's '"practical" use is to overstep the immediate reality to depict a condition whose clear desirability draws us on, like a magnet' (ibid.). In this essay, I want to introduce the reader to a book which has drawn me on like a magnet. Beatriz Preciado's *contrasexual manifesto* has attracted me since I held it in my hands for the first time. From time to time I go to my bookshelf and pull it out, browse and remain on a page for a while. I am convinced that Preciado's *dildotopia* (or godotopia),[2] which forms a large part of the *contrasexual manifesto*, is a form of utopia because 'utopia challenges by supplying alternatives, certainly. It shows what could be. But its most persistent function, the real source of its subversiveness, is as a critical commentary on the arrangements of society' (ibid.: 87–8). Preciado wants her *manifesto* to be read as a tool to interrogate knowledge and desire; a means to partially, constantly temporally question the 'givens' of society and its very preconditions; it is a critical commentary on the arrangements of a phallocentric and heteronormative society. Kumar notes that some utopians were convinced that 'utopias ... may be realized "in principle or in spirit" rather than in detail or *in toto*' (ibid.: 71). 'Utopia,' as Kumar notes, 'confronts reality not with a measured assessment of the possibilities of change but with the demand for change' (ibid.: 107). This is why for me the *manifesto* is related to utopianism: the demand for change. This demand, of course, also relates to anarchism. In the following essay, I map out how I see these relationships and how they can be put in larger theoretical contexts. I therefore will first look into the relevance of taking up sexuality as an anarchist project to then connect poststructuralist theories to post(-)anarchist thinking. As I see power as the central issue in both projects, I will briefly touch upon it, yet I will use the genealogical looking-glass of sexuality in order to explain the connection I see between Preciado's *manifesto*, its ally, the post-human cyborg, and post(-)anarchist thinking.

Jamie Heckert, anarchist queer theorist, argues for the inclusion of sexual politics in anarchist politics because in his understanding there can be no theorisation of an anarchist non-hierarchical society or practical anarchist strategies without the consideration of sexuality (Heckert 2004). Heckert hereby refers to the poststructuralist deconstruction of binaries and argues accordingly that sexuality has to be regarded as socially constructed. He stresses that 'any attempt to build a society where people are comfortable with themselves and each other *must* include a radical reorganization of sexuality' (ibid.: 101). Heckert also promotes the famous feminist claim that the personal is political and states that 'sexuality is not separate from these other issues which are more commonly considered political' (ibid.). Therefore, he reasons that 'we should understand anarchism as a theory and practice that promotes the development of non-hierarchical social organization' also with regard to sexuality (ibid.: 103). Following on from Heckert, I will argue in this essay that anarchist thinking or theorising also has to acknowledge the political character of psychoanalytic concepts of subjectivity, embodiment and desire. Moreover, these powerful concepts govern our concept of sexuality and entail the notion of the supposed ahistorical naturalness of sexuality. As I show in this essay, a queer critique can be anarchist and anarchist thinking can become queered (to the extent that they are not already intrinsically interconnected and interdependent).

Only recently, so-called post(-)anarchists started to work explicitly on and with poststructuralist thinkers such as Michel Foucault, Gilles Deleuze, Jacques Lacan, Jacques Derrida and others. The notion of classical anarchism and its relationship to its own version of 'post' has already been discussed very critically (e.g. Cohn 2002; Cohn and Wilbur 2011; Franks 2007, 2011).[3] I favour the approach of Jason Adams, who wrote about the relation between poststructuralism and anarchism, reclaims poststructuralism as an intrinsically anarchist movement of thinking and argues that most poststructuralist thinkers have or had a great affinity with anarchist thought. Poststructuralism, in Adams' notion, is born out of the political movements of the 1970s and 1980s and was therefore always already part of radical movements:

> 'Postanarchism' has emerged recently as a term that could be used to describe the phenomenon whereby this radically anti-authoritarian poststructuralist theory has developed and mutated and split off into dozens of hybrid critical theories over the past three decades, finally coming back to inform and extend the theory and practice of one of its primary roots.
>
> (Adams, quoted in Franks 2007: 132)

By interpreting the development of a number of poststructuralist theories in the light of an anti-authoritarian (maybe post(-)anarchist) motivation it should be possible to once again hunt down the politics in poststructuralism. In the following section I want to touch briefly on the main tropes in anarchist thinking that can be read as underpinning Adams' point. Moreover, in this essay I aim to add one more of these 'hybrid critical theories' to anarchist agendas and theories by reading the *contrasexual manifesto*, which is to a great extent based on poststructuralist theories, as a possibly post(-)anarchist approach to desire and embodiment.

At the heart of the question of how poststructuralism and anarchism could form a convincing union, or of how they may already be always already interconnected, is the notion of power. It is the question of where power acts, what power actually is and where, therefore, resistance can be located. Post(-)anarchists of all stripes have brooded over this and have debated this issue heatedly. While the most renowned post(-)anarchists, Saul Newman, Lewis Call and Todd May, have been criticised for not being accurate in their definition of power and for using various notions interchangeably and inconsistently, they have also attempted to fuse postmodern or poststructuralist notions of power in a positive way with anarchist thinking and politics (e.g. Cohn 2002; Cohn and Wilbur 2011). If one defines power as domination, then it can and should be resisted, but if one defines power as being everywhere and as an integral part of any society, then it cannot be resisted – at least not straightforwardly. This constitutes a theoretical and practical dilemma for anarchism which can be made productive.

What explicitly poststructuralist post(-)anarchist approaches have accomplished is that they challenge the overemphasis on the state and capitalism and emphasise the intersections of hierarchical social relations, including gender, race and ethnicity. These power relations work therefore on different levels, which can be called levels of micro-power and macro-power.[4] I agree with Deleuze, who says that every politics is at the same time a macro-politics and micro-politics (Deleuze and Guattari 2004: 213) and any distinction made has to be aware of micro-political theory that remodels traditional understandings of macro-political structures. The concept of post(-)anarchism debatably 'views capitalism and statism not as causes but as effects, not as diseases but as symptoms', and it 'challenges an entire psychology and an entire semiotic structure which underwrite the dominant system of political economy' (Call 2002: 117–18). In this essay, I focus on this 'micro-political' psychological level – the level of subjectivity and the symbolic – because I see them as connected to the concept of sexuality. Since these symbolic or psychological 'powers' are diffuse and everywhere, they require a form of resistance that is equally 'everywhere' – in our very psychological and physical make-up as humans – against certain traditional understandings of our 'make-up as humans'. With Preciado's *manifesto*, I argue for resistance in the forms of non-heteronormative, psycho-political strategies of embodiment and desire.

Where does anarchism come into poststructuralism and vice versa?

It has been argued that Friedrich Nietzsche can be reclaimed as an anarchist because his writing reflects *an anarchy of thought*. Lewis Call, for example, notes that Nietzsche's 'writing attacks hierarchy not only at the political level but at the philosophical level as well, undermining the very foundations of the deeply entrenched metaphysics of domination upon which the West has come to rely' (Call 2002: 2; see also Moore and Sunshine 2005).[5] In terms of the attacks on the 'deeply entrenched metaphysics of domination' the affinity with post(-)anarchist thinking seems rather obvious.

The works of Michel Foucault (1965, 1976, 1977, 1978), who has radicalised Nietzsche's thought by developing genealogy into a method with a specific political dimension, is central to many post(-)anarchist theories. Genealogy is a method to interrogate the production of knowledge in the context of multiple power vectors and can therefore contribute to the analysis of power/knowledge complexes rather than ignoring them or taking them for granted as traditional historical methods have done. In fact, Todd May states that the method of genealogy which seeks to trace the emergence of its object in relation to power structures can be considered the anarchist method *par excellence* (May 1994: 90). Foucault, Call states, is interested in genealogy as a strategy for the subversion of discipline as well as psychological discourses about sexuality (Call 2002: 3). Therefore, a genealogical method is promising when trying to articulate the intersections of social practices with bodies and sexualities which, in turn, are both products and practices of power. Bodies and the concept of sexuality are not ahistorical facts; the knowledge which is produced about and through them is immersed in political, social and cultural frameworks. Genealogy therefore operates in the context of certain epistemological arrangements which Foucault has called 'regimes of truth' (Foucault 1980: 131). To interrogate the categories of gender identity or sexual identity from a genealogical perspective therefore means to consider the notion of truth in relation to its exclusionary and disciplining effects. The construction of a homosexual identity category at the end of the nineteenth century, for example, shows us more about the political anxieties concerning the distinction between the sphere of production and reproduction and heteronormativity than about actual desire and sexual practices. Or, using a different example: I only become 'white' or 'female' in a society in which there are (bio-)political relations such as 'black' and 'male' to produce my being located in these particular identity frames. Power/knowledge creates our sense of ourselves and assigns us positions of identity in the socio-political context – and this can be done otherwise.

Post(-)anarchism, as I argue here, can be seen as a set of conscious practices and action through which one can reinvent everyday life and identities accordingly. Poststructuralist political theory replaces the orthodox anarchist approaches to politics and power as oppressive with the idea that power has a 'positivity or creativity' (May 1994: 87). As Foucault puts it, 'power is employed and exercised through a net-like organization. And not only do individuals circulate between its threads; they are always in the position of simultaneously undergoing and exercising this power' (Foucault 1980: 98). This is also the case with regard to sexual practices and 'identities' – but instead of subjecting ourselves to the heteronormative matrix (i.e. a phallogocentric conceptualisation of the unconscious and a constitutive lack) we could resist creatively and try to become otherwise!

Becoming resisting: a note on agency

Post(-)anarchist thinking 'prioritises the value and necessity of difference over identity' as Heckert (2011: 200) states. Similarly, Saul Newman, in his paper 'War on the State' (2001), details how according to Max Stirner the individual needs to overthrow her_his[6] own identity in order to begin the constant process of becoming *not* oneself. Deleuze agrees and, as Newman states,

> rejects the unity and essentialism of the subject, seeing it as a structure that constrains desire. He too sees *becoming* – becoming other than Man, other than human – as a force of resistance. He proposes a notion of subjectivity which privileges multiplicity, plurality and difference over unity and flux over the stability and essentialism of identity.
>
> (Newman 2001: 159)

This perspective is quite the contrary to the essentialist view of identity, which conceives of categories such as sex/gender, race, ethnicity, age, (dis)ability and so on as located on and in the body. These categories are thought of as being the crucial factors to make us what we *are*. This notion of *being* somebody relies on narratives of coherence, unity and independence: bodies are supposedly single, coherent entities which function independently from each other.

Identities are rigidly composed of these hermetical and unifying discourses about the various aspects of our social relations. However, poststructuralist theories on identity and the body have formulated wide-reaching critiques of this (Cartesian) conceptualisation. Post(-)anarchist conceptualisations of society also offer resistance on the basis that this notion of *being* lacks reference to the interconnectedness of human subjects and social relations.

And it is here where I see the possible connections between queer theory, anarchist thinking and poststructuralism. Poststructuralism can show how political oppression is always linked to larger cultural processes of knowledge production and cultural representations. The central aims of poststructuralism and queer theory are to deconstruct totalising conceptualisations of identities, bodies and power. As Andrew Koch states, poststructuralism's 'liberating potential derives from the deconstruction of any concept that makes oppression appear rational' (Koch 1993: 348) and can therefore be a valuable tool to queer and anarchist thinking. Because identity is one of the categories through which oppression works, anarchist thinking combined with queer critique of identity categories could work towards a different form of coalition building. A precondition is, according to Michelle Bastian, to 'foster nonessentialist attitudes toward identity and recognize identities not as natural or innate but rather as influenced throughout by systems of coercion' (Bastian 2006: 1040). In a heteronormative society, one of the most influential categories is a so-called sexual identity which is presumably stable and fixed and either homo or hetero. Interestingly, these highly politically invested categories find a resonance in psychoanalytical theories.

The Law of the Father vs *dildotopia*: a symbolic struggle?

Jacques Lacan's concepts of desire, the phallus and the Law of the Father (also known as the Name of the Father) have a profound influence on our conceptualisation of identity and subjectivity (Lacan 1989).[7] While controversial (see, e.g., Robinson 2005), Lacan's psychoanalytical conceptualisation of authority and resistance has been adapted for anarchist radical politics (e.g. Newman 2004). Such a reception has been possible because Lacan provides a counter-discourse to the Cartesian notion of 'reason' as being *the* constitutive factor of the subject. Lacan launches what Call terms a 'devastating attack upon the conventional Cartesian concept of subjectivity' (Call 2002: 3) by installing desire instead of the logos as the foundational working of the psyche. However, from a queer feminist perspective this conceptualisation of desire is highly problematic because it is phallogocentric, meaning that the phallus is the final (symbolic) arbiter of a possible and limited range of desires and identities.

For Lacan, the Law/Name of the Father is a symbolic formation and has a key role in the symbolic order. The Law/Name of the Father represents power and control which can never be reached by the infant. The phallus would thereby be the (master) signifier of mastery; the child has to identify with the 'father' in order to be able to participate in social/sexual relations. This 'father' is not any individual person but a signifier that only gains its relevance from a network of signifiers which include the 'law' or the phallus. This process is marked by the entrance into a linguistic system in which 'male' and 'female' can only be understood in relation to each other in a system of language and in relation to the ontological claim of a 'constitutive lack'. This ontological claim has been criticised by post(-)anarchists, namely Andrew Robinson, as a 'reintroduction of myth and essentialism into political theory' (Robinson 2005: 1). Robinson even goes as far as saying that the essential claim inherent in Lacan's theory of the subject is shallow and empty since one is not supposed to really understand it but to simply 'accept' it, 'under pain of invalidation' (ibid.). With regard to political theory, Robinson argues, rightly, that any assumption of an absolute event of absence (which the Law/Name of the Father implies) leads to depoliticisation. Most troubling in Lacanian thinking is the 'idea of a founding negativity', posited as an 'ahistorical absolute' instead of an 'autonomous positive or affirmative force' (ibid.: 7). Indispensable for the conceptualisation of the Law of the Father in Lacan's theory is the phallus – or rather its absence in some bodies. Postmodern feminism as much as postmodern anarchism has been concerned with creating strategies for the subversion of this law as an epistemological, linguistic and psychological force (Call 2002: 6) because the specific theoretical strategies which they employ question any static concept of subjectivity as well as the 'simultaneous deployment of fluid, flexible postmodern subjectivities' (ibid.). The rejection of the Law of the Father as conceived by Lacan would permit the rejection of any kind of law emanating from the state, economy or any other symbolic order. This fundamental rejection of the concept of law opens up new possibilities to radically criticise the processes of subjectivation. Judith Butler has argued: 'As opposed to the founding Law of the Symbolic that fixes identity in advance, we might reconsider the history of constitutive identification without the presupposition of a fixed and founding Law' (Butler 1990: 72). One might even go further and argue alongside Félix Guattari that

> psychoanalysis transforms and deforms the unconscious by forcing it to pass through the grid of its system of inscription and representation. For psychoanalysis, the unconscious is always already there, genetically programmed, structured, and finalized on objectives of conformity to social norms.
>
> (Guattari 1996: 206)

Guattari seems to suggest that we can do away with psychoanalysis completely. Rather than rejecting psychoanalysis wholesale, however, I think it is possible to open up a space between psychoanalysis and an anarchist expression of agency within daily sexual life. In order to sketch out this possible reformulation of psychoanalysis and agency I draw on the concepts of *contrasexuality* and *dildotopia* by Beatriz Preciado (2003), the *post-human* by Judith Halberstam and Ira Livingston (1995) and the *cyborg* by Donna Haraway (1991).

These works offer methods of resistance to heteronormative/hierarchical power structures as well as rich resources for constructing a critique of the hierarchies of body parts and gender identities. They offer useful ways of reconfiguring the relationship between post(-)anarchist theory, psychoanalysis and poststructuralist queer or feminist theory, and consequently hold a specific potential for further queer anarchist developments of theory and activism. In particular, Preciado's debatably ironic construction of *dildotopia* is helpful in identifying some difficulties in, but also raising novel possibilities for, the relation between queer theory and anarchism. To exemplify this, I will provide a narrative of the affinity between Haraway's utopian concept of the *cyborg* and its *posthuman* sexuality toward a reconceptualisation of the anarchist subject with regard to its desires, pleasures, embodiments and politics. I even suggest that my reading of these utopian concepts could stimulate anarchist alternatives. As Tadzio Mueller states, 'anarchism is a scream, not one of negation, but of affirmation: it is about going beyond rejecting, about starting to create an alternative in the present to that which triggered the scream in the first place' (Mueller 2003: 123). Mueller calls the creation of an alternative 'prefigurative politics'. In the *manifesto* I see such prefigurative politics happen.

Contrasexuality

English speakers are likely to be unfamiliar with Beatriz Preciado's *contrasexual manifesto*, which has been published in Spanish (2000), French (2000) and German (translation in 2003).[8] Since its publication, the *manifesto* has been discussed widely and received with a high degree of controversy in France, Spain and Germany. I want to propose that Preciado's *manifesto* should be read in line with post(-)anarchist theories and politics to interrogate the possibilities of reclaiming the body, the psyche and especially desire from power structures which prevent anarchism as a mode of living.

Preciado's concept of *contrasexuality* seeks to interrogate the production of knowledge about gender, sex and sexuality, and should be understood as a specific way of questioning the production of knowledge, desire and their interconnections. It is also a theoretical practice, a way to think practically. Indeed, the *manifesto* is based on a genealogy of the production of gender differences as well as sexual differences which are produced by a heterosexual social contract – the heterosexual matrix. This heterosexual social contract is reaffirmed by normative performances which inscribe themselves as biological truths on to bodies (Butler 1990). Preciado, in line with this Butlerian notion, considers nature to be a social contract which could be replaced by a *contrasexual* contract (Preciado 2003: 10). This *contrasexual* contract is based on the theoretical process of *contrasexuality*, which claims that desire, sexual arousal and the orgasm are only 'retroactive products of a certain sexual technology' (ibid.: 12). This certain sexual technology produces the perception and conceptualisation of reproductive organs as sexual organs. This discursive production results in a sexualisation of a bodily totality, which Riki Wilchins and David Valentine describe by means of the fact that 'genitals accounts for only 1 percent of the body's surface area' but these genitals still 'carry an enormous amount of cultural weight in the meaning that are attached to them' and constitute much of what individuals and society 'come to understand and assume about the body's sex and gender' (Valentine and Wilchins 1997: 215). This could be translated as: in an organism all organs are equal, but some are more equal than others because they determine the meaning of the whole body; it is a *pars pro toto* logic which constitutes gender through sexuality (i.e. penis/vagina equals man/woman). Sexual organs are used to represent the body-totality of men and women and therefore the binary sex/gender system.[9] Therefore, a body always becomes sexualised – it is assigned to either male or female from the beginning of its existence only because our frameworks of perception limit us to the dichotomous interpretation of bodies.[10] Yet, we can become differently!

Preciado's use of the concept *contrasexuality* is indirectly derived from Foucault's analysis of the possibility of resisting the disciplining production of sexuality not by struggling against the prohibition but by elaborating a contra- or counter-productivity. Preciado wants her *manifesto* to be understood in terms of a Foucauldian counter-discourse: *contrasexual* practices are 'technologies of resistance' and 'forms of a contra-discipline' (Preciado 2003: 11). This counter-discourse, as I read it, is for Foucault a practical engagement in political struggles: a space in which the formerly voiceless might begin to speak (Deleuze and Foucault 1977: 209). I argue that this voicelessness concerns the difference of bodies; only the presumed binary homogeneity of bodies can be heard in a heteronormative system. That is to say that we learn to understand bodies only as either male or female. There is no possibility of creating from scratch something new which exists entirely outside the discourse in which we are living. What we *can* do to resist or to produce a counter-discourse is reclaim or twist traditional notions in order to place them in new contexts. In depriving language or symbols of their referent and providing them with new contexts, hegemonic discourses lose their meaning. Preciado refers to Butler's analysis of the reclaiming of the term 'queer' as a productive self-identification. Butler's notion of reiteration (in particular concerning gender) makes possible a positive resignification and re-appropriation of identities, discourses and certain aspects of lived processes and actualities (Butler 1993: 315). Preciado understands sexual identity, in line with Butler, as a repetitive act of inscription of sexual practices, and in this repetition or subversive reiteration of, for example, the derogative term 'queer' lies the possibility of undermining hegemonic forms of sexual identity. I read Preciado's work as an act of creating spaces within a discourse from which a counter-discourse can emerge. The method of *contrasexuality* impacts upon notions of sexuality by decontextualising the 'quotation' of the *dildo* and twisting the position of declaration (Preciado 2003: 16). The *dildo* is one among many organic and non-organic machines such as hands, whips, penises, chastity belts, condoms and tongues (ibid.: 60). Therefore 'quoting the *dildo*' means implying the possibility of ceasing to assign the power of the phallus (the Law/Name of the Father) to an arbitrary organ. This arbitrary organ – the penis – then ceases to be the signifier of sexual/gender difference. The reiteration of the *dildo* is subversive because the *dildo* comes before the penis, as *contrasexuality* claims (ibid.: 12). This means that quoting the *dildo* displaces the origin of the penis as a male sexual organ. Sexual/gender difference, which is based on the difference of having or not having a penis, is replaced by the *dildo*. The *dildo* is a supplement which produces what it completes. The practice of 'quoting the dildo' on a head, any other body part or a tool that is involved in the *contrasexual* practice could be understood as a reference which is mediated through a metaphor but exceeds the function of a metaphor in the sense that the *dildo* becomes the body part or tool on which it is projected. This is referring to the workings of the phallus which, whenever quoted, implies the penis as the marker of sexual/gender difference. Quoting the *didlo* messes up the supposed direct relationship between the psyche and the make-up of bodies. By introducing the reader to the practice of a repetitive quotation of the *dildo*, Preciado seeks to reclaim sexuality from the heterosexual social contract. *Contrasexuality* is a practice of de-heterosexualising. It is about showing that there can be an end to the social construction of certain social relations as natural, such as the heterocentric social contract of regarding sexuality as the natural expression of so-called male and female bodies (ibid.: 10).

Preciado, in a first reflexive approach to the *dildo*, places the *dildo* as the precursor of the penis, which retroactively produces the penis (ibid.: 61). And the *dildo*, as a Derridean supplement, replaces the penis as if it was replacing a void; the *dildo* substitutes the penis in a form the penis never has; the *dildo* aims the penis against itself (although even a penis can be the *dildo*). The second approach to the *dildo* places it in the position of 'sexual excellence' (ibid.: 64) to be able to transgress or 'transcend' sexual difference. And in the third phase of this 'discursive reflexivity' (ibid.: 64) the *dildo* is made to come back to the body but only to *contrasexualise* it. Organs and quotations move horizontally (not vertically like in the hierarchical heterosexual order – the *dildo* can be everything and not just the penis or its lack) and therefore is 'multiple effect and not a single origin' (ibid.: 64). Preciado states that the penis is not the phallus but it is commonly associated with it, which is why 'masculinity' is powerful. The invention of the *dildo* is the end of the penis as a marker of sexual difference – everything can become *dildo*! The subversive repetition of the quotation of the *dildo* on any kind of body part proves and represents its performativity. The *dildo* positions a logic which will later betray it because it is not localisable, as it is not there to distinguish bodies by its presence or its absence. The *dildo* signifies sexuality but not sexual difference. The *dildo* remains invisible in *contrasexual* practices, Preciado proposes. *Contrasexuality* relies on the *dildo* to *think* about and challenge heterosexuality; therefore it is not the *dildo* as we think of it (as being the better penis because it is always erect), but it is the resignification of the phallus, inverted and subverted by its reproduction in other body parts. Preciado seems to warn us: the *dildo* can be everything. In this claim she takes a similar line to Butler (1993) when she says the phallus can be every (lesbian) body part. However, the *dildo* is not the phallus, neither does it represent the phallus, precisely because the phallus does not exist. The phallus only emerges as a form of power and as a psychoanalytical construction which can be subverted and ultimately replaced without leaving a trace.

By means of the genealogical method, Foucault provided a foundation for the rewriting of histories of sexuality and, in line with him, Preciado claims that the body is an 'organic archive of the history of humankind' (Preciado 2003: 15). But Preciado dismantles this history as one of naturalisation, where codes are constantly renegotiated, leading to cycles of omission, elimination and inclusion according to the coordinates of masculinity and femininity. The insight that these coordinates penetrate any production of knowledge allows Preciado to disrobe and dismantle sexual organs as products of hierarchically organised space (ibid.: 18). In a dichotomously organised heteronormative society the sexual organs are used to speak for the totality of the body's identity and their relationship is organised in a patriarchal space. This space is produced by technologies of gendered/sexualised relations which organise body parts and practices and judge them as private and public, institutional or domestic, social or intimate (ibid.: 18). This specific kind of discursive and material management/administration is extended onto the body, where we find body parts also organised according to hierarchically organised, binary structures: sexual and non-sexual, reproductive and non-reproductive, sensual and less sensual, intimate and public. Preciado concludes that 'the bodily architecture is political' (ibid.), which has important implications for anarchism, for which articulating and confronting the history of power and governance have always been central subjects. It is crucial that sexualities and bodies, as well as their functions and fragmentations, are included within this agenda.

Preciado explores this 'bodily architecture' through an analysis of the history of the orgasm, which she argues is embedded within the history of medical-sexual technology: she traces the technologies and discourses which are employed in the making of the intersexualised and transsexualised body. The performative 'operation theatre', which every body is subjected to in the process of being sexualised, is dismantled as inherently heterosexualising. In Preciado's argumentation, intersexualised bodies block the mechanical work of the performative 'operation theatre'; they dismantle the arbitrary character of categories and the 'heterodesign' of bodies (ibid.: 96). The de-construction and de-fragmentation which are at work in these processes recur in Preciado's analysis of the prosthesis, which will eventually take her to the reclaiming of the technologies of sex through the *cyborg*. For an exemplification of how Preciado proceeds in her genealogy of the sexualising of bodies I draw on her history of the female orgasm (ibid.: 69–88). Preciado tells the story of the medicalised and pathologised female body, whereby the 'treatment' of hysteria sometimes included the burning and cutting of the clitoris. Various technologies applied to the genitals were engineered to prevent masturbation (e.g. chastity belts as tools for enforcing governance).[11] In other cases of adult and married women, the woman's body was perceived as an uncontrollable object whose energetic activity needed to be regulated with the help of mechanical apparatuses; this could even include being forcibly masturbated by a vibrator. Preciado states that 'female pleasure has always been problematic, since it doesn't seem to have a precise function either in biological theories or religious doctrines, according to which the objective of sexuality is the reproduction of the species' (ibid.: 92). Clearly our current conception of women's orgasms is coloured by this history, and must engage with these understandings. The notion of a woman's orgasm is deeply rooted in processes of naturalisation, medicalisation and control. It therefore seems plausible to read the history of humankind as the history of technologies, as Preciado does. The medically actualised 'female orgasm' is nothing more than the paradoxical result of the work of divergent technologies for repressing masturbation and at the same time producing the 'hysterical crisis'. It needs reclaiming! For Preciado,

> sex is no precise biological spot, and no natural force either as an organ or as a practice. Indeed, sex is a technology of heterosocial government, which reduces the body to erogenous zones. For this it avails itself of an asymmetrical re-distribution of power according to gender (feminine/masculine) so that specific affects[12] fall together with certain organs and certain perceptions fuse with certain anatomical reactions.
>
> (Preciado 2003: 14)

Heterosexual society therefore is a social apparatus for the production of femininity and masculinity which operates by a separation and fragmentation of the body. Freudian and Lacanian psychoanalysis retells the story of fragmentation in a different framework and with different terms. The conceptualisation of the emergence of the bodily ego (Freud 1961 [1914]) and imaginary body parts (Lacan 1989) has fostered a focus on the genitals as the locus of gender identification and sexual pleasure. The psychoanalytical traditions which have taken these concepts for granted have reinscribed these hierarchical relations with regard to sex, gender and sexuality. Only recently, feminist and queer theorists have started to deconstruct these theories and proposed different readings (e.g. Mitchell and Rose 1982; Butler 1990;

Campbell 2000). Preciado's *manifesto*, however, is the most undutiful daughter in this endeavour since she eclectically intertwines psychoanalytical and non-psychoanalytical aspects.

Thinking the *dildo*

As Preciado might have asked when she started to think the *dildo*, is there a way to subversively undermine the power of the phallus if we still remain in the framework in which it came to birth? Do we need to refer to morphology at all when we construct and interrogate desire? Do we need to refer to psychoanalysis if we want to (theoretically) change the structure of desire? As Gallop says, the psychologically informed reader cannot 'be separated from the subject that can mistake the phallus for a penis (with its "turgidity" and its fluids that participate in "generation")' (Gallop 1985: 156). This inevitable reading implies the erect penis as a morphological 'locus' of desire and generation, as heterosexual reproduction, which makes it essentialist and heterosexist. Preciado adapts Butler's 'aggressive reterritorialization' described in 'The Lesbian Phallus' (1993) but bans the phallus, both as a metaphor and signifier. Preciado installs the *dildo* in a different territory; she is not concerned with the emergence and the maintenance of the bodily ego or its possible psychoanalytical heritage. Preciado, in her unorthodox rewriting and reclaiming of our psychoanalytically constructed bodily identities and pleasures, disrupts any linear and coherent narrative of these powerfully installed control and production mechanisms. She seems to ask: if the phallus is mobile and can even signify 'lesbian bodily parts', then why should it still carry the history of its origin and its name, which is patriarchal, heteronormative and essentialist. The *dildo* as being non-organic, detached from the body, but at the same time as being able to become any part of the body or the body in its entirety provides Preciado with a tool that has a non-coherent narrative. The *dildo* can effectively undermine hegemonic structures of desire, pleasure and bodies when applied as a subversive quotation. Quoting the *dildo* on any body part (or the entirety of the body) means to question the body as a sexual context; it questions the possibility of framing or defining the context. The practice of quoting the *dildo* demarcates flexible bodily borders and subverts the heteronormative arrangements of bodies and their parts. With the *dildo*, the impossibility of arranging body parts and bodies in a hierarchical space with regard to sexuality and sexual/gender difference emerges. The *dildo* is the centre of the *contrasexual* genealogy that seeks to demystify the concept of an ahistorical sexuality. Preciado does not deconstruct one specific discourse but draws on a wide range of technologies and discourses which have produced knowledge about the body and its (sexual) practices. However, as much as the *lesbian phallus* holds more of an 'interesting than satisfying' quality for Butler (Butler 1993: 57), the *dildo* for Preciado is characterised as critical rather than practical (in its application) even though it needs to be practiced.

The subversion of the phallus is dependent on new actions and definitions, which will create new frames of reference. By placing the *dildo* in the position of the phallus, Preciado installs a new relationship between body parts (namely genitals), sexual interconnections between bodies and the forms of power which are enacted. Only by re-appropriation can this relationship be made fruitful for the deconstruction of the heterosexual matrix which produces specific organs as the origin of pleasure (Preciado 2003: 60–7). The focus on genitals to which we are subjected is the basis for the interconnection between sexuality and reproduction. The idea of genitals being opposite and complementary at the same time is at the heart of the ongoing reiteration of sexual/gender difference. Preciado seeks to untie the supposedly linear relation between sexual pleasure, sexuality (and orientation) and procreation, and replaces this nexus with the idea of *dildotopia*. The symbolic order that can produce such a proposal and make it seem plausible is at the same time the foundation for its resistance. The ironic undertone employed throughout by Preciado allows us to analyse the orders we are living in and therefore it serves to find out what *not* to do in an anarchist sense, that is, subjecting oneself and one's body and desire to hierarchical structures and architectures. *Dildotopia* destroys the hierarchies between body parts with regard to sexual pleasure: all body parts are equal; therefore, it is rather an anti-cracy with regard to bodily features and pleasures. Preciado proposes that philosophy needs to learn from the *dildo* (ibid.: 10) and I would suggest that maybe academics need to learn from irony, subversion and disobedience. The *dildo* does not exist; it just opens up new possibilities for doing philosophy. Rosi Braidotti has stated that 'one of the forms taken by the feminist cultural practice of "as if" is irony. Irony is a systematically applied dose of de-bunking; an endless teasing; a healthy deflation of over-heated rhetoric' (Braidotti 1998: 127). In my reading, the *dildo* is an anarchist scream not of negation but of avowal by using this 'endless teasing' strategy that Braidotti describes. Preciado's *manifesto* can be read as a very basic form of ironic irritation that could be adapted by contemporary anarchism to be able to imagine it as a rupture in power structures.

The second part of the *manifesto* is a description of the *practices of contrasexual inversion*. In short: the *practices of contrasexual inversion* are various and infinitely extendable, re-workable and re-thinkable. They are based on *dildotectonics*, which is the 'contra-science' that 'explores the appearance, development and application of the dildo' (Preciado 2003: 37). *Dildotectonics* is derived from *tecton*, the constructor, the creator who has to work around medical and psychological definitions to be able to understand the body as a terrain of dislocation (ibid.: 37). Basically, in the outline of the practices there are the 'workers of the anus', who have to sign a contract in which they state that their contract-bodies are not understood as man and woman but as subjects (a copy of the contract is printed in the book). The workers of the anus are 'the new proletarians of a possible *contrasexual* revolution' (ibid.: 18) because their bodies are equal in desire and practice and their architecture cannot be separated hierarchically. Moreover, the *dildo* can work with these workers of the anus in different but equal ways. The *contrasexual* society is devoted to the systematic deconstruction and the de-naturalisation of sexual practices as well as the order of gender. The *contrasexual* genealogical project proclaims the equality, not the sameness, of all speaking body-subjects, which conform to the terms of the *contrasexual* contract to investigate lust, desire and knowledge (ibid.: 10). The anus is for Preciado the centre for the 'work of a *contrasexual* deconstruction' (ibid.: 18) for every body has one. Moreover, the anus is not intelligible within a 'heterocentristic economy'. The anus (as well as the mouth) can easily be reclaimed as a centre of lust and pleasure without being tied to reproduction or heteronormative romantic relationships (ibid.: 19). Michael O'Rourke argues correspondingly 'that the anus is indifferent to gender and cuts across orientations' (O'Rourke 2005). The idea of the contract is derived from SM practices, where partners, through signing the contract, decipher the erotic power structures, which in a heteronormative society are enforced as 'nature'. Preciado also states thirteen principles of the contrasexual society and uses cartoons and explicit descriptions and guidelines of how to practice *contrasexuality*. Preciado hereby draws on art performances and specific technologies, as well as a serious application of humour to philosophy. Opening up the space of bodily architecture and perceiving the concept of sexuality as a genealogy of technologies means to rearrange the conceptualisation of 'the human'.

The posthuman cyborg in dildotopia

For an anarchist society to emerge, I argue, the idea of 'the human' needs to be replaced by a *posthuman dildotopian* citizen; *per* – the *cyborg*.[13] This draws upon Donna Haraway's ironic myth of the *cyborg*, which, it should be noted, is only one possible conception, although one which has been theoretically well developed. Haraway has asked 'what kind of politics could embrace partial, contradictory, permanently unclosed constructions of personal and collective selves and still be faithful, effective – and, ironically, socialist-feminist?' (Haraway 1991: 157). What is termed here 'socialist-feminist' could as well be termed 'queerly post(-)anarchist' because what is envisioned is a liberated society built on personal and collective freedom. In answer to her own question, Haraway introduced the concept of the *cyborg*, which has the potential to be liberating in terms of the freedom from essentialist, humanist and identity-focused discourses. *Cyborgs* are hybrids; *cyborgs* do not have an origin or a truth to themselves but a variety of histories and narratives on which they can draw to construct themselves and to construct a political agenda which could be read as post(-)anarchist:

> There is no drive in cyborgs to produce total theory, but there is an intimate experience of boundaries, their construction and deconstruction.

> There is a myth system waiting to become a political language to ground one way of looking at science and technology and challenging the informatics of domination – in order to act potently.
>
> (Haraway 1991: 181)

Cyborgs are an undissolvable arrangement of technologies, organic parts, discourses, images, relations, histories, artificial intelligences, psychological heritages and many more features. The idea of the *cyborg* is appealing as it offers a radical way of thinking about bodies and power. Human bodies are 'topographies of power' (ibid.). This, I argue, resonates with Preciado's statement that 'the bodily architecture is political' (Preciado 2003: 18). The *cyborg* is no exception to this, but the *cyborg* accepts it and plays with it. Following Haraway, who proposed this category of fragmented, partial identification, we need to engage with this utopia/myth to be able to be politically effective. One of the preconditions is that we have to accept the cyborg as our ontology; the cyborg is a means by which we can study our existence, just as the *dildo* is the means by which we can interrogate our desires. The cyborg is genealogy as is the *dildo*. Such a perception can enable us to interrogate our ongoing construction through distinctions which function on the mechanisms and workings of power. The *cyborg* is the marker of the collapsing of three boundaries: first, the ideology of biological determinism; second, the ideology of technological determinism (assumed distinction between animal-human and the machine); and, third, the distinction between physicality and non-physicality (*cyborgs* are ether, they are quintessence) (Haraway 1991: 153). Human nature can be (re) conceived as an effect of power which is rearticulated and re-produced permanently by the negotiation of the boundaries between human and animal, body and machine. The *cyborg* is a process because it consists of the ongoing transgression of these boundaries. The rearticulating and reinstalling of these boundaries happen according to the heteronormative technologies of the naturalisation of sex. Haraway's *cyborg* resists

> the plot of original unity, out of which difference must be produced and enlisted in a drama of escalating domination of woman/nature. The *cyborg* skips the step of original unity, of identification with nature in the Western sense.
>
> (Haraway 1991: 151)

This echoes Preciado's claim to replace the social contract of nature (the hierarchisation of the bodily architecture with regard to reproduction) with another contract – here the *contrasexual* contract. The *cyborg* is the *contrasexual* citizen, which becomes its own genealogy.

Probably most important for the anarchist project is Haraway's concept of non-identity (and) politics, which claims political processes as processes of affinity. Affinity is a relationship grounded in choice, not identity. Affinity is not about kinship but about desire. 'Affinity instead of identity' is the *cyborg*'s processual, temporary and spatial specific strategy of forming coalitions. *Cyborgs* do not need a natural matrix of unity and accept that no one construction can hold the whole. This links to the concept of resistance, as I have discussed it earlier, as well as to the concept of contra-productivity, which assumes that practices are always exercising power, even when they are aimed at the hegemonic structure of power relations. Any kind of action derives from the formerly existing framework of power and only works in its boundaries. Theoretical and political actions necessarily have to refer to the discourses they emerge from, but there is the possibility of undermining them and contradicting them (just as with the quotation of the *dildo*). The *cyborg* has chosen the form of myth to open up new possibilities of identification and to escape restraining psychoanalytical narratives. The *cyborg* does not expect to be saved by her father through the production of a heterosexual partner – there is no imaginary unity/wholeness for the *cyborg* to be promised by the organic family or the oedipal project. Haraway's *cyborg* myth is

> an effort to contribute to social-feminist culture and theory in a postmodernist, non-naturalist mode and in the utopian tradition of imagining a world without gender, which is perhaps a world without genesis, but maybe also a world without end. The *cyborg* incarnation is outside salvation history. Nor does it mark time on an oedipal calendar, attempting to heal the terrible cleavages of gender in an oral symbiotic utopia or post-oedipal apocalypse.
>
> (Haraway 1991: 150)

Cyborgs are non-oedipal narratives with a different logic of repression, which we need to understand for our survival. The *cyborg* is a monster because it has to be fragmented and newly composed; it is both collective and individual. The *cyborg* does not have a problem with contradictions – they cannot be resolved. *Cyborgs* recount, re-narrate the narratives of origin. *Cyborg* politics means to fight for language but, in the same vein, to fight against perfect communication. It means to fight against the central dogma of phallogocentrism, which is the one code that translates everything accurately and accordingly. The *cyborg* does not derive from or draw on any enlightened or logical narrative, *per* is a contra-production.

The *posthuman* subject, as Judith Halberstam and Ira Livingston have conceptualised it, is in the same situation as the *cyborg*: it cannot be thought of as 'human'; it is a hybrid, multiple and decentred. It has no outside and no inside; its desires are splattered, perverse, deviant: 'Posthuman bodies are not slaves to master-discourses', Halberstam and Livingston state (1995: 2). They rather 'emerge at nodes where nodes, bodies of discourse, and discourse of bodies intersect to foreclose any easy distinction between actor and stage, between sender/receiver, channel, code, message, context' (Halberstam and Livingston

1995: 2). These post-human bodies, Haraway's *cyborg* and Preciado's *contrasexuality*, as I argue, subscribe to a 'feminist embodiment [which] is not about fixed locations in a reified body, female or otherwise, but about nodes in fields, inflections in orientations ... Embodiment is significant prosthesis' (Haraway 1991: 195). Prosthesis as embodiment places the body outside anything supposedly natural and therefore apolitical. Even the orgasm, as Preciado states, is the result of technologies. Yet, this panorama is not as bleak as it sounds; instead it opens up new possibilities of configuring ourselves, our bodies, our desires. The reclaimed concept of technology reappears in the *posthuman* as it does in the *cyborg*:

> posthuman bodies are the causes and effects of postmodern relations of power and pleasure, virtuality and reality, sex and its consequences. The posthuman body is a technology, a screen, a projected image; it is a body under the sign of AIDS, a contaminated body, a deadly body, a techno-body; it is as we shall see, a queer body. The human body itself is no longer part of 'the family of man' but of a zoo of posthumanities.
>
> (Halberstam and Livingston 1995: 3)

This scattered notion of the origin of the body is very much in line with the interrogative practice of *contrasexuality*. However, the *posthuman* body incorporates the dissolution of a 'direction/orientation' towards the desired object because it has no source or beginning. As Kenneth Dean and Brian Massumi write, 'liberation is never of the human, it is only ever from it' (Dean and Massumi 1992: 167). Thereby, they testify to the contra-productivity of the genealogical *cyborg* who can rearrange per own embodiment, desires and practices in resisting moments – perhaps with the quotation of the *dildo*.

Therefore, the anarchised *posthuman* citizen and *per*'s relation to *perself* and others is based on 'becoming' in the Deleuzian sense because it recognises its emergences as utterly genealogical. This genealogy of the *posthuman* takes into account the questions which it produces. The relationship of the *posthuman* to desire becomes clear when Halberstam and Livingston talk about sex, or rather turn-ons:

> Sex only has currency when it becomes a channel for something besides its own drive for pleasure. Turn-ons are not sexual; sexuality is a dispersed relation between bodies and things: some bodies (such as male lesbians, female cockwearers, baby butches, generationalists, sadofethishists, women with guns) and some things (dildos, pistols, vegetables, ATM cards, computers, phones, books, phonebooks). Some turn-ons: women in suits looking like boys, women in suits wearing dildo looking like and being men, men without dicks, dicks without men, virtual bodyparts, interactive fantasy. What is bodily about sex? What is sexual about sex? What is gendered? Are posthuman bodies postgender? Is anything post

> anymore, or is this the beginning? The search for origins stops here because we are the origins at which imagined reality, virtual reality, gothic reality are all up for grabs. You are not human until you are posthuman. You were never human.
>
> (Halberstam and Livingston 1995: 8)

This argument relates to and fits neatly with Preciado's description of the *contrasexual* subject, which I have translated into the *cyborg* and its emergence and also its homeland of *dildotopia*. The posthuman (or postgender) body is composed of all the 'interactive fantasies' which we can draw on to constitute our desires and pleasures. The *contrasexual manifesto* is composed to enable body subjects to interrogate knowledge and desire to be able to develop a contra-productive theory of *contrasexuality*, which is

> a theory of the body which positions itself outside of the oppositions of masculine/feminine, homo/heterosexual. It defines sexuality as technology and views the different elements of the sex/gender system 'man', 'woman', 'homosexual', 'heterosexual', 'transsexual' as well as their practices and sexual identities – as machines, products, tools, apparatuses, gadgets, prosthetics, nets, applications, programs, interconnections, energy and information flows, disruptions and disruptors, keys, laws of circulation, boundaries, necessities, designs, logics, equipments, formats, accidents, trash, mechanism, exertions, re-dedication (devotion).
>
> (Preciado 2003: 11)

In this sense, sexuality is derived from anything supposedly natural. It becomes pure practice that is open to change and de-hierarchisation through the constant negotiations between the participants. These participants recognise and accept themselves as *posthuman cyborgs* who do not subject *perselves* to the Law of the Father and who neglect the reign or the lack of the phallus. They celebrate the quotation of the *dildo* by recognising that they are their own genealogies, which they use to embody and live an anti-identitarian and anarchist *contrasexuality*. They are constantly becoming different.

Anarchise perself!

The discussion offered throughout this essay has been based on three premises. First, sex, gender and sexuality are produced by societal practices, technologies and discourses. Second, the bodily and psychological structures which emerge from these productions are governed and organised by hierarchical symbolic power structures (such as the phallus). Third, if we take into account that we are no longer 'humans' but rather 'becomings', we might be able to conceptualise ourselves as non-hierarchically organised (internally as well as externally). This opens the possibly of 'becoming-resisting'. The re-conceptualisation of identity or subjectivity in terms of its interconnectedness and dependency on social and technological relations could result in a post(-)anarchist self-conceptualisation as *cyborg*. The reclaiming of the body as a non-hierarchical structure might enable us to re-figure body parts with equal functions or characteristics in relation to erotogenicity, desire and pleasure. The discourses which are linked to a heterosexualised/gendered and naturalised hegemonic position are substantial, as Preciado shows for the orgasm, the *cyborg* and prosthetics. But in rewriting their history we might be able to reconstruct a materialising discourse which does not rely on identitarian, naturalising narratives of subjectivities, bodies and desires. This may function via the reclaiming of the body and the imaginary ego which is conceptualised by the phallus; and if we replace the phallus with the *dildo*, the phallogocentric symbolic structure and the hegemonic position of the genitals may be disrupted. The body's political architecture (organised by the hegemonic role of the phallus) could be reorganised in a non-hierarchical way with the help of the critical potential of the *dildo*. The subject of the *cyborg* might be situated in *dildotopia*, where *per* could develop a bodily ego and a bodily materalisation that is not hierarchically organised. The *cyborg* might be able to create a non-hierarchical relationship within *perself* but also in relation with other *cyborg* subjects/bodies: an anarchised way of living might be slowly activated and achieved by the *cyborg*. But we are not at this point yet; we still have to rewrite our (psychological) history to be able to reconstruct the body, subjectivity and sexuality in a different anarchist fashion. In this essay, I attempted a utopian critical commentary on the arrangements of society and I have offered an alternative conceptualisation of sex, gender and sexuality which does not claim to be coherent; rather it attempts to rearrange certain narratives. I recommend familiarising *perself* with *contrasexuality*, one of many ways to anarchise *perself*.

Notes

1 This is an adaptation of the title of Saul Newman's article 'The War on the State: Stirner's and Deleuze's Anarchism' (Newman 2001).

2 The term dildotopia does not appear in Preciado's manifesto. The term that does appear (in the German translation) in the content page is Godotopia. Gode is the French word for dildo. It does not reappear in the (German) text. There is also a short film called *Godotopia*, referring to Preciado's manifesto, shot by Frédéric de Carlo and Frédéric Gies. It is called *B-Visible = Q-Visible? #1: Godotopia*. Interview with the artists to be found on http://www.sarma.be/nieuw/bvisible/.%5Cbvisible%5Cdecarlogies2.htm (accessed 10 July 2010).

3 The prefix 'post', which engendered significant debates with regards to post-modernity, post-structuralism, even post-feminism, of course also troubles post(-)anarchists. Following Stuart Sim's classification of different strands of 'post-Marxism', Benjamin Franks identifies three types of post(-)anarchism. First there is *post*-anarchism, which is basically not anarchism any more. Theorists coming from this angle reject 'traditional anarchist concerns', and instead propose the implementation of new

critical approaches and tactics that have broken largely with anarchist thinking; they may even be 'antipathetic to traditional anarchism' (Franks 2007: 131). These theorists basically argue that the key concepts and methodologies of 'classical' anarchism are no longer relevant and need to be replaced and overcome. Second, Franks identifies a 'redemptive post*anarchism*' that 'seeks the adoption into anarchism of poststructural theory to enrich and enliven existing practices, one which sees "anarchism" as it currently stands as lacking, but amenable to change' (Franks 2007: 131). This postanarchism seeks to update anarchism by the inclusion of new theoretical developments such as (feminist) poststructuralism and postcolonialism. Third, Franks describes a postmodern anarchism 'that reapplies anarchist analyses and methods to the new globalized political economy, and concentrates on the actions of oppressed subjects' (Franks 2007: 131). In this case, then, the 'post-' of post(-)anarchism means a resituating and an alteration, an updating of the classical anarchist core within postmodern culture. Of course all these variations do not exist hermetically but are combined by their users and developers mainly through an anarchist analysis of contemporary cultural movements. As I understand Franks' three approaches to post(-)anarchism, they all see anarchism as being distinct from poststructuralism and discuss the possibility of a fertile interaction between the two.

4 This distinction demarcates that it is subjectivation on a micro-level (being gendered/sexed or racialised, etc.) that makes it possible for macro-power structures to work on individuals. So, it could be said that the internalisation of hierarchy and domination on a structural, symbolic and psychological level is produced by micropower (our production as subjects) and the power exercised on an institutional level could be considered as operating on a macro-power level (including administrative, institutional [state] structures). Even though I have a slight aversion towards this distinction because the terms 'macro' and 'micro' seem to imply a quality in intensity or impact, this is (at the time) a valuable division that might help to approach power differently from a variety of perspectives.

5 I want to add here that Nietzsche's work has been received very differently in Anglophone contexts in comparison to German contexts. In Germany Nietzsche's philosophy has often been problematised because his '*Herrenmenschentum*' (usually translated as the 'superman') has been adapted for nationalist and fascist propaganda. Due to the translation of a certain body of work, the Anglophone reception has been different and certain aspects of Nietzsche's philosophy have been neglected.

6 I use the _ in order to make space for individuals who do not identify as male or female. The terms s_he, him_her, and his_her designate a space by the _ that includes people who do not feel that the pronouns or the pronominal adjectives of he/she, his/her, him/her denote their identities. This is done in line with the author 's_he' who published an article called 'Performing the Gap – Queere Gestalten und geschlechtliche Aneignung' in the German magazine *arranca* 28 (http://arranca.nadir.org). Further down I will replace the _ with the unifying yet unlimited pronoun of *per* to press ahead with my agenda in this essay.

7 It is not possible due to the length of this essay to make clear the differences between identity and subjectivity. The reader may forgive me if I use these two terms interchangeably even though they have been used in very distinct ways by a variety of researchers. However, identity could be understood as a socio-political concept of a person's position in society and subjectivity could be seen as a more psychological concept which derives from the contextualisation of personal experience and psychological make-up.

8 Since there is no English publication yet all the translations are my translations based on the 2003 German edition.

9 In order to understand this logic one has to look into the processes of intersexualisation. The surgical treatment of intersexualised people includes the logic of either 'poking a hole or building a pole' in order to make the intersexualised child a viable member of society, i.e. either a penis-man or a vagina-woman (see Holmes 2008 for this quotation by a surgeon).

10 Butler has also worked on this through the Althusserian notion of interpellation (Butler 1990). Concerning the gendering and sexualisation of the subject it is the announcement at birth, 'It's a boy/it's a girl'. Preciado convincingly shows that this interpellation is a performative operation theatre in which all babies are ascribed an identity. Even those babies who block this machinery of ascription do not escape some form of identity: they become intersexual babies.

11 For a historical account on the technology of orgasm, see also Maines (2001).

12 The German text uses the word '*Affekt*', which is why I translated it directly. The term affect, however, could here better be replaced by the words 'emotions', 'feelings', 'desires' and/or 'attractions'.

13 The ungendered pronoun 'per' is derived from Marge Piercy's novel *Woman on the Edge of Time* (1978) and replaces the personal gendered pronouns him_her, he_she with the short form of the ungendered 'per-son'. For Donna Haraway the concept of the cyborg carries the pronoun she/her because the cyborg is intrinsically feminist and located in a feminist politics which still has to fight essentialist tendencies. In this essay I want to use the pronoun *per* because it enables us to conceive of the cyborg as non-gendered, at least in regard to the basic workings of language.

References

Adams, J. 'Postanarchism in a Nutshell'. Online. Available HTTP: http://aporiajournal.tripod.com/postanarchism.htm/ (accessed 9 July 2010).

Amster, R. (2001) 'Chasing Rainbows? Utopian Pragmatics and the Search for Anarchist Communities,' *Anarchist Studies* 9: 29–52.

Bastian, M. (2006) 'Haraway's Lost Cyborg and the Possibilities of Transversalism', *Signs: Journal of Women in Culture and Society* 31(4): 1027–49.

Braidotti, R. (1998) 'Cyberfeminism with a Difference', in S. Eiblmayr (ed.), *Steirischer Herbst, exhibition catalogue Zones of Disturbance*, Graz.

Butler, J. (1990) *Gender Trouble*, New York: Routledge.

——(1993) *Bodies that Matter: On the Discursive Limits of 'Sex'*, New York: Routledge.

Butler, J., Laclau, E. and Zizek, S. (2000) *Contingency, Hegemony, Universality: Contemporary Dialogues on the Left*, London: Verso.

Call, L. (2002) *Postmodern Anarchism*, Oxford/New York: Lexington.

Campbell, J. (2000) *Arguing with the Phallus: Feminist, Queer and Postcolonial Theory: A Psychoanalytic Contribution*, London, Zed Books.

Cohn, J. (2002) 'What Is Postanarchism "Post"?', review of: Saul Newman, *From Bakunin to Lacan: Anti-Authoritarianism and the Dislocation of Power*, Lanham, MD: Lexington, 2001, *Postmodern Culture* 13(1).

Cohn, J. and Wilbur, S. (2011) 'What's Wrong with Postanarchism?', in D. Rousselle and S. Evren (eds), *Post-anarchism: A Reader*, Ann Arbor, MI/London: Pluto Press. Online. Available HTTP: http://www.anarchist-studies.org/article/articleview/26/1/1 (accessed 22 May 2010).

Dean, K. and Massumi, B. (1992) *First and Last Emperors: The Absolute State and the Body of the Despot*, New York: Autonomedia.

Deleuze, G. and Foucault, M. (1977) 'Intellectuals and Politics', in D. F. Bouchard (ed.), *Language, Counter-Memory, and Practice*, Ithaca, NY: Cornell University Press.

Deleuze, G. and Guatarri, F. (1977) *Anti-Oedipus. Capitalism and Schizophrenia*, New York: Viking Press.

——(2004) *A Thousand Plateaus: Capitalism and Schizophrenia*, London: Continuum.

Foucault, M. (1965) *Madness and Civilization: A History of Insanity in the Age of Reason*, New York: Pantheon Books.

——(1976) *The Birth of the Clinic*, London: Routledge.

——(1977) *Discipline and Punish: The Birth of the Prison*, New York: Vintage Books.

——(1978) *The History of Sexuality*, vol. I: *An Introduction*, London: Penguin Books.

——(1980) *Power/Knowledge: Selected Interviews and Other Writings 1972–1977*, ed. C. Gordon, New York: Pantheon.

Franks, B. (2007) 'Postanarchism: A Critical Assessment', *Journal of Political Ideologies* 12(2): 127–45.

——(2011) 'Postanarchism: A Partial Account', in D. Rousselle and S. Evren (eds), *Post-anarchism: A Reader*, Ann Arbor, MI/London: Pluto Press.

Freud, S. (1961 [1914]) 'On Narcissism: An Introduction', in *The Standard Edition of the Complete Psychological Works of Sigmund Freud*. vol. 14 (trans. and ed. James Strachey), London: Hogarth.

Gallop, J. (1985) *Reading Lacan*, Ithaca, NY/London: Cornell University Press.

Gerrie, J. (2003) 'Was Foucault a Philosopher of Technology?', *Techné: Research in Philosophy and Technology* 7(2): 14–26.

Guattari, F. (1996 [1979]) 'A Liberation of Desire', in Gary Genosko (ed.), *The Guattari Reader*, Cambridge, MA: Blackwell Publishers.

Halberstam, J. and Livingston, I. (eds) (1995) *Posthuman Bodies*, Bloomington, IN: Indiana University Press.

Haraway, D. (1991) *Simians, Cyborgs, and Women: the Re-Invention of Nature*, London: Routledge.

Heckert, J. (2004) 'Sexuality/Identity/Politics', in J. Purkis and J. Bowden (eds), *Changing Anarchism. Anarchist Theory and Practice in a Global Age*, Manchester/New York: Manchester University Press.

——(2011) 'Sexuality as State-form', in D. Rousselle and S. Evren (eds), *Post-anarchism: A Reader* Ann Arbor, MI/London: Pluto Press.

Holmes, M. (2008) *Intersex. A Perilous Difference*, Selinsgrove, PA: Susquehanna University Press.

Koch, A. (1993) 'Poststructuralism and the Epistemological Basis of Anarchism', *Philosophy of the Social Sciences* 23: 327–51.

Kumar, K. (1991) *Utopianism*, Buckingham: Open University Press.

Lacan, J. (1989) *Écrits: A Selection*, London/New York: Routledge.

Maines, R. (2001) *The Technology of Orgasm: "Hysteria," the Vibrator, and Women's Sexual Satisfaction*, Baltimore, MD: The Johns Hopkins University Press.

May, T. (1994) *The Political Philosophy of Poststructuralist Anarchism*, University Park, PA: Pennsylvania State University Press.

Mitchell, J. and Rose, J. (1982) *Feminine Sexuality: Jaques Lacan and the école freudienne*, New York/London: Pantheon Books.

Moore, J. and Sunshine, S. (eds) (2005) *I Am Not a Man, I Am Dynamite: Friedrich Nietzsche and the Anarchist Tradition*, New York: Autonomedia.

Mueller, T. (2003) 'Empowering Anarchy: Power, Hegemony, and Anarchist Strategy', *Anarchist Studies* 11(2): 122–49.

Newman, S. (2001) 'War on the State: Stirner's and Deleuze's Anarchism', *Anarchist Studies* 9(2): 147–64.

——(2004) 'Interrogating the Master: Lacan and Radical Politics', *Journal for the Psychoanalysis of Culture & Society* 9(3): 298–314.

Niman, M. (1997) *People of the Rainbow: A Nomadic Utopia*, Knoxville, TN: University of Tennessee Press.

O'Rourke, M. (2005) 'On the Eve of a Queer–Straight Future: Notes toward an Antinormative Heteroerotics', *Feminism and Psychology* 15(1): 111–16.

Preciado, B. (2003) *kontrasexuelles manifest*, Berlin: b_books.

Robinson, A. (2005) 'The Political Theory of Constitutive Lack: A Critique', *Theory and Event* 8(1). Online. Available HTTP: http://muse.jhu.edu/journals/theory_and_event/v008/8.1robinson.html.

Valentine, D. and Wilchins, R. (1997) 'One Percent on the Burn Chart: Gender, Genitals, and Hermaphrodites with Attitude', *Social Text* 52/53: 215–22.

Chapter 5

On anarchism

An interview with Judith Butler[1]

Jamie Heckert

JH: A number of scholars have drawn on your work in developing anarchist theory, including myself and several other contributors to this volume (particularly Lena Eckert). This has been enabled by recent developments, variously labelled 'postanarchism', 'poststructuralist anarchism' and 'postmodern anarchism', in which the writings of figures such as Foucault, Deleuze and Guattari, Lyotard and Baudrillard are read as continuous with (and perhaps superseding) anarchist traditions of theory and praxis. (Are you familiar with this body of literature, by the way?) Reading your work in an anarchist light has also been enabled by your public statements, including a recent interview in which I heard you refer to yourself as a 'provisional anarchist'.[2] Could you say a bit more about your relationship with anarchist identity?

JB: I am not sure I understand anarchism as an identity, but rather as a movement, one that does not always function in a "continuous" fashion. There are at least two points of reference within contemporary politics for my concerns. The one has to do with Anarchists Against the Wall. The other has to do with the way in which queer anarchism poses an important alternative to the rising movement of gay libertarianism. Although I am sure that the anarchists against the wall in Israel/Palestine are interested in the history of the anarchist movement, it seems to me that this is a case in which direct action against a military force and a segregationist politics is a very powerful event. If you follow, for instance, the weekly demonstrations at Bi'lin, you can see that human bodies are put into the path of machines that are building the separation wall, are exposing themselves to tear gas, and literally producing an interruption and redirection of military power. The point is to enter into the scene, the building, the movements, to stop them, to redirect them, but also to deploy the body as an instrument of resistance. Of course, it is important that there are cameras there, on the scene, and these machines function as counter-machines, documenting Israeli state violence, but also interrupting its effort to control media coverage of its own actions. Since racism is at the basis of this segregation wall, we see as well the "scandal" of violence being done against Israeli activists. Of course, the outrage is much greater against those sorts of injuries and deaths than against any that are inflicted against Palestinians or, indeed, other internationals on the scene. There is an important "queer anarchist" component to these demonstrations, and it has to do with episodic, direct action, drawing on older traditions from ACT UP, for instance. But it also has to do with exposing and stopping the violence of an ostensibly legal authority.

I think this last is important to point out, since when the legal regime is itself a violent regime, and legal violence consumes all recourse to due process or legal intervention, then anarchism becomes the way of contesting and opposing the violent operation of the state.

Compare this with new forms of gay libertarianism that we have seen emerging in places like the UK, Belgium, and the Netherlands. There the clearly racist opposition to new immigration and the phobic relations to populations from North Africa or the Middle East, mainly Muslim, have recruited gay advocates who espouse personal freedom, the right to private property, and market relations. Although libertarian views such as these usually subscribe to a minimal or "private" state apparatus, these proponents of gay libertarianism invariably do the bidding of the state, supporting anti-immigration efforts, and defending forms of nationalism or Eurocentrism that are patently exclusionary and racist. In this way, gay libertarians befriend the state, are even recruited by them, and help to sustain state violence against other minorities. It is important to recognize here that "freedom" means personal liberty, and it is in no way linked with the struggle for equality or the struggle against state violence. But any minority has to make allies among those who are subject to arbitrary and devastating forms of state violence. It is in this way that I think queer anarchism is "smarter" about state power, and legal violence in particular. Gay libertarianism imagines it is defending the rights of individuals, but fails to see that individualism is a social form which, under conditions of capitalism, depends upon both social inequality and the violent power of the state. This last becomes clear in anti-immigration politics.

So anarchism in the sense that interests me has to do with contesting the "legal" dimensions of state power, and posing disturbing challenges about state legitimacy. The point is not to achieve anarchism as a state or as a final form for the political organization of society. It is a disorganizing effect which takes power, exercises power, under conditions where state violence and legal violence are profoundly interconnected. In this sense, it always has an object, and a provisional condition, but it is not a way of life or an "end" in itself.

JH: Thank you for that thoughtful and thought-provoking response. I am particularly moved by the clear appreciation of compassion and equality I read in your critique of building walls around nations or identities. To follow on from your last statement, can I ask here how you conceptualise the state? I'm thinking of Foucault's writing on governmentality and how it was prefigured by the Jewish anarchist philosopher Gustav Landauer when he wrote: "The state is not something which can be destroyed by a revolution, but is a condition, a certain relationship between human beings, a mode of human behaviour; we destroy it by contracting other relationships, by behaving differently." In this way, I wonder, is the practice of disrupting state violence, of troubling state power and the individualised identities with which it is intertwined, not also a way of living, of relating differently? In other words, is the undermining or overflowing of walls and borders not potentially a "continuous" process?

JB: My one worry about this formulation is that it can be taken to mean that the state is permanent. We can say that the state is permanent, but certain state formations are not. But maybe it is equally true to say that because there is no "state" that is not at once a state formation, states are the kinds of arrangements that come into being, alter, and are dissolved. It seems to me that the right to revolution depends on the possibility of the state being dissolved by the concerted will of the people. This is a certain power that popular sovereignty has over state sovereignty, and I want to hold on to this notion. It is true that certain states project their permanence, even try to institute that permanence, but they can only do this through fortifying the effects of their legitimacy and, of course, their armed power – army and police alike. So does it not make more sense to say that the state is always in the process of re-instituting its effect of permanence, and that critical interventions can be made at the various sites where that re-institution takes place. In other words, that re-institution is not guaranteed, and that lack of guarantee can be exposed by strategies we call anarchist.

JH: Is there a connection between your conception of anarchism as intervening in the re-institution of the state and your earlier work on the performativity of gender?

JB: Perhaps the question is actually about the relationship between reiterative performatives and Walter Benjamin's influential distinction between law-preserving and law-founding violence. My sense is that every time law is reiterated, it is "re-founded" and "re-instituted." This becomes most important in relation to the general strike, that is, the strike that is not protected by law, but which aims to bring to a standstill an existing regime of law. One could say that we are sometimes under an obligation to pull the brake of emergency on gender norms. I suppose Irigaray meant something like this when she suggested we jam the machinery of sexual difference.

JH: I'm asking this because for many of us, particularly queer anarchists and anarcha-feminists, anarchism is simultaneously about interrupting or halting the institutionalisation of the state in favour of popular sovereignty *and* subverting everyday disciplinary identities and hierarchical relationships. It seems to me the latter has long been a theme in your work.

JB: Yes, it is. I would also point out that there is an operation of freedom and agency which is not the same as that which is stipulated as the personal liberty of the individual under liberal democratic regimes. Of course, I want legal protections for certain kinds of freedoms, but if the version of freedom produced by the idea of legal protection becomes all we think of freedom, then surely we are constrained in some unacceptable ways. It is important to point out that various forms of gender regulation and social hierarchy and exclusion work through domains of power that are not reducible to law, but this also means that the forms of resistance and claims to freedom we make cannot be fully conceptualized within the rubric of law. This is one way to insist that the claims of a radical social movement must exceed those of legal reform, even if those legal reforms are sometimes useful for that movement. My sense is that anarchism is an important mode of thought and action precisely when we have to figure out where and how to enter into regimes of power, what opportunities exist for their subversion. To some extent, this is a function of a contingent situation and the possibilities it opens, but this also means that agency is not always institutionalized or institutionalizable. In fact, if political agency is to remain critical, it must weigh the costs of institutionalization and resist any full institutionalization. This does not mean that we have to avoid all institutional practices, but only that they not become the restrictive norm for radical political change.

JH: I'm in agreement about the value of doing subversive work within institutional settings and also very aware of the challenges, emotional and political. Are there particular aspects or examples of anarchist, feminist and/or queer politics you particularly appreciate for enabling these operations of freedom, or even popular sovereignty?

JB: I am impressed with Anarchists Against the Wall and other actions against the wall at Bi'lin which continue to divert the military and have solicited great support from global networks. The rallies against the confiscation of Palestinian property in East Berlin have been growing, and they are heartening to see. I am also in favor of organizations that help non-documented peoples both in the US and in Europe, especially when that assistance has to remain below the radar of the law. In a sense, such actions are below the law, outside the law, even against the law, but are fundamentally movements to change law, and to hold existing law to broader standards of justice. My sense as well is that the student movements opposing the destruction of public education in many countries right now are invariably coming up against police force, and it is crucial to find ways to resist police violence, and to expose its criminal dimensions. Similarly, squatter activism that seeks to lay claim to properties and to claim rights of inhabitation by virtue of having made that claim and set up that abode – these are critical movements. Smuggling medical aid into the Palestinian territorties when the borders are blocked has to be included among important movements of this kind. The large meetings in Chiapas against globalization a few years ago have to be included in my list, but so too do transgender activists who take to the streets with their queer allies in many countries even though it is precisely on the streets that they lack police protection or are subject to police violence. The same with unprotected sex workers (sometimes, as you know, these two groups overlap). I am hoping that in the state of Arizona there might be widespread non-compliance with the new racist laws. My hope is that every faculty member at Arizona University and Arizona State, for instance, will choose to teach Ethnic Studies courses now that they are legally banned. If everyone taught them, then the universities would be unable to enforce such a hideous law, and the law would become powerless.

JH: Now, here's a point I really want to explore: what enables the freedom of non-compliance? The way I understand it, it is not only this law which is vulnerable to non-compliance, but all law. Or, in other words, compliance is a necessary part of the re-founding and re-instituting of state power (in contrast, perhaps, to a collective reiteration of commitment to law produced through popular sovereignty, such as the EZLN[3] Revolutionary Laws). This compliance, in turn, is produced through various forms of state(-like) terrorism. As you wrote in *Bodies that Matter*, "There must be a body trembling before the law, a body whose fear can be compelled by the law, a law that produces the trembling body prepared for its inscription."[4] Is there something about anarchist(ic) practice that calms the trembling body so that you or I or anyone can act in ways unconstrained by fear of the law and the threats of violence with which it is intertwined, particularly against those bodies inscribed as subjectable to violation: women's bodies, queer bodies, brown bodies, criminal bodies, insane bodies, indigenous bodies, poor bodies, homeless bodies, undocumented bodies, animal bodies and all of the countless ways these inscriptions intersect? Or, in other words, what enables moments of, or transitions to, popular sovereignty, in spite of state claims of power?

JB: If the body trembles, it is through the tremble, as it were, that we act. It may take the trembling to submit or to act, and either one can act to calm it – the first through the fantasy that compliance will satisfy the law and leave us alone; the second through a resistance that either works furtively through the appearance of compliance or openly defies, and has to withstand the future that comes, that has to initiate whatever future comes.

JH: Since we last corresponded the Israeli military has attacked the Gaza Freedom Flotilla in international waters killing several people, wounding many more and arresting hundreds. I'm struck by the words of Avital Leibovich, an Israeli military spokeswoman, quoted in Al Jazeera: "we have the right to defend ourselves."[5] How is it that people are, at times, able to become so disconnected from their empathy for others that the delivery of food and medical supplies is to be seen as an invasion by enemies? And what effects does this have on other intimate relationships with our own bodies and the bodies of others?

JB: Of course, one has to follow a very specific paranoid sequence to understand how "self-defense" could possibly be invoked by the Israelis here. If the ship carrying food and aid breaks the blockade, then the blockade will be broken and other ships carrying guns and materials for the construction of bunkers and artilleries will arrive, and those ships will be (in part or in whole) from Iran, which means that Iran is docking in Gaza. Even so, the notion of self-defense only works if we accept the presupposition that the maritime border of Gaza ought to remain within Israel's sovereign authority, and there is no legal backing for such a claim. The other ways of justifying self-defense seem to emerge from imagining a group of "mercenaries" boarding the ship at a second location; but most of all, the self-defense claim is clearly refuted by the now highly documented and corroborated fact that the Israelis shot at the ship before boarding. So who precisely was defending themselves against attack?

For anarchism, the struggle is an important one, since we have good reasons for breaking bad laws. At the same time, when we see rogue states breaking international law, we have to respond with outrage. The point is not to be against all law, nor is it to live without any laws. The point, in my view, is to develop a critical relation to law which is, after all, a field of power, one that is differentially applied and supported. We have to be part of the struggle to make law just, but no existing law will tell us what that justice is. In this sense, we have to seek recourse to extra-legal norms and values to decide strategies in relation to law.

JH: You've spoken about anarchism a number of times in public talks, but this is the first time, I believe, you have written about it for a public audience. Could you say something about that?

JB: Actually, I wrote about it in relation to Benjamin's *A Critique of Violence*, and there I suggested that Benjamin posits an "extra-legal" perspective by which to judge criminal regimes of law.[6] When law becomes an instrument of state violence (and its coercive force is always in some ways implicated in that violence), then one has to engage forms of "disobedience" in order to call for another order of law. In this way, one has to become what Althusser called a "bad subject" or a provisional anarchist, in order to unbind the law from the process of subjectivation. This happens in the general strike when one has to fail as a worker and as a citizen in order to expose an unjust economic mode of exploitation or a violent state regime, or both. We do not have access to natural law at such a moment, but only a certain upsurge of freedom, critique, and also an exercise of a critical capacity, and a powerful negation. We might understand this upsurge as that part of popular sovereignty that is never fully codified in law, and upon which all law depends for its persistence, and which always potentially implies the dissolution of a particular legal code or regime.

JH: You've mentioned in this interview connections between anarchism and the transgression of, or halting of, gender norms. I see, too, connections with anarchism in your essay on surgical interventions done to intersex people, "Doing Justice to Someone".[7] Could you say a bit more about the connections you see between anarchism and transgender, intersex and genderqueer politics?

JB: Time and again the new political efforts to establish marriage as an issue of civic equality or "gays in the military" as an issue of unequal treatment before the law stay within the structures of conjugality and the military, and seek only to achieve political aims within those frameworks. But what happens to a movement when it ceases to question the value of the military or, indeed, of conjugality itself? It loses its critical capacity, and it breaks alliance with all those gay, lesbian, trans, queer, bi and intersex peoples who are struggling against heightened militarism, against structural racism and nationalism, against the brutality of the police in relation to sexual and gender minorities, and who are trying to find ways of living and desiring that are sustainable outside of marriage norms and free of police and psychiatric violence. This last seems to be the ultimate goal of any movement of sexual and gender minorities – one that actually thinks analytically about existing social structures and insists on producing new ones. Perhaps anarchism is in this sense linked to productive power.

JH: Do you have any other comments on links between anarchism and sexuality that we've not yet covered?

JB: Just one: that every effort, psychiatric or legal, to "regulate" sexuality causes damage and violence, but it also fails, since sexuality can be punished, but as long as the sexual person lives, sexuality cannot be extinguished by law (it would rather take "law" as its object than suffer a final death).

Notes

1 This interview took place by email between mid-March and mid-June 2010.

2 Untitled interview with Leonor Silvestri in Buenos Aires, Argentina. Online. Available HTTP: http://www.megaupload.com/?d=M16XIW8Q (accessed 30 July 2010).

3 Ejército Zapatista de Liberación Nacional (Zapatista Army of National Liberation).

4 Judith Butler (1993) *Bodies that Matter: On the Discursive Limits of 'Sex'*, London: Routledge, p. 101.

5 Aljazeera.net (2010) 'Israel Attacks Gaza Aid Fleet'. Online. Available HTTP: http://english.aljazeera.net/news/middleeast/2010/05/201053133047995359.html (accessed 1 June 2010).

6 Judith Butler (2006) 'Critique, Coercion, and Sacred Life in Benjamin's "Critique of Violence"', in Hent de Vries and Lawrence Sullivan (eds), *Political Theologies: Public Religions in a Post-Secular World*, New York: Fordham University Press.

7 Judith Butler (2001) 'Doing Justice to Someone: Sex Reassignment and Allegories of Transsexuality', *GLQ: A Journal of Lesbian and Gay Studies* 7(4): 621–6; reprinted in Judith Butler (2004) *Undoing Gender*, New York/London: Routledge.

Poetic interlude 3

REMEMBRANCE DAY

Tom Leonard

I know what it is
to be powerless

I know what it is
to be made to lie low

while the unknown enemy
invades you

what it is
not to have words

for what is happening
for grass and tree

and inanimate thing
to be

your only witness
on the clearest day

of a childhood
almost fifty years ago;

how I hate
male

fucking violence.
this day

I will wear
nor white nor red

nor account myself solitary
instead

I remember the many
who know what it is

to be made to lie low
while the enemy

known or unknown
invades

in dead of night
or in the field

that spoil of war
that
earth's oldest currency

Chapter 6

Love and revolution in Ursula Le Guin's *Four Ways to Forgiveness*[1]

Laurence Davis

Introduction

What is the connection between love and revolution? Judging by the contemporary 'common sense' understanding of these terms, the answer would appear to be 'very little'.

When people think about love, they typically think of something essentially insular and private, a mixture of sexual attraction and day-to-day caring about another person that tends to detach the individuals concerned from wider social circumstances. One of the characters in a Raymond Carver short story expresses this popular understanding of the term quite nicely when he says, 'You know the kind of love I'm talking about now. Physical love, that impulse that drives you to someone special, as well as love of the other person's being, his or her essence, as it were. Carnal love and, well, call it sentimental love, the day-to-day caring about the person' (Carver 1995: 143).

When people think about revolution, they tend to think of a form of governmental change through the violent seizure of state power. Many dictionary definitions reflect this common understanding of the term. Michael Kimmel quotes one such definition in a relatively recent sociological study of revolutions:

> The *Oxford English Dictionary* defines revolution as 'A complete overthrow of the established government in any country or state by those who were previously subject to it; a forcible substitution of a new ruler or form of government.' This definition implies that revolutions take place on the political level, involving government and rulers, and that they must be 'complete' and successful in order to count as revolutions. It also equates the imposition of a new ruler with a revolutionary transformation of society.
>
> (Kimmel 1990: 4)

From this perspective, the gap between love and revolution would appear to be unbridgeable. Love is exclusively private and personal, while revolution is entirely public and political. Love is the prerogative of two people absorbed in their relationship with one another, while revolution is the job of professional revolutionaries bent on the violent overthrow of government.

Self-proclaimed revolutionaries, too, have by and large tended to overlook the connections between love and revolution. While Sheila Rowbotham quite rightly points out that, 'despite denunciation from outside and attempts at exorcism from within, the idea of revolution and the idea of freedom in love have enjoyed a remarkably deep and long lasting relationship' (Rowbotham 1972: 46), Ulrike Heider also accurately observes that 'the history of social movements knows but few attempts to revolutionise both society and the individual simultaneously' (Heider 2000: 134). Many Marxists inspired by the Leninist model of revolutionary organisation, for example, have tended to dismiss concern with love – and indeed feeling and emotion in general – as a self-indulgent luxury of the privileged classes (Jaggar 1988: 232). Rowbotham highlights one of the unfortunate by-products of this suppression of feeling and emotion in the following telling caricature of the Leninist conception of the revolutionary leader: 'This individual militant appears as a lonely character without ties, bereft of domestic emotions, who is hard, erect, self-contained, controlled, without the time or ability to express loving passion, who cannot pause to nurture, and for whom friendship is a diversion' (Rowbotham 1979: 68). According to Rowbotham, whose reflections are based in part on her personal experiences of various activist milieux, the problem is not confined to Leninists alone. Rather, 'most' Marxian-inspired left language is constantly distinguishing itself as 'correct' and then covering itself with a determined objectivity. The problem is thus one of the 'use of the concept of science in Marxism itself' (ibid.: 40).

In contrast to their ideological cousins and sometime political rivals, liberalism and 'scientific' socialism, most anarchists – like so many feminists, pacifists, ecologists, anti-imperialists, and libertarian and utopian socialists – regard the liberation of everyday life as a defining feature of both their social ideals and the means of achieving them. The political thinker Murray Bookchin articulated this point with memorable clarity in the aftermath of the rebellions of the 1960s:

> It is plain that the goal of revolution today must be the liberation of daily life. Any revolution that fails to achieve this goal is counter-revolution. Above all, it is *we* who have to be liberated, *our* daily lives, with all their moments, hours and days, and not universals like 'History' and 'Society'.
> (Bookchin 2004 [1971]: 10)

In a similar vein, the fictional character Shevek in Ursula K. Le Guin's anarchist utopian novel *The Dispossessed: An Ambiguous Utopia*, remarks that '[y]ou cannot buy the Revolution. You cannot make the Revolution. You can only be the Revolution. It is in your spirit, or it is nowhere' (Le Guin 2001 [1974]: 301). As these quotations suggest, anarchists have not been content simply to theorise or strategise revolutionary alternatives. They have also embodied revolutionary change in their daily lives, thus spawning an enormously creative counterculture consisting of (amongst other things) free art, free schools, free media and, of course, free love.[2]

Even anarchist revolutionaries, however, have frequently failed to question or challenge the sharp dichotomy between public and private which has dominated so much of Western civilisation, and which has grown increasingly polarised and gendered with the development of capitalist societies.[3] That is to say, they have frequently failed to question or challenge the organisation of our lives

> around two realms: a private realm where women are most in evidence, where 'natural' functions like sex and the bodily functions related to procreation take place, where the affective content of relationships is primary, and a public realm where men are most in evidence, where 'culture' (books, schools, art, music, science) is produced, where money is made, work is done, and where one's efficiency at producing goods or services takes precedence over one's feelings about fellow workers.
>
> (Martin 1989, quoted in Harding 1998: 26)

As a result, they have by default acted on the basis of commonplace assumptions regarding love and revolution absorbed uncritically from existing society.

Consider as an illuminating case in point the anarchist revolutionary activities in Spain during the years of the Spanish Civil War (1936–9). On the one hand, in many areas of Spain conventional patterns of interpersonal relationships were challenged, if not 'overturned altogether' (Ackelsberg 1988: 29). Millions of people lived or worked in highly participatory and productive rural and urban collectives, marketed through cooperatives, and devised means of distributing material wealth more equally. In this revolutionary context the relations between men and women were transformed, and many women who had been particularly oppressed by illiteracy, poverty, male dominance and organised religion contributed to the revolutionary struggle as comrades. This was particularly true in the rural collectives, in a number of which women actively participated, took positions of responsibility and experienced a dramatic increase in personal freedom (Ackelsberg 1988: 35; 1993: 378).

On the other hand, in spite of frequent rhetorical criticisms of 'bourgeois' forms of marriage and sexuality, most anarchist revolutionaries in Spain continued to regard personal life and domestic arrangements as entirely private matters. They did not question the authority of males within the family, and assumed as a matter of course that women would take responsibility for domestic chores (Ackelsberg 1988: 31–6; 1993: 374–6). Still less did any but a small minority challenge the prevailing view of homosexuality as a moral corruption,[4] or consider the relationship between the social organisation of intimate life and revolutionary socio-political change. Revolutionary women were in general in advance of their male comrades in calling attention to the point that marriage and birth control arrangements, access to information about sexuality and the like were not simply private matters, but even in the wartime publications of the revolutionary anarchist women's organisation Mujeres Libres there was surprisingly little attention paid overall to issues of love and sexuality (Ackelsberg 2000: 109). Moreover, what little attention was paid to them petered out almost completely by the end of 1937, as wartime pressures and the need to cement progressive alliances made such concerns seem to be a disposable luxury. The unfortunate result, as Ackelsberg points out, was that once the initial revolutionary flurry had passed, many pre-existing oppressive societal values governing sexuality (and women's sexuality in particular) were allowed to continue intact.

Influenced by the radical anti-slavery, anarchist, pacifist, and contemporary radical and black feminist traditions, Ursula K. Le Guin's almost entirely neglected[5] science fiction 'story suite'[6] *Four Ways to Forgiveness* (Le Guin 1997 [1995]) challenges some of the assumptions about love and revolution referred to above, and shows us that they may be far more closely intertwined than is commonly imagined. My primary aims in the present essay are to elucidate this aspect of the narrative, draw out its anarchist dimensions and consider some of its political implications for our contemporary world. I will do so by means of close and politically focused textual analysis of the book's four interconnected stories, followed by concluding reflections on the historical experience of antebellum slavery that in part inspired the work, its contemporary non-fictional analogues in the revolutionary and feminist theory of bell hooks and George Lakey, and its continuing political relevance today.

'Betrayals'

The bleak setting of *Four Ways to Forgiveness* is signalled on the very first page of its opening story, 'Betrayals'. Rather than begin by describing its setting directly, this book about distant imaginary worlds opens with an image of a single individual reading a book about a distant imaginary world. On the world of Gethen, the character muses, in an incredulous and reflective pause in her reading, there has never been a war. Her incredulity indicates to us immediately that hatred and war rive her own world, Yeowe. The reflective pause – during which she speculates, 'What would that world be, a world without war? It would be the real world' (Le Guin 1997 [1995]: 7) – creates a space for the reader to reflect on the artificial political construction of violence in her or his own social 'reality'. It also suggests the futility of trying to escape from the destructive effects of political violence by retreating into a private world based on very different principles: 'Any peace one of us can make in our life is only a denial that the war is going on, a shadow of the shadow, a doubled unbelief' (ibid.: 7).

As if in tacit confirmation of the validity of these ruminations, the narrative shifts swiftly from Yoss' thoughtful reading to the tale of Wada and Eyid, two star-crossed lovers whose sad story echoes the one told by Shakespeare in his classic tragedy *Romeo and Juliet*. Like Romeo and Juliet, young Wada and Eyid are madly and passionately in love. Thanks to the kindness of Yoss they have been able to express their passion in secret for some time, but they cannot live openly in partnership because of the long-running feud between their respective families. Their passion, the narrator observes tellingly, was 'trapped in the hatred of the old' (ibid.: 9). Eventually, we discover later in the story, it is smothered by that hatred.

For all its sentimental interest, the tragic love story of Wada and Eyid is but a small tale within a much larger story. The primary focus of 'Betrayals' is another more mature and atypical love story that suggests a very different relationship between the personal and the political. As those who are familiar with the story will know, I am of course speaking of the love that blossoms between Yoss and Abberkam. Abberkam, or 'Chief Abberkam', as Yoss calls him when they first meet, is, like Yoss, a refugee from the endless war and grief that plague Yeowe. A former hero of the revolutionary liberation movement that freed Yeowe from its longstanding status as a colony of the slave-owning sister world of Werel, Abberkam is by the time we encounter him also the disgraced ex-leader of Yeowe's first World Party. Having lied, betrayed his supporters and embezzled public funds, Abberkam is not only a symbol of the fallen 'perfect politician' (as Yoss accurately describes him, with some justifiable disgust), but also an embodiment of the dominance drive evident in so many 'real world' revolutions.

In order to see this point more clearly, it may be helpful to step back from the text for a moment in order to consider Le Guin's reflections about revolution in a recent essay entitled 'A War without End' (Le Guin 2004). Near the end of this essay, Le Guin hazards an explanation of why it is that revolutions generally fail. Her explanation takes the form of a commentary on the poet Audre Lorde's observation that you can't dismantle the master's house with the master's tools: 'Revolutions generally fail. But I see their failure beginning when the attempt to rebuild the house so everybody can live in it becomes an attempt to grab all the saws and hammers, barricade Ole Massa's toolroom, and keep the others out. Power not only corrupts, it addicts' (ibid.: 217). In other words, revolutions tend to go astray because of the inclination of some revolutionaries to make use of and eventually monopolise the very mechanisms of power that their masters formerly used to oppress them.

These comments, while overstated when framed as an explanation of the root cause of revolutionary failure – there are many complex reasons why revolutions fail, and it is probably a mistake to try to identify any one root cause of the phenomenon – are nevertheless highly illuminating when interpreted more modestly as a persuasive account of one of the primary reasons why revolutions generally fail. Like George Orwell's *Animal Farm*, they remind us of the ease with which the desire to dominate may itself dominate the revolutionary process and make a mockery of its most noble ideals. They are also quite interesting for what they reveal about the unorthodox and elusive politics of *Four Ways to Forgiveness*.

Consider once more the character of Abberkam. Initially we know him only by way of his public reputation. An elected Chief of one of the principal tribes of Yeowe, he rose to prominence during the last years of revolutionary struggle against the Werelian colonisers by leading a mass movement for 'Racial Freedom'. The main aim of the movement, institutionalised in a World Party and symbolised by the image of a curved sword, was to ensure that nobody lived on Yeowe but its own people. In practice this territorialist policy entailed the exclusion not only of the slave-owning Werelians, but also of the inhabitants of other peaceful worlds opposed to slavery, including representatives of the Ekumen (a non-directive, information-gathering consortium of peaceful worlds that features repeatedly in Le Guin's science fiction writings). The policy also encouraged protracted violence even after the Liberation, as the habit of killing Werelians learned during the revolutionary struggle mutated into internecine conflict among power-hungry tribes and city chiefs. While Abberkam strove to prevent this violence, he did so not in the service of a struggle to end domination and institutionalised hierarchy,[7] but in order to secure his own position as the most powerful politician on Yeowe. As is all too frequently the case with ambitious politicians, this quest for supreme political power in turn degenerated into corruption – debauchery, embezzlement, secret plots, betrayal, etc. – and his eventual downfall and public disgrace.

The occasion for us to see beyond this one-dimensional public image comes when Yoss recognises that Abberkam is, like herself, a 'soul in pain', and is impelled to do what she can to ease his suffering. As in so many other of Le Guin's writings, love here begins in shared pain, in the conscious decision to reach out to a stranger in order to help them in a time of need. One thinks, for example, of Shevek's remarks to his boyhood friends at the end of chapter 2 of *The Dispossessed*:

> All of us here are going to know grief; if we live fifty years, we'll have known pain for fifty years. And in the end we'll die ... There are times I – I am very frightened. Any happiness seems trivial. Any yet, I wonder if it isn't all a misunderstanding – this grasping after happiness, this fear of pain ... If instead of fearing it and running from it, one could ... get through it, go beyond it. There is something beyond it. It's the self that suffers, and there's a place where the self – ceases.
>
> (Le Guin 2001 [1974]: 60–1)

Little does Shevek know when he makes these remarks that one of the friends present, young Takver, will one day become his life partner, his constant companion through times of suffering as well as joy. Similarly, Yoss has no idea when she first goes to see Abberkam at his house that the two of them will eventually form an intimate bond. She goes because she is concerned for his welfare. She remains because she finds him convulsed with a high fever, and returns because doing so apparently satisfies her desire to be 'useful'.

During these visits Yoss and Abberkam talk and get to know one another better. Love and respect do not come easily, however. Because both are exceptionally proud and strong-willed individuals accustomed to being in positions of authority, their initial interaction takes the form of a battle of wills. Abberkam tends to orate rather than communicate, except when employing his formidable charm in order to try to seduce Yoss (as he has seduced and abandoned so many other women in the past), while Yoss stubbornly refuses to admit to herself that she feels anything for Abberkam other than pity and contempt.

The point at which this awkward relationship blossoms into love is the pivotal point near the end of the story when Abberkam finally divests himself of the terrible burden of his politician's ego by risking his life on behalf of another. Specifically, when he sees from afar that Yoss' house has caught fire, he rushes heedlessly into the collapsing structure in order to save her. While she is in fact already safe, it is only thanks to his intervention that Yoss' beloved pet cat is spared from the flames. En route home to tend his injuries he encounters Yoss, informs her of what has just happened, and comforts and consoles her in her time of need. He also offers her a new home with him, as Yoss touchingly discovers when she arrives at his house and finds that the peaceful old room she had grown attached to during her sick calls has been lovingly prepared for her.

The story concludes on an open-ended note, with the possibility of a loving relationship between the two based on trust, truth, respect for the independent views and personal traits of the other, open communication and shared suffering as well as joys. The relationship may well not last, but both are at least genuinely committed to trying to make it work. The measure of Abberkam's commitment is indicated by his heartfelt confession to Yoss that while he did not 'hold to the one noble thing' in the past – he repeatedly betrayed his son's mother, other women, himself – she, Yoss, gave him the 'beautiful' opportunity to do so in the present. The redemptive nature of these remarks is almost certainly not lost on Yoss, who earlier in the story responds to Abberkam's use of the very same expression ('hold to the one noble thing') by offering to read from the religious book in which the quotation appears. In that instance, Abberkam was responding to Yoss' observation that young Wada and Eyid clung to their love for each other as if they knew that it was their only truth in a world filled with hatred and lies. The repetition of the phrase in the very different circumstances of the closing pages of the story suggests that Yoss and Abberkam may be able to forge a more lasting relationship than did the doomed young lovers because their commitment to one another extends beyond the private pursuit of pleasure. In contrast to the fearful love of Wada and Eyid, and indeed in contrast to the currently popular conception of love represented by the Raymond Carver passage quoted at the start of this chapter (p. 103), the intimate love that Yoss and Abberkam come to feel for one another is a *transformative* and healing force that helps them to overcome at least a small part of the legacy of corruption and domination left by Abberkam's betrayal of the revolution.

'Forgiveness Day'

As in 'Betrayals', love and respect do not come easily to the two central characters of 'Forgiveness Day', the whimsical and endearing second composition in Le Guin's four-part story suite. In this case the narrative unfolds on the slave-owning world of Werel, and the chief protagonists are an Ekumenical diplomat (Solly) and her Werelian military bodyguard (Teyeo).

Very cleverly, our introduction to the setting and characters of the story is initially confined to a vertiginous glimpse of the world from the perspective of the pampered and hence apparently rather callow Envoy Solly. In stark contrast to Abberkam or Yoss, or indeed any of the other characters in *Four Ways to Forgiveness*, Solly has led a remarkably privileged life. As a result of this privileged background, she is easily bored with and quick to judge those she meets. She has little time or patience for either the embassy staff or the official representatives of her host world. Her greatest ire, however, is reserved for her Werelian bodyguard, Rega (a military title, translated by her as 'Major') Teyeo. In the opening pages of the story, narrated entirely from Solly's perspective, Teyeo is described variously as as stiff and cold as rigor mortis, stiff as a stick, rigid, a stuffed shirt, controlling and an officer officially incapable of humanity. In the absence of any evidence to the contrary, it is likely that many readers (including this one, I must confess) will be inclined initially to accept this caricature, especially insofar as they empathise with Solly's plight as an enlightened feminist, humanist and secularist on a world marred by gender hierarchies, slavery and religious war.

Having been taken in by Solly's rather hasty and harsh assessment of the major, we feel for his humanity all the more deeply when the narrative perspective of the story suddenly shifts and we have an opportunity to see the world from his point of view. The ensuing character sketch of Teyeo is both utterly convincing and deeply affecting, a tribute to Le Guin's formidable powers of empathy and imagination. Among other things, we learn that Teyeo's childhood years were shaped by the stark discipline of a poor military household. His days typically began at five in the morning, and were filled with lessons and fenced with disciplines. He spent much of his time alone, and learned to value silence and good manners. Because he studied only the history and literature of his own people, he quite naturally adopted their relatively conservative attitudes towards women and foreigners. Like others of his veot-class military background, he came to value above all else self-sufficiency, competence, responsibility, courage, honour and self-respect.

The formative experience of Teyeo's life is his extended posting on Yeowe in the service of a war to put down the anti-colonial slave revolution. Tragically, as he continues to fight a losing battle against the rebels, his wife lies dying on Werel of complications related to a fever. Only when he returns to his home world after over seven years of senseless carnage does he learn that she is dead. He also discovers with great bitterness and an increasingly consuming sense of anger that the army on Yeowe in which he so loyally served has essentially been written off by his government. Insult is added to injury when, instead of honouring his sacrifice, his government and society make him feel like a useless relic of a past best forgotten. Desolate, alone, unemployed and increasingly plagued by an unfamiliar sense of self-doubt, he attempts to make himself useful in the new order of things by studying the ways and mores of the Ekumen. Le Guin's wise and infinitely compassionate narrator comments as follows: 'Not sure what he needed to know, he floundered about in the network, bewildered by the endless information available, increasingly aware that he was no intellectual and no scholar and would never understand Alien minds, but doggedly driving himself on out of his depth' (Le Guin 1997 [1995]: 65). In the process of trying to educate himself, Teyeo makes the acquaintance of a Hainish lecturer and diplomat named Old Music. The contact proves to be fortuitous, as Old Music enlists his services as a member of the Embassy Guard. It is in this capacity that he is assigned to protect a 'headstrong' young Envoy named Solly, whom he quickly comes to regard as 'an aggressive, spoiled child with the sexuality of an adult, given the responsibility of a diplomat in a dangerously unstable country' (ibid.: 69).

The idea of a relationship developing between Solly and Teyeo thus appears even more implausible than it did in the case of Yoss and Abberkam. As in 'Betrayals', however, circumstances change drastically when they are thrown together by developments outside their control, and they begin to bond in response to the impulse to mutual aid. I won't attempt to convey here the wonderfully farcical quality of Le Guin's narration of the events that unfold on the day of the Festival of Forgiveness. Suffice to say that Solly is kidnapped in a confusing melee in which the major is injured while leaping to her defence, and the two of them are imprisoned in a small, windowless room in the basement of a house.

Notwithstanding their physical proximity, at first they maintain rigid personal boundaries that neither dares to cross. Over time, however, each develops a new-found respect for the independent personality and views of the other. More specifically, Teyeo comes to respect Solly's courage and resourcefulness in the face of danger and adversity, while she begins to appreciate the value of his restraint, formality and quietness. These realisations in turn induce thoughtful critical reflection of both a personal and political nature.

Solly, for example, ponders for the very first time the implications of living one's life as a project extending over time. 'It was curious', she reflects,

> how his stiff manner, his manners, which had always shunted her aside, cut her out, here had quite another effect: his restraint and formality

> reassured her that she was still part of the world outside this room, from which they came and to which they would return, a world where people lived long lives. What did long life matter? she asked herself, and didn't know. It was nothing she had ever thought about before.
>
> (Le Guin 1997 [1995]: 87)

And again: 'I keep thinking about long life, about living long ... Something about thinking of life as long makes a difference. Like having kids does. Even thinking about having kids. It's like it changes some balance' (ibid.: 89). She also reflects on the invisible but absolute physical barriers between herself and Teyeo, and these thoughts lead her to a mature appreciation of the stultifying constraints of slave societies: 'He was only maintaining, under incredibly difficult circumstances, the rigid restraint he had always shown. Not just he ... all of them ... It was the mentality of a slave society: slaves and masters caught in the same trap of radical distrust and self-protection' (ibid.: 90). When one recalls the pampered diplomat at the beginning of the story who blithely took for granted her enormous freedom, it is difficult to escape the conclusion that the character transformation these words express is in its own small way revolutionary.

Teyeo, too, undergoes enormous changes during their captivity. When Solly endeavours to communicate with him about the terrible waste involved in maintaining the institution of slavery, he responds with a measure of honesty and critical social awareness completely at odds with his veot-class background. 'We learn to ... close ranks', he acknowledges haltingly after a long reflective pause, 'You're right, it wastes ... energy, the spirit. You are open' (ibid.: 92). Solly appears to appreciate the enormous significance of these remarks: 'His words cost him so much, she thought, not like hers that just came dancing out of the air and went back into it. He spoke from the marrow. It made what he said a solemn compliment, which she accepted gratefully' (ibid.: 92). Later, near the end of the story, Teyeo quite remarkably even contemplates the possibility of revolution on Werel.

Whether such events will ever come to pass neither he nor we can foresee at the time, but what is clear is that Teyeo has experienced a revolutionary change of consciousness in the process of forging a loving bond with Solly. As we have already seen, this transformation is not confined to his worldview alone. As he and Solly communicate their fears and dreams to one another they both change and grow together. By the end of the story they are partners in the fullest sense of the word. Like the budding partnership between Yoss and Abberkam, their relationship is rooted in trust, truth, respect for the independent views and personal traits of the other, open communication and shared suffering as well as joys. Moreover, and very importantly, their love for one another does not lead to insular self-absorption and detachment from the troubles of society. To the contrary, it cultivates respect for difference and sensitivity to the suffering of others. In Teyeo's case, it prompts him, two years after his own freedom from captivity, to free his family's assets (slaves) by an act of irrevocable manumission. In both cases, it enables them to play prominent and constructive parts in the revolutionary events described in the latter two stories of *Four Ways to Forgiveness*. Once again we see love represented as a transformative force, one that in this instance nurtures not only individual growth but principled and non-violent revolutionary social change as well.

The personal and political dimensions of the love portrayed in 'Forgiveness Day' are apparently compatible, for we are informed in a touchingly romantic coda that Solly and Teyeo eventually marry and live together in fulfilment for many years. In the narrator's words,

> In all her [Solly's] travels and posts she was accompanied by her husband, a Werelian army officer, a very handsome man, as reserved as she was outgoing. People who knew them knew their passionate pride and trust in each other. Solly was perhaps the happier person, rewarded and fulfilled in her work; but Teyeo had no regrets. He had lost his world, but he had held fast to the one noble thing.
>
> (Le Guin 1997 [1995]: 106–7)

The ending of the story would thus appear to be an unambiguously happy one.

And yet, in spite of this seeming absence of ambiguity, the reader is left pondering an unresolved question of great significance. Shortly before Solly and Teyeo are released from their captivity, and shortly after they make love to one another for the very first time, Teyeo reflects as follows on their situation:

> It was curious ... how little sex changed anything ... the only thing that was truly different was something he had no word for. Sex, comfort, tenderness, love, trust, no word was the right word, the whole word. It was utterly intimate, hidden in the mutuality of their bodies, and it changed nothing in their circumstances, nothing in the world, even the tiny wretched world of their imprisonment.
>
> (Le Guin 1997 [1995]: 104)

The troubling question this passage raises is whether something so small and socially insignificant as the love two people feel for one another can really shake the foundations of society. This is one of the primary questions to which we now turn in our analysis of the remaining two stories in Le Guin's story suite.

'A Man of the People'

While all four of the pieces in *Four Ways to Forgiveness* explore the relationship between love and revolution, the last two stories in the collection have a more overt and pronounced political focus than the first two. That is to say, they foreground the question of the nature of social revolution. According to one traditional understanding of the term explicated by Kimmel at the start of this chapter, a revolution refers to the complete overthrow of an established government by those who were previously subject to it, as well as the forcible substitution of a new ruler or form of government. True to her anarchist, pacifist and Taoist convictions, Le Guin challenges this power-centred understanding of revolutions by portraying in vivid fictional detail a radically different type of revolutionary movement concerned not with the violent seizure of political power but with the liberation of imagination, desire and human creative potential in everyday life. In stark contrast to the dogmatic, destructive, mechanically impersonal, yang-heavy revolutions of old, she provides us with an imaginative vision of a patient, constructive, organic and open-ended form of revolutionary practice ultimately rooted in a transformation of the individual spirit. She also offers us invaluable human-scale portraits of a new kind of revolutionary. The heroes of her tales are not great military leaders or ideologues, but teachers and healers, a man born and raised in a simple pueblo village and a remarkable woman who overcomes slavery and sexual abuse to campaign for the complete emancipation of women as a necessary component of social revolution.

In 'A Man of the People', the protagonist in question is Havzhiva, short for Mattinyehedarheddyuragamuruskets Havzhiva. Apart from his unpronounceable name, it is difficult to find much not to like about Havzhiva, a man with the common touch whose overriding passion in life is an unwavering commitment to truth and the ethical use of knowledge. Born in a peaceful but insular pueblo community on the planet Hain, he leads a relatively happy and contented existence until a chance encounter with a family relation who left the community many years ago to become a historian triggers in him a restless desire to do the same. The meeting of minds also unbalances him by throwing his previously unquestioned pueblo value system into disarray. His life from that point onwards becomes a kind of spiritual quest to restore his lost sense of balance and wholeness on alien worlds seemingly bereft of clear, recognisable and authoritative moral horizons.

What begins as a seemingly personal quest evolves over time into a political one as well. Initially the main preoccupation of his life is the search for knowledge that will enable to him to see beyond the restricted confines of his present. Having grown up in an environment with almost no books, he consumes them with a passion once he gains access to the voluminous libraries of the Hainish network of cities and information centres called the temple. He also eagerly pursues another less ethereal form of knowledge apparently available in great abundance outside the confines of the pueblo. As the narrator explains,

> He had been conscious mainly of his own increasingly fearless and careless transgression of what had been the rules. Not all the women wanted to

> have sex, and not all the women wanted to have sex with men, as he had soon discovered, but that still left an infinite variety ... He had sought out women from off-world; sleeping with Aliens added exoticism to transgression, or, as he put it, was an enrichment of knowledge such as every historian should seek.
>
> (Le Guin 1997 [1995]: 128)

While he has more serious loving relationships at this point in his life as well, they too are primarily products of what is then still a very personal and inward-looking quest for liberating knowledge and emotional balance. Indeed, the two great early loves of his life founder for precisely this reason. An arranged relationship in the pueblo collapses because it cannot bear the weight of his impulse to transcend local knowledge, while a far more intense relationship in his student days breaks apart because he brings to it unrealistic expectations and demands spawned by his all-consuming need for internal balance.

Having arrived at the dispiriting conclusion that he has no hope of personal joy in his life, Havzhiva resolves to find fulfilment instead in the ethical use of knowledge. An opportunity for him to do so arises when he is assigned by the Ekumenical Ambassador on Yeowe ('a clever young Terran named Solly') as Envoy to a politically tumultuous region in the south called Yotebber. There he finds himself embroiled in a revolutionary struggle, albeit of a very different sort than the violent rebellion of the Yeowen slaves against their Werelian colonial masters. In this case the revolution consists of non-violent resistance conducted by Yeowen women unwilling to accept their continued subordination in a post-colonial order run exclusively by men. As one of their representatives (Dr Yeron) explains to the sympathetic Ekumenical Envoy,

> The men think they have to be bosses. They have to stop thinking that. Well, one thing we have learned in my lifetime, you don't change a mind with a gun. You kill the boss and you become the boss ... This is a matter of education ... It will take a long time.
>
> (Le Guin 1997 [1995]: 143)

Havzhiva assists these efforts largely through subtle diplomatic pressure and encouragement. Drawing on his early experiences in the pueblo – experiences that he had previously repudiated because of their apparent parochialism – he recognises that he is able to help most not by judgementally surveying the situation and attempting to impose a quick-fix rational solution, but by patiently familiarising himself with the pattern of local custom so that he might play a supportive part in its gradual reconstruction. In his own words, '[y]ou can't change anything from outside it. Standing apart, looking down, taking the overview, you see the pattern. What's wrong, what's missing. You want to fix it. But you can't patch it. You have to be in it, weaving it. You have to be part of the weaving' (ibid.: 157). And with this wisdom comes fulfilment.

By the end of the story, which takes place many years in the future, Havzhiva has at last attained a measure of personal equilibrium. Just as Teyeo and Solly achieve a balance in their relationship between sitting still and flying, so too, by means of his unassuming political activity on behalf of the women of Yotebber, Havzhiva achieves a balance in his own person between the static values of the pueblo and the dynamic values of the historians.

'A Woman's Liberation'

The subject of Le Guin's second revolutionary portrait is even more improbable than the first. Her features are also much more fully and lovingly drawn. Indeed, it is fair to say that interesting and engaging as are all the protagonists in *Four Ways to Forgiveness*, one of them stands out above the rest for the sheer beauty and emotional resonance of her tale. Rakam, the only character in the collection accorded the respectful freedom to narrate her own life tale without the intervention of an omniscient narrator, is without a doubt the most fully developed and hauntingly memorable of Le Guin's creations in her four-part story suite.

Born a slave on the planet Werel, Rakam spends her early childhood confined in a gender-segregated slave compound owned by the wealthy and politically influential Shomeke family. Unlike the other light-skinned servants in the compound, however, Rakam is dark, similar in colour to the members of the Werelian ruling class. Although she isn't aware of the fact at the time, the reason for her unusual pigmentation is that she is the product of an exploitative sexual encounter between her lighter-skinned, asset (slave)-class mother and the dark-skinned owner of the slave compound.

Precisely because she represents a mixture of what Werelian class institutions are designed to separate, Rakam suffers at the hands of both the owners and her fellow assets. When she is a young child, older asset children taunt her by calling her 'Blackie' and 'Bossie'. Matters only get worse when, thanks to the intervention of her mother, Rakam is admitted to the Great House of the Shomeke family as a personal servant to the master's wife, Lady Tazeu Shomeke. While she is thus spared the tragic fate of those condemned to work long hours in the compound fields, she is obliged instead to become the sexual plaything of Lady Tazeu. To her credit, Le Guin describes these events with great sensitivity and care, and in such an artful manner that we are able to empathise with Rakam's plight. Because Le Guin allows her creation the freedom to tell her own tale, Rakam's mixture of fear and reverent awe is palpable when she is first introduced to Lady Tazeu. We also understand her vulnerability, and while it quickly becomes apparent that Lady Tazeu is a victim of sorts as well – like other women of wealthy or distinguished Werelian families she is regarded as the property of her husband and confined indoors – there is no doubt that the sexual relationship that develops between them is an exploitative one. As Rakam explains,

> I became the pet of Lady Tazeu Wehoma Shomeke. I slept with her almost every night. Her husband was seldom home and when he was there did not come to her, preferring bondswomen for his pleasure. Sometimes she had my mother or other, younger bondswomen come into her bed, and she sent me away at those times, until I was older, ten or eleven, when she began to keep me and have me join in with them, teaching me how to be pleasured. She was gentle, but she was the mistress in love, and I was her instrument which she played.
>
> (Le Guin 1997 [1995]: 173)

During these years Rakam seldom returns to the slave compound. When she does the children she used to play with reject her. In order to cope psychologically with this rejection, Rakam internalises the values of the race-based Werelian class system and identifies with the master class whose company she so intimately keeps.

Her first inkling that it is possible to live a life based on a very different set of values comes when Lady Tazeu presents Rakam as a gift to her son Erod on the occasion of his seventeenth birthday. A sensitive, bookish and idealistic young man who hates his father and all that he stands for, Erod does not take sexual advantage of Rakam. Instead he talks to her endlessly about the idea of revolution. Rakam is understandably sceptical:

> I had no idea what a revolution was. When Erod told me that it meant that assets on plantations in this place called Yeowe were fighting their owners, I did not understand how assets could do that. From the beginning it was ordained that there should be higher and lower beings, the Lord and the human, the man and the woman, the owner and the owned. All my world was Shomeke Estate and it stood on that one foundation. Who would want to overturn it? Everyone would be crushed in the ruins.
>
> (Le Guin 1997 [1995]: 178)

Her scepticism changes to excited anticipation when Erod's father dies and the son exercises his rights of inheritance by choosing to free all the slaves. But the excitement is short lived. Impatient to get away from the scene of his misery and begin a new life in the city working for freedom, Erod fails to ensure the safety of his charges. As soon as he and his staff depart, the owners of neighbouring estates move in and violently re-enslave the newly freed assets. Rakam's grandmother is shot, while Rakam herself is forcibly removed to the Zeskra Estate, where the owners and their guests exploit her as a sexual slave.

As a result of these experiences[8] Rakam develops very distinctive and emphatic views about love and revolution. She associates the former with sexual exploitation, and when she succeeds in escaping from Zeskra to the city she attempts to cut it out of her life altogether. In her own words,

> I was angry now at every man who looked at me as men look at women. I was angry at women who looked at me seeing me sexually ... I hated the sexual parts of myself, my genitals and breasts and the swell of my hips and belly. Ever since I was a child, I had been dressed in soft clothing made to display all that sexuality of a woman's body. When I began to be paid and could buy or make my own clothing, I dressed in hard, heavy cloth.
>
> (Le Guin 1997 [1995]: 194)

She associates revolution with mindless violence, promises betrayed and the replacement of one ruling class by another, and so when she begins her new life as a manumitted asset she embarks on a very personal quest to discover alternative paths to liberation.

Like Havzhiva, Rakam devotes herself with particular zeal to the study of history, which she too regards as a means of escaping from the slavery of the present. Whereas at Shomeke and Zeskra there was nothing but the way things were, since nobody knew anything about a time when things had been different, in her history books Rakam discovers evidence that rebellion is possible. She also learns that in history any freedom has been made by those who are subject to exploitative forms of power, not given by those who wield it. One of the triumphs of the narrative is that it enables us to see and feel just how difficult this learning process is for Rakam. We discover, for example, that she must contend with the practical motivational difficulties involved in studying after a hard day's work: 'It was hard work. Reading is hard for a grown person to learn, tired, at night, after work all day. It is much easier to let the net take one's mind over' (ibid.: 200). Even more dauntingly, she must deal with opposition from her fellow revolutionaries, who criticise her for selfishly pursuing her studies (and, later, her public lecturing and publishing) at the expense of the revolutionary struggle. Rakam responds forcefully and persuasively that she wishes to bring liberating knowledge to those who need it most. 'Everything I do is for freedom', she exclaims in a wounding argument with her friend Ahas; 'I don't put myself first – politicians and capitalists do that. I put freedom first' (ibid.: 201–2). Privately, however, she feels guilty for reading while others are engaged in the more mundane, day-to-day work of making a revolution. She also acknowledges with an admirable degree of critical self-awareness that she is not always as attuned as she might be to the political exigencies of the struggle.

Rakam's fiercest clash with her fellow revolutionaries occurs in the context of a debate about the role of women in the struggle. Erod, now 'Lord' Erod, argues at one of the revolutionary meetings that private affections must be overridden by loyalty to the cause of liberty, and that any personal issue must take second place to the primary issue of legal emancipation. Rakam responds that there is no freedom without sexual freedom. When Erod insists in reply that men must bear the responsibility for the public side of life and women the responsibility for the domestic side of life, Rakam offers the following passionate and persuasive rejoinder: 'Then will emancipation for a woman mean she's free to enter the beza, be locked in on the women's side [of the house]? ... what is freedom for a woman? Is it different from freedom for a man? Or is the free person free?' (ibid.: 204). In thus speaking from the heart, much as Shevek does before a much larger gathering of revolutionaries in chapter 9 of *The Dispossessed*, Rakam finds her own distinctive revolutionary voice and inspires other asset women to do the same.

She develops this distinctive revolutionary voice further when, thanks to the intervention of Old Music and (we may surmise) Rega Teyeo, she succeeds in eluding imminent arrest by going into exile on the ostensibly free world of Yeowe. There she discovers to her horror, as Havzhiva did in 'A Man of the People', that gender hierarchies are even more deeply entrenched on Yeowe than they are on the slave world of Werel. In many ways, her experiences on Yeowe directly mirror her earlier experiences on Werel. For example, she is initially confined with other female refugees in a gender-segregated agricultural village, from which she must flee to escape to the relative freedom of the city. However, whereas on Werel she lacked the education, imagination, and practical communication and organisational skills necessary to resist her oppressors, on Yeowe she quickly becomes a leader of the resistance. Like Dr Yeron, whom she eventually befriends, she conceives emancipation as a long-term process consisting largely of patient educational work designed to counteract the lingering Yeowen slave mentality. She acts on these convictions in the agricultural village by teaching illiterate women and children to read. Later, she shares her knowledge of history with the women in order to mobilise them to demand from the men their earned share of the proceeds of communal labour. In the city she teaches at a school staffed by men and women who 'believed with a fierce passion that only education would lead to freedom' (ibid.: 221). She also joins an educational society composed of democrats, mostly teachers, working to counteract hierarchical thinking in all spheres of life. Very interestingly, the men in the group are in general gradualists, while the women are ready for revolution, thus confirming a pattern in the story suggesting a connection between sexual oppression and social radicalism.

Having travelled such a great physical, intellectual and psychological distance in pursuit of her revolutionary freedom dreams,[9] it is hardly surprising that Rakam experiences crises of self-doubt. Perhaps the most debilitating of these is precipitated by her fear that all her educational efforts will come to naught as a result of governmental control of the influential non-print media. 'Against that', she wonders,

> what harm could a lot of teachers do? Parents who had no schooling had children who entered the net to hear and see and feel what the Chief wanted them to know: that freedom is obedience to leaders, that virtue is violence, that manhood is domination. Against the enactment of such

> truths in daily life and in the heightened sensational experience of the neareals, what good were words?
>
> (Le Guin 1997 [1995]: 222)

Help arrives fortuitously in the form of the Sub-Envoy of the Ekumen to the Yotebber Region, an alien named Yehedarhed Havzhiva. Sent by Old Music to return the books that Rakam had left behind on Werel in her haste to depart for Yeowe, Havzhiva does far more than that. He also helps to restore Rakam's confidence in her educational mission by reinforcing her waning faith in the freedom-giving power of words.

It is perhaps more accurate to say that they reinforce each other's faith in the freedom-giving power of the written word. And this common love of books facilitates a different sort of love between them, one that grows stronger and deeper as they work together to help organise a great demonstration of women. At the very end of the story the two embrace and make love, and we feel that something very profound has occurred, something that may well shake the foundations of society. For their love for one another is not simply a private affair. It is also a repudiation of the system of class, race, gender and sexuality-based domination that enslaved Rakam and inflicted on her a lifetime of sexual servitude and denial. In helping her to overcome her deepest fear, it strikes to the heart of a system that thrives above all on the propagation of terror. Rakam herself half-recognises this point when she recoils at Havzhiva's suggestion that she come home with him:

> 'Don't make me laugh!' I said, and began crying. I wept all the way back along the levee. I sobbed and thought the sobs were ceasing and then sobbed again. I cried for all my sorrows, all my shames. I cried because they were with me now and always would be. I cried because the gate was open and I could go through at last, go into the country on the other side, but I was afraid to go.
>
> (Le Guin 1997 [1995]: 233)

Having overcome this fear, Rakam gains the confidence and strength necessary to conquer other fears as well. Among other things she joins the faculty of the University of Yeowe as a teacher of history, assumes the editorship of the University Press and writes the story of her life. The final lines of that story may be interpreted as a fitting counterpoint to Teyeo's scepticism about the revolutionary significance of love:

> What is one man's and one woman's love and desire, against the history of two worlds, the great revolutions of our lifetimes, the hope, the unending cruelty of our species? A little thing. But a key is a little thing, next to the door it opens. If you lose the key, the door may never be unlocked. It is in our bodies that we lose or begin our freedom, in our

> bodies that we accept or end our slavery. So I wrote this book for my friend, with whom I have lived and will die free.
>
> (Le Guin 1997 [1995]: 234)

Conclusions

It is now commonly assumed that romantic love and revolution are fundamentally unconnected phenomena. From one such popular perspective, love is a mixture of sexual attraction and day-to-day caring about another person that tends to detach the individuals concerned from wider social circumstances; revolution is a form of governmental change through violence, and the one has nothing to do with the other. In *Four Ways to Forgiveness*, Ursula K. Le Guin challenges these assumptions. She does so first and foremost by offering us strikingly beautiful portraits of fictional characters enacting very different, and inextricably interrelated, forms of love and revolution. More specifically, she successfully embodies in her narrative forms of loving that nurture creative qualities like individual growth and transformation, and forms of non-violent social revolution both driven by and conducive to such life-affirming and fundamentally constructive expressions of the human spirit.

In the first two stories of the collection Le Guin explores the relationship between love and revolution by considering the transformative potential of love. In both of these stories, the two main characters are strong willed and very different individuals brought together by unexpected circumstances that help to generate an impulse to mutual aid. Initially they each maintain rigid personal boundaries that the other dares not cross. Pride and stubborn self-control create insurmountable obstacles to intimacy, and each treats the other as an object. Over time, however, honest communication encourages a newfound respect for the independent personality and views of the other. This mutual respect in turn opens the way to genuine intimacy, and facilitates a process of loving, mutual redefinition in which both individuals change and grow together. In contrast to the fearful and self-absorbed love of the young couple Wada and Eyid, the committed love that develops between Yoss and Abberkam, and between Solly and Teyeo, cultivates a mature and considered sensitivity to the suffering of others. In the case of Solly and Teyeo, it also leads to prominent and constructive non-violent action on behalf of revolutionary social change.

In the last two stories of the collection, Le Guin explores the relationship between love and revolution by inquiring into the nature of social revolution. True to her anarchist, Taoist and pacifist convictions, she challenges traditional power-centred understanding of revolutions by portraying in vivid fictional detail a radically different type of revolutionary movement – one concerned not with the violent seizure of political power, but with the liberation of imagination, desire and human creative potential in everyday life. Very much in the spirit of the non-violent anarchist revolutionary tradition, the imaginative vision represented is one of a patient, constructive, organic and open-ended form of revolutionary practice ultimately rooted in a transformation of the individual spirit. Hence the human-scale focus of the stories, and their depiction of revolutionary lives very different from those of the great military leaders or ideologues who typically take centre stage in both fictional and non-fictional accounts of revolution. In 'A Man of the People', the revolutionary portrait is of an unassuming man born in a simple pueblo village who achieves wisdom and balance in his life not by dominating his environment, but by patiently familiarising himself with the pattern of local custom so that he might play a supportive role in its gradual reconstruction. In 'A Woman's Liberation', it is of a remarkable woman who overcomes slavery, sexual abuse and the wounding criticisms of fellow revolutionaries to become a leader in the non-violent struggle for women's liberation. In both stories, the main characters are portrayed not as larger-than-life figures free of all imperfections, but as flawed human beings beset by ambivalence, conflict and self-doubt – individuals who must ultimately acknowledge they need the love and support of others in order to carry on.

Perhaps the closest contemporary analogues to this way of thinking about love and revolution may be found in the anarchistic, non-fictional writings of bell hooks and George Lakey. In *All About Love: New Visions*, the former adopts M. Scott Peck's definition of love as the will to extend one's self for the purpose of nurturing one's own or another's spiritual growth.[10] It follows, she argues, that love and abuse, or domination, cannot coexist. The exercise of dominating power gives one the illusion of having triumphed over fear, over the need to love. In fact, however, it leads only to alienation and separation. When we love, hooks suggests, we no longer allow our hearts to be held captive by fear. We surrender the will to domination,[11] and open ourselves to the possibility of growth and transformation through connection with another. Insofar as such loving practice is an active and creative force based on respect for difference, responsibility and sensitivity to the suffering of others, it should lead us into greater communion with the world, and the recognition that all spheres of life could and should have as their foundation a universal love ethic. hooks acknowledges the fact that most people today are deeply sceptical about the idea of love serving as such a transformative social force. But she quite rightly replies that one need only recall the words of Martin Luther King, and the relatively recent experience of the American civil rights movement, to see that loving practice is about far more than simply giving an individual greater life satisfaction.[12] It is also an essential element in the struggle to construct humane alternatives to fear-based structures of domination and oppression.

Like hooks, George Lakey makes the observation that as each of us replaces despair with love we move our world a bit closer to a living revolution. In his book *Powerful Peacemaking: A Strategy for a Living Revolution* (Lakey 1987), he refutes the antiquated belief that successful revolutionary change necessarily entails a sudden violent action to remake society, and proposes instead a developmental model of revolutionary movement that grows organically over time, with each successive stage building on the preceding one. More specifically, he identifies five core stages of what he calls a 'living revolution': cultural preparation, organisation building, propaganda of the deed, mass economic and political noncooperation, and parallel institutions. Like the German anarchist thinker Gustav Landauer – who observed that the state is 'a condition, a certain relationship among human beings, a mode of behaviour between them; we destroy it by contracting other relationships, by behaving differently toward one another' and emphasised the role of 'love' rather than violence in revolutionary change (Landauer, quoted in Marshall 1993: 411–12)[13] – Lakey recognises that meaningful social change is ultimately rooted in a loving transformation of the individual spirit. Being an eminently practical thinker, he also understands that only a strong and united people's organisation with a revolutionary programme can provide the new life that becomes the new society. Building such an organisation is hard work, involving not only social analysis and critique, but also self-awareness, self-education and the continuing creative imagination of both revolutionary goals and strategy (I would add love to this list as well). Nobody can give such skills to us. Only through popular struggle can the people gain a freedom they can keep. Governments will, of course, do everything in their power to stymie this process, not least by fomenting violence in order to discredit the revolutionary movement and justify repression. But, as Lakey accurately observes in terms that will be familiar to students of anarchist thought (see, for example, Étienne de la Boétie's classic work on the subject, *Discours de la servitude volontaire*, frequently translated into English as *Of Voluntary Servitude*),

> It is discouraging to see the impressive apparatus of repression belonging to the state, but the fact remains that the state cannot continue without the cooperation of the people. In the metaphor of a house, the foundation is the people's consent, and no matter how impressive the roof of army, police, or secret files, if the foundation gives way, the house will fall.
>
> (Lakey 1987: 55)

Very interestingly, both hooks and Lakey reserve some of their harshest criticisms for the destructive effects of patriarchal masculinity. hooks observes that in patriarchal societies men, more so than women, use lying and psychological terrorism as a means of gaining power in heterosexual relationships. Many women are complicit in these lies because they wish to be able to project onto men a fantasy image of ideal masculine strength and power. The tragic but inevitable consequence of such control-oriented deceptions is the loss of the capacity to give and receive love, because 'it is impossible to nurture one's own or another's spiritual growth when the core of one's being and identity is shrouded in secrecy and lies' (hooks 2000: 46).

Lakey too is scathing in his criticism of patriarchal masculinity, but, in contrast to hooks, focuses primarily on its social implications, and in particular on the ways in which it helps to reinforce destructive institutions such as the war system. Sexuality, we are taught by our patriarchal culture, is about domination: 'fucking', for example, means both sexual intercourse and exploitation. Men are meant to be sexually dominating. Women and gay men are perceived to be sexually subordinate. Hence men must prove that they are neither effeminate nor gay by expressing dominance. Violence, and the elaborate war system it maintains, is one way of doing so. The living revolutionary alternative, Lakey suggests, would entail equality of sexes and sexual orientations, and the abandonment of polarised sex roles.

As the four tales in Le Guin's story suite make abundantly clear, any such love-inspired, transformative social project would benefit greatly from sustained reflection on the complex historical legacy of slave societies and their mutually reinforcing systems of class, race, gender and sexuality-based oppression. In this and many other respects, the work of black feminist writers such as bell hooks, Audre Lorde, Toni Morrison, Octavia Butler and June Jordan is invaluable. Drawing on this work, the sociologist Patricia Hill Collins notes that systems of oppression frequently sustain themselves by harnessing the power of deep feelings like love and the erotic to the exigencies of domination. This is so, she contends, in the cases of both contemporary capitalism and historical slave societies (Hill Collins 2009: 162–3). I agree, and would cite as particularly compelling historical evidence of the latter the sexual economy of slavery in the United States in the nineteenth century that systematically expropriated black women's sexuality and reproductive capacity for the pleasure and profit of white slave-owners.

Specifically, not only were enslaved women the only segment of antebellum (pre-Civil War) society compelled to labour both in the fields and in the gender-segregated domestic sphere, they were also the only group forced to perform sexual and reproductive labour to satisfy the economic, political and personal interests of elite-class white men. In economic terms, the reproductive labour performed by enslaved black women in the United States was – in contrast to other slave societies in Latin America and the Caribbean, which replenished themselves primarily by means of constant influxes of new slaves from Africa – arguably the most valuable labour performed in the entire economy (Davis 2009: 221). Hence the legal rules and precedents that treated them as livestock, and stipulated that the race of the father did not alter the status of an enslaved black woman's child. Even more barbarously, as a direct result of such laws 'tens of thousands of white men were able to sexually abuse and coerce individual enslaved women without the risk that the women would bear children whose legal status would be affected in any way by their own' (ibid.: 224). Members of an enslaved workforce, black women were expected to provide sex on demand, and the resulting abuse was by no means limited to coercive sexual relations with their white masters. Slave-owners frequently compelled their slaves to 'initiate' a son or younger nephew, or pleasure a family friend, and in many cases they sold those deemed to be the most attractive (the so-called 'fancy girls', usually of lighter skin complexion) for a hefty profit. In these ways the slave system worked to thwart and manipulate the erotic power within the culture of an oppressed group that could have provided energy for social change. One of the many destructive legacies of this exercise of power as domination may be seen in the complex social power dynamics shaping African-American love and desire today, and in particular the stubborn persistence of a form of black masculinity that sometimes blurs the distinction between 'protecting' black women and controlling them (Hill Collins 2009: 169–70). Equally, however, the creative legacy of resistance to slavery has inspired the black feminist tradition and its powerful and inspirational efforts to reclaim love and the erotic as a catalyst for emancipatory social change.

Were any of the major characters in *Four Ways to Forgiveness* to read some of the analyses of love and revolution referred to above, they would no doubt find much food for thought useful to them in understanding, and acting rightly in, their own warring and divided worlds. We, the readers of Le Guin's science fiction story suite, are in a slightly different position, for her work treats ideas only insofar as they are embodied in the lives of the characters that populate her fictional narrative. Still, we may perhaps emerge from our imaginative engagements with the lives of these characters with very different perspectives on both our own individual lives and the possibilities for organised collective resistance to structures of domination. In the current climate of state-sponsored fear and terror that suffocates hope and silences expressions of human solidarity, images of a very different way of being such as are to be found in the pages of *Four Ways to Forgiveness* are sustenance for the hungry spirit. They remind us of the generous and inclusive freedom dreams historically articulated with particular poignancy by black women artists and freedom fighters, now all but forgotten in a world where dreams and desires of every shade and colour have been commodified and colonised in the service of capital and the state. By helping us to see beyond the tyranny of the present, Le Guin has, in effect, opened the gate to another and far better world. It remains to be seen whether we will have the courage to step through.

Notes

1 My thanks to Peter Stillman and Jamie Heckert for their supportive comments on an earlier draft of this essay, and to Martha Ackelsberg and Richard Cleminson for their helpful advice regarding the gender and sexual politics of the Spanish anarchists.

2 I try to give a flavour of the richness of this anarchist counterculture in the United States' context in which Bookchin and Le Guin were writing in my recent journal article 'Social Anarchism or Lifestyle Anarchism: An Unhelpful Dichotomy' (Davis 2010). For detailed accounts, see Avrich (2005, 1980), Blechman (1994), Falk (1984),

Farrell (1997), Koenig (2009), Marshall (1993), Ording (2009), Roszak (1995), Sonn (1992) and Veysey (1973).

3 To question or challenge the dichotomous and highly gendered ways in which public and private have so frequently been defined in Western civilisation does not, of course, necessarily entail rejecting the distinction between them altogether. Although my views on the subject are by no means fixed, I am currently inclined to agree with Peter Steinberger (1999) that it is helpful to distinguish between the thesis of identity (the idea that there is no real difference between public and private) and the thesis of inseparability (the idea that although public and private denote different ways of being or manners of acting in the world, they are nonetheless always and importantly connected). Whereas the former may entail jettisoning the idea of privacy altogether, along with the shelter it sometimes provides for freedom and intimacy within community, the latter enables one to criticise the idea of a separate and distinct sphere of privacy while still retaining a vocabulary in which it is possible to defend private activity against the coercive force of public opinion.

4 See on this point Richard Cleminson's piece 'Male Inverts and Homosexuals: Sex Discourse in the Anarchist *Revista Blanca*' (Cleminson 1995b). Lesbianism was discussed in the Spanish anarchist press as well, but to a lesser degree than male homosexuality. The principal work that discusses both of these issues is Cleminson's *Anarquismo y homosexualidad: Antología de artículos de la Revista Blanca, Generación Consciente, Estudios e Iniciales (1924–1935)* (Cleminson 1995a). See also Martha Ackelsberg's pioneering study of the revolutionary anarchist women's organisation Mujeres Libres, *Free Women of Spain: Anarchism and the Struggle for the Emancipation of Women* (Ackelsberg 2005 [1991]). In both this work (Ackelsberg 2005: 172) and a subsequent journal article (Ackelsberg 2000) she observes that while it was well known within Mujeres Libres circles that one of the co-initiators of the group was a lesbian who lived openly with her female partner, there is no written material from the period even acknowledging their relationship, let alone discussing and/or defending it.

5 In 1995, the second story in the collection ('Forgiveness Day') won the Asimov's Readers' Award, the Locus Readers' Award, and the Theodore Sturgeon Award. In 1996, the collection as a whole won the Locus Readers' Award. In spite of this well-deserved recognition, *Four Ways to Forgiveness* has been almost entirely neglected by scholarly critics. My research searches have uncovered a smattering of references or excerpts in science fiction anthologies and obscure journal articles, as well as brief book reviews largely confined to plot summaries, but not much else. One might reasonably expect that anarchist scholarship would prove an exception to the general rule given the strong, if subtle, anarchist influences on the story. However, this supposition is not at present supported by the evidence of publication.

6 The term is Le Guin's. She explains its *raison d'être* as follows in the foreword to her collection of stories *The Birthday of the World*:

> My book *Four Ways to Forgiveness* consists of four connected stories. Once more I plead for a name, and thus recognition, for this fictional form (which goes back at least as far as Elizabeth Gaskell's *Cranford* and has become increasingly frequent and interesting): a book of stories linked by place, characters, theme, and movement, so as to form not a novel but a whole. There's a sneering British term 'fix-up' for books by authors who, told that collections 'don't sell', patch unconnected stories together with verbal duct tape. But the real thing is not a random collection, any more than a Bach cello suite is. It does things a novel doesn't do. It is a real form, and deserves a real name. Maybe we could call it a story suite? I think I will.
>
> (Le Guin 2002: xi–xii)

Readers may be interested to know *The Birthday of the World* includes a fifth contribution to the original four-story suite. The title of the sequel story is 'Old Music and the Slave Women'. It is much darker than the other four, and is perhaps motivated in part by Le Guin's indignation at the presumption, especially common in science fiction, that slaves who do not revolt against their oppressors are either contemptible or of no consequence. See her essay 'A War without End' (Le Guin 2004) for further discussion of this particular point.

7 My use of these terms is deliberate, and influenced in part by Harold Barclay's helpful discussion of forms of power in his 'Power: Some Anthropological Perspectives' (Barclay 2005). Like Barclay, I believe that power is best understood as a continuum, at one end of which is domination and at the other the exertion of influence without domination. My criticisms of 'power' in this essay are directed at its dominating, destructive forms.

8 It is perhaps worth emphasising the point that such experiences are still all too common in the non-fictional world of our Earth. The difference, of course, is that our ruling classes are usually *lighter* in skin colour than our subordinate classes. By deliberately reversing this colour-status connection in her fiction, Le Guin challenges her readers to reflect on the completely illogical nature of racial discrimination. She thus helps to plant the seeds of a radically different way of seeing and living.

9 I borrow this expression from the title of Robin Kelley's passionately argued book, *Freedom Dreams: The Black Radical Imagination* (Kelley 2002).

10 hooks acknowledges that many people appear to be uncomfortable with the emphasis on spirituality in Peck's definition of love:

> Some folks have difficulty with Peck's definition of love because he uses the word 'spiritual'. He is referring to that dimension of our core reality where mind, body, and spirit are one. An individual does not need to be a believer in religion to embrace the idea that there is an animating principle in the self – a life force (some of us call it soul) that when nurtured enhances our capacity to be more fully self-actualized and able to engage in communication with the world around us.
>
> (hooks 2000: 13)

11 hooks tends at times to idealise and over-domesticate love. Whereas she appears to associate love with total and complete liberation from fear and the will to domination, I understand it as an ongoing emotional process integrally associated with everyday fears, pain, problems, uncertainties, dangers and complexities. Robert Solomon's criticisms of Fromm and Peck, both of whose theories heavily influence hooks' conception of love, are helpful as a corrective to this particular tendency:

> The vulgar reduction of love invites an equally vulgar inflation of love, and so we get those heaps of extravagant praise without a hint of danger, as if love were always good and not sometimes stupid, even fatal, as if the virtues of love were 'sweetness' and calm rather than exhilaration and violence of the soul. It is all well and good and perhaps even poetic to call love 'divine' and 'the answer', but as love becomes more abstract and idealized, it loses touch with the realities of passion and our everyday fears, desires, hopes and expectations.
>
> (Solomon 2006: 23)

12 hooks is more critical of the example of Martin Luther King in the final chapter of her book *Outlaw Culture: Resisting Representations* (hooks 1994). As in *All About Love: New Visions* (hooks 2000), she argues in the earlier work that without love all

our efforts to liberate ourselves and our world community from oppression and exploitation are doomed. More specifically, she suggests that without an ethic of love shaping the direction of our political visions and radical aspirations, we tend to move against domination only when we feel our self-interest directly threatened. She praises King for recognising this point, but also criticises him for advocating a reformist rather than a revolutionary love ethic. According to hooks, King's continued reformism in the face of stubborn and frequently violent white resistance to the civil rights movement opened the door to the Black Power movement and its emphasis on power rather than love: 'While King had focused on loving our enemies, Malcolm called us back to ourselves, acknowledging that taking care of blackness was our central responsibility. Even though King talked about the importance of black self-love, he talked more about loving our enemies' (hooks 1994: 244). hooks' sympathetic criticisms of King are thought provoking, and consistent with her persuasive later claim in *All About Love* that self-love is the foundation of loving practice.

13 Of course, one might also argue that in certain circumstances the use of violent force could be understood as an expression of love. The French anarchist Elisée Reclus defended such a position, and explained its rationale as follows: 'I see a cat that is tortured, a child that is beaten, a woman who is mistreated, and if I am strong enough to prevent it, I prevent it' (Reclus, quoted in Marshall 1993: 343). I take no definitive position in this essay on the question of whether some forms of (non-consensual) violence may be compatible with love, and instead refer the reader to the Raymond Carver short story cited on p. 103, in which the characters discuss and debate precisely this issue in its most intimate form.

References

Ackelsberg, M. (1988) 'Anarchist Revolution and Women's Liberation', *Society* 25(2): 29–37.

——(1993) 'Models of Revolution: Rural Women and Anarchist Collectivisation in Civil War Spain', *Journal of Peasant Studies* 20(3): 367–88.

——(2000) 'Mujeres Libres: Identity, Community, Sexuality, and Power', *Anarchist Studies* 8: 99–117.

——(2005 [1991]) *Free Women of Spain: Anarchism and the Struggle for the Emancipation of Women*, Edinburgh and Oakland, CA: AK Press.

Avrich, P. (1980) *The Modern School Movement: Anarchism and Education in the United States*, Princeton, NJ: Princeton University Press.

——(2005) *Anarchist Voices: An Oral History of Anarchism in America*, Edinburgh and Oakland, CA: AK Press.

Barclay, H. (2005) 'Power: Some Anthropological Perspectives', *Anarchist Studies* 13(2): 104–17.

Blechman, M. (ed.) (1994) *Drunken Boat: Art, Rebellion, Anarchy*, Brooklyn, NY/Seattle, WA: Autonomedia and Left Bank Books.

Bookchin, M. (2004 [1971]) *Post-Scarcity Anarchism*, Edinburgh and Oakland, CA: AK Press.

Carver, R. (1995) 'What We Talk about When We Talk about Love,' in *Where I'm Calling From: The Selected Stories*, London: Harvill.

Cleminson, R. (1995a) *Anarquismo y Homosexualidad. Antología de Artículos de la Revista Blanca, Generación Consciente, Estudios e Iniciales (1924–1935)*, Madrid: Huerga y Fierro.

——(1995b) 'Male Inverts and Homosexuals: Sex Discourse in the Anarchist *Revista Blanca*,' in Gert Hekma, Harry Oosterhuis and James Steakley (eds), *Gay Men and the Sexual History of the Political Left*, New York/London: Harrington Park Press.

Davis, A. (2009) '"Don't Let Nobody Bother Yo Principle": The Sexual Economy of American Slavery', in S. M. James, F. Smith Foster and B. Guy-Sheftall (eds), *Still Brave: The Evolution of Black Women's Studies*, New York: The Feminist Press.

Davis, L. (2010) 'Social Anarchism or Lifestyle Anarchism: An Unhelpful Dichotomy', *Anarchist Studies* 18(1): 62–82.

Davis, L. and Kinna, R. (eds) (2009) *Anarchism and Utopianism*, Manchester: Manchester University Press.

De Ligt, B. (1989 [1937]) *The Conquest of Violence: An Essay on War and Revolution*, London: Pluto Press.

Ehrlich, H. J. (1996) 'How to Get From Here to There: Building Revolutionary Transfer Culture,' in H. J. Ehrlich (ed.), *Re-inventing Anarchy, Again*, Edinburgh/San Francisco: AK Press.

Falk, C. (1984) *Love, Anarchy, and Emma Goldman*, New York: Holt, Rinehart & Winston.

Farrell, J. J. (1997) *The Spirit of the Sixties: Making Postwar Radicalism*, New York and London: Routledge.

Harding, J. (1998) *Sex Acts: Practices of Femininity and Masculinity*, London: Sage Publications.

Heider, U. (2000) 'The German Student Movement and Sexual Revolution', *Anarchist Studies* 8: 133–43.

Hill Collins, P. (2009) *Black Feminist Thought*, New York/London: Routledge.

hooks, b. (1994) *Outlaw Culture: Resisting Representations*, New York/London: Routledge.

——(2000) *All About Love: New Visions*, London: The Women's Press.

Jaggar, A. (1988) *Feminist Politics and Human Nature*, Lanham, MD: Rowman & Littlefield.

Jordan, J. (1981) *Civil Wars*, Boston, MA: Beacon.

Kelley, R. D. G. (2002) *Freedom Dreams: The Black Radical Imagination*, Boston, MA: Beacon.

Kimmel, M. S. (1990) *Revolution: A Sociological Interpretation*, Cambridge: Polity Press.

Koenig, B. (2009) 'Visions of the Future: Reproduction, Revolution and Regeneration in American Anarchist Utopian Fiction,' in L. Davis and R. Kinna (eds), *Anarchism and Utopianism*, Manchester: Manchester University Press.

de La Boétie, É. (1963 [1576]) *Discours de la servitude volontaire*, ed. M. Rat, Paris: Armand Colin.

Lakey, G. (1987) *Powerful Peacemaking: A Strategy for a Living Revolution*, Philadelphia, PA/Santa Cruz, CA: New Society Publishers.

Landauer, G. (1907) *Die Revolution*, Frankfurt am Main: Neudruck.

Le Guin, U. K. (1997 [1995]) *Four Ways to Forgiveness*, London: Vista.

——(2001 [1974]) *The Dispossessed: An Ambiguous Utopia*, New York: HarperCollins.

——(2002) *The Birthday of the World*, London: Gollancz.

——(2004) 'A War without End', in *The Wave in the Mind: Talks and Essays on the Writer, the Reader, and the Imagination*, Boston, MA: Shambhala.

Lorde, A. (1984) *Sister Outsider*, Trumansberg, NY: Crossing Press.

Marshall, P. (1993) *Demanding the Impossible: A History of Anarchism*, London: Fontana Press.

Martin, E. (1989) *The Woman in the Body: A Cultural Analysis of Reproduction*, Milton Keynes: Open University Press.
Morrison, T. (1987) *Beloved*, New York: Random House.
Ording, D. (2009) 'Intimate Fellows: Utopia and Chaos in the Early Post-Stonewall Gay Liberation Manifestos,' in L. Davis and R. Kinna (eds), *Anarchism and Utopianism*, Manchester: Manchester University Press.
Orwell, George (1945) *Animal Farm*, London: Penguin.
Roszak, T. (1995) *The Making of a Counter Culture: Reflections on the Technocratic Society and Its Youthful Opposition*, Berkeley, CA: University of California Press.
Rowbotham, S. (1972) *Women, Resistance and Revolution*, London: Penguin.
Rowbotham, S., Segal, L. and Wainwright, H. (eds) (1979) *Beyond the Fragments: Feminism and the Making of Socialism*, London: Merlin Press.
Solomon, R. C. (2006 [1994]) *About Love: Reinventing Romance for Our Times*, Indianapolis/Cambridge: Hackett Publishing.
Sonn, Richard D. (1992) *Anarchism*, New York: Twayne Publishers.
Steinberger, P. J. (1999) 'Public and Private', *Political Studies* 47(2): 292–313.
Tolstoy, L. (1915) *Social Evils and Their Remedy*, ed. H. C. Matheson, London: Methuen.
Veysey, L. (1973) *The Communal Experience: Anarchist and Mystical Communities in Twentieth-Century America*, Chicago: University of Chicago Press.

Chapter 7

Structures of desire

Postanarchist kink in the speculative fiction of Octavia Butler and Samuel Delany

Lewis Call

> It's a beautiful universe ... wondrous and the more exciting because no one has written plays and poems and built sculptures to indicate the structure of desire I negotiate every day as I move about in it.
>
> —Samuel Delany, *Stars in My Pocket Like Grains of Sand*

The problem of power is one of the major philosophical and political preoccupations of the modern West. It is a problem which has drawn the attention of some of the greatest minds of the nineteenth and twentieth centuries, including Friedrich Nietzsche and Michel Foucault. I have argued elsewhere that the philosophies of power articulated by Nietzsche and Foucault stand as prototypes of an innovative form of anarchist theory, one which finds liberatory potential in the disintegration of the modern self and its liberal humanist politics (Call 2002: chs 1 and 2). Lately this kind of theory has become known as *postanarchism.* For me, postanarchism refers to a form of contemporary anarchist theory which draws extensively upon postmodern and poststructuralist philosophy in order to push anarchism beyond its traditional boundaries. Postanarchism tries to do this by adding important new ideas to anarchism's traditional critiques of statism and capitalism. Two of these ideas are especially significant for the present essay: the Foucauldian philosophy of power, which sees power as omnipresent but allows us to distinguish between power's various forms, and the Lacanian concept of subjectivity, which understands the self to be constituted by and through its desire.

Postanarchism implies and includes a crucial sexual anarchism. Indeed, the disruption of conventional forms of sexual identity is one of the most powerful moves available to the postanarchist. When postanarchism's anti-essentialist critique is applied to sexuality, the result is queer. When that critique is applied to power, the result is kinky. Postanarchism enables a system of erotic ethics suitable for an age beyond humanism. That system endorses radical relations of erotic power up to and including consensual play-slavery. This dramatic form of erotic power exchange mimics the structure of slavery, but in a way which produces radically different subjective meaning for the participants: unlike slavery, play-slavery can be ethical and erotic. Postanarchism suggests that ethical structures of erotic power (including those of play-slavery) may actually sap the authority of their non-consensual *Doppelgängers*. I have used the term 'kink theory' to describe the body of work which explores the ethical possibilities of consensual erotic power exchange (Call 2007). I now wish to argue that when kink theory encounters postanarchism, the result is something new and interesting: an ethical position and a strategy for political action, which I propose to call postanarchist kink.

This essay examines elements of postanarchist kink in the speculative fiction of two African American authors, Octavia Butler and Samuel Delany.[1] The work of Butler and Delany is centrally concerned with the political and ethical problems of slavery. These two authors provide what amounts to a traditional anarchist critique of the historical American slave system. However, their work also endorses erotic power exchange, including forms which seem to replicate the structures of slavery. Their remarkable novels suggest that an erotic play-slavery based upon consent and mutual desire may help us overcome the crippling legacy of chattel slavery. In their most radical moments, Butler and Delany demonstrate that erotic power exchange can facilitate a breakdown of the traditional political subject; furthermore, they show that this breakdown is potentially liberating. As Sherryl Vint has recently observed, Butler and Delany are 'authors whose critical engagement with questions of sexuality and power pushes the boundaries of the current social configuration' (Vint 2009: 402). The novels of Butler and Delany suggest, counterintuitively but convincingly, that one way out of capitalist political economy may lead through the S/M dungeon: a kinky postanarchism.

The body of theory which I call postanarchist kink was born in the 1980s, alongside queer theory. In 1984, *The Advocate* published a groundbreaking interview with Michel Foucault entitled 'Sex, Power, and the Politics of Identity'. Foucault emphasised the anarchist aspects of queer politics: 'being homosexuals, we are in a struggle with the government, and the government is in a struggle with us' (Foucault 1984: 167). This bold, oppositional stance would become one of the defining features of queer theory, and Foucault's crucial contributions to that body of theory are well known. Yet Foucault's work supports more than one radical theory about sexuality. Even as he helped to create queer theory, he simultaneously contributed to a related critical discourse, which I have been calling kink theory. The latter discourse studies the set of practices known collectively as BDSM: bondage/discipline (B/D), dominance/submission (D/S) and sadomasochism (S/M). Through its study of these practices, kink theory attempts to theorise the consensual exchange of erotic power. Kink theory interprets such power exchange as a viable ethical alternative to the non-consensual power structures which permeate the modern world. 'What strikes me with regard to S&M', said Foucault, 'is how it differs from social power' (ibid.: 169). Foucault argued that social power 'is a strategic relation which has been stabilized through institutions', while S&M 'is a strategic relation, but it is always fluid' (ibid.).

For Foucault, kink was important because it showed that even in a world where power is omnipresent, *some* of that power flows in accordance with an ethics of freedom. Anarchists should be very interested in the possibility that this ethical, erotic power might be deployed as a symbolic challenge to the forms of social, economic and political power against which they struggle.

Certainly the modern liberal state has taken a strong interest in kink. Foucault's fellow kink theorist Gayle Rubin noted that the state goes to great lengths to delegitimise S/M in particular, largely by asserting that those who practice S/M are 'legally incapable of consenting' to such practices (Rubin 1984: 305).[2] So the state tries to contest S/M on precisely the same theoretical terrain where anarchism attacks the legitimacy of that state: the terrain surrounding the concept of consent. This struggle over the meaning of consent suggests that consent means one thing to the state and something very different to anarchists and kinksters. Wendy Brown has argued compellingly that within liberalism consent marks the presence of a power to which one submits (Brown 1995: 162–3). Thus the liberal form of consent actually 'marks the subordinate status of the consenting party' (ibid.: 163). Clearly, liberal consent could not provide the basis for ethical power relations, since this kind of consent requires and presumes radical inequalities between the parties. In the liberal model, an immensely powerful entity (the state) seeks consent from those who possess little if any power (political subjects, or citizens). Thus, as Brown argues, liberal consent is 'a response to power – it adds or withdraws legitimacy – but is not a mode of enacting or sharing in power' (ibid.).

Here we may draw a sharp line between liberal consent and the kind of consent which enables relations of erotic power exchange. The structures of erotic consent are deeply informed by desire, particularly embodied desire. This is rarely, if ever, the case with the structures of political consent which enable modern liberal states, or with the forms of economic consent which underwrite modern capitalism. The consent of the liberal political subject or the capitalist economic subject can be grudging, indifferent or apathetic. Relations of erotic power, by the same token, require desire. Mutual desire guarantees the ethical content of erotic power exchange, for desire ensures that the needs and wishes of the 'subordinate party' will be taken fully into account. In Lacan's famous general formulation, '*man's desire is the desire of the Other*' (Lacan 1981: 38). Kinky relations provide a particularly striking example of this. In a typical BDSM relationship, the dominant desires the desire of the submissive. The submissive's desire frequently structures negotiations and determines the shape and extent of the scene. By endorsing and emphasising the desire of the submissive, BDSM promotes a high level of equality between the participants. This equality may sometimes lie hidden behind the *apparent* inequality generated by the BDSM roles themselves, and confusion around this issue may motivate many moral critiques of kink (Highleyman 1997: para. 10). A form of consent which promotes such equality, and which fully respects the desires of all parties involved, could be compatible with anarchism, while the liberal form of consent cannot.

Perhaps the practices of kinksters, and the concept of desiring consent which stands behind those practices, represent a real challenge to the modern state and its political theories. Some anarchists have already begun to recognise this possibility. A 2002 issue of *Organise!*, the magazine of Britain's Anarchist Federation, called for 'safe, free, diverse and consensual' sex. The magazine ran an 'Interview with an Anarchist Dominatrix', one Mistress Venus. Mistress Venus clearly understands how to wield symbolic power against the dominant order. She defines the domination session as an 'escape from reality' (Anarchist Federation 2002: 8). But this does not appear to be a nihilistic 'escape' into non-reality. Rather, it looks very much like an attempt to critique the symbolic order of modern capitalism. Mistress Venus does this by developing an alternative symbolic order, one in which symbols of power are redeployed in subversive ways. If this strategy is successful, these redeployed symbols may challenge or undermine the authority of the conventional symbolic order. Mistress Venus suggests that

> the roles we play mirror the power-based capitalistic society we live in today, a society of greed, oppression and subversion, a society of force, silence and pain. This is in no way representative of the lifestyle I choose to live in as an anarchist, a society based on equality, respect and self-government. Domination is a game, the adult's version of what children call 'playing'.
> (Anarchist Federation 2002: 8)[3]

Here Mistress Venus acknowledges the crucial contribution which kink can make to anarchism. As she points out, kink reflects the non-consensual, real world power relations which anarchists universally condemn. Yet this reflection is always consensual, desired and playful. Kink performs real world power relationships in a way which simultaneously critiques those relations and offers a vital ethical alternative. As Liz Highleyman argues, S/M role-playing can be used 'to challenge illegitimate authority. Most SM players believe that such play is a parody of real world authority rather than an imitation of it' (Highleyman 1997: para. 24). The strategy here is to reproduce the structure of real world power relations, but to do so in a way that will radically alter the subjective significance of those relations. The idea, in Highleyman's wonderful formulation, is to 'subvert, pervert, and make overt the erotic subtext of power and authority' (ibid.: para. 27). This has the potential to reduce the psychological power of real world authority, and surely that is a step in the direction of anarchist liberation.

If it is to realise this potential, however, postanarchist kink must be careful not to slip back into a liberal humanist philosophy or politics. Judy Greenway has argued that

> even when sexual transgression seems to be about creating new versions of sexuality, the language of the true inner self recurs ... Sometimes, for

> instance in the debates around the limits of consensual sado-masochism, its defenders use the traditional rhetoric of civil liberties, maintaining the public/private distinction.
>
> (Greenway 1997: 8)

Indeed, this does represent a serious potential problem for postanarchist kink theory. The risk here is that kinky desire might inadvertently produce a problematic kind of identity politics. This politics would depend for its very existence upon the liberal humanist subject and the liberal state, both of which postanarchism seeks to subvert. Wendy Brown has formulated this problem quite effectively. Her analysis convincingly suggests that identity politics cannot possibly be deployed against the modern state. Brown argues eloquently that 'politicized identities generated out of liberal, disciplinary societies, insofar as they are premised on exclusion from a universal ideal, require that ideal, as well as their exclusion from it, for their own continuing existence as identities' (Brown 1995: 65). If Brown is right about this, then a kinky identity politics will be of little use to anarchism.

The source of this problem is desire; more specifically, it is the troubling way in which identity politics seem to channel desire within a liberal order. Thus Brown speaks of 'politicized identity's *desire* within liberal-bureaucratic regimes, its foreclosure of its own freedom' (ibid.: 66). For Brown this is a reactionary desire, one which grows out of a kind of Nietzschean *ressentiment*. Brown emphasises the 'structure of *desire* fueling identity-based political claims' (ibid.: 62). I believe that this term 'structure of desire' (also used by Delany) provides the key that may unlock kink's radical potential. Specifically, I suggest that we must strive to distinguish the reactionary structure of desire which Brown has ably identified from a very different structure of desire. The structure I have in mind would describe the desire of postmodern subjects: deeply embodied, without fixed or stable identities. The identities of these subjects would fluctuate too rapidly and too dramatically for identity politics to emerge. This would also be a structure of kinky desire. As Jamie Heckert has observed, the 'poststructuralist argument on the potential fluidity of the self' suggests that S/M could be used to 'redefine the meaning of power play', though Heckert rightly warns us that this project may not be for everyone, and that it should only be pursued with great care and caution (Heckert 2005: 208–9). The concept of fluidity is crucial here: kink has the potential to add flexible, fluid power relations to the fluid identity structures which poststructuralism has identified. 'SM roles are so fluid', observes Highleyman; '[a]n SM role is not predetermined on the basis of one's occupation, gender, sexual orientation, race, or class, and each partner may take on the role(s) that meet their individual or collective desires' (Highleyman 1997: para. 25). Similarly, Foucault points out that in S/M there are roles, but these can be reversed; even when the roles are stabilised, they are clearly part of a game (Foucault 1984: 169).

Certainly many kinksters identify with particular positions within the structure of erotic power relations. Many claim specific identities for themselves, often introducing themselves as tops or bottoms, dominants or submissives, masters or slaves. But many also switch (at least in my experience). Here desire takes priority over specific roles or identities. Within such a structure of desire, identities and power relations are in a constant state of flux. Because the stable subject required by liberal humanism cannot emerge from this structure of desire, I call it postanarchist.

Postanarchist kink sees power not as a problem but as a possibility. Foucault showed us that the attempt to eliminate power is absurd. Rather than attacking power, we might draw careful distinctions between different *kinds* of power. We should entertain the hypothesis that it is, after all, possible to exercise power in an ethically responsible way. Indeed, as Highleyman astutely observes, 'the idea that we can use SM to learn to use power in an ethical way remains, along with consent, the crux of the moral defense of erotic dominance and submission' (Highleyman 1997: para. 38). The key to this ethical possibility is to be found in the philosophy of consent and desire embodied in the practices of erotic power exchange. According to this philosophy, the exchange of power is ethically legitimate if and only if all persons involved consent to that exchange and desire it. These criteria permit erotic power exchange to stand as a dramatic ethical alternative to non-consensual, undesired power.

In order to gain a deeper understanding of the crucial differences between these two forms of power, I will examine a body of literature which addresses both forms: the speculative fiction of Octavia Butler and Samuel Delany. These two African American authors are deeply aware of the massive historical traumas which have resulted from the exercise of non-consensual political and economic power, particularly in the American South prior to the Civil War. (As a white male American, I experience these traumas much less directly and in a very different way. As a postanarchist historian, I believe that we can learn from these traumas.) Butler and Delany are especially aware of the problems of sexual exploitation endemic in the American slave system, an awareness they share with other well-known African American authors like Toni Morrison and Alice Walker.[4] But Butler and Delany go further than many of their peers, for they not only provide a compelling critique of the political and sexual economies of slavery, they also provide an alternative. For Butler and Delany, erotic power exchange and play-slavery provide an antidote to the ethically bankrupt institution of slavery. These two authors thus offer us a way to begin healing the wounds which chattel slavery has left upon our culture and its philosophy of ethics.

Becoming a kind of master: postanarchist kink in Octavia Butler's *Patternist* books

As an African American woman who writes science fiction, Octavia Butler speaks from a triply marginalised subject position. She is a woman writing in a field which is dominated by male authors. She is an African American writing in a field dominated by white authors. And by choosing to write science fiction, she has elected to participate in a field which is itself marginal to literature – a 'paraliterary' field, to use Delany's terminology. Since this last marginalisation, at least, represents a choice on Butler's part, we must consider the possibility that she *wants* to speak from the margins. Indeed, it is possible that Butler has things to say which can be said *only* at the margins. Butler's work deals with themes of power and slavery – hardly unusual concerns for an African American writer. But by choosing to write science fiction, Butler gives herself the opportunity to approach these themes in a way which is radically different from the approaches of mainstream literature. Certainly we find in Butler a compelling and elegant critique of socio-economic slavery, and of the forms of power which sustain that system. But there is also another kind of power at work in Butler's writing. Lauren J. Lacey argues quite convincingly that 'Butler's last three novels [*Parable of the Sower*, *Parable of the Talents* and *Fledgling*] work through the complexities of power in ways that offer possibilities for contemporary feminists – and others – to cope with and even to profit from the power formations that surround us' (Lacey 2008: 380). While Lacey is right to say that Butler's later novels show us the positive political possibilities of power, this theme is not a new one for Butler. It can also be found in her earliest published work, the *Patternist* series.

Butler quite rightly rejects the sort of power which produced master–slave relations in the antebellum American South. In her *Patternist* series, she describes these relations in terms which will make sense to a largely white science fiction audience who may not be entirely familiar with the political economy of slavery. Butler accomplishes this by locating her slave society in a future world which is ruled by a group of powerful telepaths. These telepaths share access to a grid of mental energy known as the Pattern. The Pattern is strictly hierarchical. This hierarchical structure makes the Pattern a tempting target for anarchist critique, which Butler deploys without naming it as such. The strongest telepath within the Pattern is known as the Patternmaster, and this individual has the ability to exercise non-consensual telepathic control over the other Patternists. The Patternmaster delegates power to Housemasters, who also use their power in a non-consensual way. Butler describes a Housemaster called Coransee as someone who 'radiated power in the way of a man not only confident but arrogant' (Butler 1976: 15).

The parallels between these Housemasters and nineteenth-century American plantation owners are unmistakable. Housemasters are in general very competitive, yet they 'had a tradition of returning one another's runaways' (ibid.: 75). Like their real world counterparts, Housemasters recognise that they share a common interest in maintaining the slave system. The Housemasters also reproduce the reprehensible gender relations of the plantation economy. It was, of course, common practice in the American South for slavemasters to rape their female slaves, in order to ensure the reproduction of the slave population. Similarly, Housemaster Coransee knows that 'no woman of his House had the right to refuse him' (ibid.: 158). For women Patternists especially, non-consensual, undesired power is the very essence of the Pattern. And yet these Patternist women yearn for precisely the same kind of power which has traditionally been used against them. 'I want the same thing you want', says a Patternist woman named Amber; 'My House. Mine' (ibid.: 134). One of the most painful truths about non-consensual power is that those who are victimised by such power often respond by dreaming not of a liberated and egalitarian society, but of a world in which that power flows through their hands instead of the hands of their masters. This psychological aspect of the slave system makes it fairly simple to divide the slave population and turn the slaves against one another. Distinctions are drawn in Butler's Houses between the more prestigious household slaves and the lower-ranking 'outsiders'. This closely parallels the distinction between house and field slaves in the antebellum American South. Starved of power, the outsiders often abuse the only people who are below them in the Patternist social hierarchy: those who lack telepathic powers altogether, the 'mutes'. For example, 'there was an outsider who had researched ancient methods of torture and made a hobby of trying them on mutes' (ibid.: 68).

The mutes are clearly an important part of the slave system which the *Patternist* series describes. In the profoundly hierarchical structure of the Pattern, they are the lowest of all groups. Their inequality is largely based upon their lack of telepathic power (which stands in Butler's work as a surrogate for unequal levels of economic power in the American South). But the most honest of Butler's characters understand that this inequality is also linguistic in origin. Consider this conversation between the immortal shape-shifting woman Emma (also known as Anyanwu) and Doro, patriarchal progenitor of the Pattern:

> 'Mutes!'
>
> He looked annoyed, probably with himself. 'It's a convenient term. People without telepathic voices. Ordinary people.'
>
> 'I know what it means, Doro. I knew the first time I heard Mary use it. It means nigger!'
>
> (Butler 1977: 161)

Although the Pattern is the result of an extended breeding programme carried out by the immortal Doro, he is, ironically, a mute. However, Doro does have the ability to transfer his mind into another person's body. In doing so, he permanently extinguishes that person's consciousness. Doro has lived for millennia in this way, hopping from one body to another, 'consuming' the minds which inhabit these bodies. Not surprisingly, Doro emerges in Butler's narrative as the ultimate slavemaster. He can kill at will, but he cannot be killed. His power is absolute and unquestionable. He is also completely unconcerned about the pain of others. 'It was rare for another person's pain to disturb

Doro. If the girl seemed to be dying, he would be concerned that good seed was about to be lost. But if she were merely in agony, it did not matter' (Butler 1980: 184). Indeed, Doro derives sadistic pleasure from the act of killing, especially when his victim is mentally or telepathically sensitive. Doro explains that he is able to recognise 'the kinds of people that I would get the most pleasure from if I took them. I guess you could say, the kinds of people who tasted best' (Butler 1977: 97). Thus Doro is not merely a sadist; he is a kind of psychic cannibal who enjoys consuming the mental energy of his victims.

But there is also another motivation for Doro's cruelty: 'Doro wanted an empire. He didn't call it that, but that was what he meant ... He needed tools, because an empire of ordinary people wasn't quite what he had in mind' (ibid.: 92–3). Doro's slaves are his tools. He uses them to enhance and increase his political power. Yet there is another form of power which is even more important to Doro. Foucault called it 'bio-power', that which 'brought life and its mechanisms into the realm of explicit calculations' (Foucault 1978: 143). Just as a nineteenth-century American slave owner would always be concerned about the size of his 'herd', Doro is obsessed with his breeding programme. 'Had human life ever mattered to Doro beyond his interest in human husbandry?' (Butler 1977: 55). In this context, Doro's power is largely biological in origin, since he controls the breeding programme. But again, Butler reminds us that power is always partly linguistic. '*Breed* didn't sound like the kind of word that should be applied to people. The minute he said it, though, I realized it was the right word for what he was doing' (ibid.: 96). Doro's breeding programme is partly enabled by language's reluctance to name it as such. So Butler combines a radical critique of bio-power with an almost structuralist critique of linguistic power: her project has clear Foucauldian affinities.

Like any slavemaster, Doro regards the children born to his 'breeders' not as people but as his property. 'The daughter had been his from the moment of her conception – his property as surely as though his brand were burned into her flesh. She even thought of herself as his property' (Butler 1980: 150). Doro's dehumanising breeding project thus exhibits all the worst features of nineteenth-century American slavery.

But, as Foucault reminds us, 'there are no relations of power without resistances' (Foucault 1980: 142). The nineteenth century was a time not only of slavery but of slave revolts. In the *Patternist* books, these revolts arrive in the person of Mary, the protagonist of *Mind of My Mind*. Mary is the end result of Doro's breeding programme. It is her telepathic power that establishes the Pattern itself. Her relationship with Doro ranges from tense to antagonistic, and much of this antagonism stems from Mary's resentment of Doro's power:

> 'What am I for, Doro? What are you progressing toward?'
> 'You know the answer to that.'
> 'Your race, your empire, yes, but what place is there in it for me?'
> (Butler 1977: 101)

As Mary joins with other telepaths to form the Pattern, her power increases dramatically. One of the first to notice this change is Mary's husband Karl, a strong telepath who had once dominated Mary:

> 'You're changing. I've been watching you change, wondering how far you would go.'
>
> 'Changing how?'
>
> 'Growing up perhaps. I can remember when it was easier to intimidate you.'
>
> (Butler 1977: 188)

Gradually Doro, too, comes to realise that he can no longer control Mary as he once did. Indeed, as a mute, Doro remains shut out of the Pattern. 'Together, the "Patternists" were growing into something that he could observe, hamper, or destroy but not something he could join' (ibid: 155). Naturally, this necessitates a war between Doro and Mary. Doro is immensely powerful, but Mary is more powerful still, for she has the strength of her Patternists to draw upon. Mary does not merely *have* power, 'she *was* power, strength concentrated as Doro had never felt it before – the strength of dozens, perhaps hundreds of Patternists' (ibid.: 217, emphasis added). In the end, even Doro can't stand against such strength. At the conclusion of *Mind of My Mind*, Doro is himself enslaved, then extinguished: 'He was a member of the Pattern. A Patternist. Property. Mary's property ... She consumed him slowly, drinking in his terror and his life, drawing out her own pleasure, and laughing through his soundless screams' (ibid.: 220). This is a dramatic, ironic reversal of fortune for a man who has been enslaving and consuming others for millennia.

As satisfying as it surely is to see the tables turned on Doro, however, we cannot assume that Mary will be able to escape the temptations of non-consensual power. She may be destined to become a female Doro. The tendency among feminist critics, however, has been to argue otherwise. Marleen Barr maintains that Mary 'uses her power to create a new community, a new body of men and women' (Barr 1987: 77). Similarly, Robin Roberts suggests that Mary is a kind of nurturing 'queen bee' whose community-centred values make her preferable to the patriarchal Doro (Roberts 1993: 107). Unfortunately, we don't really know for certain how Mary's regime will compare to that of Doro. Her rule is established at the very end of *Mind of My Mind*, and develops within the narrative gap which exists between that book and *Clay's Ark*. But we may reasonably imagine that Mary – a former slave herself – at least has the potential to feel sympathy for those she dominates, as Doro could not. And Butler does show us enough of Mary's relationship with the Patternists in *Mind of My Mind* to convince us that Mary does genuinely care for her telepaths, that she sees them not as breeding stock but as members of a vibrant organic community. Still, we cannot ignore the fact that while Mary's regime may be more nurturing and more organic than Doro's, it remains a non-consensual slave system nonetheless. Members of the Pattern have no choice but to participate, and all are forced to acknowledge Mary's absolute power.

It is only in the final volume of the *Patternist* series, *Wild Seed*, that Butler shows us an egalitarian relationship based upon the exchange of erotic power. Though *Wild Seed* was one of the last books to appear in the *Patternist* series, it represents the beginning of the narrative which runs through that series. (The tension between these two sequences – publication and narrative – is one way in which Butler's work refuses the too-convenient comforts of linear narrative.) *Wild Seed* tells us of Doro's origins, and of his centuries-spanning power struggle with the immortal shape-shifting woman called Anyanwu. That this is a *political* struggle is clear; Stacy Alaimo has described it as 'a battle between two modes of knowing and being: the tyrannical force of an egotistical, disembodied mind and the transformative powers of an utterly embodied woman' (Alaimo 1998: 126). In one sense, then, this is the story of the postmodern body's revenge upon the Enlightenment's mythology of human subjectivity. But *Wild Seed* is much more than that. It is also an account of the ways in which power and desire flow between Doro and Anyanwu. It is, in short, a sadomasochistic love story.

Like any dominant, Doro finds that what he wants more than anything else is Anyanwu's submission. Lacan might say Doro desires the desire of the Other. The problem is that Anyanwu is 'wild seed'. She is a genetic aberration, and not the product of Doro's selective breeding programme. She is thus quite difficult to control, but Doro hopes that, 'like no other wild seed, Anyanwu would learn to fear him and bend herself to his will' (Butler 1980: 90). He will settle for nothing less than total obedience. Anyanwu must even learn to define ethics in Doro's terms. 'She would learn that right and wrong were what he said they were' (ibid.: 92). Yet, time and time again, Doro is frustrated in his quest to gain power over Anyanwu. She remains untameable. 'What will I have to do next to teach you to obey?' Doro laments (ibid.: 176). When Anyanwu finally does begin to submit, it is only because her instincts of self-preservation are strong. She knows that Doro could kill her; to protect herself, she submits. This is not (yet) an ethical or erotic submission: she submits out of necessity, without desire. Thus 'Doro had reshaped her. She had submitted and submitted and submitted to keep him from killing her ... she had formed the habit of submission' (ibid.: 196). But that is not all she develops. Anyanwu comes to enjoy Doro's attentions: 'Anyanwu enjoyed his touches even now when she thought they were more imprisoning than caressing' (ibid.: 94). In short, she learns to eroticise the power relations which exist between her and Doro. By doing so, she alters the basic nature of their relationship.

The erotic power which begins to flow between Anyanwu and Doro becomes entirely distinct from the ethically problematic forms of power which

Butler described in the previous *Patternist* books. One crucial difference is that these power relations are based upon reciprocal desire. Another important difference is that they are reversible. Here the joke, as always, is on Doro. From the very moment that Doro attains erotic mastery over Anyanwu, he begins to develop what Hegel called a 'dependent consciousness'.[5] Doro is enslaved by his desire for Anyanwu, by his all-consuming need to dominate the one woman who could possibly be his equal. It takes Doro several centuries and an entire novel to realise that this is happening to him. Anyanwu, however, articulates her strategy on page 9 of *Wild Seed*: 'She knew some people were masters and some were slaves. That was the way it had always been ... She had become a kind of master herself. "Sometimes, one must become a master to avoid becoming a slave," she said softly' (ibid.: 9). This, then, is the dance which these two immortals perform through the centuries: 'mastering' and 'enslaving' one another in a permanent spiral of mutual desire.

The culmination of the erotic relationship between Anyanwu and Doro occurs near the end of the novel. In a scene which is deeply charged with erotic energy, Doro feeds upon Anyanwu's life essence, taking her as close to death as he can without killing her. The scene reveals the depths of Doro's desires, and the extent to which he is controlled by those desires:

> 'I had to know you that way at least once,' he said. 'I had to touch you that way.'
>
> 'Why?' she asked.
>
> 'Because it's the closest I'll ever come to you.'
>
> (Butler 1980: 259)

This remarkable kinky love scene highlights the importance of mutual, consensual desire. Doro 'wondered what she would say if he told her no one had ever before enjoyed such contact with him. No one in nearly four thousand years ... But Anyanwu had participated, had enjoyed, had even taken the initiative for a while, greatly intensifying his pleasure' (ibid.: 260). For millennia, Doro has been a psychic rapist, consuming people's consciousness against their will. Now he is astonished to discover that what he really wants and needs is not an unwilling victim but a partner, someone who genuinely enjoys the exchange of power and can participate in that exchange as an equal. Here is the supreme irony: Anyanwu has made the ultimate submission to Doro. She has offered him her life. And yet by doing so, she has gained total power over him. Through the reciprocal, consensual exchange of power and desire, Anyanwu has accomplished something truly remarkable. She has reappropriated slavery, and transformed it from an ethical abomination into something beautiful. She has discovered a kind of erotic play-slavery. *Wild Seed* presents this play-slavery as an effective strategic and symbolic challenge to Doro's ugly, empire-building slavery. A text would have to be kinky *and* postanarchist to achieve something like that.

A land of wholly inverted values: postanarchist kink in Samuel Delany's *Nevèrÿon* books

Like Butler, Samuel Delany speaks from the literary and erotic margins. Indeed, many of his most interesting ideas can be articulated *only* from a position which is marginal to mainstream literature and sexuality. Those interpretations of Delany's work which fail to recognise this are doomed to remain incomplete. In her frequently cited essay on 'Recent Feminist Utopias', for example, Joanna Russ makes the rather astonishing claim that Delany writes from an 'implicit level of freedom' simply because he is male (Russ 1981: 83). Russ chooses to disregard the ways in which Delany, a gay African American who writes S/F about S/M, is automatically relegated to the margin of the margins. As science fiction, Delany's texts are marginal to literature. There is a subtle but persistent concern for race in Delany's work, and this is certainly enough to make his project marginal to that of white literature. His elaborate articulation of gay themes makes his writing marginal to heterosexual literature. And his frequent discussions of S/M make his work marginal to vanilla literature. By focusing only on Delany's gender, Russ disregards these important margins. Damien Broderick gets a bit closer; he recognises that, as a gay black man, Delany does write about marginal experience (Broderick 1995: 120). And yet Broderick still does not give us a complete picture of Delany's work. He ends up suggesting, rather implausibly, that Delany's 'fiction is articulated about a semiotic programme which seems, at its limit, to merge with humanist, albeit highly relativist, liberal pluralism' (ibid.: 138). This misconception stems from the fact that Broderick acknowledges some of the margins which Delany occupies (gay/black) but disregards another (kinky). This is an essential omission, for it is precisely Delany's commitment to the principles of erotic power exchange that makes his work incompatible with the tradition of liberal humanism. Humanism has amply demonstrated that it has room for a great many different identities, including those of ethnic minority groups and possibly even homosexuals. But it has not, so far, shown that it has any room for kink, and the one thing it has not yet learned to tolerate is frank discussions of power. Delany's work points us not towards any liberal humanism (however pluralist), but rather towards a kinky postanarchism.

Delany is a deeply political thinker, with a strong sense of ethics. Nowhere is this more clear than in his philosophy of kink. The cornerstone of Delany's system of erotic ethics is a principle of consent informed by desire, which is something that his system has in common with many anarchist ethical philosophies. In a number of ways, in a variety of different texts, Delany makes this fundamental point: desired and consensual forms of power exchange are ethically acceptable and potentially erotic; undesired, non-consensual forms of power are intrinsically unethical and non-erotic. Delany is especially careful to articulate the vital distinction between erotic and political power: 'To assume a session of "sexual torture" between two consenting adults requires only minimal reorganization of what goes on in an actual session of political torture – and in any way manifests the same "power relations" – signs only gross ignorance of the context *and* the substance of *both* situations!' (Delany 1994: 140). It is ethics, of course, which separates the two situations. In *Stars in My Pocket Like Grains of Sand*, Delany highlights and sharpens this ethical point by describing a world in which 'all sadomasochism was hunted out and punished with barbaric singlemindedness; especially if concert [sic] was written out or clearly specified by verbal contract, which their authorities considered the ultimate disease' (Delany 1984: 215). Reading this passage, one experiences a remarkable ethical vertigo: *why* should consensual S/M be repressed *in particular*? What is it about such practices that the state might find so troubling? Perhaps it is the fact that consensual erotic power exchange threatens the state's jealously guarded (and non-consensual) power monopoly. That would be a very anarchist interpretation.

Like Butler, Delany provides extensive meditations on slavery. And like Butler, Delany understands that 'slavery' can refer either to a non-consensual set of socio-economic relations or to the consensual eroticisation of such relations. (This eroticisation represents a particular form of the more general practice of erotic power exchange.) Indeed, 'slavery' is a slippery signifier which can sometimes slide back and forth between the two meanings. Delany's Gorgik is a character who has experienced both real slavery and play-slavery; he seems to feel that one can lead to another: 'Fire, slavery, cloth, coin, and stone – these are the basis of civilized life. Sometimes it happens that one or another of them gets hopelessly involved in the most basic appetites of a woman or a man' (Delany 1979: 143). But Delany also recognises that the eroticisation of class relations represents a potentially potent threat to the dominant social order: 'The easier it is to name, survey, and pathologize the eroticization of any particular set of class relations, then the more *dangerous* that set of relations – and their eroticization – is to patriarchal *status quo* phallocentric society' (Delany 1994: 136). S/M eroticises the class relations which are such a fundamental part of chattel slavery; by this logic, S/M must be one of the most dangerous forces ever unleashed against the patriarchy. For no erotic practice has been more thoroughly catalogued, more ruthlessly medicalised. From Krafft-Ebing's vast nineteenth-century inventory of perversions to today's *Diagnostic and Statistical Manual of Mental Disorders*, erotic power exchange has remained one of psychology's great obsessions.[6] It's no wonder that the patriarchy has done everything within its considerable power to control the discourse surrounding S/M, for as long as S/M remains trapped within the psychiatric discourse, the threat which it represents is contained.

Clearly, Delany is fascinated by the politics of kink, and he has devoted considerable paraliterary effort to the exploration of these politics. Erotic power relations are at the thematic core of the multi-volume sword and sorcery epic which Delany initiated in 1979 with *Tales of Nevèrÿon*. Delany tells us that it was in these stories that he 'turned to examine some of the real (i.e., again, I mean political) problems that the idea of S/M brings up' (Delany 1999: 118). And it's clear that this exploration has a deep personal significance for him. 'Should you really want to know what this weird Delany guy is all about, *these* are the books to wrestle with', Delany assures us (ibid.: 119). But why did Delany choose the much-maligned genre of sword and sorcery fantasy as the forum in which to speak about ideas which are clearly so important to him? He recognises that sword and sorcery is 'SF's despised younger cousin' (Delany 1994: 46). Indeed, he goes out of his way to emphasise that sword and sorcery represents 'the margin of the margin' (ibid.: 71). Perhaps, then, Delany chose sword and sorcery precisely because it *is* marginal – indeed, because it exists on the margins of an already marginal paraliterary genre called science fiction. After all, such a doubly marginal genre is perfect for a discussion of that most marginal of sexual strategies, erotic power exchange. By choosing sword and sorcery, Delany is not merely accepting marginal status. He is insisting upon it.

Like almost all of Delany's books, the *Nevèrÿon* stories draw very clear lines between non-consensual socio-economic power and consensual, desired erotic power. Delany is especially careful to distinguish slavery from play-slavery. Nevèrÿon is a slave society, and Nevèrÿon's slave system reproduces the power relations of the antebellum American South, down to the last detail. Delany is careful to emphasise, for example, the special status of the favoured administrative ('house') slaves, who in Nevèrÿon wear ornate covers over their iron slave collars as a sign of relative rank. Of course, these elite slaves must contend with the inevitable feelings of guilt and complicity which result from their collaboration with slavery. Collar covers 'add far more weight to the neck than the circle of iron they cover', observes one house slave (Delany 1979: 224). Delany uses the symbol of the collar cover to illustrate the morass of moral dilemmas which slavery inevitably produces.

In order to ensure that the *Nevèrÿon* series can describe the entire history of slavery, Delany employs a clever technique of narrative acceleration. Historical developments which took centuries in the real world take decades in Nevèrÿon. This allows characters to comment on broad historical transformations. Some of these characters are able to describe the problems that emerge when slaves are emancipated. 'Freedom is not so simple a thing as that', a house slave points out when confronted with possible liberation. 'Where do you expect us to go? If we leave here, what do you expect will happen to us?' (ibid.: 221). Here Delany recognises that the transition from a traditional economy based on chattel slavery to a market economy based on formally free wage labour will not be an easy one. The former slaves who join the ranks of the impoverished urban working class may find that their lives have not improved. Indeed, another house slave argues that 'you free the labor pens into a world where, at least in the cities and the larger towns, a wage-earning populace, many of them, is worse off than here' (ibid.: 225).

Despite these potential (and, in the case of American history, very real) problems, many citizens of Nevèrÿon are willing to fight for the abolition of slavery, under the leadership of a former slave known as Gorgik the Liberator. Delany makes it easy to see why slavery arouses such intense anger. The ethical atrocities which result from this kind of non-consensual socio-economic power are clear, particularly when Delany examines the sexual dimension of the slave system. In Nevèrÿon, as in the antebellum American south, slavery encourages rape and other forms of sexual abuse. Long before he begins his campaign against slavery, Gorgik (not yet 'the Liberator') visits the slave market. 'Buy me, lord!' begs a woman slave. 'You will take me, please, away from him! We go to the desert tribes and I'll be sold there again. Do you know what they do to women slaves in the desert? I was there before. I don't want to go back' (ibid.: 135). Surely few moral crusades could be more inspirational than the campaign to end to such violations.

And yet the same narrative which contains this thorough critique of socio-economic slavery also includes a very sympathetic portrayal of consensual, desired play-slavery. Gorgik does not buy the woman at the slave market. Instead, he purchases a slave boy called Small Sarg. Sarg suggests that Gorgik should have bought the woman instead, for he could have had her work by day, her body by night. Gorgik replies, 'you think I'll get any less from you?' (ibid.: 137). At first, this sounds like another example of non-consensual sexual slavery. But in fact the relationship between Gorgik and Sarg is far more complex than that. The first time Gorgik approaches Sarg sexually, he informs Sarg that the boy must wear a slave collar this time, but that on another night Gorgik will take the collar off Sarg and put it on himself (ibid: 143). It turns out that Gorgik's sexuality is directly linked to the symbol of slavery. It doesn't matter to him which partner wears the collar, because the roles are reversible, as they often are in S/M (Foucault 1984: 169). The specific power configuration of Gorgik and Sarg's first encounter seems quite arbitrary: Gorgik refuses to wear the collar himself only because he does 'not feel like wearing it ... at least tonight' (Delany 1979: 143).

Even if we read the first encounter between Gorgik and Sarg as non-consensual, this aspect of their relationship seems to last no longer than one night. The next morning, Sarg awakes to find Gorgik asleep, the collar off. Sarg slips away and could easily have escaped. He finds a girl hiding in the bushes; the first thing she says to him is 'you're not a slave now' (ibid.: 145). Perhaps to emphasise this, Delany has the girl repeat this point twice more: 'you are a slave no longer' and 'you are not a slave any more' (ibid.: 148). This triple invocation, formulated a bit differently each time, suggests that Sarg has indeed left socio-economic slavery behind. He chooses to stay with Gorgik, shares desire with him and fights by his side. Gorgik does sometimes wear the collar; when he does, he calls Sarg 'little master' (ibid.: 234). When Gorgik tries to explain the nature of their relationship to others, he claims that 'we are both free men' (ibid.: 237). The reality, however, is that neither is free, for they are both enchained by mutual desire. By participating in a kind of play-slavery, Gorgik and Small Sarg reappropriate the symbolic structure of the socio-economic slavery which they hate, and use that structure to fulfil their erotic needs.

Certainly, Delany is well aware of the explosive danger which is contained within such play-slavery. In *Neveryóna*, the second volume of the *Nevèrÿon* series, Small Sarg turns against Gorgik. 'Before you sits a man whose every word and act is impelled by lusts as depraved as any in the nation, who would make a slave of all and anyone to satisfy them, calling such satisfaction freedom!' says Sarg of his former lover (Delany 1983: 77). We don't know what, exactly, caused Sarg to reject the relationship which he once shared with Gorgik; these developments occur 'off-stage', outside Delany's narrative. But the fact that Sarg was able to leave Gorgik is important. As Highleyman observes, a play-slave 'has an out', and this is one thing that makes his situation very different from that of African American slaves in the nineteenth century (Highleyman 1997: para. 16). Sarg tries to kill Gorgik, but Sarg himself is killed in the ensuing conflict. Yet even though Small Sarg has just tried to kill him, Gorgik will allow no ill to be spoken of his former lover. 'But that man, dead on the tile, was also a friend – once', Gorgik declares. 'Had his friendship not been so great, his hatred might have been less' (Delany 1983: 87). Gorgik still remembers Sarg fondly, and even Sarg's betrayal is not enough to dissuade Gorgik from his campaign to bring ethics to power. As always, he continues this campaign on two simultaneous fronts, waging a guerrilla campaign against the institution of slavery while also deploying erotic power relations as a dramatic ethical alternative to that institution. *Flight From Nevèrÿon*, the third volume in the series, finds Gorgik in another kinky relationship, this time with a one-eyed former mine slave called Noyeed. Gorgik and Noyeed develop their relationship consciously, with great deliberation and care. 'What we do together, you and I,' says Noyeed, 'we do very much awake' (Delany 1985: 123). Noyeed and Gorgik recognise the dangers inherent in a relationship such as theirs, and they are mindful of the example of Small Sarg. Nonetheless, they still choose erotic play-slavery, as a liberating alternative to the socio-economic slave system which they fight by day.

I must, therefore, strongly contest the interpretation advanced by Robert Elliot Fox. In his study of sexual politics in Delany's work, Fox asserts that

> one of the things which is so thoroughly repulsive about the master/slave relationship in sado-masochism is that it is a psychosexual parody of a relationship (which, to be sure, had its own psychosexual aspect) involving large masses of people, not just individuals, under conditions of the most overt compulsion.
>
> (Fox 1996: 52)

Here Fox completely fails to grasp the nature of consensual, desired play-slavery. On Delany's worlds and moons, this type of 'slavery' represents a liberation precisely because it replaces a non-consensual form of slavery – which both liberals and anarchists would probably find repulsive – with a form of play based upon consent and mutual desire. In the land of Nevèrÿon, it is not the radicalness of Gorgik's campaign against the institution of slavery that bothers the ruling class (since that institution was dying anyway, of 'natural' economic causes); '[r]ather, it was the radicalness of his appearance that had bothered the nobles, merchants, and their conservative employees – not the Liberator's practice so much as his potential; for appearances are signs of possibilities' (Delany 1985: 9). We cannot afford to discount the significance of this point, because the *Nevèrÿon* books, like much of Delany's writing, operate within a semiotic system which is informed by the poststructuralist theories of people like Foucault. Within such a semiotic system, the most significant political acts are likely to occur not on the material level of political economy, but on the level of sign and symbol. In this respect, as in many others, Delany's work is postanarchist. Jes Battis has recently noted the specifically kinky valence of Gorgik's semiotic system: 'it is through S/M sexuality ... that Gorgik stages political interventions within the gendered order of his own world' (Battis 2009: 480). A semiotic system like this demands that we take seriously arguments such as the one that Gorgik advances: 'As one word uttered in three different situations may mean three entirely different things, so the collar worn in three different situations may mean three different things. They are not the same: sex, affection, and society' (Delany 1979: 238). By developing this radically contextual theory of semiotics and symbolism, Gorgik (and Delany) resolve the apparent contradiction which Fox believes he has identified. The symbolic redemption of slavery from the semiotic and ethical abyss in which it lingers is a crucial part of Delany's project. Jeffrey Allen Tucker is right to suggest that 'Gorgik became a revolutionary who sought to attain for himself and all slaves in Nevèrÿon the power to wrest symbolic control of the slave collar from the aristocracy and the freedom to shift the significance of the collar from one context to another' (Tucker 2004: 148). This is the apex of Delany's kinky poststructuralist anarchism: freedom is defined here as the power to create context, the right to signify freely.

But if we wish to observe the full realisation of Delany's theory of erotic power, we must *Return to Nevèrÿon*. In a book by that name (originally published as *The Bridge of Lost Desire* in 1987), Delany brings his philosophy of power as close to a conclusion as such an open-ended theoretical project could come. In 'The Game of Time and Pain', a tale set shortly after the liberation of Nevèrÿon's slaves, we learn that S/M is 'one of the more common perversions in a Nevèrÿon so recently awakened from a troubling dream of slaves' (Delany 1987: 24). Here Delany makes explicit the historical connection between non-consensual socio-economic slavery and its consensual erotic reflection. This connection might seem to have ominous ethical implications for play-slavery. But here it is crucial to consider Delany's philosophy of history. In *Return to Nevèrÿon*, he assures us that history, 'despite our masters, is never inevitable, only more or less negotiable' (ibid.: 34).[7] Delany goes on to argue that history must 'be founded as richly on desire as on memory' (ibid.: 74). His argument points towards a radically subjective form of history – indeed, it suggests a kind of Lacanian history. After all, Lacan saw desire as the Freudian version of the Cartesian *cogito*: the 'nodal point' where subjectivity occurs (Lacan 1981: 154). Delany's work suggests that history is experienced by this desiring subject.[8] But what might such a negotiated, subjective, desiring history look like? Clearly, such a history would involve what Nietzsche called a 'revaluation of all values' (Nietzsche 1969: 254, 310–13). Thus Delany's Gorgik dreams of 'a land of wholly inverted values where the very sign of my servitude, the iron at my neck, would be taken by all I met as a symbol of transcendent freedom' (Delany 1987: 34).

For Gorgik and for other citizens of Nevèrÿon, such an inversion of values is inherently political. For us it is anarchist: as always, the relevant politics are the politics of consent and desire. Delany's storytelling emphatically demonstrates that non-consensual socio-economic slavery cannot be erotic. Gorgik recalls an erotic moment which he experienced when he was still a slave. Temporarily uncollared, Gorgik watched an aristocrat place a slave collar around his own neck – and Gorgik felt desire. But when the aristocrat discovered that Gorgik was watching, he quickly moved to re-collar the slave. Gorgik speaks of the collar: 'And just as I had recognized the sexual in his placing of it about his own neck, I knew that, though lust still reeled in his body and still staggered in mine, this gesture was as empty of the sexual as it is possible for a human gesture to be' (ibid.: 54). The fundamental realisation that no reconciliation is possible between socio-economic slavery and play-slavery sets Gorgik on the path to true knowledge and true freedom. For this is what Gorgik learned that night in the aristocrat's tent: 'I knew, at least for me, that the power to remove the collar was wholly involved with the freedom to place it there when I wished. And, wanting it, I knew, for the first time since I'd been brought to the mines – indeed, for the first time in my life – the self that want defined' (ibid.: 57). Here Gorgik is announcing a rather remarkable epistemological revolution. It is a revolution of the Lacanian variety, in which the self is actually constituted through desire – and, indeed, through a specifically fetishistic desire, as Georgia Johnston has noted (Johnston 2007: 54). But what is truly significant here is not merely the creation of a desiring subject, but rather the fact that through desire this self called Gorgik is set free for the first time in his life. And he is free (indeed, there is a 'he' who can be free) because he has the power to give that freedom up willingly. It is important to note that the 'he' created in this way is not the self sought by modern humanism or the liberal state, for it was Lacanian desire that brought Gorgik into existence, rather than any rationalist Cartesian *cogito*.

Perhaps the meaning of Gorgik, then, is freedom – at least for those citizens of Nevèrÿon who recognise that the ethical wound of non-consensual slavery can be healed, in part, through the consensual exchange of erotic power. For them, as for Gorgik, consent and desire are the razor-sharp blades which separate the ethical from the criminal, the erotic from the economic. As Nevèrÿon awakens from its nightmare of non-consensual slavery, its S/M community flourishes. 'When I was free,' old Gorgik tells his would-be lover, 'I learned that the power, the freedom, the pleasures you and I would indulge here tonight take place within the laws of a marginal society and an eccentric civility that allows us to grasp them, one and the other, with a stunning force and joy that whoever skulks after them like a slave cannot imagine' (Delany 1987: 65). As always, Delany celebrates marginality: explicitly, the marginality of the kinky community, but also Gorgik's and perhaps Delany's own. If Delany's work has a utopian moment, it is surely this. In liberated Nevèrÿon, Delany dreams of (and Gorgik remembers) a world in which power flows in accordance with the rules of civility and desire. It is a world which recognises the inevitability of power, and simply insists that such power be used ethically.

Delany's work, like Butler's, embodies an attempt to describe a range of ethical power relations. The basic rule for both authors is that these relations must be consensual and desired. In this sense, their projects are fundamentally anarchistic. But Butler and Delany also represent the culmination of a theoretical tradition which began when Masoch added the concept of consent to the philosophy of erotic power, thus creating the category of practices and strategies which would eventually come to be known as BDSM.[9] Of course, Butler and Delany are interesting not merely because they make innovative contributions to kink theory via the medium of paraliterary genre fiction – though that certainly would be a remarkable enough achievement in its own right. Butler and Delany also expand, enhance and refine kink theory. Surely the most significant contribution which Butler and Delany make to our understanding of power emerges from their reappropriation of the master–slave dynamic. Relationships such as that of Doro and Anyanwu, or Gorgik and Small Sarg, show, as no amount of dialectical thinking ever could, that there is, after all, a kind of mutual reciprocity to such relationships. Most crucially, Butler and Delany give us, through the principle of consent and the practice of mutual desire, a set of tools which we may use to distinguish unethical slavery from ethical play-slavery. This may well turn out to be their lasting contribution to the philosophy of power and to the erotic practices which flow from that philosophy.

Notes

1 I use the phrase 'speculative fiction' rather than 'science fiction' so that Delany's *Nevèrÿon* books, which describe vital components of his philosophy of power, may be included in the discussion.

2 Sadly, Marxism is no help here. As Rubin points out, 'the issue of consent has been clouded by an overly hasty application of Marxian critiques of bourgeois contract theory to sex law and practice' (Rubin 1982: 222). So liberalism and Marxism share the suspicion that kink can't be consensual. But the anarchist concept of consent,

which is broader, deeper and more open than those of most other political philosophies, may have room for kink.

3 Mistress Venus recognises that if there is a reactionary danger in what she does, that comes from the fact that her kink is inscribed within the structures of capitalist exchange. It is capitalism, not kink, that promotes 'body fascism' (Anarchist Federation 2002: 8).

4 See White (1985) for a good account of the enormous dilemmas which female slaves faced, especially with respect to issues of sexuality and reproduction.

5 In a well-known section from *The Phenomenology of Mind* entitled 'Lordship and Bondage', Hegel examined the richly intricate ways in which masters and slaves come to depend upon one another. He concluded that since the consciousness of the master must always be mediated through the consciousness of the slave, the master cannot attain true independence, but only a 'dependent consciousness' (Hegel 1967: 234ff).

6 Moser and Kleinplatz (2005) have argued eloquently, however, that the American Psychiatric Association should remove sexual sadism and sexual masochism from its DSM. Although the paraphilias will likely remain in the DSM, the proposed revisions to DSM-5 would distinguish paraphilias from paraphilic *disorders*. This is meant to reflect a consensus among clinicians that paraphilias such as sexual sadism or sexual masochism 'are not *ipso facto* psychiatric disorders' (American Psychiatric Association 2010).

7 The emphasis which Delany places on negotiation is not surprising. Real world S/M communities, including the California communities with which I am most familiar, often regard negotiation as one of the most important skills. Jay Wiseman calls it *the* most important (Wiseman 1996: 57). Pat Califia points out that the community uses negotiation for everything from individual scenes to entire relationships (Califia 2001: 25).

8 It's interesting to note here that Lacan said of the analytic method that 'its operations are those of history' (Lacan 1968: 19).

9 Masoch used the mechanism of the contract to explore the concept of consent in his famous erotic novel *Venus in Furs* (von Sacher-Masoch 1991 [1870]).

References

Alaimo, S. (1998) '"Skin Dreaming": The Bodily Transgressions of Fielding Burke, Octavia Butler, and Linda Hogan', in G. Gaard and P. D. Murphy (eds), *Ecofeminist Literary Criticism*, Urbana, IL: University of Illinois Press.

American Psychiatric Association (2010) 'DSM-5 Development', s.v. 302.83 Sexual Masochism. Online. Available HTTP: http://www.dsm5.org/ProposedRevisions/Pages/SexualandGenderIdentityDisorders.aspx (accessed 6 May 2010).

Anarchist Federation (2002) 'Interview with an Anarchist Dominatrix' *Organise!* 59: 7–9. Online. Available HTTP: http://www.afed.org.uk/org/org59.pdf (accessed 6 May 2010).

Barr, M. (1987) *Alien to Femininity: Speculative Fiction and Feminist Theory*, New York: Greenwood Press.

Battis, J. (2009) 'Delany's Queer Markets: *Nevèrÿon* and the Texture of Capital', *Science Fiction Studies* 36(3): 478–89.

Broderick, D. (1995) *Reading by Starlight: Postmodern Science Fiction*, New York: Routledge.

Brown, W. (1995) *States of Injury*, Princeton, NJ: Princeton University Press.

Butler, O. E. (1976) *Patternmaster*, New York: Warner Books.

——(1977) *Mind of My Mind*, New York: Avon Books.
——(1980) *Wild Seed*, New York: Warner Books.
——(1984) *Clay's Ark*, New York: St Martin's Press.
Califia, P. (2001) *Sensuous Magic*, San Francisco: Cleis Press.
Call, L. (2002) *Postmodern Anarchism*, Lanham, MD: Lexington Books.
——(2007) '"Sounds Like Kinky Business to Me": Subtextual and Textual Representations of Erotic Power in the Buffyverse', *Slayage: The Online International Journal of Buffy Studies* 6(4). Online. Available HTTP: http://slayageonline.com/ (accessed 6 May 2010).
Delany, S. R. (1979) *Tales of Nevèrÿon*, New York: Bantam Books.
——(1983) *Neveryóna, or: The Tale of Signs and Cities*, New York: Bantam Books.
——(1984) *Stars in My Pocket Like Grains of Sand*, New York: Bantam Books.
——(1985) *Flight From Nevèrÿon*, New York: Bantam Books.
——(1987) *Return to Nevèrÿon*, Hanover, NH: Wesleyan University Press.
——(1994) *Silent Interviews: On Language, Race, Sex, Science Fiction and Some Comics*, Hanover, NH: Wesleyan University Press.
——(1999) *Shorter Views: Queer Thoughts and the Politics of the Paraliterary*, Hanover, NH: Wesleyan University Press.
Foucault, M. (1978) *The History of Sexuality*, vol. I: *An Introduction*, New York: Vintage Books.
——(1980) *Power/Knowledge: Selected Interviews and Other Writings, 1972–1977*, New York: Pantheon Books.
——(1984) 'Sex, Power, and the Politics of Identity', *The Advocate* 400; reprinted in P. Rabinow (ed.) (1997) *Ethics: Subjectivity and Truth*, vol. 1 of *The Essential Works of Foucault, 1954–1984*, New York: The New Press.
Fox, R. E. (1996) 'The Politics of Desire in Delany's *Triton* and *Tides of Lust*', in J. Sallis (ed.), *Ash of Stars: On the Writing of Samuel R. Delany*, Jackson, MS: University Press of Mississippi.
Greenway, J. (1997) 'Twenty-first Century Sex', in J. Purkis and J. Bowen (eds), *Twenty-first Century Anarchism: Unorthodox Ideas for a New Millennium*, London: Cassell. Online. Available HTTP: http://www.judygreenway.org.uk/21stcenturysex/21stcenturysex.html (accessed 6 May 2010).
Heckert, J. (2005) 'Resisting Orientation: On the Complexities of Desire and the Limits of Identity Politics', unpublished PhD thesis, University of Edinburgh. Online. Available HTTP: http://sexualorientation.info/thesis/resisting%20orientation.pdf (accessed 22 July 2010).
Hegel, G. W. F. (1967) *The Phenomenology of Mind*, New York: Harper & Row.
Highleyman, L. (1997) 'Playing with Paradox: the Ethics of Erotic Dominance and Submission', in Pat Califia and Drew Campbell (eds), *Bitch Goddess*, San Francisco: Greenery Press. Online. Available HTTP: http://black-rose.com/articles-liz/bitchgoddess.html (accessed 23 June 2010).
Johnston, G. (2007) 'Discourses of Autobiographical Desires: Samuel Delany's *Nevèrÿon* Series', *Biography* 30(1): 48–60.
Lacan, J. (1968) *The Language of the Self: The Function of Language in Psychoanalysis*, Baltimore, MD: Johns Hopkins University Press.
——(1981) *The Four Fundamental Concepts of Psychoanalysis*, New York: W. W. Norton.
Lacey, L. J. (2008) 'Octavia E. Butler on Coping with Power in *Parable of the Sower*, *Parable of the Talents*, and *Fledgling*', *Critique* 49(4): 379–94.

Moser, C. and Kleinplatz, P. J. (2005) 'DSM-IV-TR and the Paraphilias: An Argument for Removal', *Journal of Psychology and Human Sexuality* 17(3/4). Online. Available HTTP: http://www2.hu-berlin.de/sexology/GESUND/ARCHIV/MoserKleinplatz.htm (accessed 6 May 2010).

Nietzsche, F. (1969) *On the Genealogy of Morals* and *Ecce Homo*, ed. W. Kaufmann, New York: Vintage Books.

Roberts, R. (1993) *A New Species: Gender and Science in Science Fiction*, Urbana, IL: University of Illinois Press.

Rubin, G. (1982) 'The Leather Menace: Comments on Politics and S/M', in Samois (ed.), *Coming to Power: Writings and Graphics on Lesbian S/M*, Boston, MA: Alyson Publications.

——(1984) 'Thinking Sex: Notes for a Radical Theory of the Politics of Sexuality', in C. S. Vance (ed.), *Pleasure and Danger: Exploring Female Sexuality*, New York: Routledge & Kegan Paul.

Russ, J. (1981) 'Recent Feminist Utopias', in M. S. Barr (ed.), *Future Females: A Critical Anthology*, Bowling Green, OH: Bowling Green State University Popular Press.

Tucker, J. A. (2004) *A Sense of Wonder: Samuel R. Delany, Race, Identity, and Difference*, Middletown, CT: Wesleyan University Press.

Vint, S. (2009) 'Thinking Sex in SF', *Science Fiction Studies* 36(3): 402–3.

von Sacher-Masoch, L. (1991 [1870]) *Venus in Furs*, New York: Zone Books.

White, D. G. (1985) *Ar'n't I a Woman? Female Slaves in the Plantation South*, New York: Norton.

Wiseman, J. (1996) *SM 101*, San Francisco: Greenery Press.

Chapter 8

Fantasies of an anarchist sex educator[1]

Jamie Heckert

> Why does one write, if not to put one's pieces together? From the moment we enter a school or church, education chops us into pieces: it teaches us to divorce soul from body and mind from heart. The fishermen of the Colombian coast must be learned doctors of ethics and morality, for they invented the word *sentipensante*, feeling-thinking, to define the language that speaks the truth.
>
> —Eduardo Galeano, *The Book of Embraces*

'A spell', says anarchist, feminist and Witch, Starhawk, 'is a story we tell ourselves that shapes our emotional and psychic world' (Starhawk 2002: 155). She brings attention to the powerful spells cast by corporate media and other authorities in the wake of September 11: stories of fear, of security through control and of the inevitability (and righteousness) of war. Stories we may come to believe and to tell ourselves, perhaps in different forms. Stories that can be resisted. 'The counterspell', she says, 'is simple: tell a different story' (ibid.).

Writing this essay has been an exercise in putting my pieces together, in telling different stories. The casting of these counterspells has been anything but simple. One night, struggling with this process, I wrote in a bedside notebook, 'It is painful to write, to speak. Silence is familiar, if not comfortable. So, too, telling stories that act as cloaks, covering the vulnerability of honest naked flesh. Holding back the flow of words, emotions, life. Disconnecting.' Stories I find easy to tell *are* simple: they are the stories I learned to tell in order to survive. These stories, simple stories, aren't working for me any more. I crave deeper sustenance, something more than survival. 'The politics worth having, the relationships worth having, demand that we delve still deeper' (Rich 2001a: 39). This delving, argues Adrienne Rich, lies in honesty. And for her, truth is never simple:

> There is no 'the truth', 'a truth' – truth is not one thing, or even a system. It is an increasing complexity. The pattern of carpet is a surface. When we looked closely, or when we became weavers, we learned of the tiny multiple threads unseen in the overall pattern, the knots on the underside of the carpet.
>
> (Rich 2001a: 32)

If truth is never simple, neither is learning to weave. To look closely at the patterns of one's own life is to find ways to resist profound forms of psychic domination, to potentially find ways to weave counterspells. To share the stories one finds reading these patterns can be an act of solidarity. That is both my hope in sharing these stories and my experience hearing and reading the stories of others. The stories of people I interviewed for my PhD research (Heckert 2005), stories of violence and desire (e.g. Allison 1993; Dunbar-Ortiz 1998), stories of friends and strangers; these are the stories that help me to imagine my own life (Le Guin 2004a), to cast my own counterspells.

I can relate to the male Latin American poets that Adrienne Rich criticised for writing as if 'the enemy is always outside the self, the struggle somewhere else' (Rich 2001b: 28). It is a practice that no longer sustains me. Now, more than ever, I feel a great affinity with the wisdom born of feminist movement,[2] that there can be no clear-cut division between the personal and the political:

> Throughout my life somebody has always tried to set the boundaries of who and what I will be allowed to be ... What is common to these boundary lines is that their most destructive power lies in what I can be persuaded to do to myself – the walls of fear, shame, and guilt I can be encouraged to build in my own mind ... I am to hide myself, and hate myself, and never risk exposing what might be true about my life. I have learned through great sorrow that all systems of oppression feed on public silence and private terrorization ... For all of us, it is the public expression of desire that is embattled, any deviation from what we are supposed to want and be, how we are supposed to behave.
>
> (Allison 1995: 117)

In writing the fantasies for this piece, I deepen my acknowledgement of the struggles within as well as those without. In sharing them, I end some of my silence.

Before beginning the sharing, I want to be clear in my agreement with the notion that there is 'no such thing as a true story' (Chödrön 2002: 17; see also, e.g., Stainton Rogers and Stainton Rogers 1997). (Or, in other words, rather than telling an absolute truth, 'story tells human truth' [Le Guin 2009: 119]). Others present at the events I describe might tell very different stories. *I* could tell different stories myself. These are the ones I choose to tell today, experiencing the dignity of speaking (only) for myself (Deleuze 1977; Tormey 2006).

I have fantasies of getting in trouble

I find myself waiting for it – the next insult, the next assault. My muscles tighten in preparation, as though I still lived in the house of my father and his drinking, as though I were still in school and a target for violence. I expect strangers, friends and lovers to realise what I imagined others knew – that I'm not good enough, that I'm not doing it right.

I remember walking home from school one day, I must have been ten, and finding a large, solid sheet of ice. I tried to carry it as a shield to protect myself; it was too heavy. Holding it, I could hardly move. I wonder, do my arms and shoulders ache because I'm holding it still?

Does my gut clench because it is still braced for a punch? Or is my belly irritable because I learned not to listen to it? What good were the signals from my body, my belly, my heart, that something wasn't right, when there was so little I could do? Better, it seemed, to ignore them, to fantasise of a better future, of other worlds. The present held little promise.

In the meantime, the tightening of muscles, the holding of breath, the freezing of myself continues, stemming the flow of emotion. Tears halt, fears burrow, fury abides. I focus, instead, on survival. Survival and escape.

The nightmares were intense when I decided to try to stay living in the UK with my new lover, thirteen years ago. I would wake us both up, terrified by visions of police chasing me through the streets. I was sure I wouldn't be allowed to stay. The authorities would know, somehow, that I was dangerous, queer, an anarchist.

I worried, too, when I started working for the council. I waited until I was 'legal', having received the first of many stamps in my passport granting me temporary 'leave to remain'. My new job was going into schools and talking with teenagers about sex. I could just imagine the tabloid headline – SEX CLASSROOM SCANDAL: QUEER FOREIGN ANARCHIST CORRUPTING OUR YOUTH.

Finishing my PhD on anarchism and sexuality, I did not believe I would get it. For so much of my life I've been in trouble for talking about sex, for questioning authority. How could I get rewarded for it now? Even as I prepared to graduate, I had visions of some university hierarch standing up, pointing at me and shouting, 'Anarchist, out!'

Writing this current chapter, I've been afraid, wondering, how will this get me in trouble?

These fantasies aren't surprising, really. I've been in trouble most of my life.

In the microcosm of the tiny Midwestern town of my childhood, I learned that difference was dangerous. Security, I was taught in so many lessons, comes from sameness. An atheist in a Christian town, I was the regular object of evangelical efforts. Why didn't I believe what they believed? When, as a teenager, I played fantasy role-playing games instead of baseball, I was warned of the dangers to my mental health as well as to my soul. When I continued to follow my own desires, rumours spread that I was a Satanist. Intertwined with this were others' anxieties about my gender/sexuality, expressed as something that was wrong with me. I was the one who was *different* (i.e. 'disgusting', 'perverted', 'gay') – an object of both fascination and contempt.

It wasn't just at school, in the so-called public sphere, that I was in trouble. My father abused alcohol when I was growing up. He was a respected member of the community, working in the local furniture store and serving on the city council. I remember once when I was young, watching him shaking hands and smiling with a customer in the store. I didn't understand how anyone could like him. Didn't they know what he was like? I don't know how I expected them to know. I just knew that I was often afraid of him. When he was angry, my mother, brother, sister and I were all potential targets. When he was angry, we were in trouble. When he was angry, it was one of us who was making trouble. He claimed the authority to define the laws, to make judgements and give out punishments. Sameness, in the forms of agreement and obedience, offered some security from his wrath. Our household was a micro-state and for the most part I played my part in a vain attempt to evade my father's violence.

Here and in school, I was assessed – in trouble when found wanting, praised when successful/compliant according to the terms of those assessing. Marshall Rosenberg refers to this state that the cultures of my school and home encouraged as 'emotional slavery', in which 'we believe ourselves responsible for the feelings of others. We think we must constantly strive to keep everyone happy. If they don't appear happy, we feel responsible and compelled to do something about it' (Rosenberg 2003: 57).

How did I survive growing up in this patriarchal household, in a small conservative town? Fantasies. One time when my father sent me to fetch him yet another beer from the refrigerator, I shook it ever so slightly. Not enough that it would actually foam all over him when he opened it, but enough that I could imagine it. When it was my turn to set the table for dinner, I gave him the odd plate or piece of cutlery when I had the chance, so that, I fantasised, he would realise he was different and unwanted and would leave us to get on with our lives in peace. I knew that being different made you want to leave. I wanted to leave. I escaped into fantasy novels. My favourites were tales of young men who were different; escaping stigma, they became heroes who saved worlds (Eddings 1982; Feist 1982).

I remember sitting in the principal's office with him, Mr Robinson, and two boys who had bullied me in the playground. We were in elementary school, maybe eight or nine years old. I remember trying to make sense of it, to deal with the pain, through fantasy. I was like Luke Skywalker, you see, and they were like Darth Vader and the evil Emperor. It was a battle of good versus evil, and I, of course, was the good guy.

About twenty years later, I went to my ten-year high school class reunion. I was terrified and had hardly slept the night before. I wanted to meet the people who had become monsters in my head, to see them as real people. And so I met the man whom my very young self had labelled 'evil Emperor'. Even while I was viscerally remembering the feeling of his fist in my gut, I listened eagerly to his criticisms of politics and capitalism. He told me about his industrial workplace in the same small town that we had both grown up in, about how people were suffering. I asked him, 'Why do you think people put up with it?' He said simply, 'Because they are afraid.'

I had another strategy. I was 'smart' (in the terms of schools). While this still got me into trouble, both with my classmates for 'being a geek' and with those teachers whose claims to intellectual authority I challenged, it also 'earned' me some respect. I learned here that different was safer when it meant better. If I couldn't get security from sameness, I could get it from success.

This became my key strategy for survival – fantasies of superiority. My 'differences' didn't make me lesser than others, they made me better. The reverse discourse of identity politics I have since rejected (Heckert 2004) was one I embraced in my youth. Homosexuality wasn't a perversion; it was radical, dangerous, *interesting*. My atheism didn't mean I was going to suffer in hell; it was a sign of my superior rationality and intellect – how I would have loved the arrogance of *The God Delusion* (Dawkins 2006). Being in trouble with my dad, well, that meant I wasn't anything like him (I wanted to believe). And being 'good' at school, that meant I could go to college and get out of that town. Then, I fantasised, I would be free.

I dreamed that life would be okay when I got out, as I counted down the days that summer after high school. If I just suffered through this, I'd be okay when I got to college. There, I wouldn't be so different. There, I could succeed. Success, I was taught, brought freedom.

I have fantasies of being an Anarchist Sex Educator

> To make a trouble was, within the reigning discourse of my childhood, something that one should never do precisely because that would get one *in* trouble. The rebellion and its reprimand seemed to be caught up in the same terms, a phenomenon that gave rise to my first critical insight into the subtle ruse of power: The prevailing law threatened one with trouble, even put one in trouble, all to keep one out of trouble. Hence, I concluded that trouble is inevitable and the task, how best to make it, what best way to be in it.
>
> (Butler 1990: vii)

> Modern schools and universities push students in the habits of depersonalised learning, alienation from nature and sexuality, obedience to hierarchy, fear of authority, self-objectification, and chilling competitiveness.
>
> (Evans 1978: 136)

I felt tremendous relief to arrive at Grinnell College. One of the wealthiest educational institutions in United States, due to its early investment in Intel, the college can easily afford the beneficence of scholarships for working-class kids who are 'good enough'. Accepted by this elite institution, I got to hold on to my fantasies of superiority and success. It was, at the same time, a place where I could let go of some of the silences I'd been carrying. I came out as gay (and how!), very quickly coming to think of myself as an activist.

I loosened my hold on intelligence as rationality, dropping chemistry for women's studies and atheism for paganism. Success took on new forms.

'If you could be the best at anything, what would it be?' A group of us were sitting in the Stonewall Resource Centre at Grinnell asking each other questions. 'Activist,' I said. 'Ah, a revolutionary!' said Ali. I hadn't thought of it like that before. Yeah, maybe revolutionary. Trouble-maker, definitely. It's who I've always been.

Four years before that, I sat on my best friend's bed agreeing that it would be cool to be sex researchers when we grew up. I never thought I really would.

Somehow, I became both: an anarchist sex researcher and educator.

Anarchism seemed so obviously *right* when I met my first anarchist; I was twenty years old at the time, studying 'abroad', in Stirling, Scotland. I was immediately hooked. (And not *just* on him.) It offered visions of other possibilities, a radical critique of the domination I (and so many others) had experienced; it fit with the feminist challenges to hierarchies of gender, class, 'race' and sexuality that I had been eagerly learning about in women's studies classrooms. I was in love.

Studying again in Scotland years later, this time in Edinburgh, I was surprised to find myself writing about anarchism and sexuality. I had thought of anarchism as something I did outside the university, something too dangerous to combine with my research on sexuality.[3] I tried to keep these fears at bay using a strategy I'd found helpful for many years: I tried to be *right*.

Like many people engaged in struggles for post-capitalist, post-state and post-patriarchal cultures, I was deeply moved and inspired reading Derrick Jensen's autobiographical book *A Language Older than Words* (Jensen 2000). I sobbed as I read his stories of familial violence and as I remembered my own. I came to identify with him and his argument. He evocatively links his experiences of domination with wider patterns: economic, political, ecological, sexual, racial and spiritual. His conclusion: civilisation depends on domination and must be stopped. I was drawn to his arguments in part because they seemed even *more radical* than my own position. I was seduced by this book and thrown into confusion. Maybe *he* was right.

Derrick Jensen wrote of his choice to end all communication with his father, which I respect at the same time as I chose otherwise.[4] What concerns me more is that Jensen not only gives up on his father, he gives up on a large proportion of humanity. Quoting Viktor Frankl, a survivor of Auschwitz who said, 'There are only two human races – the race of the decent and the race of the indecent people', Jensen continues:

> He is right of course. To restate this in terms of this book's exploration: there are those who listen and those who do not; those who value life and those who do not; and those who do not destroy and those who do. The indigenous author Jack Forbes describes those who would destroy as suffering from a literal illness, a virulent and contagious disease he calls

> *we'tiko*, or cannibal sickness, because those so afflicted consume the lives of others – human and nonhuman – for private purpose or profit, and do so with no giving back of their own lives. There are those who are well, and those who are sick. The distinction really is that stark.
>
> (Jensen 2000: 198)

A line between healthy and sick is one I've been put on the wrong side of too many times to trust any attempt to draw one. However, any concern is quickly brushed aside as the reader is encouraged to identify with the well and the decent:

> How can *those of us who are well* learn to respond effectively to those who are not? How can the decent respond to the indecent? If we fail to appreciate and answer this question, those who destroy will in the end cause the cessation of life on this planet, or at least as much of it as they can. The finitude of the planet guarantees that running away is no longer a sufficient response. Those who destroy must be stopped. The question: How?
>
> (Jensen 2000: 198–9, emphasis added)

Being a hero, one of the good guys[5], being *right*, is a common theme in activist literature like *A Language Older than Words* (see Goldberg 2005), in the survival strategies of 'adult children of alcoholics' (Crisman 1991), in academia and in my own history. While I distrust drawing these lines between the good guys and bad guys, the well and the ill, I still find myself doing it. These are the strategies I've used to survive: 'success' in institutionalised education, silences of emotions and desires that don't fit with being 'good', the sameness of being one of the (good) guys, who are at the same time 'weirdos and freaks' – the activists (Anonymous 2000: 166). While inverting conventional morality (i.e. bad is the new good) has been life saving for me at times, I worry now about its other effects. For one, it can inhibit transformations of consciousness or social relations (see, e.g., Brown 1995; S. Newman 2004). Also, identifying as an outsider has often been a great source of loneliness and isolation for me. Even in spaces with other 'outsiders', I can be afraid of losing my status as an insider among the outsiders; here, too, disciplinary labels abound: liberal, reformist, sell-out. In fear, I can silence myself.

I can also silence others. Learning from a number of painful lessons where my desire to be right had led to a loss of connection with others, I decided not to take any sessions in schools during the final period of writing up my PhD thesis. I was terrified that it wouldn't be 'good enough' (what if I wasn't right?). I knew I could easily turn sessions into a defence of my argument, being more concerned with my own needs than those of the young people. They didn't need me trying to convince them of the importance of anarchism to the everyday politics/experience of sexuality. Becoming an Anarchist Sex

Educator, as I sometimes do, I fall back on the strategy of pointing to everyday domination in the hope that if others see how bad things are, and how good they could be, it will encourage revolution. I'm not alone in finding comfort in this pattern:

> [O]ften I intended my teachings to serve as a conduit to radicalization, which I now understand to mean a certain imprisonment that conflates the terms of domination with the essence of life. Similar to the ways in which domination always already confounds our sex with all of who we are, the focus on radicalization always turns our attention to domination.
>
> (Alexander 2005: 8)

Like Jacqui Alexander, I'm concerned about the effects of continuous attention to domination rather than life itself. Is this a source of activist burnout? Of widespread and increasing depression globally? (Of my burnout, my depression?)

Letting go of fantasies of being an Anarchist Sex Educator, I'm faced with new questions. How can sex education *be anarchist*, rather than just a promotion of anarchism?

I have fantasies of anarchist sex education

> If you have come here to help me, you are wasting your time. But if you have come because your liberation is bound up with mine, then let us work together.
>
> (Lilla Watson)

> The state is a relationship between human beings, a way by which people relate to one another; and one destroys it by entering into other relationships, by behaving differently to one another.
>
> (Landauer 2005 [1910]: 165)

If anarchism is about changing relationships throughout life, then sex education could be just as much a focus of anarchist practice as G8 summits, poverty or climate change (inasmuch as any of these are really separate). Anarchist ethics of prefiguration and mutual aid, of listening and appreciating difference, seem to me to speak clearly to the challenges of sex education (broadly defined). What effects do various forms of oppression have on our capacities for sexual pleasure, for self-care, for intimacy? More specifically, how do particular patterns of domination in particular times and places affect the capacities of the people involved? What practices shift patterns in consciousness and in relationships, undermining domination, nurturing connection, in particular locations?

Sometimes, filled with despair, I have fantasies that this is impossible in schools. I look at the architecture and see in the courtyards and metal bars the shapes of prisons (Foucault 1977). I hear teachers shouting and bells ringing, demanding order. Order – on whose terms? I wince to recall a guidance teacher who encouraged us to lock the door when in the room with young people to stop any unwanted intrusions, never mind how the young people might feel about this. I remember being furious in another school where young people were subjected to a military recruiter immediately before our session. In classrooms, notices on 'appropriate' behaviour frequently equate respect with obedience. And when a young person asked me for permission to go to the toilet, I thought, 'How can I support them to feel capable of making their own decisions when it comes to sex when such basic physical needs as eating, drinking, pissing and shitting are scheduled by external authority and exceptions require permission?' One classroom sign went so far as to say, 'Unless you have a medical condition, please do not ask permission to use the toilet as refusal may cause offence.' How can I encourage listening and empathy in an institution where young people receive so little themselves? How can I nurture capacities for equality when it comes to sex when schools naturalise hierarchy? How does anyone expect institutionalised education, with its cultures of assessment, to result in people prepared to express their desires, listen to those of others and work out together, cooperatively, what to do (or not do)? What are the implications of bureaucracy for sexual health? Of spending so much time in human constructed environments? Of boredom?

I've heard horror stories of school sex education lessons. The most sickening was when young men told me they had been shown a graphic video of the surgical removal of a cancerous testicle. The use of fear seems to be a common tactic in sex education.

'Are you saying our school nurse is a terrorist?'

~ ~ ~

The experiences in the classroom I remember with the most joy are the ones where we had a connection that touched me. I was not giving it to them, giving them what I knew was good for them, giving them what I decided they needed. I was listening. I was responsive.

Touching. Listening. Responsive. Is this education, or is it sex?

'Can sex education be practical?' asked John Wilson (2003) in a controversial article. I say it always already is. My question instead: what is practised?[6]

Or, rather, how might sex education be a practice that changes the present and opens different possibilities for the future?

I have fantasies of erotic education – of learning spaces that let go of judgement, of assessment (how good are you at sex? Are you doing it right? How 'smart' are you? Are you man enough, woman enough, straight enough, gay enough? Are you thin enough? Muscular enough? Beautiful enough?); that awaken the senses; that nurture a capacity for joy in living and learning; that nurture an ever-expanding awareness of one's own embodiment–feelings–thoughts. To profoundly experience both pleasure and pain in all their complexities and flavours, to neither hold too tightly nor be held for long by either, to listen to the needs and desires of other beings as well as to one's own, to resist the will to dominate or to be dominated, to find the will to connect: these are practices for sex, for life itself.

~ ~ ~

Listening could be the place to start. Ursula Le Guin (2004b) contrasts two models of communication. The first is information transfer – from A to B or B to A – which reminds me of the policy speak of 'delivering a sex education programme'. Like it was a pizza. It's what Paulo Freire (2000) calls the banking model of education: knowledge is an object, a commodity to be transferred. The second model has more erotic potential: 'intersubjectivity', she says, 'is mutual. It is a *continuous interchange* between two consciousnesses. Instead of an alternation of roles between box A and box B, between active subject and passive object, it is a *continuous intersubjectivity that goes both ways all the time*' (Le Guin 2004b: 188). Her model for this: amoeba sex. Two bodies linking, opening to each other, giving and receiving of each other (literally, for they are sharing genetic material). Listening and telling. Telling, she reminds us, *is* listening:

> This is very similar to how people unite themselves and give each other parts of themselves – inner parts, mental not bodily parts – when they talk and listen. (You can see why I use amoeba sex not human sex as my analogy: in human hetero sex, the bits only go one way. Human hetero sex is more like a lecture than a conversation. Amoeba sex is truly mutual because amoebas have no gender and no hierarchy. I have no opinion on whether amoeba sex or human sex is more fun. We might have the edge, because we have nerve endings, but who knows?)
>
> (Le Guin 2004b: 189)

Traditional heterosex education teaches that the bits only go one way, and it does so in the form of a lecture. Well, that was my experience anyway. Maybe yours was different?

Anarchic sex education might invite the possibility that human sex could be more like amoeba sex – with (many) genders *and* with nerve endings! Anarchic sex education might be like amoeba sex, an amoeba orgy in the classroom (or in a social centre or gathering, in the pub or around the kitchen table). Not a worker delivering a pizza: a group of people making a pizza together, or even a group planning to make a pizza, while open to the possibility that it may turn into something else entirely.

But, you might say, a classroom is not like a social centre. It is a space in a hierarchical institution, a place of discipline and punishment. Maybe you remember some of the pain you experienced in school. You're right, anyway. A classroom is different. Usually.

The architecture doesn't demand authoritarian education. Institutions don't force obedience; they can't. Resistance is constrained through cajoling and rewards or threat of trouble, but it never disappears. 'Where there is power, there is resistance' (Foucault 1990: 95; see also Scott 1990). With the help of an anarchic facilitator and the willingness of a group of young people (ideally a self-selected affinity group with an ethic of free association – everyone *wants* to be there, with each other), a classroom can become a temporary autonomous zone (Bey 1991), a space for an erotic amoeba orgy when before and after it may host (more or less) orderly rows of 'students', with a 'teacher' giving it to them.

I remember clearly a moment in a school last year. It was early in a session when the group I was working with went silent. 'This isn't what you expected, is it?' I said to them. One young man looked at me and said, 'In a way, it's what we wanted. I thought we wouldn't be allowed to laugh.' 'That would suck,' I responded without thinking. 'Yeah,' he said, looking a little stunned, 'that would suck.'

What if it had been okay for him to cry, too?

> let tears come
> so we can really
> laugh together
> carve out spaces
> to dream of things better she said
> than this she said
>
> (claque 2002)

~ ~ ~

Teenagers are always in trouble. In another school session several years ago, a discussion with a group of young men on the topic of homosexuality helped me understand this. They said that they didn't want to act homophobic, but if they didn't, then they would get called gay themselves. We talked about how those things weren't separate, that by continuing to police themselves and each other they were participating in the creation of a policed environment. They were trapped in a cycle and struggled to imagine doing things differently. I asked, 'Can you talk about it?' One replied, 'No, we can't.'

I remember one of my undergraduate psychology lecturers saying that homophobia was a pathology; it's not *us* who are sick, it's *them*. I cheered with others, at the time. After years of working with young men, I see homophobia, the fear of homosexuality, as something to be listened to. It's okay to be afraid. It's okay to be angry. It's okay to *feel* anything. The question for me is, how can each of us learn to take responsibility for our own feelings, to let go of a sense of responsibility for the feelings of others (Rosenberg 2003)?

My fantasy of the school as prison, as a space antithetical to sexual health, comes in part from the pain and anger I feel remembering particular experiences I've had in schools and my great love of autonomy and equality. I also experience profound empathy for the anger I've heard from young people when they talk about their schooling. It's not the only story I could tell. I've also been inspired by the care I've seen teachers express for young people. I remember in particular how appreciative and supportive teachers in one of the Catholic schools were, aware of the challenges of our negotiating entry to the school (not always successfully). They knew how popular we were with the students and I had the impression that they genuinely cared for young people and hoped that they might experience sexual well-being and caring relationships. I am both moved by their care and pained by the patterns of control they seem to uphold in the school.

Teachers, too, are afraid of getting into trouble. After a conference talk advocating anarchism as a source of inspiration for sex education, one schoolteacher said she would love to do this, but how? Parents would be upset.

Maybe parents and teachers need to be listened to, too. Could this be one aspect of anarchist community organising?

~ ~ ~

Sessions I did in schools always included space for the young people to sit in small groups and to write questions they may have had about sex, sexuality and/or relationships. I was frequently amazed and inspired by the depth and variety of questions asked. Looking over eight years worth of collected questions, I see some interesting patterns. Young men, for example, frequently wrote questions like 'How many positions are there?' and 'What's the best position?' Safe questions in a disciplinary culture: quantify, evaluate. Questions that mimic, too, the language of men's lifestyle magazines, with their emphasis on (sexual) performance and managerialism (Tyler 2004).

At the same time, I hear something else in these questions – a desire to develop erotic imaginations.

Here, counterspells may be cast. When the telling of different stories is a listening, responsive to the needs of others as well as honestly recognising one's own needs, it is a powerful act of solidarity. (If not, it may be an imposition, a violation.) I sometimes told the story about the young men who didn't want to be homophobic to men in other schools. A deeply attentive silence was a common response.

I smile, remembering a session in a Catholic school where a young woman exclaimed, 'Oh!' when I hoped for an opening of imaginations, inviting a breakdown of heteronormative divisions between 'foreplay' and 'real sex' by discussing sex between women and the possibilities of pleasure without penetration (see, e.g., Albury 2002; Chalker 2000; Dodson 1987; F. Newman 2004).

Similarly, young men often loved stories focusing on techniques for pleasure, offering alternatives to the medicalised and reproduction-oriented narratives of most sex education. In response to their questions, we discussed techniques for slowing ejaculation and prolonging pleasure (i.e. slower breathing, condom use, squeezing the base of the cock, gently tugging the balls back down and changing activities). Learning Kegel exercises for their PC muscles[7] was also pretty popular ('for next time you're bored in Maths class'). More fraught with young men were explorations of the notion that penetrative pleasures may not only be a one-way street, even in heterosexual relationships (Morin 1998). (Even when discussions were emotionally challenging, as they often were, young men wrote appreciatively of sessions on evaluation forms.)

When young people repeated stories of the evolutionary imperatives of heterosexuality and monogamy, stories I told of the sexual habits and radically egalitarian social organisation of bonobos, of the MMF (male–male–female) triad of swans I saw on a Channel 4 documentary, or of the vast diversity of what we might call sexuality in human cultures around the world and throughout history often excited discussion. Many of the young people also appreciated opening up discussions about the relationship between health and hierarchy (see, e.g., Marmot 2004; Wilkinson 2001), particularly when these were grounded in the concrete experiences of their education and current or future employment.

One could also tell stories of erotic connections between people that were not necessarily genitally focused, opening imaginations to other possibilities in a hypersexual culture (see, e.g., Alexander, Chapter 2). I could tell, for example, the story a friend my age told me of remembering the joy of kissing for hours when he was a teenager. Rather than advocating an authoritarian, not to mention unrealistic, notion of celibacy, such stories might help young people imagine (and practice!) negotiating their own ideas of what constitutes sex, including slow sex (Honoré 2005), no sex (e.g. Packer 2002) and/or safer sex. 'Erika', one of the women I interviewed for my PhD research, described how learning to say no to sex was a crucial part of her healing after childhood sexual abuse (see also Haines 1999):

> My first really sexual experience was to decide not to have sex. To just say 'no' to sex and it came out of fear and out of confusion and out of all sorts of shit but actually it was really affirming and sexual and made me feel really sexy because I realised that I couldn't really say 'yes' to sex without knowing what it was like to say 'no.' I'm quite choosy about sex now. I very rarely enter into sex unless I've got a clear inkling that its going to be good because I'm not interested in any sex that's any less than like really, really good. I don't want boring sex anymore. I don't want any of that, or guilt sex or kind of street cred sex or … I don't want any of that. I'm not interested. I think that's one of things that I can't change, is that … that was the beginning of my sex life. I can't do

anything about that and what I can do is just make sure that its really good now, which I do.

(Erika, in Heckert 2005: 145)

~ ~ ~

Anarchist sex education might also involve sharing skills of deconstructing stories as an act of solidarity. Bronwyn Davies described how she did this with children in a primary school:

> [C]hildren can be introduced to the possibility, not of learning the culture, or new aspects of it, as passive recipients, but as producers of culture, as writers and readers who make themselves and are made within the discourses available to them. It allows them to see the intersection between themselves as fictions (albeit intensely experienced fictions) and the fictions of their culture – which are constantly being (re)spoken, (re)written and (re)lived
>
> (Davies 1993: 2)

Imagine teenagers, and older adults, learning to deconstruct the dominant sexual stories of their cultures! What shifts might occur in the classed, racialised and gendered power relationships of teenage sexuality, where young men engage critically with pornography and young women take apart the messages in lifestyle magazines (and vice versa!)? What could happen if more people questioned the disciplinary nature of state-sponsored sexual health materials? Could this be another route to becoming 'protagonists', as people in the popular movements of Argentina refer to themselves (Sitrin 2006; see also Johnstone 2010)?

Finally, imagination comes from a flexibility and openness not only of the mind, but also of the heart, of the body, as they are inseparable. Learning (and practising!) non-violent communication (NVC) improved my ability to connect emotionally with the young people I was working with, helping me let go of the security I find in intellectualisation. This applies to taking care of myself more generally: I find that the more I care for myself, the more I am able to care for others. What other practices might help (young) people (including 'sex educators') cast off the immobilising effects of fear (Lappé and Perkins 2005) and shame (Scheff 1990), to deepen bodily awareness and connection with emotions?

The nomadic creativity of social movements and grassroots cultures offers continuous sources of inspiration for anarchist sex education. What would happen if (young) people were taught queer histories of HIV/AIDS response?

> Gay people invented safe sex. We knew that alternatives – monogamy and abstinence – were *unsafe*, unsafe in the latter case because people do not abstain from sex, and if you only tell them just say no, they will have unsafe sex. We were able to invent safe sex because we have always known that sex is not, in an epidemic or not, limited to penetrative sex. Our promiscuity taught us many things, not only about the pleasures of sex, but about the great multiplicity of those pleasures. It is that psychic

> preparation, that experimentation, that conscious work on our own sexualities that has allowed many of us to change our sexual behaviours … very quickly and very dramatically.
>
> (Crimp 1987: 252–3)

In what spaces might we speak of queer erotic communities (e.g. Hutchins 2007) as well as the nonsexual practices of connection among LGBTQ folk (Sawicki 2004)?

Of course, anarchist sex education is alive and well within autonomous feminist health groups and networks (see, e.g., Anonymous 2003; Gordon and Griffiths 2007; Griffiths and Gordon 2007), including self-help groups (e.g. Shodini Collective 1997), caressing workshops (Anonymous, 2007), resources for autonomy in pregnancy and childbirth (Fannen 2001), discussions of the politics of menstruation (Lisa 2008), DIY contraception and termination, herbal gynaecology (Nelson 1976), feminist histories of reproductive autonomy (e.g. Federici 2004) and more. Another potential source of inspiration coming out of struggles for social transformation and self-care is SOMA, an anarchist group therapy combining elements of radical psychology, anarchism and capoeira angola developed by Roberto Freire in Brazil to undermine the effects of dictatorship on individuals (see Goia 2008).

Fragments of an anarchist sex education might also be found within more mainstream settings. What elements of mutual aid, of listening, of imagination are already present in popular culture (Duncombe 2007), in health promotion practices (e.g. Nutland *et al.* 2003), in schools, universities and youth clubs? Can they be observed, with these observations offered back as gifts (Graeber 2004)? How can they be nurtured, diverting energy from patterns of domination into patterns of connection and care?

I have fantasies of erotic anarchy

> What we must work on, it seems to me, is not so much to liberate our desires but to make ourselves infinitely more susceptible to pleasure.
>
> (Foucault 1989: 310)

> Eroticism is exciting, life would be a drab routine without at least that spark. That's the point. Why has all the joy and excitement been concentrated, driven into that one narrow, difficult-to-find alley of human experience, and all the rest laid to waste? There's plenty to go around within the spectrum of our lives.
>
> (Firestone 1979: 147)

The arrogant rationalism, the atheist supremacy, of my youth could not protect me from the dominant Christian values of my cultures. The day a Jehovah's Witness leaflet came through my door, I saw, to my horror, that *their* vision of heaven was remarkably like *my* ideas of an anarchist future.

Both visions might be seen as utopian projections, imagining a future that contains what the present lacks (Bloch 1986). For Bloch, utopia can act as a method of inspiring social transformation and recognising desires that are not being met. For Hakim Bey, by way of contrast, such visions may be a distraction from enacting those desires. 'Between tragic Past & impossible Future, anarchism seems to lack a Present – as if afraid to ask itself, here & now, WHAT ARE MY TRUE DESIRES? – & what can I DO before it's *too late*?' (Bey 1991: 61). While I have a deep sense of appreciation for Bloch, Bey's concern speaks strongly to the shock I felt that day. Tracing this thread of anarcho-mysticism to Rilke's biting critique of the Church helps me understand my fantasies of life after the revolution, of heaven:

> The idea that we are sinful and need to be redeemed as a prerequisite for God is more and more repugnant to a heart that has comprehended the earth. Sinning is the most wonderfully roundabout path to God – but why should *they* go wandering who have never left him? The strong, inwardly quivering bridge of the Mediator has meaning only where the abyss between God and us is admitted; but this very abyss is full of the darkness of God; and where someone experiences it, let him [sic] climb down and howl away inside it (that is more necessary than crossing it). Not until we can make even the abyss our dwelling-place will the paradise that we have sent on ahead of us turn around and will everything deeply and fervently of the here-and-now, which the Church embezzled for the Beyond, come back to us.
> (Rilke 1989: 332–3)

In my efforts to deny pain, I diminish my capacity to experience pleasure.

~ ~ ~

One spring when I was in college, I was cycling through campus when suddenly my front wheel turned sideways and I flew over the handlebar. I picked up my bike, locked it to a signpost on the roadside and went into the nearest building – computing services. I didn't feel any pain. In the men's room, I looked in the mirror and was startled by the amount of blood. I tried to clean it up with tissues. Realising it was too much for me to handle, I went to reception and said to the woman working there, who I knew, 'I think I need to go to the hospital or see a doctor or something, but I'm not sure. I'm kinda confused right now.' I remember clearly that as soon as she told me, 'Oda's coming to take you to the hospital,' my awareness switched off. Somebody else was taking care of things. I'd broken off my two front teeth and needed my forehead stitched back together again.

Sometimes, switching off is all you can do. It's a way of adapting, of surviving. In the short term, it can save your life. If it goes on, it can be hard to remember the point of living. While I've never been suicidal, I have struggled with bouts of depression. I've not always known how to feel the pain inside.

From my own memories of domestic (and other) violence to the daily struggles I see around me to the global politics of war and climate change, I feel great pain (Sullivan 2004). To cope, I regularly anaesthetise myself in various ways (moralising, intellectualising or distracting myself, with porn or political theory, television or net surfing, with ideas of 'success'). And when I do, I end up feeling worse. Numb.

> Repression takes a mammoth toll on our energy, and also on our sensitivity to the world around us. Repression is not a local anaesthetic. If we won't feel pain, we won't feel much else, either – both loves and losses are less intense, the sky less vivid, pleasure is muted. As a doctor working with Vietnam veterans observed, 'The minds pays for its deadening to the state of our world by giving up its capacity for joy and flexibility.'
>
> (Macy and Brown 1998: 34)

I don't notice that the sky has gone dull (is it a gradual change?) until a profound experience brings me back into a fuller awareness of life. Have you ever experienced that? I've had it a few times, after great sex or with psilocybin, after massage, yoga or sauna, gardening or other connecting experiences. It's such a joy to remember the beauty of the world. How did I ever forget?

Fantasies.

The continual frustration of pleasure as anticipated rather than lived, of learning to find value only in utility (Winnubst 2006); the continual fear of never being 'good enough' (Crisman 1991; Wikipedia, 2008); the continual shame of embodiment in patriarchal cultures (Lisa 2008) and inequality in hierarchical 'democracies' – all mean its switching off is sometimes the best I can imagine doing. My survival strategy of success, an inheritance of 'phallicised whiteness' (Winnubst 2006: 10) and (domestic) violence, takes me 'outside myself' (lang 1992). Caught up in goals and judgements (Success? Failure?), I disconnect again and again from the experience of presence, from the sensations of being. 'The revolutionary is like the frustrated suitor whose single-minded focus remains on wedding and bedding his beloved, failing to take advantage of the pleasures of courting' (Simpson 2004: 20). Depressed and judgemental, from 'demanding the impossible' of myself, I adopt a stance of grumpywarriorcool (starr 2007), holding tightly to my ice shields sure that if I let my guard down others will judge me as harshly as I've come to judge myself. Better to play it cool. Depressed, grumpy anarchist, seeing nothing but domination, I become like Rilke's Panther:

> His vision, from the constantly passing bars,
> has grown so weary that it cannot hold
> anything else. It seems to him there are
> a thousand bars; and behind the bars, no world.
>
> (Rilke 1989: 25)

My anarchist fantasies of the end of domination *keep* domination at the very centre of my vision. Central, yet abstracted because the pain is both ignored and held tightly, disconnecting me.

Doing so, I may be once again playing out on an individual level much larger cultural patterns. In an effort to understand why potentially radically liberating impulses transformed into a turning to the State for recognition and legislation (i.e. identity politics), Wendy Brown offers a feminist reading of Nietzsche's account of *ressentiment*, 'the moralising revenge of the powerless' (Brown 1995: 61). Resulting from the suffering of false promises of individual freedom and social equality made by liberal democracies, its effects include 'imaginary revenge' (Nietzsche 1969: 36) targeted toward a constructed enemy who is seen as responsible for the injury of inequality or a lack of freedom. Focusing on the moral outrage and the desire to return injury, the pain of the original injury is 'anaesthetised'. Shaking the beer can. Trying to bring down 'civilisation'. Demands for State protection. These efforts maintain a position of powerlessness, of permanently injured status, offering anaesthetic for the pain of wanting freedom, equality and connection. Whereas,

> all that such pain may long for – more than revenge – is the chance to be heard into a certain release, recognized into self-overcoming, incited into possibilities for triumphing over, and hence losing, itself. Our challenge, then, would be to configure a radically democratic political culture that can sustain such a project in its midst without being overtaken by it, a challenge that includes guarding against abetting the steady slide of political into therapeutic discourse, even as we acknowledge the elements of suffering and healing we might be negotiating.
>
> (Brown 1995: 74–5)

~ ~ ~

Is it anarchism that is 'trapped between a tragic past and an impossible future' or is it me? I could hold on to my anger and pain at my father, at school bullies, at capitalism and Christianity and the State, furious that my needs were/are not met. I could keep trying to make it all right, to create a world where my needs are met (all the while doing so in the name of abstract values, on behalf of others). But I'm tired.

So tired that I find it increasingly difficult to be anti-State. Not that I am pro-State; I want to have more than two choices, to resist the George Bush logic of 'you're either with us or against us' (CNN 2001). I find that logic entirely too easy to turn against myself, to judge myself not good enough, not anarchist enough. Like Landauer or Deleuze and Guattari, I see the State less as an institution that can be smashed and more as a mode of behaviour, of relating. This understanding was accentuated after attending a course on non-violent communication where I learned to see all forms of behaviour as strategies for meeting needs (Rosenberg 2003). And if the State (like capitalism, patriarchy and white supremacy) is a strategy, it is one that I have used and continue to use. It is both a source of my oppression and a resource for my strategies of survival.

I experience meditation as a letting go of thoughts, of feelings, of judgements. I cannot hold on to the stillness; I cannot *make* it happen. All I can do is let go of whatever is not stillness. So, too, mindful sex, alone or with partner(s), is a letting go of all that is not the experiences of connecting with bodies and pleasures.

Perhaps anarchy is similar. I cannot *make* it happen (and not for lack of trying!). If the State cannot be smashed, maybe it can be let go of, with practice. Only as I taste other possibilities, experience them in the fullness of bodymind, do I learn to let go of the State. Slowly, gently, I am becoming-anarchist (Heckert 2010).

Being my own lover (not just a fantasy)

> The artist does at [their] best what lovers do, which is to reveal the beloved to [themselves] and with that revelation to make freedom real.
>
> (James Baldwin, quoted in Alexander 2005: 18)

> i do it for the joy it brings
> because i'm a joyful girl
> because the world owes me nothing
> and we owe each other the world
>
> (Difranco 1996)

During the Christmas/midwinter festive season of 1992, my best friend gave me a copy of Betty Dodson's *Sex for One: The Joy of Selfloving* – a crucial moment of solidarity in my teenage years! An inheritance from feminist consciousness-raising efforts in the US, this book not only affirmed my teenage sex life with myself (including all my fantasies), it encouraged me to be my own lover in every sense of the word.

How better to practise letting go of the State than with myself? How better to be more caring, less controlling, less controlled, than by being a lover to myself?

I want to be clear, here: I'm not suggesting we all just wank our way to revolution. Rather, I'm coming to realise, again and again, that for me to practise anarchy is to care for myself, to listen to myself, to offer compassion to myself. One way of interpreting this is that 'we' should take care of ourselves in order to be more *effective* anarchists: care as a means to an end. This works as far as it goes. I do have more energy to write, to organise events, to participate in meetings the more I take care of myself. This instrumental care seems to me to be less the care of a lover and more the care of a coach or drill sergeant, training myself for revolution with a regime of healthy diet, regular exercise and plenty of rest. The care I want for myself is a means without end, without goals.

Being in touch with myself, touching myself. Letting myself receive the touch, love and appreciation of others. Letting go of the ice shield, the State of disconnection. Being gentle with myself, listening to my body, I learn to feel the pain when my desires are unsatisfied, either in the present or as memories of the past that still come to life. Muscles soften, tears flow. I don't *have* to make it okay – that's what the State does (or tries to do) with its borders and its judgements and its policing (Scott 1998). That's what I do sometimes. That's how I learned to survive. Make it okay so he doesn't get angry. Make it okay so he doesn't hit me. Make it okay so I don't feel the pain. I do not want to smash the State, because I know that I am the State sometimes. It's how I survive. I want to let it go as I develop other ways of relating to myself and the world around me. I can't do that on my own. I need help.

Asking for help is one of the aspects of anarchy I find most difficult to practise. For mutual aid to be truly mutual is to acknowledge vulnerability. Dammit, that's just not how I was raised! And to ask, rather than demand, is to accept that the answer might be 'no'. Hearing and reading feminist criticisms of macho behaviour in anarchist spaces, I know I'm not the only one facing these challenges (e.g. Osterweil 2007; Sullivan 2005, 2007). Stephen Duncombe suggests that this fear of vulnerability haunts 'progressive' politics generally, and, more importantly, can be a source of inspiration:

> If we are afraid to publicly recognise and politicise our own desires, how can we hope to speak to those of other people? But if we start to ask the questions of what our needs and desires are, and how a politics might meet them, we just might discover that, lo and behold, *our* needs are the same as *theirs*.
>
> (Duncombe 2007: 84–5)

To make myself, as Foucault suggests, more susceptible to pleasure is, it seems to me, to accept my vulnerability, my ability to be wounded. Suddenly, the challenge of radical social transformation, of letting go of the State, sounds an awful lot like how folk might describe their fears of intimacy: they might get hurt. I might get hurt. Being a coach, drill sergeant, judge, policeman or other 'male in the head' (Holland *et al.* 1998), I push myself to ignore my desires, my needs, my pain. Being my own lover, I'm there to give myself compassion, to listen to myself.

Being my own lover is an ongoing journey, with no fixed answers or correct practices. Walking, I ask questions. In doing so, I look to philosophy less as an intellectualising anaesthetic, as I sometimes do, and more as an ethos or practice of living (May 2005; McWherter 2004), as both a love of knowledge *and* a knowledge of love (Irigaray 2004). As such, it becomes one of many practices of connection in which I am able to find strength in vulnerability, in flexibility, in openness. Others might be termed spiritual practices: connecting with the rest of earth through marking the turning of the year, through gardening and gathering wild foods, through taking in the beauty and power of the sea, the forest and the sky, connecting with my embodiment and my capacities for stillness and for motion through swimming, cycling, yoga and chi gung, connecting with my own feelings and desires and those of others through meditation and non-violent communication, accepting the inevitability of death so that I embrace life more fully and with greater appreciation (Batchelor 1998), connecting with other sources of wisdom through the reading of spiritual texts (e.g. Chödrön 2002; Lao Tzu 1997; Starhawk 2005), fantasy novels (e.g. Butler 1993, 2001; Marks 2002; Donaldson 1993; Starhawk 1993) and other stories that offer me different understandings of power and possibilities (Cohn 2007; Le Guin 2009).

I imagine a reader asking, is all of this care of the self meant to be a replacement for action?[8] As a friend reminded me, 'There are women in California who do *nothing but* take care of themselves.' I want to both offer reassurance and to challenge the question. I'll challenge first: where does the emphasis on *action* or being *active* come from? My thoughts turn to a recent visit to the GUM (genito-urinary medicine) clinic for a check-up, where I was stunned by so much, including the consultant's use of the terms active and passive to describe anal sex between men. I said I preferred to use giving and receiving, thinking of those words as less inscribed with power. (She nodded, writing down the words she preferred.) However, they now remind me of a commonly cited passage from the Bible: 'It is more blessed to give than to receive' (Acts 20: 35). This in turn, takes me back to anal sex and what Michael Warner calls 'bottom shame' and the shame-induced risk-taking for men whose 'masculinity is more closely identified with insertive than with receptive anal sex' (Warner 2000: 212). I recognise, for myself, how a prioritisation of *action*, being *active* or an *activist*, is intertwined with a comfort in *giving* rather than receiving, offering care to others more often than accepting care. Again, I am not alone in this (see, e.g., Anonymous 2000; Crisman 1991; starr 2007). In emphasising practices of connection, and in starting with myself, I become more practised in the mutuality of mutual aid. In starting with myself, I reassure you (and me), that I do not end with myself. I cannot, for my self is relational (MacKenzie and Stoljar 2000): simultaneously social and ecological (e.g. Stevens 2009, 2010). Connection does not take me inside myself (i.e. navel gazing) or 'outside myself' (i.e. depression or disassociation); it allows the outside in and the inside out, blurring any supposed border. It's amoeba sex.

Being my own lover *is* action: a form of erotic direct action. In this way, I increase my susceptibility to pleasure, to connection with others; I want to experience the erotic potential of everyday life. Every day. I don't want to wait for 'after the revolution' to feel joy; indeed, perhaps there is no after. No afterlife, only life. And life, I know, is full of erotic potential. I have tasted it.

Notes

1 This essay is dedicated to my fellow workers on the sexual health team and to each of the young people I worked with over those years. This would not have been written without you. I also want to acknowledge conversations with Richard Cleminson, Liz McGregor, Rowan Cobelli, Liz Kingsnorth, Lisa Fannen, Cloudberry McLean, Sian Sullivan, Kristina Nell Weaver, Anthony McCann, Matt Wilson, Ben Franks, Lloyd Miller, Debbie Cowan, Simon Edney, Alex Jackson, Laurie Heckert, Jason Heckert, Helen Moore, Grant Denkinson, Elizabeth Barner, Jane Heckert, Larry Heckert, Rob Teixeira, Joan Robertson, Diggsy Leitch, Michael Gallagher, Ben Tura, Jane Harris, Nicky MacDonald and, of course, Paul Stevens for helping make this essay possible.

2 Following bell hooks (2000), I refer to social movement, rather than maintaining that boundaries can be placed around identifiable 'social movements'.

3 This attitude, a response to fear, changed through a number of events, including organising with a fellow anarchist worker a meeting of tutors (called TAs in North America) to threaten a strike on marking in response to a wage cut for fellow tutors, as well as discovering that others were writing anarchist theory in universities.

4 My father has stopped drinking and retrained as a drug and alcohol counsellor, while Jensen suggests that his has in no way acknowledged the harm he has done.

5 They use the masculine 'guys' purposely here to indicate what I see as the gendered nature of heroics in this case.

6 Anarchist sex education could blur any distinction between prefigurative (Franks 2003; Gordon 2008) or consequentialist ethics (May 1994), which focus on practices that bring about a different (more anarchist) future and an immediatist one focused on experiencing the present differently (e.g. Bey 1991, 1994). Both can apply simultaneously, practising practices relevant to sexual health (again, broadly defined) without necessarily being 'sexual' themselves. Mindfulness, for example, changes one's experience of the present, allowing judgements, thoughts and feelings to be acknowledged and let go of, increasing a sense of connection with oneself. Being deeply present during sex, in my experience, is profoundly pleasurable as well as both self- and other-caring.

7 The pubococcygeus muscle, or PC muscle, links the coccyx (tailbone) with the pubic bone and functions as the floor of the pelvic cavity, supporting the pelvic organs. Kegel exercises, a method for learning to flex and strengthen this muscle, are used to prevent premature ejaculation in men, to improve urinary control and to ease childbirth.

8 I see care of the self as consistent with the central theme of connection, expressed in various ways, throughout anarchist and anarchic politics: as the 'groundless solidarity' and 'affinity of affinities' of anarchism (Day 2005), as the 'politica affectiva' of horizontalism (Sitrin 2006) or the 'affective resistance' of autonomous feminism (Shukaitis, Chapter 3), as well as in the shared joys (Shepard 2009) and pains (Plaw 2005) of nurturing community.

References

Albury, K. (2002) *Yes Means Yes: Getting Explicit About Heterosex*, Sydney: Allen & Unwin.

Alexander, M. J. (2005) *Pedagogies of Crossing: Meditations on Feminism, Sexual Politics, Memory, and the Sacred*, Durham, NC/London: Duke University Press.

Allison, D. (1993) *Bastard Out of Carolina*, New York: Plume.

——(1995) *Skin: Talking About Sex, Class and Literature*, Ithaca, NY: Firebrand Books.

Anonymous (2000) 'Give up Activism', *Do or Die: Voices from the Ecological Resistance* 9: 160–6.
——(2003) 'Our Bodies, Our Lives! Feminist Health, Healing and Herbs', *Do or Die: Voices from the Ecological Resistance* 10: 183–4. Online. Available HTTP: http://www.eco-action.org/dod/no10/bodies.htm (accessed 30 July 2010).
——(2007) 'Report from a Radical Gathering of Women in Spain 21st–24th September 2006', in *Last Hours* 15. Online. Available HTTP: http://www.lasthours.org.uk/archive/articles/bootycamp-2006/ (accessed 14 March 2008).
Batchelor, S. (1998) *Buddhism without Beliefs: A Contemporary Guide to Awakening*, London: Bloomsbury.
Bey, H. (1991) *TAZ: The Temporary Autonomous Zone, Ontological Anarchy, Poetic Terrorism*, New York: Autonomedia.
——(1994) *Immediatism*, Edinburgh/San Fransisco: AK Press.
Bloch, E. (1986) *The Principle of Hope*, Cambridge, MA: MIT Press.
Brown, W. (1995) *States of Injury: Power and Freedom in Late Modernity*, Princeton, NJ: Princeton University Press.
Butler, J. (1990) *Gender Trouble: Feminism and the Subversion of Identity*, New York: Routledge.
Butler, O. (1993) *Parable of the Sower*, London: The Women's Press.
——(2001) *Wild Seed*, New York: Grand Central Publishing.
Chalker, R. (2000) *The Clitoral Truth: The Secret World at Your Fingertips*, New York: Seven Stories Press.
Chödrön, P. (2002) *Comfortable with Uncertainty: 108 Teachings on Cultivating Fearlessness and Compassion*, Boston, MA: Shambhala.
claque (2002) *Untitled* (CD), Glasgow: Big Deal Records.
CNN (2001) 'You Are Either with Us or Against Us.' Online. Available HTTP: http://archives.cnn.com/2001/US/11/06/gen.attack.on.terror/ (accessed 3 May 2008).
Cohn, J. (2007) 'What is Anarchist Literary Theory?', *Anarchist Studies* 15(2): 115–31.
Crimp, D. (1987) 'How to Have Promiscuity in an Epidemic', in D. Crimp (ed.), *AIDS: Cultural Analysis/Cultural Activism*, Cambridge, MA: MIT Press.
Crisman, W. (1991) *The Opposite of Everything Is True: Reflections on Denial in Alcoholic Families*, New York: William Morrow & Co.
Davies, B. (1993) *Shards of Glass: Children Reading and Writing beyond Gendered Identities*, Sydney: Allen & Unwin.
Dawkins, R. (2006) *The God Delusion*, Boston, MA/New York: Houghton Mifflin.
Day, R. J. F.(2005) *Gramsci Is Dead: Anarchist Currents in the Newest Social Movements*, London: Pluto Press.
Deleuze, G. (1977) 'Intellectuals & Power: A Conversation between Michel Foucault and Gilles Deleuze', in D. Bouchard (ed.), *Language, Counter-Memory, Practice*, Ithaca, NY: Cornell University Press. Online. Available HTTP: http://libcom.org/library/intellectuals-power-a-conversation-between-michel-foucault-and-gilles-deleuze (accessed 2 May 2008).
Difranco, A. (1996) 'Joyful Girl', on *Dilate* (CD), Buffalo, NY: Righteous Babe Records.
Dodson, B. (1987) *Sex for One: The Joy of Selfloving*, New York: Crown Trade Paperbacks.
Donaldson, S. (1993) *The Chronicles of Thomas Covenant the Unbeliever*, London: Collins.
Dunbar-Ortiz, R. (1998) *Red Dirt: Growing Up Okie*, London/New York: Verso.

Duncombe, S. (2007) *Dream: Re-imagining Progressive Politics in an Age of Fantasy*, New York/London: The New Press.

Eddings, D. (1982) *Pawn of Prophecy*, New York: Ballantine Books.

Evans, A. (1978) *Witchcraft and the Gay Counterculture*, Boston, MA: Fag Rag Books.

Fannen, L. (2001) *Pregnancy and Birth: In Support of Autonomy*, Glasgow: Women's Health Information Collective.

Federici, S. (2004) *Caliban and the Witch: Women, the Body and Primitive Accumulation*, New York: Autonomedia.

Feist, R. E. (1982) *Magician*, New York: Science Fiction Book Club.

Firestone, S. (1979) *The Dialectic of Sex: The Case for Feminist Revolution*, London: The Women's Press.

Foucault, M. (1977) *Discipline and Punish: The Birth of the Prison* (trans. Alan Sheridan), New York: Vintage.

——(1989) 'Friendship as a Way of Life', in S. Lotringer (ed.), *Foucault Live: Interviews, 1966–84*, New York: Semiotext(e).

——(1990 [1978]) *The History of Sexuality*, vol. 1: *An Introduction*, New York: Vintage.

Franks, B. (2003) 'The Direct Action Ethic: from 59 Upwards', *Anarchist Studies* 11(1): 13–41.

Freire, Paulo (2000) *Pedagogies of the Oppressed*, New York: Continuum.

Gallacher, L. and Gallagher, M. (2008) 'Methodological Immaturity in Childhood Research: Thinking through "Participatory Methods"', *Childhood* 15(4): 499–516.

Goia, J. (2008) 'SOMA: An Anarchist Experiment', in G. Grindon (ed.), *Aesthetics and Radical Politics*, Newcastle upon Tyne: Cambridge Scholars Press.

Goldberg, M. (2005) *Telling Mythologies: Pasts and Possible Futures in Activist Literature*, Self-published MSc thesis, Centre for Human Ecology. Online. Available HTTP: http://www.myshelegoldberg.com/academic/goldberg_thesis.pdf (accessed 30 July 2010).

Gordon, T. and Griffiths, B. (2007) 'How to Manage Your Own Health', in Trapeze Collective (ed.), *Do It Yourself: A Handbook for Changing Our World*, London/Ann Arbor, MI: Pluto Press.

Gordon, U. (2008) *Anarchy Alive! Anti-Authoritarian Politics from Practice to Theory*, Ann Arbor, MI: Pluto.

Graeber, D. (2004) *Fragments of an Anarchist Anthropology*, Chicago: Prickly Paradigm Press.

Griffiths, B. and Gordon, T. (2007) 'Why Society Is Making Us Sick', in Trapeze Collective (ed.), *Do It Yourself: A Handbook for Changing Our World*, London/Ann Arbor, MI: Pluto Press.

Haines, S. (1999) *The Survivor's Guide to Sex: How to Have an Empowered Sex Life After Child Sexual Abuse*, San Francisco: Cleis Press.

Heckert, J. (2004) 'Sexuality/Identity/Politics', in J. Purkis and J. Bowen (eds), *Changing Anarchism: Anarchist Theory and Practice in a Global Age*, Manchester: Manchester University Press.

——(2005) *Resisting Orientation: On the Complexities of Desire and the Limits of Identity Politics*, self-published PhD thesis, University of Edinburgh. Online. Available HTTP: http://sexualorientation.info/thesis/ (accessed 30 July 2010).

——(2010) 'Intimacy with Strangers/Intimacy with Self: Queer Experiences of Social Research', in K. Browne and C. Nash (eds), *Queer Methods and Methodologies: Intersecting Queer Theories and Social Science Research*, Farnham: Ashgate.

Holland, J., Ramazanoglu, C., Sharpe, S. and Thomson, R. (1998) *The Male in the Head: Young People, Heterosexuality and Power*, London: Tufnell Press.
Honoré, C. (2005) *In Praise of Slow: How a Worldwide Movement Is Challenging the Cult of Speed*, London: Orion.
hooks, b. (2000) *Feminism is for Everybody: Passionate Politics*, London: Pluto Press.
Hutchins, L. (2007) 'Playing with Sacred Fire: Building Erotic Communities', in B. Firestein (ed.), *Becoming Visible: Counseling Bisexuals Across the Lifespan*, Irvington, NY/Bognor Regis: Columbia University Press.
Irigaray, L. (2004) *The Way Of Love* (trans. Heidi Bostic and Stephen Pluhacek), London: Continuum.
Jensen, D. (2000) *A Language Older than Words*, London: Souvenir Press.
Johnstone, C. (2010) *Find Your Power: A Toolkit for Resilience & Positive Change*, East Meon, Hampshire: Permanent Publications.
Landauer, G. (2005 [1910]) 'Weak Statesmen, Weaker People,' excerpted in R. Graham (ed.), *Anarchism: A Documentary History of Libertarian Ideas*, vol. I: *From Anarchy to Anarchism (300CE–1939)*, Montreal: Black Rose Books.
lang, kd (1992) *Ingénue* (CD), New York: Sire/Warner Brothers.
Lao Tzu (1997) *Tao Te Ching: A Book about the Way and the Power of the Way* (trans. Ursula K. Le Guin), Boston, MA: Shambhala.
Lappé, F. M. and Perkins, J. (2005) *You Have the Power: Choosing Courage in a Culture of Fear*, New York: Tarcher/Penguin.
Le Guin, U. K. (2004a) 'The Operating Instructions', in *The Wave in the Mind: Talks and Essays on the Writer, the Reader, and the Imagination*, Boston, MA: Shambhala.
——(2004b) 'Telling is Listening', in *The Wave in the Mind: Talks and Essays on the Writer, the Reader, and the Imagination*, Boston, MA: Shambhala.
——(2009) *Cheek by Jowl: Talks & Essays on How & Why Fantasy Matters*, Seattle, WA: Aqueduct Press.
Lisa (2008) *Threads*, Glasgow: self-published. Available from www.threadsbook.org.
Macy, J. and Brown, M. Y. (1998) *Coming Back to Life: Practices to Reconnect Our Lives, Our World*, Gabriola Island, BC: New Society Press.
Marks, L. J. (2002) *Fire Logic*, New York: Tor.
MacKenzie, C. and Stoljar, N. (eds) (2000) *Relational Autonomy: Feminist Perspectives on Autonomy, Agency, and the Social Self*, Oxford: Oxford University Press.
McWherter, L. (2004) 'Practicing Practicing', in D. Taylor and K. Vintges (eds), *Feminism and the Final Foucault*, Urbana, IL/Chicago: University of Illinois Press.
Marmot, M. (2004) *Status Syndrome*, London: Bloomsbury.
May, T. (1994) *The Political Philosophy of Poststructuralist Anarchism*, University Park, PA: Pennsylvania State University Press.
——(2005) *Gilles Deleuze: An Introduction*, Cambridge: Cambridge University Press.
Morin, J. (1998) *Anal Pleasure & Health*, San Francisco: Down There Press.
Nelson, C. (1976) *Self Help Home Remedies*. Online. Available HTTP: http://www.womenshealthspecialists.org/default.asp?cf=self%20help/self%20help%20home%20remedies (accessed 14 April 2008).
Newman, F. (2004) *The Whole Lesbian Sex Book: A Passionate Guide for All of Us*, San Francisco: Cleis Press.
Newman, S. (2004) 'Anarchism and the Politics of Ressentiment', in J. Moore with S. Sunshine (eds), *I Am Not a Man, I Am Dynamite! Friedrich Nietzsche and the Anarchist Tradition*, New York: Autonomedia.

Nietzsche, F. (1969) *On the Genealogy of Morals* (trans. W. Kaufmann and P. J. Hollingdale), New York: Vintage.

Nutland, W., Weatherburn, P., Burnell, C., Keogh, M., Doyle, T., Watson, R. and Gault, A. (2003) *Making It Count: A Collaborative Planning Framework to Reduce the Incidence of HIV Infection during Sex between Men*, London: Sigma Research. Online. Available HTTP: http://www.sigmaresearch.org.uk/downloads/report03e.pdf (accessed 3 May 2008).

Osterweil, M. (2007) '"Becoming-Woman?" In Theory or in Practice?', in *Turbulence* (1). Online. Available HTTP: http://www.turbulence.org.uk/becoming-woman.html (accessed 3 May 2008).

Packer, T. (2002) *The Wonder of Presence: And the Way of Meditative Inquiry*, Boston, MA: Shambhala.

Plaw, A. (2005) 'Empty Hands: Communication, Pluralism, and Community in Ursula K. Le Guin's *The Dispossessed*', in Laurence Davis and Peter Stillman (eds), *The New Utopian Politics of Ursula K. Le Guin's* The Dispossessed, Oxford: Lexington Books.

Rich, A. (2001a [1975]) 'Women and Honour: Some Notes on Lying', in *Arts of the Possible: Essays and Conversations*, New York/London: Norton.

——(2001b [1971]) '"When We Dead Awaken": Writing as Re-Vision', in *Arts of the Possible: Essays and Conversations*, New York/London: Norton.

Rilke, R. M. (1989) *The Selected Poetry of Rainer Maria Rilke* (trans. Stephen Mitchell), New York: Vintage.

Rosenberg, M. B. (2003) *Nonviolent Communication: A Language of Life*, Encinitas, CA: PuddleDancer Press.

Sawicki, J. (2004) 'Foucault's Pleasures: Desexualising Queer Politics', in Diana Taylor and Karen Vintges (eds), *Feminism and the Final Foucault*, Urbana, IL/Chicago: University of Illinois Press.

Scheff, T. J. (1990) *Microsociology: Discourse, Emotion, and Social Structure*, Chicago: University of Chicago Press.

Scott, J. C. (1990) *Domination and the Arts of Resistance: The Hidden Transcript of Subordinate Groups*, New Haven, CT: Yale University Press.

——(1998) *Seeing Like a State: How Certain Schemes to Improve the Human Condition Have Failed*, New Haven, CT: Yale University Press.

Shepard, B. (2009) *Queer Political Performance and Protest: Play, Pleasure, and Social Movement*, New York: Routledge.

Shodini Collective (1997) *Touch Me, Touch-me-not: Women, Plants, and Healing*, New Delhi: Kali for Women.

Simpson, P. (2004) 'Michel Foucault on Freedom and the Politics of Experience', paper presented at 20 Years After Foucault conference. Online. Available HTTP: http://www.panopticweb.com/2004conference/4.simpson.pdf (accessed 3 May 2008).

Sitrin, M. (2006) *Horizontalism: Voices of Popular Power in Argentina*, Edinburgh/Oakland, CA: AK Press.

Stainton Rogers, W. and Stainton Rogers, R. (1997) 'Does Critical Social Psychology Mean the End of the World?', in Tomás Ibáñez and Lupicinio Íñigues (eds), *Critical Social Psychology*, London: Sage.

Starhawk (1993) *The Fifth Sacred Thing*, New York: Bantam.

——(2002) *Webs of Power: Notes from the Global Uprising*, Gabriola Island, BC: New Society Publishers.

——(2005) *The Earth Path: Grounding Your Spirit in the Rhythms of Nature*, San Francisco: Harper.

starr, a. (2007) 'Grumpywarriorcool: What Makes Our Movements White?', in S. Best and A. J. Nocella II (eds), *Igniting a Revolution: Voices in Defense of the Earth*, Edinburgh/Oakland, CA: AK Press.

Stevens, P. (2009) 'Exploring Our Physical Connections: The Role of Magnetic Fields in Restorative Environments', *Ecopsychology* 1(2): 85–92.

——(2010) 'Embedment in the Environment: A New Paradigm for Wellbeing?', *Perspectives in Public Health* 130(6): 265–269.

Sullivan, S. (2004). '"We Are Heartbroken and Furious!"(#2) Violence and the (Anti-) Globalisation Movement(s)', CSGR Working Paper No. 133/04. Online. Available HTTP: http://www2.warwick.ac.uk/fac/soc/csgr/research/workingpapers/2004/wp13304.pdf (accessed 6 May 2008).

——(2005) 'An *Other* World Is Possible? On Representation, Rationalism and Romanticism in Social Forums', *Ephemera* (5)2: 370–92. Online. Available HTTP: http://www.ephemeraweb.org/journal/5–2/5–2ssullivan.pdf (accessed 3 May 2008).

——(2007) '"Viva Nihilism!" On Militancy and Machismo in (Anti-)Globalization Protest', in R. Devetak and C. Hughes (eds), *The Globalization of Political Violence: Globalization's Shadow*, London: Routledge.

Tormey, S. (2006) '"Not in My Name": Deleuze, Zapatismo and the Critique of Representation', *Parliamentary Affairs* 1: 138–54.

Tyler, M. (2004) 'Managing between the Sheets: Lifestyle Magazines and the Management of Sexuality in Everyday Life', *Sexualities* 7(1): 81–106.

Warner, M. (2000) *The Trouble with Normal: Sex, Politics and the Ethics of Queer Life*, Cambridge, MA: Harvard University Press.

Wikipedia (2008) 'Impostor Syndrome'. Online. Available HTTP: http://en.wikipedia.org/wiki/Impostor_Syndrome (accessed 10 May 2008).

Wilkinson, R. (2001) *Mind the Gap: Hierarchies, Health, and Human Evolution*, New Haven, CT: Yale University Press.

Wilson, J. (2003) 'Can Sex Education Be Practical?', *Sex Education* 3(1): 23–32.

Winnubst, S. (2006) *Queering Freedom*, Bloomington/Indianapolis: Indiana University Press.

Zindell, D. (1993) *The Broken God*, London: Collins.

Poetic interlude 4

MANIFESTO OF A PISSED-OFF FAGGOT #2

J. Fergus Evans

WE'RE HERE
  WE'RE QUEER
    GET USED TO US!
(I repeat)
WE'RE HERE
  WE'RE QUEER
    GET USED TO US!
I repeat ...
but they still don't like me on canal street
maybe I'm not pretty enough
a bit too gritty and raw but
I won't be out-foxed by Fox, NBC, CBS or the BBC trying to tell me how to be more
  me
won't let them sell me back my stake in the gay identity
won't let channel 4 tell me how to look more like a homo and less like a hobo

do I scare them?
do I disappoint because I might not want
  an appointment at the registry office
  a husband
  2.4
  a 4x4
and I'm not a label whore. I'm just
a whore
maybe I'm not allowed through the doors of your culture club because
I'm more uppity than upwardly mobile—

a mouthy faggot who doesn't know his place
(but can place pieces of poetry in the corners of your heart that wait all night to detonate
'til you're home tonight
turn off the light
kiss your partner goodnight
and wonder when it is you started living someone else's idea of the Good Life)

See
I'm okay with the grey area
don't believe many people fit neatly into society's binaries
don't believe you'll EVER see reality on tv

and I don't believe you have to look outside yerself for a sense of authenticity.

This is a culture war
so I'm fighting back with words
gonna fan the flame of revolution like rockets in yer belly tell you
you can make a contribution to the overthrowing of outdated labels like homo and hetero
and man, I hope inciting a riot makes you hard
and horny
'cause when I suck cock it's a fucking revolution.

WILDCRAFT, LOVECRAFT

Helen Moore

When I'd like to surprise my lover
by cooking up a storm,
I relish the moments when I find
our kitchen-cupboards bare –
what else then
but to hare into the fields
and rustle up a salad?

It's so convenient to discover,
rinsed with dew and table-ready,
Dandelions and Sorrels
abundant for gleaning;
or as herbivore of hedgerows,

to browse on young Hawthorn,
pinch tender Nettle tops for soup.

Down by the lardering stream
a patch of Lady's Smock is peppery,
enticing, and the search for Brooklime
leaves me wanting more;
but Jack-by-the-hedge is easy,
brimming green with garlic mustard,
and I'm not poor for taking him.

Maybe the nooks and rides of woods
are most deliciously giving –
on my back a fur of sunlight
as I rootle among the lacy umbels,
tracing down each fragile stem
to unearth a brown-skinned Pignut;
or, taking flight with my small cargo,
how the Elders offer flowery desserts?

In my grandmother's store I recall
jars swimming with the ruby flesh of Rosehips,
and the thirteen moons of pickled eggs.
Along their rows I'd count my lineage
back to those shape-shifting Hare-women –
how from fields and hedgerows
they fed and nurtured, laid out the dead;
and the canny ways of which their daughters
were too long dispossessed.

And now to love's cuisine my roots
are reaching, thriving in the rains
of pleasure's kiss – in serving wilderness
we taste our freedom, come alive
to our most earthy flavours.

Chapter 9

Sexuality issues in the Czech anarchist movement[1]

Marta Kolářová

Introduction

Czech anarchism and sexuality – is this really an issue? Sexuality has only been minimally discussed in the Czech anarchist movement in comparison to other axes of inequality such as class, race or, recently, gender. Activists dealing with sexuality issues within anarchism have not been very visible; neither are there many of them. In addition, the historical and academic pieces on Czech anarchism (Slačálek 2002; Tomek and Slačálek 2006) do not address sexuality at all. In order to analyse this lack, I draw together some stories from the scant literature that exists. I see the connection between anarchism and sexuality in various ways – this connection implies both practice and reflection, intertwined with the issues and activism that surround both. In practice, the largely heterosexual relations in the Czech anarchist movement shape the understandings and discussions (or lack thereof) of sexuality.

Daphne (2006) describes the limited discussion of sexuality issues in the People's Global Action meeting in Lyon. According to her there is a lack of knowledge among radicals about what heterosexism is, even though people in these circles consider themselves open-minded and 'homo-friendly'. This attitude, however, makes heterosexual dominance invisible. The Czech anarchist movement, I would argue, has not even reached this stage of discussion yet.

Anarchist discourse in former Czechoslovakia and subsequently in the Czech Republic has not focused on the intersections between different kinds of inequality. The new wave of anarchism, starting in the early 1990s, addressed mostly class issues, later race (antifascism) and gender (anarcho-feminism). There has never been any specific organisation or magazine dealing with sexuality issues, and general anarchist magazines have rarely covered sexuality. Only very recently, since 2004, have sexuality, queer, LGBT and free love issues been discussed; and only in some fora and by some activists, mostly anarcho-feminists. This includes, notably, the appearance of one zine made by punk anarcho-feminist lesbians. Since 2008, some anarchists and anarcho-feminists have participated in new events organised by LGBT activists, including annual Queer Parades.

In this chapter I discuss why issues of sexuality were marginalised in Czech anarchism and I explore who raises sexuality issues, how the discourse on sexuality is shaped, what activities around sexuality issues take place and the relationship with LGBT movements. This piece is mainly empirical, drawing on my ethnographic study including long-term participant observation (2001–3), interviews with activists (Kolářová 2004) and an analysis of the movement's media (from 2000 to 2006).[2] The chapter aims to be a contribution towards raising these issues in the movement and thus strengthening the movement's theoretical and practical impact.

This issue needs to be seen in the historical context of the evolution of the Czech anarchist, feminist, LGBT and other social movements, their non-existence under state socialism and their development since the early 1990s within an Eastern European context. The Czech Republic is quite liberal, but Poland is much more restrictive, for instance, on the availability of contraceptives. Despite this liberalism, however, the queer movement has been developing rather slowly and is not connected with radical politics or anarchism in the Czech Republic.

Sexual relations in the Czech anarchist subculture

The politics of the anarchist movement are influenced by personal and intimate relationships; the Czech anarchist movement is a small community and activists know each other well. There is a low level of participation by women and an absence or invisibility of homosexual relations in the subculture.

Women usually have partners from the movement and have a wider choice than men given the gender disparity among activists. Men, then, have to choose among non-activists. They often bring their partners into the movement and this works as one method for the recruitment of women (Kolářová 2004). By the same token, relationships not only facilitate political activity but can also cause problems, especially within an organisation. For a woman, when she comes alone and single to an organisation, it can be difficult to participate: 'It is not really easy, when a woman comes to a meeting where two-thirds of people are men and they start to hit on her, for her not to take it personally' (Andrej, anarchist, male, quoted in Kolářová 2004: 9).

The anarchist movement in its praxis has been quite male dominated and recently influenced by a skinhead subculture adopted mainly by antifascists. Women can be discouraged from entering or staying in the movement by the activities or culture of some groups or the movement as a whole because of the role of violence within it. Militant antifascist groups using physical confrontation have very few women members. These organisations are said to have a 'macho image' that associates the cult of violence and roughness with men:

> These organisations attract one type of person. If you look at them, they all look the same – young men with shaved heads. They claim to have an

> anarcho-communist programme that should be open for everyone, but it does not seem to be the most attractive thing for those entering. It is something else; it is the macho image of those people, the culture of the organization.
>
> (Ruda, anarchist, male, quoted in Kolářová 2004: 8)

> We can find aggressive, tough and rowdy macho behaviour in anti-fascist groups where women cannot participate at all.
>
> (Kenský 2002: 13)

This macho image can be the reason why women do not enter the movement, or these groups in particular. While these forms of masculinity might also serve to attract some women, it seems that men in these groups do not want to accept them because of their gender. Women who eventually enter these groups are not allowed by men to express themselves; they are discouraged and may leave the group (Kolářová 2004). Also, homosexual people could feel the same way. Although some gay men could be attracted to a macho image (gay skins are found in some countries, but not in the Czech Republic), some individuals in the male groups behave in homophobic ways and make jokes about homosexuals. This behaviour, by no means practised by everyone, has not always been challenged and critiqued.

In this environment, it would be very difficult for gay people to come out. Homo/bisexual voices are not heard in the movement. From my long participation in the movement, exclusively heterosexual relationships are the only ones that are visible. Of course, there might be people who are homosexual or bisexual but who do not come out in the anarchist movement. For lesbians it would be difficult because feminists are already criticised and looked at askance in the movement by some antifascists who do not accept any critique of sexism. In general, in Czech society feminists are stigmatised and equated with lesbians. In comparison with what I have observed in the West (East Coast USA and some parts of the UK) it seems that the Czech anarchist movement constitutes a world of rather narrow displays of femininity and masculinity. Femininity is (maybe because of the fear of being criticised) defined quite traditionally, with respect to image especially (long hair, make-up, etc.). Masculinity was for many years influenced by skinhead images and behaviour as tough men and fighters connected with heterosexuality.

However, some people do question these gender norms, at least in a playful way and on some specific occasions. In certain circumstances, such as during parties or talks, some anarchist men like to dress as women (especially in pink after the wave of pink and silver activism), and sometimes a few women dress as men, as a performance. It is a marginal activity, but it seems to show the need for transgressing gender and sexuality norms.

Free love and polyamory in the Czech anarchist movement

Polyamory can be defined as a practice of having more than one intimate relationship and/or loving more than one person at the same time. All the partners involved should be aware of this situation. The word polyamory is not known in the Czech Republic and Czechs still use the term 'free love', or sometimes 'open relationships'. The evolution of these notions is interesting. The old concept of free love that Czechs know from Emma Goldman (1969) is still used, because Czech anarchism has not addressed sexuality issues and has not followed the development of new terms. While, for instance, 'gender' is a new and widely used concept in Czech society, and in the anarchist movement, polyamory has not been taken up in the same way.

Based on interviews, observation and discussion, polyamory or the practice of free love serves as more of a short-term phase between serial monogamous relationships than as a longer term alternative. When people in the movement have dated more than one person at the same time, it has usually been temporarily. Anarchists practising polyamory have been criticised by others. This form of social control in the movement has pushed multiple relationships to dissolve and shamed individuals into returning to monogamy. The Czech anarchist movement is rather conservative in this sense and short-term serial relationships are deemed more acceptable. This is subject to the all-too-common gendered double standard. When a man has more relationships, people say, 'Oh, he has another girl,' but about women they would say, 'She sleeps with everyone' (see e.g. *Bloody Mary*, no. 1 for a critique).

If we consider the old anarchist notion of 'free love' meaning relationships outside marriage and unregulated by the state or church, these predominate in the movement. Generally, Czech anarchists consider marriage to be an anachronism and people usually do not get married, even couples with children. Free love, in this sense, is not particularly exceptional in contemporary Czech society. This phenomenon, however, was very uncommon under state socialism, when very young people (between the ages of 18 and 20) got married, often as a strategic move for benefits or housing. Since the early 1990s cohabitation has become more common. Also, due to state socialism, there was never a strong hippy subculture or a sexual revolution as in the West. Sexual freedom came slowly during socialism, when sex and conjugal infidelity were an important part of leisure time, which people could not devote to study, travelling or consumption.

I would now like to present an analysis of a discussion on sexuality that I organised in Prague's anarchist info café and later on the website of the Czechoslovak Anarchist Federation in spring 2005 (www.csaf.cz, September 2005; a report on the discussion is available in Kolářová 2005). The whole discussion was influenced by the fact that we were not familiar with the concept of polyamory, and there was a lack of general clarity in the debates. I started the discussion with a short talk about the development of the term 'free love'.

Then I asked the participants (about thirty people) what free love meant to them today. Is it a meaningful concept? Does it mean to have more partners, promiscuity, as it seems to be understood by most? Can free love be more free when we already have (in euro-American society) sexual freedom, premarital sex, cohabitation, divorce and contraception? How does free love differ for men and women? To what extent it is about freedom and about responsibility (to partner/s and children)? How can jealousy be dealt with? Is it possible to love more than one person at the same time? And people of the same and the opposite sex? Is the notion of free love today still associated with social change when the sexual revolution is already under way? How is free love defined and what experience have you had of it?

In the discussion, the biggest problem was in defining free love. The people debating did not find one definition to agree on. Some argued that free love meant more partners and related it to promiscuity. For others, free love was considered to consist of more relationships, not only in the sexual but also in the emotional sense. Other people understood free love as one relationship but freed from possessive ties to the other person and from the influence of state institutions. Free love was based on openness about other relationships. Infidelity could not be considered a part of free love, because partners should communicate about their feelings and need for other partner/s. Mostly, the question of whether free love meant having more partners was discussed. Practical issues such as timing (how to be with more partners together) or housing (when the contemporary housing situation in the Czech Republic is not disposed towards community living) were discussed. For many, a cohabiting partner had priority over others; this hierarchy of relationships was also discussed. One relationship is usually considered more important and the others are seen as second-class relationships because the input of energy and time into them is less. Some people said they did not mind their partner having other relationships, but they wanted him or her to be with them when they needed them.

Many questions remained unanswered. What do you do if some of the partners do not like each other? Or when someone has a serious problem, how much time should a person devote to him/her and to the others? Or what to do when one partner wants free love and the other does not. How does a relationship change from monogamy to free love? And so on. Only a few people spoke from their very limited experiences of free love; their desires for non-monogamy were not understood or tolerated by their partners, so these relationships were only short term.

Differences between men and women were also discussed. Some argued that there is no difference regarding gender. One participant said, 'Men sometimes think that free love is great, but when their girlfriend practises it they are not able to deal with it.' Women, in particular, said that there is still double standard: a man with several girlfriends is successful, while a woman behaving similarly is a slut. The influence of the socialisation of men to be less emotional in relations was also emphasised.

The issue of children was addressed specifically. According to one participant free love is part of the parents' lifestyle and they should not change it because of their children, as they do not change other things. The biggest problem was seen to be the prejudices of the wider society, which does not accept free love. Childrearing in free communal partnerships was suggested. Some said that traumatic experiences from a divorce, fathers leaving the family or violence in the family were much worse for children than a functioning relationship with more than one partner. However, some people expressed prejudice against childrearing in either open relationships or same-sex relationships.

Homosexual experience as such was not discussed because the participants considered themselves to be heterosexual. However, potential bisexual relations in free love were considered. More women than men said that their partners would mind if they started a relationship with someone of the same sex. On other occasions outside this discussion it is possible to hear discussion about homosexual marriage (which has not been addressed by Czech anarchists at all). Most asked, 'Why do they want it when marriage itself is a bad institution?'

Participants in the debate pointed out that we are all influenced by society, the media and family education to believe that the ideal is a monogamous heterosexual relationship and the nuclear family. Contrariwise, we can see under the surface that these ideals do not work – promiscuity in society is very common. Participants criticised Czech society as hypocritical because of the frequency with which marriages or other supposedly monogamous relationships are associated with concealed infidelity. As an alternative to the patriarchal nuclear family the participants did not suggest the accumulation of partners as souvenirs, but the total removal of taboos in matters of love. Compared to existing relationships based on possessiveness, free love can have a subversive role in society. New definitions of erotics, the eradication of the beauty myth and sexual abuse, and autonomous communities based on free love and communal childrearing were all proposed. Participants also acknowledged that these alternative projects of partnerships and parenthood are influenced by the deeply embedded feelings of jealousy, betrayal and possessiveness.

In the discussion there was a strong emphasis on freedom and emancipation from negative morality. For instance, one man said:

> I understand free love as my need. As I can never know who I will desire or fall in love with, I am not interested in listening to some moralistic bullshit about what I can or cannot do. This is my rebellion against the dictatorship of capital and its destructive possessive relationships.
>
> (quoted in Kolářová 2005)

Others argued against this, understanding free love as being too individualistic, consumerist and 'bourgeois', meaning having as much as you can. Free love borders on selfishness and does not include responsibility.

Some said that we were talking about freedom most of the time, but another important aspect of anarchism was not being taken into the account – equality. Why is free and equal love not talked about? Free love without equality and responsibility is bad; it is only hedonism and extreme individualism. As we said before, in polyamorous relationships hierarchies arise and it is difficult to speak about equality. Crucially, gender inequalities in free love are far from resolved.

Sexuality in Czech anarchist and anarcho-feminist discourses

In the primary Eastern European anarchist forum, the magazine *Abolishing the Borders from Below*, there are efforts to connect the analysis of intersections of inequality based on class, gender, ethnicity, sexuality, disability and so on. *Abolishing the Borders from Below* pays attention specifically to LGBT communities, including reports from Pride marches in Russia, Romania and Poland. These parades are not organised by anarchists, but anarchists participate in and support these struggles. LGBT activists have a difficult position in these countries. Usually, Gay Pride is illegal, prohibited by the authorities (e.g. in Moscow and Bucharest). Even if the marches happen illegally, they are attacked by the police and by neo-Nazis: 'In the Serbian gay pride a few years ago fascist and religious fanatics viciously beat up the participants on the march' (Anonymous 2006: 6–7). As a reaction to that, anarchists struggling against fascism have made contact with LGBT activists. This has been most successful in Poland, where the Black Bloc supports the LGBT parades.

In contrast, in the Czech anarchist movement there was no discussion or mention of supporting LGBT movements and their struggle until 2008. Even though Czech homosexuals and transgendered people were attacked by neo-Nazi skinheads, anarchists were usually silent on this issue.[3] From the beginning of the 1990s up to 2004, homosexuality was not an issue for the Czech (non-feminist) anarchist media. I have found only two mentions of sexuality and homosexuality was not addressed in either. The first of these articles appeared as 'Anarchism and Sex' in the biggest anarchist magazine, *A-kontra* (1, 2003). It was an article translated from the British and Irish magazine *Organise!* (no. 59, winter 2002), and no original Czech discussion on this issue has yet occurred in the anarchist press. The second was an interview with a woman from the International Union of Sex Workers in *Alarm*, on the website of the former Organisation of Revolutionary Anarchists. This was also a translation and there was no information about the Czech situation.

The Czech anarchist movement had for a long time discussed mostly class and race inequalities, while gender and sexuality issues were neglected (Kolářová 2004). In recent years, there have been several attempts to put gender issues on to the agenda. The most important of these were the creation of an *Anarcho-feminist group* in autumn 2000 and *Bloody Mary* – a riot grrrl zine founded in Prague in spring 2000. While Czech anarcho-feminists have focused on connecting gender, race and sexual orientation in their speeches, they rarely cooperate with lesbian feminists or Roma women activists. Problematic as this may be, anarcho-feminists have been the only anarchist subjects who have started to pay attention to sexuality issues. The *Anarcho-feminist group* organised two discussions on constructing sexuality, including homosexuality issues, in 2004 and started to address homosexuality in their magazine *Přímá cesta* (Direct way) in 2005. Recently, some of these activists participated in organising Queer Parades together with LGBT activists.

Bloody Mary is a riot grrrl, anarcho-feminist magazine focusing on women's issues, such as women and globalisation, women's poverty, abortion, women in subcultures, prostitution, menstruation and so on. The magazine also covers alternative culture and publishes reviews of shows and exhibitions as well as interviews with bands, stories and poems. The magazine's stance is critical of men's sexist behaviour within the punk and anarchist movement. For example, it criticised double standards in anarcho-punk subcultures where punk girls are expected to sleep with anyone because punk style means to have sex without commitments. Each issue of *Bloody Mary* is devoted to a particular topic. Those issues related to sexuality were no. 3 (2000) on abortion, sterilisation and birth control; no. 7 (2002) on menstruation; and no. 8 (2003) on prostitution. Sexuality is understood as part of women's issues, such as health, masturbation and pornography, more than in the sense of the relationships between men and women. However, in a *Bloody Mary* special issue on sexuality (no. 10, 2005) the editorial discusses the connection between gender and sexuality, and particularly addresses homosexuality and transgender issues. Inside the zine there is an interview with a lesbian activist, but no connection with anarchism or feminism is made. Issue no. 11 published an interview with an Italian lesbian activist of colour. Recently, *Bloody Mary* started to focus on queer issues, and the collective organised a festival, Gender Fuck Fest, in October 2009 that was defined as a queer event. The fifteenth issue of the zine presents several reflections on this action and interviews with queer bands and activists. The organisers were inspired by Ladyfests in other countries, mostly in Germany, but wanted their action to be less 'ladylike'. They had a motto for the festival: 'Svoje pohlaví nechte doma' (Leave your sex/gender at home). The participants could listen to music by feminist, queer or punk bands – for instance the queer band Rebis from Germany – could learn how to make sex toys, p-mates[4] or DIY fashion pieces in several workshops, could discuss issues of heteronormativity, queer activities, or sexual violence in the anarchist movement, and see theatre performances and exhibitions of feminist, lesbian and queer zines. Gender Fuck Fest was a unique event in the Czech Republic, especially in linking alternative culture with radical queer and feminist politics.

The magazine *Přímá cesta*, published by the anarcho-feminist group, also focuses each issue on a particular topic, for instance on the family and the state, pornography and gender and language. *Přímá cesta* also contains theoretical essays on anarcho-feminism and articles about the history of the labour movement regarding the condition of women. The eighth issue from 2005 was titled 'Let's dissolve sexual norms'. In the editorial of this issue (p. 2) homosexuality and heterosexuality are understood not as natural, from birth, but as socially constructed. Particularly unusually for a Czech anarchist publication, it also addresses the politics of transgender identities. The editors want to transgress gendered and sexualised norms as a part of a broader anarchist project of challenging norms. They present information about homosexual movements in other countries as these are largely unknown in the Czech Republic. They sympathise with the radical wing of LGBT or queer movements abroad who also focus on other systems of oppression such as sexism, capitalism and racism. They are also crititical of more reformist LGBT movements for being too consumerist, commercial and focused on fashion. The magazine also includes writing about the definition of homophobia (without specifically referring to Czech society), about paedophilia, personal experience with rape and several pieces on sexual education in Czech primary schools. Finally, there is an interview with a fifteen-year-old gay man who seems to feel fine coming out and does not feel any discrimination from his friends and acquaintances, who are very tolerant. Before publishing this issue addressing homosexuality, *Přímá cesta* had discussed sexuality only in connection with pornography and abortion.

In 2004, the *Anarcho-feminist group* started to organise summer camps where sex education workshops for children and discussions for adults on sexuality issues, including homosexuality, took place. Also, the group used to organise counter-demonstrations against the rallies of the Pro-Life Movement every year. Anarcho-feminists and other anarchist groups are the only people who criticise and publicly demonstrate their opposition to this right-wing tendency and take a strong pro-choice position in Czech society. Abortion in the Czech Republic is not a contentious issue, however. Abortion was already legal under communism and it has been permitted for more than forty years now. The Czech Republic is different from Western countries, where the right to abortion had to be fought for. However, this cannot be said in general about other post-communist countries, such as Poland. Abortion had been legalised there under the communist regime, but after the fall of state socialism abortion was prohibited once more. Much of Polish women's or feminist activism is focused on this question. In the Czech Republic, it seems, this activity is not central, and the women's movement, apart from anarcho-feminism, does not address it.

Regarding the lack of cooperation between anarcho-feminists and lesbian activists, there are notable exceptions. There was a women-only anarchist group called 'Luna' within the squatter movements, existing from 1995 to 1998. Its focus was on women's rights, animal rights, the environment and pagan issues. It organised demonstrations against right-wing movements and parties and on the International Day for the Elimination of Violence against Women. The group was also part of a broader platform called 'Women against

Racism', where it cooperated with lesbian women's groups. Also, the editorial group of the *Bloody Mary* zine was created predominantly by women and recently they have cooperated with lesbian activists. A few anarcho-feminist activists started to define themselves as queer or came out as bisexual; they also helped to organise Queer Parades, especially in Tábor in 2009.

Homosexual and queer activism in the anarchist movement and cooperation with LGBT activists

As I have shown, it has been very difficult for the anarchist movement to cooperate with LGBT people and movements. Likewise, cooperation is not very likely from the other side. In the Czech Republic there are no radical LGBT organisations that see links between sexuality and racism or militarism. The Czech Republic only has a moderate, reformist LGBT movement. Until 2008 there was no Gay Pride or any other major public event relating to LGBT liberation, except an annual festival of lesbian culture called 'Apriles' between 1995 and 2003.

Sokolová (2006) points out that Czech society discriminates against LGBT people, so discrimination (and not identity) is what drives activism. In the Czech context, homosexuality was decriminalised in 1961, but only removed from the list of mental illnesses as recently as 1992 (Sokolová 2006). Under the socialist regime the issue was taboo in society and it was discussed largely in terms of medical discourse. The legalisation of registered partnerships and same-sex marriage came in 2006. This legislation was a result of long discussions in the Czech Parliament and pressure from the civil society Gay and Lesbian League. The Czech LGBT movement has a history of being strongly patriarchal and gay male dominated; at the same time, lesbians have been excluded from the heterosexist mainstream women's and feminist movement. Lesbian rights are not considered women's rights, and gender and sexuality issues have been separated from each other. The dominant gender discourse is based on a presumed natural duality of men and women, together with normative notions of femininity and masculinity. Furthermore, the understanding of sexualities and gender identities is highly dichotomised, leaving transgender and bisexual issues even more marginalised (Sokolová 2006).

According to Kotišová and Vampolová (2006), there has never even been any Czech lesbian movement as such, with only a few lesbian activists working in isolation from each other. Lesbian activists have also largely been disconnected (with a few exceptions) from the potential support of the anarchist or anarcho-feminist movement. They have worked alone in order to avoid the stigmatisation of being lesbian and feminists (Kotišová and Vampolová 2006), and also the stigmatisation of cooperating with anarchists or antifascists, who are frequently represented as extremists by the media.

In the case of transgender people, cooperation is even less likely. According to Spencerová, transgender people do not want to be visible politically at all.

They do not want to deal with other political issues or even with transgender issues publicly. Transsexuals want to pass as 'normal' people and are mostly politically conservative (Spencerová 2006). It is highly improbable that they would enter or cooperate with the anarchist movement. While some transgender people have been attacked by neo-Nazi skinheads, they have not been drawn to join anarchist or antifascist struggles against fascism.

Because of the communist regime there has not been any second wave feminist movement in which feminists have been connected with lesbian women or transgender people as in Western countries. The social movements from below started after the fall of communism, and the early 1990s were significant as a new beginning for the anarchist, feminist and LGBT movements. These movements, even though they are not very strong and none of them has a large membership, still have very little contact with each other. Similarly, their political analyses tend to be separate, with none of them focusing on the intersections of inequalities such as class, race, gender, sexuality, age, disability and so on.

The situation changed in 2008 when the Queer Parade, as a public demonstration of visibility of the LGBT community, started to take place in Brno. An event composed of a march and workshops, exhibitions, theatre performances and discussions has been organised annually: in 2009 in Tábor, a small town in southern Czech Republic, and in 2010 in Brno, attracting hundreds of participants. It was organised by LGBT grassroots activists together with some local gender activists, and, especially in Tábor, some anarcho-feminists helped with the organisation. The events were supported by the Minister for Human Rights, local politicians and some gay celebrities, such as the tennis player Martina Navrátilová. This action was strongly opposed by Czech nationalist and neo-Nazi movements, with huge banners saying 'No Way for Gays, No Tolerance for Deviants' and so on, and the Dělnická strana (Workers' Party – an extreme right-wing nationalist group, which was prohibited by the highest Czech court in 2010) held counter-meetings against homosexuals. As the first Queer Parade (including some anarchists who participated in the march) was attacked by neo-Nazis, the next year in Tábor a group of anarchists (mostly from the collective Kolektivně proti kapitálu [Collectively against capital] and antifascists) organised security guards to protect the parade. So, as in other Eastern European countries, the opposition against queer activities by nationalist and neo-Nazi movements has brought anarchists and antifascists together with LGBT activists.

The anarcho-feminist lesbian zine *Houpačka*

The lack of an intersectional approach in Czech anarchism has changed recently, with one project connecting multiple issues. *Houpačka* (Seesaw) is a zine created by two young anarcho-feminist lesbian women (and later more people) from a town in the northern part of the Czech Republic. They started in autumn 2005 and have published five issues. While homosexuality or transgender issues have been part of the zine since the third issue, their most important focus is women's issues. They write against discrimination, sexual harassment, sexist culture, domestic violence and other forms of violence against women, including rape.

In addition to their lesbian and feminist politics, they claim an alliance with anarchism, antifascism and the punk subculture. They strongly oppose racism, and the rise of the local neo-Nazi movement particularly. Besides that, they deal with environmental issues, animal rights, anti-election campaigns and consumer culture. While the zine is not theoretical or very information oriented, the editors present their opinions on a broad range of issues. They deal particularly with local issues and problems of everyday life, but in the context of broader politics or hierarchies in society (for instance anorexia amongst their friends at school). Their feminism is not aggressively targeted against men, but they demand that men change their behaviour towards women. They present real stories of violence against women and domestic violence from people around them and provide contact details of women's non-governmental organisations that help survivors of violence and abuse. They also think that women should speak up against violence and harassment and should unite and act in solidarity. Drawing on their experience, they show how to deal with these problems in everyday life. For example, they have reported how one of them supported some women who were harassed or how women or girls can prevent rape in toilets[5] in bars by going in groups, not alone. They comment upon their interaction with chauvinist men in pubs and bars who sexually harass young punk women, and who hate lesbians. They express anger at being criticised for their unconventional style and image, for wearing men's clothing styles and no make-up.

Since issue no. 3 (spring 2006), they have openly expressed their homosexuality in poems, stories and essays. For instance, they speak about stereotypes that their acquaintances tend to rehearse, for example that in a lesbian couple there has to be one dominant and one submissive woman. For them, the reality is very different: 'One of the reasons I became a lesbian is your [macho men's] dominance over women, which really makes me sick' (Zdendule 2006).

In this issue, they repeated a story about the question of registered partnerships, which were legalised in 2006 in the Czech Republic. The young women told the story of how they had gone to a demonstration in support of legalised partnerships in Prague, thinking it had been organised by some gay and lesbian organisation. Not many people participated and the demonstration was uneventful. To liven things up, they started to drum and sing 'free vaginas' and the organisers distanced themselves. Finally, they learned that the demonstration was organised by a governmental party, the social democrats, but they carried no leaflets or banners with their name. The girls understood the activity of the social democrats as completely opportunistic, in order to gain votes from the homosexual community, as this issue was not supported by other parties and several times the proposed legislation had been rejected by Parliament.

I have interviewed the woman who initiated the *Houpačka* project. She answered the question 'What comes to your mind when anarchism and sexuality are connected?' as follows: 'First, I define and present myself as an anarchist. Considering the fact that I am a lesbian, so the issue of sexuality affects me too.' She understands anarchism in terms of free choice, which is not possible in sexuality. It is possible to choose a partner, but not the sex of the partner. Homosexuality is a given according to her and she cannot have sex with men. She defines herself primarily as an anarchist and feminist. However, she prefers to interact with different people, not only with anarchists who have the same opinion. Besides, she criticises local anarchists for being conservative:

> In the small town where I live, I meet anarchists who have very conservative attitudes. They are scared of gay men. They behave arrogantly, as if heterosexuality was a privilege. Maybe they feel when they talk to me that people would see them as gay. Sometimes I found that they made stupid comments when introducing their partner to me. They were afraid that I would date her. I would not expect something like that from anarchists.
> (email interview, 2006)

Because of her evident punk look, she provokes discussion in various places. She mentioned struggles at work, where she defended a colleague who was threatened with being paid a lower wage by their employer. She speaks about the severe homophobic behaviour of people around her; she has found that people use the word 'lesbian' as a curse or an insult. However, she feels they changed once she explained her identity and stance.

She also openly expresses her antifascist attitude, because of which she has had serious problems. Known for her opinions and strong criticism of neo-Nazi skinheads in local pubs, she has been physically attacked, knocked to the ground, beaten and kicked by a group of fascist men several times. They also burgled her and smashed up her house, stole her money and tore her antifascist patches off her clothes. In the locality, she and her girlfriend are the only ones who stand up against neo-Nazism. Local punks and anarchists are afraid of opposing the neo-Nazis.

After the attacks, her friends contacted people from antifascist organisations in Prague and nearby, but they were quite reluctant to help because of her specific case. It is unusual for a young woman to be attacked by neo-Nazis, so antifascists were not really prepared for this. The situation may also be affected by the fact that she is openly feminist and lesbian.

Although she is lesbian and defends LGBT people, she is not interested in participating in the LGBT community. She does not feel that her sexual orientation is a basis for friendship with members of this community. They have a different lifestyle and interests. She also does not cooperate with them politically, because she is not interested in the struggle for legislation (such as same-sex marriage and adoption rights). Now that the registered partnership law has been passed, she thinks it is even more difficult for gays and lesbians to get married in a small town or village given levels of rural homophobia. She does not accept the institution of marriage. She does not even think that LGBT people should be understood like the majority heterosexual community because they are different. She feels the gay community is not interested in women's issues, is too macho and too focused on appearance. Instead of sexuality issues, she is more politically interested in the question of violence against women. She is concerned that very few lesbians consider themselves feminists.

Conclusion

Sexuality issues have been marginal for the Czech anarchist movement and, until recently, LGBT people have been absent or silenced in broader Czech society. Since the early 1990s, the anarchist movement has been male dominated and primarily heterosexual. Also, there is a general lack of cooperation between anarchists and gay or queer activists, with the exception of anarcho-feminist activists working with lesbian activists or participating more recently in Queer Parades. The lack of connection between LGBT and anarchist movements is also affected by the fragmentation of women's and LGBT movements and their fear of anarchism as extremism. There appears to be little interest among LGBT people in broadening their activities beyond sexuality issues to a wider radical politics.

With respect to anarchism, however, the situation has started to change recently. Anarcho-feminists have begun to pay more attention to sexuality, and lesbian and gay issues in particular. A specific anarcho-feminist punk lesbian zine has appeared. The *Bloody Mary* collective organised a queer cultural festival and some other anarcho-feminists became involved in the LGBT community's Queer Parades. These people connect queer, feminism and anarchism.

The struggle against neo-Nazism is an obvious potential point for the anarchist movement and LGBT activists to meet, because they are both objects of neo-Nazi hatred. The active anarchist and antifascist presence in Queer Parades recently has shown that these separate movements can cooperate as part of a widening circle of activist movements.

Notes

1 I would like to thank Richard Cleminson, Jamie Heckert, Ondřej Slačálek, Dita Jahodová and Michal Tulík for their comments on drafts of this essay.
2 This chapter is based on research material collected up to the year 2006. Since then there has been some development of this issue that I try to reflect on here, drawing on my participant observation and internet sources.
3 There is one exception: the small counter-demonstration organised by the editorial group of *A-kontra* in Karlovy Vary in 2000 against the demonstration of neo-Nazis

who protested against a gay and lesbian action. More recently, anarchists have started to participate in Queer Parades and organised security guards to protect the marches.

4 A female portable urinating device that allows women to urinate standing up.

5 It is not a very common form of violence, though.

References

Anonymous (2006) 'On the Streets Against Homophobia!', *Abolishing the Borders from Below* 25: 6–8.

Daphne, K. L. (2006) 'Understanding Heterosexism in Radical Political Scenes', *European PGA Conference Newspaper 2006*: 8–9. Online. Available HTTP: http://www.ainfos.ca/06/oct/ainfos00111.html (accessed 24 January 2011).

Goldman, E. (1969) 'Marriage and Love', in *Anarchism and Other Essays*, New York: Dover Publications.

Kenský, J. (2002) 'Angažovanost žen – změnit klima v hnutí a ve společnosti' [Women's participation – changing climate in the movement and in the society], *Akce!* [Action!] 6: 13.

Kolářová, M. (2004) *Gender in the Czech Anarchist Movement*, Prague: Subverze.

——(2005) 'Láska a svoboda: anarchistické pojetí volné lásky' [Love and freedom: anarchist notion of free love], *Přímá cesta* 8: 7–9.

Kotišová, M., and V. Vampolová (2006) 'České lesby: daleko k hnutí, daleko k feminismu' [Czech lesbians: far from a movement, far from feminism], in H. Hašková, A. Křížková and M. Linková (eds), *Mnohohlasem* [Multiple voices], Prague: Sociologický ústav.

Slačálek, O. (2002) 'Don't Trust Anybody, Not Even Us!: A Brief History of the Czech Anarchism'. Online. Available HTTP: www.csaf.cz (accessed 20 December 2002).

Sokolová, V. (2006) 'Koncepční pohled na "sexuální menšiny" aneb vše je jen otázka správné orientace ... ' [A Conceptual view on 'sexual minorities' or everything is just a matter of the right orientation ...], in H. Hašková, A. Křížková and M. Linková (eds), *Mnohohlasem* [Multiple voices], Prague: Sociologický ústav.

Spencerová, T. (2006) 'Pohlavně-identitní ilegalita: (ne)spolupráce transgenderové komunity s ženskými organizacemi' [Sex-identity illegality: (non)cooperation of the transgender community with women's organisations], in H. Hašková, A. Křížková and M. Linková (eds), *Mnohohlasem* [Multiple voices], Prague: Sociologický ústav.

Tomek, V. and O. Slačálek (2006) *Anarchismus: Svoboda proti moci* [Anarchism: Freedom against power], Prague: Vyšehrad.

Zdendule (2006) 'Father? Mother? Unclear!', *Houpačka* 3.

Other sources

A-kontra 1, 2003

Bloody Mary 1–11, 2000–2006

Houpačka [Seesaw] 1–4, 2005–2006

Přímá cesta [Direct Way] 1–8, 2001–2005

Email interview with anarcho-feminist lesbian activist, member of *Houpačka* editorial collective, October 2006.

Chapter 10

Amateurism and anarchism in the creation of autonomous queer spaces

Gavin Brown

Over the last two decades, geographers, anthropologists and architectural theorists have been writing about gay and queer space. With the exception of a body of work on cruising and public sex sites (Bell 2001; Binnie 2001; Turner 2003) and a few pieces on lesbian social networks constituted through domestic spaces (Peace 2001; Valentine 1993), most of this work has focused on gay gentrification and issues relating to the mainstream commercial gay scene (Knopp 1992; Nast 2002; Quilley 1997). In contrast, I have spent several years participating in, researching and writing about queer sites that exist outside capitalist social relations (or, at least, attempt to do so).[1] The Anarchism and Sexuality conference from which this book arises offered me the opportunity to present an intellectual analysis of these sites in front of an audience I knew would be unlike the usual audiences I speak to at academic conferences, queer or otherwise; it would include many people who would be familiar with many of the sites I was speaking about, would have participated in them and might have helped initiate and organise them. I seldom get very nervous before giving a conference paper, but this conference, despite the organisers' conscious attempts to foster a supportive environment, was an exception. I feared I would be exposed for over-intellectualising the project of claiming queer autonomy and worried how the more 'activist' elements of the audience might react to my attempt to uncover impulses towards autonomy in a range of spaces beyond activist circuits. I need not have worried. The audience engaged enthusiastically and supportively with my ideas and the discussion that followed the two papers in our session on queer autonomous spaces was by far the most engaged and inclusive discussion I have experienced at an academic conference in the last decade. I have attempted to include and reflect upon many issues raised in that discussion as I have expanded my paper into the current book chapter.

This chapter, then, is about experiments in the creation and reclamation of autonomous queer spaces. In the pages that follow, I explore those spaces that are created by self-identified activists inspired by anarchist ideals, such as the international Queeruption gatherings, fund-raising benefit parties and queer interventions in the spectacles of gay consumption. These spaces are strategically important. However, I want to complicate the discussion a little by also thinking about events and moments where other forms of queer autonomy emerge (often without any direct frame of reference to anarchist ideas or autonomous political movements). These other queer spaces that I consider range from do-it-yourself club nights that exist on the fringes of the mainstream commercial scene, to spiritual gatherings and self-organised resistance to the neglect and erasure of non-commercial public sex environments that serve as a form of (predominantly male-focused) queer commons (Brown 2009). For me, these spaces, with all of their contradictions, are also important because they offer glimpses of what a queerer life could be like in other circumstances.

Queer autonomous geographies

Before I go any further, I should make clear that 'queer', as I am using it here, is more than simply an umbrella term for all those who are 'othered' by normative heterosexuality. It is more than a synonym for any of the variety of acronyms made up from identity categories (e.g. 'LGBT'). Indeed, 'queer', in many of the spaces I am thinking about, is as opposed to homonormativity as it is to heteronormativity. Queer opposes and contests the complacent politics of mainstream gay politicians who actively work to win gay people's compliance with a depoliticised culture based on domesticity and privatised consumption. Queer celebrates gender and sexual fluidity and consciously blurs binaries. It is more of a process of trying to put into practice a set of ethical modes of engagement with sexual and gender difference than a simple identity category. As Jamie Heckert (2004) has suggested, a truly radical politics of sexuality must move beyond simple transgression and incorporate its ethical goals (for example co-operative, non-hierarchical, sex-positive relationships) into its mode of operation.

The queer autonomous spaces that I discuss in this chapter are attempts to create room for these ethics to be put into practice – indeed, in finding ways of creating these spaces, participants are engaged in a process of putting such ethics into practice. In their recent attempts to theorise the geographies of a range of experiments in social autonomy (e.g. social centres, convergence spaces and intentional communities), Jenny Pickerill and Paul Chatterton have articulated that these are '[s]paces where people desire to constitute non-capitalist, egalitarian and solidaristic forms of political, social and economic organization through a combination of resistance and creation' (Pickerill and Chatterton 2006: 730).

This constellation of sites offers small-scale workable alternatives to wage labour, capitalist consumption and representative democracy. Like Castoriadis (1991), the authors stress that autonomy is a collective process, created and sustained through reciprocal and mutually beneficial relations with other participants (Pickerill and Chatterton 2006: 733), where the tensions between individual freedom and collective self-rule are continually negotiated in practice. As such, autonomy is always incomplete, and in the process of building autonomous spaces participants must continually negotiate and confront tensions between moments of autonomy and alienated dependence on hierarchical structures: 'Autonomous spaces are an incomplete terrain where daily struggles are made and remade, both symbolically and materially, and where people live by their beliefs and face contradictions from living between worlds – the actually existing and the hoped for' (ibid.: 736–7).

Claiming autonomy and creating spaces where it can be exercised is a relational process – it is deeply contextual and is shaped by the time and place in which the experiment takes place, as well as the circumstances of the people involved (Brown and Pickerill 2009). Autonomy is not an object that can be possessed, only a process that can be worked towards in conjunction with others. Increasingly, those others may not simply be the people that are present in the physical location where autonomy is being built. Complex spatial and temporal networks exist between those engaged in the creation of autonomous experiments. Previous experiments are remembered and their lessons built upon, whilst translocal solidarity networks help experimental methods travel from one location to another across the globe (Olesen 2005). As I shall suggest later in this chapter (see p. 217), sometimes these lessons get lost in translation, when attempts are made to replicate experiments in their entirety without taking into account the specifics of the new location in which they are being enacted. However, what it is important to remember, and what is at the core of my exploration of autonomous tendencies that exist outside radical queer activist networks, is that because autonomy is an ongoing process constructed through contextual practices 'no clear boundaries between autonomous and non-autonomous processes and space exist' (Pickerill and Chatterton 2006: 737). The impulse towards autonomy is not the sole possession of radical activists and can be found anywhere people attempt to take control of their own lives and create what they desire for themselves rather than relying on others to deliver it for them. The journey towards autonomy becomes an end in itself. The process of working with the resources that are to hand at the time, and without deference towards those claiming positions of authority, can be more important than whether the end goal is ever achieved or not.

The queer autonomous spaces and experiments described in this chapter are important because they offer room for sexual dissidents and gender outlaws to exist on their own terms. Increasingly, gay life in the metropolitan centres of the Global North has become saturated by the commodity. Through an engagement with the commercial gay scene, people consume products and experiences that confirm their identity as 'gay'. Consequently people no longer relate to each other as active participants in the creation of society, but as the owners (or not) of things that are divorced from the processes by which they came into being. The social relations of production, of 'doing', are converted into 'being' (in this case, *being gay*). This is the essence of capitalism: the separating of people from their own doing (Holloway 2002). The queer autonomous spaces described here offer some respite from capitalist social relations and attempt to create spaces where sexuality is not reduced to the acquisition of commodities that have been separated from the conditions of their production, and the experiences of those that produced them. In queer autonomous spaces, sexuality is honoured, questioned and practised differently. More than this, those who are involved in the creation of these spaces have not relied on others, claiming positions of authority and power, to supply alternative spaces for them. In contrast to the experience of life on the receiving end of 'power-over', experiments in queer autonomy are about making modest, low-key attempts to re-engage our 'power-to-do' (ibid.) (which is always part of a social process of doing with others).[2] And so I return to my earlier point that 'queer' within the autonomous queer spaces I am thinking about functions more as a process enacted through the relationships between people, rather than a simple identity category. Queer is an ethical process by which (some) gender outlaws and sexual dissidents strive collectively to reclaim and develop our ability to determine the conditions of *our own* lives. It is about attempting to prefigure in the here and now, through form and process, aspects of life beyond capitalism, and beyond the limiting range of consumable identities that are currently sold to us. Queer social relationships, in this context, are produced through the very process of working collectively to create a less alienated and more empowered space in which to explore a multiplicity of sexual and gendered potentialities. As I hope is clear by now, my conception of 'queer' is very different to most common uses of the term – for me, queer happens through experiments with autonomous practices.

Anarchism, amateurism and the impulse for autonomy

Before exploring some examples of queer autonomous spaces, I want to trace two sets of ideas that influence the processes that shape the creation of these spaces. They are contemporary anarchist praxis and an inclination towards amateur modes of production. Of course, these two modes of thinking overlap and influence each other, but I want to distinguish between sites that are motivated by anarchist-inspired political activism and those that are less directly 'political' and stem from the collective endeavours of groups of like-minded friends who want to try their hands at doing something different. Of course, Kropotkin developed his theories of mutual aid and anarchism on the basis of his observations of everyday, 'amateur' practices. The connections between anarchism and amateurism have existed for a long time.

Uri Gordon (2005, 2007) has suggested that contemporary anarchism has a 'hybrid genealogy' drawing on the revival of anarchist values in a broad intersection of movements (Gordon 2005: 9). This is certainly true of the anarcha-queer networks engaged in creating some of the spaces I map in this chapter.[3] They draw influence from the anti-capitalist, direct action politics and non-hierarchical, mutualist ethics of early gay liberation, Greenham

Common and the Zapatistas, as well as practical experience from radical feminism, environmental protest, Reclaim the Streets and the social centres movement. These movements encapsulate the 'present-time politics' that Gordon ascribes to contemporary anarchism – a political approach that views revolution as an ongoing process of undermining structures of domination and systemic violence through attempts to implement a libertarian ethos within progressive movements.

Gordon (2005, 2007) notes that in recent decades anarchist resistance has been generalised such that it no longer focuses predominantly on the state and capital, but attempts to expose and undermine all forms of domination operating in society (including racism, patriarchy and heteronormativity). The goal of anarchism has shifted from the abolition and replacement of existing political institutions towards the redefinition of every aspect of social relations. It can be unsettling for many 'activists' to appreciate that this goal is unlikely ever to be achieved completely, for as the structure and functioning of society change, new forms of domination and exclusion might emerge. This should be taken not as an argument against anarchism, but rather as one in favour of an anarchism that pursues an ongoing process of fostering the most egalitarian and anti-oppressive social relations possible. As Emma Goldman recognised long ago, '[a]narchism is not … a theory of the future. It is a living force in the affairs of our life, constantly creating new conditions … the spirit of revolt, in whatever form, against everything that hinders human growth' (Goldman 1969: 63, cited in Ferrell 2001: 243).

In this context, prefigurative praxis becomes a central motivating feature for anarchist activism (Franks 2006; Gordon 2007). It creates the conditions in which those who want to can attempt to inhabit, as much as is possible within a racist, patriarchal capitalist society, the social relations that might underpin the kind of post-capitalist society anarchists aspire to create (Gordon 2005, 2007). In the process of building prefigurative experiments, the desires for personal liberation and social change motivate each other. This in turn promotes anarchism as a culture, a rhizomatic lived experience that pops up everywhere, adapting to specific situations and cultures. Even though it may not be possible to generalise these experiments (at least in the near future), it is still important to promote their development for the lessons and glimpses of freedom they offer. For Jeff Ferrell, 'this practice of spontaneity, experimentation, and playful dis-organization replicates in contemporary cultural space battles the old anarchist strategy of direct action and the notion that an inclusive process, properly unleashed, will find its own progressive direction' (Ferrell 2001: 237).

Alongside an expanding repertoire of direct action tactics that confront and undermine oppressive forms of power and domination without reliance on other forms of external authority, a tendency towards *in*direct action (McKay 1998: 9) can also be witnessed within the processes of claiming autonomous modes of living. That is the tendency towards disappearance and withdrawal from capitalist society and a refusal to adhere to its norms or engage in the practices that sustain it (Scott 2009).

If, as David Graeber has suggested, anarchism is 'less about seizing state power than about exposing, delegitimizing and dismantling mechanisms of rule' (Graeber 2002: 62), then anarcha-queer praxis is less about reclaiming lesbian and gay identities than about 'exposing, delegitimizing and dismantling' the alienated consumption of sexual identities within neoliberal economies as well as the power differentials produced through these processes.

Contemporary anarchist praxis (queer or otherwise) frequently engages creative and playful modes of resistance and prefiguration, recognising that 'a revolution that reproduces existing arrangements of authority in its execution, that draws on strategies of drudgery and domination, that offers up a new boss the same as the old boss, is no revolution at all' (Ferrell 2001: 23). In the spirit of many earlier generations of anarchists, like Emma Goldman and the early IWW (Industrial Workers of the World), and in contrast to too many contemporary mainstream gay politicians, many queers refuse to always act 'respectably' (even as many of us appreciate *being* respected much of the time).

The principle of anarchist direct action *is* do-it-yourself as an ethics of mutual aid (ibid.). Contemporary DIY culture is a form of amateur production that has its roots in punk, as well as earlier grassroots cultural movements such as skiffle[4] (McKay 1998; Spencer 2005). It stems from the desire to make a 'zine reflecting your interests or recording music primarily for yourself and then passing it on to others' (ibid.: 11), using the resources currently available to you to cross the boundary between consumer and producer. Participants in this scene tend not to be 'fixated with the promise of money, they are people who want to do something just to see it happen' (Michal Cupid, quoted in ibid.: 11). More than this, they engage in a process of community and alliance building forged through the distribution and publicity networks that they create for their DIY events and products.

George McKay has described these modes of self-production as the 'cultural politics of autonomy' and as practising 'an intuitive liberal anarchism' (McKay (1998: 23, 3). He also acknowledges that there are uncomfortable parallels between the rhetoric of do-it-yourself self-empowerment and the centrality of the individual in aspects of neoliberal ideology (ibid.: 19). Against this concern, I would stress that a key difference can be found in the reciprocal relationships (of mutual aid) and non-hierarchical forms of organisation and distribution found within these networks, alongside a host of other ethical commitments to both anti-oppressive practices and the fostering of equality, empowerment and care (for the human and non-human worlds). It is these ethical commitments that separate DIY cultural networks from many other forms of amateur production. Nevertheless, amateur endeavours still contain many features that are important to an anarchist ethic: they promote skill-sharing over professional specialisation; fluidity and horizontal forms of organisation over hierarchies; sites for learning and personal growth away from the more controlled environments of formal education; and a celebration of playful inefficiency over the earnest efficiency of alienated work. This ethics of amateurism also offers an alternative to the increasingly specialised role of 'the activist' (Bobel 2007; Heckert 2002), and serves as a reminder that experimenting with more autonomous modes of living, as much as making music, can be done by anyone.

Certainly many of the DIY queer spaces discussed in the next section of this chapter were created by individuals and collectives with an affinity with more 'activist' forms of contemporary anarchist resistance and prefigurative experimentation. However, at least one example in what follows was the result of a group of friends (none of whom identified as 'activists' or 'anarchists') reaching the realisation that something needed to be done and that they could not rely on anyone else to do it for them.

Exploring moments of queer autonomy

I now want to examine four short examples of different ways of creating queer autonomous space. In doing so, I want to highlight the diversity of these spaces, as well as to suggest how moments of queer autonomy can emerge in other situations. These spaces are not discrete sites that exist in isolation from the others. They are overlapping and relational – many participants move between them, using each space to satisfy a particular set of needs and bringing lessons from one type of queer autonomous space to inform the creation and renewal of other sites. Similar spatial interventions are often replicated over time and in different locations. In the process, spaces that look and feel superficially similar may end up fulfilling quite distinct functions and may be interpreted in substantially different ways according to their context. I begin by examining the growth of activist-led urban experiments in queer autonomy. In contrast, I then focus on a set of rural, spiritual spaces which, despite a significantly different orientation, still share much in terms of form and process with their urban counterparts. Having examined these spaces which intentionally seek to position themselves at some distance from the mainstream, I consider a range of DIY queer music and club venues that have a more complex and fluid relationship to the commercial gay scene. Finally, I recall some more spontaneous outbreaks of queer autonomy that I observed whilst researching sites of public homosex and consider what they might suggest about the potential for new forms of queer autonomy. All of these sites rely on processes and relations of 'amateur' production to some extent.

Queer Mutinies

Writing a decade ago, after the peak of the early 1990s rave culture and the period of widespread media attention on high-profile environmental direct action, but before Seattle and the period of intense summit-hopping convergences,

McKay cautioned that, '[t]he danger is that DiY Culture quietens marginalised voices and erases difference, and that, paradoxically, it achieved both of these by a loud rhetoric of inclusivity' (McKay 1998: 45).

He went on to observe an apparent invisibility of lesbians and gay people and culture in the 1990s' DIY scene. He was partly right. In the year these comments were published a group of queer anarchists in London organised the first Queeruption gathering – to offer a DIY alternative to the blandness of the commercial gay scene, to draw together and share the skills that many had acquired through an involvement in the protest movements of the time, but also to create a safe space against the homophobia and machismo that they had experienced from others in those movements (Wilkinson 2009).

An international Queeruption gathering occurred each year from 1998 to 2007 (except in 2000, when no gathering happened, and 2005, when there were two) and they have now taken place in nine cities across three continents (Vanelslander 2007). Mostly these gatherings take place in large squatted premises, although in circumstances where there is no local tradition of squatting, or where to do so might draw too much unwanted attention from state authorities and risk the safety of participants, rented space has been used. The funds to enable the convergences are raised through benefit parties held both in the host city, by the organisers, and across the international network of past and future participants. The main programme of each gathering usually lasts for about a week and consists of workshops on political and ethical issues that share skills and foster creativity, alongside protests, direct actions and, of course, parties and celebrations. Accommodation is usually located on site, and a large part of each day can be taken up with the logistics of providing cheap, nutritious vegan food (and lots of cakes) for several hundred participants.[5] At most gatherings, the priorities and practicalities of the day are shaped, on a consensus basis, by a morning plenary of as many participants as are interested in contributing to the process. At times, the consensus process has been slow and frustrating, slowed further by the need to provide translation for non-English speakers (however problematically, English has usually been the default language of these gatherings). However, facilitation skills have been actively shared amongst the participants and lessons have been carried from one gathering to another.

I have written at length elsewhere (Brown 2007a, 2007b) about both the exhilarating joys and the recurrent tensions and frustrations that can occur at Queeruptions, so do not intend to rehearse these ideas further here. However, there is one source of tension that arises year after year which warrants a brief mention (not least because it was raised in the discussion that followed this paper at the Anarchism and Sexuality conference) and that surrounds the (perceived) centrality of sex and specific notions of sex radicalism at these gatherings. These tensions often arise in relation to the sex party that occurs towards the end of most gatherings, but also in response to the flirtatious and sexually charged atmosphere that can arise within such an intense period of respite from the drudgery of quotidian life.[6] For many within this network of activists, being a 'radical queer' has become synonymous with an interest in non-monogamy, polyamory and a range of BDSM and public sex practices. The resulting assumption about others' sexual ethics and personal boundaries can be intimidating, frightening and exclusionary for some participants. Further effort is needed at future gatherings to foster mutual aid and an appreciation of difference within the context of this sex positive ethos (Rouhani forthcoming).

Occasions like Queeruption offer a specifically queer form of constructive direct action (Day 2005) – a convergence space (Routledge 2003, 2005) where radical queer activists from different countries can come together to share information, skills and community for a short period. They offer a form of community that is not based on adherence to social norms, but instead a community that is created through an 'open-ended process of mutual engagement and exploration' that is 'woven just tightly enough to offer comfort and self-determination, but always left loose enough to ensure difference' (Ferrell 2001: 32).

Another set of spatial practices that are a mainstay of these anarcha-queer activist networks operate through interventions in mainstream Pride festivals and the creation of alternative, free, grassroots community celebrations. In Britain, North America and Australia, such interventions have been motivated by the mutation of LGBT pride parades from politicised community events that protested invisibility, injustice and police harassment in the 1970s and 1980s into contemporary urban spectacles offering commercial opportunities for corporate sponsors and place-marking opportunities for local and national governments keen to demonstrate their liberal credentials and boost tourism revenues. In this context, events like the Queer Mutinies in London, Gay Shame in San Francisco and Twee Pride in Manchester have enabled local queer activists to both playfully satirise the commodification of LGBT pride events and have demonstrated a practical example of low-impact, autonomous alternatives that can engage more than just core activists in the active creation of these event-spaces. They demonstrate what a small group of 'amateurs' can achieve for next to no expense. In the process, many people learnt new skills and discovered new talents. Although it is hard work to create the events, they offer a space in which participants can rest, relax and play together[7] – which is important for the sustainability of the multiple forms of resistance in which they are engaged.

Rural encounters

The examples I have just offered are of urban political community spaces. Next I want to explore rural examples of queer autonomous spaces. To this end, I could stay focused on politicised activist spaces and talk about the queer barrios at the convergences against the G8 summits at Gleneagles in 2005 (Harvie *et al.* 2005; Pickerill and Chatterton 2006) and Heiligendam in 2007, or various Climate Camps since then. Instead, I want to think about more spiritual queer spaces. I want to think about QPC (Queer Pagan Camp), as an innovation in itself and in the context of its overlaps with Radical Faerie gatherings. None of these spaces are straightforwardly anarchist in their orientation, but they are utilising non-hierarchical, do-it-yourself models to create autonomous spaces for the exploration of specifically queer spiritual practices.

The Radical Faeries were formed in the United States in the 1970s, inspired in large part by the ideas and enthusiasm of a long-term gay activist, Harry Hay (although it is important to note that, to the extent that Hay 'founded' the Faeries, he was drawing on the experience of a series of gay men's experiments with rural and frequently communal modes of living). There are now Faerie circles and sanctuaries across North America, much of Western Europe and also in Australia (Povinelli 2006). If, as I charted earlier, contemporary anarcha-queer activism draws on a complex genealogy, then the same is true of the Radical Faeries, as Hennen demonstrates:

> Radical Faerie culture is forged from an astonishingly diverse cultural tool box that includes Marxism, feminism, paganism, Native American and New Age spirituality, anarchism, the mythopoetic men's movement, radical individualism, the therapeutic culture of self-fulfilment and self-actualization, earth-based movements in support of sustainable communities, spiritual solemnity coupled with a camp sensibility, gay liberation, and drag.
>
> (Hennen 2004: 500–1)

He goes on to position the development of the Radical Faeries very much within a desire to escape and counter the rapid commodification of urban gay culture in the wake of early gay liberation politics. The Faeries appealed to a layer of gay men who were alienated by the growing sexual objectification of men's bodies during the 1970s, and the increasing dominance within the urban gay scene of hypermasculine tropes of desirability. In contrast, Harry Hay promoted an ethics of developing 'subject–subject consciousness' on the basis that 'one must always treat others as subjects like themselves, never as objects, or as a means to some instrumental end' (ibid.: 513). For Hay, subject–object relations amongst gay men were a product of the increasing 'hetero-imitative' focus of urban gay life that accompanied the growing commodification of the gay scene. He hoped that the rural retreats, gatherings and communal 'sanctuaries' developed by men inspired by the Faeries would create space where queer men could collectively build new relationships with each other based on intimacy and an ethics of speaking from the heart. Although Radical Faerie gatherings are intended to be spiritual spaces they are very inclusive, attracting men (and, at some gatherings, also women) from a range of different spiritual paths – Pagan, Buddhist, Christian and none. How these spiritual and ethical values are put into practice will be familiar to many who have participated in prefigurative autonomous spaces that function on non-hierarchical, participatory lines and attempt to embody their vision of a post-capitalist future in contemporary practices. 'Refreshingly, Faerie culture seems to continually privilege process over results. Faerie enterprises, from preparing a meal to creating a sanctuary, are notoriously inefficient affairs – and this is just the way most Faeries like it' (ibid.: 502).

Similar 'problems' can be witnessed at QPC, which is a ten-day gathering of queer pagans that has taken place in Britain each summer since 1998. It is not wholly coincidental that QPC began the same year as the first Queeruption gathering. From the beginning, the two networks have had strong links, with several key individuals involved in organising both gatherings over the years. Many feel an affinity with both concepts and there has been a mutual sharing of skills and organisational praxis. Similar links exist with several Radical Faerie circles. As the QPC's 'vision statement' notes:

> Queer Pagan Camp grew out of the experiences of people being marginalised by wider society and other pagan or spiritual groups based on stereotypes of sexual identities and gender preferences. The first principal of Queer Paganism is respect for each other, ourselves, the Spirits and the Land, and we work on the basis of self-identification.
>
> (QPC n.d.)

In contrast to the gender polarity inherent in many forms of pagan practice, this is a defiantly queer approach (very much in the sense of queer as a relational ethics that I described earlier). This queer sensibility moves beyond attempting to create a safe space for people of all sexualities and genders, and informs a queer pagan approach to spiritual practice and ritual – 'we recognise that there are many paths to "spirit", "nature" and "magic" and we positively revel in diversity' (ibid.).

Partly out of necessity, due to lack of funds, and partly out of ethical principle (drawing on the prior involvement of many of the original organisers within feminist, queer and anarchist networks that stressed autonomous modes of organising), the camp had a participative, do-it-yourself ethos from the start. Although individuals take responsibility each year for arranging aspects of the camp (such as finding, renting and preparing the site, organising childcare and coordinating the kitchen), the group operates on the basis that the camp's organisers are those who turn up for the publicised organising meetings throughout the year. The camp aspires to operate by consensus and all campers are encouraged to take responsibility for its daily functioning – chopping firewood, raddling the compost toilets, cooking the collective evening meal, offering workshops and rituals; or bringing the camp to life with music, costume and clowning. The achievement of truly inclusive, non-hierarchical and consensus-based forms of organising at QPC is an ongoing challenge and a work in progress. After thirteen years of operation, the camp's established customs and practice can seem opaque to some newcomers and can serve to inhibit the more spontaneous expressions of a DIY ethos some hold dear. Generally, the QPC community responds reflexively to these tensions and challenges; and a strong tradition of fooling at the camp serves to prick the pretensions of those perceived to be taking themselves too seriously or attempting to accumulate too much power.

This participative and non-hierarchical approach to running the camp has come to influence its rituals, the acts of magic that take place there and the ethics of relating to the more-than-human world(s) that they foster (Abram 1996):

> As Queer Pagans we communicate directly with spirits, nature, ancestors, Gods, Goddesses or other divinities. We do not need mediators. We work consensually to create rituals. We do not need hierarchies. We welcome spirits and work with them. We do not command them. We share knowledge of different traditions and we create new ways of working. Stirring the cauldron of gender we are not limited by gender-based magical working. We believe we can all work with spiritual power, that we all can be our own healers, celebrants and guides.
>
> And a lot of fabulous dressing up and glitter too!
>
> (QPC n.d.)

Although the workshops at QPC can be a useful starting point for finding out the core beliefs and practices of different pagan traditions, many fuse traditions eclectically and, with camp élan, do not take themselves too seriously – 'enlightenment through lipstick' and 'prance dancing' being two memorable examples from recent years. Such a queer approach to magic and ritual can only come about as a result of the broader, non-hierarchical and autonomous modes of living experienced by the participants at QPC year after year.

Autonomy on the edge of the commercial scene

In contrast to the two examples I've already given, it is important to recognise that queer autonomy does not only exist outside the commercial gay scene. There are many sites that exist in a more complex and contradictory relationship to both the mainstream scene and the autonomous spaces I have already discussed. Following the emergence of punk in the mid-1970s, many gay punks found themselves caught between a growing gay bar scene that did not accommodate their musical tastes and a punk milieu that was not always welcoming of sexual difference. Their experience of feeling a partial affinity with two different sub-cultural groups, but experiencing only partial acceptance from both led to the development of the queercore music and performance scene. Since the 1980s, queer do-it-yourself networks have proliferated across much of the Global North, with the emergence of the internet strengthening connections across national borders. For Larry Bob, a long-term protagonist in the queercore scene on the West Coast of the United States, queercore offered an opportunity to engage and collaborate with a vast range of creative people:

> In general, mass entertainment happens because it's profitable. Queercore isn't profitable – people do things because they want to have the sort of experience that queercore offers. It's such a cultural niche that it's only going to happen if people do it themselves.
>
> (Larry Bob, quoted in Spencer 2005: 281)

The DIY queer scene enables people to employ their own values around gender, money and censorship. The resulting events tend to be cheap, promote occasionally obscure musicians and amateur performers (often from amongst the clubs' regulars and their extended friendship networks), and frequently attempt to create an atmosphere that is welcoming of a broader range of sexual and gender difference than the niche marketplaces of the commercial mainstream. However, there is always a danger that, by drawing so heavily on close friendship networks, these gigs and club nights can become overly dominated by small cliques and end up negating their own inclusive intentions (Culton and Holtzman 2010; Jindal 2004).

In Britain, in recent years, the do-it-yourself approach to queer entertainment and clubbing has been sustained through the events organised around Club Fag (in Cardiff), Kaffequeeria (in Manchester), Homocrime, Unskinny Bop and WANC (Women's Anarchist Nuisance Café) (in London), as well as Club Wotever (in London, Brighton and occasionally major cities throughout the rest of Europe). Some of these events take place in squatted venues and radical social centres, some do deals to bring custom to straight venues at quiet times of the week, and others (particularly Club Wotever) mostly utilise the infrastructure of the mainstream lesbian and gay bar scene. None of these events are run for profit, and most rely heavily on the enthusiasm of a small group of core organisers, even as they require the active participation of their audiences in the co-production of their events.

Homocrime was largely organised for the fun of it, to provide a space in which amateur musicians with a queer aesthetic could perform. It presented itself as a safe space for 'queers of all sexualities and genders'. The Homocrime events took place every second month (frequently alternating with dances organised by Unskinny Bop). They were an opportunity to showcase many lo-fi musicians and performers, and each night was planned to coincide with the release of a three-inch CD-R featuring related musicians. Given the amateur, do-it-yourself basis of the project, inevitably these CDs were not always finished in time, and the collective was realistic about the impact they would have:

> Doing the *Singles Club* has always been one of my favourite parts of Homocrime. There are lots of talented & unpretentious kids around, and

> it's great to be able to help get their music 'out there' (i.e. into the bedrooms of tens of other people ...).
>
> (Daniel, Homocrime 2006: 5)

The club's friendly, appreciative audience inspired many attendees to start making their own music (without worrying about the limits of their technical abilities). Performances could be shambolic, but they were usually greeted with enthusiasm and encouragement. This commitment to creating a space in which to enjoy music is shared by the Unskinny Bop DJs. Whereas Homocrime was a space in which to hear music that was absent from most gay venues, to create one's own music, to listen to friends perform and celebrate lo-fi, do-it-yourself production values, Unskinny Bop was motivated by overcoming other barriers to the full enjoyment of music:

> Unskinny Bop welcomes gals 'n' guys of all shapes and persuasions onto the dancefloor with open arms. We want you to experience the joy of dancing with wild, thrilling abandon to your favourite songs, unintimidated by fear of ridicule, evil stares and nasty comments. And we don't want it to stop here: as it is at the disco, so it shall be in life.
>
> (Unskinny Bop n.d.)

Club Wotever, although it has grown into an international phenomenon, originated in a similar DIY impulse to create a space that was more inclusive by dissolving the heteronormative gender binaries that predominate on the gay scene, as much as in the straight world. Club Wotever relies on amateur performers and a large proportion of its audience making the effort to dress up in homemade costumes for its theme nights in order to create the atmosphere that makes the club work as an alternative to the mainstream:

> We welcome all with a sense of humour – who like to dress up and flirt with all and everyone. This is a friendly place and we do our best to spread the LOVE. We are open for all genders, sexualities and expressions. The only thing we ask for is: RESPECT yourself and RESPECT others at the club, gig, screening or happening where we are. We are a non-profit organization who work hard to be able to share ourselves with you.
>
> (Club Wotever 2007)

The political implications of this commitment to the collective, participatory creation of an autonomous space that attempts to transcend and work through the exclusions frequently perpetuated in commodified venues, with a clearer distinction between the producers and consumers of entertainment, is more clearly posed in the following statement from the WANC website. Here, too, the political importance of sharing fun and laughter in the process of building prefigurative spaces of queer feminist autonomy is also reiterated:

> Women's Café is about ... using the power of music, cooking, eating and laughter as a way of understanding and uniting women from all backgrounds and walks of life, dissolving or celebrating our differences of sexuality or class. A place of mutual participation. A DIY space that is a panacea to passive consumption ... Like all places where freedom works, a structure is created and held, wherein anything can happen. It is a friendly space where anyone is accepted ... The café builds a community from our often fragmented inner city lifestyles. It anchors and roots us, providing us with positive reference points for who we are, all on our own terms, which is a political feat in itself!
>
> (WANC website, www.wanc-cafe.org.uk)

Many of the organisers of the various projects outlined in this section have an affinity with the anarcha-queer activism of the Queeruption networks and several have been active participants in shaping those gatherings and the related projects. Of all of these entertainment projects, WANC probably maintains the strongest and most obvious connections with more directly political forms of activism. It has run benefit nights to raise funds for activist initiatives and to pay off the fines imposed on activists for their participation in direct actions and protests. At one early WANC event, women from the Aldermaston Women's Peace Camp offered a skill-sharing workshop on the use of lock-on blockading techniques. Similarly, the themed café nights have often developed more improvised and spontaneous forms of entertainment, such as the 'tomboy night' that featured tree climbing in the local park and a conkers tournament. They have also more frequently breached the shell of the venue where the café has been hosted and led to performative interventions in the public sphere, for example when a flamenco theme led to the women staging a 'bull run' in the street outside.

Although the conventional gay male media have largely ignored the existence of these clubs, some elements of the lesbian media have occasionally run features promoting the existence of Club Wotever, WANC and Unskinny Bop as quirky alternatives to more traditional lesbian venues. If WANC has stayed closest in form to the autonomous spaces created through Queeruption gatherings, convergence spaces and social centres (Hodkinson and Chatterton 2006), Club Wotever has found a place for itself right on the edge of the commercial lesbian and gay scene. These clubs and cafés are situated across a broad spectrum of autonomous forms, from those that utilise squatted spaces, reclaimed materials and 'skipped' food, through to those that are more closely implicated in commercial transactions and business-like forms of organisation. Nevertheless, to some extent, they were all inspired by an amateur, DIY impulse to create a safe or inclusive space that satisfies needs and desires that are unmet on the commercial gay scene. They continue to operate on a not-for-profit basis. And, they encourage the active participation of their audiences as the co-producers of the space, rather than as consumers of a product. As such, they inhabit an autonomous queer geography.

Autonomous housekeeping

My final example is of several fleeting moments of autonomous action that I witnessed a few years ago in a 'cottage' (public toilet) in East London where men regularly cruised each other for sex (Brown 2008). This playful encounter is suggestive of what Nigel Thrift has identified as the possibilities for a politics of affect and 'tending' where the 'political imperative is to widen the potential number of interactions a living thing can enter into, [and] to widen the margin of "play"' (Thrift 2004b: 70). This is not a politics of demands or rights claims, but a politics of 'giving a chance to encounters and interactions that are partially invisible in the dominant regime and are excluded from the definition of what counts as knowledge' (Thrift 2004a: 84).

I see a glimmer of this impulse towards 'tending' in this incident. It occurred on a quiet night, when there was no cruising taking place, and in a period when the local council had neglected to clean the toilet for many weeks. In the absence of the flow of cruising men needed to keep the sexual energy of the cottage going, a small group of regulars, all of them by then friends, were huddled inside the toilet gossiping. After chatting for a while, they broke into the (abandoned) attendant's office, brought out two large jugs of detergent, mops and buckets, and started thoroughly cleaning the place.

At the time, this 'housekeeping' of the site amused me. It was certainly performed for effect. However, in hindsight this expression of care for a meaningful and strategic site by some of its users moves me in other ways. As Jon Binnie (2001) and Paul Hallam (1993) have argued, dirt and dereliction may contribute to the erotic appeal of such sites, but there are limits. At the time, the toilet was falling into a state of grimy disrepair that had moved beyond erotic frisson. As a result, despite the constant availability of access to the site and little risk of official interruption, many of the users of the site were abandoning it. There were more quiet nights than not. By taking it upon themselves to clean the site, this band of friends were performing an act of care for the site and ensuring its functional sustainability as a 'cottage' (as opposed to a semi-derelict public toilet). Their act of care-taking reveals an intuitive understanding of the importance of the fabric of the site to sustaining the potential for affective encounters between men (Brown 2008). The cruiser knows, viscerally, just how much dirt is needed to sustain the erotic potential of a public sex environment. In tending to this strategic site, I believe the men were asserting their autonomy as users of the space.

From autumn 2001 until the toilet's eventual long-term closure in 2004, there was a war of attrition between the cruisers, the police and council authorities, and some local residents who contested the increasing visibility of the site as a public sex environment. The council tried closing the site early or for long stretches of time. The police made regular, visible patrols in front of the toilet at night, occasionally looking inside (if it was open), but seldom doing more than moving men on or temporarily disrupting the cruising. Some of the local residents took matters into their own hands and, when the council suspended the evening closures for a while, turned up with their own padlocks and intimidation. In response, many of the regular cruisers actively defended *their* site, by their continuing presence, a refusal to be shamed by the police and occasional verbal confrontations with the disapproving locals. When the toilet was locked shut, it was frequently reclaimed as a cottage:

> As I walked down the steps, there was one very obvious change to the space. In addition to the horizontal shutter over the steps (that appeared some time last year, but which I have never seen shut over), there is now a very basic 'door' at the bottom of the stairs. This door is little more than a roughly trimmed sheet of plywood on a couple of hinges and with a padlock to seal it shut. This attempt to further prevent queer pleasure after dark appeared to have been as unsuccessful as all the other 'security' measures, as the door had obviously been forced open on a number of occasions and now looked only notionally secure.
>
> (Field note: The Toilet, 3 August 2002).

Of course, it is possible to argue that, at least to some extent, it was the cruisers' comfort and confidence in claiming the toilet as a public sex environment that ended up making it *too* visible, drawing unwanted attention to the site and accelerating its demise. That dynamic was certainly at work. However, something else of significance was definitely going on as well. In defending that space of multiple potentialities of pleasure, men were claiming an autonomous space. Both their appropriation of (otherwise heteronormative) public space and their tending of that space are indicative of an autonomous politics that exceeds the efforts of self-identified 'activist' networks. The men were asserting their autonomy to use a publicly owned space in a manner that asserted their right to difference. They were asserting their presence in the public realm *as a* public. As Ferrell has rhetorically enquired, paraphrasing Brecht, 'which is the worse crime, to outlaw public space, or to open public space to outlaws?' (Ferrell 2001: 224).

This minor, low-key mobilisation in defence of a politics of pleasure offers some hope in the face of increasing pessimism about the continuing viability of many public sex environments and the 'laboratories of love and friendship' that they sustain (Bell and Binnie 2000: 132). Although they are fewer and further between now than they were in the past, cottages and outdoor cruising grounds are still strategically important non-commercial spaces that can foster communality across class and ethnic distinctions. In these places actions speak louder than words, and they can serve to question and undermine rigid sexual identities and social norms. In the most secure and well established of sites, this communality begins to take the form of autonomous modes of being that demonstrate the potential for other ways of engaging with the fabric of the city and changing the means by which queer people relate to each other in queer ways.

Queer urban futures

In many ways, although these four examples have described quite a diverse range of events and spaces, all of them have arisen from groups of friends identifying unmet needs in their lives and taking collective, constructive direct action to rectify the problem or attempt to create what they desire. As a result, these spaces are directly experienced rather than mediated through the commodity. But they are not without their problems.

In this concluding section, I want to examine some of the continuing tensions and problems that exist in these spaces, but also draw out some of the potential that they offer for increasing the scope for autonomous modes of queer life in contemporary urban spaces. In doing so, I draw on elements of the wide-ranging discussion about queer autonomous spaces at the Anarchism and Sexuality conference, at which participants raised many concerns about how to overcome the limitations and persisting exclusions within sites that mean so much to so many of them. Discussants were concerned that in Western Europe and North America too many queer autonomous spaces remain predominantly 'white' environments (Jindal 2004; Starr 2006; cf. Kuntsman and Miyake 2008) and involve few people over the age of forty. Others worried that the process of experimenting with queer autonomous forms was still perceived as something 'we' do, that it has not escaped the 'activist ghetto' (Anonymous 2000a, 2000b). For some, there was concern that some activists have attempted to transplant forms of queer autonomy developed in one location, without adapting them sufficiently to the political and cultural dynamics of their own situation. In thinking about the limitations on how well experiments in queer autonomy travel, some participants voiced a concern that the hedonism, frivolity and sex-positive pleasures that have become central to Queeruption gatherings and similar spaces were not appropriate to all geographic locations. Certainly some activists stayed away from the 2006 Queeruption in Tel Aviv because they could not countenance having a sex party in a war zone (whilst others were equally adamant that the unleashing of queer exuberance was exactly the inspiration needed in such circumstances). Of course, as I have already noted, the centrality of public displays of 'sex radicalism' can be off-putting, offensive and exclusionary for some potential allies who, although queer and open to anarchist social politics, hold different sexual ethics. Although some of these concerns are specific to queer spaces, similar issues confront all of those committed to creating space for autonomous living. The ongoing process of seeking solutions to these problems is at the heart of claiming autonomy and living without deference to externally imposed norms. For example, Pickerill and Chatterton make the following observations with regard to the network of autonomous social centres operating in Britain:

> Continuing problems of internal hierarchies (of knowledge and competence) and boundaries of inclusion/exclusion exist within social centres.

> Many participants are acutely aware of outsiders' perceptions. Do they appear as ghettos that stop people from participating? Are they really connected to everyday issues? Is it easy for people to come and get involved? While no easy answers to these issues exist, addressing them is the bedrock of making autonomy. Interstitial living can also be a source of creativity, producing hybrid, flexible and transient identities, challenging the norms we live by and creating potential new interactions.
>
> (Pickerill and Chatterton 2006: 742)

Transformations of urban (or rural) space cannot be separated from the transformations of everyday life in those environments (Pinder 2005: 3). David Bell has suggested that the queer city can be found in the 'creative and wild possibilities' that are (barely) contained within the urban form (Bell 2001: 102). By exploiting these 'wild possibilities' and the gap between people's desires and their lived experience, modest alterations in the uses of the city in the here and now can reveal new forms of queer sociality, and *vice versa*.

The spaces and encounters described in this chapter, although not all directly and consciously inspired by anarchist thought, offer signposts towards a world in which more people care for themselves and others in diverse autonomous, self-organised ways. The case studies illustrate that experiments with autonomous modes of living are not the sole preserve of self-identified activists, but are enacted through a wide range of amateur endeavours that frequently start with a small group of like-minded friends, but draw wider networks of people into their processes. These amateur experiments suggest means of moving towards a more autonomous, equitable and compassionate society, without necessarily having all of the answers or solutions to how to get from 'here' to 'there'. Indeed, this approach recognises that there are no once-and-forever universal solutions, preferring instead an ongoing process of experimentation, change and adaptation. The process of creating more queer space in the city could begin with observing and interacting with what currently exists before changing anything and then attempting to make the least change for maximum effect. This might offer greater recognition of the significance of relative location to these observations and developments. The functioning of any given site is affected by what surrounds it. I hope ways can be found of extending to non-human objects and entities queer's ethical commitment to engaging with difference and relating ethically with others. In this, I would include the land upon which such experiments are built.

In their imaginative work on the diverse economy and existing post-capitalist social relations, J. K. Gibson-Graham (2006: 81) stress the importance of creating and maintaining 'commons', a process which they consider is

> by definition an ethical practice of being-in-common, one that informs material practices and social boundaries of community ... The commons

> can be seen as a community stock that needs to be maintained and replenished so that it can continue to constitute the community by providing its direct input (subsidy) to survival.
>
> (Gibson-Graham 2006: 96–7)

I would suggest that most (if not all) of the examples of queer autonomous spaces that I have offered in this chapter are important queer commons that foster alternative modes of communality, offer participants a chance to slow down, and attempt to offer cheap or free entertainment, services and support that are not dominated by capitalist social relations (Brown 2009). As such, I believe, these spaces need to be defended and extended.

So, what might a sustainable queer city look like? I hope it would be based upon spaces that promote social relations that foster 'responsibility, reciprocity, collectivism and mutuality' (Chatterton 2006: 261). The challenge ahead, for those of us who recognise the value and importance of autonomous queer spaces, is to resist imposing our (individual and collective) visions on others, but instead to invite and encourage them to experiment with the realisation of their own visions (Hern 2010).

I want to encourage a proliferation of diverse queer spaces across the urban landscape, rather than concentrating them in some 'radical' replication of 'gay ghettos'. This invitation to open forms of integration might need to be balanced or offset against an appreciation of the value and productivity of marginal spaces, identities and practices. Those who cultivate land according to permaculture principles (Whitefield 2002) recognise that the zone where different eco-systems meet (such as the edge of a forest or the rocky pools along the seashore) can often be highly fertile, innovative and productive places. Queer space does, and I hope will continue to, harness this 'edge effect'.[8] By encouraging the spread of a mosaic of queer spaces across the city, rather than concentrating and consolidating them in one space, queer people might be able to maximise the productive opportunities that arise from their interaction with other ways of living in the city (City Repair Project 2006). I hope that this would lead to a multiplicity of different modes of queer living that would exceed the limitations of what is currently on offer either on the commercial gay scene or through existing activist networks. I believe glimpses of what could be possible can be seen in a host of existing amateur networks.

Just as cruisers notice how the city's streets, buildings and open spaces resonate with particular states of mind and offer possibilities for the enactment of their erotic desires, so queer urban dwellers have the capacity to extend their repertoire of ways to observe, interact with and adapt the fabric of the city to better meet their unmet needs. Through these processes of active engagement in the (re)creation of urban space (Chatterton and Hollands 2003), queers can attempt to produce more spaces that can be directly experienced, imagined and reinvented for *queer* autonomous living.

Notes

1 At times, bringing this perspective into the realm of academic sexual geography has felt quite lonely, as few people seemed to appreciate the connections and analysis I was trying to make. Thankfully, I have been surrounded by many encouraging and supportive people along the way who have generously engaged with my work and offered constructive critiques. In particular, I would like to thank Loretta Lees, Tim Butler, Kath Browne, Jason Lim, Jamie Heckert, Carrie Hamilton, Jenny Pickerill, John Levin and Eleanor Wilkinson for all the friendly discussions over the years. I also want to remember Sam 'Tumbleweed' Roberts, who liked what I had to say, shared his own analysis of queer autonomy with me (at great length), but died horribly young in the months following the Leeds conference.

2 There is, to me, an obvious parallel between Holloway's 'power-to-do' and Starhawk's (1997) concept of 'power-with'.

3 The feminine form *anarcha* is generally used both to disrupt normative assumptions about gendered forms of (anarchist) activism and to stress the links between anarcha-queer and anarcha-feminist praxis (Dark Star 2002).

4 'Skiffle' is a form of folk jazz played on improvised instruments that was revived in the late 1950s in the UK (and USA) but had its origins in New Orleans earlier in the twentieth century.

5 Vegan food is commonly served at such events because it is cheap, does not involve the exploitation of animals and is inclusive of the dietary requirements of the largest number of participants.

6 I am willing to accept that this analysis might be too reliant on my own affective responses to participating in such gatherings. I recognise that participants may act flirtatiously in these circumstances because they are nervous and it helps them make connections with people or 'fit in', or because it helps demonstrate their 'queerness', or for a host of other reasons I have not yet considered.

7 Whilst I stand by this analysis, I thank Jamie Heckert for reminding me that participation in these types of gathering, event and action can also be physically and emotional tiring.

8 I see clear parallels between the ethics underpinning permaculture design and many contemporary visions of a society based on anarchist and autonomous principles. There is not, however, space in this chapter to fully explore either these connections or the full implications of associating queer social relations with permaculture's 'edge effect'.

References

Abram, D. (1996) *The Spell of the Sensuous*, New York: Vintage Books.

Anonymous (2000a) 'Give up Activism', *Do or Die: Voices from the Ecological Resistance* 9: 160–6.

——(2000b) 'Give up Activism: Postscript', *Do or Die: Voices from the Ecological Resistance* 9: 166–70.

Bell, D. (2001) 'Fragments for a Queer City', in D. Bell, J. Binnie, R. Holliday, R. Longhurst and R. Peace (eds), *Pleasure Zones: Bodies, Cities, Spaces*, Syracuse, NY: Syracuse University Press.

Bell, D. and Binnie, J. (2000) *The Sexual Citizen: Queer Politics and Beyond*, Cambridge: Polity Press.

Binnie, J. (2001) 'The Erotic Possibilities of the City', in D. Bell, J. Binnie, R. Holliday, R. Longhurst and R. Peace (eds), *Pleasure Zones: Bodies, Cities, Spaces*, Syracuse, NY: Syracuse University Press.

Bobel, C. (2007) '"I'm Not an Activist, Though I've Done a Lot of It": Doing Activism, Being Activist and the "Perfect Standard" in a Contemporary Movement', *Social Movement Studies* 6(2): 147–59.
Brown, G. (2007a) 'Autonomy, Affinity and Play in the Spaces of Radical Queer Activism', in K. Browne, J. Lim and G. Brown (eds), *Geographies of Sexualities: Theory, Practices and Politics*, Aldershot: Ashgate.
——(2007b) 'Mutinous Eruptions: Autonomous Spaces of Radical Queer Activism', *Environment & Planning A* 39(11): 2685–98.
——(2008) 'Ceramics, Clothing and Other Bodies: Affective Geographies of Homoerotic Cruising Encounters', *Social and Cultural Geography* 9(8): 915–32.
——(2009) 'Thinking beyond Homonormativity: Performative Explorations of Diverse Gay Economies', *Environment & Planning A* 41: 1496–510.
Brown, G. and Pickerill, J. (2009) 'Space for Emotion in the Spaces of Activism', *Emotion, Space and Society* 2(1): 24–35.
Castoriadis, C. (1991) *Philosophy, Politics, Autonomy: Essays in Political Philosophy*, Oxford: Oxford University Press.
Chatterton, P. (2006) '"Give Up Activism" and Change the World in Unknown Ways: Or, Learning to Walk with Others on Uncommon Ground', *Antipode* 38(2): 259–81.
Chatterton, P. and Hollands, R. (2003) *Urban Nightscapes: Youth Cultures, Pleasure Spaces and Corporate Power*, London: Routledge.
City Repair Project (2006) *The City Repair Project's Placemaking Guidebook: Neighbourhood Placemaking in the Public Right-of-Way*, Portland, OR: City Repair Project.
Club Wotever (2007) *Wotever World*. Online. Available HTTP: http://www.wotever-world.com (accessed 28 April 2010).
Culton, K. R. and Holtzman, B. (2010) 'The Growth and Disruption of a "Free Space": Examining a Suburban DIY Punk Scene', *Space and Culture* 13(3): 270–84.
Dark Star (eds) (2002) *Quiet Rumours. An Anarcha-feminist Reader*, Edinburgh/Oakland, CA: AK Press/Dark Star.
Day, R. J. F. (2005) *Gramsci is Dead: Anarchist Currents in the Newest Social Movements*, London/Ann Arbor, MI: Pluto Press.
Ferrell, J. (2001) *Tearing Down the Streets: Adventures in Urban Anarchy*, New York: Palgrave Macmillan.
Franks, B. (2006) *Rebel Alliances: The Means and Ends of Contemporary British Anarchisms*, Edinburgh/Oakland, CA: AK Press.
Gibson-Graham, J. K. (2006) *A Postcapitalist Politics*, Minneapolis: University of Minnesota Press.
Gordon, U. (2005) 'Anarchism and Political Theory: Contemporary Problems', unpublished DPhil thesis, University of Oxford. Online. Available HTTP: http://zinelibrary.info/files/anarchismpoliticaltheory.pdf (accessed 6 January 2011).
——(2007) *Anarchy Alive! Anti-authoritarian Politics from Practice to Theory*, London: Pluto Press.
Graeber, D. (2002) 'The New Anarchists', *New Left Review* 13: 61–73.
Hallam, P. (1993) *The Book of Sodom*, London: Verso.
Harvie, D., Milburn, K., Trott, B. and D. Watts (eds) (2005) *Shut Them Down! The G8, Gleneagles 2005 and the Movement of Movements*, Leeds: Dissent! and Autonomedia.
Heckert, J. (2002) 'Maintaining the Borders: Identity and Politics', *Greenpepper* (Autumn): 26–8.

——(2004) 'Sexuality/Identity/Politics', in J. Purkis and J. Bowen (eds), *Changing Anarchism: Anarchist Theory and Practice in a Global Age*, Manchester: Manchester University Press.

Hennen, P. (2004) 'Fae Spirits and Gender Trouble', *Journal of Contemporary Ethnography* 33(5): 499–533.

Hern, M. (2010) *Common Ground in a Liquid City: Essays in Defense of an Urban Future*, Edinburgh/Oakland, CA/Baltimore, MD: AK Press.

Hodkinson, S. and Chatterton, P. (2006) 'Autonomy in the City? Reflections on the Social Centres Movement in the UK', *City* 10(3): 305–15.

Holloway, J. (2002) *Change the World Without Taking Power*, London: Pluto Press.

Homocrime (2006) *Homospective* (self-produced zine; available from the author).

Jindal, P. (2004) 'Sites of Resistance or Sites of Racism?', in Mattilda Bernstein Sycamore (ed.), *That's Revolting! Queer Strategies for Resisting Assimilation*, New York: Soft Skull Press.

Knopp, L. (1992) 'Sexuality and the Spatial Dynamics of Capitalism', *Environment & Planning D: Society & Space* 10: 651–69.

Kuntsman, A. and Miyake, E. (eds) (2008) *Out of Place: Interrogating Silences in Queerness/Raciality*, York: Raw Nerve Books.

McKay, G. (1998) *DiY Culture: Party & Protest in Nineties Britain*, London: Verso.

Nast, H. J. (2002) 'Queer Patriarchies, Queer Racisms, International', *Antipode* 34(5): 877–909.

Olesen, T. (2005) *International Zapatismo: The Construction of Solidarity in the Age of Globalization*, London: Zed Books.

Peace, R. (2001) 'Producing Lesbians: Canonical Proprieties', in D. Bell, J. Binnie, R. Holliday, R. Longhurst and R. Peace (eds), *Pleasure Zones: Bodies, Cities, Spaces*, Syracuse, NY: Syracuse University Press.

Pickerill, J. and Chatterton, P. (2006) 'Notes towards Autonomous Geographies: Creation, Resistance and Self-management as Survival Tactics', *Progress in Human Geography* 30(6): 730–46.

Pinder, D. (2005) *Visions of the City*, Edinburgh: Edinburgh University Press.

Povinelli, E. A. (2006) *The Empire of Love: Towards a Theory of Intimacy, Genealogy and Carnality*, Durham, NC: Duke University Press.

QPC (n.d.) 'Why Queer Paganism?' Online. Available HTTP: http://www.queerpagancamp.org/ (accessed 28 April 2010).

Quilley, S. (1997) 'Constructing Manchester's "New Urban Village": Gay Space in the Entrepreneurial City', in G. B. Ingram, A.-M. Bouthillette and Y. Retter (eds), *Queers in Space: Communities/Public Places/Sites of Resistance*, Seattle, WA: Bay Press.

Rouhani, F. (forthcoming) 'The Richmond Queer Space Project: Building Bridges over Chasms We Create', *ACME: An International e-Journal for Critical Geographies*.

Routledge, P. (2003) 'Convergence Space: Process Geographies of Grassroots Globalization Nnetworks', *Transactions of the Institute of British Geographers* 28: 333–49.

——(2005) 'Grassrooting the Imaginary: Acting within the Convergence', *Ephemera: Theory and Politics in Organization* 5(4): 615–28.

Scott, J. C. (2009) *The Art of Not Being Governed: An Anarchist History of Upland Southeast Asia*, New Haven, CT: Yale University Press.

Spencer, A. (2005) *DIY: The Rise of Lo-fi Culture*, London: Marion Boyars Publishers.

Starhawk (1997) *Dreaming the Dark: Magic, Sex and Politics*, Boston, MA: Beacon Press.

Starr, A. (2006) 'Grumpywarriorcool: What Makes Our Movement So White?', in S. Best and A. J. Nocella (eds), *Igniting a Revolution: Voices in Defence of the Earth*, Edinburgh and Oakland, CA: AK Press.

Thrift, N. (2004a) 'Summoning Life', in P. Cloke, P. Crang and M. Goodwin (eds), *Envisioning Human Geographies*, London: Arnold.

——(2004b) 'Intensities of Feeling: Towards a Spatial Politics of Affect', *Geografiska Annaler* 86 B(1): 57–78.

Turner, M. W. (2003) *Backward Glances: Cruising the Queer Streets of New York and London*, London: Reaktion Books.

Unskinny Bop (n.d.) 'Mainfesto of Unskinny Bop'. Online. Available HTTP: http://www.unskinnybop.pwp.blueyonder.co.uk (accessed 28 April 2010).

Valentine, G. (1993) 'Negotiating and Managing Multiple Sexual Identities: Lesbian Time–Space Strategies', *Transactions of the Institute of British Geographers* 18(2): 237–248.

Vanelslander, B. (2007) 'Long Live Temporariness: Two Queer Examples of Autonomous Spaces', *Affinities: A Journal of Radical Theory* 1(1): 5–11. Online. Available HTTP: http://affinitiesjournal.org/index.php/affinities/article/viewFile/3/22 (accessed 28 April 2010).

WANC (n. d.) 'Why WANC?' Online. Available HTTP: http://www.wanc-cafe.org.uk (accessed 28 April 2010).

Whitefield, P. (2002) *Permaculture in a Nutshell*, East Meon, Hampshire: Permanent Publications.

Wilkinson, E. (2009) 'The Emotions Least Relevant to Politics? Queering Autonomous Activism', *Emotion, Space and Society* 2(1):36–43.

Chapter 11

Afterword

On the phenomenology of fishbowls

Kristina N. Weaver

I hitched my way to the conference in the back of an SUV captained by a military mum taking two teenagers on a grand tour of universities. The act of aiding and abetting myself, my traveling companion, and a bass guitar had been her second thought. Having passed us by, she then stopped and pulled over before entering the motorway. She had never before given a lift to a hitchhiker, but the sight of our bedraggled forms and the sparkle of her bright young daughters had encouraged her to bravery.

Once we were snug in the spare back seat (and provided with glossy gossip magazines to help us pass the time), our rescuer asked where we were headed. When I replied, "a conference about anarchism and sexuality," she gave us some sound advice: "Don't get arrested."

Not being a presenter, myself, I had expectations of the usual passive absorption typical of academic conferences—at best the chance to slot a few more nodes in my network of activist and academic contacts; at worst an encounter with the kinds of social policing so common in queer spaces. I did not think that was the kind of prison this concerned mum meant, and so I reassured her of my unarrestable status.

A few days later, my sights on the next adventure, I could confidently confirm that there had been no jail cell. I was not caught or cornered at that conference in Leeds. I was not stuck or stashed, labeled or locked away, but her predilection had not been far off. Captivated I had been, my breath frequently catching at the truths expressed, the stories witnessed, the theories spun, and the guards released. My mind had been arrested more than once by the magic of awakened life.

I subscribe to the viewpoint that we are all anarchists most of the time. We live and delight in the muddling through of mutual aid. Were this not my belief, I would not have bothered to stick out my thumb as a preferred mode of transportation to an academic conference. But I did not encounter the formal theories and practices of anarchism until my bright and early undergraduate days in the States, when the Battle of Seattle introduced me to the possibilities of effective experiments in nonhierarchy. By the time I was a postgraduate in Scotland and an attendee of the conference, I had become a seasoned participant/facilitator of marathon consensus meetings, makeshift spokescouncil sessions, real-time affinity group huddles, rebel clown army trainings, forum theater performances, and whatever other modes of radical process we could find a use for.

Conference organizer and dear friend Jamie shares my love of anarchist process, and upon meeting him in Leeds I was delighted to learn that he and Richard had designed this gathering with the express purpose of combining activist strategies for participation and discussion with the rigors and privileges of academic reflection. Collapse the binary distinction between the ivory tower and the social center, and see what survives. When Jamie asked me to facilitate one of the sessions, I was excited to be gifted a role in an experiment so many of us have dreamed of, flirted with, and squeezed into the margins of our work.

Jamie suggested a fishbowl, a prospect that scattered shivers across my skin. I had often read and heard of this methodology, used to encourage conversation capable of delving into issues and surfacing latent emotions. Anarcho-nerd that I am, I was both thrilled and terrified to be charged with setting up this process after one of the morning's panel sessions.

Jamie and I conferred briefly on the rules of the game. Variations exist, of course, but the fishbowl we devised took the following shape. After the usual panel of paper presenters, session attendees were enlisted to clear the room of all but four chairs, which we arranged in a circle in the center of the space. Participants were then invited to form a larger ring around the chairs. Three volunteers occupied the center of the circle and engaged in open discussion on the topics that had been introduced by the panelists. The rest of us were tasked with the practice of active and mindful listening. At any time, a fourth person from the audience ring could silently occupy the vacant chair in the "fishbowl." One of the original speakers would then be required to silently and promptly volunteer to leave the center, thereby sustaining a continual rotation and preserving the form of the method.

As it happened, I had never before facilitated a group experience that required so little active work on my part. If explained well and enacted by willing and present participants, the fishbowl method is truly self-facilitating. It requires a dedicated exploration of external as well as internal dynamics of power. Those who are accustomed to taking up space and using up time become very aware of the requirement to share the privilege of speaking. Those who prefer the silent margins experience the visibility of this conditioning and are encouraged to step into the experiment of being heard, of being seen.

On this particular occasion, this conscious interplay of power and engagement yielded a fascinating, complex conversation. Precisely because the discourse was bounded in such an elegant form, its circuit was liberated to follow multiple leads, to retrace steps, to falter and begin again, to dive into surprising depths. Our fishbowl covered a wide range of challenging issues. Full-time activists, many of whom had been skeptical of the value of the conference before arriving, here experienced the opportunity to speak and reflect at length, with no particular goal or intention. Many expressed gratitude for the quality of listening in the room, the active interest of others in a number of frustrations, hopes, and dreams that were not on the initial agenda. Academics commented on the simple freedom found in forming a circle of fellowship at an academic conference—a forum where hierarchy ordinarily holds sway. Panelists enjoyed the rare experience of witnessing a present-time application of the ideas they had offered up.

More than what was spoken, when I think of the Anarchism and Sexuality conference fishbowl I remember the pleasure we felt in creating it. Above all, a fishbowl requires that we take a genuine interest in one another. There was a sense of joint ownership and mutual discovery that animate the experience of learning at its best. The question and answer time allotted to that panel went at least forty minutes over schedule, until we were forced to break the trance. As participants poured out of the room into the remainder of the day, I remember marveling at shining faces, listening eyes, and a resilient quality of possibility.

Since that time, the fishbowl has become a treasured tool in my kit of anarchist praxis. I taught the method to a collective of young Nigerian activists working on issues of public health and urban development in Ibadan, one of Africa's most ancient and populous cities. They were excited to use it as a way of drawing out complex attitudes around the centralized leadership of their organization and the future direction of their work. I facilitated a fishbowl as a strategy for safely sustaining frank conversation about racism in a mixed race discussion and action group convened in a polarized city in Central Virginia. Most recently, after teaching the method to members of a forum theater collective I work with, I was delighted to experience its reinterpretation. Members of the group were inspired to craft a silent fishbowl that employed contact improvisation dance and other modes of physical theater, allowing for the nonverbal exploration of interrelational tensions, liberations, desires, and expressions.

These are reasons people come to the Academy. These are reasons people take to the Streets. I look forward to my next adventure in self-facilitated sharing, a possibility embodied for me by the Anarchism and Sexuality conference. At the end of the day and over breakfast the next morning, I heard how the experiment this conference undertook served as a much-needed success and restoration in the lives of many of its enactors. I left Leeds with the impression of shared feelings of substantial nourishment through one another, a looser grasp on my own identities and a firmer conviction in the powers of intersection, interdiscipline, and interdependence. I remain grateful for the opportunity I was offered to participate in this alchemy, and for the courage of a mother in an SUV who made the passing choice to help a few strangers get to Leeds on time.

Index

VOLUME ONE HUNDRED AND TWENTY

ADVANCES IN IMMUNOLOGY

Development and Function of Myeloid Subsets

Edited by

KENNETH M. MURPHY

Washington University, School of Medicine, St. Louis, Missouri, USA

MIRIAM MERAD

Icahn School of Medicine at Mount Sinai, New York, USA

Series Editor

FREDERICK W. ALT

Howard Hughes Medical Institute, Boston, Massachusetts, USA

ELSEVIER

AMSTERDAM • BOSTON • HEIDELBERG • LONDON
NEW YORK • OXFORD • PARIS • SAN DIEGO
SAN FRANCISCO • SINGAPORE • SYDNEY • TOKYO
Academic Press is an imprint of Elsevier

Academic Press is an imprint of Elsevier
525 B Street, Suite 1800, San Diego, CA 92101-4495, USA
225 Wyman Street, Waltham, MA 02451, USA
The Boulevard, Langford Lane, Kidlington, Oxford, OX5 1GB, UK
32 Jamestown Road, London, NW1 7BY, UK
Radarweg 29, PO Box 211, 1000 AE Amsterdam, The Netherlands

First edition 2013

ISBN: 978-0-12-417028-5
ISSN: 0065-2776

For information on all Academic Press publications
visit our website at store.elsevier.com

CONTENTS

CONTRIBUTORS

Carl E. Allen
Texas Children's Cancer Center, and Baylor College of Medicine, Houston, Texas, USA

Gabrielle T. Belz
Division of Molecular Immunology, Walter and Eliza Hall Institute of Medical Research, and Department of Medical Biology, University of Melbourne, Melbourne, Victoria, Australia

Marie-Luise Berres
Department of Oncological Sciences, Tisch Cancer Institute, and Immunology Institute, Icahn School of Medicine at Mount Sinai, New York, USA

Silvia Cerboni
Institut Curie, and INSERM U932, Paris, France

Matthew Collin
Institute of Cellular Medicine, Newcastle University, Newcastle upon Tyne, United Kingdom

Matteo Gentili
Institut Curie, and INSERM U932, Paris, France

Florent Ginhoux
Singapore Immunology Network (SIgN), Agency for Science, Technology and Research (A*STAR), Singapore

Muzlifah Haniffa
Institute of Cellular Medicine, Newcastle University, Newcastle upon Tyne, United Kingdom

Steffen Jung
Department of Immunology, Weizmann Institute of Science, Rehovot, Israel

Massimo Locati
Humanitas Clinical and Research Center, Rozzano, and Department of Medical Biotechnologies and Translational Medicine, University of Milan, Milan, Italy

Nicolas Manel
Institut Curie, and INSERM U932, Paris, France

Alberto Mantovani
Humanitas Clinical and Research Center, Rozzano, and Department of Medical Biotechnologies and Translational Medicine, University of Milan, Milan, Italy

Miriam Merad
Department of Oncological Sciences, Tisch Cancer Institute, and Immunology Institute, Icahn School of Medicine at Mount Sinai, New York, USA

Alexander Mildner
Department of Immunology, Weizmann Institute of Science, Rehovot, Israel

Kaaweh Molawi
Centre d'Immunologie de Marseille-Luminy, France, and Max Delbrueck Center for Molecular Medicine, Berlin, Germany

Kenneth M. Murphy
School of Medicine, Department of Pathology and Immunology, and Howard Hughes Medical Institute, Washington University, St. Louis, Missouri, USA

Shalin Naik
The Walter and Eliza Hall Institute, Melbourne, Australia, and Division of Immunology, The Netherlands Cancer Institute, Amsterdam, The Netherlands

Meredith O'Keeffe
Centre for Immunology, Burnet Institute, Melbourne, and Department of Immunology, Monash University, Clayton, Australia

Andrew M. Platt
Institute of Immunology, Infection and Inflammation, Glasgow Biomedical Research Centre, University of Glasgow, Glasgow, United Kingdom

Gwendalyn J. Randolph
Department of Pathology and Immunology, Washington University, St. Louis, Missouri, USA

Priyanka Sathe
The Walter and Eliza Hall Institute, Melbourne, Australia, and Immunology Institute, Mount Sinai School of Medicine, New York, USA

Cyril Seillet
Division of Molecular Immunology, Walter and Eliza Hall Institute of Medical Research, and Department of Medical Biology, University of Melbourne, Melbourne, Victoria, Australia

Ken Shortman
The Walter and Eliza Hall Institute, and Centre for Immunology, Burnet Institute, Melbourne, Australia

Antonio Sica
Humanitas Clinical and Research Center, Rozzano, Milan, and Department of Pharmaceutical Sciences, Università del Piemonte Orientale "Amedeo Avogadro", Novara, Italy

Michael H. Sieweke
Centre d'Immunologie de Marseille-Luminy, France, and Max Delbrueck Center for Molecular Medicine, Berlin, Germany

David Vremec
The Walter and Eliza Hall Institute, Melbourne, Australia

Simon Yona
Department of Immunology, Weizmann Institute of Science, Rehovot, Israel

CHAPTER ONE

Ontogeny and Functional Specialization of Dendritic Cells in Human and Mouse

Muzlifah Haniffa[*,1], **Matthew Collin**[*], **Florent Ginhoux**[†,1]
[*]Institute of Cellular Medicine, Newcastle University, Newcastle upon Tyne, United Kingdom
[†]Singapore Immunology Network (SIgN), Agency for Science, Technology and Research (A*STAR), Singapore
[1]Corresponding author: e-mail address: m.a.haniffa@ncl.ac.uk; florent_ginhoux@immunol.a-star.edu.sg

Contents

Advances in Immunology, Volume 120
ISSN 0065-2776
http://dx.doi.org/10.1016/B978-0-12-417028-5.00001-6

Abstract

Dendritic cells (DCs) are a heterogeneous group of functionally specialized antigen-presenting cells that initiate and orchestrate immune responses. Our understanding of DC immunobiology has been largely shaped by research using murine models. The relevance of murine findings on human DC organization and function is only just beginning to be investigated. In this chapter, we present the key historical developments and recent advances in human and mouse DC research to contextualize the existing knowledge on DC subset origin and functional specializations. We also propose a framework to align human and mouse DC networks to enhance our understanding of the parallel organization of DCs in both species in order to facilitate the full exploitation of our knowledge on DC biology and function for clinical therapeutic strategies.

1. INTRODUCTION

Dendritic cells (DCs) are a class of bone marrow (BM)-derived cells found in the blood, lymphoid, interstitial, and epithelial tissues. DCs are equipped with sensors to recognize pathogens, vaccines, and self-antigens; process and present the relevant antigenic moieties to lymphocytes; and direct the type, magnitude, and specificity of immune responses. Recent advances using murine models have helped to define DCs as a distinct hematopoietic lineage and to separate them from other members of the mononuclear phagocyte system (MPS), which also include blood monocytes and tissue macrophages. Ontogeny and functional specializations of different DC subsets in murine studies are beginning to be unraveled. However, the translation of these findings to human biology remains uncertain. The aim of this chapter is to present a framework to align human and mouse DC networks to facilitate the full exploitation of current knowledge on DC biology and function for clinical therapeutic strategies.

2. HISTORY OF DC IDENTIFICATION AND CHARACTERIZATION

2.1. Mouse DCs

The capacity to generate diverse and specific responses to a wide range of antigens, a hallmark of the vertebrate immune system, was well recognized in the late 1950s (Burnet, 1957). However, the initiating events that led to antigen recognition by lymphocytes puzzled many researchers. The pursuit to answer this important question gave birth to the discovery of DCs by the late Nobel Laureate Ralph Steinman in the laboratory of Zanvil Cohn in 1973 (Steinman & Cohn, 1973). The spleen was known to harbor accessory cells important to initiate antibody responses. Investigation of spleen cell suspension identified a rare cell type (<1% of all adherent cells) with probing morphology. These cells were structurally distinct from macrophages and possessed poor phagocytic capacity. The appearance of branching structures when the live cells were viewed by phase contrast microscopy gave rise to the name dendritic (from the Greek *dendron*, meaning tree) (Steinman & Cohn, 1973). The evidence that DCs were indeed the principal initiator of an immune response came several years later when they were shown to be the critical component of accessory cells that stimulated mixed leukocyte reaction (MLR) (Steinman & Witmer, 1978). Although MLR was a useful tool, it did not test the specific ability of DCs to process complex antigen and initiate an antigen-specific response. DCs were later shown to be potent inducers of antigen-specific cellular and humoral immune responses (Inaba, Steinman, Van Voorhis, & Muramatsu, 1983; Nussenzweig, Steinman, Gutchinov, & Cohn, 1980). DCs were demonstrated to present antigen using major histocompatibility complex (MHC) Class II (MHC-II) molecules on their cell surface, but importantly, unlike any other MHC-II-expressing cells, including macrophages and B cells, DCs were the principal activator of naïve T cells (reviewed in Steinman & Nussenzweig, 1980).

Splenic DCs were found to express MHC-II and the integrin CD11c (Metlay et al., 1990; Steinman, Kaplan, Witmer, & Cohn, 1979). Later, epidermal Langerhans cells (LCs) were also noted to express MHC-II (Stingl, Katz, Shevach, Wolff-Schreiner, & Green, 1978). Although Paul Langerhans had identified LCs in human epidermis in 1868, they were believed to be intraepidermal nerve endings due to their impregnation by the neuronal label gold chloride (Langerhans, 1868). LCs were also found to possess similar immunogenic functions as splenic DCs (Stingl, Katz, Clement, Green, & Shevach, 1978). This led to the idea that DCs may be more widespread than previously assumed and was proven by subsequent studies demonstrating the presence of DCs that constitutively express MHC-II in the interstitial tissues of the lung, heart, liver, thyroid, pancreas, skin, kidney, ureter, and bladder but not brain (Hart & Fabre, 1981; Sertl et al., 1986; Tse & Cooper, 1990).

DCs in peripheral tissues need to access lymph nodes (LNs) in order to deliver antigen and interact with and activate naïve T cells. LCs and interstitial tissue DCs were shown to migrate through lymphatics to reach draining LNs (Balfour, Drexhage, Kamperdijk, & Hoefsmit, 1981; Kelly, Balfour, Armstrong, & Griffiths, 1978). These early studies were followed by parallel investigations on DC migration to the spleen and LN through circulating blood (Austyn, Kupiec-Weglinski, Hankins, & Morris, 1988). These studies, collectively, highlighted the importance of the lymphatics as a conduit for peripheral tissue DCs and the blood stream as the migratory route for circulating antigen-loaded DCs to access the spleen and LN.

The ability of LCs to migrate spontaneously from the epidermis cultured *in vitro* led to the extensive use of this model to dissect the properties of peripheral DCs (Larsen et al., 1990). An important finding from these early LC studies was the need for DCs to undergo phenotypic and functional "maturation" to unleash their full immune-stimulating potential (Schuler & Steinman, 1985). Immature DCs were effective at capturing antigens, but maturation is required to activate lymphocytes to the captured antigens (Romani et al., 1989). A variety of maturation signals have been studied including microbial products (e.g., lipopolysaccharide (LPS), flagellin, and viral nucleic acids), endogenous molecules (e.g., HMGB1), cytokines, and cell surface ligands recognizing receptors on DCs (CD40L).

The demonstration of a BM precursor origin for both splenic DCs and LCs (Steinman, Lustig, & Cohn, 1974) also facilitated the development of culture protocols to generate BM-derived DCs *in vitro* (Inaba et al., 1992).

CD8 ($\alpha\alpha$ form) expression on a subset of resident splenic and thymic DCs was the first demonstration that DCs within one tissue were phenotypically heterogeneous (Vremec et al., 1992). CD8$^-$ splenic DCs were later defined by CD11b expression (Vremec & Shortman, 1997), and a further refinement to the CD11b$^+$ fraction was made by studying CD4 expression, which divides splenic DCs into CD8$^+$CD11b$^-$CD4$^-$ (CD8$^+$ DCs), CD8$^-$CD11b$^+$CD4$^+$ (CD4$^+$ DCs), and CD8$^-$CD11b$^+$CD4$^-$ (double-negative DCs) (Vremec, Pooley, Hochrein, Wu, & Shortman, 2000). More recently, high expression of endothelial cell-specific adhesion molecule (ESAM) was shown to characterize CD4$^+$ splenic DCs (Lewis et al., 2011).

Heterogeneity within interstitial nonlymphoid tissue (NLT) DCs was first demonstrated by differential expression of CD103 in the gut (Annacker et al., 2005). The lung CD103$^+$ DC transcriptome was also noted to have high expression of the C-type lectin langerin, a marker initially thought to be exclusive to LCs (Sung et al., 2006). The generation of DC depletion models that were dependent on langerin expression confirmed that langerin was restricted not only to LCs but also on a subset of dermal- and skin-draining LN DCs coexpressing CD103 and distinct from

LCs (Bursch et al., 2007; Ginhoux et al., 2007; Poulin et al., 2007). NLT DCs are now broadly divided into two subsets characterized by the mutually exclusive expression of CD103 and CD11b (Ginhoux et al., 2009), except in the lamina propria where an additional subset coexpressing CD103 and CD11b can be found (Bogunovic et al., 2009).

The discovery of human plasmacytoid DCs (pDCs) (Grouard et al., 1997; Siegal et al., 1999) prompted the search for murine pDCs, which were identified in 2001 (Asselin-Paturel et al., 2001; Bjorck, 2001; Nakano, Yanagita, & Gunn, 2001). More recently, a $CD8^{+}CX3CR1^{+}$ DC subset related to pDCs was identified in mouse spleen (Bar-On et al., 2010).

In addition to steady-state DCs described so far, inflammation results in the influx of distinct populations that are presumed to arise from circulating monocytes. There are two distinct types of murine "inflammatory DCs" described. The first type was observed in the spleen of mice infected with *Listeria monocytogenes* and is characterized by the production of vast quantities of TNF-α and iNOS (Tip-DCs) (Serbina, Salazar-Mather, Biron, Kuziel, & Pamer, 2003). The second type, identified more recently, was found in the LN following LPS treatment (Cheong et al., 2010).

2.2. Human DCs

The two most accessible human tissues to study leukocytes are the peripheral blood and skin. This was in contrast to the lymphoid tissues (LTs), such as the spleen and LN, as the early focus of murine DC studies. In 1982, the search for DCs similar to those of mouse lymphoid organs in human peripheral blood identified a rare population of cells (<1% of mononuclear cells) with cytological features as mouse DCs, expressing MHC-II and potent allo-activators (Van Voorhis, Hair, Steinman, & Kaplan, 1982). Human DCs express high levels of MHC-II (HLA-DR) and lack typical lineage markers CD3 (T cell), CD19/20 (B cell), and CD56 (natural killer (NK) cell). The classical descriptions of DCs as HLA-DR^{+} $lineage^{-}$ cells have been refined to exclude monocytes expressing CD14 and CD16 but include a number of positive DC lineage markers (Ziegler-Heitbrock et al., 2010). Current nomenclature describes two myeloid DC subsets characterized by the expression of CD1c/BDCA-1 and CD141/BDCA-3 in human peripheral blood (MacDonald et al., 2002; Ziegler-Heitbrock et al., 2010).

Human epidermal LC was the first tissue DC to be described. LCs are positive for CD36, ATPase, and FcεR1 (reviewed in Romani, Brunner, & Stingl, 2012). Intracellular tennis racket-shaped Birbeck granules are visible by electron microscopy. LCs are now identified as CD1a bright cells coexpressing the C-type lectin langerin, EpCAM, and E-cadherin (reviewed in Romani et al., 2012). The first description of dermal DC was made in 1983 as a HLA-DR$^+$ "indeterminate cell" (Czernielewski, Schmitt, Faure, & Thivolet, 1983). In the early 1990s, two dermal DC subsets characterized by the expression of CD1a and CD14 were characterized (Lenz, Heine, Schuler, & Romani, 1993; Nestle, Zheng, Thompson, Turka, & Nickoloff, 1993). CD1a$^+$ dermal DCs distinct from CD1a^{++} epidermal LCs were identified from digested dermal preparations (Lenz et al., 1993). Studies on spontaneously migrating cells from dermal explants cultured *ex vivo* identified the presence of CD14$^+$ dermal DCs in addition to CD1a$^+$ DCs (Nestle et al., 1993). Although CD14 has been historically used in histopathology analysis to identify macrophages, the spontaneous migratory property of the CD14$^+$ cells from skin explants resulted in their classification as DCs. In situ, the CD14$^+$ DC is not easily distinguishable from dermal macrophages (Zaba, Fuentes-Duculan, Steinman, Krueger, & Lowes, 2007), but flow cytometry of dermal cell suspension allows the separation of SSC^{hi} autofluorescent dermal macrophages from CD14$^+$ DCs (Haniffa et al., 2009).

The different nomenclature used to define blood and tissue DCs has made it difficult to unify the human DC network. We recently showed that by using the same flow cytometry analysis of blood and cell suspension from the skin, liver, and lung, two myeloid DC subsets identical to blood CD1c$^+$ and CD141$^+$ DCs can be identified in human peripheral tissues (Haniffa et al., 2012). In addition, human tissues also contain CD14$^+$ DCs, which do not have a counterpart in peripheral blood (Haniffa et al., 2012). As CD1a is an antigen expressed by interstitial DCs in human skin but not in other tissues and all dermal CD1a$^+$ DCs coexpress CD1c (Haniffa et al., 2012; Zaba et al., 2007), we will refer to these cells as CD1c$^+$ migratory DCs hereafter.

The logistical difficulties of studying primary human blood and tissue DCs were eased by the discovery in the early 1990s of *in vitro* DC generation protocols from blood monocytes, using granulocyte macrophage colony-stimulating factor (GM-CSF) and IL-4 (Romani et al., 1994; Sallusto & Lanzavecchia, 1994), and CD34$^+$ hematopoietic stem cells (HSCs) from cord blood (Caux et al., 1996) and BM (Reid, Stackpoole, Meager, & Tikerpae, 1992), using GM-CSF and TNF-α. These *in vitro* culture models allowed the generation of large quantities of CD1a$^+$ and CD14$^+$ DCs from

$CD34^+$ HSCs and peripheral blood monocytes. The phenotypic resemblance of the *in vitro*-generated cells to the interstitial dermal DCs resulted in their widespread use as surrogates of primary human DCs. The important role of the Fms-like tyrosine kinase 3 ligand (FLT3L) in DC hematopoiesis only became apparent later, and the more modern protocols using $CD34^+$ HSC cultures include the addition of this DC-poietin (Maraskovsky et al., 1996, 2000; McKenna, de Vries, Brasel, Lyman, & Williams, 1995; Poulin et al., 2010). Although major advances were made in understanding human DC biology using *in vitro*-generated cells, their physiological relevance and *in vivo* equivalents are still uncertain as monocyte-derived DCs appear to be distinct in function and gene expression profile from steady-state DC populations (Harman et al., 2013; Osugi, Vuckovic, & Hart, 2002; Robbins et al., 2008).

In 1997, a $Lin^-HLA\text{-}DR^+$ plasmacytoid cell distinct to known myeloid DC was identified in human LTs and peripheral blood (Grouard et al., 1997; Olweus et al., 1997). These cells were historically known as plasmacytoid T cells or plasmacytoid monocytes due to their expression of CD4, CD45RA, and morphological appearance resembling plasma cells (Grouard et al., 1997; Olweus et al., 1997). The lack of the T cell antigen, CD3, and the myeloid antigens CD11b, CD11c, CD13, and CD33 in the context of high MHC-II expression identified them as a distinct entity of leukocytes and was subsequently shown to differentiate into DCs upon culture with IL-3 and CD40L (Cella et al., 1999; O'Doherty et al., 1994; Siegal et al., 1999). pDCs are the same entity as the previously described "natural interferon-producing cells" (Cella et al., 1999; O'Doherty et al., 1994; Siegal et al., 1999).

In contrast to the major advances in murine LT DC studies, limited access to primary material hampered parallel progress on human LT DCs. Both myeloid DC subsets and pDC have been described in human LTs, in addition to a number of $CD14^+$ populations (Cox et al., 2005; Segura et al., 2012; Takahashi et al., 1998; van de Ven et al., 2011).

Inflammatory DCs have also been described in humans. TNF-α and iNOS producing DCs (Tip-DCs), 6-sulfo LacNAc expressing DCs (slan DCs), and pDCs have been demonstrated in inflamed skin (Lowes et al., 2005; Nestle et al., 2005; Zaba, Krueger, & Lowes, 2009). More recently, inflammatory DCs and macrophages have also been described in inflamed synovial and ascitic fluids (Segura et al., 2013). The origin of human inflammatory DCs and the contribution of peripheral blood monocyte subsets to tissue antigen-presenting cells remain to be defined.

2.3. Classification of mouse and human DCs

DCs can be divided into distinct subsets by anatomical location and diversity in phenotype and function. The anatomical division separates "resident" LT DCs from "migratory" NLT DCs. The latter leave peripheral tissues to enter draining LNs via afferent lymphatics. Migration of murine NLT DCs to LNs via lymphatics is regulated by the chemokine receptor CCR7 (Ohl et al., 2004). DCs migrate to LNs in the steady state and during inflammation. Steady-state migration is not accompanied by full DC maturation and can lead to immune tolerance to the antigen presented (reviewed in Steinman et al., 2003). This contrasts with migration during inflammation, accompanied by upregulation of costimulatory receptors in the presence of proinflammatory cytokines, which generates immunity. The cues driving steady-state migration *in vivo* are unknown.

In mouse, resident LT DCs are often referred to as "classical" or "conventional" DCs to distinguish them from pDCs and migratory DCs. LTs with afferent lymphatics such as LNs are populated by both resident and migratory DC subsets. Resident DCs in LNs are found along the subcapsular sinus and LN conduits, but migratory DCs aggregate in the paracortical T cell zone (Sixt et al., 2005; Villadangos & Schnorrer, 2007). The distinction between resident and migratory myeloid DCs can be made in both human and mouse by the differential expression of $CD11c^{hi}MHC\text{-}II^{lo}$ that delineates resident DCs from $CD11c^{lo}MHC\text{-}II^{hi}$ migratory DCs (Dakic et al., 2004; Haniffa et al., 2012). Human LN migratory DCs have higher expression of CD80, CD83, and CD86 compared to LN-resident DCs (Haniffa et al., 2012).

A second anatomical compartment distinguishes epithelial DCs such as epidermal LCs from interstitial DCs. The third steady-state anatomical compartment is peripheral blood. Circulating human blood DCs have a more immature phenotype and require maturation *ex vivo* to develop the full characteristics of a DC (MacDonald et al., 2002). In contrast, $MHC\text{-}II^{-}$ circulating DC precursors are found in mouse blood, which can mature into $MHC\text{-}II^{+}$ DCs in peripheral tissue (Inaba, Steinman, et al., 1992; Liu et al., 2009).

In human, MHC-II is not a DC maturation marker but is constitutively expressed even by $CD34^{+}$ HSC precursors. It is tempting to speculate that human blood DCs are in fact tissue DC precursors as was suggested by recent transcriptomic analysis and *in vitro* experiments (Haniffa et al., 2012). Human blood DCs are also not in active cell cycle reminiscent of mouse circulating classical DC precursors (pre-DCs) in contrast to tissue DCs, which appear to enter cell cycle locally (Haniffa et al., 2009, 2012). Comparative assessment of the mouse blood compartment to interrogate the homology between mouse pre-DCs and human blood DCs will be revealing.

A second classification of DC stems from their diversity in phenotype and function and is described by the current nomenclature to define DC subsets as detailed in the previous sections. In addition, the terminology "myeloid" DCs is also used to contrast all LT and NLT DCs from pDCs, which were originally described as "lymphoid" due to their secretory morphology that resembles plasma cells. The terminology "lymphoid" is confusing and is no longer used in DC nomenclature.

3. RECENT ADVANCES IN MOUSE DC IMMUNOBIOLOGY: LESSONS FROM A RODENT

As described earlier, the heterogeneity of murine DC populations has only been recently unraveled. The efforts to delineate the relationships between LT and NLT DC subsets were resolved by combining common developmental requirements (genetic approach) and immune specializations (functional approach). The key concepts that have emerged from these studies are the following: firstly, DCs arise from a unique hematopoietic lineage independently of monocytes; secondly, DC heterogeneity is developmentally determined; and thirdly, ontogeny imprints functional specialization of DC populations. An excellent case in point is the common developmental origin and functional properties of $CD8^+$ and $CD103^+$ DCs despite their apparent phenotypic differences. In the following section, we summarize the characteristic phenotype, distribution, origin, function, and developmental relationships of murine DC subsets. Figure 1.1 shows the origin and organization of mouse and human DC networks.

3.1. Origin and differentiation of mouse DCs

Recent studies on DC ontogeny have begun to shed light on the organization of murine DC lineage and the relationships between the various subsets. Identification of the progenitors that contribute to steady-state DCs has outlined a DC-restricted lineage that originates from the BM to give rise to all DCs (for review, Geissmann et al., 2010), apart from LCs, which derive from embryonic precursors (Hoeffel et al., 2012; Fig. 1.1). The macrophage and DC precursor (MDP; phenotype: Lin^-Sca1^--$IL7R\alpha^-c\text{-}kit^+CX3CR1^+CD115^+$) gives rise to monocytes and to the common DC precursor (CDP; phenotype:

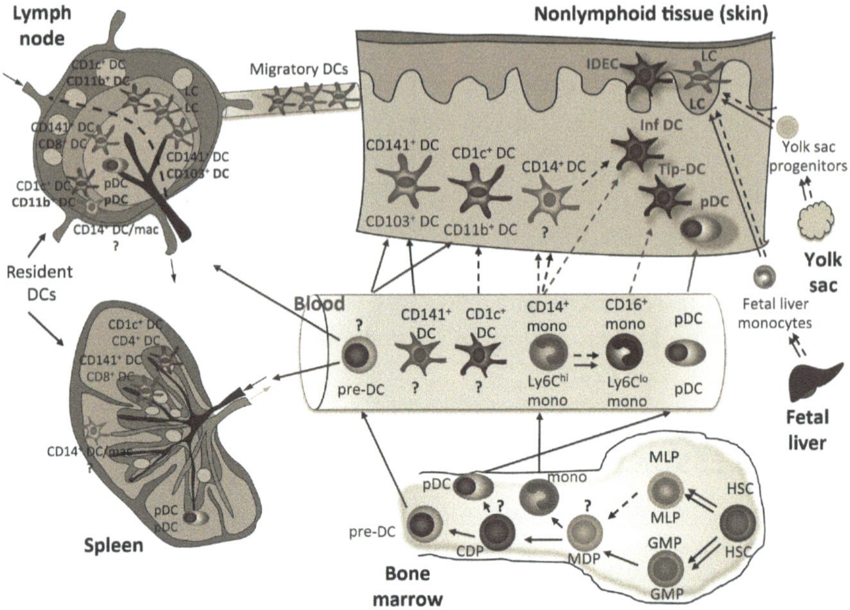

Figure 1.1 Origin and organization of human and mouse dendritic cell networks. Precursors, monocytes, and DC subsets are annotated in black for human. The mouse homologues of human subsets are annotated in blue underneath the cell type or human terminology. Question mark indicates unknown identity for the relevant species, black for human and blue for mouse. Origin and relationship of precursors, monocytes, and DC subsets to one another are indicated by black arrows (human) and blue arrows (mouse). Proven origin and relationships are indicated by solid arrows and speculative relationships by dashed arrows. Changes during inflammation are indicated by red text and arrows. HSC, hematopoietic stem cells; MLP, mixed lymphoid progenitors; GMP, granulocyte macrophage progenitors; MDP, macrophage/DC precursor; CDP, common DC precursor; pre-DC, DC precursor; pDCs, plasmacytoid DCs; mac, macrophage; mono, monocytes; inf DC, inflammatory DCs; IDEC, inflammatory dendritic epidermal cell; Tip-DC, TNF-α and iNOS-producing DC. (See color plate.)

Lin$^-$Sca1$^-$IL7Rα^-CD16/32^{lo}c-kit^{int}CD115$^+$CD135$^+$), which has lost monocyte/macrophage differential potential and gives rise exclusively to DCs, via a circulating precursor, the pre-DC (phenotype: Lin$^-$c-kit$^-$CD16/32$^-$CX3CR1$^+$CD135$^+$CD11c$^+$ MHC-II$^-$CD45RA^{lo}CD43^{int} SIRPa^{int}CD4$^-$CD8$^-$) (Liu et al., 2009). Pre-DCs migrate from the BM through the blood to the lymphoid (Liu et al., 2009) and nonlymphoid (Ginhoux et al., 2009) organs, where they differentiate into both CD8$^+$ and CD4$^+$CD11b$^+$ DCs and the CD103$^+$ and CD11b$^+$ DC populations, respectively. These findings underline the common lineage of both LT and NLT DCs.

Recently, the expression of the transcription factor (TF) Zbtb46 (BTBD4) was identified in pre-DCs and classical DCs but not in monocytes and macrophages (Meredith et al., 2012; Satpathy et al., 2012). The Zbtb46 reporter mouse and DTR model have unequivocally delineated the common DC lineage shared by LT and NLT DCs and their committed precursors from pDCs, monocytes, macrophages, and other lymphoid or myeloid lineages (Meredith et al., 2012; Satpathy et al., 2012).

The similar developmental program of LT and NLT DCs can also be seen by their shared cytokine/receptor and TF requirements. The key cytokines shown to play a role in DC hematopoiesis in mice include the Fms-like tyrosine kinase 3 ligand (FLT3L), and granulocyte-macrophage colony-stimulating factor (CSF2/GM-CSF). Each murine DC subset is regulated by specific cytokines, which control their proliferation and differentiation and likely influence their immune functions.

FLT3L and its receptor (FLT3) play an instructive role in the commitment of hematopoietic progenitors into the DC-restricted lineage and their development. FLT3L is sufficient to drive DC differentiation from mouse and human precursors *in vitro* (Brasel, De Smedt, Smith, & Maliszewski, 2000). FLT3L is ubiquitously secreted by stromal and endothelial cells in various tissues and by activated T cells (Lyman & Jacobsen, 1998; Lyman et al., 1995; Miloud, Fiegler, Suffner, Hammerling, & Garbi, 2012), while the expression of the receptor for FLT3 is restricted to the DC lineage. Mice that are deficient in FLT3 and FLT3L have reduced numbers of pre-DCs in LTs and NLTs (Ginhoux et al., 2009; Liu et al., 2009) and pDCs and DCs in LTs (McKenna et al., 2000; Waskow et al., 2008). In the NLTs of mice lacking FLT3, CD103$^+$ DCs were absent and CD11b$^+$ DCs were partially reduced (Ginhoux et al., 2009). FLT3L is also required for DC differentiation from HSC precursors and homeostatic proliferation of peripheral DC (Waskow et al., 2008). The downstream signaling pathway of FLT3 signaling involves STAT3. Mice lacking STAT3 have marked reductions in DCs that cannot be rescued by FLT3L administration (Laouar, Welte, Fu, & Flavell, 2003).

CSF-2/GM-CSF is a key cytokine for the differentiation of hematopoietic progenitors (Caux, Dezutter-Dambuyant, Schmitt, & Banchereau, 1992) and monocytes (Sallusto & Lanzavecchia, 1994) into DCs *in vitro* in mice and humans. Initially, GM-CSF was described to play a crucial role in the development of DCs in lymphoid organs during inflammation (Naik et al., 2006), leading to the concept that GM-CSF mainly controls the development of inflammatory DCs. However, more recent studies identify the need for GM-CSF in NLT CD103$^+$ and CD11b$^+$ DC survival but not for LT DCs

(King, Kroenke, & Segal, 2010; Kingston et al., 2009). In fact, GM-CSF was recently shown to be dispensable for the differentiation and function of inflammatory DCs during acute injuries but critical for the survival and homeostasis of NLT CD103$^+$ and CD11b$^+$ DCs (Greter, Helft, et al., 2012). GM-CSF is also involved in the terminal differentiation of CD8$^+$ DC differentiation and acquisition of cross-presentation functions (Zhan et al., 2011).

Macrophage colony stimulating factor (CSF-1/M-CSF) is known as a key cytokine for macrophage development. Mice deficient for CSF-1 or its receptor CSF-1R (also known as c-fms and CD115) lack several macrophage populations and develop osteopetrosis due to the absence of osteoclasts (Dai et al., 2002; Yoshida et al., 1990). CSF-1 is secreted by endothelial, stromal cells, osteoblasts, and macrophages. It is detectable in serum in the steady state and is elevated upon inflammation (Hamilton, 2008). CSF-1R is expressed by various precursors of the DC lineage (Geissmann et al., 2008) and by CD11b$^+$ DCs (Ginhoux et al., 2009). It is likely that CSF-1 has a role in DC precursor differentiation but not in terminal DC differentiation and peripheral DC homeostasis. This is supported by the observation of partial CSF-1 dependence of CD11b$^+$ DCs now confirmed to be due to contaminating MHC-II$^+$CD11b$^+$ monocyte/macrophage cells (Schlitzer et al., 2013). The development of LCs is also dependent on CSF-1R but paradoxically independent of CSF-1 suggesting the existence for an alternative ligand for CSF-1R. The alternative ligand, IL-34, signals through CSF-1R and has now been shown to regulate LC development. Mice lacking IL-34 are profoundly deficient in LCs, but monocytes, dermal, and LT macrophages are spared (Greter, Lelios, et al., 2012).

Lymphotoxin-β is required for CD11b$^+$ splenic DC differentiation, but its role in NLT DC differentiation has not been studied (Kabashima et al., 2005; Wang, Kim, Wang, Yu, & Fu, 2005).

These findings, collectively, highlight the dependence of all bona fide DCs on FLT3, and heterogeneity in FLT3 and CSF-1R dependence simply reflects contamination by monocytes/macrophages within the population studied. Surface markers to distinguish bona fide DCs from monocytes/macrophages will be discussed later in the chapter.

3.2. CD8$^+$/CD103$^+$ DC lineage

The observation of CD8 expression on a subset of resident splenic, LN, and thymic DCs enabled early studies on the specific functions of DC subsets. Unfortunately, CD8 expression is only shared by murine resident LN

DCs but not shared by any murine NLT or human DCs, preventing the extrapolation of $CD8^+$ splenic/LT DC studies to other NLT tissues.

The NLT counterpart of $CD8^+$ DCs (Vremec et al., 1992), characterized by the expression of CD103, was only identified 15 years later (Bursch et al., 2007; del Rio, Rodriguez-Barbosa, Kremmer, & Forster, 2007; Edelson et al., 2010; Ginhoux et al., 2009; Sung et al., 2006). The NLT migratory $CD103^+$ DCs and $CD8^+$ LT DCs are now considered together as a distinct DC lineage based on their shared criteria despite phenotypic differences. $CD8^+$/$CD103^+$ DCs are both dependent upon FLT3 as detailed in the earlier text and, more importantly, have overlapping requirement for common TFs and possess similar immune functions.

TFs involved in $CD8^+$/$CD103^+$ DC differentiation include interferon regulatory factor 8 (IRF8), inhibitor of DNA binding 2 (ID2), and the basic leucine zipper transcription factor, ATF-like 3 (BATF3). IRF8 belongs to the family of (IRF) proteins (formerly also called PU.1 interaction partner, Pip, or interferon consensus sequence binding protein, ICSBP). IRF8-deficient mice have reduced pDCs and LT $CD8^+$ DCs but intact LT $CD8^-$ DCs (Aliberti et al., 2003), while mice that carry the BXH2 hypomorphic IRF8 mutation have a defect in the development of $CD8^+$ DCs but not LT $CD8^-$ DCs or pDCs (Tailor, Tamura, Morse, & Ozato, 2008). Strikingly, $IRF8^{-/-}$ mice and mice that carry the IRF8 BXH2 mutation completely lacked NLT $CD103^+$ DCs and exhibited myeloproliferation (Ginhoux et al., 2009).

ID2 plays a critical role in the differentiation of several hematopoietic lineages. Mice lacking ID2 have a severe reduction of LT $CD8^+$ DCs (Hacker et al., 2003). Similar to $IRF8^{-/-}$ mice, $ID2^{-/-}$ mice also lack $CD103^+$ DCs in the peripheral organs, but $CD11b^+$ DCs were not affected (Ginhoux et al., 2009).

The TF BATF3 is highly expressed in DCs compared to other hematopoietic and non-hematopoietic cells. BATF3-deficient mice have a selective loss of spleen $CD8^+$ DCs and peripheral organ $CD103^+$ $CD11b^-$ DCs but intact LT and NLT $CD11b^+$ DCs (Edelson et al., 2010; Hildner et al., 2008).

Furthermore, $CD8^+$/$CD103^+$ DCs share a similar expression profile. Both populations are $CD11b^{lo}$, $DEC205^+$, and $langerin^+$, although langerin intensity is variable across tissues (Ginhoux et al., 2009). $CD8^+$/$CD103^+$ DCs share common receptors such as the chemokine receptor XCR1 (Crozat et al., 2011), NECL2 (Galibert et al., 2005), and the lectin receptor CLEC9A (Caminschi et al., 2008; Huysamen, Willment, Dennehy, & Brown, 2008; Sancho et al., 2009) as well as the apoptotic cell scavenging receptor CD36 (Ren, Silverstein, Allen, & Savill, 1995).

In the spleen, $CD8^+$ DCs are located in the marginal zone, but in the LN, they can be found in the subcapsular sinus and LN conduits where they are ideally located to sample blood and lymph-borne antigens (Idoyaga, Suda, Suda, Park, & Steinman, 2009).

$CD8^+/CD103^+$ DCs respond to TLR3 stimulation, secrete IL-12p70, and are endowed with superior ability to cross-present antigen during viral infections, tumor, and self-antigen models (del Rio, Bernhardt, Rodriguez-Barbosa, & Forster, 2010; den Haan & Bevan, 2002; Edelson et al., 2010). Cross-presentation allows exogenous antigen to be processed for presentation on MHC Class I molecules to activate $CD8^+$ cytotoxic T cells, with cross-priming referring to naïve $CD8^+$ T cells activation by this process. Cross-presentation is an important function that explains how DCs can generate cytotoxic responses to cancer and viral antigens in the absence of cytoplasmic generation of cancer antigens by DCs or direct infection of DCs by the virus (Rock, 2003).

The role of $CD8^+/CD103^+$ DCs in activating $CD4^+$ T cells has not been completely defined. Their ability to produce IL-12p70 would suggest a role in Th1 polarization, but recent studies employing genetically deficient or depleting models involving $CD8^+/CD103^+$ DCs show conflicting evidence for their requirement in $CD4^+$ T cell priming upon fungal, viral, and tumor challenge (reviewed in Merad, Sathe, Helft, Miller, & Mortha, 2013). $CD8^+/CD103^+$ DCs have also been shown to participate in peripheral tolerance (Idoyaga et al., 2013; Qiu et al., 2009). Current available murine models to study this DC lineage cannot selectively deplete $CD8^+$ or $CD103^+$ preventing the independent evaluation of $CD8^+$ and $CD103^+$ DCs in immunity.

3.3. $CD11b^+$ DCs

$CD11b^+$ DCs are found in LTs and NLTs. In the spleen, CD4 expression distinguishes $CD4^+CD11b^+$ DCs from $CD4^-CD11b^+$ DCs, and the term splenic $CD11b^+$ DCs is used to refer to the former subset. $CD11b^+$ DCs are $CX3CR1^+$, SIRP-α^+, $BTLA^+$, $F4/80^+$, $CD14^-$, and $CD64^-$. The TFs IRF2, IRF4, IKAROS, RELB, and members of the NOTCH pathway such as NOTCH2 and RBP/J have been shown to regulate $CD11b^+$ DC development (reviewed in Hashimoto, Miller, & Merad, 2011).

Interestingly, IRF4-deficient mice have reduced LT $CD8^-$ DCs and slightly reduced pDCs, while $CD8^+$ DCs are unaffected (Suzuki et al., 2004; Tamura et al., 2005). A recent study reported an increased proportion of both $CD11b^+$ and $CD103^+$ DCs in the dermis of IRF4-deficient mice (Bajana, Roach, Turner, Paul, & Kovats, 2012). However, we did not detect any major defect in the splenic or dermal DC network of IRF4 mixed BM chimeras or in mice lacking IRF4 in the DC lineage (using the DC-specific CRE recombinase mouse CD11c-CRE (Caton, Smith-Raska, & Reizis, 2007) crossed with a mouse where the *Irf4* gene is flanked by loxP sites (Klein et al., 2006)), compared to the full IRF4 KO mice. Nevertheless, we recently described IRF4-dependent $CD11b^+$ DCs in murine lung and small intestine using IRF4 KO mixed BM chimeras or in mice lacking IRF4 in the DC lineage (Schlitzer et al., 2013), suggesting that either the molecular mechanism of action of IRF4 is different in these tissues or an additional cell type is involved and confers the observed phenotype in the dermis (Bajana et al., 2012) and the spleen of the full IRF4 KO mice (Suzuki et al., 2004; Tamura et al., 2005).

NLT and LT $CD11b^+$ DCs were shown to be heterogeneous in both origin and differentiation. NLT $CD11b^+$ DCs can be derived from BM DC-specific progenitors and monocytes in steady state (Ginhoux et al., 2009) with partial dependence on both FLT3 and CSF-1R (Ginhoux et al., 2009). Both CSF-1R KO mice and CSF-1R KO chimeric mice show a partial reduction in $CD11b^+$ DCs. In addition, mouse spleen $CD8^-CD11b^+$ DCs were found to be composed of $ESAM^+CD4^+$ and a potentially monocyte-derived $ESAM^-CD4^-$ fraction (Lewis et al., 2011), although the $ESAM^-CD4^-$ fraction was independent of CSF-1R (Schlitzer et al., 2013). These evidence point to heterogeneity within the NLT $CD11b^+$ DC fraction and suggest possible contamination with a monocyte/macrophage-like cells similar to splenic $CD11b^+$ DCs. CD64 (FcγR1) expression has been shown to distinguish NLT $CD11b^+$ bona fide DCs from contaminating monocytes or macrophages in the lung (Plantinga et al., 2013), muscle (Langlet et al., 2012), and gut (Tamoutounour et al., 2012). We recently showed that within the $CD11b^+MHC\text{-}II^+CD11c^+$ fractions of the lung and small intestine lamina propria, mutually exclusive expression of the "heat-stable antigen" CD24 and CD64 distinguished FLT3-dependent $CD24^+CD64^-$ DCs from contaminating CSF-1R-dependent $CD24^-CD64^+$ macrophages (Schlitzer et al., 2013). The $CD24^+CD64^-$ DCs in the lamina propria overlap with the $CD103^+CD11b^+$ DCs that are dependent on NOTCH2 and FLT3 (Lewis et al., 2011), unlike the $CD64^+CD103^-CD11b^+$ monocyte/macrophage cells, which are dependent on CSF-1R (Bogunovic et al., 2009; Schlitzer et al., 2013). In line with these observations, transcriptome analysis of lung $CD11b^+$ DCs suggests that the

$CD24^+CD64^-$ cells have the expression profile of DCs in contrast to the expression profile of $CD24^-CD64^+$ cells within the $CD11b^+$ fraction, which resembled that of macrophages (Gautier et al., 2012). These observations are further supported by the high expression of the DC lineage-restricted TF zbtb46 in the $CD24^+$ fraction of lung $MHC\text{-}II^+CD11c^+CD11b^+$ and gut LP $MHC\text{-}II^+CD11c^+CD11b^+CD103^+$ populations (Satpathy et al., 2012).

Migratory $CD11b^+$ DCs in draining LN are found in the T cell zone within the paracortex. In the spleen, $CD4^+CD11b^+$ DCs are located in the marginal zone and bridging channels (Dudziak et al., 2007).

The immune specializations of $CD11b^+$ DCs have been unclear likely due to heterogeneity within the population confounding earlier studies. The recent delineation of bona fide DCs from monocyte/macrophage cells will facilitate fine dissection of their specialized functions. Nevertheless, $CD11b^+$ DCs have higher expression of MHC-II presentation machinery than $CD8^+$ DCs and are more effective at antigen presentation to $CD4^+$ T cells in the steady state and inflammation (Dudziak et al., 2007). Although $CD11b^+$ DCs are inferior to $CD8^+/CD103^+$ DCs in priming naïve $CD8^+$ T cells, they have a crucial role in $CD8^+$ T cell restimulation during memory response (Wakim, Waithman, van Rooijen, Heath, & Carbone, 2008). However, the relative roles of steady-state $CD11b^+$ DCs and infiltrating inflammatory $CD11b^+$ DCs in activating memory $CD8^+$ T cell response have not been delineated (Wakim et al., 2008). $CD11b^+$ DCs in the skin and $CD103^+CD11b^+$ lamina propria DCs have been reported to induce peripheral regulatory T cell differentiation using a mechanism involving retinoic acid metabolism and the enzyme aldehyde dehydrogenase (Coombes et al., 2007; Guilliams et al., 2010; Sun et al., 2007). In our hands, IRF4-dependent $CD11b^+$ DCs in murine lung and small intestine were critical for the induction of Th17 immunity (Schlitzer et al., 2013).

3.4. Plasmacytoid DCs

Murine pDCs are $MHC\text{-}II^+$ but $CD11c^{lo}$ and are characterized by the expression of CD4, SiglecH, BST2, and B220/CD45RA. pDCs are found circulating in the blood and LTs in the steady state and are recruited during inflammation. pDCs were initially reported to be derived from CDPs, although at a low yield compared to conventional DCs. A recent study has now identified pDC-specific precursors as the $CD115^-$ cells within the CDP fraction (Onai et al., 2013). The key lineage commitment for pDC differentiation is the upregulation of the basic helix-loop-helix transcription factor (E protein), E2-2, which is accompanied by low expression of ID2, which drives myeloid/classical DC differentiation. E2-2 deletion in mature pDCs results in their spontaneous conversion to myeloid/classical DCs (Cisse et al., 2008).

The origin of pDCs is still a contentious issue. Early studies demonstrated a lymphoid rather than a myeloid origin supported by the findings of RAG1 expression and D-J rearrangements of IgH genes (Corcoran et al., 2003; Pelayo et al., 2005). However, the clear demonstration of CDP derivation of pDCs indicates a myeloid origin (Liu et al., 2009). In addition, both common myeloid progenitors (CMPs) and common lymphoid progenitors (CLPs) have been shown to be capable of generating pDCs upon adoptive transfer into irradiated mice (D'Amico & Wu, 2003; Manz, Traver, Miyamoto, Weissman, & Akashi, 2001). Similar pDC-producing capacity by CMPs and CLPs has also been demonstrated in humans (Ishikawa et al., 2007).

pDCs express high levels of the nucleic acid sensors TLR7 and TLR9, secrete vast quantities of type I interferon, and interact with NK cells during viral infection (reviewed in Reizis, Bunin, Ghosh, Lewis, & Sisirak, 2011). pDCs can prime and cross-prime antigens and induce Th1 polarization. TLR activation is required for efficient antigen presentation and T cell activation. The fate of pDCs after activation is under debate with suggestion of plasticity in fate with a capacity to convert into myeloid/classical DCs (Reizis et al., 2011).

3.5. Langerhans cells

Although murine epidermal LCs have been extensively studied, their exact immunological role is still unclear. There are conflicting reports using depletion models if LCs are required, dispensable, or redundant in initiating contact hypersensitivity reaction (reviewed in Kaplan, Kissenpfennig, & Clausen, 2008). Recent evidence show LCs promoting Th17 responses upon cutaneous challenge with *Candida albicans* (Igyarto et al., 2011). Current consensus opinion on LC role suggests a flexible *modus operandi* that is dictated by environmental cues, pathogen, and inflammatory signals (reviewed in Romani et al., 2012).

The origin of LCs is unique and distinct to all other DC subsets. In the mouse, LCs arise from embryonic hematopoietic precursors, largely from fetal liver monocytes (Hoeffel et al., 2012), that seed the skin before BM hematopoiesis begins (Romani, Schuler, & Fritsch, 1986). The origin of human LCs appears to be tantalizingly similar as LCs can be detected in 6–7-week-old human embryonic skin and as immature langerin-expressing cells in the epidermis in 9–10-week-old embryos (Foster, Holbrook, & Farr, 1986; Schuster et al., 2009).

3.6. Inflammatory DCs

Inflammatory DCs are MHC-II$^+$, CD11c^{int}, and CD11b$^+$ and may be phenotypically difficult to distinguish from steady-state CD11b$^+$ DCs and activated recruited monocytes. Although inflammatory DCs express the monocyte marker Ly6C, this is very rapidly downregulated. However, the use of CD64 and the high affinity IgE receptor FcεR1 expression to identify inflammatory DCs was recently reported (Plantinga et al., 2013). There are two distinct types of murine "inflammatory DCs" described: Tip-DCs that are not affected in Zbtb46-DTR mice treated with DT (Meredith et al., 2012) and inflammatory DCs observed in murine LN following LPS injection that express CD209, CD206, and the DC TF Zbtb46, are absent in FLT3$^{-/-}$ mice, and have potent cross-presentation capacity (Cheong et al., 2010; Meredith et al., 2012). It remains to be proven if inflammatory DCs arise purely from monocytes or can be derived from HSC precursors undergoing an alternative DC differentiation program during inflammation. The fate of inflammatory DCs, their functional roles, and how they complement resident steady-state DCs in maintaining and resolving inflammation are important areas for future research.

4. RECENT ADVANCES IN HUMAN DC IMMUNOBIOLOGY

Studies on human tissue DCs are technically challenging. Much of what we know about the various human DC subsets is from studies of NLT primarily skin DCs and also blood DCs.

4.1. Origin and differentiation of human DCs

Human DCs arise from BM precursors that undergo a series of restricted differentiation programs. Current evidence of DC differentiation in human is limited to the demonstration that both granulocyte macrophage precursors (GMPs) and multilymphoid progenitors (MLPs) can give rise to DCs (Doulatov et al., 2010). The human equivalents, if they exist, of mouse MDPs, CDPs, and immediate precursors of tissue DCs remain elusive (Fig. 1.1). The ready expression of MHC-II on human CD34$^+$ HSCs adds to the difficulties in identifying DC precursors, as lack of MHC-II expression is a crucial determinant of mouse DC precursors. The potential of human blood DCs as circulating DC precursors remains to be definitively proven. A detailed account on the phenotype, distribution, function, and relationships of the recognized human DC subsets will be provided in the following section.

Similar to murine models, there is evidence that CSF-1, FLT3L, and GM-CSF are required for human DC differentiation. Administration of FLT3L in patients expands both myeloid DCs and pDCs (Maraskovsky et al., 2000; Marroquin et al., 2002; Morse et al., 2000). Human CD141$^+$ DCs, CD1c$^+$ DCs, and pDCs express FLT3 and GM-CSFR (Haniffa et al., 2012; Poulin et al., 2010; and unpublished). Human CD14$^+$ DCs on the other hand express CSF-1R (Haniffa, unpublished). *In vitro* culture techniques to generate CD141$^+$ DCs from human CD34$^+$ progenitors require the presence of FLT3L, GM-CSF, and IL-4 (Poulin et al., 2012).

Human immunodeficiency syndromes affecting DCs and monocytes have provided useful insight into DC development. In DC, monocyte, B, and NK lymphoid (DCML) deficiency syndrome, heterozygous mutations in *GATA2* results in complete loss of DCs and monocytes in peripheral blood and tissue (Bigley et al., 2011). As the name suggests, profound defects in B and NK cells also occur in these patients. Serum FLT3L is markedly elevated demonstrating further evidence for its role in human DC development. In the BM, GMPs are diminished and MLPs are absent suggesting an early precursor defect (Bigley et al., 2011). This also suggests that human DCs arise from either GMPs, MLPs, or both progenitor types.

TFs that have been shown to affect human DC differentiation include Ikaros, PU.1, GFi1, IRF8, BATF3, and ID2. Ikaros and GFi1 defects in humans appear to have much broader hematopoietic defects than would be expected by murine models (Hashimoto et al., 2011; Watowich & Liu, 2010; and reviewed in Collin, Bigley, Haniffa, & Hambleton, 2011). The autosomal recessive K108E IRF8 mutation results in total loss of myeloid DCs and pDCs with severe reduction in circulating monocytes (Hambleton et al., 2011). Serum FLT3L is elevated and myeloproliferation with expanded GMP and MLP fractions is seen in the BM. The heterozygous T80A mutation unexpectedly showed a reduction only in myeloid CD1c$^+$ DCs without any defects in CD141$^+$ DCs and pDCs (Hambleton et al., 2011). IRF4 expression can be detected in *in vitro*-derived DCs (Ahn et al., 2002), but its role in DC differentiation *in vivo* is unknown. In humans, BATF3 affects *in vitro* CD141$^+$ DC differentiation, but cellular defects were not observed in humanized mice transplanted with BATF3$^{-/-}$ CD34$^+$ progenitors (Poulin et al., 2012).

An interesting feature observed in DCML and biallelic IRF deficiency is the relative preservation of tissue macrophages in the absence of circulating monocytes. This is in keeping with the monocyte-independence of murine tissue macrophages (Hashimoto, Chow, Noizat, Pearline, & Beasley, 2013; Yona et al., 2013).

4.2. Myeloid CD141^{hi} DCs

CD141 (BDCA-3) or thrombomodulin was found to be expressed on ~10% of blood myeloid DCs (0.1% of mononuclear cells) characterizing the minor myeloid DC population in humans (Dzionek et al., 2000). In tissue, CD141 is also expressed on endothelial cells and in the skin (Jongbloed et al., 2010), by other tissue DC subsets including migratory CD14^{+} DCs (Chu et al., 2012; Haniffa et al., 2012). The rarity of CD141^{hi} DCs and the promiscuity of CD141 expression in tissues made their identification in situ difficult. They do not express CD14 and have lower expression of CD11b and CD11c (Haniffa et al., 2012; Poulin et al., 2010) and are distinct from CD14^{+} DCs coexpressing CD141 as was recently described in the skin (Chu et al., 2012). The combined markers of CD141^{hi}CD11c^{lo} or CD141^{hi}CD11b^{lo} distinguishes them from CD1c^{+} DCs. Comparative biology approaches have identified CLEC9A (Caminschi et al., 2008; Huysamen et al., 2008; Sancho et al., 2009), XCR1 (Dorner et al., 2009), NECL2 (Galibert et al., 2005), and TRL3 (Schulz et al., 2005) as shared markers of CD141^{hi} DCs and their murine counterpart CD8^{+}/CD103^{+} DCs. DEC205, a marker of CD8^{+} mouse DCs, is expressed on human CD141^{+} DCs and also CD1c^{+} DCs. Unlike mouse CD8^{+}/CD103^{+} DCs, CD141^{hi} cells are langerin negative. The development of CD141^{+} DCs probably requires FLT3L and is less dependent on CSF-1, in accordance with their higher expression of FLT3 compared to CD1c^{+} DCs. This is in agreement with the strict dependence on FLT3 by the murine CD8^{+}/CD103^{+} lineage (Ginhoux et al., 2009).

CD141^{hi} DCs can be found in human LN, tonsil, spleen, and BM (Jongbloed et al., 2010; Mittag et al., 2011; Poulin et al., 2010; Segura et al., 2012) as well as NLTs such as the skin, lung, and liver (Haniffa et al., 2012). CD141^{hi} cells are located in the paracortical T cell zone of skin-draining LNs, interdigitating between lymphocytes (van de Ven et al., 2011).

CD141^{hi} DCs are regarded as the human cross-presenting DCs. They have an enhanced ability to take up dead or necrotic cells via CLEC9A (Bachem et al., 2010; Sancho et al., 2009), sense viral nucleic acids with TLR 3 and 8, and cross-present antigen to CD8^{+} T cells *in vitro* (Crozat,

Guiton, Contreras, et al., 2010; Haniffa et al., 2012; Jongbloed et al., 2010; Poulin et al., 2010). This function is similar to their murine homologue $CD8^+$/$CD103^+$ DCs. However, gene transcripts controlling Class I presentation are less enriched in blood $CD141^+$ DCs compared to mouse $CD8^+$ DCs (Crozat, Guiton, Guilliams, et al., 2010). Blood and skin $CD141^+$ DCs secrete TNF-α and CXCL10 upon stimulation (Haniffa et al., 2012; Jongbloed et al., 2010). Similar to $CD8^+$ splenic DCs, $CD141^+$ human blood DCs also produce high levels of the antiviral cytokine IFNλ upon treatment with poly I:C (Lauterbach et al., 2010). IL-12p70 can be produced by blood $CD141^+$ DCs (Jongbloed et al., 2010; Poulin et al., 2010) although IL-12p70 is not detectable from skin DCs. The amount of IL-12p70 produced by blood $CD141^+$ DCs is modest compared to *in vitro* monocyte-derived DCs, which are also able to cross-present (Ebner et al., 2001). Whether IL-12p70 directly promotes human DC cross-presentation function remains uncertain. Skin and blood $CD141^{hi}$ DCs are as efficient as $CD1c^+$ DCs in activating allogeneic $CD4^+$ T cell response (Jongbloed et al., 2010).

4.3. Myeloid $CD1c^+$ DCs

In addition to CD1c (Dzionek et al., 2000), this DC subset is also characterized by the expression of CD11c, CD13, CD33, CD172 (SIRP-α), and CD45RO (Cella et al., 1999; MacDonald et al., 2002; Mittag et al., 2011). $CD1c^+$ DCs also express CD11b, the latter antigen characterizing its murine $CD11b^+$ DC counterpart. Dermal $CD1c^+$ DCs can be distinguished from LCs in transit by the expression of langerin, EpCAM, and higher CD1a on LCs (Angel, Lala, et al., 2007).

Human tissue $CD1c^+$ DCs appear phenotypically more activated expressing higher levels of CD80, CD83, CD86, and CD40 than their blood counterparts (Angel, Lala, et al., 2007; McLellan, Heiser, Sorg, Fearnley, & Hart, 1998). Tissue homing receptors such as CLA and CD62L are downregulated, but the LN homing chemokine receptor, CCR7, is upregulated (Haniffa et al., 2009, 2012; Harman et al., 2013).

$CD1c^+$ DCs are found in the blood, NLTs (skin, liver, lung, and gut), and LTs (spleen and LN). They comprise ~1% of blood mononuclear cells, usually slightly lower than pDCs. In NLTs, they occupy the connective tissue space and form the major DC subset in the steady state. In LNs, $CD1c^+$ DCs probably migrate to form "interdigitating cells" found in the T cell areas (Rausch, Kaiserling, & Goos, 1977). Variable expression of CD1a and langerin in skin-draining nodes suggests that both CD1c$^+$ DCs and LCs contribute to the migratory LN DC compartment (Geissmann et al., 2002; Segura et al., 2012; Takahashi et al., 1998). The tonsil and spleen also contain resident CD1c$^+$ DCs of blood-borne origin (Mittag et al., 2011; Segura et al., 2012; Summers, Hock, McKenzie, & Hart, 2001).

CD1c$^+$ DCs possess a wide range of immune receptors for antigen uptake, transport, and presentation. Blood and skin CD1c$^+$ DCs express TLRs 1–9. TLR10, which is unique to human, is also expressed by blood CD1c$^+$ DCs. Dectin-1 (CLEC7A) and Dectin-2 (CLEC6A) are highly expressed (Harman et al., 2013; Lundberg et al., 2013), but DEC205 (CD205; CLEC13B) and the macrophage mannose receptor CD206 (CLEC13D) are variable (Segura et al., 2012). Skin CD1c$^+$ DCs secrete TNF-α, IL-8, IL-10, and IL-23 when stimulated (Haniffa et al., 2012; Morelli et al., 2005). IL-12p70 is produced by blood DCs upon stimulation with the TLR7/8 agonist, CL075, but is undetectable in the skin even using the same stimulus (Schlitzer et al., 2013). The functional consequence of CD1c$^+$ DC capacity to produce both IL-23 and IL-12p70 is unclear but may imply plasticity for Th1 and Th17 response induction in different contexts. Isolated CD1c$^+$ DCs are good stimulators of naïve CD4$^+$ T cells but have inferior capacity to cross-present antigen to CD8$^+$ T cells in most reports (Bachem et al., 2010; Crozat, Guiton, Contreras, et al., 2010; Haniffa et al., 2009, 2012; Jongbloed et al., 2010; Morelli et al., 2005). Blood and lung CD1c$^+$ DCs were superior to other DC subsets at inducing autologous Th17 polarization following DC stimulation with *Aspergillus fumigatus* (Schlitzer et al., 2013). The possibility that blood DCs are recruited to inflamed tissues and LNs and contribute to the inflammatory DC pool has not been tested. The role of CD1c$^+$ DCs in activating CD1c- and CD1a-restricted T cells is a largely unexplored area.

4.4. CD14$^+$ DCs

Human LTs and NLTs contain a third subset of myeloid DC characterized by the expression of CD14 and were originally identified from cells migrated from human skin explant cultured ex vivo (Nestle et al., 1993). They were subsequently referred to as "interstitial-type" or "dermal-type" DCs, but these terms do not do justice to the major population of interstitial CD1c$^+$ DCs (Klechevsky et al., 2009, 2008). CD14$^+$ DCs have an intermediate phenotype between DCs and monocyte/macrophages. These cells are

MHC-II^{hi} and CD11c^{hi} but express the monocyte/macrophage markers such as CD163, CD11b, CX3CR1, FXIIIa, and CD209 (DC-SIGN) and are CCR7^{-} (Angel, Lala, et al., 2007; de Gruijl et al., 2006; Haniffa et al., 2009; Ochoa, Loncaric, Krutzik, Becker, & Modlin, 2008). Their phenotype can be recapitulated by culturing blood CD14^{+} monocytes in the presence of vitamin D3 and IL-10 (Chu et al., 2012). They are difficult to separate by surface antigen expression from interstitial macrophages, but unlike macrophages, they have low side scatter properties and are not auto-fluorescent (Haniffa et al., 2009). Skin CD14^{+} DCs have low expression of CD1c and can upregulate CD141 expression in culture but should not be mistaken for CD141^{hi} cross-presenting DCs, which do not express CD14 or macrophage markers. CD14^{+} DCs have lower expression of CD80 and CD86 than CD1c^{+} DCs and do not express CD83 (Angel, Lala, et al., 2007; de Gruijl et al., 2006). TLRs 1–9 are expressed by CD14^{+} DCs (Matthews, Chung, Klasse, Moore, & Sanders, 2012).

CD14^{+} DCs are found in NLTs and LTs. In LNs, CD14^{+} DCs can be detected in the medullary cords and paracortex, although their distinction from LN macrophages is unclear (Angel et al., 2009). CD14^{+} DCs secrete IL-1β, IL-6, IL-8, and IL-10 (Klechevsky et al., 2008). They do not stimulate naïve T cells efficiently and have often been referred to as "less mature" than CD1c^{+} DCs (Angel et al., 2006; de Gruijl et al., 2006; Penel-Sotirakis, Simonazzi, Peguet-Navarro, & Rozieres, 2012). Like monocytes, CD14^{+} DCs have been shown to differentiate into LC-like or DC-like cells *in vitro* although the *in vivo* relevance of this is unclear (Larregina et al., 2001).

As CD14^{+} DCs do not express CCR7, it is questionable whether they migrate to LNs (Angel et al., 2006; Haniffa et al., 2012). Although CD14^{+}CD209^{+} cells can be detected in LN, they may be blood-derived and cannot be distinguished from macrophages, which they morphologically resemble (Angel et al., 2009; Segura et al., 2012). Transcriptomic analysis shows the dermal CD14^{+} DC expression profile to be related to blood monocytes and dermal macrophages (Haniffa et al., 2012 and Haniffa unpublished). However, their turnover following BM transplantation is rapid, unlike long-lived macrophages (Haniffa et al., 2009).

Intriguingly, CD14^{+} DCs play an important role in the formation of follicular helper T cells (Klechevsky et al., 2008) and induce antibody-secreting B cell differentiation (Matthews et al., 2012). Dermal CD14^{+} DCs and their *in vitro* monocyte treated with vitamin D3 derivative can induce regulatory T cells (Chu et al., 2012).

The phenotypic, transcriptomic, and functional resemblance of $CD14^+$ DCs to monocytes/macrophages suggests an origin that is distinct from $CD1c^+$ and $CD141^+$ DCs. $CD14^+$ DCs are more tolerogenic and functionally resemble monocyte-derived DCs that have been exposed to vitamin D3 or IL-10. One possibility is that these cells are classical monocytes that have extravasated during steady state. It is therefore conceivable that human microbiota and environmental pathogens that induce a tonic inflammatory stimulus that drives the generation of $CD14^+$ DCs, in contrast to the specific pathogen-free (SPF) mice environment. The evidence for T cell immune modulation by skin and gut commensals highlights the need to explore commensal microbial influence on tissue DC composition and function (Hand et al., 2012; Naik et al., 2012). The putative murine equivalent of $CD14^+$ DC is under investigation and may be the monocyte-/macrophage-like population contaminating murine NLT $CD11b^+$ fraction (Langlet et al., 2012; Plantinga et al., 2013; Schlitzer et al., 2013) or inflammatory DCs not observed in SPF mice.

4.5. Plasmacytoid DCs

pDCs can be distinguished from myeloid DCs and other cells by the surface markers CD123 (IL-3R), CD303 (CLEC4C: BDCA-2), and CD304 (neuropilin: BDC-4) (Dzionek et al., 2000). pDCs form ~1% of blood mononuclear cells and constitute ~50% of blood DCs (MacDonald et al., 2002). They are found in the LN T cell zones and form 20% of $MHC\text{-}II^+$ cells (Cox et al., 2005). They are also present in HEV suggesting direct recruitment from blood into LN. In the tonsil, pDCs are located in the T cell-rich extrafollicular areas and not in the germinal centers (Grouard et al., 1997). pDCs are rare in healthy peripheral tissues but are rapidly recruited upon inflammation (Haniffa et al., 2012; Zaba et al., 2007).

The formation of pDCs is regulated by FLT3L and is critically dependent upon the basic helix-loop-helix transcription factor E2-2 and the Ets factor Spi-B (Cisse et al., 2008; Reizis, 2010). Humans with Pitt–Hopkins syndrome caused by heterozygous mutation of E2-2 have pDCs with abnormal phenotype and impaired interferon secretion capacity (Cisse et al., 2008). E2-2 knockdown or overexpression in human hematopoietic progenitors results in reduced or increased pDC development *in vitro*, respectively (Cisse et al., 2008).

pDCs have a variety of proinflammatory and tolerogenic functions (reviewed in Reizis et al., 2011). The propensity of pDCs to release type 1 interferon in response to viruses was the first specialized DC function to be described (Perussia, Fanning, & Trinchieri, 1985; Siegal et al., 1999). pDCs are unique in expressing high levels of TLR 7 and 9 that can recognize ssRNA and ssDNA, respectively, and transduce signals upon sensing viral and self nucleic acids (reviewed in Gilliet, Cao, & Liu, 2008). Freshly isolated blood pDCs are immature and require maturation stimulus before they can prime naïve T cells efficiently (Grouard et al., 1997; O'Doherty et al., 1994; Siegal et al., 1999). They can polarize Th1 or Th2 $CD4^+$ responses in a context-dependent manner (Rissoan et al., 1999). pDCs have also been reported to induce $CD4^+CD25^+Foxp3^+$ Tregs and IL-10 producing T cells related to their ability to sense type B CpG ODN and notable expression of ICOSL (Ito et al., 2007; Moseman et al., 2004) and to cross-present *in vitro* (Hoeffel et al., 2007). Failure of pDCs to maintain tolerance to self nucleic acids is linked to autoimmune diseases such as systemic lupus erythematosus and psoriasis (reviewed in Gilliet et al., 2008).

4.6. Langerhans cells

LCs are found in the suprabasal epidermis where they form a network in the interstices of keratinocytes. LCs are $CD11c^{lo}$ compared to $CD1c^+$ and $CD14^+$ dermal DCs. LCs have also been described in stratified squamous epithelia (bronchus, oral, and genital mucous membrane). Migrated LCs are readily detected in draining LNs especially in inflammatory skin disorders where they occupy the paracortical areas and can be seen interdigitating between T cells (Rausch et al., 1977).

The unique homeostasis of LCs in contrast to other DCs in human is reminiscent of murine findings. There is clear evidence for persistence and self-renewing capacity for human LCs (Czernielewski & Demarchez, 1987; Kanitakis, Morelon, Petruzzo, Badet, & Dubernard, 2011; Kanitakis, Petruzzo, & Dubernard, 2004). Epidermal LCs were found to remain limb donor-derived up to 10 years after a human limb transplant (Kanitakis et al., 2011, 2004). This is supported by the observed preservation of LCs in human DC and monocyte deficiency syndromes. Moreover, dissection of the fate of human epidermal LCs after HSC transplantation revealed that 90% of LCs were of donor origin after 100 days (Collin et al., 2006). Although at first glance this appears to contradict earlier studies on LC persistence, it in fact highlights the impact of inflammatory conditioning regimens and graft versus host disease on the survival of recipient LCs and is in agreement with the observation from earlier murine studies (Frelinger, Hood, Hill, & Frelinger, 1979; Katz, Tamaki, & Sachs, 1979; Merad et al., 2002). These findings collectively demonstrate the shared properties of human and murine LCs *in vivo*. TGF-β, Axl, and NOTCH signaling appear to be important in human LC differentiation (Bauer et al., 2012; Strobl et al., 1996).

LCs have been described as the "prototype DC" and extensively studied. Most of our initial knowledge on migratory DCs is based on studying LCs. LCs were initially thought to be the initiators of all immunogenic skin responses, but more recent literature suggest that they may also be tolerogenic upon glucocorticoid treatment (Stary et al., 2011) and maintain cutaneous immune homeostasis by activating dermal regulatory T cells (Seneschal, Clark, Gehad, Baecher-Allan, & Kupper, 2012). Interestingly, LCs do not express TLRs 2, 4, and 5 and respond poorly to Gram-negative bacteria stimulation (van der Aar et al., 2007). LCs have also been shown to be capable of presenting nonpeptide antigens to CD1a-restricted T cells (Hunger et al., 2004).

There have been inconclusive reports of LC cross-presentation *in vitro*. While it is clear that CD34-derived LC-like cells are better at cross-presenting compared to $CD14^+$ CD34-derived cells (Klechevsky et al., 2008), these may not be the same as primary LCs isolated from the epidermis. A more recent study (van der Vlist et al., 2011) found that primary LCs are not efficient at cross-presentation. Our data also suggests that primary LCs were much less efficient than *in vitro*-derived LCs at cross-presentation (Haniffa et al., 2012).

The current consensus on LC functions relates to maintaining epidermal biology and that LC-mediated immune functions are adaptable and determined by the nature of the environmental stimuli and the adjacent keratinocytes (reviewed in Romani et al., 2012).

4.7. Slan DCs

Slan DCs refer to a subset of blood $CD16^+$ monocytes that express 6-sulfo LacNAc (slan), a carbohydrate modification of the P-selectin glycoprotein ligand-1 (PSGL-1). These cells have been shown to secrete large amounts of TNF-α, IL-1-β, and IL-12 and respond rapidly to inflammatory stimuli (Hansel et al., 2011; Schakel et al., 2002, 2006). However, recent findings suggest that slan DCs are indistinguishable from $CD16^+$ monocytes (Cros et al., 2010). Slan DCs and $CD16^+$ monocytes cluster together by transcriptomic analysis and appear distinct to blood DCs (Cros et al., 2010; Haniffa et al., 2012). Slan DCs have been found in steady state and inflamed skin (Gunther, Starke, Zimmermann, & Schakel, 2012).

4.8. Inflammatory DCs

Human inflammatory DCs have only recently been characterized (Hansel et al., 2011; Lowes et al., 2005; Segura et al., 2013). These cells are invariably MHC-II^{hi} and CD11c^{hi} but different phenotypes exist. Tip-DCs and slan DCs, both of which are CD14^{-}CD1c^{-}, have been found in psoriatic skin. Their phenotype contrasts the CD14^{+}CD1c^{+} inflammatory DCs recently identified in synovitis and malignant ascites (Segura et al., 2013). The latter also express CD206, CD1a, CD11b, SIRP-α, and FcεR1 (Segura et al., 2013), and it is currently unclear if they are simply activated resident CD1c^{+} DCs or arise from a separate lineage such as monocytes. Inflammatory epidermal dendritic cells (IDECs) expressing CD11c, CD206, CD1a, CD11b, FcεR1, and CD209 but lacking Birbeck granules have also been described in the skin of atopic dermatitis patients (Wollenberg, Kraft, Hanau, & Bieber, 1996; Zaba et al., 2009).

Tip-DCs and slan DCs produce TNF-α and iNOS (reviewed in Zaba et al., 2009) in tissues and have been proposed to be the same entity. All three inflammatory DCs except IDECs drive Th17 polarization (Hansel et al., 2011; Lowes et al., 2005; Segura et al., 2013). The functional properties of IDECs are currently unknown.

5. HUMANIZED MICE

An alternative resource to study human DCs is humanized mice. Humanized mouse models are derived by transplanting human cells/tissues into immunodeficient mice that are receptive to the xenograft. The available models have evolved from nude mice, which lack T cells alone, to SCID mice, which cannot make functional T and B lymphocytes to the widely used NOD/SCID/IL-2R$\gamma^{-/-}$ (NSG) strain, which lacks T and B lymphocytes and NK cells. Reconstitution of NSG mice with CD34^{+} HSCs from various sources including fetal liver results in successful reconstitution of the lymphoid compartment (reviewed in Manz & Di Santo, 2009). However, the myeloid compartment especially monocytes and macrophages shows poor reconstitution due to lack of interspecies cross-reactivity of critical cytokines such as CSF-1 necessary for their differentiation (reviewed in Manz & Di Santo, 2009). A recent refinement to the NSG mouse model is the transient (Chen, Khoury, & Chen, 2009) or permanent (Rathinam et al., 2011) introduction of human cytokines and growth factors such as GM-CSF, CSF-1, and FLT3L to enhance myeloid lineage reconstitution. DCs, monocytes, and macrophages have been demonstrated in humanized mouse peripheral blood, spleen, BM, lung, and kidney (Poulin et al., 2012; Tanaka et al., 2012; Yu et al., 2013) but are undetectable in human skin and gut in NSG mice (Haniffa and Ginhoux, unpublished). DCs and macrophages from humanized mice can phagocytose, secrete human cytokines upon stimulation, and activate T cells (Tanaka et al., 2012; Yu et al., 2013). Interestingly, lung CD1c^{+} DCs from humanized mice were recently shown to specialize in regulating mucosal CD8^{+} T cell differentiation (Yu et al., 2013). The main drawback of humanized mouse models is the lack of HLA Class I and Class II systems and poor cross-reactivity of critical molecules required for robust functional cellular and humoral responses. Attempts to integrate human HLA transgenes into these mouse models are currently underway. Nevertheless, humanized mice provide a useful *in vivo* model to study human DC differentiation and homeostasis.

6. MATCHING MICE AND MEN

Human and murine DC research has for many years advanced along two separate but parallel routes. This was put down to irreconcilable differences arising from 80 million years of independent evolution separating mice and man. There were several major obstacles that prevented researchers from aligning human and mouse DC subsets. Firstly, a unified network and nomenclature for human DC subsets were not evident. The observation of phenotypically distinct myeloid DC subsets between peripheral blood (CD1c^{+} DC and CD141^{+} DCs) and tissues (CD1c^{+} DCs and CD14^{+} DCs) prevented the establishment of a unified myeloid DC network in human. Secondly, the focus on LTs (spleen and LN) for mouse DC research compared to blood and skin for human DC research created a gulf dividing the two species further apart. The limited knowledge on mouse blood DCs (O'Keeffe et al., 2003) prevented alignment with their well-studied human counterparts. Interspecies correlation was easily identified for pDCs and epidermal LCs but proved problematic for the myeloid DC subsets.

The first suggestion of interspecies homologous relationship for myeloid DCs was between human tissue CD1c^{+} DCs and murine tissue CD103^{+} DCs (Klechevsky et al., 2009). This initial proposition is at a glance unlikely as CD103^{+} DCs are a minor population compared to CD11b^{+} DCs in contrast to human CD1c^{+} DCs being the major population compared to CD14^{+} DCs. Moreover, the phenotypic and nomenclature differences between mouse and human DCs as a consequence of using surface markers such as CD8, CD4, and CD103 do not translate easily across species. These differences questioned the relevance and utility of using murine models to study DC biology and prevented clinical translation and exploitation of murine *in vivo* findings.

6.1. Interspecies parallels

The homology predicted by transcriptomic analysis and later by phenotype and functional analyses between mouse LT CD8$^+$ DCs with human blood CD141$^+$ DCs was a major breakthrough in the pursuit of interspecies unification (Bachem et al., 2010; Crozat, Guiton, Guilliams, et al., 2010; Jongbloed et al., 2010; Poulin et al., 2010; Robbins et al., 2008). The subsequent identification and functional characterization of human tissue CD141$^+$ DCs enabled the unification of the human blood and tissue myeloid DC system and functionally harmonized the human and mouse interspecies NLT DC networks (Haniffa et al., 2012). Transcriptional profiling has been an instrumental tool to separate DCs from other members of the MPS and to identify interspecies homologies (Crozat, Guiton, Guilliams, et al., 2010; Gautier et al., 2012; Haniffa et al., 2012; Miller et al., 2012; Robbins et al., 2008). The power of this approach is that it offers an unbiased assessment of relationships between cells rather than reliance upon a small selection of markers. Principal component analysis has simplified multidimensional data presentation. This analysis has revealed that (1) primary human DCs form discrete populations separate from monocytes and *in vitro* monocyte-derived DCs and (2) there is no currently available *in vitro* system able to capture the transcriptional profile of primary human DCs (Crozat, Guiton, Guilliams, et al., 2010; Robbins et al., 2008). An important consideration with this approach is the ability to identify tissue-related transcripts that could prevent alignment of comparable DC subsets across different tissues. Tissue-related transcripts result in DC subsets clustering by tissue and maneuvers to overcome this are required to establish unified DC networks within and across species. There are several approaches that can be employed: (1) identification of gene sets unique to a DC subset from a fluid-phase tissue such as blood and using these gene sets to probe DCs isolated from other tissues (Crozat, Guiton, Guilliams, et al., 2010; Robbins et al., 2008) and (2) removal of tissue-specific transcripts annotated in established tissue datasets or transcripts that are not shared across tissue before identifying gene sets unique to a DC subset (Haniffa et al., 2012). Homology between mouse splenic $CD8^+$ DCs and human blood $CD141^+$ DCs could only be identified by removing the potential confounding effects of tissue-related transcripts (Crozat, Guiton, Guilliams, et al., 2010; Robbins et al., 2008). Removal of tissue-related transcript effects was also critical in the identification of the human blood and tissue $CD141^+$ DC lineage and the demonstration of its murine $CD103^+/CD8^+$ homologue (Haniffa et al., 2012). Interspecies alignment allows the extrapolation of functional experiments in mouse to human immunology. In addition, it also predicts heterogeneity within the current mouse tissue $CD11b^+$ DC classification to include human CD1c-like and CD14-like components (Haniffa et al., 2012), which revealed to be true (Plantinga et al., 2013; Schlitzer et al., 2013). However, it remains to be ascertained if the murine CD14-like cells are monocytes, macrophages, or monocyte-derived inflammatory DCs.

Interestingly, although *in vitro* monocyte-derived DCs do not reflect primary human DCs, inflammatory DCs isolated directly from human synovial and ascitic fluid possess monocyte-related signatures (Segura et al., 2013) and could parallel the contribution of murine monocyte-derived DCs during inflammation.

Phenotypically conserved surface markers of DCs that transcend species barriers include BTLA, XCR1, CD135/FLT3R, CX3CR1, CD172-α, CD14, CD11b, and CLEC9A. Figure 1.2 shows the surface markers that characterize the different DC subsets in human and mouse. Murine $CD8^+/CD103^+$ DC subset is endowed with superior ability to cross-prime and cross-present. Human blood $CD141^+$ DCs, the counterparts of $CD8^+$ DCs, are also similarly superior at cross-presentation (Bachem et al., 2010; Jongbloed et al., 2010; Poulin et al., 2010). More recently, human tissue $CD141^+$ DCs were found to be superior at cross-presenting soluble antigen to cytotoxic $CD8^+$ T cells (Haniffa et al., 2012). While these human *in vitro* cross-presentation studies have been informative in supporting functional conservation between murine $CD8^+/CD103^+$ DCs and human $CD141^+$ DCs, *in vivo* proof and evidence for cross-priming is still lacking. The type of antigen delivered in human studies that ranges from long peptide, soluble whole antigen, to necrotic cell-derived antigen may also influence the ability of different DC subsets to cross-present and account for the observation of cross-presentation capacity by blood $CD1c^+$ DCs and epidermal LCs.

Murine $CD11b^+$ DCs are superior at activating $CD4^+$ T cell responses through antigen presentation on MHC Class II molecules (Dudziak et al., 2007). We recently identified an IRF4-dependent $CD11b^+$ DC subset in

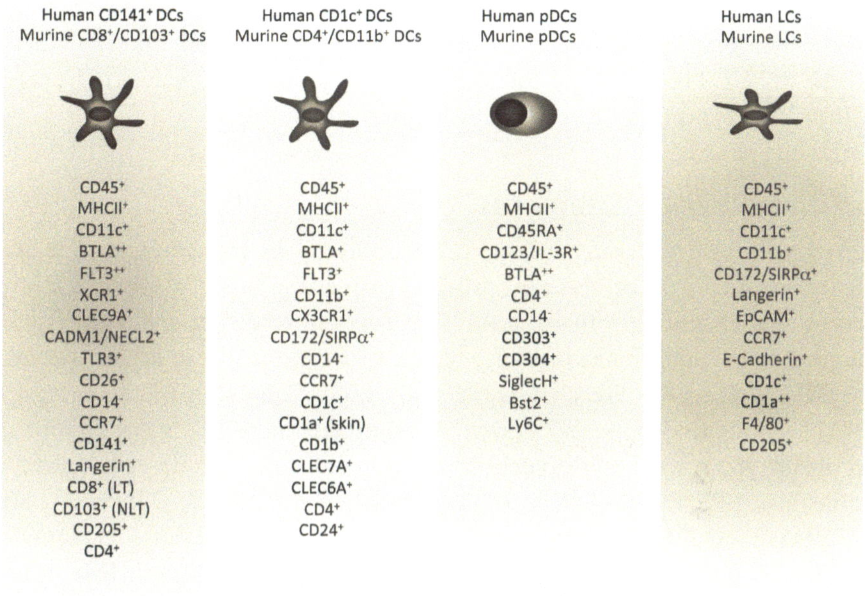

Figure 1.2 Phenotypic markers of human and mouse DC subsets. Markers in red are shared between species, markers in black are restricted to human, and markers in blue are restricted to mouse. (See color plate.)

mouse mucosal tissues responsible for Th17 immune responses. $CD1c^+$ DCs, the human homologue of murine $CD11b^+$ DCs, similarly expressed IRF4 and higher levels of the Th17 polarizing cytokine IL-23 in the steady state. Additionally, we found potent induction of IL-17 expression on $CD4^+$ T cells by *Aspergillus hyphae*-activated lung $CD1c^+$ DCs (Schlitzer et al., 2013).

Altogether, the comparative biology studies have revealed the parallel organization of DC networks in human and mouse (Fig. 1.1). There are two main DC subsets in both species: human $CD141^+$ DC lineage with shared homology to mouse cross-presenting $CD8^+/CD103^+$ DCs and human $CD1c^+$ DC lineage homologous to mouse $CD4^+$ splenic DCs. Recent data also show that both human lung $CD1c^+$ DCs and their murine lung $CD11b^+$ DC homologue are endowed with Th17 polarizing capabilities (Schlitzer et al., 2013). In addition, human tissues contain a $CD14^+$ DC subset with monocyte/macrophage characteristics. The murine counterpart of human CD14^{+} DCs is currently unknown. It is tempting to speculate that the contaminating monocyte/macrophage cells within the murine tissue MHC-II^{+}CD11c^{+}CD11b^{+} fraction are the functional equivalent of human CD14^{+} DCs although this requires further validation.

6.2. Interspecies differences

Selective pressures from pathogens encountered in the environment are strong evolutionary drivers separating human and mouse. While it is fascinating that DC subset organization is broadly conserved, there are likely to be phenotypic and functional adaptations that are not shared across species.

All murine DCs are characterized by high expression of the integrin CD11c. This molecule also known as complement receptor 4 is involved in phagocytosis and has a diverse array of ligands that include cell adhesion molecules, LPS, fibrinogen, and collagen (Sadhu et al., 2007). The exact role of CD11c on DCs is unclear but blocking antibody against CD11c was shown to inhibit human LC antigen presentation activity (Meunier, Bohjanen, Voorhees, & Cooper, 1994). In humans, CD11c is highly expressed by CD1c^{+} DCs, but lower expression intensity is observed on blood and tissue CD141^{+} DCs. Both murine and human epidermal LCs also have lower expression of CD11c. CD8 is another molecule that is differentially regulated. CD8 is not expressed on any human DC subsets, but CD4 appears to be a pan-DC and monocyte marker in human with the highest expression observed on pDCs (MacDonald et al., 2002; Jardine et al., personal communication). In contrast, CD4 is only expressed by mouse CD4^{+} splenic DC and pDCs. Langerin is expressed by both human and mouse LCs, but while langerin expression characterizes mouse CD8^{+} and CD103^{+} DCs, their human CD141^{+} DC counterpart lacks this marker (Haniffa et al., 2012). Low-level langerin expression is observed on a subset of human skin CD1c^{+} DCs (van de Ven et al., 2011; Bigley and Collin, unpublished).

Mouse CD8^{+}/CD103^{+} DCs are the main synthesizers of IL-12, but studies on human blood DCs show that IL-12 production is not restricted to blood CD141^{+} DCs but is also secreted by CD1c^{+} DCs (Mittag et al., 2011). IL-12 was not detected when skin DCs were cultured with a wide range of stimuli including TLR3 and TLR7/8 agonists (Haniffa et al., 2012). However, human *in vitro* monocyte-derived DCs are known to secrete vast amounts of IL-12p70 upon stimulation (Ebner et al., 2001).

7. THE RELATIONSHIP OF DCs TO MONOCYTES AND MACROPHAGES

The discovery of DC as an independent cell type distinct to monocytes and macrophages has sparked controversy regarding its "pedigree." The classical view of DCs, monocytes, and macrophages asserts that all three cell types belong to the MPS and have overlapping phenotype and function. Monocytes are also perceived as the precursors of both DCs and macrophages. There is a good line of evidence now to separate DCs from macrophages. Firstly, most LT and NLT mouse DCs in the steady state are derived from a distinct lineage as clearly demonstrated by the Zbtb46 reporter and DTR mouse models, which delineates DCs and its immediate precursors from the rest of the MPS (Liu & Nussenzweig, 2010; Meredith et al., 2012; Satpathy et al., 2012).

Secondly, recent evidence suggests that murine tissue macrophages in steady state are not monocyte-derived but are seeded by precursors from the yolk sac and fetal liver and maintained throughout life (Hashimoto et al., 2013; Yona et al., 2013; Ginhoux et al., 2010). However, macrophages in specialized niches, where local conditioning by microbiota and tonic inflammatory stimuli are present, such as the gut lamina propria, are monocyte-derived (Zigmond et al., 2012). Whether monocytes give rise to DCs in the steady state remains to be definitively proven. Thirdly, the use of transcriptome analysis has enabled the generation of molecular signatures to separate DCs from monocytes and macrophages in mouse and human (Crozat, Guiton, Guilliams, et al., 2010; Gautier et al., 2012; Haniffa et al., 2012; Miller et al., 2012; Robbins et al., 2008). This approach enabled identification of distinct functional markers and attributes for all three cell types.

Finally, an important functional distinction of macrophages is their resident/fixed nature within tissues compared to NLT DCs that have the ability to migrate to the afferent lymphatics. We recently showed that only $CD11b^+$ bona fide DCs could migrate to lung-draining LN but interstitial macrophages were tissue-resident (Schlitzer et al., 2013). In human skin, macrophages are only found within digested dermal suspension, but not within the dermal-migrated fraction (Haniffa et al., 2009). CCR7, the chemokine receptor critical in lymphatic migration, is concomitantly absent on macrophages but expressed on DCs (reviewed in Merad et al., 2013). The distinction between DC and macrophages is also reflected in their differential renewal rates in the mouse steady state (Ginhoux et al., 2009; Jenkins et al., 2011; Schlitzer et al., 2013; Veres et al., 2013) and corroborates the observation in human after stem cell transplantation *in vivo* (Haniffa et al., 2009).

8. NEXT STEPS AHEAD

There has been tremendous progress in our understanding of DC network organization and functional diversity in the last 40 years since their discovery. We are now able to demonstrate the conservation of DC subset organization between mouse and human and evaluate functional divergence and/or redundance between species. One of the main impetus that has precipitated this progress is the move from simple phenotypic evaluation to the use of the transcriptome as molecular signatures to define DC subsets. This strategy has enabled the evaluation of relationship of DC subsets (1) within the DC lineage, (2) with other members of the MPS, and (3) within and across species. It has provided evidence for the role of DC subset developmental specificity in determining functional specialization. There are, however, obvious gaps in our knowledge, particularly in relation to human DC development and function that need to be addressed. Can we use the existing knowledge on murine DC precursors to predict the identity of human DC precursors? Would it be possible to define the identity of pathological cell types in relation to known DC subsets? A case in point is the origin of langerin-expressing cell characteristic of LC histiocytosis. Langerin and bright CD1a expression were evidence for its origin from LCs, but there is doubt within the field that this is indeed the case as langerin is also expressed by DCs from other lineage. The reliance on limited markers can easily constraint our ability to evaluate the complete portrait of a cell, and the new tools we have allow more in-depth evaluations to be constructed.

In contrast to the steady-state DCs, inflammatory monocytes appear to differentiate into highly plastic progenies. Inflammatory monocyte-derived progenies also demonstrate a degree of developmental and functional convergence with DCs and macrophages. Gene expression studies are beginning to define these monocyte-derived cells in inflammation and will also reveal the effect of the nature of pathogenic/inflammatory challenge on inflammatory DC differentiation and function. The precise functions and ultimate fate of these cells during inflammation and its resolution remain unresolved.

Other exciting avenues to explore include the possibility of using human inducible pluripotent stem cells (iPSCs) to produce $CD34^+$ hematopoietic precursors with selective loss of genes known to be involved in myeloid differentiation. This strategy combined with the use of humanized mouse models provides a powerful approach to define human DC hematopoiesis. We still have far to go in evaluating the *in vivo* significance and relevance of human *in vitro* DC functional studies. In addition, the impact of adjacent leukocytes, nonleukocytes, and regional microorganisms in modulating DC composition and functions needs to be dissected. A precise understanding of human DC hematopoiesis and functional diversity will bring us closer to exploit the full potential of using DCs in clinical immunotherapeutic strategies.

9. DISCLOSURE STATEMENT

The authors have no conflict of interests to declare.

ACKNOWLEDGMENTS

We would like to thank Andreas Schlitzer for critical input into the manuscript and Katja Fink and Venetia Bigley for assistance with illustrations. We apologize to colleagues whose work we have not cited, through either ignorance or space restrictions. M.H. is funded by a Wellcome Intermediate Fellowship, F.G. by Singapore A*STAR Singapore Immunology Network (SIgN) Core Funding, and M.C. by Leukaemia Research and Bright Red.

REFERENCES

Ahn, J. H., Lee, Y., Jeon, C., Lee, S. J., Lee, B. H., Choi, K. D., et al. (2002). Identification of the genes differentially expressed in human dendritic cell subsets by cDNA subtraction and microarray analysis. *Blood, 100*(5), 1742–1754.

Aliberti, J., Schulz, O., Pennington, D. J., Tsujimura, H., Reis e Sousa, C., Ozato, K., et al. (2003). Essential role for ICSBP in the in vivo development of murine CD8alpha+ dendritic cells. *Blood, 101*(1), 305–310.

Angel, C. E., Chen, C. J., Horlacher, O. C., Winkler, S., John, T., Browning, J., et al. (2009). Distinctive localization of antigen-presenting cells in human lymph nodes. *Blood, 113*(6), 1257–1267.

Angel, C. E., George, E., Brooks, A. E., Ostrovsky, L. L., Brown, T. L., & Dunbar, P. R. (2006). Cutting edge: CD1a+ antigen-presenting cells in human dermis respond rapidly to CCR7 ligands. *Journal of Immunology, 176*(10), 5730–5734.

Angel, C. E., George, E., Ostrovsky, L. L., & Dunbar, P. R. (2007). Comprehensive analysis of MHC-II expression in healthy human skin. *Immunology & Cell Biology, 85*(5), 363–369.

Angel, C. E., Lala, A., Chen, C. J., Edgar, S. G., Ostrovsky, L. L., & Dunbar, P. R. (2007). CD14+ antigen-presenting cells in human dermis are less mature than their CD1a+ counterparts. *International Immunology, 19*(11), 1271–1279.

Annacker, O., Coombes, J. L., Malmstrom, V., Uhlig, H. H., Bourne, T., Johansson-Lindbom, B., et al. (2005). Essential role for CD103 in the T cell-mediated regulation of experimental colitis. *The Journal of Experimental Medicine, 202*(8), 1051–1061.

Asselin-Paturel, C., Boonstra, A., Dalod, M., Durand, I., Yessaad, N., Dezutter-Dambuyant, C., et al. (2001). Mouse type I IFN-producing cells are immature APCs with plasmacytoid morphology. *Nature Immunology, 2*(12), 1144–1150.

Austyn, J. M., Kupiec-Weglinski, J. W., Hankins, D. F., & Morris, P. J. (1988). Migration patterns of dendritic cells in the mouse. Homing to T cell-dependent areas of spleen, and binding within marginal zone. *The Journal of Experimental Medicine, 167*(2), 646–651.

Bachem, A., Guttler, S., Hartung, E., Ebstein, F., Schaefer, M., Tannert, A., et al. (2010). Superior antigen cross-presentation and XCR1 expression define human CD11c+CD141+ cells as homologues of mouse CD8+ dendritic cells. *The Journal of Experimental Medicine, 207*(6), 1273–1281.

Bajana, S., Roach, K., Turner, S., Paul, J., & Kovats, S. (2012). IRF4 promotes cutaneous dendritic cell migration to lymph nodes during homeostasis and inflammation. *Journal of Immunology, 189*(7), 3368–3377.

Balfour, B. M., Drexhage, H. A., Kamperdijk, E. W., & Hoefsmit, E. C. (1981). Antigen-presenting cells, including Langerhans cells, veiled cells and interdigitating cells. *Ciba Foundation Symposium, 84*, 281–301.

Bar-On, L., Birnberg, T., Lewis, K. L., Edelson, B. T., Bruder, D., Hildner, K., et al. (2010). CX3CR1+ CD8alpha+ dendritic cells are a steady-state population related to plasmacytoid dendritic cells. *Proceedings of the National Academy of Sciences of the United States of America, 107*(33), 14745–14750.

Bauer, T., Zagorska, A., Jurkin, J., Yasmin, N., Koffel, R., Richter, S., et al. (2012). Identification of Axl as a downstream effector of TGF-beta1 during Langerhans cell differentiation and epidermal homeostasis. *The Journal of Experimental Medicine, 209*(11), 2033–2047.

Bigley, V., Haniffa, M., Doulatov, S., Wang, X. N., Dickinson, R., McGovern, N., et al. (2011). The human syndrome of dendritic cell, monocyte, B and NK lymphoid deficiency. *The Journal of Experimental Medicine, 208*(2), 227–234.

Bjorck, P. (2001). Isolation and characterization of plasmacytoid dendritic cells from Flt3 ligand and granulocyte-macrophage colony-stimulating factor-treated mice. *Blood, 98*(13), 3520–3526.

Bogunovic, M., Ginhoux, F., Helft, J., Shang, L., Hashimoto, D., Greter, M., et al. (2009). Origin of the lamina propria dendritic cell network. *Immunity, 31*(3), 513–525.

Brasel, K., De Smedt, T., Smith, J. L., & Maliszewski, C. R. (2000). Generation of murine dendritic cells from flt3-ligand-supplemented bone marrow cultures. *Blood, 96*(9), 3029–3039.

Burnet, F. M. (1957). A modification of Jerne's theory of antibody production using the concept of clonal selection. *The Australian Journal of Science, 20*(3), 67–69.

Bursch, L. S., Wang, L., Igyarto, B., Kissenpfennig, A., Malissen, B., Kaplan, D. H., et al. (2007). Identification of a novel population of Langerin+ dendritic cells. *The Journal of Experimental Medicine, 204*(13), 3147–3156.

Caminschi, I., Proietto, A. I., Ahmet, F., Kitsoulis, S., Shin Teh, J., Lo, J. C., et al. (2008). The dendritic cell subtype-restricted C-type lectin Clec9A is a target for vaccine enhancement. *Blood, 112*(8), 3264–3273.

Caton, M. L., Smith-Raska, M. R., & Reizis, B. (2007). Notch-RBP-J signaling controls the homeostasis of CD8− dendritic cells in the spleen. *The Journal of Experimental Medicine, 204*(7), 1653–1664.

Caux, C., Dezutter-Dambuyant, C., Schmitt, D., & Banchereau, J. (1992). GM-CSF and TNF-alpha cooperate in the generation of dendritic Langerhans cells. *Nature, 360*(6401), 258–261.

Caux, C., Vanbervliet, B., Massacrier, C., Dezutter Dambuyant, C., de Saint-Vis, B., Jacquet, C., et al. (1996). CD34+ hematopoietic progenitors from human cord blood differentiate along two independent dendritic cell pathways in response to GM-CSF+ TNF alpha. *The Journal of Experimental Medicine, 184*(2), 695–706.
Cella, M., Jarrossay, D., Facchetti, F., Alebardi, O., Nakajima, H., Lanzavecchia, A., et al. (1999). Plasmacytoid monocytes migrate to inflamed lymph nodes and produce large amounts of type I interferon. *Nature Medicine, 5*(8), 919–923.
Chen, Q., Khoury, M., & Chen, J. (2009). Expression of human cytokines dramatically improves reconstitution of specific human-blood lineage cells in humanized mice. *Proceedings of the National Academy of Sciences of the United States of America, 106*(51), 21783–21788.
Cheong, C., Matos, I., Choi, J. H., Dandamudi, D. B., Shrestha, E., Longhi, M. P., et al. (2010). Microbial stimulation fully differentiates monocytes to DC-SIGN/CD209(+) dendritic cells for immune T cell areas. *Cell, 143*(3), 416–429.
Chu, C.-C., Ali, N., Karagiannis, P., Di Meglio, P., Skowera, A., Napolitano, L., et al. (2012). Resident CD141 (BDCA3)+ dendritic cells in human skin produce IL-10 and induce regulatory T cells that suppress skin inflammation. *The Journal of Experimental Medicine, 209*(5), 935–945.
Cisse, B., Caton, M. L., Lehner, M., Maeda, T., Scheu, S., Locksley, R., et al. (2008). Transcription factor E2-2 is an essential and specific regulator of plasmacytoid dendritic cell development. *Cell, 135*(1), 37–48.
Collin, M., Bigley, V., Haniffa, M., & Hambleton, S. (2011). Human dendritic cell deficiency: The missing ID? *Nature Reviews Immunology, 11*(9), 575–583.
Collin, M. P., Hart, D. N., Jackson, G. H., Cook, G., Cavet, J., Mackinnon, S., et al. (2006). The fate of human Langerhans cells in hematopoietic stem cell transplantation. *The Journal of Experimental Medicine, 203*(1), 27–33.
Coombes, J. L., Siddiqui, K. R., Arancibia-Carcamo, C. V., Hall, J., Sun, C. M., Belkaid, Y., et al. (2007). A functionally specialized population of mucosal CD103+ DCs induces Foxp3+ regulatory T cells via a TGF-beta and retinoic acid-dependent mechanism. *The Journal of Experimental Medicine, 204*(8), 1757–1764.
Corcoran, L., Ferrero, I., Vremec, D., Lucas, K., Waithman, J., O'Keeffe, M., et al. (2003). The lymphoid past of mouse plasmacytoid cells and thymic dendritic cells. *Journal of Immunology, 170*(10), 4926–4932.
Cox, K., North, M., Burke, M., Singhal, H., Renton, S., Aqel, N., et al. (2005). Plasmacytoid dendritic cells (PDC) are the major DC subset innately producing cytokines in human lymph nodes. *Journal of Leukocyte Biology, 78*(5), 1142–1152.
Cros, J., Cagnard, N., Woollard, K., Patey, N., Zhang, S. Y., Senechal, B., et al. (2010). Human CD14dim monocytes patrol and sense nucleic acids and viruses via TLR7 and TLR8 receptors. *Immunity, 33*(3), 375–386.
Crozat, K., Guiton, R., Contreras, V., Feuillet, V., Dutertre, C. A., Ventre, E., et al. (2010). The XC chemokine receptor 1 is a conserved selective marker of mammalian cells homologous to mouse CD8alpha+ dendritic cells. *The Journal of Experimental Medicine, 207*(6), 1283–1292.
Crozat, K., Guiton, R., Guilliams, M., Henri, S., Baranek, T., Schwartz-Cornil, I., et al. (2010). Comparative genomics as a tool to reveal functional equivalences between human and mouse dendritic cell subsets. *Immunological Reviews, 234*(1), 177–198.
Crozat, K., Tamoutounour, S., Vu Manh, T. P., Fossum, E., Luche, H., Ardouin, L., et al. (2011). Cutting edge: Expression of XCR1 defines mouse lymphoid-tissue resident and migratory dendritic cells of the CD8{alpha}+ type. *Journal of Immunology, 187*(9), 4411–4415.
Czernielewski, J. M., & Demarchez, M. (1987). Further evidence for the self-reproducing capacity of Langerhans cells in human skin. *The Journal of Investigative Dermatology, 88*(1), 17–20.

Czernielewski, J. M., Schmitt, D., Faure, M. R., & Thivolet, J. (1983). Functional and phenotypic analysis of isolated human Langerhans cells and indeterminate cells. *British Journal of Dermatology*, *108*(2), 129–138.

D'Amico, A., & Wu, L. (2003). The early progenitors of mouse dendritic cells and plasmacytoid predendritic cells are within the bone marrow hemopoietic precursors expressing Flt3. *The Journal of Experimental Medicine*, *198*(2), 293–303.

Dai, X. M., Ryan, G. R., Hapel, A. J., Dominguez, M. G., Russell, R. G., Kapp, S., et al. (2002). Targeted disruption of the mouse colony-stimulating factor 1 receptor gene results in osteopetrosis, mononuclear phagocyte deficiency, increased primitive progenitor cell frequencies, and reproductive defects. *Blood*, *99*(1), 111–120.

Dakic, A., Shao, Q. X., D'Amico, A., O'Keeffe, M., Chen, W. F., Shortman, K., et al. (2004). Development of the dendritic cell system during mouse ontogeny. *Journal of Immunology*, *172*(2), 1018–1027.

de Gruijl, T. D., Sombroek, C. C., Lougheed, S. M., Oosterhoff, D., Buter, J., van den Eertwegh, A. J., et al. (2006). A postmigrational switch among skin-derived dendritic cells to a macrophage-like phenotype is predetermined by the intracutaneous cytokine balance. *Journal of Immunology*, *176*(12), 7232–7242.

del Rio, M. L., Bernhardt, G., Rodriguez-Barbosa, J. I., & Forster, R. (2010). Development and functional specialization of CD103+ dendritic cells. *Immunological Reviews*, *234*(1), 268–281.

del Rio, M. L., Rodriguez-Barbosa, J. I., Kremmer, E., & Forster, R. (2007). CD103− and CD103+ bronchial lymph node dendritic cells are specialized in presenting and cross-presenting innocuous antigen to CD4+ and CD8+ T cells. *Journal of Immunology*, *178*(11), 6861–6866.

den Haan, J. M., & Bevan, M. J. (2002). Constitutive versus activation-dependent cross-presentation of immune complexes by CD8(+) and CD8(−) dendritic cells in vivo. *The Journal of Experimental Medicine*, *196*(6), 817–827.

Dorner, B. G., Dorner, M. B., Zhou, X., Opitz, C., Mora, A., Guttler, S., et al. (2009). Selective expression of the chemokine receptor XCR1 on cross-presenting dendritic cells determines cooperation with CD8+ T cells. *Immunity*, *31*(5), 823–833.

Doulatov, S., Notta, F., Eppert, K., Nguyen, L. T., Ohashi, P. S., & Dick, J. E. (2010). Revised map of the human progenitor hierarchy shows the origin of macrophages and dendritic cells in early lymphoid development. *Nature Immunology*, *11*(7), 585–593.

Dudziak, D., Kamphorst, A. O., Heidkamp, G. F., Buchholz, V. R., Trumpfheller, C., Yamazaki, S., et al. (2007). Differential antigen processing by dendritic cell subsets in vivo. *Science*, *315*(5808), 107–111.

Dzionek, A., Fuchs, A., Schmidt, P., Cremer, S., Zysk, M., Miltenyi, S., et al. (2000). BDCA-2, BDCA-3, and BDCA-4: Three markers for distinct subsets of dendritic cells in human peripheral blood. *Journal of Immunology*, *165*(11), 6037–6046.

Ebner, S., Ratzinger, G., Krosbacher, B., Schmuth, M., Weiss, A., Reider, D., et al. (2001). Production of IL-12 by human monocyte-derived dendritic cells is optimal when the stimulus is given at the onset of maturation, and is further enhanced by IL-4. *Journal of Immunology*, *166*(1), 633–641.

Edelson, B. T., KC, W., Juang, R., Kohyama, M., Benoit, L. A., Klekotka, P. A., et al. (2010). Peripheral CD103+ dendritic cells form a unified subset developmentally related to CD8alpha+ conventional dendritic cells. *The Journal of Experimental Medicine*, *207*(4), 823–836.

Foster, C. A., Holbrook, K. A., & Farr, A. G. (1986). Ontogeny of Langerhans cells in human embryonic and fetal skin: Expression of HLA-DR and OKT-6 determinants. *The Journal of Investigative Dermatology*, *86*(3), 240–243.

Frelinger, J. G., Hood, L., Hill, S., & Frelinger, J. A. (1979). Mouse epidermal Ia molecules have a bone marrow origin. *Nature*, *282*, 321–323.

Galibert, L., Diemer, G. S., Liu, Z., Johnson, R. S., Smith, J. L., Walzer, T., et al. (2005). Nectin-like protein 2 defines a subset of T-cell zone dendritic cells and is a ligand for class-I-restricted T-cell-associated molecule. *Journal of Biological Chemistry*, *280*(23), 21955–21964.

Gautier, E. L., Shay, T., Miller, J., Greter, M., Jakubzick, C., Ivanov, S., et al. (2012). Immunological Genome Consortium. Gene-expression profiles and transcriptional regulatory pathways that underlie the identity and diversity of mouse tissue macrophages. *Nature Immunology*, *13*(11), 1118–1128. http://dx.doi.org/10.1038/ni.2419. Epub 2012 Sep 30.

Geissmann, F., Auffray, C., Palframan, R., Wirrig, C., Ciocca, A., Campisi, L., et al. (2008). Blood monocytes: Distinct subsets, how they relate to dendritic cells, and their possible roles in the regulation of T-cell responses. *Immunology & Cell Biology*, *86*(5), 398–408.

Geissmann, F., Dieu-Nosjean, M. C., Dezutter, C., Valladeau, J., Kayal, S., Leborgne, M., et al. (2002). Accumulation of immature Langerhans cells in human lymph nodes draining chronically inflamed skin. *The Journal of Experimental Medicine*, *196*(4), 417–430.

Geissmann, F., Manz, M. G., Jung, S., Sieweke, M. H., Merad, M., & Ley, K. (2010). Development of monocytes, macrophages, and dendritic cells. *Science*, *327*(5966), 656–661.

Gilliet, M., Cao, W., & Liu, Y. J. (2008). Plasmacytoid dendritic cells: Sensing nucleic acids in viral infection and autoimmune diseases. *Nature Reviews Immunology*, *8*(8), 594–606.

Ginhoux, F., Collin, M. P., Bogunovic, M., Abel, M., Leboeuf, M., Helft, J., et al. (2007). Blood-derived dermal langerin+ dendritic cells survey the skin in the steady state. *The Journal of Experimental Medicine*, *204*(13), 3133–3146.

Ginhoux, F., Greter, M., Leboeuf, M., Nandi, S., See, P., Gokhan, S., Mehler, M. F., et al. (2010). Fate mapping analysis reveals that adult microglia derive from primitive macrophages. *Science*, *330*(6005), 841–845.

Ginhoux, F., Liu, K., Helft, J., Bogunovic, M., Greter, M., Hashimoto, D., et al. (2009). The origin and development of nonlymphoid tissue CD103+ DCs. *The Journal of Experimental Medicine*, *206*(13), 3115–3130.

Greter, M., Helft, J., Chow, A., Hashimoto, D., Mortha, A., Agudo-Cantero, J., et al. (2012). GM-CSF controls nonlymphoid tissue dendritic cell homeostasis but is dispensable for the differentiation of inflammatory dendritic cells. *Immunity*, *36*(6), 1031–1046.

Greter, M., Lelios, I., Pelczar, P., Hoeffel, G., Price, J., Leboeuf, M., et al. (2012). Stroma-derived interleukin-34 controls the development and maintenance of langerhans cells and the maintenance of microglia. *Immunity*, *37*(6), 1050–1060.

Grouard, G., Rissoan, M. C., Filgueira, L., Durand, I., Banchereau, J., & Liu, Y. J. (1997). The enigmatic plasmacytoid T cells develop into dendritic cells with interleukin (IL)-3 and CD40-ligand. *The Journal of Experimental Medicine*, *185*(6), 1101–1111.

Guilliams, M., Crozat, K., Henri, S., Tamoutounour, S., Grenot, P., Devilard, E., et al. (2010). Skin-draining lymph nodes contain dermis-derived CD103(−) dendritic cells that constitutively produce retinoic acid and induce Foxp3(+) regulatory T cells. *Blood*, *115*(10), 1958–1968.

Gunther, C., Starke, J., Zimmermann, N., & Schakel, K. (2012). Human 6-sulfo LacNAc (slan) dendritic cells are a major population of dermal dendritic cells in steady state and inflammation. *Clinical and Experimental Dermatology*, *37*(2), 169–176.

Hacker, C., Kirsch, R. D., Ju, X. S., Hieronymus, T., Gust, T. C., Kuhl, C., et al. (2003). Transcriptional profiling identifies Id2 function in dendritic cell development. *Nature Immunology*, *4*(4), 380–386.

Hambleton, S., Salem, S., Bustamante, J., Bigley, V., Boisson-Dupuis, S., Azevedo, J., et al. (2011). IRF8 mutations and human dendritic-cell immunodeficiency. *The New England Journal of Medicine*, *365*(2), 127–138.

Hamilton, J. A. (2008). Colony-stimulating factors in inflammation and autoimmunity. *Nature Reviews Immunology*, *8*(7), 533–544.

Hand, T. W., Dos Santos, L. M., Bouladoux, N., Molloy, M. J., Pagan, A. J., Pepper, M., et al. (2012). Acute gastrointestinal infection induces long-lived microbiota-specific T cell responses. *Science, 337*(6101), 1553–1556.

Haniffa, M., Ginhoux, F., Wang, X. N., Bigley, V., Abel, M., Dimmick, I., et al. (2009). Differential rates of replacement of human dermal dendritic cells and macrophages during hematopoietic stem cell transplantation. *The Journal of Experimental Medicine, 206*(2), 371–385.

Haniffa, M., Shin, A., Bigley, V., McGovern, N., Teo, P., See, P., et al. (2012). Human tissues contain CD141(hi) cross-presenting dendritic cells with functional homology to mouse CD103(+) nonlymphoid dendritic Cells. *Immunity, 37*(1), 60–73.

Hansel, A., Gunther, C., Ingwersen, J., Starke, J., Schmitz, M., Bachmann, M., et al. (2011). Human slan (6-sulfo LacNAc) dendritic cells are inflammatory dermal dendritic cells in psoriasis and drive strong TH17/TH1 T-cell responses. *The Journal of Allergy and Clinical Immunology, 127*(3), 787–794, e1–9.

Harman, A. N., Bye, C. R., Nasr, N., Sandgren, K. J., Kim, M., Mercier, S. K., et al. (2013). Identification of lineage relationships and novel markers of blood and skin human dendritic cells. *Journal of Immunology, 190*(1), 66–79.

Hart, D. N., & Fabre, J. W. (1981). Demonstration and characterization of Ia-positive dendritic cells in the interstitial connective tissues of rat heart and other tissues, but not brain. *The Journal of Experimental Medicine, 154*(2), 347–361.

Hashimoto, D., Chow, A., Noizat, C., Pearline, T., & Beasley, M. B. (2013). Tissue-resident macrophages self-maintain locally throughout adult life with minimal contribution from circulating monocytes. *Immunity, 38*(4), 792–804.

Hashimoto, D., Miller, J., & Merad, M. (2011). Dendritic cell and macrophage heterogeneity in vivo. *Immunity, 35*(3), 323–335.

Hildner, K., Edelson, B. T., Purtha, W. E., Diamond, M., Matsushita, H., Kohyama, M., et al. (2008). Batf3 deficiency reveals a critical role for CD8alpha+ dendritic cells in cytotoxic T cell immunity. *Science, 322*(5904), 1097–1100.

Hoeffel, G., Ripoche, A. C., Matheoud, D., Nascimbeni, M., Escriou, N., Lebon, P., et al. (2007). Antigen cross-presentation by human plasmacytoid dendritic cells. *Immunity, 27*(3), 481–492.

Hoeffel, G., Wang, Y., Greter, M., See, P., Teo, P., Malleret, B., et al. (2012). Adult Langerhans cells derive predominantly from embryonic fetal liver monocytes with a minor contribution of yolk sac-derived macrophages. *The Journal of Experimental Medicine, 209*(6), 1167–1181.

Hunger, R. E., Sieling, P. A., Ochoa, M. T., Sugaya, M., Burdick, A. E., Rea, T. H., et al. (2004). Langerhans cells utilize CD1a and langerin to efficiently present nonpeptide antigens to T cells. *The Journal of Clinical Investigation, 113*(5), 701–708.

Huysamen, C., Willment, J. A., Dennehy, K. M., & Brown, G. D. (2008). CLEC9A is a novel activation C-type lectin-like receptor expressed on BDCA3+ dendritic cells and a subset of monocytes. *Journal of Biological Chemistry, 283*(24), 16693–16701.

Idoyaga, J., Fiorese, C., Zbytnuik, L., Lubkin, A., Miller, J., Malissen, B., et al. (2013). Specialized role of migratory dendritic cells in peripheral tolerance induction. *The Journal of Clinical Investigation, 123*(2), 844–854.

Idoyaga, J., Suda, N., Suda, K., Park, C. G., & Steinman, R. M. (2009). Antibody to Langerin/CD207 localizes large numbers of CD8alpha+ dendritic cells to the marginal zone of mouse spleen. *Proceedings of the National Academy of Sciences of the United States of America, 106*(5), 1524–1529.

Igyarto, B. Z., Haley, K., Ortner, D., Bobr, A., Gerami-Nejad, M., Edelson, B. T., et al. (2011). Skin-resident murine dendritic cell subsets promote distinct and opposing antigen-specific T helper cell responses. *Immunity, 35*(2), 260–272.

Inaba, K., Inaba, M., Romani, N., Aya, H., Deguchi, M., Ikehara, S., et al. (1992). Generation of large numbers of dendritic cells from mouse bone marrow cultures supplemented with granulocyte/macrophage colony-stimulating factor. *The Journal of Experimental Medicine, 176*(6), 1693–1702.

Inaba, K., Steinman, R. M., Pack, M. W., Aya, H., Inaba, M., Sudo, T., et al. (1992). Identification of proliferating dendritic cell precursors in mouse blood. *The Journal of Experimental Medicine, 175*(5), 1157–1167.

Inaba, K., Steinman, R. M., Van Voorhis, W. C., & Muramatsu, S. (1983). Dendritic cells are critical accessory cells for thymus-dependent antibody responses in mouse and in man. *Proceedings of the National Academy of Sciences of the United States of America, 80*(19), 6041–6045.

Ishikawa, F., Niiro, H., Iino, T., Yoshida, S., Saito, N., Onohara, S., et al. (2007). The developmental program of human dendritic cells is operated independently of conventional myeloid and lymphoid pathways. *Blood, 110*(10), 3591–3660.

Ito, T., Yang, M., Wang, Y. H., Lande, R., Gregorio, J., Perng, O. A., et al. (2007). Plasmacytoid dendritic cells prime IL-10-producing T regulatory cells by inducible costimulator ligand. *The Journal of Experimental Medicine, 204*(1), 105–115.

Jardine, L., Barge, D., Ames-Draycott, A., Pagan, S., Cookson, S., Spickett, G., et al. CD4 is a lineage marker for human antigen presenting cells that facilitates rapid enumeration of peripheral blood monocytes and dendritic cells. Personal communication.

Jenkins, S. J., Ruckerl, D., Cook, P. C., Jones, L. H., Finkelman, F. D., van Rooijen, N., et al. (2011). Local macrophage proliferation, rather than recruitment from the blood, is a signature of TH2 inflammation. *Science, 332*(6035), 1284–1288.

Jongbloed, S. L., Kassianos, A. J., McDonald, K. J., Clark, G. J., Ju, X., Angel, C. E., et al. (2010). Human CD141+ (BDCA-3)+ dendritic cells (DCs) represent a unique myeloid DC subset that cross-presents necrotic cell antigens. *The Journal of Experimental Medicine, 207*(6), 1247–1260.

Kabashima, K., Banks, T. A., Ansel, K. M., Lu, T. T., Ware, C. F., & Cyster, J. G. (2005). Intrinsic lymphotoxin-beta receptor requirement for homeostasis of lymphoid tissue dendritic cells. *Immunity, 22*(4), 439–450.

Kanitakis, J., Morelon, E., Petruzzo, P., Badet, L., & Dubernard, J. M. (2011). Self-renewal capacity of human epidermal Langerhans cells: Observations made on a composite tissue allograft. *Experimental Dermatology, 20*(2), 145–146.

Kanitakis, J., Petruzzo, P., & Dubernard, J. M. (2004). Turnover of epidermal Langerhans' cells. *The New England Journal of Medicine, 351*(25), 2661–2662.

Kaplan, D. H., Kissenpfennig, A., & Clausen, B. E. (2008). Insights into Langerhans cell function from Langerhans cell ablation models. *European Journal of Immunology, 38*(9), 2369–2376.

Katz, S. I., Tamaki, K., & Sachs, D. H. (1979). Epidermal Langerhans cells are derived from cells originating in bone marrow. *Nature, 282*(5736), 324–336.

Kelly, R. H., Balfour, B. M., Armstrong, J. A., & Griffiths, S. (1978). Functional anatomy of lymph nodes. II. Peripheral lymph-borne mononuclear cells. *Anatomical Record, 190*(1), 5–21.

King, I. L., Kroenke, M. A., & Segal, B. M. (2010). GM-CSF-dependent, CD103+ dermal dendritic cells play a critical role in Th effector cell differentiation after subcutaneous immunization. *The Journal of Experimental Medicine, 207*(5), 953–961.

Kingston, D., Schmid, M. A., Onai, N., Obata-Onai, A., Baumjohann, D., & Manz, M. G. (2009). The concerted action of GM-CSF and Flt3-ligand on in vivo dendritic cell homeostasis. *Blood, 114*(4), 835–843.

Klechevsky, E., Liu, M., Morita, R., Banchereau, R., Thompson-Snipes, L., Palucka, A. K., et al. (2009). Understanding human myeloid dendritic cell subsets for the rational design of novel vaccines. *Human Immunology, 70*(5), 281–288.

Klechevsky, E., Morita, R., Liu, M., Cao, Y., Coquery, S., Thompson-Snipes, L., et al. (2008). Functional specializations of human epidermal langerhans cells and CD14+ dermal dendritic cells. *Immunity, 29*(3), 497–510.

Klein, U., Casola, S., Cattoretti, G., Shen, Q., Lia, M., Mo, T., et al. (2006). Transcription factor IRF4 controls plasma cell differentiation and class-switch recombination. *Nature Immunology*, 7(7), 773–782.

Langerhans, P. (1868). Uber die Nerven der menschlichen Haut. *Virchows Archives of Pathological Anatomy*, *44*, 325–337.

Langlet, C., Tamoutounour, S., Henri, S., Luche, H., Ardouin, L., Gregoire, C., et al. (2012). CD64 expression distinguishes monocyte-derived and conventional dendritic cells and reveals their distinct role during intramuscular immunization. *Journal of Immunology*, *188*(4), 1751–1760.

Laouar, Y., Welte, T., Fu, X. Y., & Flavell, R. A. (2003). STAT3 is required for Flt3L-dependent dendritic cell differentiation. *Immunity*, *19*(6), 903–912.

Larregina, A. T., Morelli, A. E., Spencer, L. A., Logar, A. J., Watkins, S. C., Thomson, A. W., et al. (2001). Dermal-resident CD14+ cells differentiate into Langerhans cells. *Nature Immunology*, *2*(12), 1151–1158.

Larsen, C. P., Steinman, R. M., Witmer-Pack, M., Hankins, D. F., Morris, P. J., & Austyn, J. M. (1990). Migration and maturation of Langerhans cells in skin transplants and explants. *The Journal of Experimental Medicine*, *172*(5), 1483–1493.

Lauterbach, H., Bathke, B., Gilles, S., Traidl-Hoffmann, C., Luber, C. A., Fejer, G., et al. (2010). Mouse CD8alpha+ DCs and human BDCA3+ DCs are major producers of IFN-lambda in response to poly IC. *The Journal of Experimental Medicine*, *207*(12), 2703–2717.

Lenz, A., Heine, M., Schuler, G., & Romani, N. (1993). Human and murine dermis contain dendritic cells. Isolation by means of a novel method and phenotypical and functional characterization. *The Journal of Clinical Investigation*, *92*(6), 2587–2596.

Lewis, K. L., Caton, M. L., Bogunovic, M., Greter, M., Grajkowska, L. T., Ng, D., et al. (2011). Notch2 receptor signaling controls functional differentiation of dendritic cells in the spleen and intestine. *Immunity*, *35*(5), 780–791.

Liu, K., & Nussenzweig, M. C. (2010). Origin and development of dendritic cells. *Immunological Reviews*, *234*(1), 45–54.

Liu, K., Victora, G. D., Schwickert, T. A., Guermonprez, P., Meredith, M. M., Yao, K., et al. (2009). In vivo analysis of dendritic cell development and homeostasis. *Science*, *324*(5925), 392–397.

Lowes, M. A., Chamian, F., Abello, M. V., Fuentes-Duculan, J., Lin, S. L., Nussbaum, R., et al. (2005). Increase in TNF-alpha and inducible nitric oxide synthase-expressing dendritic cells in psoriasis and reduction with efalizumab (anti-CD11a). *Proceedings of the National Academy of Sciences of the United States of America*, *102*(52), 19057–19062.

Lundberg, K., Albrekt, A. S., Nelissen, I., Santegoets, S., de Gruijl, T. D., Gibbs, S., et al. (2013). Transcriptional profiling of human dendritic cell populations and models—Unique profiles of in vitro dendritic cells and implications on functionality and applicability. *PLoS One*, *8*(1), e52875.

Lyman, S. D., & Jacobsen, S. E. (1998). c-kit ligand and Flt3 ligand: Stem/progenitor cell factors with overlapping yet distinct activities. *Blood*, *91*(4), 1101–1134.

Lyman, S. D., James, L., Escobar, S., Downey, H., de Vries, P., Brasel, K., et al. (1995). Identification of soluble and membrane-bound isoforms of the murine flt3 ligand generated by alternative splicing of mRNAs. *Oncogene*, *10*(1), 149–157.

MacDonald, K. P., Munster, D. J., Clark, G. J., Dzionek, A., Schmitz, J., & Hart, D. N. (2002). Characterization of human blood dendritic cell subsets. *Blood*, *100*(13), 4512–4520.

Manz, M. G., & Di Santo, J. P. (2009). Renaissance for mouse models of human hematopoiesis and immunobiology. *Nature Immunology*, *10*(10), 1039–1042.

Manz, M. G., Traver, D., Miyamoto, T., Weissman, I. L., & Akashi, K. (2001). Dendritic cell potentials of early lymphoid and myeloid progenitors. *Blood, 97*(11), 3333–3341.
Maraskovsky, E., Brasel, K., Teepe, M., Roux, E. R., Lyman, S. D., Shortman, K., et al. (1996). Dramatic increase in the numbers of functionally mature dendritic cells in Flt3 ligand-treated mice: Multiple dendritic cell subpopulations identified. *The Journal of Experimental Medicine, 184*(5), 1953–1962.
Maraskovsky, E., Daro, E., Roux, E., Teepe, M., Maliszewski, C. R., Hoek, J., et al. (2000). In vivo generation of human dendritic cell subsets by Flt3 ligand. *Blood, 96*(3), 878–884.
Marroquin, C. E., Westwood, J. A., Lapointe, R., Mixon, A., Wunderlich, J. R., Caron, D., et al. (2002). Mobilization of dendritic cell precursors in patients with cancer by flt3 ligand allows the generation of higher yields of cultured dendritic cells. *Journal of Immunotherapy, 25*(3), 278–288.
Matthews, K., Chung, N. P., Klasse, P. J., Moore, J. P., & Sanders, R. W. (2012). Potent induction of antibody-secreting B cells by human dermal-derived CD14+ dendritic cells triggered by dual TLR ligation. *Journal of Immunology, 189*(12), 5729–5744.
McKenna, H. J., de Vries, P., Brasel, K., Lyman, S. D., & Williams, D. E. (1995). Effect of flt3 ligand on the ex vivo expansion of human CD34+ hematopoietic progenitor cells. *Blood, 86*(9), 3413–3420.
McKenna, H. J., Stocking, K. L., Miller, R. E., Brasel, K., De Smedt, T., Maraskovsky, E., et al. (2000). Mice lacking flt3 ligand have deficient hematopoiesis affecting hematopoietic progenitor cells, dendritic cells, and natural killer cells. *Blood, 95*(11), 3489–3497.
McLellan, A. D., Heiser, A., Sorg, R. V., Fearnley, D. B., & Hart, D. N. (1998). Dermal dendritic cells associated with T lymphocytes in normal human skin display an activated phenotype. *The Journal of Investigative Dermatology, 111*(5), 841–849.
Merad, M., Manz, M. G., Karsunky, H., Wagers, A., Peters, W., Charo, I., et al. (2002). Langerhans cells renew in the skin throughout life under steady-state conditions. *Nature Immunology, 3*(12), 1135–1141.
Merad, M., Sathe, P., Helft, J., Miller, J., & Mortha, A. (2013). The dendritic cell lineage: Ontogeny and function of dendritic cells and their subsets in the steady state and the inflamed setting. *Annual Review of Immunology, 31*, 563–604.
Meredith, M. M., Liu, K., Darrasse-Jeze, G., Kamphorst, A. O., Schreiber, H. A., Guermonprez, P., et al. (2012). Expression of the zinc finger transcription factor zDC (Zbtb46, Btbd4) defines the classical dendritic cell lineage. *The Journal of Experimental Medicine, 209*(6), 1153–1165.
Metlay, J. P., Witmer-Pack, M. D., Agger, R., Crowley, M. T., Lawless, D., & Steinman, R. M. (1990). The distinct leukocyte integrins of mouse spleen dendritic cells as identified with new hamster monoclonal antibodies. *The Journal of Experimental Medicine, 171*(5), 1753–1771.
Meunier, L., Bohjanen, K., Voorhees, J. J., & Cooper, K. D. (1994). Retinoic acid upregulates human Langerhans cell antigen presentation and surface expression of HLA-DR and CD11c, a beta 2 integrin critically involved in T-cell activation. *The Journal of Investigative Dermatology, 103*(6), 775–779.
Miller, J. C., Brown, B. D., Shay, T., Gautier, E. L., Jojic, V., Cohain, A., et al. (2012). Deciphering the transcriptional network of the dendritic cell lineage. *Nature Immunology, 13*(9), 888–899.
Miloud, T., Fiegler, N., Suffner, J., Hammerling, G. J., & Garbi, N. (2012). Organ-specific cellular requirements for in vivo dendritic cell generation. *Journal of Immunology, 188*(3), 1125–1135.
Mittag, D., Proietto, A. I., Loudovaris, T., Mannering, S. I., Vremec, D., Shortman, K., et al. (2011). Human dendritic cell subsets from spleen and blood are similar in phenotype and function but modified by donor health status. *Journal of Immunology, 186*(11), 6207–6217.

Morelli, A. E., Rubin, J. P., Erdos, G., Tkacheva, O. A., Mathers, A. R., Zahorchak, A. F., et al. (2005). CD4+ T cell responses elicited by different subsets of human skin migratory dendritic cells. *Journal of Immunology*, *175*(12), 7905–7915.
Morse, M. A., Nair, S., Fernandez-Casal, M., Deng, Y., St Peter, M., Williams, R., et al. (2000). Preoperative mobilization of circulating dendritic cells by Flt3 ligand administration to patients with metastatic colon cancer. *Journal of Clinical Oncology*, *18*(23), 3883–3893.
Moseman, E. A., Liang, X., Dawson, A. J., Panoskaltsis-Mortari, A., Krieg, A. M., Liu, Y. J., et al. (2004). Human plasmacytoid dendritic cells activated by CpG oligodeoxynucleotides induce the generation of CD4+ CD25+ regulatory T cells. *Journal of Immunology*, *173*(7), 4433–4442.
Naik, S., Bouladoux, N., Wilhelm, C., Molloy, M. J., Salcedo, R., Kastenmuller, W., et al. (2012). Compartmentalized control of skin immunity by resident commensals. *Science*, *337*(6098), 1115–1119.
Naik, S. H., Metcalf, D., van Nieuwenhuijze, A., Wicks, I., Wu, L., O'Keeffe, M., et al. (2006). Intrasplenic steady-state dendritic cell precursors that are distinct from monocytes. *Nature Immunology*, 7(6), 663–671.
Nakano, H., Yanagita, M., & Gunn, M. D. (2001). CD11c(+)B220(+)Gr-1(+) cells in mouse lymph nodes and spleen display characteristics of plasmacytoid dendritic cells. *The Journal of Experimental Medicine*, *194*(8), 1171–1178.
Nestle, F. O., Conrad, C., Tun-Kyi, A., Homey, B., Gombert, M., Boyman, O., et al. (2005). Plasmacytoid predendritic cells initiate psoriasis through interferon-alpha production. *The Journal of Experimental Medicine*, *202*(1), 135–143.
Nestle, F. O., Zheng, X. G., Thompson, C. B., Turka, L. A., & Nickoloff, B. J. (1993). Characterization of dermal dendritic cells obtained from normal human skin reveals phenotypic and functionally distinctive subsets. *Journal of Immunology*, *151*(11), 6535–6545.
Nussenzweig, M. C., Steinman, R. M., Gutchinov, B., & Cohn, Z. A. (1980). Dendritic cells are accessory cells for the development of anti-trinitrophenyl cytotoxic T lymphocytes. *The Journal of Experimental Medicine*, *152*(4), 1070–1084.
O'Doherty, U., Peng, M., Gezelter, S., Swiggard, W. J., Betjes, M., Bhardwaj, N., et al. (1994). Human blood contains two subsets of dendritic cells, one immunologically mature and the other immature. *Immunology*, *82*(3), 487–493.
O'Keeffe, M., Hochrein, H., Vremec, D., Scott, B., Hertzog, P., Tatarczuch, L., et al. (2003). Dendritic cell precursor populations of mouse blood: Identification of the murine homologues of human blood plasmacytoid pre-DC2 and CD11c+ DC1 precursors. *Blood*, *101*(4), 1453–1459.
Ochoa, M. T., Loncaric, A., Krutzik, S. R., Becker, T. C., & Modlin, R. L. (2008). "Dermal dendritic cells" comprise two distinct populations: CD1(+) dendritic cells and CD209(+) macrophages. *The Journal of Investigative Dermatology*, *128*(9), 2225–2231.
Ohl, L., Mohaupt, M., Czeloth, N., Hintzen, G., Kiafard, Z., Zwirner, J., et al. (2004). CCR7 governs skin dendritic cell migration under inflammatory and steady-state conditions. *Immunity*, *21*(2), 279–288.
Olweus, J., BitMansour, A., Warnke, R., Thompson, P. A., Carballido, J., Picker, L. J., et al. (1997). Dendritic cell ontogeny: A human dendritic cell lineage of myeloid origin. *Proceedings of the National Academy of Sciences of the United States of America*, *94*(23), 12551–12556.
Onai, N., Kurabayashi, K., Hosoi-Amaike, M., Toyama-Sorimachi, N., Matsushima, K., Inaba, K., et al. (2013). A clonogenic progenitor with prominent plasmacytoid dendritic cell developmental potential. *Immunity*, *38*(5), 943–957.
Osugi, Y., Vuckovic, S., & Hart, D. N. (2002). Myeloid blood CD11c(+) dendritic cells and monocyte-derived dendritic cells differ in their ability to stimulate T lymphocytes. *Blood*, *100*(8), 2858–2866.

Pelayo, R., Hirose, J., Huang, J., Garrett, K. P., Delogu, A., Busslinger, M., et al. (2005). Derivation of 2 categories of plasmacytoid dendritic cells in murine bone marrow. *Blood*, *105*(11), 4407–4415.

Penel-Sotirakis, K., Simonazzi, E., Peguet-Navarro, J., & Rozieres, A. (2012). Differential capacity of human skin dendritic cells to polarize CD4+ T cells into IL-17, IL-21 and IL-22 producing cells. *PLoS One*, 7(11), e45680.

Perussia, B., Fanning, V., & Trinchieri, G. (1985). A leukocyte subset bearing HLA-DR antigens is responsible for in vitro alpha interferon production in response to viruses. *Natural Immunity and Cell Growth Regulation*, *4*(3), 120–137.

Plantinga, M., Guilliams, M., Vanheerswynghels, M., Deswarte, K., Branco-Madeira, F., Toussaint, W., et al. (2013). Conventional and monocyte-derived CD11b(+) dendritic cells initiate and maintain T helper 2 cell-mediated immunity to house dust mite allergen. *Immunity*, *38*(2), 322–335.

Poulin, L. F., Henri, S., de Bovis, B., Devilard, E., Kissenpfennig, A., & Malissen, B. (2007). The dermis contains langerin+ dendritic cells that develop and function independently of epidermal Langerhans cells. *The Journal of Experimental Medicine*, *204*(13), 3119–3131.

Poulin, L. F., Reyal, Y., Uronen-Hansson, H., Schraml, B. U., Sancho, D., Murphy, K. M., et al. (2012). DNGR-1 is a specific and universal marker of mouse and human Batf3-dependent dendritic cells in lymphoid and nonlymphoid tissues. *Blood*, *119*(25), 6052–6062.

Poulin, L. F., Salio, M., Griessinger, E., Anjos-Afonso, F., Craciun, L., Chen, J. L., et al. (2010). Characterization of human DNGR-1+BDCA3+ leukocytes as putative equivalents of mouse CD8alpha+ dendritic cells. *The Journal of Experimental Medicine*, *207*(6), 1261–1271.

Qiu, C. H., Miyake, Y., Kaise, H., Kitamura, H., Ohara, O., & Tanaka, M. (2009). Novel subset of CD8{alpha}+ dendritic cells localized in the marginal zone is responsible for tolerance to cell-associated antigens. *Journal of Immunology*, *182*(7), 4127–4136.

Rathinam, C., Poueymirou, W. T., Rojas, J., Murphy, A. J., Valenzuela, D. M., Yancopoulos, G. D., et al. (2011). Efficient differentiation and function of human macrophages in humanized CSF-1 mice. *Blood*, *118*(11), 3119–3128.

Rausch, E., Kaiserling, E., & Goos, M. (1977). Langerhans cells and interdigitating reticulum cells in the thymus-dependent region in human dermatopathic lymphadenitis. *Virchows Archiv. B: Cell Pathology*, *25*(4), 327–343.

Reid, C. D., Stackpoole, A., Meager, A., & Tikerpae, J. (1992). Interactions of tumor necrosis factor with granulocyte-macrophage colony-stimulating factor and other cytokines in the regulation of dendritic cell growth in vitro from early bipotent CD34+ progenitors in human bone marrow. *Journal of Immunology*, *149*(8), 2681–2688.

Reizis, B. (2010). Regulation of plasmacytoid dendritic cell development. *Current Opinion in Immunology*, *22*(2), 206–211.

Reizis, B., Bunin, A., Ghosh, H. S., Lewis, K. L., & Sisirak, V. (2011). Plasmacytoid dendritic cells: Recent progress and open questions. *Annual Review of Immunology*, *29*, 163–183.

Ren, Y., Silverstein, R. L., Allen, J., & Savill, J. (1995). CD36 gene transfer confers capacity for phagocytosis of cells undergoing apoptosis. *The Journal of Experimental Medicine*, *181*(5), 1857–1862.

Rissoan, M. C., Soumelis, V., Kadowaki, N., Grouard, G., Briere, F., de Waal Malefyt, R., et al. (1999). Reciprocal control of T helper cell and dendritic cell differentiation. *Science*, *283*(5405), 1183–1186.

Robbins, S. H., Walzer, T., Dembele, D., Thibault, C., Defays, A., Bessou, G., et al. (2008). Novel insights into the relationships between dendritic cell subsets in human and mouse revealed by genome-wide expression profiling. *Genome Biology*, *9*(1), R17.

Rock, K. L. (2003). The ins and outs of cross-presentation. *Nature Immunology*, *4*(10), 941–943.
Romani, N., Brunner, P. M., & Stingl, G. (2012). Changing views of the role of Langerhans cells. *The Journal of Investigative Dermatology*, *132*(3 Pt 2), 872–881.
Romani, N., Gruner, S., Brang, D., Kämpgen, E., Lenz, A., Trockenbacher, B., et al. (1994). Proliferating dendritic cell progenitors in human blood. *The Journal of Experimental Medicine*, *180*(1), 83–93.
Romani, N., Koide, S., Crowley, M., Witmer-Pack, M., Livingstone, A. M., Fathman, C. G., et al. (1989). Presentation of exogenous protein antigens by dendritic cells to T cell clones. Intact protein is presented best by immature, epidermal Langerhans cells. *The Journal of Experimental Medicine*, *169*(3), 1169–1178.
Romani, N., Schuler, G., & Fritsch, P. (1986). Ontogeny of Ia-positive and Thy-1-positive leukocytes of murine epidermis. *The Journal of Investigative Dermatology*, *86*(2), 129–133.
Sadhu, C., Ting, H. J., Lipsky, B., Hensley, K., Garcia-Martinez, L. F., Simon, S. I., et al. (2007). CD11c/CD18: Novel ligands and a role in delayed-type hypersensitivity. *Journal of Leukocyte Biology*, *81*(6), 1395–1403.
Sallusto, F., & Lanzavecchia, A. (1994). Efficient presentation of soluble antigen by cultured human dendritic cells is maintained by granulocyte/macrophage colony-stimulating factor plus interleukin 4 and downregulated by tumor necrosis factor alpha. *The Journal of Experimental Medicine*, *179*(4), 1109–1118.
Sancho, D., Joffre, O. P., Keller, A. M., Rogers, N. C., Martinez, D., Hernanz-Falcon, P., et al. (2009). Identification of a dendritic cell receptor that couples sensing of necrosis to immunity. *Nature*, *458*(7240), 899–903.
Satpathy, A. T., KC, W., Albring, J. C., Edelson, B. T., Kretzer, N. M., Bhattacharya, D., et al. (2012). Zbtb46 expression distinguishes classical dendritic cells and their committed progenitors from other immune lineages. *The Journal of Experimental Medicine*, *209*(6), 1135–1152.
Schakel, K., Kannagi, R., Kniep, B., Goto, Y., Mitsuoka, C., Zwirner, J., et al. (2002). 6-Sulfo LacNAc, a novel carbohydrate modification of PSGL-1, defines an inflammatory type of human dendritic cells. *Immunity*, *17*(3), 289–301.
Schakel, K., von Kietzell, M., Hansel, A., Ebling, A., Schulze, L., Haase, M., et al. (2006). Human 6-sulfo LacNAc-expressing dendritic cells are principal producers of early interleukin-12 and are controlled by erythrocytes. *Immunity*, *24*(6), 767–777.
Schlitzer, A., McGovern, N., Teo, P., Zelante, T., Atarashi, K., Low, D., et al. (2013). IRF4 transcription factor-dependent CD11b$^+$ dendritic cells in human and mouse control mucosal IL-17 cytokine responses. *Immunity*, *38*, 970–983.
Schuler, G., & Steinman, R. M. (1985). Murine epidermal Langerhans cells mature into potent immunostimulatory dendritic cells in vitro. *The Journal of Experimental Medicine*, *161*(3), 526–546.
Schulz, O., Diebold, S. S., Chen, M., Naslund, T. I., Nolte, M. A., Alexopoulou, L., et al. (2005). Toll-like receptor 3 promotes cross-priming to virus-infected cells. *Nature*, *433*(7028), 887–892.
Schuster, C., Vaculik, C., Fiala, C., Meindl, S., Brandt, O., Imhof, M., et al. (2009). HLA-DR+ leukocytes acquire CD1 antigens in embryonic and fetal human skin and contain functional antigen-presenting cells. *The Journal of Experimental Medicine*, *206*(1), 169–181.
Segura, E., Touzot, M., Bohineust, A., Cappuccio, A., Chiocchia, G., Hosmalin, A., et al. (2013). Human inflammatory dendritic cells induce th17 cell differentiation. *Immunity*, *38*(2), 336–348.
Segura, E., Valladeau-Guilemond, J., Donnadieu, M.-H., Sastre-Garau, X., Soumelis, V., & Amigorena, S. (2012). Characterization of resident and migratory dendritic cells in human lymph nodes. *The Journal of Experimental Medicine*, *209*(4), 653–660.

Seneschal, J., Clark, R. A., Gehad, A., Baecher-Allan, C. M., & Kupper, T. S. (2012). Human epidermal langerhans cells maintain immune homeostasis in skin by activating skin resident regulatory T cells. *Immunity*, *36*(5), 873–884.
Serbina, N. V., Salazar-Mather, T. P., Biron, C. A., Kuziel, W. A., & Pamer, E. G. (2003). TNF/iNOS-producing dendritic cells mediate innate immune defense against bacterial infection. *Immunity*, *19*(1), 59–70.
Sertl, K., Takemura, T., Tschachler, E., Ferrans, V. J., Kaliner, M. A., & Shevach, E. M. (1986). Dendritic cells with antigen-presenting capability reside in airway epithelium, lung parenchyma, and visceral pleura. *The Journal of Experimental Medicine*, *163*(2), 436–451.
Siegal, F. P., Kadowaki, N., Shodell, M., Fitzgerald-Bocarsly, P. A., Shah, K., Ho, S., et al. (1999). The nature of the principal type 1 interferon-producing cells in human blood. *Science*, *284*(5421), 1835–1837.
Sixt, M., Kanazawa, N., Selg, M., Samson, T., Roos, G., Reinhardt, D. P., et al. (2005). The conduit system transports soluble antigens from the afferent lymph to resident dendritic cells in the T cell area of the lymph node. *Immunity*, *22*(1), 19–29.
Stary, G., Klein, I., Bauer, W., Koszik, F., Reininger, B., Kohlhofer, S., et al. (2011). Glucocorticosteroids modify Langerhans cells to produce TGF-beta and expand regulatory T cells. *Journal of Immunology*, *186*(1), 103–112.
Steinman, R. M., & Cohn, Z. A. (1973). Identification of a novel cell type in peripheral lymphoid organs of mice. I. Morphology, quantitation, tissue distribution. *The Journal of Experimental Medicine*, *137*(5), 1142–1162.
Steinman, R. M., Hawiger, D., Liu, K., Bonifaz, L., Bonnyay, D., Mahnke, K., et al. (2003). Dendritic cell function in vivo during the steady state: A role in peripheral tolerance. *Annals of the New York Academy of Sciences*, *987*, 15–25.
Steinman, R. M., Kaplan, G., Witmer, M. D., & Cohn, Z. A. (1979). Identification of a novel cell type in peripheral lymphoid organs of mice. V. Purification of spleen dendritic cells, new surface markers, and maintenance in vitro. *The Journal of Experimental Medicine*, *149*(1), 1–16.
Steinman, R. M., Lustig, D. S., & Cohn, Z. A. (1974). Identification of a novel cell type in peripheral lymphoid organs of mice. 3. Functional properties in vivo. *The Journal of Experimental Medicine*, *139*(6), 1431–1445.
Steinman, R. M., & Nussenzweig, M. C. (1980). Dendritic cells: Features and functions. *Immunological Reviews*, *53*, 127–147.
Steinman, R. M., & Witmer, M. D. (1978). Lymphoid dendritic cells are potent stimulators of the primary mixed leukocyte reaction in mice. *Proceedings of the National Academy of Sciences of the United States of America*, *75*(10), 5132–5136.
Stingl, G., Katz, S. I., Clement, L., Green, I., & Shevach, E. M. (1978). Immunologic functions of Ia-bearing epidermal Langerhans cells. *Journal of Immunology*, *121*(5), 2005–2013.
Stingl, G., Katz, S. I., Shevach, E. M., Wolff-Schreiner, E., & Green, I. (1978). Detection of Ia antigens on Langerhans cells in guinea pig skin. *Journal of Immunology*, *120*(2), 570–578.
Strobl, H., Riedl, E., Scheinecker, C., Bello-Fernandez, C., Pickl, W. F., Rappersberger, K., et al. (1996). TGF-beta 1 promotes in vitro development of dendritic cells from CD34+ hemopoietic progenitors. *Journal of Immunology*, *157*(4), 1499–1507.
Summers, K. L., Hock, B. D., McKenzie, J. L., & Hart, D. N. (2001). Phenotypic characterization of five dendritic cell subsets in human tonsils. *American Journal of Pathology*, *159*(1), 285–295.
Sun, C. M., Hall, J. A., Blank, R. B., Bouladoux, N., Oukka, M., Mora, J. R., et al. (2007). Small intestine lamina propria dendritic cells promote de novo generation of Foxp3 T reg cells via retinoic acid. *The Journal of Experimental Medicine*, *204*(8), 1775–1785.
Sung, S. S., Fu, S. M., Rose, C. E. J., Gaskin, F., Ju, S. T., & Beaty, S. R. (2006). A major lung CD103 (alphaE)-beta7 integrin-positive epithelial dendritic cell population

expressing Langerin and tight junction proteins. *Journal of Immunology, 176*(4), 2161–2172.

Suzuki, S., Honma, K., Matsuyama, T., Suzuki, K., Toriyama, K., Akitoyo, I., et al. (2004). Critical roles of interferon regulatory factor 4 in CD11bhighCD8alpha– dendritic cell development. *Proceedings of the National Academy of Sciences of the United States of America, 101*(24), 8981–8986.

Tailor, P., Tamura, T., Morse, H. C., & Ozato, K. (2008). The BXH2 mutation in IRF8 differentially impairs dendritic cell subset development in the mouse. *Blood, 111*(4), 1942–1945.

Takahashi, K., Asagoe, K., Zaishun, J., Yanai, H., Yoshino, T., Hayashi, K., et al. (1998). Heterogeneity of dendritic cells in human superficial lymph node: In vitro maturation of immature dendritic cells into mature or activated interdigitating reticulum cells. *American Journal of Pathology, 153*(3), 745–755.

Tamoutounour, S., Henri, S., Lelouard, H., de Bovis, B., de Haar, C., van der Woude, C. J., et al. (2012). CD64 distinguishes macrophages from dendritic cells in the gut and reveals the Th1-inducing role of mesenteric lymph node macrophages during colitis. *European Journal of Immunology, 42*(12), 3150–3166.

Tamura, T., Tailor, P., Yamaoka, K., Kong, H. J., Tsujimura, H., O'Shea, J. J., et al. (2005). IFN regulatory factor-4 and -8 govern dendritic cell subset development and their functional diversity. *Journal of Immunology, 174*(5), 2573–2581.

Tanaka, S., Saito, Y., Kunisawa, J., Kurashima, Y., Wake, T., Suzuki, N., et al. (2012). Development of mature and functional human myeloid subsets in hematopoietic stem cell-engrafted NOD/SCID/IL2rgammaKO mice. *Journal of Immunology, 188*(12), 6145–6155.

Tse, Y., & Cooper, K. D. (1990). Cutaneous dermal Ia+ cells are capable of initiating delayed type hypersensitivity responses. *The Journal of Investigative Dermatology, 94*(3), 267–272.

van de Ven, R., van den Hout, M. F., Lindenberg, J. J., Sluijter, B. J., van Leeuwen, P. A., Lougheed, S. M., et al. (2011). Characterization of four conventional dendritic cell subsets in human skin-draining lymph nodes in relation to T-cell activation. *Blood, 118*(9), 2502–2510.

van der Aar, A. M., Sylva-Steenland, R. M., Bos, J. D., Kapsenberg, M. L., de Jong, E. C., & Teunissen, M. B. (2007). Loss of TLR2, TLR4, and TLR5 on Langerhans cells abolishes bacterial recognition. *Journal of Immunology, 178*(4), 1986–1990.

van der Vlist, M., de Witte, L., de Vries, R. D., Litjens, M., de Jong, M. A., Fluitsma, D., et al. (2011). Human Langerhans cells capture measles virus through Langerin and present viral antigens to CD4(+) T cells but are incapable of cross-presentation. *European Journal of Immunology, 41*(9), 2619–2631.

Van Voorhis, W. C., Hair, L. S., Steinman, R. M., & Kaplan, G. (1982). Human dendritic cells. Enrichment and characterization from peripheral blood. *The Journal of Experimental Medicine, 155*(4), 1172–1187.

Veres, T. Z., Voedisch, S., Spies, E., Valtonen, J., Prenzler, F., & Braun, A. (2013). Aeroallergen challenge promotes dendritic cell proliferation in the airways. *Journal of Immunology, 190*(3), 897–903.

Villadangos, J. A., & Schnorrer, P. (2007). Intrinsic and cooperative antigen-presenting functions of dendritic-cell subsets in vivo. *Nature Reviews Immunology*, 7(7), 543–555.

Vremec, D., Pooley, J., Hochrein, H., Wu, L., & Shortman, K. (2000). CD4 and CD8 expression by dendritic cell subtypes in mouse thymus and spleen. *Journal of Immunology, 164*(6), 2978–2986.

Vremec, D., & Shortman, K. (1997). Dendritic cell subtypes in mouse lymphoid organs: Cross-correlation of surface markers, changes with incubation, and differences among thymus, spleen, and lymph nodes. *Journal of Immunology, 159*(2), 565–573.

Vremec, D., Zorbas, M., Scollay, R., Saunders, D. J., Ardavin, C. F., Wu, L., et al. (1992). The surface phenotype of dendritic cells purified from mouse thymus and spleen: Investigation of the CD8 expression by a subpopulation of dendritic cells. *The Journal of Experimental Medicine*, *176*(1), 47–58.
Wakim, L. M., Waithman, J., van Rooijen, N., Heath, W. R., & Carbone, F. R. (2008). Dendritic cell-induced memory T cell activation in nonlymphoid tissues. *Science*, *319*(5860), 198–202.
Wang, Y. G., Kim, K. D., Wang, J., Yu, P., & Fu, Y. X. (2005). Stimulating lymphotoxin beta receptor on the dendritic cells is critical for their homeostasis and expansion. *Journal of Immunology*, *175*(10), 6997–7002.
Waskow, C., Liu, K., Darrasse-Jeze, G., Guermonprez, P., Ginhoux, F., Merad, M., et al. (2008). The receptor tyrosine kinase Flt3 is required for dendritic cell development in peripheral lymphoid tissues. *Nature Immunology*, *9*(6), 676–683.
Watowich, S. S., & Liu, Y. J. (2010). Mechanisms regulating dendritic cell specification and development. *Immunological Reviews*, *238*(1), 76–92.
Wollenberg, A., Kraft, S., Hanau, D., & Bieber, T. (1996). Immunomorphological and ultrastructural characterization of Langerhans cells and a novel, inflammatory dendritic epidermal cell (IDEC) population in lesional skin of atopic eczema. *The Journal of Investigative Dermatology*, *106*(3), 446–453.
Yona, S., Kim, K. W., Wolf, Y., Mildner, A., Varol, D., Breker, M., et al. (2013). Fate mapping reveals origins and dynamics of monocytes and tissue macrophages under homeostasis. *Immunity*, *38*(1), 79–91.
Yoshida, H., Hayashi, S., Kunisada, T., Ogawa, M., Nishikawa, S., Okamura, H., et al. (1990). The murine mutation osteopetrosis is in the coding region of the macrophage colony stimulating factor gene. *Nature*, *345*(6274), 442–444.
Yu, C. I., Becker, C., Wang, Y., Marches, F., Helft, J., Leboeuf, M., et al. (2013). Human CD1c dendritic cells drive the differentiation of CD103 CD8 mucosal effector T cells via the cytokine TGF-beta. *Immunity*, *38*(4), 818–830.
Zaba, L. C., Fuentes-Duculan, J., Steinman, R. M., Krueger, J. G., & Lowes, M. A. (2007). Normal human dermis contains distinct populations of CD11c+BDCA-1+ dendritic cells and CD163+FXIIIA+ macrophages. *The Journal of Clinical Investigation*, *117*(9), 2517–2525.
Zaba, L. C., Krueger, J. G., & Lowes, M. A. (2009). Resident and "inflammatory" dendritic cells in human skin. *The Journal of Investigative Dermatology*, *129*(2), 302–308.
Zhan, Y., Carrington, E. M., van Nieuwenhuijze, A., Bedoui, S., Seah, S., Xu, Y., et al. (2011). GM-CSF increases cross-presentation and CD103 expression by mouse CD8 (+) spleen dendritic cells. *European Journal of Immunology*, *41*(9), 2585–2595.
Ziegler-Heitbrock, L., Ancuta, P., Crowe, S., Dalod, M., Grau, V., Hart, D. N., et al. (2010). Nomenclature of monocytes and dendritic cells in blood. *Blood*, *116*(16), e74–e80.
Zigmond, E., Varol, C., Farache, J., Elmaliah, E., Satpathy, A. T., Friedlander, G., et al. (2012). Ly6C hi monocytes in the inflamed colon give rise to proinflammatory effector cells and migratory antigen-presenting cells. *Immunity*, *37*(6), 1076–1090.

CHAPTER TWO

Dendritic Cell Migration Through the Lymphatic Vasculature to Lymph Nodes

Andrew M. Platt[*,1], **Gwendalyn J. Randolph**[†,1]
[*]Institute of Immunology, Infection and Inflammation, Glasgow Biomedical Research Centre, University of Glasgow, Glasgow, United Kingdom
[†]Department of Pathology and Immunology, Washington University, St. Louis, Missouri, USA
[1]Corresponding author: e-mail address: andrew.platt@glasgow.ac.uk; grandolph@path.wustl.edu

Contents

Abstract

The mobilization of antigen-presenting dendritic cells (DCs) from peripheral tissues to draining lymph nodes drives the initiation of adaptive immune responses. Recent advances have been made in understanding how and where DCs enter the lymphatic vasculature and what mechanisms control this process. In this chapter, we highlight these advances. Delineating DC–lymphatic vessel interactions is critical for our fundamental understanding of DC trafficking in states of health and disease and for efforts to manipulate DC mobilization for immunotherapy and vaccination.

Dendritic cells (DCs) are the most potent antigen-presenting cells in the body and are critical for acquiring and processing antigen in the periphery and initiating adaptive immune responses. DCs act as sentinels in peripheral tissues where they are present in high numbers especially in tissues with abundant antigen exposure such as the skin and mucosal surfaces. Upon activation in the periphery, DCs mobilize through lymphatic vessels to draining lymph nodes (LNs). Lymph-trafficking DCs include $CD103^+$ and $CD11b^+$

Advances in Immunology, Volume 120
ISSN 0065-2776
http://dx.doi.org/10.1016/B978-0-12-417028-5.00002-8

DC subsets (Miller et al., 2012) and can also include monocyte-derived cells that closely resemble DCs (Hohl et al., 2009; Randolph, Inaba, Robbiani, Steinman, & Muller, 1999). Upon arrival in the LN, activated DCs join the so-called LN-resident DCs—close counterparts to the $CD103^+$ and $CD11b^+$ DCs that populate lymphoid organs continuously. In LNs, these precursors arrive via the high endothelial venules (HEVs) (Liu et al., 2009). In the absence of inflammation, LN-resident DCs dominate (Jakubzick et al., 2008) but inflammatory conditions can greatly expand the proportion of lymph-derived DCs, as DC transit increases in lymph by an order of magnitude or more (MacPherson, Jenkins, Stein, & Edwards, 1995). Lymph-derived and LN-resident DCs work together to present antigen to specific T cells and influence their differentiation to shape the immune response initiated (Jakubzick et al., 2008). The extent of and mechanisms underlying the cooperation between DCs that arrive in LNs by different routes remain to be fully characterized and may differ depending upon the nature of the stimulus that fuels the immune response. In general, the failure of DCs to emigrate to LNs is associated with poor induction of immunity (Itano et al., 2003), even when soluble antigen still arrives through the lymph for presentation by LN-resident DCs. Thus, despite the emergence of a new paradigm in recent years that LNs are populated with DCs through precursors that arrive from the blood vasculature, there remains much interest in understanding how DC entry into the lymphatic vasculature is controlled. Indeed, as it has recently emerged that lymph-migratory DCs are critical in regulating development and maturation of the HEVs in LNs (Girard, Moussion, & Forster, 2012; Moussion & Girard, 2011), lymph-derived DCs ultimately regulate the population of LNs by resident DCs derived from blood.

1. STRUCTURE AND FUNCTION OF THE LYMPHATIC VASCULATURE

Lymphatic vessels are found in all tissues with the exception of the bone marrow and central nervous system (Tammela & Alitalo, 2010). The lymphatic system is organized such that absorptive initial lymphatic capillaries with blind-ended termini are positioned in most organs (Schmid-Schonbein, 1990). Lymphatic capillaries consist of a single layer of lymphatic endothelial cells (LECs). They are not uniform in size, but instead range widely in width from 10 to 80 μm in diameter (Fischer et al., 1996; Spiegel et al., 1992). LECs of capillaries express high levels of the membrane glycoprotein lymphatic vessel endothelial hyaluronan receptor-1 (LYVE-1). LYVE-1 is dispensable for normal lymphatic development and DC mobilization to LNs (Gale et al., 2007), but as a receptor for hyaluronan, it likely participates importantly in the regulation of immunity and inflammation (Jackson, 2009).

The endothelial cells of lymphatic capillaries exhibit an oak leaf shape with overlapping flaps at their border, which account for their absorptive nature (Fig. 2.1; Baluk et al., 2007). These "button-like" junctions between endothelial cells possess the same junctional proteins as junctions between blood endothelial cells, so it is not their molecular composition but rather their organization that distinguishes them (Baluk et al., 2007). We will discuss in the succeeding text the critical organization of these junctions in the promotion of DC entry into lymphatic vessels.

As lymphatics extend toward LNs, the initial lymphatic capillaries converge into larger collecting lymphatic vessels (Schmid-Schonbein, 1990). In mice, these vessels express little if any LYVE-1 (Makinen et al., 2005) and the LECs of collecting vessels are spindle-shaped. Their distinct features include luminal valves that ensure unidirectional flow and an organized mural wall composed of specialized muscle cells (Muthuchamy & Zawieja, 2008). Collecting vessels consist of bulb-like segments called lymphangions that, driven by the muscle cells, contract in a coordinated manner so that lymph pushed through one lymphangion is thrust into the next as the valve closes to prevent fluid backflow. Collecting vessels possess an inherent leakiness (Scallan & Huxley, 2010) that means that some of the contents of lymph are lost in transit. In contrast to lymphatic capillaries, the intercellular junctions between LECs of collecting vessels have a "zipper-like" appearance, more closely resembling those between endothelial cells lining blood vessels and are thus not considered to be absorptive (Baluk et al., 2007). Deep collecting lymphatic vessels are embedded in the perinodal adipose tissue, contact the subcapsular sinus of the LN, and transition into smaller terminal lymphatic capillaries that terminate at the LN capsule (Randolph, Angeli, & Swartz, 2005). Lymph and the cells within it then pass through and around the capsule, with different cell types finding distinct positions in which to enter the LN parenchyma—T cells enter the parenchyma after passing along the sinus toward the medulla, but DCs progress to the medulla near the sites along the sinus where they enter the LN (Braun et al., 2011). Lymph exits the LN through the efferent lymphatic vessel with apparent similar properties as the afferent collecting vessel and can travel through several LNs before returning to the blood circulation via the thoracic duct.

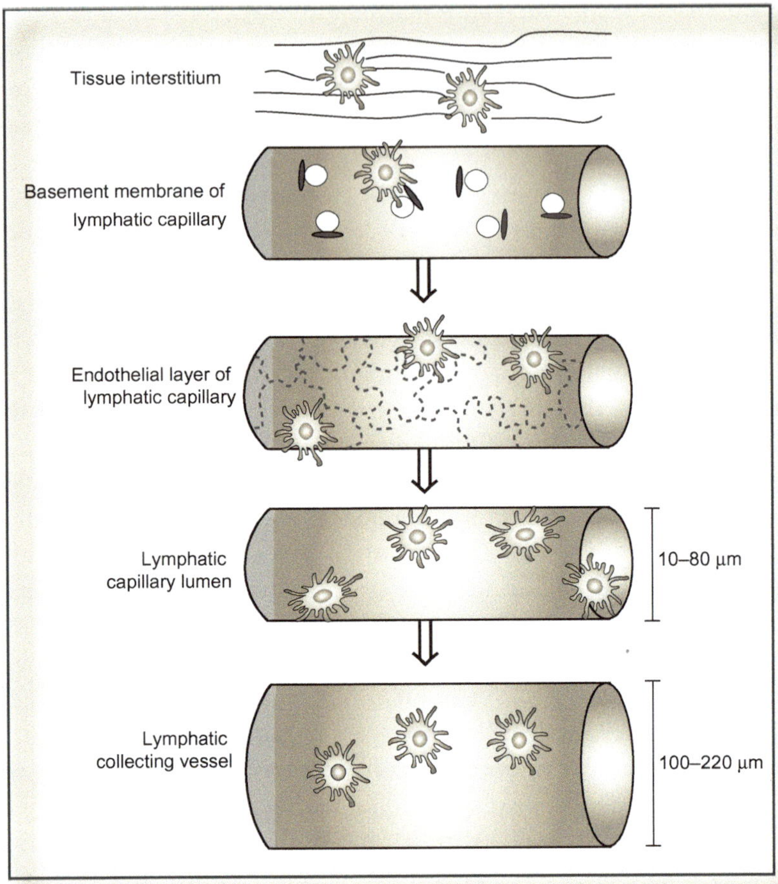

Figure 2.1 A depiction of the journey of DCs from the tissue interstitium to the draining LN through the lymphatic network. After navigation through the extracellular matrix, DCs must traverse the lymphatic basement membrane that contains "pre-formed portals" (white; ~1–2 μm diameter), commonly associated with CCL21 puncta (in red). DCs must then squeeze through the gaps in the "button-like" junctions (in red) between oak leaf-shaped lymphatic endothelial cells (LECs) before entering into the lumen of the vessel. The gaps between these junctions are 2–3 μm. Once inside, DCs continue to interact with the luminal side of LECs in a process termed "intralymphatic" crawling, likely facilitated by the flat cross section of these vessels (10–80 μm diameter). When DCs reach collecting vessels, the increased diameter (100–220 μm) and flow rate contribute to a 200-fold faster flow through this region compared with the initial capillaries. (For interpretation of the references to color in this figure legend, the reader is referred to the online version of this chapter.)

When the lymphatic system is defective, there is an accumulation of protein-rich interstitial fluid in the peripheral tissue that drives chronic inflammation. This, in turn, is thought to be linked to fibrosis and impaired immune responses (Lister, Black, Calonje, & Burnand, 1997; Mallon, Powell, Mortimer, & Ryan, 1997; Rockson, 2001), but little is known regarding the sequence of events or causes of adverse changes. Although primary or congenital lymphedema is relatively rare, the condition is profoundly debilitating. Further, secondary or acquired lymphedema is far more common and is particularly frequent during filariasis and following breast cancer surgery in industrialized countries (Harwood & Mortimer, 1995). Although the lymphatic defects during lymphedema clearly lead to fluid accumulation, until recently, how they impact the capacity of DCs to mobilize from the periphery to draining LNs remained unexplored.

2. DC MIGRATION INTO LYMPHATICS AND THE REQUIREMENT FOR SPECIALIZED LYMPHATIC CAPILLARIES

We know that DC mobilization to LNs is a constitutive process because DCs can be recovered from lymph in the steady state (Brand, Hunziker, & Braathen, 1992; Bujdoso, Hopkins, Dutia, Young, & McConnell, 1989; Pugh, MacPherson, & Steer, 1983) and the putative skin-derived MHC-II^{hi} DCs are consistently present in skin-draining LNs. Further, using mice transgenic for the photoswitchable protein, Kaede, demonstrated that approximately 5% of LN DCs per 24 h are derived from the skin in the steady state (Tomura et al., 2008). The caveat here is that photoactivation is likely an inflammatory stimulus. The identification of selective lymphatic vessel markers fueled recent research on how and where DCs cross the lymphatic endothelial barrier to enter lymphatic vessels. First, DCs must navigate their way through the interstitium to reach lymphatic capillaries. In some cases, such as for Langerhans cells residing in the epidermis, they must penetrate a basement membrane prior to entering into the lymphatic-containing tissue. Although lymphatic capillaries are the branch of lymphatics most distal from the LN, they may not be the first channels that DCs must travel along *en route* to LNs. Indeed, flow fields, termed pre-lymphatic channels, exist, which are created by the interstitial fluid being pulled in the direction of the lymphatic capillary lumen (Boardman & Swartz, 2003; Schmid-Schonbein, 1990). These channels are influenced by anchoring filaments, under tension by interstitial fluid pressure, which pull LECs apart and force lymph to flow into the lymphatic capillary (Schmid-Schonbein, 2003). Even if the direction of flow within fluid channels facilitates the route to the lymphatic vessel, guidance to the lymphatic capillary is still an active process involving the sensing of a CCL21 gradient established by the lymphatic vessel (Weber et al., 2013). Once in close proximity to the lymphatic capillary, DCs preferentially seek out regions of terminal lymphatic capillaries with gaps or "portals" in the basement membrane (Pflicke & Sixt, 2009) and enter initial lymphatic capillaries through flaps that are created between the so-called "button-like" junctions between endothelial cells only in the proximal half of the initial lymphatic capillaries (Fig. 2.1; Baluk et al., 2007). These junctions generate hinges such that the endothelial border between hinges generates a flap akin to a door closing a passage into the lymphatic vasculature. As both the basement membrane portals and the endothelial flaps are preexisting, DCs enter lymphatic vessels rapidly by squeezing through these portals in an integrin- and proteolysis-independent manner (Baluk et al., 2007; Lammermann et al., 2008; Pflicke & Sixt, 2009). Integrin-independent amoeboid movement requires a 3D structure that lends support, though not direct binding, to the emigrating DC (Buch et al., 2009). There appear to be scenarios in the succeeding text when such support is insufficient and alternative mechanisms become relevant.

Until recently, a formal demonstration of the dependency on specialized lymphatic capillaries for DC mobilization was lacking. Recent studies have now investigated whether DCs can emigrate to LNs in the absence of lymphatic capillaries in mouse strains that retain downstream lymphatic collecting vessels. In support of the expected outcome that DC migration would fail in the absence of lymphatic capillaries, emigration of DCs from skin to skin-draining LNs is completely abolished under both resting and stimulated conditions in K14-VEGFR3 Ig mice (Thomas et al., 2012), whose skin lymphatic vasculature regresses before birth (Makinen et al., 2001). A similar result was expected in the so-called *Chy* mice bearing a mutant VEGFR3 (Karkkainen et al., 2001). Indeed, in body extremities that include limbs, tail, and ear skin, no lymphatic capillaries were found and DC migration was ablated (Platt et al., 2013). However, on the thicker body trunk skin, residual lymphatic capillaries were retained. The overall lymphatic density was nonetheless greatly reduced by ~90%. Surprisingly, DC traffic to LNs was intact, occurring in *Chy* mice without kinetic delay or reduction in proportion recovered in LNs (Platt et al., 2013). Thus, although lymphatic capillary density is surprisingly not rate-limiting for DC mobilization, it seems that these vessels are critical for this process to occur. It is unlikely that prelymphatic fluid channels (Schmid-Schonbein, 1990) evolved to greater efficiency in *Chy* mice, because this would be expected to translate into improved lymphatic transport of macromolecules. However, we found that drainage of soluble lymphatic tracers was markedly reduced in *Chy* mice, arguing against compensatory modifications in processes associated with both molecular and cellular transport. Thus, we propose that lymphatic capillaries in WT mouse skin evolved to the density they did in order to allow for optimal molecular transport and that the threshold of lymphatic density needed to support the migration of actively motile DCs is far lower.

This study brings up the vexing issue of how best to quantify DC migration to LNs from upstream tissues like the skin. In the past, we have found that as LN cellularity increases, DC entry/retention in those LNs proportionally increases (Angeli et al., 2006; Qu et al., 2004). In the *Chy* mice, LNs were smaller than in controls (by about half, not 90% smaller), so the net number of emigrated DCs was lower (Platt et al., 2013). However, since this reduction in total emigrated DCs would also be observed in small, WT LN, it is not possible to conclude that DC migration is reduced in *Chy* mice. It remains absolutely unclear how stimulated DCs from the same surface area of the skin give rise to emigration that is proportional to LN cellularity rather than the area of skin stimulated. In the *Chy* mouse, one might ask why LNs are smaller than in controls. This question remains unanswered. An interesting clue might come back to the role that lymph-derived DCs have in maintaining the HEVs within LNs and in recruiting T lymphocytes through these HEVs (Girard et al., 2012; Moussion & Girard, 2011; Wendland et al., 2011). Thus, one way to view the results in *Chy* mice is that the reduced lymphatic density in the steady state sets up an LN environment that is appropriately calibrated to the upstream tissue: the lower density of lymphatic vessels means that fewer DCs can truly access them, but the immune system is able to keep interactions between lymphocytes and DCs—both resident and migratory—in proportional balance by establishing and maintaining a smaller LN. Proportion and overall organization of LNs that promote efficient encounters between lymphocytes and DCs are likely more important than overall LN cellularity. The smaller LNs in *Chy* mice appear as efficient as WT LN in supporting humoral immunity, even though *Chy* mice were unable to support LN hypertrophy in response to CFA due to poor induction of LN lymphangiogenesis, which is required for LN hypertrophy (Platt et al., 2013).

After DCs enter specialized lymphatic capillaries, they continue to interact with the luminal wall, termed "intra-lymphatic crawling" (Tal et al., 2011). The flat cross section and slow flow rate of initial lymphatics likely facilitate such persistent DC–lymphatic vessel interactions. However, the role of intralymphatic crawling remains to be determined, although it is possible that DCs continue to receive signals from the lymphatic endothelium once inside the vessel. Studies so far indicate that when DCs reach the level of collecting vessels, they begin to flow freely in the lymph traveling 200-fold faster than through the initial lymphatic capillaries (Tal et al., 2011), but far less work has been done to be sure that this is true under all conditions. DCs then transmigrate through the floor of the subcapsular sinus on the afferent side and migrate into the T cell zone of the LN parenchyma (Braun et al., 2011). Although few DCs have been found in efferent lymph (Cavanagh et al., 2005), the scarcity of DCs in efferent lymph and in the subsequent LN along the chain (Braun et al., 2011) suggests that the journey for the vast majority of DCs culminates in the primary LN where they will die.

3. DC MOBILIZATION TO LNs: THE ROLE OF CCR7

DC migration assays have demonstrated the importance of numerous chemokines and their receptors, particularly CCR7, in the mobilization of DCs to LNs. DC migration to LNs appears strictly dependent upon CCR7 and it ligands in both the steady state and during inflammation (Forster et al., 1999; Ohl et al., 2004), and accordingly, CCR7 KO DCs fail to migrate to LNs or drive T cell responses (MartIn-Fontecha et al., 2003). Both of the CCR7 ligands, CCL21 and CCL19, are important for DC migration to LNs (Robbiani et al., 2000; Saeki, Moore, Brown, & Hwang, 1999); however, CCL21 is sufficient in the absence of CCL19 (Britschgi, Favre, & Luther, 2010). CCL21 is heparan sulfate-binding and is expressed on initial lymphatic capillaries (de Paz et al., 2007), whereas CCL19 is a soluble mediator produced by DCs themselves and by various stromal cells (Luther, Tang, Hyman, Farr, & Cyster, 2000; Ngo, Tang, & Cyster, 1998). However, upon contact *in vitro*, DCs truncate the anchoring residues of CCL21, releasing it in soluble form where it performs similar functions to CCL19 (Schumann et al., 2010). In addition, two isoforms of CCL21 exist, one containing a leucine residue (CCL21-Leu) at position 65 and the other a serine (CCL21-Ser) (Vassileva et al., 1999). CCL21-Leu is expressed in peripheral tissues, while CCL21-Ser is located in LNs

(Chen et al., 2002), and the naturally occurring *plt* (paucity of LN T cells) mouse lacks CCL19 and CCL21-Ser but retains expression of CCL21-Leu in the periphery (Luther et al., 2000). It is secreted apparently exclusively by LECs, which contain relatively large amounts of CCL21 in intracellular stores that appear as puncta in fixed and permeabilized tissue. However, extracellular CCL21 is not arranged in puncta, but a soluble gradient culminating at the lymphatic vessel is observed. The gradient is maintained by the binding of CCL21 to heparan sulfates in the extracellular matrix and functionally extends for about 90 μm (Weber et al., 2013). It would be interesting to determine if this distance is increased or not in *Chy* mice, where the distance between DCs and lymphatics would be increased.

In summary, CCR7 and its ligands, especially CCL21, have multiple roles in mediating DC transit from skin to the LN parenchyma. First, it controls DC chemotaxis toward lymphatic capillaries and docking on the vessel itself (Tal et al., 2011; Weber et al., 2013). Once in the LN subcapsular sinus, it is again critical for correct localization to the T cell zone, with CCR7-deficient DCs exiting the sinus more slowly and remaining in adjacent cortical regions (Braun et al., 2011).

4. DC MOBILIZATION TO LNs: THE MACHINERY FOR LOCOMOTION

DCs utilize complex machinery to mobilize to LNs. Absence of both of the Rho family triphosphatases, Rac1 and Rac2, decreases the ability of DCs to migrate from the skin to draining LNs (Benvenuti et al., 2004). Further, the signaling adaptor Eps8 is critical for DCs to polarize, form migratory protrusions, and for migration to LNs *in vivo* (Frittoli et al., 2011), and DC migration to LNs is reduced in mice deficient for the Wiskott–Aldrich syndrome protein, important for actin cytoskeletal remodeling (de Noronha et al., 2005).

Upon arrival at the vessel wall, it has been shown that semaphorin 3A, expressed by lymphatic vessels, binds the Plexin-1A-Neuropilin 1 receptor complex on DCs and drives myosin IIA phosphorylation and uropod contraction needed to cross the lymphatic endothelium (Takamatsu et al., 2010). Further, a recent study also reported the role of interactions between CLEC2 on DCs and podoplanin on lymphatics in regulating DC cytoskeletal rearrangement, cell motility, and transit to the LN (Acton et al., 2012). The role of adhesive integrins in DC mobilization is complex and seemingly dependent on the inflammatory conditioning of the lymphatic vasculature.

In the steady state, lymphatic capillaries express little to no ICAM-1 and VCAM-1 (Johnson et al., 2006) and adoptively transferred integrin-deficient DCs migrate to the LN normally (Lammermann et al., 2008). However, ICAM-1 and VCAM-1 are upregulated during inflammation (Johnson et al., 2006) and are needed for optimal migration of DCs to LNs during contact sensitization (Johnson et al., 2006; Ma, Wang, Guo, Sy, & Bigby, 1994; Xu et al., 2001), along with other adhesive cues (Fig. 2.2). Delineating the distinct requirements for DC migration under inflammatory and resting conditions and the underlying reasons why the requirements are different under these conditions requires more research. Interestingly, although also expressed by LECs, expression of junctional adhesion molecule-A by DCs themselves limits DC migration (Cera et al., 2004).

5. LYMPHANGIOGENESIS AND DC TRAFFICKING DURING INFLAMMATION

Turning to the changes in the lymphatic vasculature in conditions of inflammation, it is clear that interstitial fluid transport increases by more than 10-fold (Brand et al., 1992; Olszewski et al., 2001) and lymph contains greater amounts of inflammatory cytokines (Olszewski et al., 2001). A local expansion of the lymphatic vessel network sometimes occurs in chronic inflammation (Alitalo, Tammela, & Petrova, 2005) through the process of lymphangiogenesis that entails endothelial cell sprouting from existing vessels (He et al., 2004). During inflammation, cells such as macrophages and granulocytes produce large amounts of VEGF-C and VEGF-D that drive lymphangiogenesis (Kataru et al., 2009). Further, the diameter of lymphatic capillaries increases substantially during inflammation (Baluk et al., 2007), and the molecular weight requirements for entry of molecules into lymphatic capillaries may also change during inflammation, as can occur during increased flow (Ikomi, Hunt, Hanna, & Schmid-Schonbein, 1996). However, whether lymphangiogenesis during inflammation is beneficial or deleterious remains unclear (von der Weid, Rehal, & Ferraz, 2011). Indeed, lymphatic function has been shown to be impaired despite an increased lymphatic density in Crohn's disease and chronic skin inflammation (Geleff, Schoppmann, & Oberhuber, 2003; Heatley, Bolton, Hughes, & Owen, 1980; Huggenberger et al., 2011). One important problem may be that the new lymphatic vessels in chronically inflamed states do not exhibit button-like junctions that are thought to facilitate DC entry into the lymphatic capillary. Indeed, the junctions have the more sealed character of the

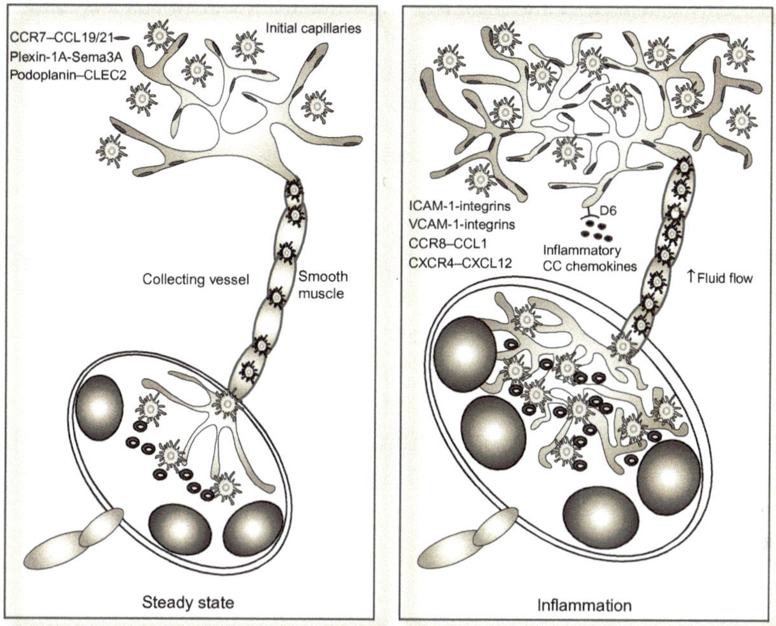

Figure 2.2 The migration of DCs through lymphatics, the pathways involved, and how these are altered during inflammation. Initial lymphatic capillaries, most distal from the LN, express high levels of CCL21 in a punctate pattern (in red). DCs primarily utilize the CCR7–CCL21/19 axis to enter capillaries; however, other pathways such as the Plexin-1A-Neuropilin 1 receptor complex (Plexin-1A) and CLEC2 on DCs binding semaphorin 3A (Sema3A) and podoplanin on lymphatic vessels, respectively, are also involved. Collecting vessels have a layer of smooth muscle (red) that facilitates contractility and pumping of lymph downstream. DCs traffic constitutively in the steady state, continually seeding the T cell area of LNs in a process likely important for the maintenance of immunological tolerance. In contrast, after the onset of inflammation, lymphangiogenesis occurs in the tissue and in the draining LN itself, and more DCs enter the peripheral tissue. This, together with an increased expression of CCL21 and other chemokine (CCR8–CCL1 and CXCR4–CXCL12) and integrin (ICAM-1 and VCAM-1, both binding numerous integrins) pathways, drives increased transit of DCs to the LN. The decoy chemokine receptor, D6, is expressed by LECs and binds inflammatory CC chemokines and prevents "crowding" of the lymphatic interface with inflammatory cells. Fluid flow and inflammatory cytokines in the lymph are also markedly increased during inflammation that perpetuates lymphadenopathy in the downstream LN. (For interpretation of the references to color in this figure legend, the reader is referred to the online version of this chapter.)

so-called zipper-like junctions (Yao, Baluk, Srinivasan, Oliver, & McDonald, 2012).

Several studies have attempted to address the net effect of lymphatics in the inflammatory response. VEGFR3 blockade exacerbates UVB-induced skin inflammation in K14-VEGF-A transgenic mice (Kajiya & Detmar, 2006), and locally injected VEGF-$C^{cys156ser}$ (which only binds to VEGFR3 and not VEGFR2) decreases edema (Kajiya, Sawane, Huggenberger, & Detmar, 2009). Using both K14-VEGF-C and K14-VEGF-D transgenic mice, which have an expanded lymphatic network and enhanced lymphatic drainage, lymphatic vessels were shown to limit inflammation in oxazolone- and UVB-induced acute inflammatory models (Huggenberger et al., 2011). Interestingly, VEGFR3 expression by LECs is reduced during acute inflammation (Huggenberger et al., 2011; Vigl et al., 2011). Further, in a model of chronic inflammation where oxazolone is applied to the skin of K14-VEGF-A transgenic mice, inhibition of VEGFR3 inhibited lymphangiogenesis but increased inflammation (Huggenberger et al., 2010). Taken together, these findings suggest that lymphatic vessels are important to limit both acute and chronic inflammation; however, despite their increased density during the latter, their function is impaired (Huggenberger et al., 2010) and reversal of this impairment may have therapeutic potential. This impairment of lymphatic function seems contradictory to increased flow seen during contact dermatitis and rheumatoid arthritis (Brand et al., 1992; Olszewski et al., 2001). Differences between reports could represent distinct modes of lymphangiogenesis in various chronic inflammatory conditions and/or assays used to measure lymphatic function. These unresolved issues raise important questions regarding inflammation-associated lymphangiogenesis: are the *de novo* lymphatic vessels hypo- or hyperfunctional and what structural alterations may drive this? How do they relate to preexisting lymphatics and can DCs utilize them for entry into the lymphatic vasculature? Do they aid or hinder the resolution of inflammation and is this context-dependent?

Despite these studies on lymphatic function during inflammation, information about how inflammation affects DC mobilization is scarce. The fact that there are more lymphatic vessels means that DCs have a shorter distance to travel to the lymphatic wall, which also expresses higher levels of CCL21 in response to inflammatory cytokines (Fig. 2.2; MartIn-Fontecha et al., 2003). Further, dermal DCs increase their motility after inciting inflammation (Tal et al., 2011), and thus, DCs should enter lymphatics more rapidly and likely in higher numbers. Although this study did not quantify DCs, the first correlative finding suggesting DC migration through lymphatic vessels might be increased during inflammation is that lymph cellularity increases with flow, which increases during inflammation (Ikomi et al., 1996). Subsequently, a study demonstrated that DCs or inflammatory cytokines administered 6–8 h prior to a subsequent DC transfer increase the number of DCs that mobilize to the LN and correlate with increased lymphatic expression of CCL21 (MartIn-Fontecha et al., 2003). Further, a somewhat increased local skin network and a vastly expanded lymphatic network within the downstream LN augments DC mobilization to LNs (Angeli et al., 2006).

6. CONCLUDING REMARKS

Technological advances in imaging DCs in situ have paved the way for a greatly improved understanding of the recruitment of DCs into lymphatic vessels in recent years. We have focused on many of these advances here, and we have given special attention to the lymphatic vessel itself, as progress in the area of lymphatic biology begins to explode. It is the connection to the lymphatic vasculature that makes the LN such an elegant, beautiful organ and the DCs within it so intriguing. In the past, the prevailing model was that DC migration through lymphatic vessels was an essential component of a productive immune response within LNs. However, with the revelation that so many of the DCs in a LN are not derived from the lymphatic route, we believe that this paradigm needs to be further refined, so we have purposely avoided perpetuation of this viewpoint. With new information that migratory DCs condition the LN for recruitment of other cells across the HEV, we begin to see how elegantly the LN is designed and a new role for lymph-derived DCs emerges. The lymph-migratory DC not only carries antigen to the LN through the lymphatic vasculature for presentation of that antigen to T cells or for sharing with other DCs (Allan et al., 2006; Angeli et al., 2006), but it serves as the chief traffic patrol officer, ensuring that the two traffic routes that converge in the LN remain appropriately balanced. We look forward to further research on this new role for lymph-migratory DCs.

REFERENCES

Acton, S. E., Astarita, J. L., Malhotra, D., Lukacs-Kornek, V., Franz, B., Hess, P. R., et al. (2012). Podoplanin-rich stromal networks induce dendritic cell motility via activation of the C-type lectin receptor CLEC-2. *Immunity*, *37*, 276.

Alitalo, K., Tammela, T., & Petrova, T. V. (2005). Lymphangiogenesis in development and human disease. *Nature*, *438*, 946.

Allan, R. S., Waithman, J., Bedoui, S., Jones, C. M., Villadangos, J. A., Zhan, Y., et al. (2006). Migratory dendritic cells transfer antigen to a lymph node-resident dendritic cell population for efficient CTL priming. *Immunity*, *25*, 153.

Angeli, V., Ginhoux, F., Llodra, J., Quemeneur, L., Frenette, P. S., Skobe, M., et al. (2006). B cell-driven lymphangiogenesis in inflamed lymph nodes enhances dendritic cell mobilization. *Immunity*, *24*, 203.

Baluk, P., Fuxe, J., Hashizume, H., Romano, T., Lashnits, E., Butz, S., et al. (2007). Functionally specialized junctions between endothelial cells of lymphatic vessels. *The Journal of Experimental Medicine*, *204*, 2349.

Benvenuti, F., Hugues, S., Walmsley, M., Ruf, S., Fetler, L., Popoff, M., et al. (2004). Requirement of Rac1 and Rac2 expression by mature dendritic cells for T cell priming. *Science*, *305*, 1150.

Boardman, K. C., & Swartz, M. A. (2003). Interstitial flow as a guide for lymphangiogenesis. *Circulation Research*, *92*, 801.

Brand, C. U., Hunziker, T., & Braathen, L. R. (1992). Isolation of human skin-derived lymph: Flow and output of cells following sodium lauryl sulphate-induced contact dermatitis. *Archives of Dermatological Research*, *284*, 123.

Braun, A., Worbs, T., Moschovakis, G. L., Halle, S., Hoffmann, K., Bolter, J., et al. (2011). Afferent lymph-derived T cells and DCs use different chemokine receptor CCR7-dependent routes for entry into the lymph node and intranodal migration. *Nature Immunology*, *12*, 879.

Britschgi, M. R., Favre, S., & Luther, S. A. (2010). CCL21 is sufficient to mediate DC migration, maturation and function in the absence of CCL19. *European Journal of Immunology*, *40*, 1266.

Buch, M. H., Boyle, D. L., Rosengren, S., Saleem, B., Reece, R. J., Rhodes, L. A., et al. (2009). Mode of action of abatacept in rheumatoid arthritis patients having failed tumour necrosis factor blockade: A histological, gene expression and dynamic magnetic resonance imaging pilot study. *Annals of the Rheumatic Diseases*, *68*, 1220.

Bujdoso, R., Hopkins, J., Dutia, B. M., Young, P., & McConnell, I. (1989). Characterization of sheep afferent lymph dendritic cells and their role in antigen carriage. *The Journal of Experimental Medicine*, *170*, 1285.

Cavanagh, L. L., Bonasio, R., Mazo, I. B., Halin, C., Cheng, G., van der Velden, A. W., et al. (2005). Activation of bone marrow-resident memory T cells by circulating, antigen-bearing dendritic cells. *Nature Immunology*, *6*, 1029.

Cera, M. R., Del Prete, A., Vecchi, A., Corada, M., Martin-Padura, I., Motoike, T., et al. (2004). Increased DC trafficking to lymph nodes and contact hypersensitivity in junctional adhesion molecule-A-deficient mice. *Journal of Clinical Investigation*, *114*, 729.

Chen, S. C., Vassileva, G., Kinsley, D., Holzmann, S., Manfra, D., Wiekowski, M. T., et al. (2002). Ectopic expression of the murine chemokines CCL21a and CCL21b induces the formation of lymph node-like structures in pancreas, but not skin, of transgenic mice. *Journal of Immunology*, *168*, 1001.

de Noronha, S., Hardy, S., Sinclair, J., Blundell, M. P., Strid, J., Schulz, O., et al. (2005). Impaired dendritic-cell homing in vivo in the absence of Wiskott–Aldrich syndrome protein. *Blood*, *105*, 1590.

de Paz, J. L., Moseman, E. A., Noti, C., Polito, L., von Andrian, U. H., & Seeberger, P. H. (2007). Profiling heparin–chemokine interactions using synthetic tools. *ACS Chemical Biology*, *2*, 735.

Fischer, M., Franzeck, U. K., Herrig, I., Costanzo, U., Wen, S., Schiesser, M., et al. (1996). Flow velocity of single lymphatic capillaries in human skin. *American Journal of Physiology*, *270*, H358.

Forster, R., Schubel, A., Breitfeld, D., Kremmer, E., Renner-Muller, I., Wolf, E., et al. (1999). CCR7 coordinates the primary immune response by establishing functional microenvironments in secondary lymphoid organs. *Cell*, *99*, 23.

Frittoli, E., Matteoli, G., Palamidessi, A., Mazzini, E., Maddaluno, L., Disanza, A., et al. (2011). The signaling adaptor eps8 is an essential actin capping protein for dendritic cell migration. *Immunity*, *35*, 388.

Gale, N. W., Prevo, R., Espinosa, J., Ferguson, D. J., Dominguez, M. G., Yancopoulos, G. D., et al. (2007). Normal lymphatic development and function in mice deficient for the lymphatic hyaluronan receptor LYVE-1. *Molecular and Cellular Biology*, *27*, 595.

Geleff, S., Schoppmann, S. F., & Oberhuber, G. (2003). Increase in podoplanin-expressing intestinal lymphatic vessels in inflammatory bowel disease. *Virchows Archiv*, *442*, 231.

Girard, J. P., Moussion, C., & Forster, R. (2012). HEVs, lymphatics and homeostatic immune cell trafficking in lymph nodes. *Nature Reviews Immunology*, *12*, 762.

Harwood, C. A., & Mortimer, P. S. (1995). Causes and clinical manifestations of lymphatic failure. *Clinics in Dermatology*, *13*, 459.

He, Y., Rajantie, I., Ilmonen, M., Makinen, T., Karkkainen, M. J., Haiko, P., et al. (2004). Preexisting lymphatic endothelium but not endothelial progenitor cells are essential for tumor lymphangiogenesis and lymphatic metastasis. *Cancer Research*, *64*, 3737.

Heatley, R. V., Bolton, P. M., Hughes, L. E., & Owen, E. W. (1980). Mesenteric lymphatic obstruction in Crohn's disease. *Digestion*, *20*, 307.

Hohl, T. M., Rivera, A., Lipuma, L., Gallegos, A., Shi, C., Mack, M., et al. (2009). Inflammatory monocytes facilitate adaptive CD4 T cell responses during respiratory fungal infection. *Cell Host & Microbe*, *6*, 470.

Huggenberger, R., Siddiqui, S. S., Brander, D., Ullmann, S., Zimmermann, K., Antsiferova, M., et al. (2011). An important role of lymphatic vessel activation in limiting acute inflammation. *Blood*, *117*, 4667.

Huggenberger, R., Ullmann, S., Proulx, S. T., Pytowski, B., Alitalo, K., & Detmar, M. (2010). Stimulation of lymphangiogenesis via VEGFR-3 inhibits chronic skin inflammation. *The Journal of Experimental Medicine*, *207*, 2255.

Ikomi, F., Hunt, J., Hanna, G., & Schmid-Schonbein, G. W. (1996). Interstitial fluid, plasma protein, colloid, and leukocyte uptake into initial lymphatics. *Journal of Applied Physiology: Respiratory, Environmental and Exercise Physiology*, *81*, 2060.

Itano, A. A., McSorley, S. J., Reinhardt, R. L., Ehst, B. D., Ingulli, E., Rudensky, A. Y., et al. (2003). Distinct dendritic cell populations sequentially present antigen to CD4 T cells and stimulate different aspects of cell-mediated immunity. *Immunity*, *19*, 47.

Jackson, D. G. (2009). Immunological functions of hyaluronan and its receptors in the lymphatics. *Immunological Reviews*, *230*, 216.

Jakubzick, C., Bogunovic, M., Bonito, A. J., Kuan, E. L., Merad, M., & Randolph, G. J. (2008). Lymph-migrating, tissue-derived dendritic cells are minor constituents within steady-state lymph nodes. *The Journal of Experimental Medicine*, *205*, 2839.

Johnson, L. A., Clasper, S., Holt, A. P., Lalor, P. F., Baban, D., & Jackson, D. G. (2006). An inflammation-induced mechanism for leukocyte transmigration across lymphatic vessel endothelium. *The Journal of Experimental Medicine*, *203*, 2763.

Kajiya, K., & Detmar, M. (2006). An important role of lymphatic vessels in the control of UVB-induced edema formation and inflammation. *Journal of Investigative Dermatology*, *126*, 919.

Kajiya, K., Sawane, M., Huggenberger, R., & Detmar, M. (2009). Activation of the VEGFR-3 pathway by VEGF-C attenuates UVB-induced edema formation and skin inflammation by promoting lymphangiogenesis. *Journal of Investigative Dermatology*, *129*, 1292.

Karkkainen, M. J., Saaristo, A., Jussila, L., Karila, K. A., Lawrence, E. C., Pajusola, K., et al. (2001). A model for gene therapy of human hereditary lymphedema. In: *Proceedings of the National Academy of Sciences of the United States of America*, *98*, 12677.

Kataru, R. P., Jung, K., Jang, C., Yang, H., Schwendener, R. A., Baik, J. E., et al. (2009). Critical role of CD11b+ macrophages and VEGF in inflammatory lymphangiogenesis, antigen clearance, and inflammation resolution. *Blood, 113*, 5650.
Lammermann, T., Bader, B. L., Monkley, S. J., Worbs, T., Wedlich-Soldner, R., Hirsch, K., et al. (2008). Rapid leukocyte migration by integrin-independent flowing and squeezing. *Nature, 453*, 51.
Lister, R. K., Black, M. M., Calonje, E., & Burnand, K. G. (1997). Squamous cell carcinoma arising in chronic lymphoedema. *British Journal of Dermatology, 136*, 384.
Liu, K., Victora, G. D., Schwickert, T. A., Guermonprez, P., Meredith, M. M., Yao, K., et al. (2009). In vivo analysis of dendritic cell development and homeostasis. *Science, 324*, 392.
Luther, S. A., Tang, H. L., Hyman, P. L., Farr, A. G., & Cyster, J. G. (2000). Coexpression of the chemokines ELC and SLC by T zone stromal cells and deletion of the ELC gene in the plt/plt mouse. In: *Proceedings of the National Academy of Sciences of the United States of America, 97*, 12694.
Ma, J., Wang, J. H., Guo, Y. J., Sy, M. S., & Bigby, M. (1994). In vivo treatment with anti-ICAM-1 and anti-LFA-1 antibodies inhibits contact sensitization-induced migration of epidermal Langerhans cells to regional lymph nodes. *Cellular Immunology, 158*, 389.
MacPherson, G. G., Jenkins, C. D., Stein, M. J., & Edwards, C. (1995). Endotoxin-mediated dendritic cell release from the intestine. Characterization of released dendritic cells and TNF dependence. *Journal of Immunology, 154*, 1317.
Makinen, T., Adams, R. H., Bailey, J., Lu, Q., Ziemiecki, A., Alitalo, K., et al. (2005). PDZ interaction site in ephrinB2 is required for the remodeling of lymphatic vasculature. *Genes & Development, 19*, 397.
Makinen, T., Jussila, L., Veikkola, T., Karpanen, T., Kettunen, M. I., Pulkkanen, K. J., et al. (2001). Inhibition of lymphangiogenesis with resulting lymphedema in transgenic mice expressing soluble VEGF receptor-3. *Nature Medicine, 7*, 199.
Mallon, E., Powell, S., Mortimer, P., & Ryan, T. J. (1997). Evidence for altered cell-mediated immunity in postmastectomy lymphoedema. *British Journal of Dermatology, 137*, 928.
MartIn-Fontecha, A., Sebastiani, S., Hopken, U. E., Uguccioni, M., Lipp, M., Lanzavecchia, A., et al. (2003). Regulation of dendritic cell migration to the draining lymph node: Impact on T lymphocyte traffic and priming. *The Journal of Experimental Medicine, 198*, 615.
Miller, J. C., Brown, B. D., Shay, T., Gautier, E. L., Jojic, V., Cohain, A., et al. (2012). Deciphering the transcriptional network of the dendritic cell lineage. *Nature Immunology, 13*, 888.
Moussion, C., & Girard, J. P. (2011). Dendritic cells control lymphocyte entry to lymph nodes through high endothelial venules. *Nature, 479*, 542.
Muthuchamy, M., & Zawieja, D. (2008). Molecular regulation of lymphatic contractility. *Annals of the New York Academy of Sciences, 1131*, 89.
Ngo, V. N., Tang, H. L., & Cyster, J. G. (1998). Epstein–Barr virus-induced molecule 1 ligand chemokine is expressed by dendritic cells in lymphoid tissues and strongly attracts naive T cells and activated B cells. *The Journal of Experimental Medicine, 188*, 181.
Ohl, L., Mohaupt, M., Czeloth, N., Hintzen, G., Kiafard, Z., Zwirner, J., et al. (2004). CCR7 governs skin dendritic cell migration under inflammatory and steady-state conditions. *Immunity, 21*, 279.
Olszewski, W. L., Pazdur, J., Kubasiewicz, E., Zaleska, M., Cooke, C. J., & Miller, N. E. (2001). Lymph draining from foot joints in rheumatoid arthritis provides insight into local cytokine and chemokine production and transport to lymph nodes. *Arthritis and Rheumatism, 44*, 541.

Pflicke, H., & Sixt, M. (2009). Preformed portals facilitate dendritic cell entry into afferent lymphatic vessels. *The Journal of Experimental Medicine, 206*, 2925.

Platt, A. M., Rutkowski, J. M., Martel, C., Kuan, E. L., Ivanov, S., Swartz, M. A., et al. (2013). Normal dendritic cell mobilization to lymph nodes under conditions of severe lymphatic hypoplasia. *Journal of Immunology, 190*, 4608.

Pugh, C. W., MacPherson, G. G., & Steer, H. W. (1983). Characterization of non-lymphoid cells derived from rat peripheral lymph. *The Journal of Experimental Medicine, 157*, 1758.

Qu, C., Edwards, E. W., Tacke, F., Angeli, V., Llodra, J., Sanchez-Schmitz, G., et al. (2004). Role of CCR8 and other chemokine pathways in the migration of monocyte-derived dendritic cells to lymph nodes. *The Journal of Experimental Medicine, 200*, 1231.

Randolph, G. J., Angeli, V., & Swartz, M. A. (2005). Dendritic-cell trafficking to lymph nodes through lymphatic vessels. *Nature Reviews Immunology, 5*, 617.

Randolph, G. J., Inaba, K., Robbiani, D. F., Steinman, R. M., & Muller, W. A. (1999). Differentiation of phagocytic monocytes into lymph node dendritic cells in vivo. *Immunity, 11*, 753.

Robbiani, D. F., Finch, R. A., Jager, D., Muller, W. A., Sartorelli, A. C., & Randolph, G. J. (2000). The leukotriene C(4) transporter MRP1 regulates CCL19 (MIP-3beta, ELC)-dependent mobilization of dendritic cells to lymph nodes. *Cell, 103*, 757.

Rockson, S. G. (2001). Lymphedema. *American Journal of Medicine, 110*, 288.

Saeki, H., Moore, A. M., Brown, M. J., & Hwang, S. T. (1999). Cutting edge: Secondary lymphoid-tissue chemokine (SLC) and CC chemokine receptor 7 (CCR7) participate in the emigration pathway of mature dendritic cells from the skin to regional lymph nodes. *Journal of Immunology, 162*, 2472.

Scallan, J. P., & Huxley, V. H. (2010). In vivo determination of collecting lymphatic vessel permeability to albumin: A role for lymphatics in exchange. *The Journal of Physiology, 588*, 243.

Schmid-Schonbein, G. W. (1990). Microlymphatics and lymph flow. *Physiological Reviews, 70*, 987.

Schmid-Schonbein, G. W. (2003). The second valve system in lymphatics. *Lymphatic Research and Biology, 1*, 25.

Schumann, K., Lammermann, T., Bruckner, M., Legler, D. F., Polleux, J., Spatz, J. P., et al. (2010). Immobilized chemokine fields and soluble chemokine gradients cooperatively shape migration patterns of dendritic cells. *Immunity, 32*, 703.

Spiegel, M., Vesti, B., Shore, A., Franzeck, U. K., Becker, F., & Bollinger, A. (1992). Pressure of lymphatic capillaries in human skin. *American Journal of Physiology, 262*, H1208.

Takamatsu, H., Takegahara, N., Nakagawa, Y., Tomura, M., Taniguchi, M., Friedel, R. H., et al. (2010). Semaphorins guide the entry of dendritic cells into the lymphatics by activating myosin II. *Nature Immunology, 11*, 594.

Tal, O., Lim, H. Y., Gurevich, I., Milo, I., Shipony, Z., Ng, L. G., et al. (2011). DC mobilization from the skin requires docking to immobilized CCL21 on lymphatic endothelium and intralymphatic crawling. *The Journal of Experimental Medicine, 208*, 2141.

Tammela, T., & Alitalo, K. (2010). Lymphangiogenesis: Molecular mechanisms and future promise. *Cell, 140*, 460.

Thomas, S. N., Rutkowski, J. M., Pasquier, M., Kuan, E. L., Alitalo, K., Randolph, G. J., et al. (2012). Impaired humoral immunity and tolerance in K14-VEGFR-3-Ig mice that lack dermal lymphatic drainage. *Journal of Immunology, 189*, 2181.

Tomura, M., Yoshida, N., Tanaka, J., Karasawa, S., Miwa, Y., Miyawaki, A., et al. (2008). Monitoring cellular movement in vivo with photoconvertible fluorescence protein "Kaede" transgenic mice. In: *Proceedings of the National Academy of Sciences of the United States of America, 105*, 10871.

Vassileva, G., Soto, H., Zlotnik, A., Nakano, H., Kakiuchi, T., Hedrick, J. A., et al. (1999). The reduced expression of 6Ckine in the plt mouse results from the deletion of one of two 6Ckine genes. *The Journal of Experimental Medicine, 190*, 1183.
Vigl, B., Aebischer, D., Nitschke, M., Iolyeva, M., Rothlin, T., Antsiferova, O., et al. (2011). Tissue inflammation modulates gene expression of lymphatic endothelial cells and dendritic cell migration in a stimulus-dependent manner. *Blood, 118*, 205.
von der Weid, P. Y., Rehal, S., & Ferraz, J. G. (2011). Role of the lymphatic system in the pathogenesis of Crohn's disease. *Current Opinion in Gastroenterology, 27*, 335.
Weber, M., Hauschild, R., Schwarz, J., Moussion, C., de Vries, I., Legler, D. F., et al. (2013). Interstitial dendritic cell guidance by haptotactic chemokine gradients. *Science, 339*, 328.
Wendland, M., Willenzon, S., Kocks, J., Davalos-Misslitz, A. C., Hammerschmidt, S. I., Schumann, K., et al. (2011). Lymph node T cell homeostasis relies on steady state homing of dendritic cells. *Immunity, 35*, 945.
Xu, H., Guan, H., Zu, G., Bullard, D., Hanson, J., Slater, M., et al. (2001). The role of ICAM-1 molecule in the migration of Langerhans cells in the skin and regional lymph node. *European Journal of Immunology, 31*, 3085.
Yao, L. C., Baluk, P., Srinivasan, R. S., Oliver, G., & McDonald, D. M. (2012). Plasticity of button-like junctions in the endothelium of airway lymphatics in development and inflammation. *American Journal of Pathology, 180*, 2561.

CHAPTER THREE

A Close Encounter of the Third Kind: Monocyte-Derived Cells

Alexander Mildner, Simon Yona[1], Steffen Jung[2]
Department of Immunology, Weizmann Institute of Science, Rehovot, Israel
[1]Current address: Division of Medicine, University College London, London, United Kingdom
[2]Corresponding author: e-mail address: s.jung@weizmann.ac.il

Contents

Abstract

Recent insights into discrete myeloid developmental pathways have provided critical information about the organization of the murine mononuclear phagocyte compartment. Short-lived dendritic cells (DCs) have been shown to continuously arise from dedicated bone marrow-derived precursors. In contrast, it is now appreciated that most tissue macrophage populations are established before birth and subsequently maintain themselves throughout adulthood by longevity and limited self-renewal. Both of these classical tissue-resident mononuclear phagocyte compartments can be complemented on demand by monocyte infiltrates giving rise to macrophage or DC-like cells, depending on the tissue context they encounter upon extravasation. Monocytes hence have emerged as a versatile emergency squad that can be rapidly recruited to sites of injury to provide a transient supplement with proinflammatory or resolving activities for local mononuclear phagocytes.

Advances in Immunology, Volume 120
ISSN 0065-2776
http://dx.doi.org/10.1016/B978-0-12-417028-5.00003-X

1. DENDRITIC CELL AND MACROPHAGES

The mononuclear phagocyte system has historically been subdivided into two families of tissue-resident mononuclear phagocytes, that is, macrophages and dendritic cells (DCs). In this chapter, we will summarize findings from studies in the mouse that established that these two cell types descend from distinct lineages. As both classical DC (cDC) and macrophages are also the topic of accompanying articles in this volume, we will therefore limit our discussion of these cells and apologize in advance for omitting some of the literature.

1.1. Classical macrophages

The discovery of phagocytosis and macrophages is attributed to Ilya Mechnikov in the course of his ingenious intravital studies with pricked starfish larvae at the end of the nineteenth century (Metchnikoff, 1887).

Macrophages are strategically distributed throughout the body. They are specialized in ingesting and processing dead cells, debris, and foreign materials, as well as the recruitment of other immune cells to sites of injury in response to inflammatory signals (Gordon & Taylor, 2005). Macrophages also adjust to the particular tissues they reside in. Thus, recent gene expression profiling studies suggest that tissue macrophages undergo significant imprinting in their respective microenvironment adopting tissue-specific expression profiles and specialized characteristics beyond the prototype macrophage signature (Gautier et al., 2012). Importantly, the resident macrophages *raison d'être* evidently includes responsibilities beyond their role in immune defense and inflammation, such as important homeostatic developmental functions together with their specialized role as immune sentinels deployed throughout the body.

Macrophages are long-lived cells, as opposed to the ephemeral DC that will be discussed in the succeeding text. Earlier work had suggested that tissue macrophages originate from primitive hematopoietic progenitors that arise in the yolk sac during embryonic development (Alliot, Godin, & Pessac, 1999). Recent studies involving Cre-lox-based fate-mapping approaches and the use of mutant animals have substantiated this notion (Ginhoux et al., 2010; Schulz et al., 2012; Yona et al., 2013). Thus, most peripheral tissue macrophages populations are indeed seeded by primitive macrophages that arise independent of the transcription factor Myb (Schulz et al., 2012) or fetal liver-derived cells prenatally. These cells subsequently maintain themselves during adulthood through longevity and limited local self-renewal and are thus independent from further input. Maintenance of these tissue macrophage compartments is independent of monocytes and Myb-dependent definitive hematopoiesis in steady-state conditions. Tissue macrophages can undergo vigorous proliferation during specific T_H2-biased inflammatory conditions, for example, infection of the pleural cavity with the nematode *Litomosoides sigmodontis* (Jenkins et al., 2011). In this setting, resident tissue macrophages are able to locally proliferate in an IL-4-dependent manner, and the local compartments expand independent of monocyte influx (Jenkins et al., 2011).

Macrophage differentiation and survival were shown to be regulated by the transcription factor PU.1 (Tondravi et al., 1997) and the receptor for the macrophage colony-stimulating factor 1, Csf1R (also known as M-CSFR, CD115). Deletion of Csf1R leads to an almost complete absence of tissue macrophage development in various organs (Wiktor-Jedrzejczak et al., 1992). This finding was for a long time in conflict with the minor defect of tissue macrophage development observed in Csf1 (also known as M-CSF)-deficient mice, a known ligand for Csf1R (Yeung, Jubinsky, Sengupta, Yeung, & Stanley, 1987). However, recently a new ligand for Csf1R was identified, namely, IL-34 (Lin et al., 2008), which is expressed in a tissue-restricted pattern (Greter et al., 2012; Wang et al., 2012). Therefore, IL-34 controls—in synergy with Csf1—the maintenance and homeostasis of tissue macrophages in these tissues, especially the survival of Langerhans cells in the skin and microglia in the central nervous system (CNS) (Greter et al., 2012; Wang et al., 2012).

1.2. Classical dendritic cells

DCs were originally reported in the mid-1970s by Ralph Steinman, who discovered among splenocytes unique populations of cells with "veiled" morphology and unrivalled potential to prime naïve T cells (Steinman & Witmer, 1978). Subsequent studies added to these features a pronounced and tightly regulated migratory potential for these cells (Caux et al., 2000). cDCs have been shown to exist in distinct activation states, often termed "immature" and "mature," that are believed to support antigen uptake and T-cell priming, respectively. As opposed to the sessile macrophages, DCs are uniquely specialized to act as peripheral sentinels that carry antigen into tissue-draining lymph nodes (LN) and trigger T-cell activation. However, ever since their original discovery, the question of whether DCs constitute a separate lineage or rather another subset of macrophages has provided ample fodder for heated debates. A major advance towards the realization that cDCs are indeed an independent entity came with the discovery of a dedicated macrophage and DC precursors (MDP) by the Geissman group (Fogg et al., 2006). Upon adoptive transfer into unmanipulated or cDC-deleted recipient mice, MDP efficiently gave rise to splenic cDC (Varol et al., 2007). Moreover, intra-bone marrow (BM) engraftment established MDP as immediate precursors of monocytes (Varol et al., 2007). Surprisingly however, monocytes failed to reconstitute cDC in cDC-deleted recipient mice (Varol et al., 2007). These studies coincided with work from a number of laboratories (Liu et al., 2009; Naik et al., 2006; Onai et al., 2007) that collectively culminated in the identification of DC-committed precursors, the preDC, and an intermediate, the CDP, that maintains—as opposed to preDC—the potential to give rise to plasmacytoid DC (PDC) (Fig. 3.1).

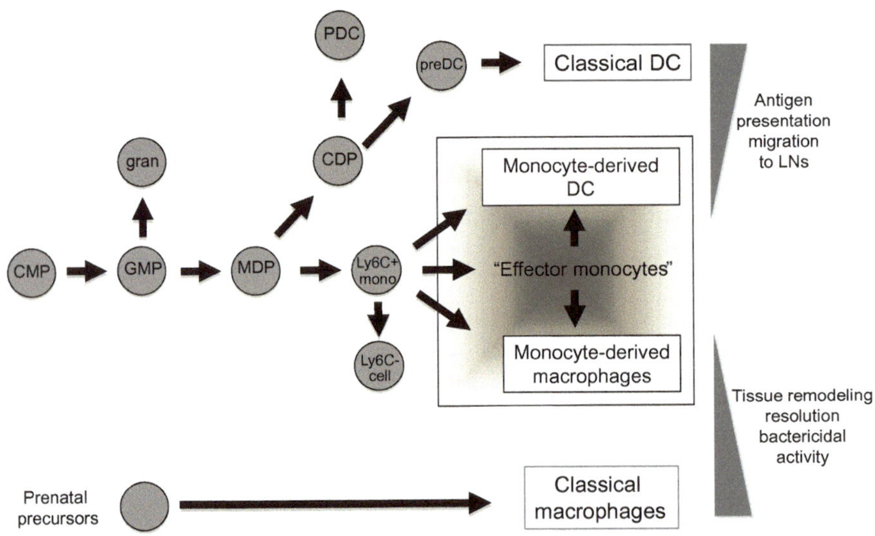

Figure 3.1 The tripartite nature of the mononuclear phagocyte system. Classical tissue macrophage compartments are established before birth from prenatal precursors and subsequently self-maintaining. Classical dendritic cells are short-lived and continuously replaced from BM-derived precursor cells. Both compartments exist in the steady state. Monocyte-derived cells are only called in case of exceptional challenges, injury, or infection. Ly6C^{+} monocytes that enter tissues are highly versatile and can adopt-depending on the tissue context they encounter-fates ranging from proinflammatory effector monocytes to resolving macrophage- and DC-like cells. (For color version of this figure, the reader is referred to the online version of this chapter.)

Notably, cDC can be further divided into distinct subpopulations that differ with respect to phenotype, function, and dependence on specific transcription factors (BatF3, Notch, and IRF4/8), as discussed in detail by Gabriela Belz (Chapter 8) and Kenneth Murphy (Chapter 10) in this volume. While most of these data were originally established for spleen resident cDC, they have now been extended to tissue-resident subsets (Helft, Ginhoux, Bogunovic, & Merad, 2010).

Collectively, these studies now suggest that cDCs, including the CD103^{+}/CD8-α^{+} and CD11b^{+} subsets, arise in a developmental pathway that is governed by the growth factor Fms-related tyrosine kinase 3 ligand (Flt3L) (Waskow et al., 2008). In fact, cDCs constitute together with PDC the major peripheral Flt3L sink, in whose absence serum Flt3L titers significantly rise and thereby cause a myeloproliferative disorder (Bar-On, Birnberg, Kim, & Jung, 2011; Birnberg et al., 2008; Hochweller et al., 2009). Conversely, exogenous Flt3L application results in the significant expansion of cDC (Maraskovsky et al., 1996), a criterion that has been used to define DC in tissues (Waskow et al., 2008). Moreover, differentiation of cDC from BM precursors can be recapitulated *in vitro* under the aegis of Flt3L. FLt3L-cultured BM cells develop into PDC, as well as CD24^{-} and CD24^{+} DC, which represent the equivalents of classical CD4 and CD8 DC, respectively (Naik et al., 2005). FLt3L-driven cultures thus provide a critical complement to earlier established granulocyte macrophage colony-stimulating factor 2 (Csf2, also known as GM-CSF)-driven BM cultures (Lutz et al., 1999; Sallusto & Lanzavecchia, 1994) that probably yield equivalents of monocyte-derived DC (moDC) (see in the succeeding text). This strict developmental dependence on Flt3L distinguishes DC from macrophages and can be therefore used experimentally (e.g., in a mixed BM chimera experiment) for the clarification of ontogenies (Anandasabapathy et al., 2011; Waskow et al., 2008).

Most recently, the zinc finger transcription factor zbtb46 has been proposed as a DC lineage marker and seems to be involved in negatively controlling DC maturation states, but not DC development per se (Meredith, Liu, Darrasse-Jeze, et al., 2012; Meredith, Liu, Kamphorst, et al., 2012; Satpathy et al., 2012).

2. MONOCYTES, THE MONONUCLEAR PHAGOCYTES OF THE BLOOD COMPARTMENT

Monocytes are the third subgroup of mononuclear phagocyte system and can be found in the peripheral circulation. Historically, it was postulated that monocytes act as a bridge, linking mononuclear phagocyte precursors in the BM with terminally differentiated tissue-resident mononuclear phagocytes. Here, we describe the emerging theme that circulating monocytes are effector cells in their own right, as the *third kind* of mononuclear phagocyte, which can *encounter* pathogens when they enter the host. Monocytes display a prominent array of scavenger and pattern recognition receptors that recognizes lipids and dying cells, which enables them to react to danger, as well as pathogenic stimuli. In response to these triggers, they can produce large quantities of effector molecules involved in the defense against pathogens and injury (Strauss-Ayali, Conrad, & Mosser, 2007).

In humans, monocytes are identified based on morphology and cytochemistry (i.e., monocyte-specific esterase), as well as surface markers, such as the LPS coreceptor CD14. Monocyte heterogeneity was first reported by the group of Ziegler-Heitbrock who identified among human monocytes a minor population of CD16 (FcγRIII)-expressing cells (Passlick, Flieger, & Ziegler-Heitbrock, 1989). The main human subset, the $CD14^{hi}$ $CD16^{-}$ cells, represents 90–95% of the total monocytes in a healthy person and was hence termed "classical" monocytes. The minor subset of $CD14^{dim}$ $CD16^{+}$ monocytes is less phagocytic compared to $CD14^{hi}$ $CD16^{-}$ cells and does not produce ROS or cytokines in response to cell-surface Toll-like receptor (TLR) engagement. Instead, $CD14^{dim}$ $CD16^{+}$ cells selectively secrete TNF-α, IL-1β, and CCL3 in response to viruses and immune complexes containing nucleic acids, via a proinflammatory TLR7-TLR8-MyD88-MEK pathway (Cros et al., 2010).

Discrete reporter gene expression in CX_3CR1^{gfp} knock-in animals (Jung et al., 2000) led to the discovery of the corresponding mouse monocyte subsets that are identified by their expression of Csf1R (Geissmann, Jung, & Littman, 2003; Palframan et al., 2001). Mouse monocytes comprise CX_3CR1^{int} $Ly6C^{+}$ and CX_3CR1^{hi} $Ly6C^{-}$ cells. Comparative gene expression analysis suggests that CX_3CR1^{int} $Ly6C^{+}$ cells are the correlate of human $CD14^{hi}$ $CD16^{-}$ monocytes, while CX_3CR1^{hi} $Ly6C^{-}$ cells are the mouse equivalent of human $CD14^{dim}$ $CD16^{+}$ monocytes (Cros et al., 2010; Ingersoll et al., 2010). However, interspecies differences remain. Of note, CX_3CR1^{hi} $Ly6C^{-}$ monocytes represent, for instance, about half of circulating monocytes in mice, but $CD14^{dim}$ $CD16^{+}$ monocytes account for only less than 15% in healthy humans (Passlick et al., 1989).

CX_3CR1^{int} $Ly6C^{+}$ monocytes exhibit classical monocyte functions. They express a large battery of chemokine receptors, most prominently CCR2, and are accordingly poised to traffic to sites of infection and inflammation (Geissmann et al., 2003; Palframan et al., 2001).

CX_3CR1^{int} $Ly6C^+$ monocytes have an exceedingly short circulation half-life of 0.8 days (19 h) (Yona et al., 2013), which is comparable to that of neutrophils (Basu, Hodgson, Katz, & Dunn, 2002).

Functions of CX_3CR1^{hi} $Ly6C^-$ monocytes remain less well understood. In a seminal study, Geissmann and colleagues showed that these cells adhere and crawl along the luminal surface of endothelial cells (Auffray et al., 2007). Likewise, human $CD14^{dim}$ $CD16^+$ monocytes share this LFA-1-dependent feature, as was shown in cross-species adoptive transfer studies (Cros et al., 2010). It has been proposed that these "patrolling" cells might be critical for the surveillance of endothelial integrity and recent data supports this notion (Carlin et al., 2013).

Both, CX_3CR1^{int} $Ly6C^+$ and CX_3CR1^{hi} $Ly6C^-$ cells derive from MDP (Varol et al., 2007). Some observations however suggested that CX_3CR1^{int} $Ly6C^+$ monocytes can give rise to CX_3CR1^{hi} $Ly6C^-$ monocytes and that these cells thus form a developmental sequence (Sunderkotter et al., 2004; Varol et al., 2007). More recently, BrdU pulse-labeling studies combined with conditional cell ablation established that blood-resident CX_3CR1^{hi} $Ly6C^-$ monocytes indeed derive in steady state from CX_3CR1^{int} $Ly6C^+$ monocytes (Yona et al., 2013). Moreover, CX_3CR1^{hi} $Ly6C^-$ monocytes were shown to display an extended circulation half-life of 2 days, which under conditions of CX_3CR1^{int} $Ly6C^+$ monocyte precursor deprivation was extended to up to 2 weeks (Yona et al., 2013). These features suggest that rather than representing a second bona fide circulating monocyte subset with DC and macrophage precursor potential (see in the succeeding text), CX_3CR1^{hi} $Ly6C^-$ cells might be terminally differentiated blood-resident macrophages. Nevertheless, when cultured *in vitro* with Csf1 or Csf2, both CX_3CR1^{int} $Ly6C^+$ and CX_3CR1^{hi} $Ly6C^-$ monocytes can differentiate into macrophage-like and DC-like cells, respectively (Jung, *unpublished observation*). However, direct demonstrations that CX_3CR1^{hi} $Ly6C^-$ cells, when isolated from the blood, can give rise to tissue-resident mononuclear phagocytes *in vivo* are missing. Rather when compared side by side for this potential, CX_3CR1^{int} $Ly6C^+$ monocytes efficiently gave rise to intestinal macrophages (see in the succeeding text), whereas CX_3CR1^{hi} $Ly6C^-$ monocytes failed to do so (Varol et al., 2009). In light of these findings, we propose that CX_3CR1^{hi} $Ly6C^-$ blood monocytes represent the homeostatic default product of short-lived $Ly6C^+$ monocytes and likely fulfill a macrophage function in the maintenance of vessel integrity.

Collectively, CX_3CR1^{int} $Ly6C^+$ monocytes and CX_3CR1^{hi} $Ly6C^-$ cells are mononuclear phagocytes found in the circulation where they represent a dynamic, rapidly recruitable cell pool contributing to inflammation and might ensure integrity of blood vessel walls under physiological conditions. However, specific activities in the unique blood compartment remain to be clearly defined.

In fact, monocytes are best known for their second life, that is, their potential to give rise to tissue-resident mononuclear phagocytes upon extravasation. Of note, however, and as argued in the preceding text, the available experimental evidence suggests that this feature probably applies exclusively to classical CX_3CR1^{int} $Ly6C^+$ monocytes and probably can be extrapolated to their human $CD14^{hi}$ $CD16^-$ monocyte counterpart.

3. MONOCYTES, AS PRECURSORS OF TISSUE MONONUCLEAR PHAGOCYTES

CX_3CR1^{int} $Ly6C^+$ monocytes and $CD14^{hi}$ $CD16^-$ monocytes express a vast array of chemokine receptors (Geissmann et al., 2003) and are hence highly sensitive to alert signals that recruit them to sites of injury and challenge. Accordingly, monocyte infiltrates are a hallmark of inflammation.

Meeting the complex functional requirements for robust and, yet, balanced inflammatory responses involves the detection of tissue injury, inflammatory reaction, and finally resolution, as well as potential establishment of an immunological memory. Monocytes seem perfectly suited for this task since they are highly plastic. Emerging data indicate that the context and time, when the monocyte enters the site of injury, will determine its skewing towards specific effector cell fate, towards a phenotype with more (DC-like) antigen presentation and T-cell priming properties, or towards (macrophage-like) tissue-repair capacities (Fig. 3.1). However, the definition of this dynamic trinity of monocytes and their descendants poses a major challenge for the scientific community. Different terms, different time points of analysis, and different detection methods have been used for the identification and description of monocyte-derived cells and have thus muddied the waters for drawing of a unified picture. In an attempt to streamline these challenges and better our understanding, throughout this chapter, we will use three definitions for monocyte descendants, depending on their functional properties: effector monocytes, moDC-like cells, and monocyte-derived macrophages.

3.1. Effector monocytes

Infections and tissue damage draw a rapid influx of CX_3CR1^{int} $Ly6C^+$ monocytes into the affected tissue (Geissmann et al., 2003). This holds true for autoimmune diseases, such as experimental autoimmune encephalomyelitis (EAE) and rheumatoid arthritis (Bruhl et al., 2007; King, Dickendesher, & Segal, 2009; Mildner et al., 2009), breaches of the intestinal barrier integrity resulting in commensal exposure (Bain et al., 2012; Zigmond et al., 2012), and bacterial challenges, such as *Listeria monocytogenes* infections (Serbina, Salazar-Mather, Biron, Kuziel, & Pamer, 2003). In particular, the monocyte-derived cells reported to accumulate in the latter scenario are characterized by their high production of TNF-α and iNOS and were hence named "TNF-α and iNOS-producing DC" (TipDC) (Serbina et al., 2003), a term that has been widely applied. The nomenclature "DC" refers to higher expression of the DC markers CD11c and MHCII but does not imply a direct contribution in antigen presentation or the like. In this regard, it was shown that in the absence of $Ly6C^{+}$ monocytes and resulting impairment of TipDC formation during *L. monocytogenes* infection, the $CD4^{+}$ and $CD8^{+}$ T-cell response was unaffected indicating a negligible role of TipDC in T-cell priming (Serbina et al., 2003). It is also arguable, whether the name TipDC should really be applied to all monocyte descendants, especially if the latter do not produce TNF-α and iNOS, or only minute amounts of the factors. While TNF-α and iNOS are effector molecules with important roles in antimicrobial responses to infections, they likely play less prominent parts in sterile inflammatory settings, such as autoimmune diseases as discussed in the succeeding text. Therefore, we propose to use the more neutral term "effector monocytes" for monocyte infiltrates, which show a prominent proinflammatory expression signature, causing collateral damage, thereby promoting pathology.

3.2. Monocyte-derived dendritic cells

The notion that monocytes can develop *in vivo* into a DC-like population was already suggested last century (Randolph, Inaba, Robbiani, Steinman, & Muller, 1999). In that study, fluorescent-labeled beads were subcutaneously injected into mice and the appearance of bead-containing cells within the skin-draining LN was followed. A migratory phagocytotic cell population was identified within the LN that was characterized by high amounts of MHCII molecules and low levels of the surface integrin CD11c, which was distinct from LN-resident cDC. Support for the monocytic origin of the newly differentiated DC-like subset came from studies involving op/op mice, a natural occurring null mutation in Csf1 (Marks & Lane, 1976). Op/op mice are characterized by a nearly complete absence of tissue macrophages and circulating monocytes, whereas DC development is reportedly unaffected (Wiktor-Jedrzejczak et al., 1992). When fluorescently labeled beads were injected into op/op animals, no bead-bearing CD11c^{int} DC-like cells were observed (Randolph et al., 1999). Of note, this study was performed in the absence of bacterial products as adjuvants, indicating that mere bead phagocytosis might suffice for the generation of CD11c^{int} moDC. In fact, it was later reported that intradermal coinjecton of beads with whole bacteria or bacterial products abolished the migration of moDC to the draining LN and their local differentiation (Rotta et al., 2003). These data emphasize that the absence or presence of inflammatory stimuli, such as bacterial compounds, seems to bias monocytes towards moDC or effector monocyte activities, respectively (Fig. 3.2). As such, they highlight the importance of the tissue context on the ensuing monocytes fates.

After these initial studies, numerous groups focused on the role and development of moDC under various circumstances and indirectly implied—just by their usage of the DC term—that these cells can critically contribute DC-like functions. Unfortunately though, in most cases, the cells were solely defined based on intermediate expression of the DC marker CD11c and high levels of the panmyeloid marker CD11b. Also Ly-6C^{-} monocytes are CD11b^{+} CD11c^{int} (Mildner et al., 2007). Moreover, preDC-derived cDC subpopulations express CD11b (Liu et al., 2009) and may downregulate CD11c during activation (Singh-Jasuja et al., 2013). The exclusive use of these integrin markers alone is hence clearly insufficient to attribute to monocyte descendants cDC characteristics, such as potential of antigen presentation and T-cell priming in secondary lymphoid organs. Rather, we will in this chapter refer with the term "moDC" to cells, which show phagocytic activity and the ability to process antigens and subsequently participate in the priming of naïve T cells or in the reactivation of antigen-experienced T cells.

3.3. Monocyte-derived macrophages

Inflammation is a crucial component of the host defense against injury and infection. Prolonged and chronic inflammatory responses can however be detrimental for the host causing considerable collateral damage (Nathan & Ding, 2010). Rather than relying on passive restoration of homeostasis with time, nature evolved mechanisms that actively promote the resolution of inflammatory reaction and thereby efficiently curb and prevent immunopathology (Serhan et al., 2007). Overt inflammatory reactions are hence

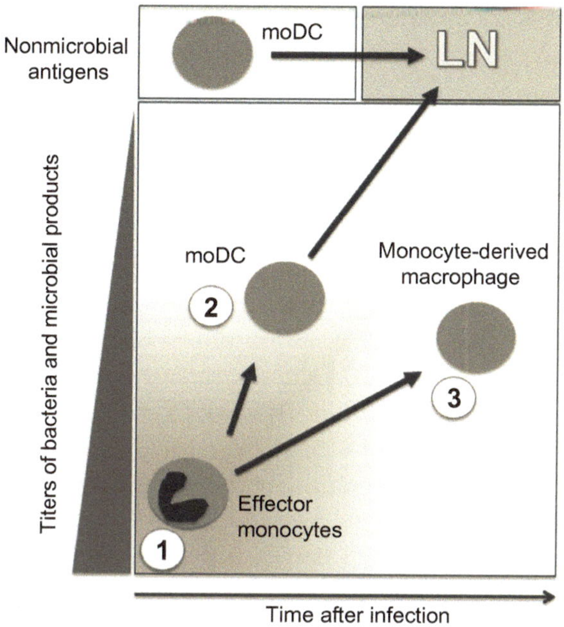

Figure 3.2 Time and context dependence of monocyte fates. Monocytes enter inflammatory lesions at different time points. If they infiltrate early during an infection when bacterial titers are high and microbial products are present (time point #1), monocytes might give rise preferentially to effector monocytes (the TipDC equivalent). At this early inflammatory stage, direct development of monocytes to monocyte-derived dendritic cells (moDCs) seems unlikely since the presence of bacterial products was reported to block moDC generation. With decreasing bacterial titers and with time the inflammatory milieu will change potentially favoring effector monocyte differentiation into moDC. Under these circumstances, the direct differentiation of newly infiltrated monocytes into moDC is possible (timepoint #2). Also, specific areas within the inflammatory lesion, such as its borders with lower bacterial concentrations, might facilitate the development of moDC. During the resolution stage monocyte-derived macrophages dominate the tissue, which are characterized by an anti-inflammatory gene expression signature and high phagocytotic activity. Monocyte infiltration at this stage of disease may lead to a direct conversion into monocyte-derived macrophages (timepoint #3) as it does in the steady-state-intestine. (For color version of this figure, the reader is referred to the online version of this chapter.)

followed by phases of tissue remodeling and repair that aim to restore tissue integrity back to steady state. During this time, accumulated cell debris has to be removed and specific anti-inflammatory gene expression signatures can be observed in monocyte-derived cells that facilitate tissue regeneration (Ramachandran et al., 2012; Stables et al., 2011). Examples of such scenarios where mainly Ly6C$^+$ monocytes are recruited to the resolving tissue and are polarized towards an anti-inflammatory/proresolution phenotype with tissue-repair capacity are found in atherosclerosis (Tacke et al., 2007), allergic skin reactions (Egawa et al., 2013), fibrosis regression (Ramachandran et al., 2012), and spinal cord injury (Shechter et al., 2009). However, whether monocyte-derived macrophages integrate into the resident phagocyte network following the resolution of tissue damage remains to be shown and probably will depend on the context. Thus, CNS-infiltrating monocyte-derived cells have been shown to vanish with time (Ajami, Bennett, Krieger, McNagny, & Rossi, 2011), while data from a peritonitis model suggest that there can be some long-term integration (Yona et al., 2013). Interestingly, the intestinal lamina propria macrophage compartment seems to constitute an exception since it seems to rely in its entirety on monocytes for maintenance, as discussed in the succeeding text (Bogunovic et al., 2009; Varol et al., 2009).

In the sections in the succeeding text, we will discuss three tissue settings where collective efforts have yielded sufficient comprehensive insight into the fate of monocytes and their descendants under inflammatory, as well as steady-state conditions. Specifically, we will focus on monocyte fates in the inflamed peritoneum and the brain, as well as the intestine.

4. MONOCYTE-DERIVED CELLS IN THE INFLAMED PERITONEUM

The naïve peritoneal cavity is predominately populated by resident macrophages. Under resting conditions, these cells act as sentinels of their microenvironment, contributing to the maintenance of tissue homeostasis, for example, clearance of senescent cells and tissue remodeling. Peritoneal macrophages originate prenatally (Yona et al., 2013); in the first 2 weeks of life, they undergo an intense period of proliferation (Davies et al., 2011) and in absence of challenge subsequently maintain themselves by longevity and self-renewal (Yona et al., 2013). In recent years, it has become apparent that the resident macrophage network in the peritoneum is divided into two distinct populations, characterized as large F4/80^{hi} MHCII^{-} and small F4/80^{lo} MHCII^{+} macrophages (Ghosn et al., 2010). F4/80^{lo} MHCII^{+} macrophages efficiently present antigen to T cells, while the F4/80^{hi}MHCII^{-} large peritoneal macrophages are capable of clearing apoptotic cells. Yet, both populations share the ability to phagocytose bacteria (Ghosn et al., 2010; Nguyen, Tran, Muller, & Jack, 2012).

In response to trauma or microbial invasion, resident peritoneal macrophages initiate an inflammatory cascade (Cailhier et al., 2005). By the release of vasoactive amines, eicosanoids, cytokines, and chemokines, they coordinate and regulate vascular changes resulting in inflammatory cell recruitment, in particular the mobilization of circulating neutrophils. Curiously, neutrophil extravasation is accompanied with a steep decline in resident macrophage numbers, termed the "macrophage disappearance reaction" (Barth, Hendrzak, Melnicoff, & Morahan, 1995; Nelson & Boyden, 1963; van Furth, Diesselhoff-den Dulk, & Mattie, 1973). The fate of these macrophages remains an issue of some contention. Suggested explanations include cell adhesion to the serosal mucosa, as a consequence of the coagulation system activation (Serra et al., 2000) or rapid draining to LN (Bellingan, Caldwell, Howie, Dransfield, & Haslett, 1996) or potentially to the omentum (Ansel, Harris, & Cyster, 2002).

Monocyte infiltration during acute peritonitis was proposed to be biphasic. Thus, shortly after challenge with heat-killed *L. monocytogenes* (<2 h), a rapid influx of Ly6C$^-$ monocytes has been observed that displayed transient production of TNF-α and IL-1β (Auffray et al., 2007), preceding the arrival of neutrophils. However, this early Ly6C$^-$ monocyte infiltrate has so far not been reported for other systems and it remains to be shown whether it is a general feature of the inflammatory cascade. The main wave of monocyte recruitment involves Ly6C$^+$ monocytes and is linked with various sequential temporal functions including proinflammatory cytokine/chemokine production and antigen presentation and culminating in the clearance of apoptotic neutrophils (Fadok et al., 1998), ultimately leading to the restoration of tissue homeostasis. Interestingly, Soehnlein and colleagues demonstrated that the recruitment of Ly6C$^+$ monocytes is a granulocyte-driven event, in which inflammatory neutrophils release antimicrobial peptides and heparin-binding protein that specifically mobilize Ly6C$^+$ monocytes to sites of inflammation (Soehnlein et al., 2008). In the advance state of inflammation, the peritoneal cavity hosts a complex makeup of cells including infiltrating Ly6C$^+$ effector monocytes (Geissmann et al., 2003; Sunderkotter et al., 2004; Takahashi, Galligan, Tessarollo, & Yoshimura, 2009), returning resident macrophages (Yona et al., 2013), and IL-12 producing moDC (Geissmann et al., 2003; Goldszmid et al., 2012). The proportion of each subpopulation is likely time- and stimuli-dependent (see Fig. 3.2) and precise effector functions of each subpopulation remain to be fully explored.

Subsequently, the release of lipid mediators and cytokines at this stage of the response orchestrates the resolution of inflammation (Lawrence, Willoughby, & Gilroy, 2002). Apoptotic neutrophil clearance by resident macrophages stimulates the expression of 12/15 lipoxygenase, establishing an autocrine feedback loop, which coordinates the nonphlogistic phagocytosis of apoptotic neutrophils, termed efferocytosis, by resident macrophages and blocks inflammatory monocyte-derived macrophage phagocytosis, helping to maintain immunological tolerance (Ariel & Serhan, 2012; Uderhardt et al., 2012). Specifically, resident macrophages express high levels of the phosphatidylserine (PS) receptor TIM-4 and low levels of milk fat globule-EGF factor 8 protein (MFG-E8), the PS bridging molecule, which enables apoptotic cells to bind to the phagocytic integrin $\alpha_v\beta_3$ (Hanayama et al., 2002). In contrast, inflammatory monocyte-derived macrophages express high levels of MFG-E8 and low levels of TIM-4. 12/15 lipoxygenase expressed by resident macrophages mediates the oxidization of phosphatidylethanolamine that outcompetes the binding of MFG-E8 required for monocyte-derived macrophage phagocytosis. Thus, 12/15 lipoxygenase favors resident macrophage phagocytosis of apoptotic cells. Moreover, monocyte-derived macrophages seem to acquire additional resolving activities that are the focus of intense research (Schif-Zuck et al., 2011; Serhan et al., 2007; Stables et al., 2011). As the cavity recovers and the resolution phase is in full swing, a significant proportion of infiltrating cells drain to the LN (Bellingan et al., 1996), while the resident macrophages proliferate to repopulate the cavity (Davies et al., 2011). Interestingly, a recent Cre-lox-based fate-mapping approach revealed that at least a fraction of monocyte-derived macrophages seems to permanently integrate (>2 months) into the resident macrophage pool, accompanied by a phenotypic shift to $MHCII^{lo}F4/80^{hi}$ cells (Yona et al., 2013). Finally, it should be noted that in certain situations, such as helminth-associated T_H2 cell milieus, IL-4 alone drives the proliferation of the resident macrophage pool without the influx of blood monocytes (Jenkins et al., 2011).

Most of the data available on monocyte fates in the peritoneum have focused on macrophage activities. A rare exception is an intriguing study involving the adjuvants alum (aluminum hydroxide) (Kool et al., 2008). Under these conditions, infiltrating monocytes differentiated into moDC that migrated from the peritoneum to the mediastinal and ipsilateral LN initiating Th2 responses. Interestingly, the authors showed that the alum challenge involves the generation of uric acid, which triggers inflammasome activation and might thereby have an impact on the monocyte fates in this setting (Kool et al., 2008).

5. MONOCYTE-DERIVED CELLS IN THE INFLAMED BRAIN

The healthy brain is seeded by a unique type of macrophage, the microglia, which displays a distinct gene expression profile (Gautier et al., 2012) most likely associated with their sequestration in the unique neuronal/macroglial context. Steady-state microglia are evenly distributed throughout the CNS, including brain and spinal cord, although there is evidence for region-specific differences in density, phenotype, and responsiveness (Olah et al., 2012). As immune cells, microglia are sensors of injury and pathological conditions (Hanisch & Kettenmann, 2007). In addition, emerging evidence indicates that microglia contribute to CNS development and brain homeostasis (Tremblay et al., 2011).

Microglia are established before birth from a primitive hematopoietic wave derived from the yolk sac (Alliot et al., 1999; Ginhoux et al., 2010) and subsequently maintain themselves throughout adulthood through longevity and limited self-renewal. They share this prenatal establishment with other resident tissue macrophages (Yona et al., 2013); however, the latter seem to be less secluded and more promiscuous with respect to the incorporation of monocytic cells derived from the fetal liver or during challenge (Hoeffel et al., 2012; Yona et al., 2013). This difference between microglia and peripheral tissue macrophages might be due to the unique location of microglia beyond the blood–brain barrier, a multilayer cell barrier formed by astroglial processes, pericytes, and endothelial cells (Owens, Bechmann, & Engelhardt, 2008), which restricts CNS entry of immune cells. Only during early embryonic development, that is, before establishment of the barrier, or during inflammatory reactions, when the barrier integrity is impaired, CNS infiltration by mononuclear cells is observed. Multiple sclerosis (MS) and its animal model, EAE (Mendel, Kerlero de Rosbo, & Ben-Nun, 1995), are such disorders associated with prominent blood–brain barrier breakdown.

Brain antigens are efficiently secluded from the peripheral organs in the healthy organism. Moreover, rare brain antigen exposure to antigen-presenting cells (APCs) in the absence of costimulatory molecules probably energizes neuroantigen-reactive T cells. However, autoreactive T cells can be activated by APC presenting viral antigens mimicking brain-specific myelin antigens (molecular mimicry) or by bystander-activated APC during brain injury (Owens & Bennett, 2012). After priming in peripheral secondary lymphoid organs, these autoreactive T cells require reactivation in the CNS by local APC. A population that could fulfill this task was recently identified in two tissue layers surrounding the brain parenchyma—the meninges and the choroid plexus (Anandasabapathy et al., 2011). These Flt3L-depending cDC could provide the critical restimulation and induce T-cell production of chemo- and cytokines that recruit further leukocytes, including monocytes, thus potentially driving the effector phase of the autoimmune neuroinflammation.

Monocytes may contribute in a number of ways to MS and EAE development. First, they could give rise to moDC that prime naïve autoreactive T cells in the periphery. For the induction of EAE, animals are immunized subcutaneously with peptides derived from myelin oligodendrocyte glycoprotein (MOG) or proteolipid protein (PLP) emulsified in complete, heat-killed bacteria containing Freund's adjuvant (Mendel et al., 1995; Paterson, 1966). The current scheme holds that skin-associated DCs at the injection site phagocytose and process the antigen and—after migration to the local draining LN—present it to self-reactive naïve CD4 T cells. These encephalitogenic T cells undergo clonal expansion, before infiltrating the CNS, where they require reactivation mediated by CNS-resident APCs as mentioned earlier. According to this scheme, cDC would be indispensible for EAE induction and indeed results from studies in MHCII-deficient mice support this notion (Slavin et al., 2001). Furthermore, when encephalitogenic T cells were adoptively transferred into mice, which only express MHCII molecules on CD11c-expressing cells, EAE symptoms similar to controls could be observed (Greter et al., 2005), indicating a crucial role of CNS-resident, CD11c-expressing DC in the reactivation of autoreactive T cells. Surprisingly, however, mice that were conditionally depleted of cDC using the diphtheria toxin (DTx) receptor (DTR) system do develop EAE indistinguishable from controls, suggesting redundancy in the priming of encephalitogenic T cells (Isaksson, Lundgren, Ahlgren, Kampe, & Lobell, 2012; Yogev et al., 2012). In these cases, Ly-6C^{+} monocytes that were recruited from the circulation to the site of immunization might have carried processed autoantigen to the draining LN (Palframan et al., 2001). Although CD11c-DTR transgenic moDCs are generally sensitive to the DTx regimen (Kool et al., 2008), in the particular experiments, some of these cells might have escaped DTx-induced cell death due to low CD11c expression (Isaksson et al., 2012; Randolph et al., 1999; Serbina et al., 2003). MoDCs have been shown to be able to activate naïve T cells, when the cDC compartment is functionally impaired, as, for instance, in CCL19/CCL20-deficient *plt* mice, in which cDC migration is compromised (Nakano et al., 2009). MoDC can also stimulate antigen-specific naïve CD4 T cells in other scenarios, including the *Listeria* and *Aspergillus fumigatus* infection models (Hohl et al., 2009; Serbina et al., 2003). However, transient depletion of Ly-6C^{+} monocytes during the priming phase in MOG-immunized mice did not reduce clinical symptoms (Mildner et al., 2009), arguing that moDCs are dispensable for naïve CD4 T-cell priming. Notably, the autoantigen MOG used in the EAE protocol is emulsified in complete Freund's adjuvant containing heat-killed *Mycobacteria*. MoDC differentiation and migration to the draining LN was however reported to be impaired in presence of bacteria or bacterial products (Rotta et al., 2003). The EAE-inducing procedures might hence be rather unfavorable for the generation of moDC that could contribute migratory APC activities.

The idea that monocytes and their descendants play an essential role in the development of EAE was first suggested by the fact that CCR2-deficient mice are resistant to disease induction (Fife, Huffnagle, Kuziel, & Karpus, 2000; Gaupp, Pitt, Kuziel, Cannella, & Raine, 2003; Izikson, Klein, Charo, Weiner, & Luster, 2000). Moreover, even transfer of autoreactive wt T cells to CCR2$^{-/-}$ mice failed to restore EAE susceptibility (Fife et al., 2000). Direct proof that the EAE phenotype of CCR2$^{-/-}$ mice results from reduced numbers of circulating Ly-6C^{+} monocytes was provided when Mildner and colleagues depleted Ly6C^{+} monocytes in MOG-immunized wt mice using an antibody that ablates CCR2-expressing cells in a CD16/32 FC-receptor-dependent manner (Mildner et al., 2009). Treatment of the animals at the peak of EAE symptoms caused a significant amelioration of the disease, accompanied with a complete absence of blood and—time-delayed—monocytic CNS infiltrates. Similar results were obtained taking a different approach involving the use of clodronate liposomes (King et al., 2009).

CNS-infiltrating Ly-6C^{+} monocytes upregulate CD11c and MHCII and also acquire a certain amount of TNF-α and iNOS expression, thus fulfilling the criteria of TipDC (King et al., 2009; Mildner et al., 2009). However, the functional importance of monocyte-derived TNF-α and iNOS in the context of EAE remains to be determined. TNF-α has long been discussed as critical regulator of MS pathology (Sharief & Hentges, 1991) and its critical proinflammatory role was shown in various EAE models (Kassiotis et al., 1999; Korner, Lemckert, Chaudhri, Etteldorf, & Sedgwick, 1997). Immunized TNF-α$^{-/-}$ mice develop no initial EAE symptoms but suffer from severe relapses during chronic autoimmunity

(Kassiotis & Kollias, 2001). These relapses, which might be associated with abnormal prolonged self-reactivity of peripheral CD4 T cells, suggest a dual, beneficial, and deleterious role of TNF-α in EAE development—a finding that might explain the failure of anti-TNF-α therapy in MS patients (van Oosten et al., 1996). Furthermore, the second TipDC product, iNOS, might not be responsible for the pathogenicity of CNS-infiltrated effector monocytes since iNOS-deficient mice are highly susceptible to EAE induction and develop aggravated clinical symptoms (Dalton & Wittmer, 2005; Fenyk-Melody et al., 1998; Sahrbacher et al., 1998). An anti-inflammatory role of iNOS could be explained by its apoptosis-inducing properties and indeed reduced apoptotic CD4 T cells were found in the CNS of immunized iNOS-deficient animals (Dalton & Wittmer, 2005). The production of NO also inhibits the proliferation of T cells *in vitro* (MacMicking et al., 1997; Mazzoni et al., 2002) and prevents the secretion of IL-12 by macrophages, thereby blocking IFN-γ production by T cells (Huang et al., 1998).

In light of the preceding text, it is unlikely that TNF-α and iNOS are the main pathogenic factors produced by effector monocytes in EAE; the physical depletion of monocytic infiltrates should otherwise have resulted in exacerbated clinical symptoms, rather than their amelioration (Mildner et al., 2009). Of note, CNS-effector monocytes also produce IL-23, IL-12, IL-6, and TGF-β1, besides TNF-α and iNOS (King et al., 2009; Miller, McMahon, Schreiner, & Bailey, 2007), that is, cytokines essential for T-cell polarization towards the Th17 fate (Bettelli, Baeten, Jager, Sobel, & Kuchroo, 2006; Veldhoen, Hocking, Flavell, & Stockinger, 2006). CNS-effector monocytes were in fact reported to be superior to other myeloid cells, when tested for their potential to induce Th17 differentiation (Bailey, Schreiner, McMahon, & Miller, 2007), and these cells could hence, once recruited to the CNS, directly support the generation of pathogenic Th17 cells. This might partially explain why effector monocytes are important players in EAE development (King et al., 2009; Mildner et al., 2009).

A major cause of disease progression is believed to be the fact that T-cell reactivity shifts from the disease-initiating epitope(s) to distinct noncross-reactive epitopes (Vanderlugt et al., 2000). Interestingly, emerging evidence suggests that during the later stages of EAE development, moDCs are critically involved in this epitope spreading. Thus, when different APCs were isolated from the CNS of PLP peptide$_{178-191}$, immunized mice were cocultured with PLP$_{139-151}$-specific CD4 T cells, only CD11b^{+} CD11c^{+}

cells were potent stimulators of T-cell proliferation (Bailey et al., 2007; McMahon, Bailey, Castenada, Waldner, & Miller, 2005).

Interestingly, presentation of exogenous antigens to CD8 T cells was also demonstrated for moDC. When mice were intradermally immunized with measles virus nucleoprotein, which induces a specific CD8 T-cell response without CD4 T-cell help, a strong dermal infiltration of Ly6C$^+$ monocytes was observed (Le Borgne et al., 2006). This monocytic infiltrate gave rise to moDC that induced CD8 T-cell responses (Le Borgne et al., 2006). This result was recently confirmed in the EAE model. Here, antibodies against MHCI-restricted myelin epitopes were used to identify a CNS-infiltrating cell population in healthy and in EAE-inflicted mice that could induce myelin-specific CD8 T-cell responses (Ji, Castelli, & Goverman, 2013). Of note, cells that presented myelin antigens in the MHCI context were phenotypically similar to tissue-infiltrating moDC. They may hence contribute during the transition from acute to chronic pathologies by epitope spreading. If these moDCs develop directly from newly recruited Ly6C$^+$ monocytes or transdifferentiate from effector monocytes requires further investigation.

In summary, these results indicate that CNS-infiltrating monocytes can give rise to either effector monocyte or moDC, maybe dependent on the time when they entered the tissue and the cytokine milieu that educates them (Fig. 3.2).

MS is a remitting, relapsing disease in which inflammatory lesions can be regenerated. It is therefore likely that monocyte-derived cells facilitate tissue repair at later stages of disease, thereby complementing the resident microglia network. Such a scenario has already been demonstrated in a mouse model of spinal cord injury, where the secretion of IL-10 from monocyte-derived macrophages but not microglia was critical for motor function recovery (Shechter et al., 2009). However, differential contributions of microglia and monocyte-derived cells remain poorly understood and insights will have to await the development of novel experimental approaches.

The long-term fate of monocytes and their descendants after the infiltration to the injured brain was addressed by the group of Rossi using an adoptive cell transfer experiment involving CX_3CR1^{GFP} cells (Ajami et al., 2011). Two weeks after engraftment—when GFP$^+$ donor cells were still present in the circulation—EAE was induced and the brain was analyzed at different time points after immunization. Surprisingly, while GFP$^+$ cells were found in the brain up to 2 weeks after EAE induction, no infiltrate was present 3 month after immunization, that is, by the time the recipients had fully recovered from clinical symptoms (Ajami et al., 2011). These data demonstrate that even after a prominent trauma-associated influx of myeloid cells into the injured CNS, a steady state relying solely on microglia seems to be restored and a stable, long-term (>2 weeks) integration of infiltrated myeloid cells into the microglial network is hence unlikely.

6. MONOCYTE-DERIVED CELLS IN THE INTESTINE

The emerging theme concerning the organization of the mononuclear phagocyte system holds that the relatively hard-wired tissue-resident cell network is complemented during injury or challenge by cells that arise from monocytes mobilized from the blood circulation, as a transient "emergency squad." As short-lived, highly plastic cells monocytes are extreme versatile and have the potential to contribute both pro- and anti-inflammatory activities, depending on the time and route of their arrival to tissues.

The gastrointestinal tract presents a notable exception from this clear dichotomy of homeostatic quiescence and conditions of challenge. The gut lumen harbors a myriad of commensal bacteria that assist its host in digestion. Efficient food uptake is ensured by a monolayer of intestinal epithelial cells that separates the lumen from deeper tissue. This scenario poses a unique challenge to the organism since the latter has to tolerate the beneficial but foreign symbionts and the constant exposure to their microbial products. Rather than remaining unresponsive, the host actively engages the commensal microflora and regulates its composition through secretion of antimicrobial peptides and immunoglobulins (Mukherjee, Vaishnava, & Hooper, 2008; Peterson, McNulty, Guruge, & Gordon, 2007). Conversely, microbiota encounter is essential for the development of functional gut-associated immune system (Rakoff-Nahoum, Paglino, Eslami-Varzaneh, Edberg, & Medzhitov, 2004) and defined intestinal commensals, such as *Clostridium*, critically shape the prevalence of distinct helper and regulatory T-cell populations (Hooper, Littman, & Macpherson, 2012). While engaging the commensal microbes, the organism has to remain sensitive to deviations from this "primed homeostasis" and rapidly respond to invading enteropathogens or injuries causing epithelial damage. Failure to maintain this exquisite balance and hyper-responsiveness in genetically predisposed individuals is likely associated with the development of chronic inflammatory bowel disorders (IBD), such as Crohn's disease and ulcerative colitis.

A critical feature of the intestinal landscape is its dynamic nature involving constant tissue renewal and adaptation. The epithelial cell layer is replaced weekly from crypt-resident stem cells (van der Flier & Clevers, 2009) and also the composition of the immune cells residing in the subepithelial connective tissue, the *lamina propria*, constantly adjusts to the local microflora challenge. Thus, the balance of regulatory and effector T cells, or DC and macrophages, differs between the small and large intestine, likely in response to local cues (Denning et al., 2011).

Intestinal CX_3CR1^{hi} macrophages match these dynamics with a unique short half-life of 3 weeks and are, unlike most other tissue macrophages, in their entirety derived from $Ly6C^+$ blood monocytes (Bogunovic et al., 2009; Varol et al., 2009). Given the general propensity of monocytes to be recruited to sites of inflammation, this is likely due to a tonic, low inflammatory stimulus provided by the commensal microflora and its products. Recent work from our laboratory indicates that the recruited monocytes are locally imprinted by yet-to-be-defined microenvironmental cues to acquire a robust noninflammatory expression profile, which resembles that of nonmigratory tissue macrophages (Rivollier, He, Kole, Valatas, & Kelsall, 2012; Zigmond et al., 2012). In the differentiation process, monocytes and macrophages likely sense bacterial products, for instance, by virtue of transepithelial dendrites (Niess et al., 2005; Rescigno et al., 2001), but likely sense also factors derived from the epithelium (Artis, 2008). Interestingly, expression signatures of monocyte-derived CX_3CR1^{hi} macrophages significantly differ between the small and large intestine (Jung, *unpublished observation*), suggesting special functional contributions of monocyte-derived macrophages in these neighboring, but anatomically distinct tissues. Rapid establishment of the noninflammatory macrophage expression signature is critical to maintain the unique dynamic equilibrium of the epithelium, microbiota, and immune cells residing in the *lamina propria*. Emerging evidence suggests that monocyte education is important for maintenance of metastable gut homeostasis. Disturbances, such as antibiotic-induced dysbiosis (Diehl et al., 2013), or genetic impairment of sensory components of the CX_3CR1^{hi} macrophages, such as the IL-10R (Zigmond et al., *unpublished observation*), can lead to potentially harmful deviations from the steady state, such as expression of CCR7 and migration to the LN or induction of proinflammatory cytokines in response to exposure to bacterial products.

The healthy gut environment imprints $Ly6C^+$ blood monocytes to acquire a macrophage signature that renders the cells compatible with the unique requirements in the gut and probably endows the cells with an exclusive capacity to communicate with the resident lymphocytes, such as T regulatory cells (Coombes et al., 2007; Denning, Wang, Patel, Williams, & Pulendran, 2007).

Interesting though, when Ly6C$^+$ blood monocytes enter the inflamed intestine, they adopt distinct fates. Analysis of CX$_3$CR1^{gfp} reporter animals (Jung et al., 2000) challenged with dextran sodium sulfate (DSS), a well-established colitis model (Okayasu et al., 1990), revealed a population of cells in the colon that displayed intermediate levels of CX$_3$CR1 and transiently dominated the *lamina propria* (Platt, Bain, Bordon, Sester, & Mowat, 2010). These CX$_3$CR1/GFP^{int} cells were also found in the T-cell transfer colitis model and shown to display proinflammatory gene expression signatures (Weber, Saurer, Schenk, Dickgreber, & Mueller, 2011). Adoptive transfer experiments established that, like the resident CX$_3$CR1^{hi} macrophages, the CX$_3$CR1^{int} cells were also derived from Ly6C$^+$ blood monocytes (Rivollier et al., 2012; Zigmond et al., 2012). Highlighting their proinflammatory potential, *in vitro* exposure of these cells to bacterial TLR or NOD-like receptor ligands, but not of resident CX$_3$CR1^{hi} macrophages triggered expression of proinflammatory cytokines (Zigmond et al., 2012). Moreover, using a conditional cell ablation strategy, depletion of CCR2-expressing CX$_3$CR1^{int} cells alongside their immediate Ly6C$^+$ monocyte precursors was found to ameliorate DSS-induced colitis (Zigmond et al., 2012). This establishes CX$_3$CR1^{int} cells as proinflammatory effector monocytes that actively drive inflammation and suggests that monocyte manipulation might have therapeutic value for the management of IBD flares. Notably, proinflammatory monocyte-derived cells have also been detected in the mesenteric LN of colitic mice, though these cells probably entered the LN from the blood (Siddiqui, Laffont, & Powrie, 2010) and the relation to lamina propria-resident cells remains to be explored.

Resident intestinal CX$_3$CR1^{hi} macrophages do not leave the lamina propria and are absent from lymphatics in the healthy state (Schulz et al., 2009). Together with morphological features and their expression profile, this nonmigratory behavior served as an argument for the classification of these cells as macrophages (Rivollier et al., 2012). Interesting though, recent data suggest that under inflammatory conditions, a small fraction of Ly6C$^+$ monocytes can also give rise to a migratory CCR7-expressing CX$_3$CR1^{int} Ly6C^{lo} cell population (Fig. 3.2). These cells could be considered moDC, as they seem to have a capacity to prime T cells toward the T$_H$1 or T$_H$17 lineage (Cerovic et al., 2013; Zigmond et al., 2012); of note, these cells do not display TNF-α or iNOS expression. Ly6C$^+$ derived CX$_3$CR1^{int}

Ly6C^{lo} cells display a "DC-like" phenotype including higher expression of CD11c and lower expression of CD64 (Bain et al., 2012; Rivollier et al., 2012). Moreover, a fraction of them expresses the newly described DC marker Zbtb46 (Meredith, Liu, Darrasse-Jeze, et al., 2012; Satpathy et al., 2012). Interestingly, also activated monocytes stimulated *in vitro* with Csf2 have been shown to express this transcription factor (Meredith, Liu, Darrasse-Jeze, et al., 2012; Satpathy et al., 2012). These data thus suggest that some monocytes initiate in the inflamed gut context a transcription program that enforces DC-like features while extinguishing the expression of alternate myeloid growth factor receptors (Satpathy et al., 2012).

Collectively, in the intestine, monocytes adopt—depending on the context they land in—three distinct fates. In the healthy gut, CX_3CR1^{int} Ly6C$^+$ monocytes give rise to noninflammatory monocyte-derived macrophages, whereas under inflammatory conditions, the same cells differentiate into Ly6C$^+$ proinflammatory effector monocytes and migratory Ly6C$^-$ cells displaying DC features.

7. DEVELOPMENT OF MONOCYTE-DERIVED CELLS

The developmental pathways leading to monocyte-derived cells remain poorly understood. Given the seminal discovery that human monocytes develop into DC-like cells when cultured with Csf2 and IL-4 (Sallusto & Lanzavecchia, 1994), Csf2 was long considered one of the major players in monocyte-derived cell development. Animal models for pathogen infection, involving, for instance, *L. monocytogenes* or influenza virus (Huang et al., 2011; Zhan, Lieschke, Grail, Dunn, & Cheers, 1998), and for autoimmune diseases, such as EAE and collagen-induced arthritis (Campbell, Bendele, Smith, & Hamilton, 1997; McQualter et al., 2001), are strictly dependent on Csf2 signaling. Since all these models are associated with a prominent monocytic infiltrates, an essential role of Csf2 in monocyte-derived cell development was suggested. The most comprehensive data set exists for MOG-immunized Csf2$^{-/-}$ mice and we therefore will discuss the Csf2-dependence of monocytes and their descendants exemplary within this autoimmunity model.

Csf2$^{-/-}$ mice are resistant to active EAE induction (McQualter et al., 2001). Moreover, transfer of Csf2-deficient encephalitogenic T cells does not induce passive EAE despite the normal ability of these cells to secrete IFN-γ, TNF-α, IL-4, and IL-5 and to undergo antigen-specific proliferation *in vitro* (Ponomarev et al., 2007). Subsequent studies showed that the Th17-specific transcription factor RORγt in T cells drives the production of Csf2

(Codarri et al., 2011), which, in turn, promotes local neuroinflammation by the recruitment and activation of myeloid cells. MOG immunization was shown to boost the generation and mobilization of monocytes from the BM (King et al., 2009). This phenomenon is Csf2 dependent, as it can be prevented by neutralization of this cytokine. Moreover, anti-Csf2 treatment also prevents disease induction (King et al., 2009). Collectively, these results argue for an essential and direct role of Csf2 during the development of effector monocytes and moDC. However, a recent study challenged this hypothesis (Greter et al., 2012). Specifically, these authors generated mixed BM chimeras in which Csf2R$^{-/-}$ cells had to compete with wild-type cells. Surprisingly, when challenged with a whole panel of different pathogens or subjected to the EAE protocol, monocyte-derived cells in these chimeras developed equally well, no matter, if the cells were Csf2R-proficient or Csf2R-deficient (Greter et al., 2012). Furthermore, the production of TNF-α and iNOS was indistinguishable between the two genotypes, confirming that even these functional properties are Csf2-independent.

The discrepancy between data obtained from Csf2$^{-/-}$ and Csf2R$^{-/-}$ mice at least in EAE might be due to differential involvement of brain resident macrophages, the microglia. Thus, Ponomarev and colleagues showed that after transfer of autoreactive Csf2-deficient T cells, microglia are not activated, whereas the small amount of infiltrating monocytes displayed induction of costimulatory molecules (Ponomarev et al., 2007). The impaired microglia activation might be responsible for the protection from EAE. Microglial activation by intracerebral LPS injection was found to restore clinical EAE symptoms after transfer of Csf2$^{-/-}$ encephalitogenic T cells (Ponomarev et al., 2007). These data indicate that Csf2 may not directly act on monocytes to facilitate their further differentiation to effector cells or moDC, but rather affect other CNS-resident cells like microglia, which then might—after Csf2 encounter—provide essential factors to support the generation of monocyte-derived cells. This assumption can be tested by the transfer of wt BM cells into irradiated Csf2R$^{-/-}$ mice or the microgial-specific deletion of Csf2R and clearly, further experiments are required to define the functional contributions of Csf2 signaling to disease development.

The early report of Randolph and colleagues showed that Csf1 signaling is essential for moDC development (Randolph et al., 1999), most likely by ensuring sufficient circulating moDC precursors, the monocytes. Similar results were obtained, when tamoxifen-inducible Csf1R deficient mice were investigated for the development of moDC (Greter et al., 2012). An advantage of these mice over *op/op* mice is that in the former only Ly6C^{-}

monocytes are affected, whereas the Ly6C^{+} pool, which constitutes the moDC precursors, is unimpaired. This is likely due to the extended half-life and increased dependence on survival factors (Landsman et al., 2009) of Ly6C^{-} monocytes, compared to short-lived Ly6C^{+} monocytes (Yona et al., 2013). When tamoxifen-induced Csf1R-deficient mice were treated with LPS or infected with influenza virus, their Ly6C^{+} monocytes accumulated in the investigated tissues as wild-type controls (Greter et al., 2012). However, Csf1R$^{-/-}$ mice displayed a significant impaired development of monocytes into effector cells or moDC. Csf1R signaling seems hence dispensable for the accumulation of Ly-6C^{hi} monocytes in the inflamed tissue, but might be crucial for subsequent differentiation or survival of monocyte-derived cells.

8. PERSPECTIVE

From a bird's-eye view, the mononuclear phagocyte compartment has three major components. Two of them, namely, macrophages and DC, are relatively static and ensure housekeeping and maintenance under steady-state conditions. A third one, linked to monocytes, is highly dynamic and versatile, reserved for exceptional challenges. Classical sessile macrophages ensure tissue integrity during physiological turnover, silently removing debris and clearing potentially harmful agents. cDCs, on the other hand, seem to serve mainly to bridge innate and adaptive immunity and ensure the immune defense through building immunological memory. DCs are migratory, but their trajectories are limited, usually directed towards the next lymphoid organ. Despite local fine-tuning, developmental pathways of classical macrophages and DCs seem predetermined. These resident homeostatic networks are complemented on demand by an additional layer of cells that circulates in the blood stream and are hence strategically positioned to rapidly reach any destination throughout the organism. Once these monocytes are called in, they read local cues and acquire flavors and activities that likely cannot be provided by the resident cells, either with respect to location, time of recruitment, quality, or mere quantity. Monocytes and their descendants control both the initiation and the resolution of inflammation. Monocytes are hence central players in virtual any immunopathology. The challenge ahead is to define their contributions in pathological setting, as well as the molecular cues that guide their plasticity towards specific fates. Manipulation of monocytes activities bears a considerable potential to harness these proinflammatory and resolving activities for therapeutic purposes.

ACKNOWLEDGMENT

This work was supported by the Deutsche Forschungsgemeinschaft (DFG) Research Unit (FOR) 1336. S.J. is a Helmsley Scholar at the Crohn's & Colitis Foundation of America. A.M. was a fellow of the Minerva Foundation.

REFERENCES

Ajami, B., Bennett, J. L., Krieger, C., McNagny, K. M., & Rossi, F. M. (2011). Infiltrating monocytes trigger EAE progression, but do not contribute to the resident microglia pool. *Nature Neuroscience*, *14*, 1142–1149.

Alliot, F., Godin, I., & Pessac, B. (1999). Microglia derive from progenitors, originating from the yolk sac, and which proliferate in the brain. *Brain Research. Developmental Brain Research*, *117*, 145–152.

Anandasabapathy, N., Victora, G. D., Meredith, M., Feder, R., Dong, B., Kluger, C., et al. (2011). Flt3L controls the development of radiosensitive dendritic cells in the meninges and choroid plexus of the steady-state mouse brain. *The Journal of Experimental Medicine*, *208*, 1695–1705.

Ansel, K. M., Harris, R. B., & Cyster, J. G. (2002). CXCL13 is required for B1 cell homing, natural antibody production, and body cavity immunity. *Immunity*, *16*, 67–76.

Ariel, A., & Serhan, C. N. (2012). New lives given by cell death: Macrophage differentiation following their encounter with apoptotic leukocytes during the resolution of inflammation. *Frontiers in Immunology*, *3*, 4.

Artis, D. (2008). Epithelial-cell recognition of commensal bacteria and maintenance of immune homeostasis in the gut. *Nature Reviews Immunology*, *8*, 411–420.

Auffray, C., Fogg, D., Garfa, M., Elain, G., Join-Lambert, O., Kayal, S., et al. (2007). Monitoring of blood vessels and tissues by a population of monocytes with patrolling behavior. *Science*, *317*, 666–670.

Bailey, S. L., Schreiner, B., McMahon, E. J., & Miller, S. D. (2007). CNS myeloid DCs presenting endogenous myelin peptides 'preferentially' polarize CD4+ T(H)-17 cells in relapsing EAE. *Nature Immunology*, *8*, 172–180.

Bain, C. C., Scott, C. L., Uronen-Hansson, H., Gudjonsson, S., Jansson, O., Grip, O., et al. (2012). Resident and pro-inflammatory macrophages in the colon represent alternative context-dependent fates of the same Ly6C(hi) monocyte precursors. *Mucosal Immunology*, *6*, 498–510.

Bar-On, L., Birnberg, T., Kim, K. W., & Jung, S. (2011). Dendritic cell-restricted CD80/86 deficiency results in peripheral regulatory T-cell reduction but is not associated with lymphocyte hyperactivation. *European Journal of Immunology*, *41*, 291–298.

Barth, M. W., Hendrzak, J. A., Melnicoff, M. J., & Morahan, P. S. (1995). Review of the macrophage disappearance reaction. *Journal of Leukocyte Biology*, *57*, 361–367.

Basu, S., Hodgson, G., Katz, M., & Dunn, A. R. (2002). Evaluation of role of G-CSF in the production, survival, and release of neutrophils from bone marrow into circulation. *Blood*, *100*, 854–861.

Bellingan, G. J., Caldwell, H., Howie, S. E., Dransfield, I., & Haslett, C. (1996). In vivo fate of the inflammatory macrophage during the resolution of inflammation: Inflammatory macrophages do not die locally, but emigrate to the draining lymph nodes. *Journal of Immunology*, *157*, 2577–2585.

Bettelli, E., Baeten, D., Jager, A., Sobel, R. A., & Kuchroo, V. K. (2006). Myelin oligodendrocyte glycoprotein-specific T and B cells cooperate to induce a Devic-like disease in mice. *Journal of Clinical Investigation*, *116*, 2393–2402.

Birnberg, T., Bar-On, L., Sapoznikov, A., Caton, M. L., Cervantes-Barragan, L., Makia, D., et al. (2008). Lack of conventional dendritic cells is compatible with normal

development and T cell homeostasis, but causes myeloid proliferative syndrome. *Immunity, 29*, 986–997.
Bogunovic, M., Ginhoux, F., Helft, J., Shang, L., Hashimoto, D., Greter, M., et al. (2009). Origin of the lamina propria dendritic cell network. *Immunity, 31*, 513–525.
Bruhl, H., Cihak, J., Plachy, J., Kunz-Schughart, L., Niedermeier, M., Denzel, A., et al. (2007). Targeting of Gr-1+, CCR2+ monocytes in collagen-induced arthritis. *Arthritis and Rheumatism, 56*, 2975–2985.
Cailhier, J. F., Partolina, M., Vuthoori, S., Wu, S., Ko, K., Watson, S., et al. (2005). Conditional macrophage ablation demonstrates that resident macrophages initiate acute peritoneal inflammation. *Journal of Immunology, 174*, 2336–2342.
Campbell, I. K., Bendele, A., Smith, D. A., & Hamilton, J. A. (1997). Granulocyte-macrophage colony stimulating factor exacerbates collagen induced arthritis in mice. *Annals of the Rheumatic Diseases, 56*, 364–368.
Carlin, L. M., Stamatiades, E. G., Auffray, C., Hanna, R. N., Glover, L., Vizcay-Barrena, G., et al. (2013). Nr4a1-dependent Ly6C(low) monocytes monitor endothelial cells and orchestrate their disposal. *Cell, 153*(2), 362–375.
Caux, C., Ait-Yahia, S., Chemin, K., de Bouteiller, O., Dieu-Nosjean, M. C., Homey, B., et al. (2000). Dendritic cell biology and regulation of dendritic cell trafficking by chemokines. *Springer Seminars in Immunopathology, 22*, 345–369.
Cerovic, V., Houston, S. A., Scott, C. L., Aumeunier, A., Yrlid, U., Mowat, A. M., et al. (2013). Intestinal CD103(−) dendritic cells migrate in lymph and prime effector T cells. *Mucosal Immunology, 6*, 104–113.
Codarri, L., Gyulveszi, G., Tosevski, V., Hesske, L., Fontana, A., Magnenat, L., et al. (2011). RORgammat drives production of the cytokine GM-CSF in helper T cells, which is essential for the effector phase of autoimmune neuroinflammation. *Nature Immunology, 12*, 560–567.
Coombes, J. L., Siddiqui, K. R., Arancibia-Carcamo, C. V., Hall, J., Sun, C. M., Belkaid, Y., et al. (2007). A functionally specialized population of mucosal CD103+ DCs induces Foxp3+ regulatory T cells via a TGF-beta and retinoic acid-dependent mechanism. *The Journal of Experimental Medicine, 204*, 1757–1764.
Cros, J., Cagnard, N., Woollard, K., Patey, N., Zhang, S. Y., Senechal, B., et al. (2010). Human CD14dim monocytes patrol and sense nucleic acids and viruses via TLR7 and TLR8 receptors. *Immunity, 33*, 375–386.
Dalton, D. K., & Wittmer, S. (2005). Nitric-oxide-dependent and independent mechanisms of protection from CNS inflammation during Th1-mediated autoimmunity: Evidence from EAE in iNOS KO mice. *Journal of Neuroimmunology, 160*, 110–121.
Davies, L. C., Rosas, M., Smith, P. J., Fraser, D. J., Jones, S. A., & Taylor, P. R. (2011). A quantifiable proliferative burst of tissue macrophages restores homeostatic macrophage populations after acute inflammation. *European Journal of Immunology, 41*, 2155–2164.
Denning, T. L., Norris, B. A., Medina-Contreras, O., Manicassamy, S., Geem, D., Madan, R., et al. (2011). Functional specializations of intestinal dendritic cell and macrophage subsets that control Th17 and regulatory T cell responses are dependent on the T cell/APC ratio, source of mouse strain, and regional localization. *Journal of Immunology, 187*, 733–747.
Denning, T. L., Wang, Y. C., Patel, S. R., Williams, I. R., & Pulendran, B. (2007). Lamina propria macrophages and dendritic cells differentially induce regulatory and interleukin 17-producing T cell responses. *Nature Immunology, 8*, 1086–1094.
Diehl, G. E., Longman, R. S., Zhang, J. X., Breart, B., Galan, C., Cuesta, A., et al. (2013). Microbiota restricts trafficking of bacteria to mesenteric lymph nodes by CX3CR1hi cells. *Nature, 494*, 116–120.

Egawa, M., Mukai, K., Yoshikawa, S., Iki, M., Mukaida, N., Kawano, Y., et al. (2013). Inflammatory monocytes recruited to allergic skin acquire an anti-inflammatory M2 phenotype via basophil-derived interleukin-4. *Immunity*, *38*, 570–580.

Fadok, V. A., Bratton, D. L., Konowal, A., Freed, P. W., Westcott, J. Y., & Henson, P. M. (1998). Macrophages that have ingested apoptotic cells in vitro inhibit proinflammatory cytokine production through autocrine/paracrine mechanisms involving TGF-beta, PGE2, and PAF. *Journal of Clinical Investigation*, *101*, 890–898.

Fenyk-Melody, J. E., Garrison, A. E., Brunnert, S. R., Weidner, J. R., Shen, F., Shelton, B. A., et al. (1998). Experimental autoimmune encephalomyelitis is exacerbated in mice lacking the NOS2 gene. *Journal of Immunology*, *160*, 2940–2946.

Fife, B. T., Huffnagle, G. B., Kuziel, W. A., & Karpus, W. J. (2000). CC chemokine receptor 2 is critical for induction of experimental autoimmune encephalomyelitis. *The Journal of Experimental Medicine*, *192*, 899–905.

Fogg, D. K., Sibon, C., Miled, C., Jung, S., Aucouturier, P., Littman, D. R., et al. (2006). A clonogenic bone marrow progenitor specific for macrophages and dendritic cells. *Science*, *311*, 83–87.

Gaupp, S., Pitt, D., Kuziel, W. A., Cannella, B., & Raine, C. S. (2003). Experimental autoimmune encephalomyelitis (EAE) in CCR2(−/−) mice: Susceptibility in multiple strains. *American Journal of Pathology*, *162*, 139–150.

Gautier, E. L., Shay, T., Miller, J., Greter, M., Jakubzick, C., Ivanov, S., et al. (2012). Gene-expression profiles and transcriptional regulatory pathways that underlie the identity and diversity of mouse tissue macrophages. *Nature Immunology*, *13*, 1118–1128.

Geissmann, F., Jung, S., & Littman, D. R. (2003). Blood monocytes consist of two principal subsets with distinct migratory properties. *Immunity*, *19*, 71–82.

Ghosn, E. E., Cassado, A. A., Govoni, G. R., Fukuhara, T., Yang, Y., Monack, D. M., et al. (2010). Two physically, functionally, and developmentally distinct peritoneal macrophage subsets. *Proceedings of the National Academy of Sciences of the United States of America*, *107*, 2568–2573.

Ginhoux, F., Greter, M., Leboeuf, M., Nandi, S., See, P., Gokhan, S., et al. (2010). Fate mapping analysis reveals that adult microglia derive from primitive macrophages. *Science*, *330*, 841–845.

Goldszmid, R. S., Caspar, P., Rivollier, A., White, S., Dzutsev, A., Hieny, S., et al. (2012). NK cell-derived interferon-gamma orchestrates cellular dynamics and the differentiation of monocytes into dendritic cells at the site of infection. *Immunity*, *36*, 1047–1059.

Gordon, S., & Taylor, P. R. (2005). Monocyte and macrophage heterogeneity. *Nature Reviews Immunology*, *5*, 953–964.

Greter, M., Helft, J., Chow, A., Hashimoto, D., Mortha, A., Agudo-Cantero, J., et al. (2012). GM-CSF controls nonlymphoid tissue dendritic cell homeostasis but is dispensable for the differentiation of inflammatory dendritic cells. *Immunity*, *36*, 1031–1046.

Greter, M., Heppner, F. L., Lemos, M. P., Odermatt, B. M., Goebels, N., Laufer, T., et al. (2005). Dendritic cells permit immune invasion of the CNS in an animal model of multiple sclerosis. *Nature Medicine*, *11*, 328–334.

Hanayama, R., Tanaka, M., Miwa, K., Shinohara, A., Iwamatsu, A., & Nagata, S. (2002). Identification of a factor that links apoptotic cells to phagocytes. *Nature*, *417*, 182–187.

Hanisch, U. K., & Kettenmann, H. (2007). Microglia: Active sensor and versatile effector cells in the normal and pathologic brain. *Nature Neuroscience*, *10*, 1387–1394.

Helft, J., Ginhoux, F., Bogunovic, M., & Merad, M. (2010). Origin and functional heterogeneity of non-lymphoid tissue dendritic cells in mice. *Immunological Reviews*, *234*, 55–75.

Hochweller, K., Miloud, T., Striegler, J., Naik, S., Hammerling, G. J., & Garbi, N. (2009). Homeostasis of dendritic cells in lymphoid organs is controlled by regulation of their precursors via a feedback loop. *Blood*, *114*, 4411–4421.

Hoeffel, G., Wang, Y., Greter, M., See, P., Teo, P., Malleret, B., et al. (2012). Adult Langerhans cells derive predominantly from embryonic fetal liver monocytes with a minor contribution of yolk sac-derived macrophages. *The Journal of Experimental Medicine, 209*, 1167–1181.
Hohl, T. M., Rivera, A., Lipuma, L., Gallegos, A., Shi, C., Mack, M., et al. (2009). Inflammatory monocytes facilitate adaptive CD4 T cell responses during respiratory fungal infection. *Cell Host & Microbe, 6*, 470–481.
Hooper, L. V., Littman, D. R., & Macpherson, A. J. (2012). Interactions between the microbiota and the immune system. *Science, 336*, 1268–1273.
Huang, F. P., Niedbala, W., Wei, X. Q., Xu, D., Feng, G. J., Robinson, J. H., et al. (1998). Nitric oxide regulates Th1 cell development through the inhibition of IL-12 synthesis by macrophages. *European Journal of Immunology, 28*, 4062–4070.
Huang, F. F., Barnes, P. F., Feng, Y., Donis, R., Chroneos, Z. C., Idell, S., et al. (2011). GM-CSF in the lung protects against lethal influenza infection. *American Journal of Respiratory and Critical Care Medicine, 184*, 259–268.
Ingersoll, M. A., Spanbroek, R., Lottaz, C., Gautier, E. L., Frankenberger, M., Hoffmann, R., et al. (2010). Comparison of gene expression profiles between human and mouse monocyte subsets. *Blood, 115*, e10–e19.
Isaksson, M., Lundgren, B. A., Ahlgren, K. M., Kampe, O., & Lobell, A. (2012). Conditional DC depletion does not affect priming of encephalitogenic Th cells in EAE. *European Journal of Immunology, 42*, 2555–2563.
Izikson, L., Klein, R. S., Charo, I. F., Weiner, H. L., & Luster, A. D. (2000). Resistance to experimental autoimmune encephalomyelitis in mice lacking the CC chemokine receptor (CCR)2. *The Journal of Experimental Medicine, 192*, 1075–1080.
Jenkins, S. J., Ruckerl, D., Cook, P. C., Jones, L. H., Finkelman, F. D., van Rooijen, N., et al. (2011). Local macrophage proliferation, rather than recruitment from the blood, is a signature of TH2 inflammation. *Science, 332*, 1284–1288.
Ji, Q., Castelli, L., & Goverman, J. M. (2013). MHC class I-restricted myelin epitopes are cross-presented by Tip-DCs that promote determinant spreading to CD8(+) T cells. *Nature Immunology, 14*, 254–261.
Jung, S., Aliberti, J., Graemmel, P., Sunshine, M. J., Kreutzberg, G. W., Sher, A., et al. (2000). Analysis of fractalkine receptor CX(3)CR1 function by targeted deletion and green fluorescent protein reporter gene insertion. *Molecular and Cellular Biology, 20*, 4106–4114.
Kassiotis, G., Bauer, J., Akassoglou, K., Lassmann, H., Kollias, G., & Probert, L. (1999). A tumor necrosis factor-induced model of human primary demyelinating diseases develops in immunodeficient mice. *European Journal of Immunology, 29*, 912–917.
Kassiotis, G., & Kollias, G. (2001). Uncoupling the proinflammatory from the immunosuppressive properties of tumor necrosis factor (TNF) at the p55 TNF receptor level: Implications for pathogenesis and therapy of autoimmune demyelination. *The Journal of Experimental Medicine, 193*, 427–434.
King, I. L., Dickendesher, T. L., & Segal, B. M. (2009). Circulating Ly-6C+ myeloid precursors migrate to the CNS and play a pathogenic role during autoimmune demyelinating disease. *Blood, 113*, 3190–3197.
Kool, M., Soullie, T., van Nimwegen, M., Willart, M. A., Muskens, F., Jung, S., et al. (2008). Alum adjuvant boosts adaptive immunity by inducing uric acid and activating inflammatory dendritic cells. *The Journal of Experimental Medicine, 205*, 869–882.
Korner, H., Lemckert, F. A., Chaudhri, G., Etteldorf, S., & Sedgwick, J. D. (1997). Tumor necrosis factor blockade in actively induced experimental autoimmune encephalomyelitis prevents clinical disease despite activated T cell infiltration to the central nervous system. *European Journal of Immunology, 27*, 1973–1981.

Landsman, L., Bar-On, L., Zernecke, A., Kim, K. W., Krauthgamer, R., Shagdarsuren, E., et al. (2009). CX3CR1 is required for monocyte homeostasis and atherogenesis by promoting cell survival. *Blood, 113*, 963–972.

Lawrence, T., Willoughby, D. A., & Gilroy, D. W. (2002). Anti-inflammatory lipid mediators and insights into the resolution of inflammation. *Nature Reviews Immunology, 2*, 787–795.

Le Borgne, M., Etchart, N., Goubier, A., Lira, S. A., Sirard, J. C., van Rooijen, N., et al. (2006). Dendritic cells rapidly recruited into epithelial tissues via CCR6/CCL20 are responsible for CD8+ T cell crosspriming in vivo. *Immunity, 24*, 191–201.

Lin, H., Lee, E., Hestir, K., Leo, C., Huang, M., Bosch, E., et al. (2008). Discovery of a cytokine and its receptor by functional screening of the extracellular proteome. *Science, 320*, 807–811.

Liu, K., Victora, G. D., Schwickert, T. A., Guermonprez, P., Meredith, M. M., Yao, K., et al. (2009). In vivo analysis of dendritic cell development and homeostasis. *Science, 324*, 392–397.

Lutz, M. B., Kukutsch, N., Ogilvie, A. L., Rossner, S., Koch, F., Romani, N., et al. (1999). An advanced culture method for generating large quantities of highly pure dendritic cells from mouse bone marrow. *Journal of Immunological Methods, 223*, 77–92.

MacMicking, J. D., North, R. J., LaCourse, R., Mudgett, J. S., Shah, S. K., & Nathan, C. F. (1997). Identification of nitric oxide synthase as a protective locus against tuberculosis. *Proceedings of the National Academy of Sciences of the United States of America, 94*, 5243–5248.

Maraskovsky, E., Brasel, K., Teepe, M., Roux, E. R., Lyman, S. D., Shortman, K., et al. (1996). Dramatic increase in the numbers of functionally mature dendritic cells in Flt3 ligand-treated mice: Multiple dendritic cell subpopulations identified. *The Journal of Experimental Medicine, 184*, 1953–1962.

Marks, S. C., Jr., & Lane, P. W. (1976). Osteopetrosis, a new recessive skeletal mutation on chromosome 12 of the mouse. *Journal of Heredity, 67*, 11–18.

Mazzoni, A., Bronte, V., Visintin, A., Spitzer, J. H., Apolloni, E., Serafini, P., et al. (2002). Myeloid suppressor lines inhibit T cell responses by an NO-dependent mechanism. *Journal of Immunology, 168*, 689–695.

McMahon, E. J., Bailey, S. L., Castenada, C. V., Waldner, H., & Miller, S. D. (2005). Epitope spreading initiates in the CNS in two mouse models of multiple sclerosis. *Nature Medicine, 11*, 335–339.

McQualter, J. L., Darwiche, R., Ewing, C., Onuki, M., Kay, T. W., Hamilton, J. A., et al. (2001). Granulocyte macrophage colony-stimulating factor: a new putative therapeutic target in multiple sclerosis. *Journal of Experimental Medicine, 194*, 873–882.

Mendel, I., Kerlero de Rosbo, N., & Ben-Nun, A. (1995). A myelin oligodendrocyte glycoprotein peptide induces typical chronic experimental autoimmune encephalomyelitis in H-2b mice: Fine specificity and T cell receptor V beta expression of encephalitogenic T cells. *European Journal of Immunology, 25*, 1951–1959.

Meredith, M. M., Liu, K., Darrasse-Jeze, G., Kamphorst, A. O., Schreiber, H. A., Guermonprez, P., et al. (2012). Expression of the zinc finger transcription factor zDC (Zbtb46, Btbd4) defines the classical dendritic cell lineage. *The Journal of Experimental Medicine, 209*, 1153–1165.

Meredith, M. M., Liu, K., Kamphorst, A. O., Idoyaga, J., Yamane, A., Guermonprez, P., et al. (2012). Zinc finger transcription factor zDC is a negative regulator required to prevent activation of classical dendritic cells in the steady state. *The Journal of Experimental Medicine, 209*, 1583–1593.

Metchnikoff, E. (1887). Ueber den Kampf der Zellen gegen Erypselkokken, ein Beitrag zur Phagocytenlehre. *Virchows Archiv. A, Pathological Anatomy and Histology, 107*, 209–249.

Mildner, A., Mack, M., Schmidt, H., Bruck, W., Djukic, M., Zabel, M. D., et al. (2009). CCR2+Ly-6Chi monocytes are crucial for the effector phase of autoimmunity in the central nervous system. *Brain, 132*, 2487–2500.

Mildner, A., Schmidt, H., Nitsche, M., Merkler, D., Hanisch, U. K., Mack, M., et al. (2007). Microglia in the adult brain arise from Ly-6ChiCCR2+ monocytes only under defined host conditions. *Nature Neuroscience, 10*, 1544–1553.

Miller, S. D., McMahon, E. J., Schreiner, B., & Bailey, S. L. (2007). Antigen presentation in the CNS by myeloid dendritic cells drives progression of relapsing experimental autoimmune encephalomyelitis. *Annals of the New York Academy of Sciences, 1103*, 179–191.

Mukherjee, S., Vaishnava, S., & Hooper, L. V. (2008). Multi-layered regulation of intestinal antimicrobial defense. *Cellular and Molecular Life Sciences, 65*, 3019–3027.

Naik, S. H., Metcalf, D., van Nieuwenhuijze, A., Wicks, I., Wu, L., O'Keeffe, M., et al. (2006). Intrasplenic steady-state dendritic cell precursors that are distinct from monocytes. *Nature Immunology, 7*, 663–671.

Naik, S. H., Proietto, A. I., Wilson, N. S., Dakic, A., Schnorrer, P., Fuchsberger, M., et al. (2005). Cutting edge: Generation of splenic CD8+ and CD8− dendritic cell equivalents in Fms-like tyrosine kinase 3 ligand bone marrow cultures. *Journal of Immunology, 174*, 6592–6597.

Nakano, H., Lin, K. L., Yanagita, M., Charbonneau, C., Cook, D. N., Kakiuchi, T., et al. (2009). Blood-derived inflammatory dendritic cells in lymph nodes stimulate acute T helper type 1 immune responses. *Nature Immunology, 10*, 394–402.

Nathan, C., & Ding, A. (2010). Nonresolving inflammation. *Cell, 140*, 871–882.

Nelson, D. S., & Boyden, S. V. (1963). The loss of macrophages from peritoneal exudates following the injection of antigens into guinea-pigs with delayed-type hypersensitivity. *Immunology, 6*, 264–275.

Nguyen, H. H., Tran, B. T., Muller, W., & Jack, R. S. (2012). IL-10 acts as a developmental switch guiding monocyte differentiation to macrophages during a murine peritoneal infection. *Journal of Immunology, 189*, 3112–3120.

Niess, J. H., Brand, S., Gu, X., Landsman, L., Jung, S., McCormick, B. A., et al. (2005). CX3CR1-mediated dendritic cell access to the intestinal lumen and bacterial clearance. *Science, 307*, 254–258.

Okayasu, I., Hatakeyama, S., Yamada, M., Ohkusa, T., Inagaki, Y., & Nakaya, R. (1990). A novel method in the induction of reliable experimental acute and chronic ulcerative colitis in mice. *Gastroenterology, 98*, 694–702.

Olah, M., Amor, S., Brouwer, N., Vinet, J., Eggen, B., Biber, K., et al. (2012). Identification of a microglia phenotype supportive of remyelination. *Glia, 60*, 306–321.

Onai, N., Obata-Onai, A., Schmid, M. A., Ohteki, T., Jarrossay, D., & Manz, M. G. (2007). Identification of clonogenic common Flt3+M-CSFR+ plasmacytoid and conventional dendritic cell progenitors in mouse bone marrow. *Nature Immunology, 8*, 1207–1216.

Owens, T., Bechmann, I., & Engelhardt, B. (2008). Perivascular spaces and the two steps to neuroinflammation. *Journal of Neuropathology and Experimental Neurology, 67*, 1113–1121.

Owens, G. P., & Bennett, J. L. (2012). Trigger, pathogen, or bystander: The complex nexus linking Epstein-Barr virus and multiple sclerosis. *Multiple Sclerosis, 18*, 1204–1208.

Palframan, R. T., Jung, S., Cheng, G., Weninger, W., Luo, Y., Dorf, M., et al. (2001). Inflammatory chemokine transport and presentation in HEV: A remote control mechanism for monocyte recruitment to lymph nodes in inflamed tissues. *The Journal of Experimental Medicine, 194*, 1361–1373.

Passlick, B., Flieger, D., & Ziegler-Heitbrock, H. W. (1989). Identification and characterization of a novel monocyte subpopulation in human peripheral blood. *Blood, 74*, 2527–2534.

Paterson, P. Y. (1966). Experimental allergic encephalomyelitis and autoimmune disease. *Advances in Immunology, 5*, 131–208.
Peterson, D. A., McNulty, N. P., Guruge, J. L., & Gordon, J. I. (2007). IgA response to symbiotic bacteria as a mediator of gut homeostasis. *Cell Host & Microbe, 2*, 328–339.
Platt, A. M., Bain, C. C., Bordon, Y., Sester, D. P., & Mowat, A. M. (2010). An independent subset of TLR expressing CCR2-dependent macrophages promotes colonic inflammation. *Journal of Immunology, 184*, 6843–6854.
Ponomarev, E. D., Shriver, L. P., Maresz, K., Pedras-Vasconcelos, J., Verthelyi, D., & Dittel, B. N. (2007). GM-CSF production by autoreactive T cells is required for the activation of microglial cells and the onset of experimental autoimmune encephalomyelitis. *Journal of Immunology, 178*, 39–48.
Rakoff-Nahoum, S., Paglino, J., Eslami-Varzaneh, F., Edberg, S., & Medzhitov, R. (2004). Recognition of commensal microflora by toll-like receptors is required for intestinal homeostasis. *Cell, 118*, 229–241.
Ramachandran, P., Pellicoro, A., Vernon, M. A., Boulter, L., Aucott, R. L., Ali, A., et al. (2012). Differential Ly-6C expression identifies the recruited macrophage phenotype, which orchestrates the regression of murine liver fibrosis. *Proceedings of the National Academy of Sciences of the United States of America, 109*, E3186–E3195.
Randolph, G. J., Inaba, K., Robbiani, D. F., Steinman, R. M., & Muller, W. A. (1999). Differentiation of phagocytic monocytes into lymph node dendritic cells in vivo. *Immunity, 11*, 753–761.
Rescigno, M., Urbano, M., Valzasina, B., Francolini, M., Rotta, G., Bonasio, R., et al. (2001). Dendritic cells express tight junction proteins and penetrate gut epithelial monolayers to sample bacteria. *Nature Immunology, 2*, 361–367.
Rivollier, A., He, J., Kole, A., Valatas, V., & Kelsall, B. L. (2012). Inflammation switches the differentiation program of Ly6Chi monocytes from antiinflammatory macrophages to inflammatory dendritic cells in the colon. *The Journal of Experimental Medicine, 209*, 139–155.
Rotta, G., Edwards, E. W., Sangaletti, S., Bennett, C., Ronzoni, S., Colombo, M. P., et al. (2003). Lipopolysaccharide or whole bacteria block the conversion of inflammatory monocytes into dendritic cells in vivo. *The Journal of Experimental Medicine, 198*, 1253–1263.
Sahrbacher, U. C., Lechner, F., Eugster, H. P., Frei, K., Lassmann, H., & Fontana, A. (1998). Mice with an inactivation of the inducible nitric oxide synthase gene are susceptible to experimental autoimmune encephalomyelitis. *European Journal of Immunology, 28*, 1332–1338.
Sallusto, F., & Lanzavecchia, A. (1994). Efficient presentation of soluble antigen by cultured human dendritic cells is maintained by granulocyte/macrophage colony-stimulating factor plus interleukin 4 and downregulated by tumor necrosis factor alpha. *The Journal of Experimental Medicine, 179*, 1109–1118.
Satpathy, A. T., Kc, W., Albring, J. C., Edelson, B. T., Kretzer, N. M., Bhattacharya, D., et al. (2012). Zbtb46 expression distinguishes classical dendritic cells and their committed progenitors from other immune lineages. *The Journal of Experimental Medicine, 209*, 1135–1152.
Schif-Zuck, S., Gross, N., Assi, S., Rostoker, R., Serhan, C. N., & Ariel, A. (2011). Saturated-efferocytosis generates pro-resolving CD11b low macrophages: Modulation by resolvins and glucocorticoids. *European Journal of Immunology, 41*, 366–379.
Schulz, C., Gomez Perdiguero, E., Chorro, L., Szabo-Rogers, H., Cagnard, N., Kierdorf, K., et al. (2012). A lineage of myeloid cells independent of Myb and hematopoietic stem cells. *Science, 336*, 86–90.
Schulz, O., Jaensson, E., Persson, E. K., Liu, X., Worbs, T., Agace, W. W., et al. (2009). Intestinal CD103+, but not CX3CR1+, antigen sampling cells migrate in lymph

and serve classical dendritic cell functions. *The Journal of Experimental Medicine, 206*, 3101–3114.

Serbina, N. V., Salazar-Mather, T. P., Biron, C. A., Kuziel, W. A., & Pamer, E. G. (2003). TNF/iNOS-producing dendritic cells mediate innate immune defense against bacterial infection. *Immunity, 19*, 59–70.

Serhan, C. N., Brain, S. D., Buckley, C. D., Gilroy, D. W., Haslett, C., O'Neill, L. A., et al. (2007). Resolution of inflammation: State of the art, definitions and terms. *The FASEB Journal, 21*, 325–332.

Serra, M. F., Diaz, B. L., Barreto, E. O., Cordeiro, R. S., Nazare Meirelles, M. N., Williams, T. J., et al. (2000). Mechanism underlying acute resident leukocyte disappearance induced by immunological and non-immunological stimuli in rats: Evidence for a role for the coagulation system. *Inflammation Research: Official Journal of the European Histamine Research Society, 49*, 708–713.

Sharief, M. K., & Hentges, R. (1991). Association between tumor necrosis factor-alpha and disease progression in patients with multiple sclerosis. *The New England Journal of Medicine, 325*, 467–472.

Shechter, R., London, A., Varol, C., Raposo, C., Cusimano, M., Yovel, G., et al. (2009). Infiltrating blood-derived macrophages are vital cells playing an anti-inflammatory role in recovery from spinal cord injury in mice. *PLoS Medicine, 6*, e1000113.

Siddiqui, K. R., Laffont, S., & Powrie, F. (2010). E-cadherin marks a subset of inflammatory dendritic cells that promote T cell-mediated colitis. *Immunity, 32*, 557–567.

Singh-Jasuja, H., Thiolat, A., Ribon, M., Boissier, M. C., Bessis, N., Rammensee, H. G., et al. (2013). The mouse dendritic cell marker CD11c is down-regulated upon cell activation through Toll-like receptor triggering. *Immunobiology, 218*, 28–39.

Slavin, A. J., Soos, J. M., Stuve, O., Patarroyo, J. C., Weiner, H. L., Fontana, A., et al. (2001). Requirement for endocytic antigen processing and influence of invariant chain and H-2M deficiencies in CNS autoimmunity. *Journal of Clinical Investigation, 108*, 1133–1139.

Soehnlein, O., Zernecke, A., Eriksson, E. E., Rothfuchs, A. G., Pham, C. T., Herwald, H., et al. (2008). Neutrophil secretion products pave the way for inflammatory monocytes. *Blood, 112*, 1461–1471.

Stables, M. J., Shah, S., Camon, E. B., Lovering, R. C., Newson, J., Bystrom, J., et al. (2011). Transcriptomic analyses of murine resolution-phase macrophages. *Blood, 118*, e192–e208.

Steinman, R. M., & Witmer, M. D. (1978). Lymphoid dendritic cells are potent stimulators of the primary mixed leukocyte reaction in mice. *Proceedings of the National Academy of Sciences of the United States of America, 75*, 5132–5136.

Strauss-Ayali, D., Conrad, S. M., & Mosser, D. M. (2007). Monocyte subpopulations and their differentiation patterns during infection. *Journal of Leukocyte Biology, 82*, 244–252.

Sunderkotter, C., Nikolic, T., Dillon, M. J., Van Rooijen, N., Stehling, M., Drevets, D. A., et al. (2004). Subpopulations of mouse blood monocytes differ in maturation stage and inflammatory response. *Journal of Immunology, 172*, 4410–4417.

Tacke, F., Alvarez, D., Kaplan, T. J., Jakubzick, C., Spanbroek, R., Llodra, J., et al. (2007). Monocyte subsets differentially employ CCR2, CCR5, and CX3CR1 to accumulate within atherosclerotic plaques. *Journal of Clinical Investigation, 117*, 185–194.

Takahashi, M., Galligan, C., Tessarollo, L., & Yoshimura, T. (2009). Monocyte chemoattractant protein-1 (MCP-1), not MCP-3, is the primary chemokine required for monocyte recruitment in mouse peritonitis induced with thioglycollate or zymosan A. *Journal of Immunology, 183*, 3463–3471.

Tondravi, M. M., McKercher, S. R., Anderson, K., Erdmann, J. M., Quiroz, M., Maki, R., et al. (1997). Osteopetrosis in mice lacking haematopoietic transcription factor PU.1. *Nature, 386*, 81–84.

Tremblay, M. E., Stevens, B., Sierra, A., Wake, H., Bessis, A., & Nimmerjahn, A. (2011). The role of microglia in the healthy brain. *Journal of Neuroscience*, *31*, 16064–16069.

Uderhardt, S., Herrmann, M., Oskolkova, O. V., Aschermann, S., Bicker, W., Ipseiz, N., et al. (2012). 12/15-lipoxygenase orchestrates the clearance of apoptotic cells and maintains immunologic tolerance. *Immunity*, *36*, 834–846.

van der Flier, L. G., & Clevers, H. (2009). Stem cells, self-renewal, and differentiation in the intestinal epithelium. *Annual Review of Physiology*, *71*, 241–260.

van Furth, R., Diesselhoff-den Dulk, M. C., & Mattie, H. (1973). Quantitative study on the production and kinetics of mononuclear phagocytes during an acute inflammatory reaction. *The Journal of Experimental Medicine*, *138*, 1314–1330.

van Oosten, B. W., Barkhof, F., Truyen, L., Boringa, J. B., Bertelsmann, F. W., von Blomberg, B. M., et al. (1996). Increased MRI activity and immune activation in two multiple sclerosis patients treated with the monoclonal anti-tumor necrosis factor antibody cA2. *Neurology*, *47*, 1531–1534.

Vanderlugt, C. L., Neville, K. L., Nikcevich, K. M., Eagar, T. N., Bluestone, J. A., & Miller, S. D. (2000). Pathologic role and temporal appearance of newly emerging autoepitopes in relapsing experimental autoimmune encephalomyelitis. *Journal of Immunology*, *164*, 670–678.

Varol, C., Landsman, L., Fogg, D. K., Greenshtein, L., Gildor, B., Margalit, R., et al. (2007). Monocytes give rise to mucosal, but not splenic, conventional dendritic cells. *The Journal of Experimental Medicine*, *204*, 171–180.

Varol, C., Vallon-Eberhard, A., Elinav, E., Aychek, T., Shapira, Y., Luche, H., et al. (2009). Intestinal lamina propria dendritic cell subsets have different origin and functions. *Immunity*, *31*, 502–512.

Veldhoen, M., Hocking, R. J., Flavell, R. A., & Stockinger, B. (2006). Signals mediated by transforming growth factor-beta initiate autoimmune encephalomyelitis, but chronic inflammation is needed to sustain disease. *Nature Immunology*, 7, 1151–1156.

Wang, Y., Szretter, K. J., Vermi, W., Gilfillan, S., Rossini, C., Cella, M., et al. (2012). IL-34 is a tissue-restricted ligand of CSF1R required for the development of Langerhans cells and microglia. *Nature Immunology*, *13*, 753–760.

Waskow, C., Liu, K., Darrasse-Jeze, G., Guermonprez, P., Ginhoux, F., Merad, M., et al. (2008). The receptor tyrosine kinase Flt3 is required for dendritic cell development in peripheral lymphoid tissues. *Nature Immunology*, *9*, 676–683.

Weber, B., Saurer, L., Schenk, M., Dickgreber, N., & Mueller, C. (2011). CX3CR1 defines functionally distinct intestinal mononuclear phagocyte subsets which maintain their respective functions during homeostatic and inflammatory conditions. *European Journal of Immunology*, *41*, 773–779.

Wiktor-Jedrzejczak, W., Ratajczak, M. Z., Ptasznik, A., Sell, K. W., Ahmed-Ansari, A., & Ostertag, W. (1992). CSF-1 deficiency in the op/op mouse has differential effects on macrophage populations and differentiation stages. *Experimental Hematology*, *20*, 1004–1010.

Yeung, Y. G., Jubinsky, P. T., Sengupta, A., Yeung, D. C., & Stanley, E. R. (1987). Purification of the colony-stimulating factor 1 receptor and demonstration of its tyrosine kinase activity. *Proceedings of the National Academy of Sciences of the United States of America*, *84*, 1268–1271.

Yogev, N., Frommer, F., Lukas, D., Kautz-Neu, K., Karram, K., Ielo, D., et al. (2012). Dendritic cells ameliorate autoimmunity in the CNS by controlling the homeostasis of PD-1 receptor(+) regulatory T cells. *Immunity*, *37*, 264–275.

Yona, S., Kim, K. W., Wolf, Y., Mildner, A., Varol, D., Breker, M., et al. (2013). Fate mapping reveals origins and dynamics of monocytes and tissue macrophages under homeostasis. *Immunity*, *38*, 79–91.

Zhan, Y., Lieschke, G. J., Grail, D., Dunn, A. R., & Cheers, C. (1998). Essential roles for granulocyte-macrophage colony-stimulating factor (GM-CSF) and G-CSF in the sustained hematopoietic response of Listeria monocytogenes-infected mice. *Blood*, *91*, 863–869.

Zigmond, E., Varol, C., Farache, J., Elmaliah, E., Satpathy, A. T., Friedlander, G., et al. (2012). Ly6C hi monocytes in the inflamed colon give rise to proinflammatory effector cells and migratory antigen-presenting cells. *Immunity*, *37*, 1076–1090.

CHAPTER FOUR

Plasmacytoid Dendritic Cell Development

Ken Shortman[*,§,1], **Priyanka Sathe**[*,†], **David Vremec**[*], **Shalin Naik**[*,‡], **Meredith O'Keeffe**[§,¶]

[*]The Walter and Eliza Hall Institute, Melbourne, Australia
[†]Immunology Institute, Mount Sinai School of Medicine, New York, USA
[‡]Division of Immunology, The Netherlands Cancer Institute, Amsterdam, The Netherlands
[§]Centre for Immunology, Burnet Institute, Melbourne, Australia
[¶]Department of Immunology, Monash University, Clayton, Australia
[1]Corresponding author: e-mail address: shortman@wehi.edu.au

Contents

Abstract

Interferon-producing plasmacytoid dendritic cells (pDC) are a specialized branch of the dendritic cell (DC) family, and their differentiation in mice is closely linked to that of conventional DC (cDC). Several different developmental pathways retain the potential to form pDC and are likely to contribute to the steady-state pDC population. A lymphoid pathway to DC development produces mainly pDC as a branch otherwise leading to B-cell development; such pDC may carry relics of a lymphoid past such as DJ rearrangements of immunoglobulin heavy chain (IgH) genes. The myeloid pathway to pDC and cDC is better known, but recent reassessment has revealed several substreams of development with separate DC-committed precursors. One substream has a lymphoid-like aspect, involving a precursor expressing RAG-1 and producing pDC with IgH gene rearrangements. Another more biased to cDC production produces

Advances in Immunology, Volume 120
ISSN 0065-2776
http://dx.doi.org/10.1016/B978-0-12-417028-5.00004-1

pDC without such IgH gene rearrangements. Finally, there is the production of interferon-producing pDC-like cells that are not pDC but appear to be cDC precursors; these do not express key pDC markers such as CCR9. Initiation of the DC and then the pDC developmental program overrides any surface marker-expressed developmental bias to other myeloid or lymphoid lineages, resulting in an apparent convergent differentiation to the pDC form. A DC fate is sometimes imprinted early in development, upstream of identifiable myeloid, or lymphoid precursors. This suggests that DC, including pDC, represent a distinct hematopoietic lineage separate from conventional myeloid or lymphoid cells.

1. BACKGROUND

Plasmacytoid dendritic cells (pDC) presented a paradox from their first identification as a novel human cell type (Siegal et al., 1999). Although they had the appearance of lymphoid cells, and often of plasma cells, when activated in culture, they presented a dendritic appearance and some of the antigen presentation properties of conventional dendritic cells (cDC). Their singular feature was a remarkable capacity to produce type I interferon (IFN-I) when stimulated by viruses or viral components. The identification of the equivalent cell type in mice (Asselin-Paturel et al., 2001) opened the door to closer experimental study, but the paradox continued. Mouse pDC expressed surface markers associated with cDC (CD11c), with B cells (B220) and with T cells (CD4 and CD8). Activation of mouse pDC by appropriate TLR ligands again induced strong IFN-I production, along with a shift from a lymphoid to a dendritic morphology. Although there are many reports of a dendritic cell (DC)-like role in tolerance and immunity, pDC circulate somewhat like lymphocytes and their antigen processing and regulation of their MHC class II expression resembles that of B cells rather than cDC (Young et al., 2008). Despite these contradictory properties, pDC are now established as a distinct element of the immune defense system (Colonna, Trinchieri, & Liu, 2004; Liu, 2005, Shortman & Liu, 2002; Swiecki, Gilfillan, Vermi, Wang, & Colonna, 2010).

Given the background in the preceding text, it is not surprising that the hematopoietic development of pDC also has paradoxical aspects. Development of pDC is generally linked to that of lymphoid tissue-resident cDC, but not to inflammatory, monocyte-derived DC, a justification for including pDC in the DC family (Shortman & Naik, 2007). In contrast to cDC where a late precursor exits bone marrow (BM) for final development in the periphery, differentiation to a functional pDC is generally completed within BM itself. There was early evidence not only of myeloid-biased early BM precursors common to pDC and cDC but also of lymphoid-biased BM precursors common to pDC and B cells (D'Amico & Wu, 2003). Divergent developmental pathways then appeared to converge to produce the distinctive pDC cell type. In this chapter, we consider these several developmental routes to cells classified as pDC.

2. MARKERS FOR pDC IDENTIFICATION

In common with DC in general, no individual surface marker alone serves to uniquely define pDC, so identification depends on the patterned expression of a series of such markers. Mouse pDC express the common DC marker CD11c (although generally at lower levels that cDC), together with CD45R (B220), CD45RA, Sca-1, Siglec-H, Bst2, and the chemokine receptor CCR9 (Blasius et al., 2006; O'Keeffe, Hochrein, Vremec, Caminschi, et al., 2002; Wendland et al., 2007; Zhang et al., 2006). A full complement of these markers may be needed to distinguish true pDC from some related cells in BM (O'Keeffe et al., 2012; Schlitzer et al., 2011). Additional surface markers appear on mouse pDC as they mature in BM and in the peripheral tissues; so far, these appear to be maturation markers rather than defining distinct sublineages of pDC. Such markers include Ly6C (Vremec et al., 2007), Ly49Q (Kamogawa-Schifter et al., 2005; Omatsu et al., 2005), CD4, and CD8 (O'Keeffe, Hochrein, Vremec, Caminschi, et al., 2002). Human pDC are usually distinguished from other DC by expression of BDCA2 (CD303), BDCA4 (CD304), and IL-3R-α (CD123) and the lack of expression of CD11c.

The basic functional property of pDC is their capacity to produce large quantities of IFN-I when stimulated by viral infections or by an appropriate TLR ligand, such as CpG-ODN (Gilliet, Cao, & Liu, 2008; Liu, 2005; Swiecki & Colonna, 2010). This for many is the defining feature of pDC and leads to their alternate name as interferon-producing cells (IPC). Some care is required in using this functional test, since transfer of certain pDC to fresh medium for IFN production assay can lead to such rapid pDC death that no IFN production is obtained (Sathe, Vremec, Wu, Corcoran, & Shortman, 2013). A negative response must therefore be accompanied with evidence that the candidate cells remained viable. Apart from IFN-I, it is also now apparent that pDC are major producers of

IFN-III (IL-28 and IL-29, also called IFN-lambda) in response to TLR7 or TLR9 ligands and to many viruses (Ank et al., 2008; Lauterbach et al., 2010).

3. CYTOKINES PROMOTING pDC DEVELOPMENT

Analysis of the cytokine requirements for the development of particular DC subsets has helped delineate distinct DC sublineages and serves as a guide to their developmental pathways (Merad & Manz, 2009; Schmid, Kingston, Boddupalli, & Manz, 2010). The development of pDC, along with the lymphoid tissue-resident type of cDC, is markedly influenced by the cytokine fms-like tyrosine kinase-3 (Flt3) ligand (Flt3L) (Gilliet et al., 2002; Karsunky, Merad, Cozzio, Weissman, & Manz, 2003; McKenna et al., 2000; O'Keeffe, Hochrein, Vremec, Pooley, et al., 2002). Mice genetically deficient in Flt3L have reduced (but not zero) levels of pDC and cDC. Raising the level of Flt3L in the bloodstream by repeated injection of mice with Flt3L increases the level of pDC, along with that of the $CD8^+$ type of cDC. Injecting humans with Flt3L produces similar results (Pulendran et al., 2000). It is not yet clear whether Flt3L regulates the level of pDC in the periphery by inducing limited expansion as it does the $CD8^+$ cDC (Waskow et al., 2008). In addition, Flt3L may promote the survival of pDC in the periphery as it does *in vitro*. However, the main effect of Flt3L on pDC development seems to be in promoting their generation in BM. Culture of mouse BM cells for 5–9 days with Flt3L as the only exogenously added cytokine produces a good yield of pDC, along with cDC, but produces few other hematopoietic cells (Brasel, De Smedt, Smith, & Maliszewski, 2000; Naik et al., 2005). The expression of the receptor Flt3 is a major determinant of whether BM precursors are able to produce pDC and cDC (D'Amico & Wu, 2003; Karsunky et al., 2003). Enforced expression of Flt3 in $Flt3^-$ BM precursors, and even in $Flt3^-$ erythrocyte/megakaryocyte restricted precursors, induces a capacity to produce pDC and cDC (Onai, Obata-Onai, Tussiwand, Lanzavecchia, & Manz, 2006). The intensity of the signals transmitted via Flt3 may also determine the balance between pDC and cDC production, high intensity favoring the former. This provides an explanation of the IFN-I promotion of pDC production (Vollstedt et al., 2006), since it upregulates Flt3 expression and so increases the intensity of Flt3L induced signaling (Lee et al., 2013).

This dominant effect of Flt3L as a pDC poietin initially obscured the role of the "myeloid" cytokine M-CSF as an effective additional promoter of pDC development. However, M-CSF was found to efficiently promote pDC (and cDC) development in BM cultures (Fancke, Suter, Hochrein, & O'Keeffe, 2008). This is in contrast to the other myeloid cytokine GM-CSF that inhibits pDC development if administered at the level that promotes development of myeloid cells (Esashi et al., 2008), although low levels of GM-CSF do enhance the production of pDC and cDC promoted by Flt3L (Kingston et al., 2009; Sathe et al., 2011). The effect of M-CSF on pDC development is much like Flt3L. The pDC produced in response to M-CSF appear similar in surface markers to those generated by Flt3L, and these pDC are efficient producers of IFN-α when stimulated with the appropriate TLR ligands. As found for Flt3L, M-CSF is also a pDC poietin *in vivo*. Mice deficient in M-CSF have reduced levels of pDC (albeit not as extensive a reduction as mice lacking Flt3L), and repeated injection of mice with M-CSF raises the level of pDC (Fancke et al., 2008), albeit much less efficiently than Flt3L. These findings are not so surprising since the DC-restricted precursors in BM express both Flt3 and the M-CSF receptor c-fms (MacDonald et al., 2005). However, M-CSF promotion of pDC development is via interaction with c-fms and occurs in Flt3L-deficient mice, indicating that it involves a signaling event independent of Flt3 engagement (Fancke et al., 2008).

Another cytokine promoting pDC development is thrombopoietin (TPO), better known for its role in megakaryocyte/platelet production. In combination with Flt3L, TPO promotes the development of pDC from human precursor cells (Chen et al., 2004; Proietto, Mittag, Roberts, Sprigg, & Wu, 2012). TPO also further promotes the development of pDC, but not cDC, in Flt3L-stimulated mouse BM cultures. Flt3L was found to induce the expression of c-mpl (a TPO receptor) on DC precursors, so providing an explanation for the synergistic effects of the two cytokines (Onai et al., 2013).

In line with the myeloid/lymphoid ambiguity of pDC, the "lymphoid" cytokine IL-7 also appears to promote pDC development (Vogt, Link, Perrin, Finke, & Luther, 2009). DC in general, including pDC, are reduced in total number in IL-7-deficient mice and increased in total number in mice overexpressing this cytokine; since this roughly parallels changes in lymphoid cells, this effect might have been indirect. However, the development of pDC from IL-7R-α-deficient BM is reduced even in the presence of normal BM in mixed BM chimeras, pointing to an inherent reduction in pDC development in the absence of IL-7/IL-7R signaling. This deficit appears to be at the level of development in BM, rather than survival or expansion in the periphery.

4. TRANSCRIPTION FACTORS DETERMINING pDC DEVELOPMENT

The network of transcription factors involved in development of DC is considered in detail elsewhere in this volume, but those specifically governing pDC development should be mentioned here since they underpin the cellular pathways that are the subject of this review. Flt3L signaling proceeds via the transcription activator STAT3 (Laouar, Welte, Fu, & Flavell, 2003) so this factor is common to the development of all DC. Mice deficient in IRF8 (previously called ICSBP) were found to have a selective loss of both pDC and the $CD8^+$ subset of cDC, pointing to a developmental link between these DC types in accordance with their common dependence on Flt3L (Tsujimura, Tamura, & Ozato, 2003). However, this linkage is broken in mice with the BXH2 mutation in IRF8, since although deficient in $CD8^+$ cDC, these mice maintain pDC development (Tailor, Tamura, Morse, & Ozato, 2008). One interpretation is that different interaction partners of IRF8, such as the BATF factors (Tussiwand et al., 2012), are involved in pDC and $CD8^+$ cDC development. The transcription factor that is specifically required for pDC development in both humans and mice is E2-2, a member of the basic helix-loop-helix family (Cisse et al., 2008; Ghosh, Cisse, Bunin, Lewis, & Reizis, 2010; Nagasawa, Schmidlin, Hazekamp, Schotte, & Blom, 2008). E2-2 activates other transcription factors essential for pDC development, including IRF8 and SpiB, and continuous expression is required to maintain pDC phenotype. Dependence on E2-2 is a common feature of all pathways to pDC development, since in the absence of E2-2, no pDC are formed. As discussed later, E2-2 dependence also serves to link pDC to a series of pDC-related precursors and pDC-related product cells that must now be distinguished from normal pDC.

5. EARLY INVESTIGATION OF THE MYELOID VERSUS LYMPHOID ORIGIN OF pDC

A milestone in hematopoiesis was the separation from mouse BM of distinct precursor populations restricted to the myeloid or the lymphoid lineages, the common myeloid precursors (CMP) and the common lymphoid precursors (CLP), respectively (Akashi, Traver, Miyamoto, & Weissman, 2000; Kondo, Weissman, & Akashi, 1997). This was considered to demonstrate an early differentiation step in a divergent, branching process leading from multipotent stem cells to the many specialized blood cell elements. Even though current models of hematopoiesis envisage a more gradual, multistep, and stochastic process of lineage commitment, this basic pathway bifurcation remains a central concept. It was therefore surprising when it was found that cDC, considered a myeloid cell type, could be generated efficiently from CLP and CMP when these precursors were transferred into irradiated recipient mice (Manz, Traver, Miyamoto, Weissman, & Akashi, 2001; Traver et al., 2000; Wu et al., 2001). Human BM myeloid and lymphoid precursors were also shown capable of DC generation (Chicha, Jarrossay, & Manz, 2004). This demonstrated that the potential to form cDC was retained in both lineage precursors and could be revealed in the extreme conditions of blood cell regeneration following irradiation, or in culture. Most work since then has suggested that in normal steady state, most cDC are indeed derived from CMP. The only exception appears to be the $CD8^+$ cDC subset generated within the thymus (Corcoran et al., 2003).

Subsequent studies showed that pDC could also be generated from both CMP and CLP when these precursors were transferred into irradiated recipients (D'Amico & Wu, 2003) and from human myeloid and lymphoid precursors in culture (Chicha et al., 2004). In view of the similarities between pDC and cells of the B-cell lineage, generation of pDC from CLP was less of a surprise than for cDC. However, for both pDC and cDC, it was only those precursors expressing the receptor Flt3 (CD135) that were able to generate DC (D'Amico & Wu, 2003; Karsunky et al., 2003). The $Flt3^+$ cells represented the major subset of CLP but only the minor subset of CMP. This accorded nicely with the finding that Flt3L was the dominant cytokine governing production of both pDC and cDC and demonstrated the close developmental relationship between pDC and cDC. However, these studies using irradiated recipient mice left open the question of the developmental origin of pDC in normal mice in steady state.

6. MARKERS OF pDC OF LYMPHOID ORIGIN?

Rearrangement of immunoglobulin heavy chain (IgH) genes is initiated even in non-B cells of lymphoid origin; T cells bear DJ, but not VDJ, rearrangements in half of their IgH gene DNA. This indelible marker of a lymphoid-related developmental history was used to assess if any pDC in the spleen or thymus of steady-state mice could be of lymphoid origin (Corcoran et al., 2003). Indeed, the DNA from such pDC contained DJ IgH gene rearrangements; although quantitation of the PCR reaction is not accurate, the results suggested around half of all pDC could have such a lymphoid developmental history. In contrast, the cDC from spleen or lymph nodes retained all their IgH gene DNA in germline configuration, in line with a myeloid origin; only the $CD8^+$ cDC subset of the thymus, endogenously generated from thymus-seeding precursors, displayed such IgH gene DJ rearrangements.

A related marker of a lymphoid history is the expression of enzymes involved in Ig gene rearrangement, measured by expression of green fluorescent protein (GFP) under the RAG-1 promoter. Although such fluorescence fades after RAG-1 synthesis ceases, sufficient levels may be retained to detect and sort individual cells with a lymphoid past. Using such RAG-1-GFP knock-in mice, it was possible to detect and sort two categories of pDC from BM and spleen, those with and those without a history of RAG-1 expression. Only the former, the GFP^+ pDC, had IgH gene DJ rearrangements (Pelayo et al., 2005). These studies reinforced the concept that some pDC are of lymphoid and some of myeloid origin.

However, this apparently solid evidence for a lymphoid pathway to pDC had an alternative interpretation (Shigematsu et al., 2004). When pDC were produced by transfer of restricted precursors into irradiated recipient mice, IgH gene DJ rearrangements were detected not only in the pDC derived from CLP but also in the pDC derived from CMP. Thus, "lymphoid associated" events had occurred even within pDC derived via what was considered a myeloid route. It was suggested that since pDC utilize certain lymphoid gene programs, initiation of pDC development "ectopically" results in expression of RAG-1 and other genes involved in IgH gene rearrangement, even within a myeloid pathway. This would not occur with cDC from the same precursors. This explanation assumed that CMP were, according to the definition, precursors completely restricted to production of myeloid cells. Although myeloid cells were clearly the dominant product of this precursor population, a low-level production of B cells had been observed both *in vitro* and upon transfer of the CMP population into irradiated recipients (Akashi et al., 2000; D'Amico & Wu, 2003). Thus, there remained a possibility that the CMP population retained some lymphoid potential, expressed as B cells and pDC with rearranged IgH genes.

7. CDP AND THE CONSENSUS MYELOID PATHWAY TO pDC

The possible lymphoid pathway to pDC became neglected when a clear myeloid route to DC production via a common dendritic cell precursor (CDP) downstream of CMP was established. Mouse BM was shown to contain precursor cells essentially restricted to the production of DC, specifically pDC and the lymphoid tissue-resident $CD8^{+}$ and $CD8^{-}$ cDC (Naik et al., 2007; Onai et al., 2007). These CDP (also termed pro-DC) were isolated from BM as $Lin^{-}c\text{-}Kit^{int/lo}Flt3^{+}M\text{-}CSFR^{+}$ cells. A similar DC-restricted precursor was isolated from cultures of BM stimulated with Flt3L without the use of the M-CSFR marker (Naik et al., 2007). An important aspect of these studies was the clonal evidence that capacity to form other hematopoietic lineages was lost (or in the case of macrophages, extensively reduced) and that many individual CDP had a capacity to produce both cDC and pDC.

There is consensus on the development of cDC from BM CDP. Clonal culture analysis demonstrated many individual CDP already producing only cDC without pDC, suggesting commitment to cDC was already occurring within the CDP population (Naik et al., 2007). A precursor population downstream of CDP, already expressing CD11c but not yet expressing surface MHC class II, was found in BM (Diao, Winter, Chen, Cantin, & Cattral, 2004) then isolated from spleen and termed pre-DC (Naik et al., 2006); this was an immediate precursor of cDC but had lost capacity to form pDC. Such pre-cDC were shown to be the cDC precursors that left BM to maintain via the bloodstream the resident cDC population of lymphoid organs (Liu et al., 2009).

The pathway from CDP to pDC was less well documented. It was assumed that pDC arose from CDP within BM, since BM is a rich source of pDC, and that fully formed and functional pDC then left BM to populate the periphery. pDC were assumed to branch off from CDP prior to pre-cDC formation. However, by clonal culture analysis, it was rare to find individual CDP producing predominantly pDC (Naik et al., 2007). A recurrent problem was the low yield of pDC from BM CDP, apparently out of balance with the steady-state cDC to pDC ratio. Was this what was to be expected in line with the slower turnover of pDC compared to cDC (O'Keeffe, Hochrein, Vremec, Caminschi, et al., 2002), or was there an additional source of pDC?

8. REASSESSMENT OF THE LYMPHOID PATHWAY TO pDC

The relatively low output of pDC from CDP was one reason for again considering a lymphoid source of pDC. A further reason was the low frequency of clones containing only pDC on culture of individual CDP, compared to the high frequency of pDC alone clones when earlier, multipotent precursor cells (LSK fraction) were cultured (Naik et al., 2007). It was argued that the immediate precursors of such pDC-dominated clones must be on a developmental branch apart from CDP, perhaps on a lymphoid branch (Sathe et al., 2013).

The deficit in pDC production in the absence of normal signaling from the lymphoid cytokine IL-7 is one new argument for significant pDC generation via a lymphoid route (Vogt et al., 2009). The pDC deficit in IL-7R-α null mice is at the level of pDC generation and is inherent to the BM precursors themselves, and only the lymphoid precursors in BM appear to be affected. One problem with the conclusion that many pDC are therefore of lymphoid origin is that these results would predict a similar origin for many spleen and lymph node cDC but there are no markers of a lymphoid past in peripheral cDC. However, additional factors in normal mice might bias a lymphoid route of DC production towards pDC and away from cDC.

Further support for a lymphoid route to pDC production has come from studies on the pDC deficit in mice lacking the IFN-I receptor and in mice where the downstream signaling from this receptor is impaired (Lee et al., 2013). Although both CDP and CLP are reduced in numbers in such mice, the production of pDC from CLP in culture is particularly impaired. This has been attributed to the reduced expression of Flt3 on CLP in the absence of signals from IFN-I, a consequent reduction in intensity of Flt3L signaling and a resulting bias away from pDC production (Lee et al., 2013). The output of pDC versus cDC from a lymphoid route may therefore depend on this IFN-I/Flt3L signaling interaction.

The Flt3L-stimulated BM culture system has been used recently to track in detail the developmental pathways leading to pDC (Sathe et al., 2013). Apart from the high levels of Flt3L used, this system reflects many of the features of steady-state DC development, combining the BM and spleen stages. A CDP or pro-DC precursor is prominent after 5 days of culture and cDC production peaks around day 8. The pDC are generated as a broad peak over 5–8 days, so many are generated much earlier than cDC and apparently too early to be products of CDP.

When CLP or CMP isolated from BM were introduced into these Flt3L-stimulated cultures, the CLP generated a peak of pDC but very few cDC around day 6, whereas CMP generated a peak of pDC at days 7–8, along with many cDC. Thus, there appeared to be separate lymphoid and myeloid routes to pDC in these cultures (Fig. 4.1).

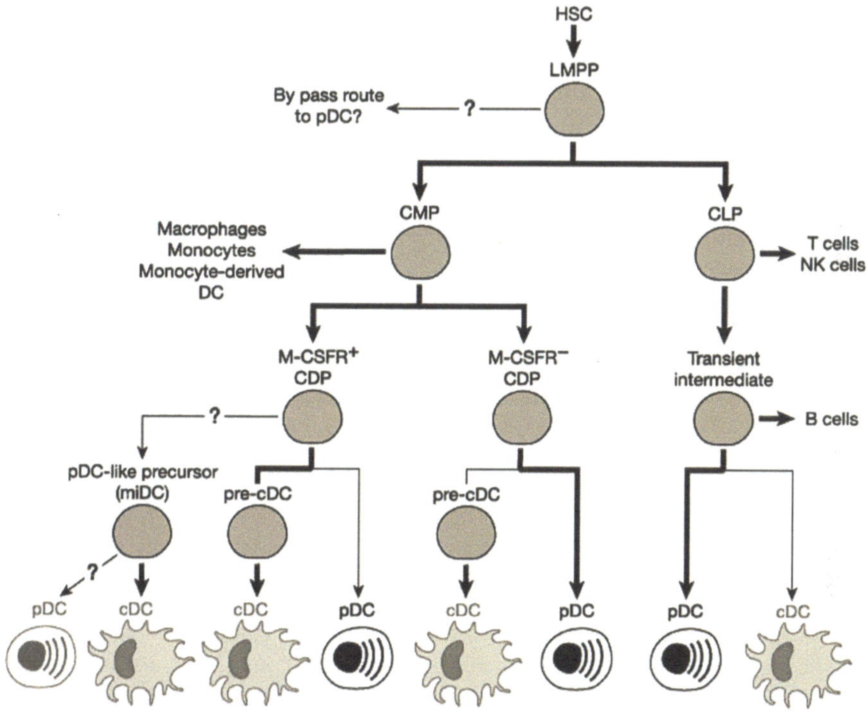

Figure 4.1 Possible developmental pathways to plasmacytoid cells. Major (heavy arrows) and minor (light arrows) hematopoietic pathways found to have a potential to produce plasmacytoid dendritic cells (pDC) or conventional dendritic cells (cDC) are outlined. The intermediate precursors are: HSS, hematopoietic stem cells; LMPP, lymphocyte primed multipotent precursors; CMP, common myeloid precursors; CLP, common lymphoid precursors: CDP, common dendritic precursors; pre-cDC, precursors of cDC; miDC, myeloid interferon-producing DC. The relative importance of different pathways and the pDC to cDC ratio will vary with environmental conditions. The routes to pDC from CLP and from M-CSFR$^-$ CDP may involve RAG-1 expression and pDC with IgH gene DJ rearrangements; the route to pDC from M-CSFR$^+$ CDP does not involve expression of these "lymphoid" markers. It is not yet clear whether a degree of early DC commitment at the LMPP stage proceeds via the pathways illustrated or represents a more direct "bypass" pathway.

Downstream of CLP a Bst2$^+$CD11c$^-$ transient intermediate was detected with potential to form pDC and B cells but which differed from CLP in lacking full capacity to form NK cells or T cells; a similar precursor was detected in normal BM (Sathe et al., 2013). A B lineage-related intermediate capable of producing DC had been described earlier (Izon et al., 2001). These results linked pDC development to B-cell development (Fig. 4.1).

The pDC produced in culture from CLP had at all time points the characteristic surface markers of pDC (Fig. 4.2). They were also capable of secreting IFN-α when stimulated with CpG in media that sustained their viability, although less efficiently than the CMP-derived pDC (Sathe et al., 2013). One clear difference from CMP-derived pDC was their rapid death when transferred into fresh culture medium; the factors required for survival have not been elucidated. Overall, a clear B-cell-related lymphoid route to pDC production occurs in these cultures, and these lymphoid-derived products meet the surface marker and functional criteria of pDC.

9. IMPLICATIONS OF RAG-1 EXPRESSION AND IgH GENE REARRANGEMENTS IN pDC

The Flt3L-stimulated BM culture system allowed a closer analysis of the significance of the "lymphoid" markers in pDC (Sathe et al., 2013). Importantly, the pDC produced in these cultures show a similar pattern of RAG-1 expression and IgH gene DJ rearrangements to the pDC from mouse spleen, and as in spleen, the cDC show no signs of these markers. As expected, the DNA of the pDC produced from CLP in this culture system contained a high level of DJ rearrangements of the IgH genes. However, in agreement with the adoptive transfer results, the pDC derived from CMP also displayed some DJ IgH gene rearrangements.

The CMP fraction from BM was itself examined more closely (Sathe et al., 2013). A small proportion of the CMP population was found to express RAG-1 and these were entirely within the Flt3$^+$ subset known to contain the DC precursors. These RAG-1$^+$ Flt3$^+$ CMP were nevertheless myeloid precursors and distinct from CLP, since they readily produced macrophages when cultured with GM-CSF. As expected, the pDC and cDC progeny of the RAG-1$^-$Flt3$^+$CMP did not display RAG-1 linked GFP fluorescence. By contrast, the pDC progeny of the RAG-1$^+$Flt3$^+$CMP displayed RAG-1 fluorescence and also contained IgH gene DJ rearrangements. However, the cDC progeny of the same

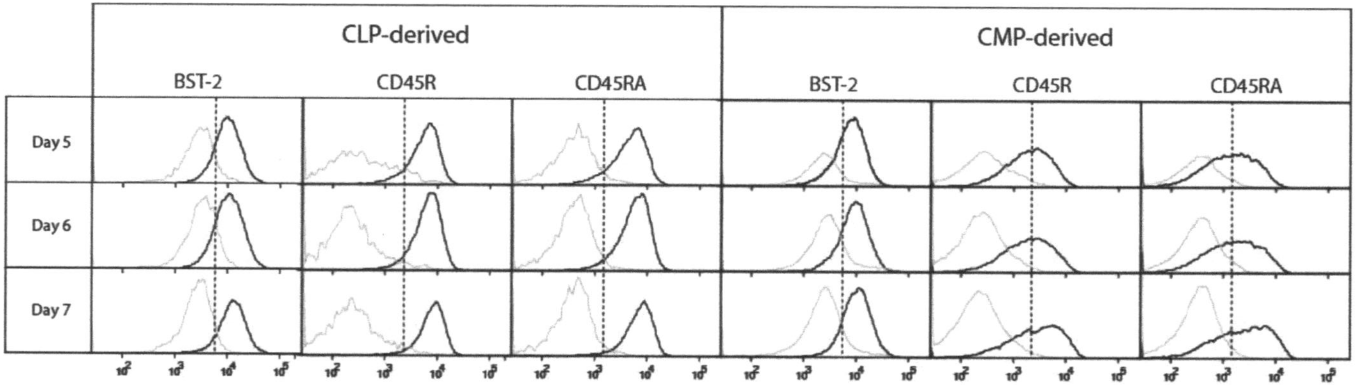

Figure 4.2 Surface phenotype of plasmacytoid-like cells generated in culture from CLP or CMP. The CLP and CMP were isolated from BM and cultured for the times shown with Flt3L (Sathe et al., 2013). The pDC-like cells produced were gated as CD11c$^+$SiglecH$^+$ and analyzed for the other surface markers shown. pDC-like cells (also termed miDC), low in expression of CD45 and CD45RA, were generated only from CMP. (For color version of this figure, the reader is referred to the online version of this chapter.)

RAG-1^{+}Flt3^{+}CMP did not display either RAG-1 fluorescence or IgH gene rearrangements.

These findings have two implications. First, as originally proposed (Corcoran et al., 2003; Pelayo et al., 2005), the presence of IgH gene DJ rearrangements and residual RAG-1 expression in pDC is generally a sound marker of origin from a precursor with a lymphoid bias; however, although this generally means lymphoid precursors such as CLP, it must now also include the subset of CMP retaining some lymphoid potential and able to express RAG-1. Second, as had also been proposed (Shigematsu et al., 2004), there is something additional in the final development of pDC that promotes persistence of RAG-1 expression and allows DJ rearrangements of IgH genes, since the cDC derived from the same RAG-1 expressing CMP show no signs of these markers.

10. EXTENSION OF THE CDP DEFINITION TO INCLUDE NEW pDC PRECURSORS

The relatively low yield of pDC from CDP as originally defined prompted a search for new pDC precursors down the myeloid route. In a recent careful study, a new precursor giving predominantly pDC, but still some cDC, has been isolated from BM; it is Lin^{-}c-Kit $^{int/lo}$Flt3^{+} like CDP but does not express the M-CSFR (Onai et al., 2013). The myeloid-derived pDC expressing RAG-1 and having IgH gene rearrangements arise from this new precursor, rather than from the conventional M-CSFR^{+} CDP. In retrospect, the pro-DC or "CDP" population previously isolated from Flt3L-stimulated BM cultures and not segregated by M-CSFR expression had given a good yield of pDC, suggesting it included this new precursor population (Naik et al., 2007). Thus, there are two parallel pathways from what may be considered an extended CDP population, one from M-CSFR^{+} precursors producing predominantly cDC and this new pathway from M-CSFR^{-} precursors producing predominantly pDC (Fig. 4.1).

11. A DIFFERENT NON-pDC BUT pDC-LIKE PRODUCT OF THE MYELOID PATHWAY

Two recent studies have demonstrated that not all cells in BM bearing pDC-like markers are pDC or even obligate precursors of the type of pDC eventually circulating in the periphery (O'Keeffe et al., 2012; Schlitzer et al.,

2011). This has been a cause of confusion in previous investigations. The pointer to this situation was the earlier observation that cells within BM identified as pDC were able on virus infection to differentiate into functional CD11b$^+$ cDC; it was significant that pDC from spleen were unable to do this (Zuniga, McGavern, Pruneda-Paz, Teng, & Oldstone, 2004). This now fits with the identification in BM of a population of "pDC-like precursors," Siglec-H$^+$Bst2$^+$ like pDC but low for CD45R (B220), and, notably not expressing CCR9, the chemokine receptor characteristic of peripheral pDC. These pDC-like cells, obtained from Flt3L-treated mice, were able on transfer to form cDC, particularly the CD11b$^+$ CD8$^-$ cDC subtype but also some cDC bearing CD8 (Schlitzer et al., 2012). They were considered as a precursor that, like pre-DC, would leave BM to populate peripheral tissues, the nature of the product DC depending on the local environment; it was argued that in some environments, they could produce pDC (Schlitzer et al., 2012). The same pDC-like population was identified in normal BM in a separate study and termed miDC (myeloid interferon-producing DC) to distinguish it from pDC (O'Keeffe et al., 2012). In this study, the role of these miDC as interferon-producing immune response elements within the BM itself was emphasized, and there was little evidence they served as pDC precursors. It remains to be firmly established whether the cells obtained from Flt3L-treated mice (Schlitzer et al., 2012) are the exact cells obtained from untreated mice (O'Keeffe et al., 2012) or whether the former may contain additional pDC precursors amplified with Flt3L treatment.

These new immune system cells share the Siglec-H and Bst2 markers with pDC (albeit slightly lower expression of both), and they are also remarkably efficient producers of IFN-I and IFN-III when stimulated by TLR7 and 9 ligands (O'Keeffe et al., 2012; Schlitzer et al., 2011). However, their survival *in vitro* is superior to that of pDC and they respond to viral stimulation more like cDC than pDC (O'Keeffe et al., 2012). Their close developmental relationship with pDC is emphasized by their common dependence on the transcription factor E2-2. However, unlike pDC, the miDC all lack Rag-I expression as determined by their lack of GFP fluorescence in RAG-GFP knock-in mice (O'Keeffe et al., 2012). These pDC-like BM cells appear to be of myeloid rather than lymphoid origin, since they are apparent as a CD45R^{lo}CD45RA^{lo} fraction of the Siglec-H positive cells developing from CMP in Flt3L stimulated cultures, but are not seen when CLP are the precursors (Fig. 4.2). The lack of Rag-1 expression suggests they are most closely related to the M-CSFR$^+$ CDP-derived sublineage (Fig. 4.1).

Some minor DC populations previously identified in the spleen seem likely to be derived from or related to these BM cells. The $B220^+CCR9^-$ spleen DC that are able on transfer to become cDC may be downstream products of these BM precursors (Segura, Wong, & Villadangos, 2009). However, caution is required when applying CCR9 expression to define pDC since others have demonstrated the downregulation of CCR9 when pDC are activated (Hadeiba et al., 2008, 2012). The $CX_3CR1^+CD8^+$ DC of spleen, sometimes termed the CD8 "look-alike" cDC population, already known to be dependent on E2-2 but not a direct product of pDC, may have a similar origin (Bar-On et al., 2010).

12. TRACKING pDC DEVELOPMENT USING CELLULAR "BARCODING"

Most information on the pathway of pDC development has come from adoptive transfer of precursor populations into recipient mice or from bulk or clonal studies on Flt3L-stimulated BM cultures. A new approach, termed cellular barcoding, allows all the progeny of individual precursor cells to be tracked *in vivo*. A library of unique DNA stretches are introduced into precursor cells by lentiviral transduction, then the uniquely marked progeny of individual precursor cells determined various times after transfer of precursors into mice. A high-resolution version of this approach has recently been applied to DC differentiation (Naik et al., 2013). When this approach was used with hematopoietic stem cell preparations, the individual precursors responsible for most of the reconstitution generally generated all the hematopoietic cell types assayed; these precursors were multipotent, as expected. However, a different result was obtained with the "lymphoid-primed multipotent progenitor" (LMPP) BM fraction, downstream of hematopoietic stem cells but upstream of CMP and CLP, and previously considered as a multipotent precursor (Adolfsson et al., 2005). The barcoding approach showed progeny of individual LMPP cells was frequently restricted to particular hematopoietic lineages. The developmental fate of these precursors appeared to be "imprinted" at this early developmental stage rather than being a consequence of the precursors developing in a particular environmental niche. DC were a striking example of this early commitment effect. At least a proportion of these LMPPs were imprinted towards a DC fate (both pDC and cDC) as demonstrated with clone splitting experiments where siblings of many single LMPPs demonstrated the same DC fate. The developmental relationship between pDC and cDC was strongly supported by these findings. The basis of this early imprinting of a DC fate and whether it is programmed, stochastic, or imposed by the environment remains to be elucidated; however, it is pertinent that LMPP precursors express Flt3, so have one of the requirements of DC precursors. Based on this striking finding, a distinct and separate DC-lineage beginning with these early precursors was proposed. Gene expression data of both murine and human DC subtypes also fit the idea that pDC and cDC form a distinct lineage from the classic myeloid and lymphoid pathways (Robbins et al., 2008). It is not yet clear whether these DC-imprinted cells immediately deflect to a DC form or whether DC commitment is initially cryptic and development continues via the conventional myeloid or lymphoid precursor intermediates (Fig. 4.1).

13. SOME CONCLUSIONS

This chapter commenced with the attempts to fit pDC development into the standard hematopoiesis model of divergent myeloid and lymphoid pathways. Although the final balance in steady-state mice is not yet clear, it seems likely that both routes contribute to the final complement of peripheral pDC. The previously neglected lymphoid route so far appears straightforward, but the well-accepted myeloid route is clearly complex, with a lymphoid-like precursor component, with parallel developmental routes with differing pDC to cDC bias, and with the generation of a related group of pDC-like IPC leading to cDC rather than pDC production. These multiple and initially divergent routes then appear to converge to produce a common peripheral pDC type with the characteristic set of surface markers and with the same basic functions, including the central function of IFN-I production. These pDC may contain functionally irrelevant relics of their past, such as IgH gene rearrangements. Whether the developmental origin determines important detailed functions, such as the pattern and extent of cytokine production as some studies indicate (Bjorck, Leong, & Engleman, 2011; Pelayo et al., 2005; Yang et al., 2005), needs further investigation to ensure these do not reflect maturation stages or loss of viability in the assay medium.

However, tracking pDC development in this way using the conventional sets of surface markers on hematopoietic precursors is clearly missing the central elements governing pDC development. If the previous pathways leading to other blood cells had not been so well established as a precedent, we would be seeking as a pDC precursor a mononuclear cell-expressing Flt3 and with the capacity to express the key transcription factors such as E2-2, and we would be discounting the currently employed surface markers of the myeloid or lymphoid streams. The gene sets and transcription factors that govern DC development in general, and pDC development in particular, seem to override the factors that bias developing hematopoietic cells towards other fates. The finding of very early commitment of some precursors to a DC fate serves to emphasize this developmental dominance of the DC program.

REFERENCES

Adolfsson, J., Mansson, R., Buza-Vidas, N., Hultquist, A., Liuba, K., Jensen, C. T., et al. (2005). Identification of Flt3+ lympho-myeloid stem cells lacking erythro-megakaryocytic potential a revised road map for adult blood lineage commitment. *Cell, 121*, 295–306.

Akashi, K., Traver, D., Miyamoto, T., & Weissman, I. L. (2000). A clonogenic common myeloid progenitor that gives rise to all myeloid lineages. *Nature, 404*, 193–197.

Ank, N., Iversen, M. B., Bartholdy, C., Staeheli, P., Hartmann, R., Jensen, U. B., et al. (2008). An important role for type III interferon (IFN-lambda/IL-28) in TLR-induced antiviral activity. *The Journal of Immunology, 180*, 2474–2485.

Asselin-Paturel, C., Boonstra, A., Dalod, M., Durand, I., Yessaad, N., Dezutter-Dambuyant, C., et al. (2001). Mouse type I IFN-producing cells are immature APCs with plasmacytoid morphology. *Nature Immunology, 2*, 1144–1150.

Bar-On, L., Birnberg, T., Lewis, K. L., Edelson, B. T., Bruder, D., Hildner, K., et al. (2010). CX3CR1+ CD8alpha+ dendritic cells are a steady-state population related to plasmacytoid dendritic cells. *Proceedings of the National Academy of Sciences of the United States of America, 107*, 14745–14750.

Bjorck, P., Leong, H. X., & Engleman, E. G. (2011). Plasmacytoid dendritic cell dichotomy: Identification of IFN-alpha producing cells as a phenotypically and functionally distinct subset. *The Journal of Immunology, 186*, 1477–1485.

Blasius, A. L., Giurisato, E., Cella, M., Schreiber, R. D., Shaw, A. S., & Colonna, M. (2006). Bone marrow stromal cell antigen 2 is a specific marker of type I IFN-producing cells in the naive mouse, but a promiscuous cell surface antigen following IFN stimulation. *The Journal of Immunology, 177*, 3260–3265.

Brasel, K., De Smedt, T., Smith, J. L., & Maliszewski, C. R. (2000). Generation of murine dendritic cells from flt3-ligand-supplemented bone marrow cultures. *Blood, 96*, 3029–3039.

Chen, W., Antonenko, S., Sederstrom, J. M., Liang, X., Chan, A. S., Kanzler, H., et al. (2004). Thrombopoietin cooperates with FLT3-ligand in the generation of plasmacytoid dendritic cell precursors from human hematopoietic progenitors. *Blood, 103*, 2547–2553.

Chicha, L., Jarrossay, D., & Manz, M. G. (2004). Clonal type I interferon-producing and dendritic cell precursors are contained in both human lymphoid and myeloid progenitor populations. *The Journal of Experimental Medicine, 200*, 1519–1524.

Cisse, B., Caton, M. L., Lehner, M., Maeda, T., Scheu, S., Locksley, R., et al. (2008). Transcription factor E2-2 is an essential and specific regulator of plasmacytoid dendritic cell development. *Cell, 135*, 37–48.

Colonna, M., Trinchieri, G., & Liu, Y. J. (2004). Plasmacytoid dendritic cells in immunity. *Nature Immunology, 5*, 1219–1226.

Corcoran, L., Ferrero, I., Vremec, D., Lucas, K., Waithman, J., O'Keeffe, M., et al. (2003). The lymphoid past of mouse plasmacytoid cells and thymic dendritic cells. *The Journal of Immunology, 170*, 4926–4932.

D'Amico, A., & Wu, L. (2003). The early progenitors of mouse dendritic cells and plasmacytoid predendritic cells are within the bone marrow hemopoietic precursors expressing Flt3. *The Journal of Experimental Medicine, 198*, 293–303.

Diao, J., Winter, E., Chen, W., Cantin, C., & Cattral, M. S. (2004). Characterization of distinct conventional and plasmacytoid dendritic cell-committed precursors in murine bone marrow. *The Journal of Immunology, 173*, 1826–1833.

Esashi, E., Wang, Y. H., Perng, O., Qin, X. F., Liu, Y. J., & Watowich, S. S. (2008). The signal transducer STAT5 inhibits plasmacytoid dendritic cell development by suppressing transcription factor IRF8. *Immunity, 28*, 509–520.

Fancke, B., Suter, M., Hochrein, H., & O'Keeffe, M. (2008). M-CSF: A novel plasmacytoid and conventional dendritic cell poietin. *Blood, 111*, 150–159.

Ghosh, H. S., Cisse, B., Bunin, A., Lewis, K. L., & Reizis, B. (2010). Continuous expression of the transcription factor E2-2 maintains the cell fate of mature plasmacytoid dendritic cells. *Immunity, 33*, 905–916.

Gilliet, M., Boonstra, A., Paturel, C., Antonenko, S., Xu, X. L., Trinchieri, G., et al. (2002). The development of murine plasmacytoid dendritic cell precursors is differentially regulated by FLT3-ligand and granulocyte/macrophage colony-stimulating factor. *The Journal of Experimental Medicine, 195*, 953–958.

Gilliet, M., Cao, W., & Liu, Y. J. (2008). Plasmacytoid dendritic cells: Sensing nucleic acids in viral infection and autoimmune diseases. *Nature Reviews Immunology, 8*, 594–606.

Hadeiba, H., Lahl, K., Edalati, A., Oderup, C., Habtezion, A., Pachynski, R., et al. (2012). Plasmacytoid dendritic cells transport peripheral antigens to the thymus to promote central tolerance. *Immunity, 36*, 438–450.

Hadeiba, H., Sato, T., Habtezion, A., Oderup, C., Pan, J., & Butcher, E. C. (2008). CCR9 expression defines tolerogenic plasmacytoid dendritic cells able to suppress acute graft-versus-host disease. *Nature Immunology, 9*, 1253–1260.

Izon, D., Rudd, K., DeMuth, W., Pear, W. S., Clendenin, C., Lindsley, R. C., et al. (2001). A common pathway for dendritic cell and early B cell development. *The Journal of Immunology, 167*, 1387–1392.

Kamogawa-Schifter, Y., Ohkawa, J., Namiki, S., Arai, N., Arai, K., & Liu, Y. (2005). Ly49Q defines 2 pDC subsets in mice. *Blood, 105*, 2787–2792.

Karsunky, H., Merad, M., Cozzio, A., Weissman, I. L., & Manz, M. G. (2003). Flt3 ligand regulates dendritic cell development from Flt3+ lymphoid and myeloid-committed progenitors to Flt3+ dendritic cells in vivo. *The Journal of Experimental Medicine, 198*, 305–313.

Kingston, D., Schmid, M. A., Onai, N., Obata-Onai, A., Baumjohann, D., & Manz, M. G. (2009). The concerted action of GM-CSF and Flt3-ligand on in vivo dendritic cell homeostasis. *Blood, 114*, 835–843.

Kondo, M., Weissman, I. L., & Akashi, K. (1997). Identification of clonogenic common lymphoid progenitors in mouse bone marrow. *Cell, 91*, 661–672.

Laouar, Y., Welte, T., Fu, X. Y., & Flavell, R. A. (2003). STAT3 is required for Flt3L-dependent dendritic cell differentiation. *Immunity, 19*, 903–912.

Lauterbach, H., Bathke, B., Gilles, S., Traidl-Hoffmann, C., Luber, C. A., Fejer, G., et al. (2010). Mouse CD8alpha+ DCs and human BDCA3+ DCs are major producers of IFN-lambda in response to poly IC. *The Journal of Experimental Medicine, 207*, 2703–2717.

Lee, C.-K., Chen, Y.-L., Chen, T.-T., Pac, L.-M., Wesoly, J., & Bluyssen, H. A. R. (2013). A type 1 IFN/Flt3 ligand axis augments plasmacytoid dendritic cell development from common lymphoid progenitors. Submitted for publication.

Liu, Y. J. (2005). IPC: Professional type 1 interferon-producing cells and plasmacytoid dendritic cell precursors. *Annual Review of Immunology, 23*, 275–306.

Liu, K., Victora, G. D., Schwickert, T. A., Guermonprez, P., Meredith, M. M., Yao, K., et al. (2009). In vivo analysis of dendritic cell development and homeostasis. *Science, 324*, 392–397.

MacDonald, K. P., Rowe, V., Bofinger, H. M., Thomas, R., Sasmono, T., Hume, D. A., et al. (2005). The colony-stimulating factor 1 receptor is expressed on dendritic cells during differentiation and regulates their expansion. *The Journal of Immunology, 175*, 1399–1405.

Manz, M. G., Traver, D., Miyamoto, T., Weissman, I. L., & Akashi, K. (2001). Dendritic cell potentials of early lymphoid and myeloid progenitors. *Blood, 97*, 3333–3341.

McKenna, H. J., Stocking, K. L., Miller, R. E., Brasel, K., De Smedt, T., Maraskovsky, E., et al. (2000). Mice lacking flt3 ligand have deficient hematopoiesis affecting hematopoietic progenitor cells, dendritic cells, and natural killer cells. *Blood, 95*, 3489–3497.

Merad, M., & Manz, M. G. (2009). Dendritic cell homeostasis. *Blood, 113*, 3418–3427.

Nagasawa, M., Schmidlin, H., Hazekamp, M. G., Schotte, R., & Blom, B. (2008). Development of human plasmacytoid dendritic cells depends on the combined action of the basic helix-loop-helix factor E2-2 and the Ets factor Spi-B. *European Journal of Immunology, 38*, 2389–2400.

Naik, S. H., Metcalf, D., van Nieuwenhuijze, A., Wicks, I., Wu, L., O'Keeffe, M., et al. (2006). Intrasplenic steady-state dendritic cell precursors that are distinct from monocytes. *Nature Immunology, 7*, 663–671.

Naik, S. H., Perie, L., Swart, E., Gerlach, C., van Rooij, N., de Boer, R. J., et al. (2013). Diverse and heritable lineage imprinting of early haematopoietic progenitors. *Nature, 496*, 229–232.

Naik, S. H., Proietto, A. I., Wilson, N. S., Dakic, A., Schnorrer, P., Fuchsberger, M., et al. (2005). Cutting edge: Generation of splenic CD8+ and CD8− dendritic cell equivalents in Fms-like tyrosine kinase 3 ligand bone marrow cultures. *The Journal of Immunology, 174*, 6592–6597.

Naik, S. H., Sathe, P., Park, H.-Y., Metcalf, D., Proietto, A. I., Dakic, A., et al. (2007). Development of plasmacytoid and conventional dendritic cell subtypes from single precursor cells derived in vitro and in vivo. *Nature Immunology, 8*, 1217–1226.

O'Keeffe, M., Fancke, B., Suter, M., Ramm, G., Clark, J., Wu, L., et al. (2012). Non-plasmacytoid, high IFN-alpha-producing, bone marrow dendritic cells. *The Journal of Immunology, 188*, 3774–3783.

O'Keeffe, M., Hochrein, H., Vremec, D., Caminschi, I., Miller, J. L., Anders, E. M., et al. (2002). Mouse plasmacytoid cells: Long-lived cells, heterogeneous in surface phenotype and function, that differentiate into CD8(+) dendritic cells only after microbial stimulus. *The Journal of Experimental Medicine, 196*, 1307–1319.

O'Keeffe, M., Hochrein, H., Vremec, D., Pooley, J., Evans, R., Woulfe, S., et al. (2002). Effects of administration of progenipoietin 1, Flt-3 ligand, granulocyte colony-stimulating factor, and pegylated granulocyte-macrophage colony-stimulating factor on dendritic cell subsets in mice. *Blood, 99*, 2122–2130.

Omatsu, Y., Iyoda, T., Kimura, Y., Maki, A., Ishimori, M., Toyama-Sorimachi, N., et al. (2005). Development of murine plasmacytoid dendritic cells defined by increased expression of an inhibitory NK receptor, Ly49Q. *The Journal of Immunology, 174*, 6657–6662.

Onai, N., Kurabayashi, K., Hosoi-Amaike, M., Toyama-Sorimachi, N., Matsusima, K., Inaba, K., et al. (2013). A clonogenic progenitor with prominent plasmacytoid dendritic cell potential. *Immunity, 38*(5), 943–957.

Onai, N., Obata-Onai, A., Schmid, M. A., Ohteki, T., Jarrossay, D., & Manz, M. G. (2007). Identification of clonogenic common Flt3+M-CSFR+ plasmacytoid and conventional dendritic cell progenitors in mouse bone marrow. *Nature Immunology, 8*, 1207–1216.

Onai, N., Obata-Onai, A., Tussiwand, R., Lanzavecchia, A., & Manz, M. G. (2006). Activation of the Flt3 signal transduction cascade rescues and enhances type I interferon-producing and dendritic cell development. *The Journal of Experimental Medicine, 203*, 227–238.

Pelayo, R., Hirose, J., Huang, J., Garrett, K. P., Delogu, A., Busslinger, M., et al. (2005). Derivation of 2 categories of plasmacytoid dendritic cells in murine bone marrow. *Blood, 105*, 4407–4415.

Proietto, A. I., Mittag, D., Roberts, A. W., Sprigg, N., & Wu, L. (2012). The equivalents of human blood and spleen dendritic cell subtypes can be generated in vitro from human CD34(+) stem cells in the presence of fms-like tyrosine kinase 3 ligand and thrombopoietin. *Cellular and molecular immunology, 9*, 446–454.

Pulendran, B., Banchereau, J., Burkeholder, S., Kraus, E., Guinet, E., Chalouni, C., et al. (2000). Flt3-ligand and granulocyte colony-stimulating factor mobilize distinct human dendritic cell subsets in vivo. *The Journal of Immunology, 165*, 566–572.

Robbins, S. H., Walzer, T., Dembele, D., Thibault, C., Defays, A., Bessou, G., et al. (2008). Novel insights into the relationships between dendritic cell subsets in human and mouse revealed by genome-wide expression profiling. *Genome Biology, 9*, R17.

Sathe, P., Pooley, J., Vremec, D., Mintern, J., Jin, J. O., Wu, L., et al. (2011). The acquisition of antigen cross-presentation function by newly formed dendritic cells. *The Journal of Immunology, 186*, 5184–5192.

Sathe, P., Vremec, D., Wu, L., Corcoran, L., & Shortman, K. (2013). Convergent differentiation: Myeloid and lymphoid pathways to murine plasmacytoid dendritic cells. *Blood, 121*, 11–19.

Schlitzer, A., Heiseke, A. F., Einwachter, H., Reindl, W., Schiemann, M., Manta, C. P., et al. (2012). Tissue-specific differentiation of a circulating CCR9− pDC-like common dendritic cell precursor. *Blood, 119*, 6063–6071.

Schlitzer, A., Loschko, J., Mair, K., Vogelmann, R., Henkel, L., Einwachter, H., et al. (2011). Identification of CCR9− murine plasmacytoid DC precursors with plasticity to differentiate into conventional DCs. *Blood, 117*, 6562–6570.

Schmid, M. A., Kingston, D., Boddupalli, S., & Manz, M. G. (2010). Instructive cytokine signals in dendritic cell lineage commitment. *Immunology Reviews, 234*, 32–44.

Segura, E., Wong, J., & Villadangos, J. A. (2009). Cutting edge: B220+ CCR9− dendritic cells are not plasmacytoid dendritic cells but are precursors of conventional dendritic cells. *The Journal of Immunology, 183*, 1514–1517.

Shigematsu, H., Reizis, B., Iwasaki, H., Mizuno, S., Hu, D., Traver, D., et al. (2004). Plasmacytoid dendritic cells activate lymphoid-specific genetic programs irrespective of their cellular origin. *Immunity, 21*, 43–53.

Shortman, K., & Liu, Y. J. (2002). Mouse and human dendritic cell subtypes. *Nature Reviews Immunology, 2*, 151–161.

Shortman, K., & Naik, S. H. (2007). Steady-state and inflammatory dendritic-cell development. *Nature Reviews Immunology, 7*, 19–30.

Siegal, F. P., Kadowaki, N., Shodell, M., Fitzgerald-Bocarsly, P. A., Shah, K., Ho, S., et al. (1999). The nature of the principal type 1 interferon-producing cells in human blood. *Science, 284*, 1835–1837.

Swiecki, M., & Colonna, M. (2010). Unraveling the functions of plasmacytoid dendritic cells during viral infections, autoimmunity, and tolerance. *Immunology Reviews, 234*, 142–162.

Swiecki, M., Gilfillan, S., Vermi, W., Wang, Y., & Colonna, M. (2010). Plasmacytoid dendritic cell ablation impacts early interferon responses and antiviral NK and CD8(+) T cell accrual. *Immunity, 33*, 955–966.

Tailor, P., Tamura, T., Morse, H. C., 3rd., & Ozato, K. (2008). The BXH2 mutation in IRF8 differentially impairs dendritic cell subset development in the mouse. *Blood, 111*, 1942–1945.

Traver, D., Akashi, K., Manz, M., Merad, M., Miyamoto, T., Engleman, E. G., et al. (2000). Development of CD8α-positive dendritic cells from a common myeloid progenitor. *Science, 290*, 2152–2154.

Tsujimura, H., Tamura, T., & Ozato, K. (2003). Cutting edge: IFN consensus sequence binding protein/IFN regulatory factor 8 drives the development of type I IFN-producing plasmacytoid dendritic cells. *The Journal of Immunology, 170*, 1131–1135.

Tussiwand, R., Lee, W.-L., Murphy, T. L., Mashayekhi, M., Kc, W., Albring, J. C., et al. (2012). Compensatory dendritic cell development mediated by BATF–IRF interactions. *Nature, 490*, 502–507.

Vogt, T. K., Link, A., Perrin, J., Finke, D., & Luther, S. A. (2009). Novel function for interleukin-7 in dendritic cell development. *Blood, 113*, 3961–3968.

Vollstedt, S., O'Keeffe, M., Ryf, B., Glanzmann, B., Hochrein, H., & Suter, M. (2006). The long-term but not the short-term antiviral effect of IFN-α depends on Flt3 ligand and pDC. *European Journal of Immunology, 36*, 1231–1240.

Vremec, D., O'Keeffe, M., Hochrein, H., Fuchsberger, M., Caminschi, I., Lahoud, M., et al. (2007). Production of interferons by dendritic cells, plasmacytoid cells, natural killer cells, and interferon-producing killer dendritic cells. *Blood, 109*, 1165–1173.

Waskow, C., Liu, K., Darrasse-Jeze, G., Guermonprez, P., Ginhoux, F., Merad, M., et al. (2008). The receptor tyrosine kinase Flt3 is required for dendritic cell development in peripheral lymphoid tissues. *Nature Immunology, 9*, 676–683.

Wendland, M., Czeloth, N., Mach, N., Malissen, B., Kremmer, E., Pabst, O., et al. (2007). CCR9 is a homing receptor for plasmacytoid dendritic cells to the small intestine. *Proceedings of the National Academy of United States of America, 104*, 6347–6352.

Wu, L., D'Amico, A., Hochrein, H., O'Keeffe, M., Shortman, K., & Lucas, K. (2001). Development of thymic and splenic dendritic cell populations from different hemopoietic precursors. *Blood, 98*, 3376–3382.

Yang, G. X., Lian, Z. X., Kikuchi, K., Moritoki, Y., Ansari, A. A., Liu, Y. J., et al. (2005). Plasmacytoid dendritic cells of different origins have distinct characteristics and function: Studies of lymphoid progenitors versus myeloid progenitors. *The Journal of Immunology, 175*, 7281–7287.

Young, L. J., Wilson, N. S., Schnorrer, P., Proietto, A., ten Broeke, T., Matsuki, Y., et al. (2008). Differential MHC class II synthesis and ubiquitination confers distinct antigen-presenting properties on conventional and plasmacytoid dendritic cells. *Nature Immunology, 9*, 1244–1252.

Zhang, J., Raper, A., Sugita, N., Hingorani, R., Salio, M., Palmowski, M. J., et al. (2006). Characterization of Siglec-H as a novel endocytic receptor expressed on murine plasmacytoid dendritic cell precursors. *Blood, 107*, 3600–3608.

Zuniga, E. I., McGavern, D. B., Pruneda-Paz, J. L., Teng, C., & Oldstone, M. B. (2004). Bone marrow plasmacytoid dendritic cells can differentiate into myeloid dendritic cells upon virus infection. *Nature Immunology, 5*, 1227–1234.

CHAPTER FIVE

Pathological Consequence of Misguided Dendritic Cell Differentiation in Histiocytic Diseases

Marie-Luise Berres[*,†,‡,1,2], **Carl E. Allen**[§,¶,1], **Miriam Merad**[*,†,‡]
[*]Department of Oncological Sciences, Icahn School of Medicine at Mount Sinai, New York, USA
[†]Tisch Cancer Institute
[‡]Immunology Institute
[§]Texas Children's Cancer Center, Houston, Texas, USA
[¶]Baylor College of Medicine, Houston, Texas, USA
[1]These authors equally contributed to the manuscript.
[2]Corresponding author: e-mail address: marie.berres@mssm.edu

Contents

Advances in Immunology, Volume 120
ISSN 0065-2776
http://dx.doi.org/10.1016/B978-0-12-417028-5.00005-3

Abstract

Histiocytic disorders represent a group of complex pathologies characterized by the accumulation of histiocytes, an old term for tissue-resident macrophages and dendritic cells. Langerhans cell histiocytosis is the most frequent of histiocytosis in humans and has been thought to arise from the abnormal accumulation of epidermal dendritic cells called Langerhans cells. In this chapter, we discuss the origin and differentiation of Langerhans cells and dendritic cells and present accumulated evidence that suggests that Langerhans cell histiocytosis does not result from abnormal Langerhans cell homeostasis but rather is a consequence of misguided differentiation programs of myeloid dendritic cell precursors. We propose reclassification of Langerhans cell histiocytosis, juvenile xanthogranuloma, and Erdheim–Chester disease as inflammatory myeloid neoplasias.

1. THE MONONUCLEAR PHAGOCYTE SYSTEM

The term mononuclear phagocyte systems (MPSs) was first proposed by Ralph van Furth to describe hematopoietic cells determined by a mononuclear morphology (as opposed to polymorphonuclear granulocytes) and high phagocytic activity (Linz et al., 2007). The MPS comprises circulating monocytes and tissue-resident macrophages and dendritic cells (DCs) that populate all tissues. Besides their crucial role in tissue homeostasis, they are critically implicated in inflammation, autoimmunity, and cancer. Most cell types within the MPS share a common origin with a commitment to the MPS lineage at the stage of the macrophage and DC progenitor (MDP) (Fogg et al., 2006), yet their defined phenotype and function at the mature stage is highly distinctive.

Within this chapter, we will specifically discuss the differentiation program of the DC lineage. Moreover, we will provide evidence that human histiocytoses—a complex of disorders with a broad manifestation spectrum and potential fatal outcome—are the pathophysiological consequence of a dysregulated differentiation of the MPS emphasizing the importance of tight regulation of this process *in vivo*.

2. THE DC LINEAGE

DCs are a heterogeneous group of hematopoietic cells that reside in all tissues but are particularly enriched in interface tissues and lymphoid organs. They were first described in the early 1970s by Ralph Steinman and Zanvil

Cohn and distinguished from macrophages by their explicit morphology and superior capacity to activate T cells in an antigen-specific manner (Steinman & Cohn, 1973, 1974). DCs can be classified into two main subsets that comprise plasmacytoid DCs (pDCs) and classical DCs. pDCs exert only limited phagocytic and antigen-presenting activity and are, in the absence of inflammation, mostly restricted to lymphoid tissue. Upon activation, pDCs produce high levels of type 1 interferon and are closely implicated during viral infections and autoimmune diseases. This chapter will mainly discuss the development and differentiation of classical DCs. The origin and development of pDCs is comprehensively discussed in a recent review by Reizis (2010).

In contrast to pDCs, classical DCs can be found in steady-state conditions in all lymphoid, connective, and interface tissues. With respect to their primary localization, they can generally be divided into lymphoid organ-resident and nonlymphoid tissue-resident DCs. In addition to lymphoid-resident DCs, peripheral lymph nodes (LNs) also harbor tissue-resident migratory DCs that have migrated to the LN via the lymphatic vessels and are characterized by high expression of MHCII but intermediate CD11c expression. Migration of tissue-resident DCs to the LN is constitutive and occurs at slow rate in the steady state, dramatically increases during inflammatory conditions, and depends on the expression of the chemokine receptor CCR7 and its ligands (Ohl et al., 2004). During inflammation, an additional DC population deriving from blood monocytes and called inflammatory DC, which includes a subpopulation termed TNF–iNOS-expressing DCs (Tip DC), transiently infiltrates the injured tissue and dissipates when the injury resolves (Merad, Sathe, Helft, Miller, & Mortha, 2013).

Due to their potent endocytosis activity and migratory capacity, DCs are dedicated to sample peripheral tissue antigens, process and present antigens, migrate to the LNs, and initiate a specific T-cell-mediated immune response against invading pathogens while maintaining tolerance to self-antigens (Idoyaga et al., 2013; Mellman & Steinman, 2001; Steinman, Hawiger, & Nussenzweig, 2003).

In addition to their specific morphology, DCs are phenotypically defined by the expression of CD45, high amounts of major histocompatibility class II antigens (MHCII), and the integrin CD11c while lacking other hematopoietic lineage markers. This definition is limited by the promiscuous expression of the markers MHCII and CD11c within the hematopoietic lineages. High MHCII expression levels are shared by B cells and activated macrophages, while CD11c is expressed on activated T cells, B cells, NK cells, and distinct macrophage populations. Additional DC marker, for example, the tyrosine kinase receptor fms-like tyrosine kinase 3 (Flt3, also expressed on hematopoietic stem cells and DC precursor), is useful to distinguish DC from tissue macrophages; however, their applicability is limited due to sensitivity to collagenase digestion, a technique that is often required for the isolation of nonlymphoid tissue DCs (Miller et al., 2012). The very recent identification that the zinc finger transcription factor zbtb46 is a marker specific for the DC lineage within the MPS represents an exciting prospect in terms of DC identification and manipulation using zbtb49 DTR mouse models (Meredith et al., 2012; Satpathy et al., 2012).

3. ORIGIN AND REGULATION OF DC DIFFERENTIATION

Similar to other hematopoietic cells, the homeostasis of DCs in lymphoid and nonlymphoid tissue depends on the dynamic balance between local division of terminally differentiated cells, cell survival, and replenishment by circulating precursors. In addition, tissue-resident DCs contribute to the DC pool in the LNs where they present antigen to T cells (Randolph, Angeli, & Swartz, 2005).

Differentiated DCs display only very low proliferation rates within the tissue (Ginhoux et al., 2009; Kabashima et al., 2005; Waskow et al., 2008), which is tightly regulated by Flt3 and the cytokine lymphotoxin-β receptor (Ginhoux et al., 2009; Kabashima et al., 2005; Waskow et al., 2008). Additionally, Flt3 could be implicated in cell survival (Singh et al., 2012) and local Csf-2, which seems to exert antiapoptotic effects in nonlymphoid tissue (Greter, Helft, et al., 2012; Hirata, Egea, Dann, Eckmann, & Kagnoff, 2010).

Parabiotic mouse models demonstrated that DCs, with the exception of Langerhans cells (LCs), are rapidly replaced in the tissue by cells derived of the parabiont partner supporting the hypothesis of a rapid turnover of differentiated DCs even in the steady state with a constant reconstitution mediated by circulating precursors (Ginhoux et al., 2009; Liu et al., 2007; Merad et al., 2002). In the past decade, several studies have greatly contributed to the understanding of the origin and regulation of these specific precursors.

In humans and mice, monocytes/macrophages and DCs share a common precursor named macrophage–dendritic cell progenitor (MDP; Fig. 5.1), which has lost granulocytic potential and marks the stage of commitment to the MPS during development (Fogg et al., 2006). MDPs give rise to monocytes and a DC-restricted precursor termed common DC precursor

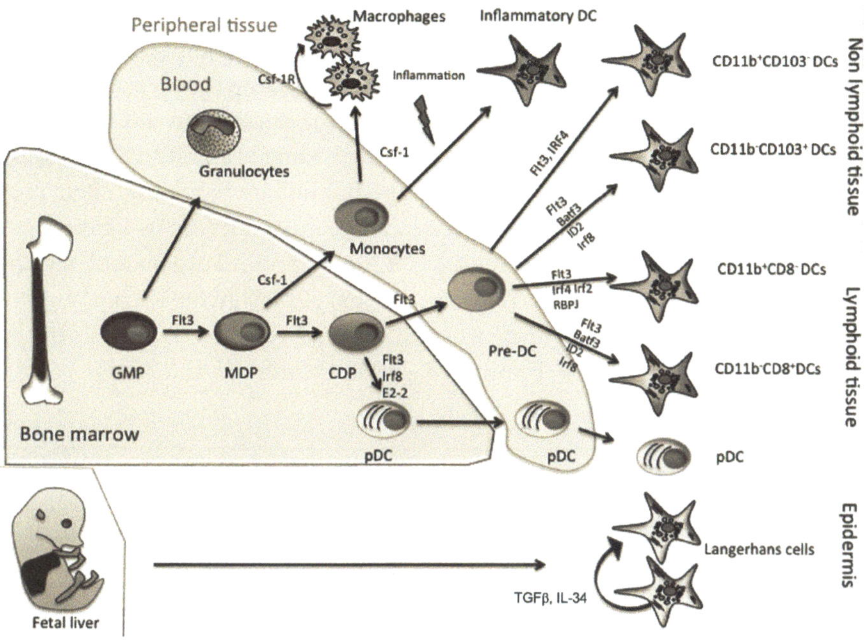

Figure 5.1 Origin and developmental regulation of the mononuclear phagocyte system (MPS) in mice: With the exemption of Langerhans cells, which derive from early embryonic progenitors in the fetal liver and maintain themselves locally throughout life, monocyte and dendritic cell subpopulations in lymphoid and nonlymphoid tissues share a common developmental origin arising from bone marrow-resident hematopoietic precursors. The lineage commitment to the MPS is thereby marked by the differentiation of the granulocyte and macrophage progenitors (GMP) to macrophage DC progenitors (MDP), which have lost granulocyte potential and exclusively give rise to monocytes and dendritic cells. MDPs differentiate into common DC progenitors, which give rise to pre-DCs and plasmacytoid DC (pDC) that egress the bone marrow after differentiation and mainly repopulate lymphoid tissues in the steady state. Circulating pre-DCs represent the common precursor also for all DC subpopulations within the lymphoid and nonlymphoid tissue. Transcription factors and cytokines involved in the regulation of specific differentiation pathways are indicated. (See color plate.)

or CDP. CDPs have lost monocyte–macrophage differential potential and give rise exclusively to pDCs and circulating precursors of classical DCs—the pre-DC (Liu et al., 2009; Naik et al., 2007; Onai et al., 2007)—which migrate to the tissue and differentiate into lymphoid tissue $CD4^{-}CD8\alpha^{+}$ and $CD4^{+}CD8\alpha^{-}$ DCs (Liu et al., 2009) and nonlymphoid tissue $CD103^{+}CD11b^{-}$ and $CD103^{+}CD11b^{+}$ DC (Bogunovic et al., 2009; Ginhoux et al., 2009). The commitment of hematopoietic progenitors to the DC lineage is strongly dependent on the receptor fms-like tyrosine kinase 3 (Flt3) and its ligand Flt3L as loss of Flt3 expression in these progenitors results in the loss of DC differentiation potential, whereas enforcement of its expression in Flt3-negative progenitors restores their DC potential (Merad & Manz, 2009). As depicted in the preceding text, Flt3 and its ligand also contribute to the homeostasis of peripheral DC by regulating their proliferation and survival in tissues. Mice lacking either Flt3 or its ligand have strongly reduced numbers of pDCs and DCs in lymphoid organs and peripheral tissues (Ginhoux et al., 2009; Waskow et al., 2008), whereas injection of Flt3L in mice and humans leads to substantial increase of these cells in the blood and different tissues (Fong et al., 2001; Manfra et al., 2003).

4. DC HETEROGENEITY

Due to their differential functional properties and their requirement of distinct transcription factors during development, lymphoid-resident and tissue-resident DCs can further be classified into two major subpopulations commonly distinguished based on the expression of different antigen or integrin on the cell surface (Miller et al., 2012). One subset of DC present in lymphoid and nonlymphoid tissue is dependent on the transcription factor inhibitor of DNA binding 2 (ID2), interferon-regulatory factor 8 (IRF8), and basic leucine zipper transcriptional factor ATF-like (BATF), and the second subpopulation differentiates independently of these factors in lymphoid and nonlymphoid tissue.

5. BATF–IRF8–ID2-DEPENDENT DC LINEAGE

Batf3$^{-/-}$ mice entirely lack a distinct population of DCs in LNs and spleen in steady state that express the CD8 antigen but not the CD11b integrin, or other macrophage markers, while CD8^{-} DCs in lymphoid tissues are unaffected (Hildner et al., 2008). CD8^{+} DCs account for 20–40% of total DC in lymphoid organs and are phenotypically immature in the steady state (Shortman & Heath, 2010). Besides Batf3, their differentiation is strongly dependent on Flt3l (Ginhoux et al., 2009), IRF8 (Schiavoni et al., 2002), and ID2 (Hacker et al., 2003). In addition, the mammalian target of rapamycin promotes the differentiation of CD8^{+} DC; while the loss of its negative regulator, the tumor suppressor gene PTEN leads to expansion of CD8^{+} cells in murine lymphoid tissue (Sathaliyawala et al., 2010).

In nonlymphoid tissues, the correlate to the lymphoid-resident $CD8^+$ DCs with regard to origin and function is represented by DCs expressing the integrin CD103 but lacking CD8 markers (Helft, Ginhoux, Bogunovic, & Merad, 2010). $CD103^+$ DCs populate most connective tissues and express low levels of CD11b or other macrophage marker. CD103 expression on DC is modulated by the tissue environment especially by local production of the cytokine Csf-2 (Edelson et al., 2011; Greter, Helft, et al., 2012; Zhan et al., 2011). Moreover, most $CD103^+$ cells express the C-type lectin receptor langerin with exception of intestinal $CD103^+$ cells (Merad, Ginhoux, & Collin, 2008).

$CD103^+CD11b^-$ nonlymphoid tissue DCs share the same differentiation requirements in terms of transcription factors and regulators as lymphoid-resident $CD8^+$ DCs (Edelson et al., 2010; Ginhoux et al., 2009). Their dependence on Flt3 during differentiation is even more pronounced as they are completely absent in Flt3-deficient bone marrow chimeras, while $CD8^+$ DCs are only reduced by one-third in lymphoid tissues (Ginhoux et al., 2009). It is important to note that in infected mice, tissue-resident $CD103^+$ DCs and $CD8^+$ lymphoid-resident DCs can still form in the absence of Batf3. The development of $Batf3^{-/-}$ $CD103^+$ and $CD8^+$ DC is dependent on the related transcription factors Batf and Batf2 that compensate for the lack of Batf3 in a cytokine-driven manner and mediate the physiological expansion of the DC subpopulations based on their common capacity to interact with other transcription factors such as IRF8 (Tussiwand et al., 2012).

In the intestine, an additional $CD103^+$ DC population resides in the lamina propria and displays high expression levels of CD11b. Lamina propria $CD103^+CD11b^+$ DCs develop independently of Batf3, IRF8, or ID2 and must therefore be regarded as a separate entity (M. Bogunovic and M. Merad (unpublished data); Edelson et al., 2010).

In addition to sharing the same precursor and differentiation program, lymphoid-resident $CD8^+$ DCs and tissue-resident $CD103^+CD11b^-$ DC share a similar transcriptome in the steady state (Miller et al., 2012). They express similar levels of pattern recognition receptors (e.g., high levels of the toll-like receptor TLR3) to sense double-stranded viral RNA and exhibit comparable repertoires of lectin-like receptors and distinct chemokine receptors (e.g., XCR1) (Hashimoto, Miller, & Merad, 2011).

Their phenotypical resemblance is mirrored by their common functional specialization. Batf3-dependent DCs excel in presenting microbial antigen and cell-associated antigen to $CD8^+$ T cells (Bedoui et al., 2009; den Haan,

Lehar, & Bevan, 2000; Helft et al., 2012; Hildner et al., 2008). Their critical and nonredundant role in the induction of a specific $CD8^+$ T-cell immune response is primarily based on their superior ability to cross present exogenously acquired antigen on MHCI molecules. $CD8^+$ DCs express, for instance, the GTPase Rac2 that restricts phagosomal protease activity, thus allowing the transfer of intact peptide to the cytosol for sufficient presentation on MHCI molecules (Savina et al., 2009). Besides, Batf3-dependent DCs are very potent producers of IL-12 and IL-15 (Mattei, Schiavoni, Belardelli, & Tough, 2001; Sung et al., 2006), two cytokines involved in the differentiation of cytotoxic $CD8^+$ T cells. Of note, Batf3-dependent DCs also exclusively express the chemokine receptor XCR1, which ligand XCL1 is produced by naive $CD8^+$ T cell establishing an additional link between these DC subpopulation and $CD8^+$ T cells (Dorner et al., 2009).

In addition to efficiently mounting a cytotoxic $CD8^+$ T-cell response to pathogens and tumor antigens, Batf3-dependent DCs have also been implicated in peripheral tolerance in the steady state by promoting deletional tolerance of antigen-specific CD8+ T cells (Qiu et al., 2009) and inducing antigen-specific regulatory T cells (Idoyaga et al., 2013).

6. BATF3–ID2–IRF8-INDEPENDENT DC LINEAGE

Although DCs of the Batf3–ID2–IRF8-independent lineage share high CD11b expression while lacking CD8 expression, they are phenotypically highly heterogeneous both in lymphoid tissue and in nonlymphoid tissue with regard to the expression of markers like CD103, CD172a, F4/80, and CX3CR1 (Helft et al., 2010). This heterogeneity is also reflected by a differential dependence on specific transcription factors, for example, IRF4, IFR 2, and RBPJ, and cytokines during differentiation. A significant portion of lymphoid $CD11b^+$ DCs, for instance, develop independently of Flt3 and Flt3L (McKenna et al., 2000; Waskow et al., 2008) and require the macrophage cytokine Csf-1 suggesting that $CD11b^+$ $MHCII^+$ $CD11c^+$ cells refer to mixed cell populations that likely contain macrophages and DCs (Bogunovic et al., 2009).

Given the diverse origins of $CD11b^+$ DCs, significant effort has recently been invested in further refining the phenotypical and functional subclassifications of this lineage. The expression of the high-affinity IgG receptor FcγRI, also termed CD64, and the macrophage marker Mertk differentiates $CD11b^+$ DCs from macrophages (Cerovic et al., 2013; Gautier et al., 2012; Langlet et al., 2012; Tamoutounour et al., 2012).

$CD11b^+$ DCs have been mainly implicated in MHCII presentation to $CD4^+$ T cells, which is in line with their enhanced expression of MHCII-antigenic pathway-associated proteins (Merad, Sathe, Helft, Miller, & Mortha, 2013). In an influenza infection model, $CD11b^+$ predominantly presents antigen to $CD4^+$ T cells *ex vivo* (Kim & Braciale, 2009). Moreover, antigen delivery specifically to $CD11b^+$ DCs induces a more efficient $CD4^+$ T-cell response *in vivo* in steady state than a CD8 T cell response. (Dudziak et al., 2007; Idoyaga et al., 2013).

7. MONOCYTE-DERIVED DCs AND INFLAMMATORY DCs

In vitro, human monocytes efficiently differentiate into DCs in the presence of Csf-2 (Sallusto & Lanzavecchia, 1994) and had therefore originally been considered to be the immediate precursor of all DC before this hypothesis was challenged by the discovery of the common DC progenitors, the CDPs (Onai et al., 2007).

During inflammation, however, monocytes do give rise to cells expressing intermediate levels of MHCII and CD11c (Dominguez & Ardavin, 2010). However, it remains unclear whether these cells represent bona fide DCs or rather constitute inflammatory antigen-presenting cells. In addition, evidence has accumulated over the last years that some inflammatory DCs might also directly derive from tissue-resident hematopoietic progenitors (Takizawa, Boettcher, & Manz, 2012).

8. THE LC EXCEPTION

LCs are DCs that reside in the outer layer of the epidermis of the skin. Phenotypically, LCs are characterized by lower MHCII expression levels, intermediate CD11c levels, and high expression of langerin (CD207), which is associated with the formation of characteristic intracytoplasmatic Birbeck granules. Moreover, LCs express the markers CD11b and F4/80, the sialoglycoprotein CD24, the adhesion molecule E-cadherin, and the epithelial cell adhesion molecule EpCAM and lack the chemokine receptor CX3CR1 (Borkowski, Nelson, Farr, & Udey, 1996; Merad et al., 2008; Stutte, Jux, Esser, & Forster, 2008; Tang, Amagai, Granger, Stanley, & Udey, 1993).

In contrast to all other DC populations, LCs do not arise from adult bone marrow-resident myeloid progenitor cell, but from embryonic precursors—mostly fetal liver-derived monocytes (Hoeffel et al., 2012) that populate the skin prior to birth and maintain themselves locally throughout life in steady-state conditions (Merad et al., 2002). However, upon severe inflammatory injury such as UV light exposure, LCs are replaced by circulating Gr-1^{hi} blood monocytes (Ginhoux et al., 2006). Nevertheless, it remains elusive if these blood-borne monocyte-derived LCs during inflammation are equivalent to steady-state LCs in terms of function and turnover in the tissue.

In line with their distinctive ontogeny compared to other DCs, LCs are independent of Flt3 and develop normally in Flt3 and Flt3L-deficient mice (Ginhoux et al., 2009) but require Csf-1 receptor (Csf-1R) for their development (Ginhoux et al., 2006). Strikingly, LC can still form in the absence of Csf-1 but fail to develop in the absence of IL-34, a recently identified cytokine in humans, mice, and birds shown to bind the Csf-1R with higher affinity than Csf-1 (Greter, Lelios, et al., 2012; Wang et al., 2012). These results are consistent with recent data showing that IL-34 is the only Csf-1R ligand expressed in the epidermis of mice and humans, whereas both Csf-1 and IL-34 are produced in mouse and human dermis (Greter, Lelios, et al., 2012). Interestingly, we found that IL-34 was not required for the recruitment and differentiation of monocytes into LCs in skin exposed to UV light but was required to maintain monocyte-derived LC in the epidermis once the inflammation resolves (Greter, Lelios, et al., 2012). In addition to IL-34, autocrine production of TGF-β controls LC homeostasis and is essential for the retention of LCs in the epidermal tissue (Bobr et al., 2012; Borkowski, Letterio, Farr, & Udey, 1996; Kaplan et al., 2007; Zahner et al., 2011).

The functional role of epidermal LCs during immune responses to pathogens and peripheral tolerance varies with regard to the type of inflammatory signal and its localization. One additional confounder hereby is certainly, especially in older studies, the insufficient discrimination of LC from other skin DCs, especially the langerin-expressing dermal $CD103^+$ DCs.

Upon *Candida albicans* infection, epidermal LCs fail to induce Th1 or $CD8^+$T-cell response in *C. albicans* infection model but promote strong Th17 differentiation (Igyarto et al., 2011). However, migratory LCs were also shown to mount a $CD4^+$T-cell response after immunization with recombinant hen egg lysozyme–MCC protein, although less efficient when dermal DCs were absent (Shklovskaya, Roediger, &

Fazekas de St Groth, 2008). Additionally, our group showed that host LCs are sufficient to prime allogeneic T-cell responses to induce skin graft-versus-host disease (Merad et al., 2004).

In the context of contact hypersensitivity, specific deletion of LCs resulted in enhanced immune responses (Kaplan, Jenison, Saeland, Shlomchik, & Shlomchik, 2005). These results are in line with human studies revealing a fundamental role of LCs in the homeostasis of skin-resident regulatory T cells (Seneschal, Clark, Gehad, Baecher-Allan, & Kupper, 2012),

9. THE HUMAN DC LINEAGE

The differentiation program and functional specializations of human DCs and their subpopulation are significantly less understood than those of their murine counterparts due to the limited accessibility to human tissue. It is mainly based on studies on skin and blood DCs or DC derived from tissue explants, obtained in the setting of specific pathologies like malignant transformation and/or chronic tissue injury that likely affect DC composition and biology.

Analogous to murine DCs, human DCs are defined as hematopoietic cells expressing high levels of MHCII and CD11c while lacking other specific lineage markers. In humans, however, CD11c seems to be more promiscuous as it is also expressed on most monocytes and macrophages (O'Doherty et al., 1994).

In the human blood, the two DC subsets are defined by either expression of the marker CD1c (also termed BDCA1) or CD141 (or BDCA3) (Dzionek et al., 2000; MacDonald et al., 2002). $CD141^+$ DCs only account for a minor population of DCs in the blood. CD1c+ and CD141+ DCs have also been identified not only in the human spleen and LN (McIlroy et al., 2001; Poulin et al., 2012; Segura et al., 2012; Velasquez-Lopera, Correa, & Garcia, 2008) but also in the bronchoalveolar lavage fluid, lung, tonsils, decidua, and kidney (Ban, Kong, Qu, Yang, & Ma, 2008; Demedts, Brusselle, Vermaelen, & Pauwels, 2005; Fiore et al., 2008; Haniffa et al., 2012; Jongbloed et al., 2010; Lindstedt, Lundberg, & Borrebaeck, 2005; Tsoumakidou, Tzanakis, Papadaki, Koutala, & Siafakas, 2006; Yu et al., 2013).

In human skin, DCs are present throughout the epidermal ad dermal layers. LCs in the human epidermis not only share the expression of CD45, MHCII, EpCAM, and langerin with their murine counterparts but also express high levels of CD1a, which is absent from murine LCs (Hunger et al., 2004; Valladeau et al., 1999). Earlier studies have showed that the dermis contains CD1a$^+$ CD14$^-$ DCs and the CD1a$^-$CD14$^+$ DCs (Nestle, Zheng, Thompson, Turka, & Nickoloff, 1993). Accumulated evidence suggests that the CD1a$^-$CD14$^+$ DCs do not represent a homogeneous DC population, but are contaminated by dermal macrophages that express CD163 in addition to CD14 (Zaba, Fuentes-Duculan, Steinman, Krueger, & Lowes, 2007). More recent studies revealed that the dermis also contains CD141$^+$ DCs that are related to CD141$^+$ DC identified in the blood, whereas CD1a+CD14$^-$ DCs also express CD1c and are related to circulating CD1c+ DCs the present suggest (Haniffa et al., 2012).

Interestingly, CD141$^+$ DCs uniquely express the markers XCR1 and Clec9A as well as high levels of TLR3, excel in the production of IL-12 and type 1 and type 3 interferon upon stimulation with a TLR3 agonist, and efficiently cross present cell-associated and soluble antigen to CD8$^+$ T cells, implying a phenotypical and functional proximity to murine CD8+ DCs (Bachem et al., 2010; Haniffa et al., 2012; Harman et al., 2013; Huysamen, Willment, Dennehy, & Brown, 2008; Lauterbach et al., 2010). This conclusion was supported by a recent gene chip meta-analysis of the transcriptome of human and murine DC subsets, which revealed a close relationship between human CD141$^+$ DC and murine CD8$^+$ DCs, while the transcriptome of human CD1c$^+$ DCs is more related to mouse CD11b$^+$ DCs (Robbins et al., 2008).

CD141$^+$ DCs also express Batf3 and IRF8, while lacking IRF4 (Robbins et al., 2008), and inhibition of Batf3 in cultures of human hematopoietic progenitors abolishes the differentiation of CD141$^+$ DCs but not CD1c$^+$ DCs (Poulin et al., 2012), implying also a similar regulation of human and murine DC subset differentiation. In contrast, specific IRF8 mutations in immunodeficient patients are associated either with a total absence of DCs and monocytes or with a depletion of blood CD1c$^+$ rather than CD141$^+$ DCs (Hambleton et al., 2011). Additionally, CD1c$^+$ DCs also seem to be able to produce high amount of IL-12 and to cross prime CD8$^+$ T cells (Mittag et al., 2011).

Taken together, these findings elucidate fundamental differences between human and murine DC subsets despite significant overlaps emphasizing the need of further detailed characterization of DC subsets and their biology in the human setting during steady state and pathology.

10. HUMAN HISTIOCYTOSES AS A RESULT OF DYSREGULATED DIFFERENTIATION OF THE HUMAN MYELOID COMPARTMENT

Histiocytic disorders are diseases arising from abnormal development or function of "histiocytes." Literal translation of *histiocyte* is "tissue cell." Although histiocyte refers only to tissue-resident DCs and macrophages, classification committees remain loyal to the archaic nomenclature for "histiocytosis" that is meant to encompass all cells of the mononuclear phagocytic system (Chu et al., 1987; Favara et al., 1997). Histiocytic diseases are characterized by presumed lineage and biological behavior into DC disorders, macrophage-related disorders, and malignant histiocytic disorders (Favara et al., 1997; Jaffe, Weiss, & Facchetti, 2005; Table 5.1). With the caveat that the phenotype of mononuclear phagocytes may be dynamic and influenced by environmental stimuli, the cellular origins of pathological histiocytes may be inferred according to cell-surface markers and histologic characteristics (Table 5.2; Fig. 5.1). The "histiocytic" umbrella therefore

Table 5.1 Classification of histiocytic disorders

Dendritic cell related
Langerhans cell histiocytosis
Juvenile xanthogranuloma/Erdheim–Chester disease
Macrophage related
Hemophagocytic syndromes
Primary hemophagocytic lymphohistiocytosis
Secondary hemophagocytic syndromes
Rosai–Dorfman disease
Malignant diseases
Monocyte-related leukemias
Extramedullary monocytic tumor (myeloid sarcoma)
Macrophage-related histiocytic sarcoma
Dendritic cell neoplasms (malignant histiocytosis)

For detailed review on the classification of histiocytosis, see references (Favara et al., 1997; Jaffe et al., 2005; Pileri et al., 2002).

Table 5.2 Phagocyte characteristics among histiocytic disorders

	Langerhans cell histiocytosis	**Juvenile xanthogranuloma**	**Erdheim–Chester disease**	**Rosai–Dorfman disease**	**Hemophagocytic lymphohistiocytosis**	**Malignant histiocytosis**
HLA-DR	++	−	−	+	+	+
CD1a	++	−	−	−	−	−
CD207 (langerin)	+++	−	−	−	−	−
Birbeck granules	+	−	−	−	−	−
CD14	+/−	++	++	++	++	−
CD68	+/−	++	++	++	++	+/−
CD163	−	−	−	++	++	−
Factor XIIIa	−	++	++	−	−	−
Fascin	−	++	++	+	+/−	++
Hemophagocytosis	+/−	−	−	−	+/−	−
Clonality	+ (−) in some adult pulmonary LCH	+	+/−	−	− reactive macrophages	+
BRAFV600E	57%[a]	+[b]	54%[c]	0%[a,c]		

[a]Badalian-Very et al. (2010).
[b]Unpublished observation.
[c]Haroche et al. (2012).

covers a wide range of disorders, from physiological reaction to pathological inflammatory stimuli to bona fide malignancy, with the common link of abnormal phagocytes. Understanding of the pathogenesis of histiocytic disorders and the identities of the myeloid culprits is advancing rapidly along with improved experimental technologies and molecular characterization of normal and pathological myelomonocytic populations.

10.1. Langerhans cell histiocytosis

10.1.1 Clinical overview

Langerhans cell histiocytosis (LCH), the most common histiocytic disease in humans, is estimated to occur in 5 children per million, which is similar incidence as acute myelogenous leukemia or Hodgkin lymphoma (Guyot-Goubin et al., 2008; Salotti et al., 2009; Stalemark et al., 2008). The majority of cases are in children, but LCH does occur *de novo* in approximately 1 adult per million (Baumgartner, von Hochstetter, Baumert, Luetolf, & Follath, 1997). The clinical presentations of LCH are highly variable, from a trivial self-resolving lesion to aggressive, life-threatening multisystem disease. Infrequent occurrence and overlapping presenting symptoms with more common pediatric conditions make LCH a challenging diagnosis to consider. However, once biopsy is performed, diagnosis is generally straightforward as inflammatory lesions with infiltrating CD1a+/CD207+ histiocytes are specific to LCH (Table 5.2; Fig. 5.2).

LCH is generally categorized according to extent of disease (single lesion vs. multifocal) and organ systems involved ("nonrisk" vs. lung, liver, spleen, or bone marrow "risk"). Lesions in the skull merit special consideration: Lesions of the facial bones and skull base are associated with increased risk of subsequent development of diabetes insipidus and other pituitary endocrinopathies as well as LCH-associated neurodegenerative disease (Grois et al., 2010). Overall survival was nearly 100% in patients with lesions limited to nonrisk organs, where 5-year survival was 74% for patients with risk organ involvement on the Histiocyte Society LCH-II trial (Gadner et al., 2008).

Due to incomplete understanding of the pathogenesis of LCH, treatment strategies have relied on empiric observation and cooperative clinical trials. Treatment for most isolated bony lesions is surgical resection or curettage. The current frontline standard of care for most children with multifocal, multisystem LCH is vinblastine and prednisone, though this strategy is poorly tolerated in adults (Cantu et al., 2012). Recurrent or refractory disease is relatively common, with one registry study reporting

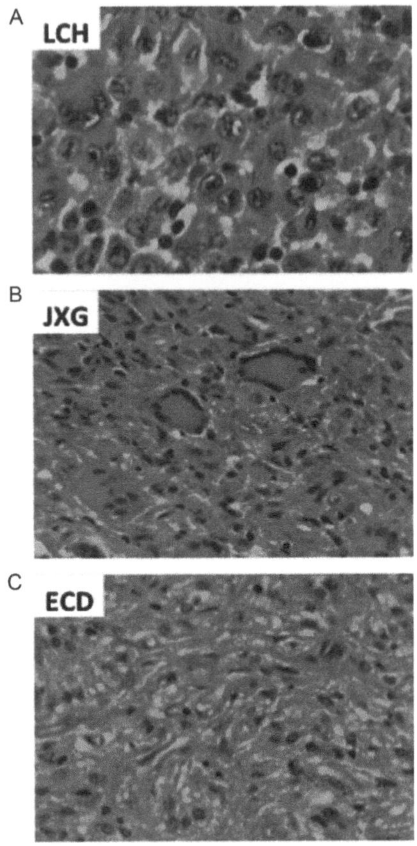

Figure 5.2 Histology of Langerhans cell histiocytosis, juvenile xanthogranuloma, and Erdheim–Chester lesions. (A) LCH: H&E stain demonstrates classic clusters of histiocytes with reniform nuclei with a background of mixed inflammatory cells, including lymphocytes, eosinophils, and macrophages. (B) JXG: Lesions are composed of smaller histiocytes with folded bland nuclei and vacuolated cytoplasm. Xanthomatous Touton giant cells (arrow) with a wreath of nuclei are observed in a majority of cases. An inflammatory infiltrate is also present. (C) ECD: ECD lesions may be histologically indistinguishable from JXG. Lesions are interogeneous with foamy histiocytes and an inflammatory infiltrate. *Images courtesy of Dr. John Hicks, Baylor College of Medicine.* (For color version of this figure, the reader is referred to the online version of this chapter.)

46% reactivation rate within five years of initial response to therapy in patients with multisystem LCH (Minkov et al., 2008). Many patients who fail to achieve a durable response to vinblastine/prednisone do respond to salvage therapies that include agents with efficacy in treatment of acute myelogenous leukemia, including cytarabine, cladribine, and clofarabine (Cantu et al., 2012; Egeler, de Kraker, & Voute, 1993; Rodriguez-Galindo, Jeng,

Khuu, McCarville, & Jeha, 2008; Weitzman et al., 2009). Some patients with progressive disease despite chemotherapy have been cured with allogeneic hematopoietic stem cell transplant (Akkari et al., 2003; Cooper et al., 2008; Steiner et al., 2005).

10.2. LCH pathogenesis

10.2.1 A brief history

LCH has a complicated history and remains an enigmatic disorder. What has come to be known as LCH first appeared in medical literature around the turn of the 1900s with reports of children with combinations of lytic bone lesions, mucosal lesions, and diabetes insipidus. Other case reports followed describing infants with hepatosplenomegaly, lymphadenopathy, and anemia along with lytic granulomatous bone lesions (reviewed in Arceci, 1999). Hand–Christian–Schüller disease came to describe patients with multifocal eosinophilic granulomas, and Letterer–Siwe disease described a fulminant, lethal disorder including histiocytic infiltration of bone marrow, liver, and spleen. In 1953, Dr. Lichtenstein observed common histology of the many eponymous classifications of what we now recognize as LCH and hypothesized that they represent a spectrum of a common disorder, which he proposed to be collectively named histiocytosis X (Lichtenstein, 1953). The "X" indicated incomplete knowledge of pathogenesis and cell of origin. With the advent of electron microscopy, Drs. Nezelof and Basset recognized a common cytoplasmic structure, the pentilaminar Birbeck granule, in both epidermal LCs and histiocytes in histiocytosis X lesions (Nezelof, Basset, & Rousseau, 1973). This disorder was then rebranded "Langerhans cell histiocytosis."

10.2.2 Genetic inheritance and LCH

One family registry study indicated that rare LCH patients may have first-degree relatives with LCH, though it is not clear if this is significantly greater than one would expect by chance. Interestingly, monozygotic twins were observed to share a higher risk of multisystem risk LCH than presumed fraternal twins (92% vs. 10%), which was interpreted as evidence for inherited risk factors (Arico, Scappatici, & Danesino, 2005). Common precursor cells in shared fetal circulation of monozygotic twins may also explain the observation. Of over 900 patients seen at the Texas Children's Histiocytosis Clinic, there have been only one family with nontwin sibling LCH patients and one with a parent and child both having LCH. While it remains plausible that potential risk alleles such as tumor necrosis factor gene promoter polymorphisms (McClain, Laud, Wu, & Pollack, 2003) or exposures such as parental occupational exposure to metal (Jubran, Marachelian, Dorey, & Malogolowkin, 2005) may be shared by siblings, Mendelian inheritance of penetrant LCH "genes" in the majority of cases seems unlikely. Additional reported associations from family studies that may inform LCH pathogenesis include increased risk of other cancers in LCH patients (Egeler et al., 1998) and increased risk of family history of thyroid disease (Bhatia et al., 1997).

10.3. Immunological disorder or cancer?

The designation "Langerhans cell" histiocytosis assumes a model in which LCH arises from aberrant epidermal LCs (Nezelof et al., 1973). Two possibilities for pathogenesis that have been considered and debated over the past decades include immune dysregulation versus malignant transformation of epidermal LCs.

10.3.1 Immune dysregulation in LCH

Examination of LCH biopsy under the microscope reveals a complex inflammatory process, and LCH lesions are often described as granulomas. In addition to the pathognomonic "Langerhans" cells, inflammatory infiltrate typically includes lymphocytes, macrophages, and eosinophils (Fig. 5.1). Despite early suggestions of a viral etiology for LCH, more recent investigations fail to identify LCH-associated pathogens (Jeziorski et al., 2008), and LCH patients have not been reported to have clinically evident immunodeficiency or specific susceptibility to infectious agents (Nezelof & Basset, 2004).

The lesional LCH cells have some features of immature epidermal LCs, including expression of high levels of the lectin langerin (CD207) and the antigen CD1a and lack of migration to draining LNs. However, like activated DCs, CD207+ cells that accumulate in LCH lesions express high levels of T-cell costimulatory molecules and proinflammatory cytokines (Allen et al., 2010; Geissmann et al., 2001; Laman, Leenen, Annels, Hogendoorn, & Egeler, 2003). Dozens of cytokines, chemokines, and cytokine and chemokine receptors have been hypothesized to play roles in LCH pathogenesis, though the mechanisms by which the pathological LCs orchestrate inflammation within the lesions remain to be fully defined (reviewed in Allen et al., 2010; Geissmann et al., 2001; Laman et al., 2003). In addition to the local "cytokine storm" within LCH lesions, many studies also report increased levels of plasma and serum proinflammatory cytokines and chemokines in patients with active LCH, including tumor necrosis factor alpha, soluble interleukin-2 receptor alpha, RANK ligand, and osteoprotegerin (Coury et al., 2008; Rosso et al., 2003; Rosso, Roy, Zelazko, & Braier, 2002). One study reported interleukin-17A (IL17A) production by LCH cells resulting in elevated systemic levels of IL17A, though this observation has not been reproduced (Allen & McClain, 2009; Coury et al., 2008; Makras et al., 2012; Peters, McClain, & Allen, 2011). Interestingly, regulatory $CD4^{+}CD25^{+}$ T cells (Tregs) are enriched in LCH lesions, and patients with LCH may have impaired skin delayed-type hypersensitivity responses (Senechal et al., 2007).

While immunological trigger for LCH remains to be proven, the immune function in patients with LCH is not normal, and inflammation accounts for many of the clinical manifestations of the disease. The clinical efficacy of thalidomide in some patients demonstrates the therapeutic potential for therapies targeting the inflammatory cascades set in motion by pathological DCs in LCH (McClain & Kozinetz, 2007).

10.3.2 LCH as a neoplastic disorder

In parallel with a search for an inflammatory etiology for LCH, investigators have examined the possibility that LCH may arise from malignant transformation of the epidermal LC. A major finding supporting the neoplastic hypothesis is the observation that CD1a+ cells from LCH lesions are clonal (Yu et al., 1994; Willman et al., 1994). An exception to this observation may be smoking-associated isolated pulmonary LCH in adults, where infiltrating histiocytes may be polyclonal (Yousem, Colby, Chen, Chen, & Weiss, 2001). Despite clonality, LCH is not a classic malignancy. The pathological DCs do not appear dysplastic. Mitoses are rarely seen in LCH lesions, with Ki67 positive by immunohistochemistry in fewer than 2% of cells (Senechal et al., 2007). It is also possible that clonality represents reactive proliferation of a local progenitor, as regional clonality has been shown in normal epidermal LCs under physiological conditions (Merad et al., 2002; Waskow et al., 2008). Cells from LCH lesions are not viable without growth factor *in vitro*, and no successful xenograft models have been reported (Nezelof & Basset, 2004). Karyotypes from LCH biopsies are typically normal. While genetic lesions have been reported in some cases of LCH, a study using array CGH and single-nucleotide polymorphism arrays with DNA from purified CD1a+ LCH lesion cells failed to identify gross chromosomal abnormalities (da Costa et al., 2009). While no recurrent genetic deletions or translocations have been reported, the activating *BRAFV600E* point mutation was discovered in the majority of a series of LCH lesions, further supporting classification of LCH as a myeloid neoplastic disorder (Badalian-Very et al., 2010).

Adding to the complexity of deciphering the pathogenesis of LCH, as biological understanding has LCH evolved, so have the definitions of "cancer" (Hanahan & Weinberg, 2011). Some "hallmarks of cancer" observed in LCH include mutated *BRAF*, (Badalian-Very et al., 2010), avoiding immune destruction through increased Treg infiltrate and TGF production (Allen et al., 2010; Egeler, Favara, van Meurs, Laman, & Claassen, 1999; Favara & Steele, 1997; Senechal et al., 2007), tumor-promoting inflammation through local and systemic cytokine storm (Allen et al., 2010; Laman et al., 2003), activating invasion and metastasis through expression of metalloproteases (Allen et al., 2010; da Costa et al., 2005; Hayashi et al., 1997), and resisting cell death through overexpression of *BCL21* and *BAX* by CD207+ cells (Allen et al., 2010; Amir & Weintraub, 2008; Schouten et al., 2002).

10.4. Cousins of LCH: juvenile xanthogranuloma and Erdheim–Chester Disease

10.4.1 Juvenile xanthogranuloma

Juvenile xanthogranuloma (JXG) is a histiocytic disorder, most common in early childhood, characterized by lesions composed of cells phenotypically similar to the dermal dendrocyte: $CD14^+$, $CD68^+$, $fascin^+$, and factor $XIIIa^+$ (Figure 5.2, Table 5.2). The lipid-laden multinucleated "Touton" giant cells have a characteristic macrophage morphology (Fig. 5.2). The incidence is not proven, but may be estimated at 1 case per million children (Janssen & Harms, 2005). JXG typically manifests as self-limited skin lesions in the neck, trunk, and head. However, almost any organ system can be involved, including orbit and brain (Dehner, 2003). Skin lesions in children generally resolve spontaneously over time. However, large retroperitoneal masses, liver lesions, bone marrow involvement, or brain tumors may be progressive and potentially life-threatening. LCH-based chemotherapy strategies have been effective in some patients with systemic JXG (Stover, Alapati, Regueira, Turner, & Whitlock, 2008).

The etiology of JXG and basis for prevalence in children and tissue distribution is not known. In a single patient, HUMARA assay analysis of a single lesion suggested the cells (90% histiocytes) were clonal (Janssen, Folster-Holst, Harms, & Klapper, 2007). Interesting associations have been reported between patients with JXG, neurofibromatosis (types 1 and 2), and juvenile chronic myelogenous leukemia that potentially implicates Ras pathway hyperactivity as shared pathogenesis among these hematologic disorders (Iyengar, Golomb, & Schachner, 1998; Tan & Tay, 1998; Winh & Sweet, 2002).

10.4.2 Erdheim–Chester disease

Erdheim–Chester disease (ECD) is an extremely rare histiocytic disorder of adults, with fewer than 500 cases reported in the literature. Histologically, ECD can be indistinguishable from the foamy macrophages of JXG: CD14+, CD68+, CD1a−, and CD207− (Figure 5.2, Table 5.2) (Winh & Sweet, 2002). Patients with ECD develop characteristic multifocal osteosclerotic lesions of long bones and may also develop extraskeletal histiocytic infiltrates at other sites. Like LCH, patients may develop pituitary involvement with diabetes insipidus. Retroperitoneal, renal, and cardiac involvement are unique features of ECD. Mean survival from time of diagnosis is 3 years (Veyssier-Belot et al., 1996).

As with LCH and JXG, the etiology of ECD remains elusive. Lesions have characteristic inflammatory infiltrate. Proinflammatory cytokines are expressed within ECD lesions, and increased expression of IFN-α, interleukin-6, interleukin-12, and monocyte chemotactic protein-1 has been observed in serum from ECD patients, interpreted as a systemic Th1 response (Arnaud et al., 2011; Stoppacciaro et al., 2006). Therapy with interferon-alpha (IFN-α) or recombinant interleukin-1 receptor-α (IL-1Rα) has been effective in some patients. Like LCH, significant cellular proliferation is not observed within ECD lesions (Stoppacciaro et al., 2006). Results from clonality studies are mixed with reports of monoclonal and polyclonal pathological histiocytes within lesions (Al-Quran, Reith, Bradley, & Rimsza, 2002; Chetritt et al., 1999; Vencio et al., 2007). Differences may be due to technical issues or possibly disease subgroups. The recent finding of frequent *BRAFV600E* mutations in the majority of ECD patients is consistent with a common precursor cell in patients with the somatic mutation (Haroche et al., 2012). *BRAFV600E* in ECD may also indicate common mechanisms of pathogenesis with LCH.

10.4.3 BRAF in histiocytic diseases

The activating mutation *BRAFV600E* had first been described in 57% of LCH lesions in cohort of patients with different manifestations of LCH (Badalian-Very et al., 2010) Subsequently, these findings were confirmed in a second cohort showing an enrichment of the mutation enriched in the $CD1a^{+}$ fraction of the lesions and extended by the identification of two additional potential activating *BRAF* mutations (Kansal et al., 2013; Satoh et al., 2012) BRAF is a central kinase of the RAS/RAF/MEK pathway, which is essentially involved in numerous cell functions including cell proliferation and migration and is frequently mutated in cancer cells (Davies et al., 2002). The *BRAFV600E* mutation leads to a constitutive activation of the downstream kinases extracellular signal-regulated kinase (ERK) and mitogen-activated protein kinase/ERK kinase (MEK) (Maurer, Tarkowski, & Baccarini, 2011). Both downstream kinases are highly activated in LCH cells as shown by immunofluorescence staining supporting the functional relevance of the mutation in LCH cells (Badalian-Very et al., 2010). Besides LCH, *BRAF* mutations are common in lesions of patients with the ECD (54% of all lesions analyzed), but have not yet been reported in other histiocytoses (Haroche et al., 2012). We have identified *BRAFV600E* in lesions from two patients with combined LCH and JXG (unpublished). However, further studies with extended samples sizes are required to establish the role of specific *BRAF* mutations or other oncogenic mutations in the spectrum of histiocytic disorders.

Not only does the identification of *BRAF* mutations in LCH and ECD support a neoplastic origin of these histiocytoses and further understanding of their pathophysiology, it also sets the stage for new therapeutic strategies. Specific BRAF inhibition has been shown to be highly efficient in the treatment of BRAFV600E-expressing malignancies, for example, melanoma and hairy-cell leukemia (Bollag et al., 2010; Dietrich et al., 2012). A very recent case report on the treatment of three patients with advanced multisystemic ECD with concurrent LCH with the BRAF inhibitor vemurafenib documented dramatic therapeutic response rate within the first months of treatment (Haroche et al., 2013). However, it remains to be proven if these responses are sustained or only transient, as frequently observed in the treatment of melanoma with BRAF inhibitors (Poulikakos & Rosen, 2011). Moreover, although no major adverse events occurred during the brief courses of the treatment in this small study (Haroche et al., 2013), large-scale trials in melanoma with prolonged treatment protocols report complex side effect profile including minor grade events (e.g., arthralgia, fatigue, and pruritus) and severe reactions (e.g., rashes and the development of cutaneous squamous cell carcinoma) (da Rocha Dias et al., 2013). A detailed risk–benefit calculation will be essential to determine LCH patients for whom BRAF inhibition would be an appropriate therapy, especially considering the young age of most patients, minimal toxicity of current chemotherapy, and relatively low mortality from LCH. Strategies to specifically target downstream pathways, such as MEK inhibition, may decrease the overall risks for these patients. We advocate the use of targeted inhibition in the context of clinical trials to prove efficacy and safety of BRAF inhibitory approaches in the treatment of advanced ECD and LCH.

10.5. Inflammatory myeloid neoplasms: histiocytic diseases arise from misguided myeloid precursors

The cell of origin of LCH has been assumed to be the epidermal LC, and models for pathogenesis have focused on maturation, activation, or transformation of this cell. However, the transcriptome of CD207$^+$ cells from LCH lesions is most consistent with an immature myeloid DC phenotype relative to the control epidermal LC (CD207$^+$) transcriptome (Allen et al., 2010). Furthermore, expression of CD207 in mice and humans is more promiscuous than initially anticipated (Chikwava & Jaffe, 2004; Ginhoux et al., 2007; Helft et al., 2010; Poulin et al., 2007; Segerer et al., 2008), opening up the possibility that LCH could arise from a number of lineages. Intriguingly, CD207$^+$ DCs are detected in the steady state within the same lymphoid and nonlymphoid tissues where LCH lesions arise, in contrast to the restricted tropism for epidermis and LN of the LC. Furthermore, DC maturation may be heterogeneous within lesions, with variable CD1a+/ CD207− subpopulations (Chikwava & Jaffe, 2004; Coury et al., 2008; Peters et al., 2011). Extended immunofluorescence staining with BRAFV600E-specific antibodies also revealed that the mutations are not entirely limited to CD207$^+$ cells within the lesions, but could be detected in CD207$^-$ cells (Sahm et al., 2012). These observations are essential in the understanding of the origin of LCH cells, as epidermal LCs and other CD207$^+$ DCs do not share a common ontogenetic program. Reports of patients with concurrent or serial histiocytic lesions of more than one phenotype also support the potential for a common precursor for LCH, JXG, and ECD (Haroche et al., 2013; Hoeger, Diaz, Malone, Pritchard, & Harper, 2001; Patrizi et al., 2004; Tsai, Tsou, Hung, Wu, & Chang, 2010).

As discussed in the preceding text, LCs derive from fetal liver monocytes (Hoeffel et al., 2012) populating the skin prior to birth and maintain themselves locally throughout life in steady-state conditions (Merad et al., 2002), whereas CD207$^+$ DCs outside the epidermis arise from circulating precursors known as pre-DCs (Naik et al., 2007). Together, these observations support a model of LCH pathogenesis in which accumulation of langerin^{+} cells in the lesions arises from dysregulated differentiation and/or recruitment of precursor cells of the DC lineage than proliferation or accumulation of dysregulated mature epidermal LCs.

Given new discoveries in DC biology and pathogenesis of histiocytic disorders, we propose that the "inflammation versus malignancy" debate for LCH may be misguided. LCH and JXG and ECD have both inflammatory and neoplastic characteristics. We hypothesize that *BRAFV600E* or other stimuli may influence lineage commitment, migration, and proliferation of myeloid DC precursors. Once precursors migrate to sites of lesions, they recruit and activate "bystander" cells in the inflammatory lesions that define the diseases. We therefore propose that LCH, JXG, and ECD be classified as *inflammatory myeloid neoplasms.*

11. CONCLUSION AND PERSPECTIVE

In mice and humans, DCs comprise a heterogeneous group of phagocytic active, antigen-presenting cells with distinct origin, differentiation, and functional specialization in steady state and inflammation. In the recent decade, evidence has accumulated strongly supporting the hypothesis that the disease complex of human histiocytosis represents the pathophysiological consequence of a dysregulated differentiation of the myeloid lineage greatly contributing to the understanding of the pathophysiology and diversity of histiocytosis.

The identification of the oncogenic mutation *BRAFV600E* in LCH and ECD, along with increasing evidence for a clonal DC precursor, prompts us to propose a reclassification of these diseases as *inflammatory myeloid neoplasms* and opens new perspectives for functional studies and therapeutic strategies. Future studies of histiocytic disorders will dissect the functional consequences of the mutations for DC differentiation, maturation, and effector function that will inform our understanding of physiological DC biology and also elucidate novel diagnostic and therapeutic strategies for patients.

ACKNOWLEDGMENTS

The authors would like to thank Dr. M. John Hicks for biopsy images and Dr. Kenneth McClain for critical review and helpful discussions. CEA is supported in part by the National Institutes of Health R01 (CA154489) and has no financial conflicts to disclose. MLB is supported in part by a grant of the German Research Association (Deutsche Forschungsgemeinschaft, BE 4818/1-1). MM is supported by NIH grants CA154947A AI10008 AI089987.

REFERENCES

Akkari, V., Donadieu, J., Piguet, C., Bordigoni, P., Michel, G., Blanche, S., et al. (2003). Hematopoietic stem cell transplantation in patients with severe Langerhans cell histiocytosis and hematological dysfunction: Experience of the French Langerhans Cell Study Group. *Bone Marrow Transplantation, 31*(12), 1097–1103.

Al-Quran, S., Reith, J., Bradley, J., & Rimsza, L. (2002). Erdheim–Chester disease: Case report, PCR-based analysis of clonality, and review of literature. *Modern Pathology, 15*(6), 666–672.

Allen, C. E., Li, L., Peters, T. L., Leung, H. C., Yu, A., Man, T. K., et al. (2010). Cell-specific gene expression in Langerhans cell histiocytosis lesions reveals a distinct profile compared with epidermal Langerhans cells. *Journal of Immunology, 184*(8), 4557–4567.

Allen, C. E., & McClain, K. L. (2009). Interleukin-17A is not expressed by CD207(+) cells in Langerhans cell histiocytosis lesions. *Nature Medicine, 15*(5), 483–484.

Amir, G., & Weintraub, M. (2008). Association of cell cycle-related gene products and NF-kappaB with clinical parameters in Langerhans cell histiocytosis. *Pediatric Blood & Cancer, 50*(2), 304–307.

Arceci, R. J. (1999). The histiocytoses: The fall of the Tower of Babel. *European Journal of Cancer, 35*(5), 747–767.

Arico, M., Scappatici, S., & Danesino, C. (2005). The genetics of Langerhans cell histiocytosis. In S. Weitzman & R. M. Egeler (Eds.), *Histiocytic disorders of children and adults* (pp. 83–94). Cambridge: Cambridge Press.

Arnaud, L., Gorochov, G., Charlotte, F., Lvovschi, V., Parizot, C., Larsen, M., et al. (2011). Systemic perturbation of cytokine and chemokine networks in Erdheim–Chester disease: A single-center series of 37 patients. *Blood, 117*(10), 2783–2790.

Bachem, A., Guttler, S., Hartung, E., Ebstein, F., Schaefer, M., Tannert, A., et al. (2010). Superior antigen cross-presentation and XCR1 expression define human CD11c+CD141+ cells as homologues of mouse CD8+ dendritic cells. *The Journal of Experimental Medicine, 207*(6), 1273–1281.

Badalian-Very, G., Vergilio, J. A., Degar, B. A., MacConaill, L. E., Brandner, B., Calicchio, M. L., et al. (2010). Recurrent BRAF mutations in Langerhans cell histiocytosis. *Blood, 116*(11), 1919–1923.

Ban, Y. L., Kong, B. H., Qu, X., Yang, Q. F., & Ma, Y. Y. (2008). BDCA-1+, BDCA-2+ and BDCA-3+ dendritic cells in early human pregnancy decidua. *Clinical and Experimental Immunology, 151*(3), 399–406.

Baumgartner, I., von Hochstetter, A., Baumert, B., Luetolf, U., & Follath, F. (1997). Langerhans'-cell histiocytosis in adults. *Medical and Pediatric Oncology, 28*(1), 9–14.

Bedoui, S., Whitney, P. G., Waithman, J., Eidsmo, L., Wakim, L., Caminschi, I., et al. (2009). Cross-presentation of viral and self antigens by skin-derived CD103+ dendritic cells. *Nature Immunology, 10*(5), 488–495.

Bhatia, S., Nesbit, M. E., Jr., Egeler, R. M., Buckley, J. D., Mertens, A., & Robison, L. L. (1997). Epidemiologic study of Langerhans cell histiocytosis in children. *Journal of Pediatrics, 130*(5), 774–784.

Bobr, A., Igyarto, B. Z., Haley, K. M., Li, M. O., Flavell, R. A., & Kaplan, D. H. (2012). Autocrine/paracrine TGF-beta1 inhibits Langerhans cell migration. *Proceedings of the National Academy of Sciences of the United States of America, 109*(26), 10492–10497.

Bogunovic, M., Ginhoux, F., Helft, J., Shang, L., Hashimoto, D., Greter, M., et al. (2009). Origin of the lamina propria dendritic cell network. *Immunity, 31*(3), 513–525.

Bollag, G., Hirth, P., Tsai, J., Zhang, J., Ibrahim, P. N., Cho, H., et al. (2010). Clinical efficacy of a RAF inhibitor needs broad target blockade in BRAF-mutant melanoma. *Nature, 467*(7315), 596–599.

Borkowski, T. A., Letterio, J. J., Farr, A. G., & Udey, M. C. (1996). A role for endogenous transforming growth factor beta 1 in Langerhans cell biology: The skin of transforming

growth factor beta 1 null mice is devoid of epidermal Langerhans cells. *The Journal of Experimental Medicine*, *184*(6), 2417–2422.
Borkowski, T. A., Nelson, A. J., Farr, A. G., & Udey, M. C. (1996). Expression of gp40, the murine homologue of human epithelial cell adhesion molecule (Ep-CAM), by murine dendritic cells. *European Journal of Immunology*, *26*(1), 110–114.
Cantu, M. A., Lupo, P. J., Bilgi, M., Hicks, M. J., Allen, C. E., & McClain, K. L. (2012). Optimal therapy for adults with Langerhans cell histiocytosis bone lesions. *PLoS One*, 7(8), e43257.
Cerovic, V., Houston, S. A., Scott, C. L., Aumeunier, A., Yrlid, U., Mowat, A. M., et al. (2013). Intestinal CD103(−) dendritic cells migrate in lymph and prime effector T cells. *Mucosal Immunology*, *6*(1), 104–113.
Chetritt, J., Paradis, V., Dargere, D., Adle-Biassette, H., Maurage, C. A., Mussini, J. M., et al. (1999). Chester–Erdheim disease: A neoplastic disorder. *Human Pathology*, *30*(9), 1093–1096.
Chikwava, K., & Jaffe, R. (2004). Langerin (CD207) staining in normal pediatric tissues, reactive lymph nodes, and childhood histiocytic disorders. *Pediatric and Developmental Pathology: The Official Journal of the Society for Pediatric Pathology and the Paediatric Pathology Society*, 7(6), 607–614.
Chu, T., D'Angio, G. J., Favara, B. E., Ladisch, S., Nesbit, M., & Pritchard, J. (1987). Histiocytosis syndromes in children. *Lancet*, *2*(8549), 41–42.
Cooper, N., Rao, K., Goulden, N., Webb, D., Amrolia, P., & Veys, P. (2008). The use of reduced-intensity stem cell transplantation in haemophagocytic lymphohistiocytosis and Langerhans cell histiocytosis. *Bone Marrow Transplantation*, *42*(Suppl 2), S47–S50.
Coury, F., Annels, N., Rivollier, A., Olsson, S., Santoro, A., Speziani, C., et al. (2008). Langerhans cell histiocytosis reveals a new IL-17A-dependent pathway of dendritic cell fusion. *Nature Medicine*, *14*(1), 81–87.
da Costa, C. E., Annels, N. E., Faaij, C. M., Forsyth, R. G., Hogendoorn, P. C., & Egeler, R. M. (2005). Presence of osteoclast-like multinucleated giant cells in the bone and nonostotic lesions of Langerhans cell histiocytosis. *The Journal of Experimental Medicine*, *201*(5), 687–693.
da Costa, C. E., Szuhai, K., van Eijk, R., Hoogeboom, M., Sciot, R., Mertens, F., et al. (2009). No genomic aberrations in Langerhans cell histiocytosis as assessed by diverse molecular technologies. *Genes, Chromosomes & Cancer*, *48*(3), 239–249.
da Rocha Dias, S., Salmonson, T., van Zwieten-Boot, B., Jonsson, B., Marchetti, S., Schellens, J. H., et al. (2013). The European Medicines Agency review of vemurafenib (Zelboraf(R)) for the treatment of adult patients with BRAF V600 mutation-positive unresectable or metastatic melanoma: Summary of the scientific assessment of the Committee for Medicinal Products for Human Use. *European Journal of Cancer*, *49*(7), 1654–1661.
Davies, H., Bignell, G. R., Cox, C., Stephens, P., Edkins, S., Clegg, S., et al. (2002). Mutations of the BRAF gene in human cancer. *Nature*, *417*(6892), 949–954.
Dehner, L. P. (2003). Juvenile xanthogranulomas in the first two decades of life: A clinicopathologic study of 174 cases with cutaneous and extracutaneous manifestations. *The American Journal of Surgical Pathology*, *27*(5), 579–593.
Demedts, I. K., Brusselle, G. G., Vermaelen, K. Y., & Pauwels, R. A. (2005). Identification and characterization of human pulmonary dendritic cells. *American Journal of Respiratory Cell and Molecular Biology*, *32*(3), 177–184.
den Haan, J. M., Lehar, S. M., & Bevan, M. J. (2000). CD8(+) but not CD8(−) dendritic cells cross-prime cytotoxic T cells in vivo. *The Journal of Experimental Medicine*, *192*(12), 1685–1696.
Dietrich, S., Glimm, H., Andrulis, M., von Kalle, C., Ho, A. D., & Zenz, T. (2012). BRAF inhibition in refractory hairy-cell leukemia. *The New England Journal of Medicine*, *366*(21), 2038–2040.

Dominguez, P. M., & Ardavin, C. (2010). Differentiation and function of mouse monocyte-derived dendritic cells in steady state and inflammation. *Immunological Reviews*, *234*(1), 90–104.
Dorner, B. G., Dorner, M. B., Zhou, X., Opitz, C., Mora, A., Guttler, S., et al. (2009). Selective expression of the chemokine receptor XCR1 on cross-presenting dendritic cells determines cooperation with CD8+ T cells. *Immunity*, *31*(5), 823–833.
Dudziak, D., Kamphorst, A. O., Heidkamp, G. F., Buchholz, V. R., Trumpfheller, C., Yamazaki, S., et al. (2007). Differential antigen processing by dendritic cell subsets in vivo. *Science*, *315*(5808), 107–111.
Dzionek, A., Fuchs, A., Schmidt, P., Cremer, S., Zysk, M., Miltenyi, S., et al. (2000). BDCA-2, BDCA-3, and BDCA-4: Three markers for distinct subsets of dendritic cells in human peripheral blood. *Journal of Immunology*, *165*(11), 6037–6046.
Edelson, B. T., Bradstreet, T. R., Kc, W., Hildner, K., Herzog, J. W., Sim, J., et al. (2011). Batf3-dependent CD11b(low/−) peripheral dendritic cells are GM-CSF-independent and are not required for Th cell priming after subcutaneous immunization. *PLoS One*, *6*(10), e25660.
Edelson, B. T., Kc, W., Juang, R., Kohyama, M., Benoit, L. A., Klekotka, P. A., et al. (2010). Peripheral CD103+ dendritic cells form a unified subset developmentally related to CD8alpha+ conventional dendritic cells. *The Journal of Experimental Medicine*, *207*(4), 823–836.
Egeler, R. M., de Kraker, J., & Voute, P. A. (1993). Cytosine-arabinoside, vincristine, and prednisolone in the treatment of children with disseminated Langerhans cell histiocytosis with organ dysfunction: Experience at a single institution. *Medical and Pediatric Oncology*, *21*(4), 265–270.
Egeler, R. M., Favara, B. E., van Meurs, M., Laman, J. D., & Claassen, E. (1999). Differential In situ cytokine profiles of Langerhans-like cells and T cells in Langerhans cell histiocytosis: Abundant expression of cytokines relevant to disease and treatment. *Blood*, *94*(12), 4195–4201.
Egeler, R. M., Neglia, J. P., Arico, M., Favara, B. E., Heitger, A., Nesbit, M. E., et al. (1998). The relation of Langerhans cell histiocytosis to acute leukemia, lymphomas, and other solid tumors. The LCH-Malignancy Study Group of the Histiocyte Society. *Hematology/Oncology Clinics of North America*, *12*(2), 369–378.
Favara, B. E., Feller, A. C., Pauli, M., Jaffe, E. S., Weiss, L. M., Arico, M., et al. (1997). Contemporary classification of histiocytic disorders. The WHO committee on histiocytic/reticulum cell proliferations. Reclassification working group of the histiocyte society. *Medical and Pediatric Oncology*, *29*(3), 157–166.
Favara, B. E., & Steele, A. (1997). Langerhans cell histiocytosis of lymph nodes: A morphological assessment of 43 biopsies. *Pediatric Pathology & Laboratory Medicine*, *17*(5), 769–787.
Fiore, N., Castellano, G., Blasi, A., Capobianco, C., Loverre, A., Montinaro, V., et al. (2008). Immature myeloid and plasmacytoid dendritic cells infiltrate renal tubulointerstitium in patients with lupus nephritis. *Molecular Immunology*, *45*(1), 259–265.
Fogg, D. K., Sibon, C., Miled, C., Jung, S., Aucouturier, P., Littman, D. R., et al. (2006). A clonogenic bone marrow progenitor specific for macrophages and dendritic cells. *Science*, *311*(5757), 83–87.
Fong, L., Hou, Y., Rivas, A., Benike, C., Yuen, A., Fisher, G. A., et al. (2001). Altered peptide ligand vaccination with Flt3 ligand expanded dendritic cells for tumor immunotherapy. *Proceedings of the National Academy of Sciences of the United States of America*, *98*(15), 8809–8814.
Gadner, H., Grois, N., Potschger, U., Minkov, M., Arico, M., Braier, J., et al. (2008). Improved outcome in multisystem Langerhans cell histiocytosis is associated with therapy intensification. *Blood*, *111*(5), 2556–2562.

Gautier, E. L., Shay, T., Miller, J., Greter, M., Jakubzick, C., Ivanov, S., et al. (2012). Gene-expression profiles and transcriptional regulatory pathways that underlie the identity and diversity of mouse tissue macrophages. *Nature Immunology*, *13*(11), 1118–1128.

Geissmann, F., Lepelletier, Y., Fraitag, S., Valladeau, J., Bodemer, C., Debre, M., et al. (2001). Differentiation of Langerhans cells in Langerhans cell histiocytosis. *Blood*, *97*(5), 1241–1248.

Ginhoux, F., Collin, M. P., Bogunovic, M., Abel, M., Leboeuf, M., Helft, J., et al. (2007). Blood-derived dermal langerin+ dendritic cells survey the skin in the steady state. *The Journal of Experimental Medicine*, *204*(13), 3133–3146.

Ginhoux, F., Liu, K., Helft, J., Bogunovic, M., Greter, M., Hashimoto, D., et al. (2009). The origin and development of nonlymphoid tissue CD103+ DCs. *The Journal of Experimental Medicine*, *206*(13), 3115–3130.

Ginhoux, F., Tacke, F., Angeli, V., Bogunovic, M., Loubeau, M., Dai, X. M., et al. (2006). Langerhans cells arise from monocytes in vivo. *Nature Immunology*, 7(3), 265–273.

Greter, M., Helft, J., Chow, A., Hashimoto, D., Mortha, A., Agudo-Cantero, J., et al. (2012). GM-CSF controls nonlymphoid tissue dendritic cell homeostasis but is dispensable for the differentiation of inflammatory dendritic cells. *Immunity*, *36*(6), 1031–1046.

Greter, M., Lelios, I., Pelczar, P., Hoeffel, G., Price, J., Leboeuf, M., et al. (2012). Stroma-derived interleukin-34 controls the development and maintenance of langerhans cells and the maintenance of microglia. *Immunity*, *37*(6), 1050–1060.

Grois, N., Fahrner, B., Arceci, R. J., Henter, J. I., McClain, K., Lassmann, H., et al. (2010). Central nervous system disease in Langerhans cell histiocytosis. *Journal of Pediatrics*, *156*(6), 873–881.

Guyot-Goubin, A., Donadieu, J., Barkaoui, M., Bellec, S., Thomas, C., & Clavel, J. (2008). Descriptive epidemiology of childhood Langerhans cell histiocytosis in France, 2000–2004. *Pediatric Blood & Cancer*, *51*(1), 71–75.

Hacker, C., Kirsch, R. D., Ju, X. S., Hieronymus, T., Gust, T. C., Kuhl, C., et al. (2003). Transcriptional profiling identifies Id2 function in dendritic cell development. *Nature Immunology*, *4*(4), 380–386.

Hambleton, S., Salem, S., Bustamante, J., Bigley, V., Boisson-Dupuis, S., Azevedo, J., et al. (2011). IRF8 mutations and human dendritic-cell immunodeficiency. *The New England Journal of Medicine*, *365*(2), 127–138.

Hanahan, D., & Weinberg, R. A. (2011). Hallmarks of cancer: The next generation. *Cell*, *144*(5), 646–674.

Haniffa, M., Shin, A., Bigley, V., McGovern, N., Teo, P., See, P., et al. (2012). Human tissues contain CD141hi cross-presenting dendritic cells with functional homology to mouse CD103+ nonlymphoid dendritic cells. *Immunity*, *37*(1), 60–73.

Harman, A. N., Bye, C. R., Nasr, N., Sandgren, K. J., Kim, M., Mercier, S. K., et al. (2013). Identification of lineage relationships and novel markers of blood and skin human dendritic cells. *Journal of Immunology*, *190*(1), 66–79.

Haroche, J., Charlotte, F., Arnaud, L., von Deimling, A., Helias-Rodzewicz, Z., Hervier, B., et al. (2012). High prevalence of BRAF V600E mutations in Erdheim–Chester disease but not in other non-Langerhans cell histiocytoses. *Blood*, *120*(13), 2700–2703.

Haroche, J., Cohen-Aubart, F., Emile, J. F., Arnaud, L., Maksud, P., Charlotte, F., et al. (2013). Dramatic efficacy of vemurafenib in both multisystemic and refractory Erdheim–Chester disease and Langerhans cell histiocytosis harboring the BRAF V600E mutation. *Blood*, *121*(9), 1495–1500.

Hashimoto, D., Miller, J., & Merad, M. (2011). Dendritic cell and macrophage heterogeneity in vivo. *Immunity*, *35*(3), 323–335.

Hayashi, T., Rush, W. L., Travis, W. D., Liotta, L. A., Stetler-Stevenson, W. G., & Ferrans, V. J. (1997). Immunohistochemical study of matrix metalloproteinases and their

tissue inhibitors in pulmonary Langerhans' cell granulomatosis. *Archives of Pathology & Laboratory Medicine, 121*(9), 930–937.
Helft, J., Ginhoux, F., Bogunovic, M., & Merad, M. (2010). Origin and functional heterogeneity of non-lymphoid tissue dendritic cells in mice. *Immunological Reviews, 234*(1), 55–75.
Helft, J., Manicassamy, B., Guermonprez, P., Hashimoto, D., Silvin, A., Agudo, J., et al. (2012). Cross-presenting CD103+ dendritic cells are protected from influenza virus infection. *The Journal of Clinical Investigation, 122*(11), 4037–4047.
Hildner, K., Edelson, B. T., Purtha, W. E., Diamond, M., Matsushita, H., Kohyama, M., et al. (2008). Batf3 deficiency reveals a critical role for CD8alpha+ dendritic cells in cytotoxic T cell immunity. *Science, 322*(5904), 1097–1100.
Hirata, Y., Egea, L., Dann, S. M., Eckmann, L., & Kagnoff, M. F. (2010). GM-CSF-facilitated dendritic cell recruitment and survival govern the intestinal mucosal response to a mouse enteric bacterial pathogen. *Cell Host & Microbe*, 7(2), 151–163.
Hoeffel, G., Wang, Y., Greter, M., See, P., Teo, P., Malleret, B., et al. (2012). Adult Langerhans cells derive predominantly from embryonic fetal liver monocytes with a minor contribution of yolk sac-derived macrophages. *The Journal of Experimental Medicine, 209*(6), 1167–1181.
Hoeger, P. H., Diaz, C., Malone, M., Pritchard, J., & Harper, J. I. (2001). Juvenile xanthogranuloma as a sequel to Langerhans cell histiocytosis: A report of three cases. *Journal of Clinical and Experimental Dermatology, 26*(5), 391–394.
Hunger, R. E., Sieling, P. A., Ochoa, M. T., Sugaya, M., Burdick, A. E., Rea, T. H., et al. (2004). Langerhans cells utilize CD1a and langerin to efficiently present nonpeptide antigens to T cells. *The Journal of Clinical Investigation, 113*(5), 701–708.
Huysamen, C., Willment, J. A., Dennehy, K. M., & Brown, G. D. (2008). CLEC9A is a novel activation C-type lectin-like receptor expressed on BDCA3+ dendritic cells and a subset of monocytes. *The Journal of Biological Chemistry, 283*(24), 16693–16701.
Idoyaga, J., Fiorese, C., Zbytnuik, L., Lubkin, A., Miller, J., Malissen, B., et al. (2013). Specialized role of migratory dendritic cells in peripheral tolerance induction. *The Journal of Clinical Investigation, 123*(2), 844–854.
Igyarto, B. Z., Haley, K., Ortner, D., Bobr, A., Gerami-Nejad, M., Edelson, B. T., et al. (2011). Skin-resident murine dendritic cell subsets promote distinct and opposing antigen-specific T helper cell responses. *Immunity, 35*(2), 260–272.
Iyengar, V., Golomb, C. A., & Schachner, L. (1998). Neurilemmomatosis, NF2, and juvenile xanthogranuloma. *Journal of the American Academy of Dermatology, 39*(5 Pt 2), 831–834.
Jaffe, R., Weiss, L. M., & Facchetti, F. (2005). *Tumors derived from Langerhans cells.* Lyon: IARC Press p. 358.
Janssen, D., Folster-Holst, R., Harms, D., & Klapper, W. (2007). Clonality in juvenile xanthogranuloma. *The American Journal of Surgical Pathology, 31*(5), 812–813.
Janssen, D., & Harms, D. (2005). Juvenile xanthogranuloma in childhood and adolescence: A clinicopathologic study of 129 patients from the Kiel pediatric tumor registry. *The American Journal of Surgical Pathology, 29*(1), 21–28.
Jeziorski, E., Senechal, B., Molina, T. J., Devez, F., Leruez-Ville, M., Morand, P., et al. (2008). Herpes-virus infection in patients with Langerhans cell histiocytosis: A case-controlled sero-epidemiological study, and in situ analysis. *PLoS One, 3*(9), e3262.
Jongbloed, S. L., Kassianos, A. J., McDonald, K. J., Clark, G. J., Ju, X., Angel, C. E., et al. (2010). Human CD141+ (BDCA-3)+ dendritic cells (DCs) represent a unique myeloid DC subset that cross-presents necrotic cell antigens. *The Journal of Experimental Medicine, 207*(6), 1247–1260.
Jubran, R. F., Marachelian, A., Dorey, F., & Malogolowkin, M. (2005). Predictors of outcome in children with Langerhans cell histiocytosis. *Pediatric Blood & Cancer, 45*(1), 37–42.

Kabashima, K., Banks, T. A., Ansel, K. M., Lu, T. T., Ware, C. F., & Cyster, J. G. (2005). Intrinsic lymphotoxin-beta receptor requirement for homeostasis of lymphoid tissue dendritic cells. *Immunity*, *22*(4), 439–450.

Kansal, R., Quintanilla-Martinez, L., Datta, V., Lopategui, J., Garshfield, G., & Nathwani, B. N. (2013). Identification of the V600D mutation in Exon 15 of the BRAF oncogene in congenital, benign langerhans cell histiocytosis. *Genes, Chromosomes & Cancer*, *52*(1), 99–106.

Kaplan, D. H., Jenison, M. C., Saeland, S., Shlomchik, W. D., & Shlomchik, M. J. (2005). Epidermal langerhans cell-deficient mice develop enhanced contact hypersensitivity. *Immunity*, *23*(6), 611–620.

Kaplan, D. H., Li, M. O., Jenison, M. C., Shlomchik, W. D., Flavell, R. A., & Shlomchik, M. J. (2007). Autocrine/paracrine TGFbeta1 is required for the development of epidermal Langerhans cells. *The Journal of Experimental Medicine*, *204*(11), 2545–2552.

Kim, T. S., & Braciale, T. J. (2009). Respiratory dendritic cell subsets differ in their capacity to support the induction of virus-specific cytotoxic CD8+ T cell responses. *PLoS One*, *4*(1), e4204.

Laman, J. D., Leenen, P. J., Annels, N. E., Hogendoorn, P. C., & Egeler, R. M. (2003). Langerhans-cell histiocytosis 'insight into DC biology'. *Trends in Immunology*, *24*(4), 190–196.

Langlet, C., Tamoutounour, S., Henri, S., Luche, H., Ardouin, L., Gregoire, C., et al. (2012). CD64 expression distinguishes monocyte-derived and conventional dendritic cells and reveals their distinct role during intramuscular immunization. *Journal of Immunology*, *188*(4), 1751–1760.

Lauterbach, H., Bathke, B., Gilles, S., Traidl-Hoffmann, C., Luber, C. A., Fejer, G., et al. (2010). Mouse CD8alpha+ DCs and human BDCA3+ DCs are major producers of IFN-lambda in response to poly IC. *The Journal of Experimental Medicine*, *207*(12), 2703–2717.

Lichtenstein, L. (1953). Histiocytosis X: Integration of eosinophilic granuloma of bone, Letterer–Siwe disease, and Schuller–Christian disease as related manifestations of a single nosologic entity. *A.M.A. Archives of Pathology*, *56*(1), 84–102.

Lindstedt, M., Lundberg, K., & Borrebaeck, C. A. (2005). Gene family clustering identifies functionally associated subsets of human in vivo blood and tonsillar dendritic cells. *Journal of Immunology*, *175*(8), 4839–4846.

Linz, B., Balloux, F., Moodley, Y., Manica, A., Liu, H., Roumagnac, P., et al. (2007). An African origin for the intimate association between humans and *Helicobacter pylori*. *Nature*, *445*(7130), 915–918.

Liu, K., Victora, G. D., Schwickert, T. A., Guermonprez, P., Meredith, M. M., Yao, K., et al. (2009). In vivo analysis of dendritic cell development and homeostasis. *Science*, *324*(5925), 392–397.

Liu, K., Waskow, C., Liu, X., Yao, K., Hoh, J., & Nussenzweig, M. (2007). Origin of dendritic cells in peripheral lymphoid organs of mice. *Nature Immunology*, *8*(6), 578–583.

MacDonald, K. P., Munster, D. J., Clark, G. J., Dzionek, A., Schmitz, J., & Hart, D. N. (2002). Characterization of human blood dendritic cell subsets. *Blood*, *100*(13), 4512–4520.

Makras, P., Polyzos, S. A., Anastasilakis, A. D., Terpos, E., Papatheodorou, A., & Kaltsas, G. A. (2012). Is serum IL-17A a useful systemic biomarker in patients with Langerhans cell histiocytosis? *Molecular Therapy*, *20*(1), 6–7.

Manfra, D. J., Chen, S. C., Jensen, K. K., Fine, J. S., Wiekowski, M. T., & Lira, S. A. (2003). Conditional expression of murine Flt3 ligand leads to expansion of multiple dendritic cell subsets in peripheral blood and tissues of transgenic mice. *Journal of Immunology*, *170*(6), 2843–2852.

Mattei, F., Schiavoni, G., Belardelli, F., & Tough, D. F. (2001). IL-15 is expressed by dendritic cells in response to type I IFN, double-stranded RNA, or lipopolysaccharide and promotes dendritic cell activation. *Journal of Immunology*, *167*(3), 1179–1187.
Maurer, G., Tarkowski, B., & Baccarini, M. (2011). Raf kinases in cancer-roles and therapeutic opportunities. *Oncogene*, *30*(32), 3477–3488.
McClain, K. L., & Kozinetz, C. A. (2007). A phase II trial using thalidomide for Langerhans cell histiocytosis. *Pediatric Blood & Cancer*, *48*(1), 44–49.
McClain, K. L., Laud, P., Wu, W. S., & Pollack, M. S. (2003). Langerhans cell histiocytosis patients have HLA Cw7 and DR4 types associated with specific clinical presentations and no increased frequency in polymorphisms of the tumor necrosis factor alpha promoter. *Medical and Pediatric Oncology*, *41*(6), 502–507.
McIlroy, D., Troadec, C., Grassi, F., Samri, A., Barrou, B., Autran, B., et al. (2001). Investigation of human spleen dendritic cell phenotype and distribution reveals evidence of in vivo activation in a subset of organ donors. *Blood*, *97*(11), 3470–3477.
McKenna, H. J., Stocking, K. L., Miller, R. E., Brasel, K., De Smedt, T., Maraskovsky, E., et al. (2000). Mice lacking flt3 ligand have deficient hematopoiesis affecting hematopoietic progenitor cells, dendritic cells, and natural killer cells. *Blood*, *95*(11), 3489–3497.
Mellman, I., & Steinman, R. M. (2001). Dendritic cells: Specialized and regulated antigen processing machines. *Cell*, *106*(3), 255–258.
Merad, M., Ginhoux, F., & Collin, M. (2008). Origin, homeostasis and function of Langerhans cells and other langerin-expressing dendritic cells. *Nature Reviews Immunology*, *8*(12), 935–947.
Merad, M., Hoffmann, P., Ranheim, E., Slaymaker, S., Manz, M. G., Lira, S. A., et al. (2004). Depletion of host Langerhans cells before transplantation of donor alloreactive T cells prevents skin graft-versus-host disease. *Nature Medicine*, *10*(5), 510–517.
Merad, M., & Manz, M. G. (2009). Dendritic cell homeostasis. *Blood*, *113*(15), 3418–3427.
Merad, M., Manz, M. G., Karsunky, H., Wagers, A., Peters, W., Charo, I., et al. (2002). Langerhans cells renew in the skin throughout life under steady-state conditions. *Nature Immunology*, *3*(12), 1135–1141.
Merad, M., Sathe, P., Helft, J., Miller, J., & Mortha, A. (2013). The dendritic cell lineage: Ontogeny and function of dendritic cells and their subsets in the steady state and the inflamed setting. *Annual Review of Immunology*, *31*, 563–604.
Meredith, M. M., Liu, K., Darrasse-Jeze, G., Kamphorst, A. O., Schreiber, H. A., Guermonprez, P., et al. (2012). Expression of the zinc finger transcription factor zDC (Zbtb46, Btbd4) defines the classical dendritic cell lineage. *The Journal of Experimental Medicine*, *209*(6), 1153–1165.
Miller, J. C., Brown, B. D., Shay, T., Gautier, E. L., Jojic, V., Cohain, A., et al. (2012). Deciphering the transcriptional network of the dendritic cell lineage. *Nature Immunology*, *13*(9), 888–899.
Minkov, M., Steiner, M., Potschger, U., Arico, M., Braier, J., Donadieu, J., et al. (2008). Reactivations in multisystem Langerhans cell histiocytosis: Data of the international LCH registry. *Journal of Pediatrics*, *153*(5), 700–705.
Mittag, D., Proietto, A. I., Loudovaris, T., Mannering, S. I., Vremec, D., Shortman, K., et al. (2011). Human dendritic cell subsets from spleen and blood are similar in phenotype and function but modified by donor health status. *Journal of Immunology*, *186*(11), 6207–6217.
Naik, S. H., Sathe, P., Park, H. Y., Metcalf, D., Proietto, A. I., Dakic, A., et al. (2007). Development of plasmacytoid and conventional dendritic cell subtypes from single precursor cells derived in vitro and in vivo. *Nature Immunology*, *8*(11), 1217–1226.
Nestle, F. O., Zheng, X. G., Thompson, C. B., Turka, L. A., & Nickoloff, B. J. (1993). Characterization of dermal dendritic cells obtained from normal human skin reveals phenotypic and functionally distinctive subsets. *Journal of Immunology*, *151*(11), 6535–6545.

Nezelof, C., & Basset, F. (2004). An hypothesis Langerhans cell histiocytosis: The failure of the immune system to switch from an innate to an adaptive mode. *Pediatric Blood & Cancer*, *42*(5), 398–400.
Nezelof, C., Basset, F., & Rousseau, M. F. (1973). Histiocytosis X histogenetic arguments for a Langerhans cell origin. *Biomedicine*, *18*(5), 365–371.
O'Doherty, U., Peng, M., Gezelter, S., Swiggard, W. J., Betjes, M., Bhardwaj, N., et al. (1994). Human blood contains two subsets of dendritic cells, one immunologically mature and the other immature. *Immunology*, *82*(3), 487–493.
Ohl, L., Mohaupt, M., Czeloth, N., Hintzen, G., Kiafard, Z., Zwirner, J., et al. (2004). CCR7 governs skin dendritic cell migration under inflammatory and steady-state conditions. *Immunity*, *21*(2), 279–288.
Onai, N., Obata-Onai, A., Schmid, M. A., Ohteki, T., Jarrossay, D., & Manz, M. G. (2007). Identification of clonogenic common Flt3+M-CSFR+ plasmacytoid and conventional dendritic cell progenitors in mouse bone marrow. *Nature Immunology*, *8*(11), 1207–1216.
Patrizi, A., Neri, I., Bianchi, F., Guerrini, V., Misciali, C., Paone, G., et al. (2004). Langerhans cell histiocytosis and juvenile xanthogranuloma. Two case reports. *Dermatology*, *209*(1), 57–61.
Peters, T. L., McClain, K. L., & Allen, C. E. (2011). Neither IL-17A mRNA nor IL-17A protein are detectable in Langerhans cell histiocytosis lesions. *Molecular Therapy*, *19*(8), 1433–1439.
Pileri, S. A., Grogan, T. M., Harris, N. L., Banks, P., Campo, E., Chan, J. K., et al. (2002). Tumours of histiocytes and accessory dendritic cells: An immunohistochemical approach to classification from the International Lymphoma Study Group based on 61 cases. *Histopathology*, *41*(1), 1–29.
Poulikakos, P. I., & Rosen, N. (2011). Mutant BRAF melanomas—Dependence and resistance. *Cancer Cell*, *19*(1), 11–15.
Poulin, L. F., Henri, S., de Bovis, B., Devilard, E., Kissenpfennig, A., & Malissen, B. (2007). The dermis contains langerin+ dendritic cells that develop and function independently of epidermal Langerhans cells. *The Journal of Experimental Medicine*, *204*(13), 3119–3131.
Poulin, L. F., Reyal, Y., Uronen-Hansson, H., Schraml, B. U., Sancho, D., Murphy, K. M., et al. (2012). DNGR-1 is a specific and universal marker of mouse and human Batf3-dependent dendritic cells in lymphoid and nonlymphoid tissues. *Blood*, *119*(25), 6052–6062.
Qiu, C. H., Miyake, Y., Kaise, H., Kitamura, H., Ohara, O., & Tanaka, M. (2009). Novel subset of CD8{alpha}+ dendritic cells localized in the marginal zone is responsible for tolerance to cell-associated antigens. *Journal of Immunology*, *182*(7), 4127–4136.
Randolph, G. J., Angeli, V., & Swartz, M. A. (2005). Dendritic-cell trafficking to lymph nodes through lymphatic vessels. *Nature Reviews Immunology*, *5*(8), 617–628.
Reizis, B. (2010). Regulation of plasmacytoid dendritic cell development. *Current Opinion in Immunology*, *22*(2), 206–211.
Robbins, S. H., Walzer, T., Dembele, D., Thibault, C., Defays, A., Bessou, G., et al. (2008). Novel insights into the relationships between dendritic cell subsets in human and mouse revealed by genome-wide expression profiling. *Genome Biology*, *9*(1), R17.
Rodriguez-Galindo, C., Jeng, M., Khuu, P., McCarville, M. B., & Jeha, S. (2008). Clofarabine in refractory Langerhans cell histiocytosis. *Pediatric Blood & Cancer*, *51*(5), 703–706.
Rosso, D. A., Ripoli, M. F., Roy, A., Diez, R. A., Zelazko, M. E., & Braier, J. L. (2003). Serum levels of interleukin-1 receptor antagonist and tumor necrosis factor-alpha are elevated in children with Langerhans cell histiocytosis. *Journal of Pediatric Hematology/Oncology*, *25*(6), 480–483.

Rosso, D. A., Roy, A., Zelazko, M., & Braier, J. L. (2002). Prognostic value of soluble interleukin 2 receptor levels in Langerhans cell histiocytosis. *British Journal of Haematology, 117*(1), 54–58.
Sahm, F., Capper, D., Preusser, M., Meyer, J., Stenzinger, A., Lasitschka, F., et al. (2012). BRAFV600E mutant protein is expressed in cells of variable maturation in Langerhans cell histiocytosis. *Blood, 120*(12), e28–e34.
Sallusto, F., & Lanzavecchia, A. (1994). Efficient presentation of soluble antigen by cultured human dendritic cells is maintained by granulocyte/macrophage colony-stimulating factor plus interleukin 4 and downregulated by tumor necrosis factor alpha. *The Journal of Experimental Medicine, 179*(4), 1109–1118.
Salotti, J. A., Nanduri, V., Pearce, M. S., Parker, L., Lynn, R., & Windebank, K. P. (2009). Incidence and clinical features of Langerhans cell histiocytosis in the UK and Ireland. *Archives of Disease in Childhood, 94*(5), 376–380.
Sathaliyawala, T., O'Gorman, W. E., Greter, M., Bogunovic, M., Konjufca, V., Hou, Z. E., et al. (2010). Mammalian target of rapamycin controls dendritic cell development downstream of Flt3 ligand signaling. *Immunity, 33*(4), 597–606.
Satoh, T., Smith, A., Sarde, A., Lu, H. C., Mian, S., Trouillet, C., et al. (2012). B-RAF mutant alleles associated with Langerhans cell histiocytosis, a granulomatous pediatric disease. *PLoS One*, 7(4), e33891.
Satpathy, A. T., KC, W., Albring, J. C., Edelson, B. T., Kretzer, N. M., Bhattacharya, D., et al. (2012). Zbtb46 expression distinguishes classical dendritic cells and their committed progenitors from other immune lineages. *Journal of Experimental Medicine, 209*, 1135–1152.
Savina, A., Peres, A., Cebrian, I., Carmo, N., Moita, C., Hacohen, N., et al. (2009). The small GTPase Rac2 controls phagosomal alkalinization and antigen crosspresentation selectively in CD8(+) dendritic cells. *Immunity, 30*(4), 544–555.
Schiavoni, G., Mattei, F., Sestili, P., Borghi, P., Venditti, M., Morse, H. C., 3rd., et al. (2002). ICSBP is essential for the development of mouse type I interferon-producing cells and for the generation and activation of CD8alpha(+) dendritic cells. *The Journal of Experimental Medicine, 196*(11), 1415–1425.
Schouten, B., Egeler, R. M., Leenen, P. J., Taminiau, A. H., van den Broek, L. J., & Hogendoorn, P. C. (2002). Expression of cell cycle-related gene products in Langerhans cell histiocytosis. *Journal of Pediatric Hematology/Oncology, 24*(9), 727–732.
Segerer, S., Heller, F., Lindenmeyer, M. T., Schmid, H., Cohen, C. D., Draganovici, D., et al. (2008). Compartment specific expression of dendritic cell markers in human glomerulonephritis. *Kidney International, 74*(1), 37–46.
Segura, E., Valladeau-Guilemond, J., Donnadieu, M. H., Sastre-Garau, X., Soumelis, V., & Amigorena, S. (2012). Characterization of resident and migratory dendritic cells in human lymph nodes. *The Journal of Experimental Medicine, 209*(4), 653–660.
Senechal, B., Elain, G., Jeziorski, E., Grondin, V., Patey-Mariaud de, S. N., Jaubert, F., et al. (2007). Expansion of regulatory T cells in patients with Langerhans cell histiocytosis. *PLoS Medicine, 4*(8), e253.
Seneschal, J., Clark, R. A., Gehad, A., Baecher-Allan, C. M., & Kupper, T. S. (2012). Human epidermal Langerhans cells maintain immune homeostasis in skin by activating skin resident regulatory T cells. *Immunity, 36*(5), 873–884.
Shklovskaya, E., Roediger, B., & Fazekas de St Groth, B. (2008). Epidermal and dermal dendritic cells display differential activation and migratory behavior while sharing the ability to stimulate CD4+ T cell proliferation in vivo. *Journal of Immunology, 181*(1), 418–430.
Shortman, K., & Heath, W. R. (2010). The CD8+ dendritic cell subset. *Immunological Reviews, 234*(1), 18–31.
Singh, G., Hashimoto, D., Yan, X., Helft, J., Park, P. J., Ma, G., et al. (2012). R-Ras is required for murine dendritic cell maturation and CD4+ T-cell priming. *Blood, 119*(7), 1693–1701.

Stalemark, H., Laurencikas, E., Karis, J., Gavhed, D., Fadeel, B., & Henter, J. I. (2008). Incidence of Langerhans cell histiocytosis in children: A population-based study. *Pediatric Blood & Cancer, 51*(1), 76–81.

Steiner, M., Matthes-Martin, S., Attarbaschi, A., Minkov, M., Grois, N., Unger, E., et al. (2005). Improved outcome of treatment-resistant high-risk Langerhans cell histiocytosis after allogeneic stem cell transplantation with reduced-intensity conditioning. *Bone Marrow Transplantation, 36*(3), 215–225.

Steinman, R. M., & Cohn, Z. A. (1973). Identification of a novel cell type in peripheral lymphoid organs of mice. I. Morphology, quantitation, tissue distribution. *The Journal of Experimental Medicine, 137*(5), 1142–1162.

Steinman, R. M., & Cohn, Z. A. (1974). Identification of a novel cell type in peripheral lymphoid organs of mice. II. Functional properties in vitro. *The Journal of Experimental Medicine, 139*(2), 380–397.

Steinman, R. M., Hawiger, D., & Nussenzweig, M. C. (2003). Tolerogenic dendritic cells. *Annual Review of Immunology, 21*, 685–711.

Stoppacciaro, A., Ferrarini, M., Salmaggi, C., Colarossi, C., Praderio, L., Tresoldi, M., et al. (2006). Immunohistochemical evidence of a cytokine and chemokine network in three patients with Erdheim–Chester disease: Implications for pathogenesis. *Arthritis and Rheumatism, 54*(12), 4018–4022.

Stover, D. G., Alapati, S., Regueira, O., Turner, C., & Whitlock, J. A. (2008). Treatment of juvenile xanthogranuloma. *Pediatric Blood & Cancer, 51*(1), 130–133.

Stutte, S., Jux, B., Esser, C., & Forster, I. (2008). CD24a expression levels discriminate Langerhans cells from dermal dendritic cells in murine skin and lymph nodes. *The Journal of Investigative Dermatology, 128*(6), 1470–1475.

Sung, S. S., Fu, S. M., Rose, C. E., Jr., Gaskin, F., Ju, S. T., & Beaty, S. R. (2006). A major lung CD103 (alphaE)-beta7 integrin-positive epithelial dendritic cell population expressing Langerin and tight junction proteins. *Journal of Immunology, 176*(4), 2161–2172.

Takizawa, H., Boettcher, S., & Manz, M. G. (2012). Demand-adapted regulation of early hematopoiesis in infection and inflammation. *Blood, 119*(13), 2991–3002.

Tamoutounour, S., Henri, S., Lelouard, H., de Bovis, B., de Haar, C., van der Woude, C. J., et al. (2012). CD64 distinguishes macrophages from dendritic cells in the gut and reveals the Th1-inducing role of mesenteric lymph node macrophages during colitis. *European Journal of Immunology, 42*(12), 3150–3166.

Tan, H. H., & Tay, Y. K. (1998). Juvenile xanthogranuloma and neurofibromatosis 1. *Dermatology, 197*(1), 43–44.

Tang, A., Amagai, M., Granger, L. G., Stanley, J. R., & Udey, M. C. (1993). Adhesion of epidermal Langerhans cells to keratinocytes mediated by E-cadherin. *Nature, 361*(6407), 82–85.

Tsai, J. W., Tsou, J. H., Hung, L. Y., Wu, H. B., & Chang, K. C. (2010). Combined Erdheim–Chester disease and Langerhans cell histiocytosis of skin are both monoclonal: A rare case with human androgen-receptor gene analysis. *Journal of the American Academy of Dermatology, 63*(2), 284–291.

Tsoumakidou, M., Tzanakis, N., Papadaki, H. A., Koutala, H., & Siafakas, N. M. (2006). Isolation of myeloid and plasmacytoid dendritic cells from human bronchoalveolar lavage fluid. *Immunology & Cell Biology, 84*(3), 267–273.

Tussiwand, R., Lee, W. L., Murphy, T. L., Mashayekhi, M., Wumesh, K. C., Albring, J. C., et al. (2012). Compensatory dendritic cell development mediated by BATF–IRF interactions. *Nature, 490*(7421), 502–507.

Valladeau, J., Duvert-Frances, V., Pin, J. J., Dezutter-Dambuyant, C., Vincent, C., Massacrier, C., et al. (1999). The monoclonal antibody DCGM4 recognizes Langerin, a protein specific of Langerhans cells, and is rapidly internalized from the cell surface. *European Journal of Immunology, 29*(9), 2695–2704.

Velasquez-Lopera, M. M., Correa, L. A., & Garcia, L. F. (2008). Human spleen contains different subsets of dendritic cells and regulatory T lymphocytes. *Clinical and Experimental Immunology*, *154*(1), 107–114.
Vencio, E. F., Jenkins, R. B., Schiller, J. L., Huynh, T. V., Wenger, D. D., Inwards, C. Y., et al. (2007). Clonal cytogenetic abnormalities in Erdheim–Chester disease. *The American Journal of Surgical Pathology*, *31*(2), 319–321.
Veyssier-Belot, C., Cacoub, P., Caparros-Lefebvre, D., Wechsler, J., Brun, B., Remy, M., et al. (1996). Erdheim–Chester disease. Clinical and radiologic characteristics of 59 cases. *Medicine*, *75*(3), 157–169.
Wang, Y., Szretter, K. J., Vermi, W., Gilfillan, S., Rossini, C., Cella, M., et al. (2012). IL-34 is a tissue-restricted ligand of CSF1R required for the development of Langerhans cells and microglia. *Nature Immunology*, *13*(8), 753–760.
Waskow, C., Liu, K., Darrasse-Jeze, G., Guermonprez, P., Ginhoux, F., Merad, M., et al. (2008). The receptor tyrosine kinase Flt3 is required for dendritic cell development in peripheral lymphoid tissues. *Nature Immunology*, *9*(6), 676–683.
Weitzman, S., Braier, J., Donadieu, J., Egeler, R. M., Grois, N., Ladisch, S., et al. (2009). 2′-Chlorodeoxyadenosine (2-CdA) as salvage therapy for Langerhans cell histiocytosis (LCH). Results of the LCH-S-98 protocol of the Histiocyte Society. *Pediatric Blood & Cancer*, *53*(7), 1271–1276.
Willman, C. L., Busque, L., Griffith, B. B., Favara, B. E., McClain, K. L., Duncan, M. H., et al. (1994). Langerhans'-cell histiocytosis (histiocytosis X)–a clonal proliferative disease. *New England Journal of Medicine*, *331*, 154–160.
Winh, T. N., & Sweet, D. E. (2002). Erdheim–Chester disease. In C. D. M. Fletcher, K. K. Unni, & F. Mertens (Eds.), *World Health Organization Classification of tumours: Pathology and genetics of tumours of the soft tissue and bone* (p. 347). Lyon: IARC Press.
Yousem, S. A., Colby, T. V., Chen, Y. Y., Chen, W. G., & Weiss, L. M. (2001). Pulmonary Langerhans' cell histiocytosis: Molecular analysis of clonality. *The American Journal of Surgical Pathology*, *25*(5), 630–636.
Yu, C. I., Becker, C., Wang, Y., Marches, F., Helft, J., Leboeuf, M., et al. (2013). Human CD1c+ dendritic cells drive the differentiation of CD103+ CD8+ mucosal effector T cells via the cytokine TGF-beta. *Immunity*, *38*(4), 818–830.
Yu, R. C., Chu, C., Buluwela, L., & Chu, A. C. (1994). Clonal proliferation of Langerhans cells in Langerhans cell histiocytosis. *Lancet*, *343*, 767–768.
Zaba, L. C., Fuentes-Duculan, J., Steinman, R. M., Krueger, J. G., & Lowes, M. A. (2007). Normal human dermis contains distinct populations of CD11c+BDCA-1+ dendritic cells and CD163+FXIIIA+ macrophages. *The Journal of Clinical Investigation*, *117*(9), 2517–2525.
Zahner, S. P., Kel, J. M., Martina, C. A., Brouwers-Haspels, I., van Roon, M. A., & Clausen, B. E. (2011). Conditional deletion of TGF-betaR1 using Langerin-Cre mice results in Langerhans cell deficiency and reduced contact hypersensitivity. *Journal of Immunology*, *187*(10), 5069–5076.
Zhan, Y., Carrington, E. M., van Nieuwenhuijze, A., Bedoui, S., Seah, S., Xu, Y., et al. (2011). GM-CSF increases cross-presentation and CD103 expression by mouse CD8 (+) spleen dendritic cells. *European Journal of Immunology*, *41*(9), 2585–2595.

CHAPTER SIX

Macrophage Activation and Polarization as an Adaptive Component of Innate Immunity

Massimo Locati[*,†], **Alberto Mantovani**[*,†,1], **Antonio Sica**[*,‡]
[*]Humanitas Clinical and Research Center, Rozzano, Milan, Italy
[†]Department of Medical Biotechnologies and Translational Medicine, University of Milan, Milan, Italy
[‡]Department of Pharmaceutical Sciences, Università del Piemonte Orientale "Amedeo Avogadro", Novara, Italy
[1]Corresponding author: e-mail address: alberto.mantovani@humanitasresearch.it

Contents

Abstract

Innate immunity has an adaptive component, which has been referred to as "memory," "trained," "imprinted" or "adaptive." Plasticity is a hallmark of cells of the monocyte–macrophage lineage. Microbial recognition and cytokines profoundly affect macrophage function causing a range of adaptive responses including activation, priming, or tolerance. These adaptive responses of macrophages include production of humoral fluid-phase pattern recognition molecules such as the prototypic long pentraxin PTX3. These components of humoral innate immunity in turn cooperate with and regulate phagocyte function. Progress has been made in defining the molecular basis underlying the polarized activation of macrophages, including signaling mediators, transcription factors, epigenetic modifications, and the microRNA network. The definition of molecules and mechanisms associated with plasticity and polarized activation of macrophages may provide a basis for innovative diagnostic and therapeutic approaches.

Advances in Immunology, Volume 120
ISSN 0065-2776
http://dx.doi.org/10.1016/B978-0-12-417028-5.00006-5

1. INTRODUCTION

Innate immunity is classically viewed as a first line of resistance against pathogens. More recently, innate immunity receptors have emerged as sensors of tissue damage and metabolic dysfunction (Medzhitov, 2008; Verbist, Wang, & Green, 2012). Moreover, cells of the innate immune system (macrophages and neutrophils) activate, orient, and regulate adaptive responses.

The innate immune system includes a cellular and a humoral arm. In addition to acting as innate effectors, macrophages and neutrophils are a major source of humoral, fluid-phase pattern recognition molecules (Bottazzi, Doni, Garlanda, & Mantovani, 2010). These include the long pentraxin PTX3, members of the ficolin and collectin family, and serum amyloid A. The production of these functional ancestors of antibodies by phagocytes links the cellular and the humoral arm of innate immunity (Bottazzi et al., 2010).

Macrophages are probably the most plastic cells among cells of hematopoietic origin (Biswas & Mantovani, 2012; Deban et al., 2010; Gordon & Martinez, 2010; Mantovani et al., 2004; Mantovani, Sozzani, Locati, Allavena, & Sica, 2002; Martinez, Helming, & Gordon, 2009; Mosser & Edwards, 2008; Pollard, 2009; Sica & Mantovani, 2012). In tissues, macrophages acquire unique and distinct morphological and functional properties (e.g., Kupffer cells in the liver and alveolar macrophages in lungs). Moreover, immunological and microbial signals have long been known to "activate" macrophages. Macrophage activation has for a long time been considered essentially a stereotyped transient increase in effector function (antimicrobial and antitumor activity) (Adams & Hamilton, 1984; Mackaness, 1969). The discovery of an alternative form of macrophage activation by IL-4 (Stein, Keshav, Harris, & Gordon, 1992) has opened a new perspective on the diversity of macrophage activation. In response to TLR, ligands and IFN-γ or IL-4/IL-13 macrophages undergo M1 (classical) or M2 (alternative) activation, which mirror the TH1–TH2 polarization and represent extremes of a continuum in a universe of activation states (Biswas & Mantovani, 2010; Mantovani et al., 2002; Mills, Kincaid, Alt, Heilman, & Hill, 2000; Mosser & Edwards, 2008; Sica & Bronte, 2007; Sica & Mantovani, 2012).

In addition to a transient wave of "activation," microbial encounters and immunological signals shape the innate immune system and condition subsequent responses for days to months (Netea, Quintin, & van der Meer, 2011). The sharp distinction between innate and adaptive immunity is an oversimplification. Early (e.g., Kurtz, 2005; Kurtz & Franz, 2003) and more recent evidence (e.g., Kleinnijenhuis et al., 2012) indicates that microbial encounters shape the "innate" response of phagocytes independently of lymphocytes. Indeed, studies in lower organisms have provided strong unequivocal evidence for an adaptive component in phagocyte responses. This lymphocyte-independent shaping of innate immunity has been referred to as "memory" (Kleinnijenhuis et al., 2012; Kurtz, 2005; Kurtz & Franz, 2003), "adaptive" (Biswas & Mantovani, 2010; Bowdish, Loffredo, Mukhopadhyay, Mantovani, & Gordon, 2007), or "trained" (Kleinnijenhuis et al., 2012; Netea et al., 2011). Evidence suggests that epigenetic changes occurring during macrophage activation underlie the long-term imprinting of macrophage responses (adaptive innate immunity) by microbial encounters (Chen et al., 2012; Kleinnijenhuis et al., 2012; Lawrence & Natoli, 2011). Here, we will review selected aspects of activation and adaptive responses of macrophages including their importance as a source of fluid-phase pattern recognition molecules, as well as genetic and epigenetic mechanisms underlying macrophage activation and polarization.

2. ACTIVATION, PRIMING, AND TOLERANCE AS ADAPTIVE RESPONSES OF MACROPHAGES (FIG. 6.1)

It has long been known that in response to microbial components and cytokines, cells of the monocyte–macrophage lineage exhibit enhanced

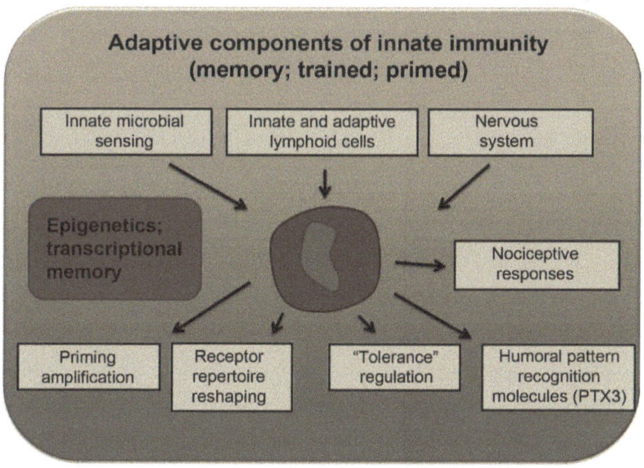

Figure 6.1 A schematic representation of adaptive responses of macrophages in innate immunity. (For color version of this figure, the reader is referred to the online version of this chapter.)

effector functions including microbicidal and tumoricidal activity (Adams & Hamilton, 1984; Mackaness, 1969; Fig. 6.1). Transcriptional profiling has added a deeper insight into the acquisition of enhanced effector function (e.g., Martinez, Gordon, Locati, & Mantovani, 2006). The wave of classical activation of mononuclear phagocyte is transient. In addition, exposure to selected cytokines (e.g., interferon-γ (IFN-γ)) primes the responsiveness of macrophages to microbial encounters (Adams & Hamilton, 1984; Nathan et al., 1984). Macrophages exposed to IFN-γ are in a primed state for several hours, with a dramatic increase in responsiveness, for instance, to lipopolysaccharide (LPS) in terms of toxic mediators (NO), cytokines (TNF-α and IL-12), and costimulatory molecules (Adams & Hamilton, 1984; Kaplan & Schreiber, 1999; Meltzer, Occhionero, & Ruco, 1982; Nathan et al., 1984). At least in human monocytes, priming is associated with sustained increased expression of pattern recognition receptors (TLR4 and MD2) and transducers (MyD88) (Bosisio et al., 2002).

Conversely, exposure to microbial signals (e.g., LPS) under appropriate conditions can result in endotoxin tolerance, that is, in hyporesponsiveness to a subsequent challenge at the macrophage and organism level. LPS tolerance generated *in vitro* reflects the immunosuppressive phenotype observed in sepsis. Moreover, tolerance represents a defense strategy to limit inflammation-related tissue damage (Medzhitov, Schneider, & Soares, 2012). Tolerance is actually a misleading definition because analysis of the macrophages transcriptome has shown that LPS tolerance is in fact expression of reorientation of macrophage function. Indeed LPS-tolerant macrophages express transcriptional profile similar to that expressed by alternatively activated (M2-polarized) macrophages (Biswas & Lopez-Collazo, 2009; Porta et al., 2009) (see in the succeeding text). These include elevated expression of interleukin-10 (IL-10), arginase 1, and the chemokines CCL17 and CCL22. Thus, what has long been known as endotoxin tolerance, far from being a form of unresponsiveness, represents an adaptive response with reorientation of macrophage function to a tissue repair and immunoregulatory phenotype.

In addition to reprogramming effector function, microbial recognition profoundly alters the spectrum of receptor repertoire expressed by mononuclear phagocyte (Bowdish et al., 2007; Willment et al., 2003). For instance, microbial recognition and cytokines regulate expression of dectin-1 and of the scavenger receptor MARCO and subsequent responses to their ligands (Bowdish et al., 2007; Willment et al., 2003). In addition to changing the levels and repertoire of macrophage surface receptors, microenvironmental signals also induce production of fluid-phase pattern recognition molecules (PRMs). These components of the humoral arm of innate immunity act as functional ancestors of antibodies ("ante-antibodies") (Bottazzi et al., 2010). Myelomonocytic cells produce a vast range of fluid-phase PRMs belonging to the collectin (e.g., mannose-binding lectin), ficolin (e.g., L-, H-, and M-ficolin), and pentraxin (e.g., PTX3) families (Bottazzi et al., 2010). PTX3 provides a paradigm of the interplay between the cellular and the humoral arm of innate immunity (Jeannin et al., 2005). This molecule is produced *de novo* in mononuclear phagocytes and is stored in a granular compartment in neutrophils. It plays an essential role in resistance against selected pathogens such as *Aspergillus fumigatus* and *Pseudomonas aeruginosa*. The effector mechanisms involve recognition and binding to microbial moieties, activation of the complement cascade, and opsonization-mediated destruction of pathogens (Bottazzi et al., 2010; Jeannin et al., 2005). In addition, PTX3 by binding to P-selectin attenuates neutrophil recruitment to sites of inflammation and thereby dampens inflammation (Deban et al., 2010). Therefore, PTX3 and other soluble PRMs produced by phagocytes have an amplification and regulatory role in phagocyte-mediated resistance and tissue damage.

The importance of microbial recognition in shaping innate immunity and macrophage function is highlighted by the phenotype of germfree mice, in terms, for instance, of cytokine production and seemingly distant pain responses (Amaral et al., 2008; Souza et al., 2004). In relation to the latter point, the neuroendocrine system and in particular the vagus axis have emerged as major regulators of macrophage function (Olofsson, Rosas-Ballina, Levine, & Tracey, 2012; Pavlov & Tracey, 2012; Fig. 6.1).

Exposure to microbial agents has long been known to be associated with increased nonspecific resistance to unrelated infectious agents (discussed in Kleinnijenhuis et al., 2012; Netea et al., 2011). Evidence from plants, invertebrates, and SCID mice strongly suggests that the increased effector function (memory or training) of the innate immune system is lymphocyte independent (Kurtz, 2005; Kurtz & Franz, 2003; Netea et al., 2011; Rodrigues, Brayner, Alves, Dixit, & Barillas-Mury, 2010). The clinical relevance of such adaptive responses of macrophages is suggested by epidemiological evidence and mechanistic analysis following BCG vaccination (Kleinnijenhuis et al., 2012). It was found that the imprinting for enhanced responses of monocytes following BCG vaccination lasted at least 3 months and was associated with increased expression of TLR4 (Kleinnijenhuis et al., 2012), a finding reminiscent of previous *in vitro* analysis of priming

(Bosisio et al., 2002). Netea and colleagues concluded that BCG-trained innate immunity is responsible for nonspecific protection and is mediated via epigenetic reprogramming (Kleinnijenhuis et al., 2012).

The lungs provide a case in point for long-term conditioning of macrophage responsiveness (Didierlaurent, Goulding, & Hussell, 2007; Didierlaurent et al., 2008; Naessens et al., 2012). Following resolution of viral infections (influenza and respiratory syncytial virus), a sustained lung macrophage desensitization lasting several months was observed (Didierlaurent et al., 2008). Interestingly, mirroring the data with *in vitro* and *in vivo* priming for enhanced responses (Bosisio et al., 2002; Kleinnijenhuis et al., 2012), the culprit for unresponsiveness rested on TLR4 desensitization. Conversely, after exposure to allergic bronchial inflammation, alveolar macrophages have been reported to exhibit increased inflammatory reactivity to TLR ligands, with acquisition of the ability to produce IFN-β (Naessens et al., 2012). Thus, evidence from different systems suggests that infectious or inflammatory conditions may imprint lung macrophages for attenuated or increased responsiveness. Understanding of the molecular basis of adaptive conditioning of lung macrophages may have a profound impact on understanding the pathogenesis of diverse clinical conditions.

3. POLARIZED ACTIVATION

The identification of an alternative (M2) form of macrophage activation by IL-4 (Stein et al., 1992) opened new vistas on the plasticity of mononuclear phagocytes. Classically and alternatively activated macrophages have been referred to as M1 and M2, mirroring Th1 and Th2 T cells characterized by differential production of the macrophage activation signals IFN-γ and IL-4. Classically activated (M1) macrophages had long been known to be induced by IFN-γ alone or in concert with microbial stimuli (e.g., LPS) or cytokines (e.g., TNF and GM-CSF). IL-4 and IL-13 were subsequently found to induce an alternative (M2) form of macrophage activation (Gordon, 2003). It is now known that other cytokines can induce M2 polarization. IL-33 is a cytokine of the IL-1 family associated with Th2 and M2 polarization (Hazlett et al., 2010; Kurowska-Stolarska et al., 2009). IL-33 amplifies IL-13-induced polarization of alveolar macrophages to an M2 phenotype characterized by the upregulation of YM1, arginase 1, CCL24, and CCL17, which mediate lung eosinophilia and inflammation

(Kurowska-Stolarska et al., 2009). IL-21 is another Th2-associated cytokine shown to drive M2 activation of macrophages (Pesce et al., 2006).

Macrophages can also be polarized into an "M2-like" state, which shares some but not all the signature features of M2 cells. In fact, various stimuli, such as antibody immune complexes together with LPS or IL-1, glucocorticoids, transforming growth factor-β (TGF-β), and IL-10, result in M2-like functional phenotypes that share properties with IL-4- or IL-13-activated macrophages (such as high expression of mannose receptor, IL-10, and angiogenic factors) (Mantovani et al., 2004). Variations on the theme of M2 polarization were also found *in vivo* (e.g., in the placenta and embryo and during helminth infection, *Listeria* infection, obesity, and cancer) (Auffray et al., 2007; Gustafsson et al., 2008; Odegaard et al., 2007; Rae et al., 2007; Raes et al., 2005). M1- and M2- or M2-like-polarized macrophages represent extremes of a continuum in a universe of functional states (Biswas & Mantovani, 2010; Mantovani et al., 2002; Mosser & Edwards, 2008; Sica & Mantovani, 2012).

In general, M1 cells are characterized by an IL-12^{high}, IL-23^{high}, and IL-10^{low} phenotype; are efficient producers of effector molecules (e.g., reactive nitrogen intermediates) and inflammatory cytokines (IL-1β, TNF, and IL-6); participate as inducer and effector cells in polarized Th1 responses; and mediate resistance against intracellular parasites and tumors. In contrast, the various forms of M2 macrophages generally express an IL-10^{high}, IL-12^{low}, and IL-23^{low} phenotype with variable capacity to produce inflammatory cytokines depending on the signal utilized. M2 cells generally have high levels of scavenger-, mannose-, and galactose-type receptors, and the arginine metabolism is shifted to ornithine and polyamines. Polarized macrophages present also differential regulation of components of the IL-1 system (Dinarello, 2005) with low IL-1β and low caspase I, high IL-1ra, and high decoy type II receptor in M2 cells. In general, M2 cells are a component of polarized Th2 responses. They contribute to parasite clearance (Noel, Raes, Hassanzadeh Ghassabeh, De Baetselier, & Beschin, 2004) and tissue remodeling (Mantovani, Biswas, Galdiero, Sica, & Locati, 2013; Wynn, 2004), promote angiogenesis and tumor progression, and have immunoregulatory functions (Biswas & Mantovani, 2010).

M1- and M2-polarized macrophages have distinct profiles in terms of chemokines and chemokine receptors. M1-polarized macrophages typically express Th1 cell-attracting chemokines such as CXCL9 and CXCL10 while polarized M2 macrophages expressing the chemokines CCL17, CCL22, and CCL24 (Mantovani, 2008; Martinez et al., 2006;

Medzhitov & Horng, 2009). Chemokines can also influence macrophage polarization, with CCL2 and CXCL4 driving macrophages to an M2-like phenotype (Gleissner, Shaked, Little, & Ley, 2010; Roca et al., 2009). Moreover, as discussed in the succeeding text, M1- and M2-polarized macrophages have distinct features in terms of the metabolism of iron, folate, and glucose (Biswas & Mantovani, 2012; Puig-Kroger et al., 2009; Recalcati et al., 2010; Rodriguez-Prados et al., 2010). The functional phenotypes expressed by macrophages *in vivo* or *ex vivo* in pathological condition such as parasite infections, allergic reaction, and many tumors mirror to a considerable extent the properties of polarized M1 and M2 cells (for review, Sica & Mantovani, 2012). In other conditions, the plasticity of mononuclear phagocytes defies simplistic classifications (see Sica & Mantovani, 2012 for discussion).

4. MOLECULAR MECHANISMS UNDERLYING MACROPHAGE POLARIZATION

Macrophage polarization is tuned by a network of signaling molecules, transcription factors, epigenetic mechanisms, and posttranscriptional regulators. Recent studies have identified key transcriptional events controlling macrophage polarization. M1-promoting signals, interferons and TLR signaling, activate the canonical IRF-STAT signaling pathways (via STAT1), whereas IL-4 and IL-13 skew macrophages toward the M2 phenotype (via STAT6) (Sica & Bronte, 2007). A key regulator of M1 polarization is IRF5, whose protein stability is regulated through the interaction with the COP9 signalosome (Korczeniewska & Barnes, 2013). IRF5 is essential for induction of cytokines (IL-12, IL-23, and TNF) involved in eliciting Th1 and Th17 responses (Krausgruber et al., 2011). Expression of M1 macrophage-associated genes is also promoted by the Notch–RBP-J axis, which induces the synthesis of IRF8 protein by selectively augmenting kinase IRAK2-dependent signaling via TLR4 to the kinase MNK1 genes (Xu et al., 2012; Fig. 6.2).

The type I and type II IL-4 receptors (Gordon & Martinez, 2010; Junttila et al., 2008) activate STAT6 (Pauleau et al., 2004), which leads the transcription of genes typical of M2 polarization (e.g., mannose receptor (*Mrc1*), resistin-like α (*Retnla* and *Fizz1*), chitinase 3-like 3 (*Chi3l3*, *Ym1*)), while IL-10 induces STAT3-mediated expression of genes (*Il10*, *Tgfb1*, and *Mrc1*) associated with an M2-like phenotype (Gordon, 2003; Lang, Patel, Morris, Rutschman, & Murray, 2002; Mantovani et al., 2002). Further,

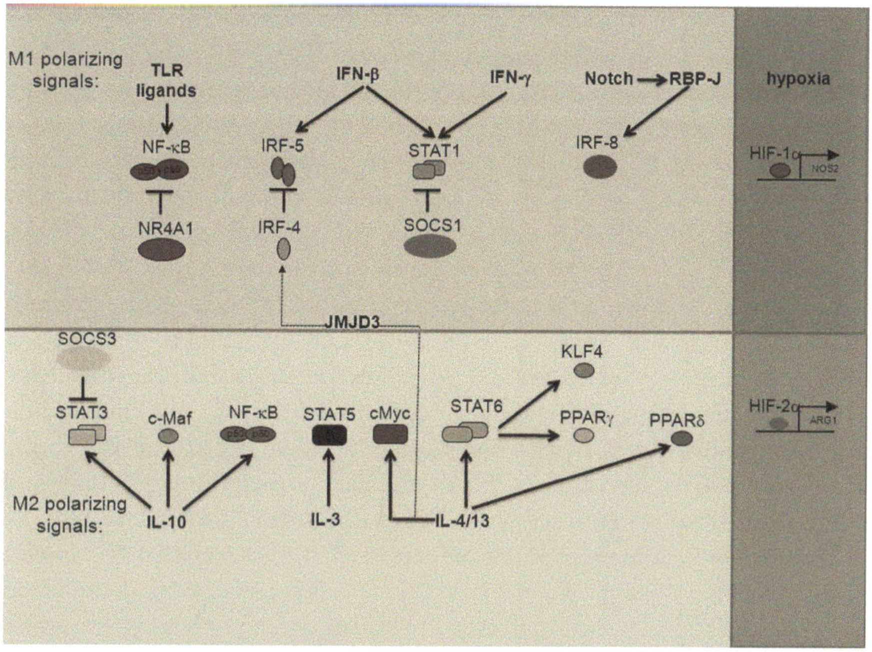

Figure 6.2 Signals and pathways of macrophage polarization. The cross talk between the M1 and M2 macrophage-polarizing pathways is also indicated. The balance between activation of STAT1 and STAT3/STAT6 finely regulates macrophage polarization and activity. These events are subject to negative regulators for M1 (NR4A1, IRF4, and SOCS1) and M1 (SOCS3) polarization. A predominance of NF-κB and STAT1 activation promotes M1 macrophage polarization, resulting in cytotoxic and inflammatory functions. In contrast, a predominance of STAT3, STAT5, and STAT6 activation results in M2 macrophage polarization, associated with immune suppression and tumor progression. PPAR-γ and PPAR-δ control distinct aspects of M2 macrophage activation and oxidative metabolism. KLF4 and KLF2 participate in the promotion of M2 macrophage functions by cooperating with STAT6 and suppressing the NF-κB-/HIF-1α-dependent transcription, respectively. IL-4 induced c-Myc activity controls a subset of M2-associated genes. IL-4 also induces the M2-polarizing JMJD3-IRF4 axis to inhibit IRF5-mediated M1 polarization. IL-10 promotes M2 polarization through the induction of p50 NF-κB homodimer, c-Maf, and STAT3 activities. (For color version of this figure, the reader is referred to the online version of this chapter.)

IL-3-mediated STAT5 activation was shown to promote M2 polarization (Kuroda et al., 2009).

Of relevance, STAT6 coordinates a panel of transcription factors orchestrating M2 polarization of macrophages. The nuclear receptors peroxisome proliferator-activated receptor (PPAR)-γ (Odegaard et al., 2007) and PPAR-δ (Kang et al., 2008; Odegaard et al., 2008) control distinct subsets of genes associated with M2 macrophage activation and oxidative metabolism (Fig. 6.1). Interestingly, STAT6 synergizes with both PPAR-γ (Szanto et al., 2010) and Krüppel-like factor 4 (KLF4) (Cao, Sun, Icli, Wara, & Feinberg, 2010; Liao et al., 2011). KLF4 cooperates with STAT6 to induce M2 genes (*Arg-1*, *Mrc1*, *Fizz1*, and *PPAR-γ*) and inhibit M1 genes (*TNF-α*, *Cox-2*, *CCL5*, and *iNOS*) via sequestration of coactivators required for NF-κB activation. KLF2 regulates macrophage activation by inhibiting the NF-κB/HIF-1α activities (Mahabeleshwar et al., 2011). IL-4 also induces c-Myc activity in human macrophages (Pello, De Pizzol, et al., 2012), which controls genes associated with M2 activation (*Scarb1*, *Alox15*, and *Mrc1*), as well as STAT6 and PPAR-γ activation (Pello, De Pizzol, et al., 2012). Accordingly, *in vivo* inhibition of c-Myc in myeloid cells impaired tumor-associated macrophage (TAM) maturation and their protumoral activities (Pello, Chevre, et al., 2012). SOCS family members are key regulators of STATs activity in macrophages. IL-4 and IFN-γ, the latter in concert with TLR stimulation, upregulate SOCS1 and SOCS3, which in turn inhibit the action of STAT1 and STAT3, respectively (Liu et al., 2008; Whyte et al., 2011). Recently, RBP-J-mediated Notch signaling has been implicated in regulating macrophage polarization in a SOCS3-dependent manner (Wang, He, et al., 2010). Further, SOCS2 and SOCS3 were demonstrated to play as key diametric regulators of M1- and M2-like macrophage polarization and inflammatory response, respectively (Spence et al., 2013).

TLR engagement leads to NF-κB activation and production of inflammatory mediators (Bonizzi & Karin, 2004) associated with M1 macrophages. However, NF-κB activation also activates a genetic program essential for resolution of inflammation (Lawrence & Gilroy, 2007) and for M2 polarization of TAMs (Hagemann et al., 2008). In this regard, nuclear accumulation of p50 NF-κB homodimers, as observed in both TAM and LPS-tolerant macrophages, is essential for M2 polarization *in vitro* and *in vivo* (Porta et al., 2009). A differential expression of the hypoxia-inducible factors HIF-1α and HIF-2α was observed in M1- versus M2-polarized macrophages (Takeda et al., 2010) and regulates inducible NOS2 (M1) and arginase 1 (M2), respectively. JNK activation is required for proinflammatory macrophage polarization, and mice with macrophage-specific JNK deficiency were protected against insulin resistance (Han et al., 2013). The NR4A1 (Nur77) nuclear receptor, which is expressed in macrophages and within atherosclerotic lesions, was recently found to act as a negative regulator of M1 inflammation, by inhibiting activation of the p65 subunit of NF-κB in macrophages (Hanna et al., 2012).

5. EPIGENETIC REGULATION OF MACROPHAGE POLARIZATION

Epigenetic changes define modifications of histones, or other chromatin proteins, controlling the tissue and context specific expression of information encoded in DNA. These events comprise posttranscriptional modifications, such as methylation, acetylation, and phosphorylation, which together set the "histone code," to control interaction and functions of selected transcription factors (Ivashkiv, 2013). New evidence indicates that different chromatin states of relevant gene loci control macrophage polarization (Medzhitov & Horng, 2009; Natoli, Ghisletti, & Barozzi, 2011; Smale, 2010). In particular: (a) a repressed transcriptional state is associated with trimethylation of histone 3 on lysine 9 (H3K9), H3K27, and H3K79; (b) an intermediate transcriptional state is characterized by the simultaneous presence of activating (H3K4me3, H3K9, and 14-Ac) and repressive histone marks (H3K9me3 and H3K27me3); and (c) an active transcriptional state is characterized by open chromatin configuration associated with trimethylation of histone 3 lysine 4 (H3K4) (Barski et al., 2007; Medzhitov & Horng, 2009; Wei et al., 2009).

This epigenetic remodeling affects macrophage differentiation, responsiveness, and polarization. As an example, reduced global DNA methylation is associated with increased myeloid commitment from hematopoietic stem cells (Takeuch & Akira, 2011). Further, during macrophage differentiation, the PU.1 and CCAAT/enhancer binding protein (C/EBP)-α bind and open the regulatory regions of several M1 genes, which are induced in response to TLR ligands (e.g., TNF-α, IL-1β, IL-6, IL-12p40, and CXCL10). TLR stimulation also promotes dissociation of repressors (e.g., BCL6) from relevant gene loci and promotes demethylases, such as JMJD3, JMJD2d, PHF2, and AOF1, that impair the activity of negative histone marks (De Santa et al., 2009; Stender et al., 2012; Zhu, van Essen, & Saccani, 2012). Histone acetylation is recognized by the bromodomain and extracellular domain (BET) family proteins, to stimulate transcriptional elongation by RNA polymerase II (Jang et al., 2005; Yang et al., 2005). Thus, targeting proteins that recognize posttranslationally modified histones may represent a new strategy for innovative immunomodulatory drugs. In this regard, a synthetic compound (I-BET), interfering with the recognition of acetylated histones by BET family members, disrupted chromatin complexes responsible for the expression of key M1 inflammatory genes in LPS-activated macrophages and conferred protection against LPS-induced endotoxic shock and bacteria-induced sepsis (Nicodeme et al., 2010). Moreover, compounds that inhibit the jumonji H3K27 demethylase (JMJD3) and related demethylases suppressed the LPS-induced inflammatory cytokine production by human primary macrophages (Kruidenier et al., 2012). Histone methylation is controlled also by oxygen availability. In particular, in macrophages, hypoxia promotes loss of jumonji histone demethylases activity, resulting in accumulation of repressive marks (H3K9me2/me3) and the consequent inhibition of chemokine (Ccl2) and chemokine receptor (Ccr1 and Ccr5) genes (Tausendschon, Dehne, & Brune, 2011). Noteworthy, IFN-γ induces M1 macrophage polarization through activation of STAT1-mediated chromatin opening and remodeling (Chen & Ivashkiv, 2010). On the contrary, the IL-4-induced upregulation of the JMJD3/IRF4 axis promotes chromatin modifications, driving M2 polarization and inhibition of M1 genes (Satoh et al., 2010; Sica & Mantovani, 2012). IL-4-induced M2 polarization is counteracted by HDAC3, which deacetylates enhancers of IL-4-inducible genes (Mullican et al., 2011). The glucocorticoid receptor (GR) is one of the most potent anti-inflammatory drugs and regulates transcription by binding to glucocorticoid response elements (Glass & Saijo, 2010). It was recently observed that TLR4 activation dramatically remodels the GR cistrome in macrophages, to a remodeled and inflammatory cistrome (Uhlenhaut et al., 2013). Interestingly, negative GR enhancers selectively utilize the corepressor function of GRIP1, antagonize IRF3 activity, and display reduced histones acetylation, thus impairing the inflammatory response (Uhlenhaut et al., 2013).

6. POSTTANSCRIPTIONAL REGULATION IN MACROPHAGE ACTIVATION AND POLARIZATION

MicroRNA (miRs) are small noncoding RNA molecules that control gene expression targeting mRNA 3′UTRs (Bartel, 2009). As a large number of miRNA have been identified and each single miRNA targets and controls several mRNA transcripts, this posttranscriptional mechanism is emerging as a major player in the control of several biological processes. Evidence indicates their involvement also in the regulation of the gene expression profile, characterizing distinct macrophage polarities. In particular, in both human and murine macrophages, TLR triggering has been associated to the regulation of a distinct set of miR that operates a multiple-targeting mechanism controlling key molecules in macrophage activation and tip the balance of pro- and anti-inflammatory processes. The best characterized proinflammatory miR is miR-155, which has been shown to increase TNF-α transcript stability (Bala et al., 2011), promotes antiviral immunity by downregulating SOCS1 (Wang, Hou, et al., 2010), and promotes atherosclerosis by targeting BCL6 (Nazari-Jahantigh et al., 2012). On the opposite, miR-146a, which was the first miR shown to be induced by TLR triggering in macrophages, operates as a negative regulator during macrophage activation by direct targeting the TLR signaling molecules IRAK-1 and TRAF6 (Taganov, Boldin, Chang, & Baltimore, 2006). Experimental evidence has then clearly defined its role of negative regulator of inflammation (Jurkin et al., 2010) and its involvement in LPS tolerance (Nahid, Pauley, Satoh, & Chan, 2009). Other miRs induced in macrophages by TLR triggering include miR-9 (Rossato et al., 2012), miR-21 (Sheedy et al., 2010), and miR-147 (Liu et al., 2009), all of which have been involved in the control of NF-κB activity, either by direct targeting of NF-κB1 (miR-9) or by indirect effects (PDCD4 targeting by miR-21). In this context, miR-125a and b, which are also regulated during macrophage activation, play a dual role as they decrease the TNF-α transcript stability (Tili et al., 2007) but at the same time also sustain inflammation enhancing NF-κB signaling by targeting A20 (Kim et al., 2012) and IRF4 (Chaudhuri et al., 2011). Finally, miR-187, recently reported as the first IL-10-regulated miR, contributes to inflammation resolution by direct targeting transcripts for TNF-α and NF-κBIZ, a positive transcriptional regulator of IL-6 and IL-12p40 (Rossato et al., 2012). Interestingly, we recently described miR-146b as a second IL-10-dependent miR and show its ability to dampen production of inflammatory cytokines by targeting key elements in the TLR signaling pathway (Curtale et al., 2013).

A clear role of miR is also emerging in macrophage polarization. The proinflammatory miR-155 targets the IL-13 receptor-α chain, thus likely interfering with M2 polarization, and indeed, its overexpression in M2 macrophages results in downregulation of the well-known M2 markers arginase 1 and CHI3I3 as a consequence of C/EBP-β targeting (He, Xu, Ding, Kuang, & Zheng, 2009). Similarly, miR-125 and miR-29b interfere with M2 activation by targeting IRF4 and sustain M1 activation unleashing NF-κB signaling as a consequence of A20 downregulation (Chaudhuri et al., 2011; Graff, Dickson, Clay, McCaffrey, & Wilson, 2012). Conversely, two intronic miRs are coregulated with their host M2 genes and are thus upregulated in response to alternative activation. MiR-378 is hosted in the first intron of the PPAR-γ gene and operates a negative feedback loop

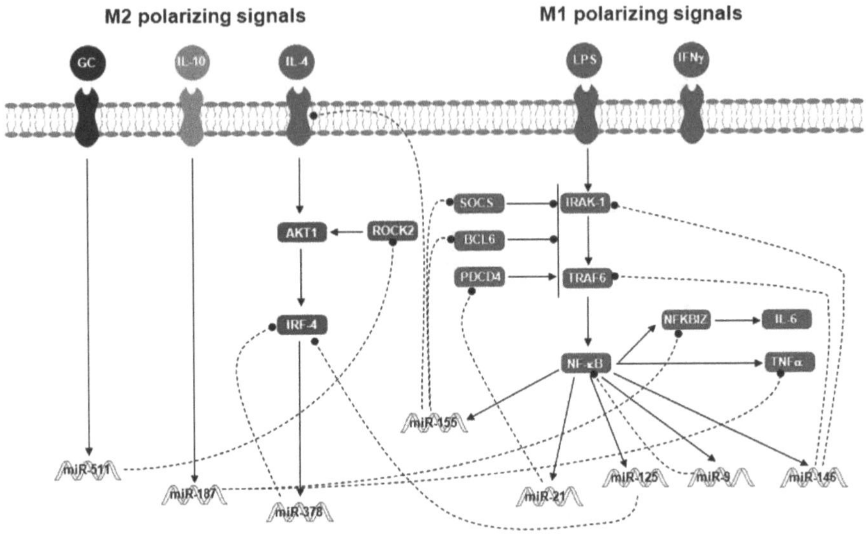

Figure 6.3 The microRNA network in macrophage activation and polarization. The network of microRNA induced by different polarizing agents and their targets is shown. Arrows indicate induction/activation, bullet-end lines indicate negative regulatory elements, and dotted lines represent miR targets. (For color version of this figure, the reader is referred to the online version of this chapter.)

as it targets the IL-4 signal transducer AKT1 (Ruckerl et al., 2012). MiR-511 is hosted in the fifth intron of the mannose receptor 1 gene (also known as CD206) and is highly expressed in M2 and TAM and controls expression levels of a number of associated genes at least in part by the selective down-regulation of ROCK2 (Squadrito et al., 2012; Fig. 6.3). Finally, a recent report identified a set of miR specifically enriched in distinct subsets of alternative macrophages (M2a—miR-222 and M2b—miR-27a, miR-27a*, miR-125a-3p, and miR-125a-5p) and M1 (miR-29b, miR-29b-1*, and miR-155) and showed evidence for their influence on their cytokine profile (Graff et al., 2012).

7. CONCLUDING REMARKS

Plasticity and flexibility are key features of mononuclear phagocytes and of their activation states. Individual tissue microenvironments shape the phenotype and function of cells of the monocyte–macrophage lineage. The integration of tissue-specific cues, microbial encounters, and cytokines dictates differentiation and activation of these cells.

Specific targeting of macrophages, their subsets, or activation states remains a holy grail for therapeutic intervention. Drugs not specifically designed to target macrophages, including PPAR-γ inhibitors, statins, zoledronic acid, and glucocorticoid hormones, are likely to act to a large extent by affecting the function of cells of the monocyte–macrophage lineage (for discussion, see Sica & Mantovani, 2012). For instance, recent evidence suggests that depletion of TAMs is a major determinant of the clinically approved anticancer agent trabectedin (Germano et al., 2013). A better understanding of molecular mechanisms and molecules associated with macrophage plasticity and polarized activation may pave the way to the design of innovative diagnostic and therapeutic strategies targeted to activation states and functions of cells of the monocyte–macrophage lineage.

ACKNOWLEDGMENTS

Alberto Mantovani is supported by AIRC (Investigator Grant and 5x1000 Grant) and the European Commission (FP7-HEALTH-2011-ADITEC-280873).

REFERENCES

Adams, D. O., & Hamilton, T. A. (1984). The cell biology of macrophage activation. *Annual Review of Immunology*, *2*, 283.

Amaral, F. A., Sachs, D., Costa, V. V., Fagundes, C. T., Cisalpino, D., Cunha, T. M., et al. (2008). Commensal microbiota is fundamental for the development of inflammatory pain. *Proceedings of the National Academy of Sciences of the United States of America*, *105*, 2193.

Auffray, C., Fogg, D., Garfa, M., Elain, G., Join-Lambert, O., Kayal, S., et al. (2007). Monitoring of blood vessels and tissues by a population of monocytes with patrolling behavior. *Science*, *317*, 666.

Bala, S., Marcos, M., Kodys, K., Csak, T., Catalano, D., Mandrekar, P., et al. (2011). Up-regulation of microRNA-155 in macrophages contributes to increased tumor necrosis factor alpha (TNF{alpha}) production via increased mRNA half-life in alcoholic liver disease. *Journal of Biological Chemistry*, *286*, 1436.

Barski, A., Cuddapah, S., Cui, K., Roh, T. Y., Schones, D. E., Wang, Z., et al. (2007). High-resolution profiling of histone methylations in the human genome. *Cell*, *129*, 823.

Bartel, D. P. (2009). MicroRNAs: Target recognition and regulatory functions. *Cell*, *136*, 215.

Biswas, S. K., & Lopez-Collazo, E. (2009). Endotoxin tolerance: New mechanisms, molecules and clinical significance. *Trends in Immunology*, *30*, 475.

Biswas, S. K., & Mantovani, A. (2010). Macrophage plasticity and interaction with lymphocyte subsets: Cancer as a paradigm. *Nature Immunology*, *11*, 889.

Biswas, S. K., & Mantovani, A. (2012). Orchestration of metabolism by macrophages. *Cell Metabolism*, *15*, 432.

Bonizzi, G., & Karin, M. (2004). The two NF-kappaB activation pathways and their role in innate and adaptive immunity. *Trends in Immunology*, *25*, 280.

Bosisio, D., Polentarutti, N., Sironi, M., Bernasconi, S., Miyake, K., Webb, G. R., et al. (2002). Stimulation of toll-like receptor 4 expression in human mononuclear phagocytes by interferon-gamma: A molecular basis for priming and synergism with bacterial lipopolysaccharide. *Blood*, *99*, 3427.

Bottazzi, B., Doni, A., Garlanda, C., & Mantovani, A. (2010). An integrated view of humoral innate immunity: Pentraxins as a paradigm. *Annual Review of Immunology, 28*, 157.

Bowdish, D. M., Loffredo, M. S., Mukhopadhyay, S., Mantovani, A., & Gordon, S. (2007). Macrophage receptors implicated in the "adaptive" form of innate immunity. *Microbes and Infection, 9*, 1680.

Cao, Z., Sun, X., Icli, B., Wara, A. K., & Feinberg, M. W. (2010). Role of Kruppel-like factors in leukocyte development, function, and disease. *Blood, 116*, 4404.

Chaudhuri, A. A., So, A. Y., Sinha, N., Gibson, W. S., Taganov, K. D., O'Connell, R. M., et al. (2011). MicroRNA-125b potentiates macrophage activation. *Journal of Immunology, 187*, 5062.

Chen, X., Barozzi, I., Termanini, A., Prosperini, E., Recchiuti, A., Dalli, J., et al. (2012). Requirement for the histone deacetylase Hdac3 for the inflammatory gene expression program in macrophages. *Proceedings of the National Academy of Sciences of the United States of America, 109*, E2865.

Chen, J., & Ivashkiv, L. B. (2010). IFN-gamma abrogates endotoxin tolerance by facilitating Toll-like receptor-induced chromatin remodeling. *Proceedings of the National Academy of Sciences of the United States of America, 107*, 19438.

Curtale, G., Mirolo, M., Renzi, T., Rossato, M., Bazzoni, F., & Locati, M. (2013). Negative regulation of toll-like receptor 4 signaling by the IL-10 dependent microRNA-146b. *Proceedings of the National Academy of Sciences of the United States of America, 110*, 11499.

De Santa, F., Narang, V., Yap, Z. H., Tusi, B. K., Burgold, T., Austenaa, L., et al. (2009). Jmjd3 contributes to the control of gene expression in LPS-activated macrophages. *EMBO Journal, 28*, 3341.

Deban, L., Russo, R. C., Sironi, M., Moalli, F., Scanziani, M., Zambelli, V., et al. (2010). Regulation of leukocyte recruitment by the long pentraxin PTX3. *Nature Immunology, 11*, 328.

Didierlaurent, A., Goulding, J., & Hussell, T. (2007). The impact of successive infections on the lung microenvironment. *Immunology, 122*, 457.

Didierlaurent, A., Goulding, J., Patel, S., Snelgrove, R., Low, L., Bebien, M., et al. (2008). Sustained desensitization to bacterial Toll-like receptor ligands after resolution of respiratory influenza infection. *The Journal of Experimental Medicine, 205*, 323.

Dinarello, C. A. (2005). Blocking IL-1 in systemic inflammation. *The Journal of Experimental Medicine, 201*, 1355.

Germano, G., Frapolli, R., Belgiovine, C., Anselmo, A., Pesce, S., Liguori, M., et al. (2013). Role of macrophage targeting in the antitumor activity of trabectedin. *Cancer Cell, 23*, 249.

Glass, C. K., & Saijo, K. (2010). Nuclear receptor transrepression pathways that regulate inflammation in macrophages and T cells. *Nature Reviews. Immunology, 10*, 365.

Gleissner, C. A., Shaked, I., Little, K. M., & Ley, K. (2010). CXC chemokine ligand 4 induces a unique transcriptome in monocyte-derived macrophages. *Journal of Immunology, 184*, 4810.

Gordon, S. (2003). Alternative activation of macrophages. *Nature Reviews. Immunology, 3*, 23.

Gordon, S., & Martinez, F. O. (2010). Alternative activation of macrophages: Mechanism and functions. *Immunity, 32*, 593.

Graff, J. W., Dickson, A. M., Clay, G., McCaffrey, A. P., & Wilson, M. E. (2012). Identifying functional microRNAs in macrophages with polarized phenotypes. *Journal of Biological Chemistry, 287*, 21816.

Gustafsson, C., Mjosberg, J., Matussek, A., Geffers, R., Matthiesen, L., Berg, G., et al. (2008). Gene expression profiling of human decidual macrophages: Evidence for immunosuppressive phenotype. *PLoS One, 3*, e2078.

Hagemann, T., Lawrence, T., McNeish, I., Charles, K. A., Kulbe, H., Thompson, R. G., et al. (2008). "Re-educating" tumor-associated macrophages by targeting NF-kappaB. *The Journal of Experimental Medicine*, *205*, 1261.
Han, M. S., Jung, D. Y., Morel, C., Lakhani, S. A., Kim, J. K., Flavell, R. A., et al. (2013). JNK expression by macrophages promotes obesity-induced insulin resistance and inflammation. *Science*, *339*, 218.
Hanna, R. N., Shaked, I., Hubbeling, H. G., Punt, J. A., Wu, R., Herrley, E., et al. (2012). NR4A1 (Nur77) deletion polarizes macrophages toward an inflammatory phenotype and increases atherosclerosis. *Circulation Research*, *110*, 416.
Hazlett, L. D., McClellan, S. A., Barrett, R. P., Huang, X., Zhang, Y., Wu, M., et al. (2010). IL-33 shifts macrophage polarization, promoting resistance against *Pseudomonas aeruginosa* keratitis. *Investigative Ophthalmology and Visual Science*, *51*, 1524.
He, M., Xu, Z., Ding, T., Kuang, D. M., & Zheng, L. (2009). MicroRNA-155 regulates inflammatory cytokine production in tumor-associated macrophages via targeting C/EBPbeta. *Cellular and Molecular Immunology*, *6*, 343.
Ivashkiv, L. B. (2013). Epigenetic regulation of macrophage polarization and function. *Trends in Immunology*, *34*, 216.
Jang, M. K., Mochizuki, K., Zhou, M., Jeong, H. S., Brady, J. N., & Ozato, K. (2005). The bromodomain protein Brd4 is a positive regulatory component of P-TEFb and stimulates RNA polymerase II-dependent transcription. *Molecular Cell*, *19*, 523.
Jeannin, P., Bottazzi, B., Sironi, M., Doni, A., Rusnati, M., Presta, M., et al. (2005). Complexity and complementarity of outer membrane protein A recognition by cellular and humoral innate immunity receptors. *Immunity*, *22*, 551.
Junttila, I. S., Mizukami, K., Dickensheets, H., Meier-Schellersheim, M., Yamane, H., Donnelly, R. P., et al. (2008). Tuning sensitivity to IL-4 and IL-13: Differential expression of IL-4Ralpha, IL-13Ralpha1, and gammac regulates relative cytokine sensitivity. *The Journal of Experimental Medicine*, *205*, 2595.
Jurkin, J., Schichl, Y. M., Koeffel, R., Bauer, T., Richter, S., Konradi, S., et al. (2010). miR-146a is differentially expressed by myeloid dendritic cell subsets and desensitizes cells to TLR2-dependent activation. *Journal of Immunology*, *184*, 4955.
Kang, K., Reilly, S. M., Karabacak, V., Gangl, M. R., Fitzgerald, K., Hatano, B., et al. (2008). Adipocyte-derived Th2 cytokines and myeloid PPARdelta regulate macrophage polarization and insulin sensitivity. *Cell Metabolism*, *7*, 485.
Kaplan, D. H., & Schreiber, R. D. (1999). The interferons: Biochemistry and biology. In J. Thèze (Ed.), *The cytokine network and immune functions* (p. 11). New York, NY: Oxford University Press.
Kim, S. W., Ramasamy, K., Bouamar, H., Lin, A. P., Jiang, D., & Aguiar, R. C. (2012). MicroRNAs miR-125a and miR-125b constitutively activate the NF-kappaB pathway by targeting the tumor necrosis factor alpha-induced protein 3 (TNFAIP3, A20). *Proceedings of the National Academy of Sciences of the United States of America*, *109*, 7865.
Kleinnijenhuis, J., Quintin, J., Preijers, F., Joosten, L. A., Ifrim, D. C., Saeed, S., et al. (2012). Bacille Calmette–Guerin induces NOD2-dependent nonspecific protection from reinfection via epigenetic reprogramming of monocytes. *Proceedings of the National Academy of Sciences of the United States of America*, *109*, 17537.
Korczeniewska, J., & Barnes, B. J. (2013). The COP9 signalosome interacts with and regulates IRF5 protein stability. *Molecular and Cellular Biology*, *33*, 1124.
Krausgruber, T., Blazek, K., Smallie, T., Alzabin, S., Lockstone, H., Sahgal, N., et al. (2011). IRF5 promotes inflammatory macrophage polarization and TH1–TH17 responses. *Nature Immunology*, *12*, 231.
Kruidenier, L., Chung, C. W., Cheng, Z., Liddle, J., Che, K., Joberty, G., et al. (2012). A selective jumonji H3K27 demethylase inhibitor modulates the proinflammatory macrophage response. *Nature*, *488*, 404.

Kuroda, E., Ho, V., Ruschmann, J., Antignano, F., Hamilton, M., Rauh, M. J., et al. (2009). SHIP represses the generation of IL-3-induced M2 macrophages by inhibiting IL-4 production from basophils. *Journal of Immunology, 183*, 3652.

Kurowska-Stolarska, M., Stolarski, B., Kewin, P., Murphy, G., Corrigan, C. J., Ying, S., et al. (2009). IL-33 amplifies the polarization of alternatively activated macrophages that contribute to airway inflammation. *Journal of Immunology, 183*, 6469.

Kurtz, J. (2005). Specific memory within innate immune systems. *Trends in Immunology, 26*, 186.

Kurtz, J., & Franz, K. (2003). Innate defence: Evidence for memory in invertebrate immunity. *Nature, 425*, 37.

Lang, R., Patel, D., Morris, J. J., Rutschman, R. L., & Murray, P. J. (2002). Shaping gene expression in activated and resting primary macrophages by IL-10. *Journal of Immunology, 169*, 2253.

Lawrence, T., & Gilroy, D. W. (2007). Chronic inflammation: A failure of resolution? *International Journal of Experimental Pathology, 88*, 85.

Lawrence, T., & Natoli, G. (2011). Transcriptional regulation of macrophage polarization: Enabling diversity with identity. *Nature Reviews. Immunology, 11*, 750.

Liao, X., Sharma, N., Kapadia, F., Zhou, G., Lu, Y., Hong, H., et al. (2011). Kruppel-like factor 4 regulates macrophage polarization. *Journal of Clinical Investigation, 121*, 2736.

Liu, G., Friggeri, A., Yang, Y., Park, Y. J., Tsuruta, Y., & Abraham, E. (2009). miR-147 a microRNA that is induced upon Toll-like receptor stimulation regulates murine macrophage inflammatory responses. *Proceedings of the National Academy of Sciences of the United States of America, 106*, 15819.

Liu, Y., Stewart, K. N., Bishop, E., Marek, C. J., Kluth, D. C., Rees, A. J., et al. (2008). Unique expression of suppressor of cytokine signaling 3 is essential for classical macrophage activation in rodents in vitro and in vivo. *Journal of Immunology, 180*, 6270.

Mackaness, G. B. (1969). The influence of immunologically committed lymphoid cells on macrophage activity in vivo. *The Journal of Experimental Medicine, 129*, 973.

Mahabeleshwar, G. H., Kawanami, D., Sharma, N., Takami, Y., Zhou, G., Shi, H., et al. (2011). The myeloid transcription factor KLF2 regulates the host response to polymicrobial infection and endotoxic shock. *Immunity, 34*, 715.

Mantovani, A. (2008). From phagocyte diversity and activation to probiotics: Back to Metchnikoff. *European Journal of Immunology, 38*, 3269.

Mantovani, A., Biswas, S. K., Galdiero, M. R., Sica, A., & Locati, M. (2013). Macrophage plasticity and polarization in tissue repair and remodelling. *The Journal of Pathology, 229*, 176.

Mantovani, A., Sica, A., Sozzani, S., Allavena, P., Vecchi, A., & Locati, M. (2004). The chemokine system in diverse forms of macrophage activation and polarization. *Trends in Immunology, 25*, 677.

Mantovani, A., Sozzani, S., Locati, M., Allavena, P., & Sica, A. (2002). Macrophage polarization: Tumor-associated macrophages as a paradigm for polarized M2 mononuclear phagocytes. *Trends in Immunology, 23*, 549.

Martinez, F. O., Gordon, S., Locati, M., & Mantovani, A. (2006). Transcriptional profiling of the human monocyte-to-macrophage differentiation and polarization: New molecules and patterns of gene expression. *Journal of Immunology, 177*, 7303.

Martinez, F. O., Helming, L., & Gordon, S. (2009). Alternative activation of macrophages: An immunologic functional perspective. *Annual Review of Immunology, 27*, 451.

Medzhitov, R. (2008). Origin and physiological roles of inflammation. *Nature, 454*, 428.

Medzhitov, R., & Horng, T. (2009). Transcriptional control of the inflammatory response. *Nature Reviews. Immunology, 9*, 692.

Medzhitov, R., Schneider, D. S., & Soares, M. P. (2012). Disease tolerance as a defense strategy. *Science, 335*, 936.

Meltzer, M. S., Occhionero, M., & Ruco, L. P. (1982). Macrophage activation for tumor cytotoxicity: Regulatory mechanisms for induction and control of cytotoxic activity. *Federation Proceedings*, *41*, 2198.
Mills, C. D., Kincaid, K., Alt, J. M., Heilman, M. J., & Hill, A. M. (2000). M-1/M-2 macrophages and the Th1/Th2 paradigm. *Journal of Immunology*, *164*, 6166.
Mosser, D. M., & Edwards, J. P. (2008). Exploring the full spectrum of macrophage activation. *Nature Reviews. Immunology*, *8*, 958.
Mullican, S. E., Gaddis, C. A., Alenghat, T., Nair, M. G., Giacomin, P. R., Everett, L. J., et al. (2011). Histone deacetylase 3 is an epigenomic brake in macrophage alternative activation. *Genes & Development*, *25*, 2480.
Naessens, T., Vander Beken, S., Bogaert, P., Van Rooijen, N., Lienenklaus, S., Weiss, S., et al. (2012). Innate imprinting of murine resident alveolar macrophages by allergic bronchial inflammation causes a switch from hypoinflammatory to hyperinflammatory reactivity. *American Journal of Pathology*, *181*, 174.
Nahid, M. A., Pauley, K. M., Satoh, M., & Chan, E. K. (2009). miR-146a is critical for endotoxin-induced tolerance: Implication in innate immunity. *Journal of Biological Chemistry*, *284*, 34590.
Nathan, C. F., Prendergast, T. J., Wiebe, M. E., Stanley, E. R., Platzer, E., Remold, H. G., et al. (1984). Activation of human macrophages. Comparison of other cytokines with interferon-gamma. *The Journal of Experimental Medicine*, *160*, 600.
Natoli, G., Ghisletti, S., & Barozzi, I. (2011). The genomic landscapes of inflammation. *Genes & Development*, *25*, 101.
Nazari-Jahantigh, M., Wei, Y., Noels, H., Akhtar, S., Zhou, Z., Koenen, R. R., et al. (2012). MicroRNA-155 promotes atherosclerosis by repressing Bcl6 in macrophages. *Journal of Clinical Investigation*, *122*, 4190.
Netea, M. G., Quintin, J., & van der Meer, J. W. (2011). Trained immunity: A memory for innate host defense. *Cell Host & Microbe*, *9*, 355.
Nicodeme, E., Jeffrey, K. L., Schaefer, U., Beinke, S., Dewell, S., Chung, C. W., et al. (2010). Suppression of inflammation by a synthetic histone mimic. *Nature*, *468*, 1119.
Noel, W., Raes, G., Hassanzadeh Ghassabeh, G., De Baetselier, P., & Beschin, A. (2004). Alternatively activated macrophages during parasite infections. *Trends in Parasitology*, *20*, 126.
Odegaard, J. I., Ricardo-Gonzalez, R. R., Goforth, M. H., Morel, C. R., Subramanian, V., Mukundan, L., et al. (2007). Macrophage-specific PPARgamma controls alternative activation and improves insulin resistance. *Nature*, *447*, 1116.
Odegaard, J. I., Ricardo-Gonzalez, R. R., Red Eagle, A., Vats, D., Morel, C. R., Goforth, M. H., et al. (2008). Alternative M2 activation of Kupffer cells by PPARdelta ameliorates obesity-induced insulin resistance. *Cell Metabolism*, *7*, 496.
Olofsson, P. S., Rosas-Ballina, M., Levine, Y. A., & Tracey, K. J. (2012). Rethinking inflammation: Neural circuits in the regulation of immunity. *Immunological Reviews*, *248*, 188.
Pauleau, A. L., Rutschman, R., Lang, R., Pernis, A., Watowich, S. S., & Murray, P. J. (2004). Enhancer-mediated control of macrophage-specific arginase I expression. *Journal of Immunology*, *172*, 7565.
Pavlov, V. A., & Tracey, K. J. (2012). The vagus nerve and the inflammatory reflex—Linking immunity and metabolism. *Nature Reviews. Endocrinology*, *8*, 743.
Pello, O. M., Chevre, R., Laoui, D., De Juan, A., Lolo, F., Andres-Manzano, M. J., et al. (2012). In vivo inhibition of c-MYC in myeloid cells impairs tumor-associated macrophage maturation and pro-tumoral activities. *PLoS One*, *7*, e45399.
Pello, O. M., De Pizzol, M., Mirolo, M., Soucek, L., Zammataro, L., Amabile, A., et al. (2012). Role of c-MYC in alternative activation of human macrophages and tumor-associated macrophage biology. *Blood*, *119*, 411.

Pesce, J., Kaviratne, M., Ramalingam, T. R., Thompson, R. W., Urban, J. F., Jr., Cheever, A. W., et al. (2006). The IL-21 receptor augments Th2 effector function and alternative macrophage activation. *Journal of Clinical Investigation, 116*, 2044.
Pollard, J. W. (2009). Trophic macrophages in development and disease. *Nature Reviews. Immunology, 9*, 259.
Porta, C., Rimoldi, M., Raes, G., Brys, L., Ghezzi, P., Di Liberto, D., et al. (2009). Tolerance and M2 (alternative) macrophage polarization are related processes orchestrated by p50 nuclear factor kappaB. *Proceedings of the National Academy of Sciences of the United States of America, 106*, 14978.
Puig-Kroger, A., Sierra-Filardi, E., Dominguez-Soto, A., Samaniego, R., Corcuera, M. T., Gomez-Aguado, F., et al. (2009). Folate receptor beta is expressed by tumor-associated macrophages and constitutes a marker for M2 anti-inflammatory/regulatory macrophages. *Cancer Research, 69*, 9395.
Rae, F., Woods, K., Sasmono, T., Campanale, N., Taylor, D., Ovchinnikov, D. A., et al. (2007). Characterisation and trophic functions of murine embryonic macrophages based upon the use of a Csf1r-EGFP transgene reporter. *Developmental Biology, 308*, 232.
Raes, G., Brys, L., Dahal, B. K., Brandt, J., Grooten, J., Brombacher, F., et al. (2005). Macrophage galactose-type C-type lectins as novel markers for alternatively activated macrophages elicited by parasitic infections and allergic airway inflammation. *Journal of Leukocyte Biology, 77*, 321.
Recalcati, S., Locati, M., Marini, A., Santambrogio, P., Zaninotto, F., De Pizzol, M., et al. (2010). Differential regulation of iron homeostasis during human macrophage polarized activation. *European Journal of Immunology, 40*, 824.
Roca, H., Varsos, Z. S., Sud, S., Craig, M. J., Ying, C., & Pienta, K. J. (2009). CCL2 and interleukin-6 promote survival of human CD11b+ peripheral blood mononuclear cells and induce M2-type macrophage polarization. *Journal of Biological Chemistry, 284*, 34342.
Rodrigues, J., Brayner, F. A., Alves, L. C., Dixit, R., & Barillas-Mury, C. (2010). Hemocyte differentiation mediates innate immune memory in *Anopheles gambiae* mosquitoes. *Science, 329*, 1353.
Rodriguez-Prados, J. C., Traves, P. G., Cuenca, J., Rico, D., Aragones, J., Martin-Sanz, P., et al. (2010). Substrate fate in activated macrophages: A comparison between innate, classic, and alternative activation. *Journal of Immunology, 185*, 605.
Rossato, M., Curtale, G., Tamassia, N., Castellucci, M., Mori, L., Gasperini, S., et al. (2012). IL-10-induced microRNA-187 negatively regulates TNF-alpha, IL-6, and IL-12p40 production in TLR4-stimulated monocytes. *Proceedings of the National Academy of Sciences of the United States of America, 109*, E3101.
Ruckerl, D., Jenkins, S. J., Laqtom, N. N., Gallagher, I. J., Sutherland, T. E., Duncan, S., et al. (2012). Induction of IL-4Ralpha-dependent microRNAs identifies PI3K/Akt signaling as essential for IL-4-driven murine macrophage proliferation in vivo. *Blood, 120*, 2307.
Satoh, T., Takeuchi, O., Vandenbon, A., Yasuda, K., Tanaka, Y., Kumagai, Y., et al. (2010). The Jmjd3-Irf4 axis regulates M2 macrophage polarization and host responses against helminth infection. *Nature Immunology, 11*, 936.
Sheedy, F. J., Palsson-McDermott, E., Hennessy, E. J., Martin, C., O'Leary, J. J., Ruan, Q., et al. (2010). Negative regulation of TLR4 via targeting of the proinflammatory tumor suppressor PDCD4 by the microRNA miR-21. *Nature Immunology, 11*, 141.
Sica, A., & Bronte, V. (2007). Altered macrophage differentiation and immune dysfunction in tumor development. *Journal of Clinical Investigation, 117*, 1155.
Sica, A., & Mantovani, A. (2012). Macrophage plasticity and polarization: In vivo veritas. *Journal of Clinical Investigation, 122*, 787.
Smale, S. T. (2010). Selective transcription in response to an inflammatory stimulus. *Cell, 140*, 833.

Souza, D. G., Vieira, A. T., Soares, A. C., Pinho, V., Nicoli, J. R., Vieira, L. Q., et al. (2004). The essential role of the intestinal microbiota in facilitating acute inflammatory responses. *Journal of Immunology, 173*, 4137.

Spence, S., Fitzsimons, A., Boyd, C. R., Kessler, J., Fitzgerald, D., Elliott, J., et al. (2013). Suppressors of cytokine signaling 2 and 3 diametrically control macrophage polarization. *Immunity, 38*, 66.

Squadrito, M. L., Pucci, F., Magri, L., Moi, D., Gilfillan, G. D., Ranghetti, A., et al. (2012). miR-511-3p modulates genetic programs of tumor-associated macrophages. *Cell Reports, 1*, 141.

Stein, M., Keshav, S., Harris, N., & Gordon, S. (1992). Interleukin 4 potently enhances murine macrophage mannose receptor activity: A marker of alternative immunologic macrophage activation. *The Journal of Experimental Medicine, 176*, 287.

Stender, J. D., Pascual, G., Liu, W., Kaikkonen, M. U., Do, K., Spann, N. J., et al. (2012). Control of proinflammatory gene programs by regulated trimethylation and demethylation of histone H4K20. *Molecular Cell, 48*, 28.

Szanto, A., Balint, B. L., Nagy, Z. S., Barta, E., Dezso, B., Pap, A., et al. (2010). STAT6 transcription factor is a facilitator of the nuclear receptor PPARgamma-regulated gene expression in macrophages and dendritic cells. *Immunity, 33*, 699.

Taganov, K. D., Boldin, M. P., Chang, K. J., & Baltimore, D. (2006). NF-kappaB-dependent induction of microRNA miR-146, an inhibitor targeted to signaling proteins of innate immune responses. *Proceedings of the National Academy of Sciences of the United States of America, 103*, 12481.

Takeda, N., O'Dea, E. L., Doedens, A., Kim, J. W., Weidemann, A., Stockmann, C., et al. (2010). Differential activation and antagonistic function of HIF-{alpha} isoforms in macrophages are essential for NO homeostasis. *Genes & Development, 24*, 491.

Takeuch, O., & Akira, S. (2011). Epigenetic control of macrophage polarization. *European Journal of Immunology, 41*, 2490.

Tausendschon, M., Dehne, N., & Brune, B. (2011). Hypoxia causes epigenetic gene regulation in macrophages by attenuating Jumonji histone demethylase activity. *Cytokine, 53*, 256.

Tili, E., Michaille, J. J., Cimino, A., Costinean, S., Dumitru, C. D., Adair, B., et al. (2007). Modulation of miR-155 and miR-125b levels following lipopolysaccharide/TNF-alpha stimulation and their possible roles in regulating the response to endotoxin shock. *Journal of Immunology, 179*, 5082.

Uhlenhaut, N. H., Barish, G. D., Yu, R. T., Downes, M., Karunasiri, M., Liddle, C., et al. (2013). Insights into negative regulation by the glucocorticoid receptor from genome-wide profiling of inflammatory cistromes. *Molecular Cell, 49*, 158.

Verbist, K. C., Wang, R., & Green, D. R. (2012). T cell metabolism and the immune response. *Seminars in Immunology, 24*, 399.

Wang, Y. C., He, F., Feng, F., Liu, X. W., Dong, G. Y., Qin, H. Y., et al. (2010). Notch signaling determines the M1 versus M2 polarization of macrophages in antitumor immune responses. *Cancer Research, 70*, 4840.

Wang, P., Hou, J., Lin, L., Wang, C., Liu, X., Li, D., et al. (2010). Inducible microRNA-155 feedback promotes type I IFN signaling in antiviral innate immunity by targeting suppressor of cytokine signaling 1. *Journal of Immunology, 185*, 6226.

Wei, G., Wei, L., Zhu, J., Zang, C., Hu-Li, J., Yao, Z., et al. (2009). Global mapping of H3K4me3 and H3K27me3 reveals specificity and plasticity in lineage fate determination of differentiating CD4+ T cells. *Immunity, 30*, 155.

Whyte, C. S., Bishop, E. T., Ruckerl, D., Gaspar-Pereira, S., Barker, R. N., Allen, J. E., et al. (2011). Suppressor of cytokine signaling (SOCS)1 is a key determinant of differential macrophage activation and function. *Journal of Leukocyte Biology, 90*, 845.

Willment, J. A., Lin, H. H., Reid, D. M., Taylor, P. R., Williams, D. L., Wong, S. Y., et al. (2003). Dectin-1 expression and function are enhanced on alternatively activated and GM-CSF-treated macrophages and are negatively regulated by IL-10, dexamethasone, and lipopolysaccharide. *Journal of Immunology, 171*, 4569.

Wynn, T. A. (2004). Fibrotic disease and the T(H)1/T(H)2 paradigm. *Nature Reviews. Immunology, 4*, 583.

Xu, H., Zhu, J., Smith, S., Foldi, J., Zhao, B., Chung, A. Y., et al. (2012). Notch-RBP-J signaling regulates the transcription factor IRF8 to promote inflammatory macrophage polarization. *Nature Immunology, 13*, 642.

Yang, Z., Yik, J. H., Chen, R., He, N., Jang, M. K., Ozato, K., et al. (2005). Recruitment of P-TEFb for stimulation of transcriptional elongation by the bromodomain protein Brd4. *Molecular Cell, 19*, 535.

Zhu, Y., van Essen, D., & Saccani, S. (2012). Cell-type-specific control of enhancer activity by H3K9 trimethylation. *Molecular Cell, 46*, 408.

CHAPTER SEVEN

Terminal Differentiation of Dendritic Cells

Cyril Seillet[*,†], **Gabrielle T. Belz**[*,†,1]
[*]Division of Molecular Immunology, Walter and Eliza Hall Institute of Medical Research, Melbourne, Victoria, Australia
[†]Department of Medical Biology, University of Melbourne, Melbourne, Victoria, Australia
[1]Corresponding author: e-mail address: belz@wehi.edu.au

Contents

Abstract

Dendritic cells (DCs) are essential for the initiation of an effective immune response. Despite this, our understanding of the molecular regulation of this important cell type has lagged significantly behind that of other lymphoid populations such as B and T cells, but recent development of various tools has greatly facilitated progress in the field. Here, we review the transcription factors that drive peripheral DC subset fate decisions. While Pu.1, Ikaros, and Gfi-1 are essential for precursor DCs to give rise to monocytes, conventional DCs, and plasmacytoid DCs, the balance between E2-2 and Id2 directs committed precursors along a pDC or cDC lineage, respectively. Several transcription

Advances in Immunology, Volume 120
ISSN 0065-2776
http://dx.doi.org/10.1016/B978-0-12-417028-5.00007-7

factors such as Batf3, Nfil3, and Id2 are required for different DC subsets at steady-state and drive segregation into the individual DCs subsets late in development in the CD8 lineage. During inflammation, CD8-expressing DCs emerge that feature many of the hallmarks of classical CD8α^+ DCs but surprisingly do not depend on the same transcription factors. Thus, the immune system has developed two pathways of DC differentiation that enable it to maintain homeostatic balance and to respond rapidly to the emergency requirement for DCs that might occur during infection.

1. INTRODUCTION

Dendritic cells (DCs) are critical regulators of immune responses. They are a functionally specialized but diverse group of heterogeneous cells, in which distinct DC subsets are established through the expression of lineage-specific transcription factors (Belz & Nutt, 2012; Geissmann et al., 2010; Miller et al., 2012). Unraveling the network that guides the development of these different DC subsets has been greatly facilitated by the isolation and characterization of progenitor populations, identification of the cytokines and transcription factors that are essential for their development, and, critically, the generation of a library of genetic tools, particularly fluorescent reporter mice, to allow direct visualization of the developmental steps of DCs both *in vitro* and *in vivo*. Thus, much more has become known about the molecular signals (specific growth and transcription factors) that promote DC fate and impart the identity and tissue localization of different DC subsets.

2. DENDRITIC CELL SUBSETS

At present, DCs are generally categorized into four main groups: conventional DCs (cDCs), plasmacytoid DCs (pDCs), Langerhans cells (LCs), and monocyte-derived inflammatory DCs. These different populations arise from the common lymphoid progenitor found in the bone marrow and become progressively restricted into macrophage-DC progenitors (MDPs) (Auffray et al., 2009; Fogg et al., 2006). Subsequently, a common DC precursor that expresses high levels of Flt3 gives rise to both cDC and pDC lineages (Naik et al., 2007; Onai et al., 2007). From here, pre-cDCs, which are entirely cDC-restricted, seed the lymphoid and nonlymphoid tissues where terminal differentiation and maturation occur (Naik et al., 2006). This is distinct from the development of pDCs, which diverge from cDCs as they undergo maturation in the bone marrow (Naik et al., 2007; Onai et al., 2007).

2.1. Conventional DCs

cDCs encompass multiple subsets including the CD8α$^+$ lineage DCs (CD8α$^+$ and CD103$^+$ DCs) and non-CD8α$^+$ DCs, which includes the CD11b$^+$ and CD4$^+$ DC subsets (Henri et al., 2001; Vremec, Pooley, Hochrein, Wu, & Shortman, 2000). CD8 lineage DCs express either CD8α or CD103 (also known as αE integrin) but do not express CD11b, and they are highly efficient at presenting exogenous antigens on major histocompatibility complex (MHC) class I molecules (Bedoui et al., 2009; den Haan, Lehar, & Bevan, 2000; Jackson et al., 2011; Sung et al., 2006). Due to their dependence on a common set of transcription factors (Irf8, Id2, Nfil3, and Batf3), they have been grouped into a single family. CD4$^+$ DCs are found in spleen and are generally considered to poorly cross present antigens but are much more efficient in presenting MHC class II-restricted antigens to CD4$^+$ T cells. Their complementary subset found in peripheral tissues, the CD11b$^+$ DCs (CD103$^+$ or D103$^-$), does not express CD4 but shares many of the features of their splenic counterparts (Bogunovic et al., 2009; Ginhoux et al., 2009).

2.2. Plasmacytoid DCs

pDCs are a distinct lineage separated from the cDCs by regulation of their differentiation program by distinct transcription factors (particularly E2-2), their capacity to secrete abundant amounts of type 1 interferon (IFN-α) following viral infection, their morphology, and their poor antigen presentation capacity (Asselin-Paturel, Brizard, Pin, Briere, & Trinchieri, 2003; Grouard et al., 1997; Siegal et al., 1999). They are characterized by their expression of B220, Ly49Q, Siglec-H, and Bst2 (CD317, bone marrow stromal cell antigen 2, also known as PDCA-1) (Asselin-Paturel et al., 2003; Omatsu et al., 2005; Zhang et al., 2006) in mice or in humans BDCA2 (CD303) and BDCA4 (CD304) (Dzionek et al., 2000).

2.3. Langerhans cells

LCs are skin-resident DCs that arise from a bone marrow-derived myelomonocytic precursor and migrate to the lymph nodes to present antigens. They are developmentally dependent on signaling through the macrophage colony-stimulating factor receptor (M-CSFR) and share similarities with macrophages in their gene expression profiles (Ginhoux et al., 2006; Hume, 2011; Miller et al., 2012). When activated, however, LCs acquire features more in line with cDCs such as their enhanced migratory ability and expression of the cDC specific transcription factor (Meredith et al., 2012; Satpathy et al., 2012).

2.4. Inflammatory monocytes

During inflammation, a subset of DCs emerge and have been described as inflammatory DCs. They differentiate from Ly6C^{hi} monocytes and are recruited to the site of inflammation where they can present antigens to both CD4^{+} and CD8^{+} T cells (Leon, Lopez-Bravo, & Ardavin, 2007). These cells express a number of markers similar to macrophages including M-CSFR (or CD115) and the chemokine receptor CX3CR1 and respond to growth factors such as granulocyte–macrophage colony-stimulating factor (GM-CSF) *in vitro* or to bacterial or fungal products *in vivo* to induce the development of fully differentiated inflammatory DCs that preferentially prime Th17 responses (Cheong et al., 2010; Segura et al., 2013).

Collectively, the selective capacity of the various DC populations to adopt different functional roles has led to the notion that a division of labor amongst DC subsets could have therapeutic potential. Our increased understanding of the genetic program that guides the development of these DC subsets suggests that the capacity to induce these outcomes is preprogrammed in the terminally differentiated DC subset and are instrumental in guiding T-cell behavior.

In this chapter, we focus on the role of transcription factors in generating different DC subsets with emphasis on late differentiation events and the generation of the CD8 family of DCs. Furthermore, we highlight the elucidation of an alternative pathway of DC development in which CD8α^{+} DCs emerge under emergency or inflammatory conditions but do not rely on the classical suite of transcriptional regulators for their development pointing to an as yet largely untapped area of research in understanding how DC plasticity is achieved once steady-state homeostasis is disrupted.

3. TRANSCRIPTIONAL REGULATION OF EARLY DC DEVELOPMENT: CELLULAR DIFFERENTIATION AND SOME OF THE KEY REGULATORY MOLECULES

At present, transcription factors that determine the lineage development of DC subsets act at multiple different levels. Some transcription factors such as Ikaros, Pu.1 (Carotta et al., 2010), Gfi-1 (growth factor independent 1) transcriptional repressor, and interferon regulatory factor (Irf) 8 are broadly required for DC development but may in addition have specific effects on individual lineages. These factors generally exert a profound effect at the level of the DC progenitors. Other regulators such as E2-2 for pDCs (Cisse et al., 2008; Ghosh, Cisse, Bunin, Lewis, & Reizis, 2010) and Nfil3 (nuclear factor, interleukin-3) regulated (Kashiwada, Pham, Pewe, Harty, & Rothman, 2011) or Batf3 (basic leucine zipper (LZ) transcription factor, ATF-like 3) (Hildner et al., 2008) for $CD8\alpha^+$ and $CD103^+$ DCs have more specific effects within a population. Framing the effects of these regulators has typically occurred in terms of their capacity to act as "master regulators"—a single factor that establishes the phenotypic identity of a lineage—and is likely to be an oversimplification of the interactions that drive the formation of different DC subsets. Instead, combinations and doses of transcription factors (intrinsic regulators) coordinated with extrinsic factors such cytokines (Fms-like tyrosine kinase-3 (Flt3) and transforming growth factor-β (TGF-β)) may be important in driving DC formation in certain circumstances such as during inflammation or emergency hematopoiesis.

3.1. Ikaros

Ikaros, a member of the Kruppel family of zinc finger DNA-binding proteins, is a key factor for self-renewal activity in hemopoietic stem cells (HSC) and to direct priming the lymphoid transcriptional program (Georgopoulos et al., 1994; Nichogiannopoulou, Trevisan, Neben, Friedrich, & Georgopoulos, 1999). As a critical transcription factor for the early hematopoiesis, several mouse models have been used to explore developmental defects in Ikaros-deficient mice. Mice expressing a dominant negative form of Ikaros (Ikaros $DN^{-/-}$) that interferes with the activity of multiple Ikaros family members lack B, T, and natural killer (NK) cells as well as cDCs in spleen and thymus (Georgopoulos et al., 1994; Wu, Nichogiannopoulou, Shortman, & Georgopoulos, 1997). LCs and erythroid and myeloid lineages are not affected by the mutation. In Ikaros null mice, although differentiation of B and NK cells is severely impaired, some T-cell development occurs in adulthood (Wang et al., 1996). The mutation also leads to a complete loss of $CD8\alpha^-$ DCs and as much as a 30-fold reduction in $CD8\alpha^+$ DCs (Wu et al., 1997). In both Ikaros null and Ikaros $DN^{-/-}$ expression of the tyrosine kinase, Flt3 is absent on hematopoietic progenitors (Nichogiannopoulou et al., 1999). Signaling through Flt3 by Flt3L is essential for the differentiation of DCs from progenitors. Thus, loss of Ikaros in early DC development appears to be due to the lack of $Flt3^+$ DC precursors (D'Amico & Wu, 2003; Onai et al., 2007).

A further study in mice expressing only low levels of Ikaros due to a hypomorphic mutation showed a selective loss of pDCs in the periphery, suggesting that sustained Ikaros activity was required to maintain pDC identity (Allman et al., 2006). Indeed, comparison of gene expression in immature pDC obtained from the bone marrow of wild-type and $Ik^{L/L}$ mice showed that a large array of genes normally not found in wild-type pDCs were upregulated in $Ik^{L/L}$ pDC. Thus, it appears that Ikaros controls pDC differentiation at least in part by silencing genes that direct cDC development.

These studies suggest that Ikaros is required at multiple steps in DC development and influences both the earliest DC progenitors and mature DCs to maintain pDC identity. Furthermore, differences observed in the different mouse models imply that the graded activity of Ikaros is important for development cDC and pDC subsets. Conditional deletion of Ikaros in the DC compartment is now needed to address more precisely the role of this transcription factor in DC development.

3.2. Pu.1

Pu.1 is encoded by the *Sfpi1* gene and is a member of the E-twenty six (Ets) family. As with Ikaros, Pu.1 regulates a board range of genes within the myeloid and lymphoid lineages. It regulates commitment of adult hematopoietic progenitors and is required for the maintenance of normal hematopoietic stem cell function. Pu.1 was an attractive candidate as a key regulator in DCs because it is expressed by all DC subsets and their progenitors (Back, Allman, Chan, & Kastner, 2005; Carotta et al., 2010; Nutt, Metcalf, D'Amico, Polli, & Wu, 2005). Interestingly, high expression of Pu.1 in monocytes favors DC development at the expense of a macrophage fate by directly inhibiting expression of the macrophage factor, MafB, suggesting that Pu.1 could be an important decision factor between DC and macrophage commitment (Bakri et al., 2005).

Pu.$1^{-/-}$ mice have profound impairment in hematopoiesis and die either in late gestation or shortly after birth. This phenotype has hampered the study of Pu.1 function in DCs and led to conflicting reports describing its role in this lineage. Using Pu.$1^{-/-}$ mice, Anderson et al. (2000) concluded that all embryonic DCs failed to develop, while in a separate model, Guerriero, Langmuir, Spain, & Scott (2000) reported that fetal thymic CD8α^+ DCs were still present. The construction of mice in which Pu.1 could be conditionally deleted allowed the role of Pu.1 in early progenitors and the function of Pu.1 within mature DC lineages to be addressed (Carotta et al., 2010). Induction of

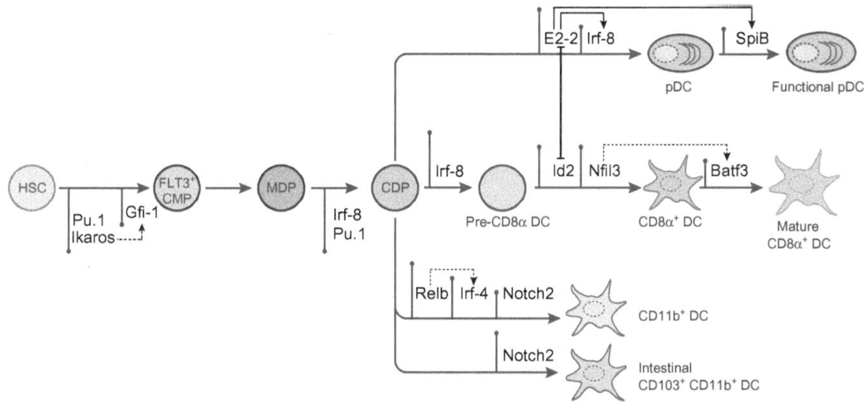

Figure 7.1 Transcription factors guiding cDC and pDC differentiation in steady-state hematopoietic stem cells (HSC) differentiate into common myeloid progenitors (CMPs), a fraction of which express FMS-related tyrosine kinase 3 (Flt3) and differentiate into more restricted macrophage and DC progenitors, MDPs, the common progenitor for monocytes and DCs. MDPs give rise to a common DC progenitor (CDP) that produce cDC and pDC subsets but in which monocyte potential is lost. The current view of transcriptional network in DC development is depicted. The coordinated action between these different factors is not yet well understood. Vertical bars indicate plausible chronological requirements for each factor between the different developmental stages. Solid arrows indicate connections that have been proven, while dotted arrows indicate hypothesized relationships. (For color version of this figure, the reader is referred to the online version of this chapter.)

deletion of Pu.1 in different hematopoietic precursors demonstrated that Pu.1 was absolutely required for DC development *in vivo* and *in vitro* in response to Flt3L. Indeed, Pu.1 directly regulated Flt3 expression on DCs and their precursors in a dose-dependent manner (Fig. 7.1; Carotta et al., 2010). Although the absence of Flt3 expression by Pu.1-deficient cells has logical consequences for DC development, Pu.1 regulates other important targets such as M-CSFR (Zhang, Hetherington, Chen, & Tenen, 1994), granulocyte-macrophage colony-stimulating factor receptor (Hohaus et al., 1995), and molecules that affect DC function such as MHC class II and co-stimulatory molecules CD80 and CD86. Thus, the role of Pu.1 is likely to be more complex than modulation of cytokine receptors expression on progenitor cells and differentiated cells, and as such, the mechanisms by which Pu.1 regulates DC lineage fate choice remain to be elucidated.

3.3. Growth factor independent-1

Growth factor independent-1 (Gfi1) is a transcriptional zinc finger repressor. Gfi1 deficiency leads to a reduction of DC precursors and consequently cDC and pDC subsets in bone marrow, spleen, and lymphoid organs (Rathinam et al., 2005). In contrast to Ikaros$^{-/-}$ mice, LC development, however, remains intact and may actually be increased. Normally, signaling *via* Flt3L and GM-CSF *in vitro* drives hematopoietic progenitors to differentiate into DCs (Kingston et al., 2009), but in the absence of Gfi1, cells are diverted to differentiate into macrophages. This shift correlated with a significant reduction of the Stat3 activity in progenitors downstream Flt3 signaling, which is required for the emergence of DC precursors (Esashi et al., 2008; Laouar, Welte, Fu, & Flavell, 2003). In multipotent progenitors, Ikaros positively regulates Gfi1 by repressing Pu.1 to promote a B-cell fate (Spooner, Cheng, Pujadas, Laslo, & Singh, 2009). It is possible that a similar pathway may be employed in DCs. However, the coordinate action of Ikaros, Pu.1, and Gfi1 during early DC development remains unclear.

4. TRANSCRIPTIONAL REGULATION OF LATE DC DEVELOPMENT AT STEADY STATE

The lineage fate of hematopoietic progenitor cells is controlled by an orchestrated expression pattern of transcription factors, yet the precise molecular mechanisms that define how these factors govern the diversification of DC progenitor cells remain largely unknown. pDCs are a distinct lineage of DCs regulated principally by the pDC master regulator E2-2 together with Spi-B. The decisions effected through E2-2, however, are balanced by the complementary interactions of the transcriptional regulator Id2. Id2 is expressed by all cDC subsets, which also express Zbtb46 and drive the development of CD8α^+ and CD103$^+$ DCs through Nfil3 and Batf3. In contrast, Irf4, RelB, and Notch are important for the formation of non-CD8 lineage DCs (Fig. 7.1). The interplay of these different transcription factors is essential to shape the rich heterogeneity of the DC family.

4.1. E2-2

E-box (or E) proteins belong to the basic helix-loop-helix (bHLH) transcription factor family, which includes E2A (encoded by *Tcf3*, producing E12, E47), HEB (encoded by *Tcf12*), and E2-2 (encoded by *Tcf4*). E proteins can form either heterodimers or homodimers and activate transcription by binding to regulatory E-box sequences on target genes (Murre, McCaw, & Baltimore, 1989; Murre, McCaw, & Vaessin, et al., 1989). Their activity is inhibited by heterodimerization with inhibitor of DNA-binding (Id proteins, class IV) helix-loop-helix proteins that lack the basic domain of E proteins. In forming a heterodimer with E proteins, they are unable to bind to DNA and thus transcription blocked.

E2-2 is highly expressed in pDC, at lower levels in B cells, and is almost undetectable in other immune cells (Cisse et al., 2008; Nagasawa, Schmidlin, Hazekamp, Schotte, & Blom, 2008). pDC formation is significantly affected when E2-2 is deleted either in the progenitor cells or by conditional deletion in $CD11c^+$ cells. Indeed, pDCs are very sensitive to E2-2 expression as pDC number and IFN-α secretion are profoundly impaired in *E2-2*$^{+/-}$ mice and in human patients with Pitt–Hopkins syndrome who have E2-2 haploinsufficiency. E2-2 directly binds to the promoter regions of pDC-expressed genes and controls the expression level of transcription factors such as *Spi-B*, *Irf8*, and *Irf7*, which are important for pDC development (Cisse et al., 2008; Ghosh et al., 2010). Induction of deletion of E2-2 in mature pDC is associated with the spontaneous acquisition of a cDC phenotype accompanied by increased expression of Id2 and the loss of pDC lineage identity. Id2, an antagonist E protein activity, is abundantly express in all cDC (Jackson et al., 2011), and its overexpression in human progenitor cells blocks pDC development *in vitro* (Spits, Couwenberg, Bakker, Weijer, & Uittenbogaart, 2000), highlighting the reciprocal balance that is mediated by E2-2 and Id2 in delineating DC fate. Thus, E2-2 appears to antagonize cDC cell fate by repressing cDC-associated genes (Ghosh et al., 2010). Intriguingly, E2-2-deficient pDCs upregulate CD8α but these cells lack other hallmarks of classical $CD8\alpha^+$ DCs such as expression of *Tlr3*, *Xcr1*, or *Itgae* genes. Thus, loss of E2-2 alone is not sufficient for bona fide cDCs formation but may give rise to related population of CD8α DCs that express CX_3CR1. $CX_3CR1^+CD8\alpha^+$ cDCs express low levels of E2-2 but require its expression for their development in the bone marrow, suggesting that they originate from committed pDC progenitors that subsequently downregulate E2-2 (Bar-On et al., 2010). When the expression of E2-2 is switched on or off to establish the fate of pDC development still remains to be fully elucidated. Indeed, exactly how E proteins and Id2 proteins are balanced during development to effect the fate decisions, or how cytokines, which induce their expression modify fate outcomes, is not clear. The discovery of E2-2 as a critical regulator of pDC lineage specification in mice and in humans, however, has greatly helped us to understand pDC development and how lineage fate decisions between pDCs and cDCs are modulated.

4.2. Spi-B

Spi-B is an Ets family member and is closely related to PU.1 with which it shares 70% sequence identity in their DNA-binding domain (DBD) (Chen et al., 1995) and appears to share many target genes at least by *in vitro* analyses (Ray-Gallet, Mao, Tavitian, & Moreau-Gachelin, 1995). Despite the similarities between Spi-B and PU.1, their expression patterns are distinct and their roles in hematopoiesis are nonredundant *in vivo*. Like E2-2, Spi-B expression is restricted to pDCs within the DC compartment (Cisse et al., 2008; Nagasawa et al., 2008; Schotte et al., 2003). The first suggestion of Spi-B involvement in pDC differentiation was indicated when ectopic expression of Spi-B in human CD34^{+} progenitor cells favored development of pDCs *in vitro* while T, B, and NK cell differentiation was inhibited (Schotte et al., 2003). Conversely, knockdown of Spi-B inhibited pDC generation from CD34^{+} precursor cells confirming an essential role for Spi-B in human pDC development (Schotte, Nagasawa, Weijer, Spits, & Blom, 2004). In mice, loss of Spi-B resulted in defects in B-cell activation and T-cell-dependent humoral immune responses (Su et al., 1997). Although *Spi-B*$^{-/-}$ mice were generated more than 15 years ago, characterization of pDC development or function has only recently been examined. Surprisingly, *Spi-B*$^{-/-}$ mice do not display a marked developmental impairment in pDCs as might be predicted from the *in vitro* studies (Sasaki et al., 2012). Bone marrow pDCs were decreased but not abolished, while pDCs in spleen and lymph nodes were increased in Spi-B$^{-/-}$ mice. Mixed bone marrow chimeras revealed that these changes were cell intrinsic. However, *Spi-B*$^{-/-}$ pDC showed profound functional alterations, with an impaired production of type I IFN and proinflammatory cytokines in response to TLR-7 or TLR-9 (Sasaki et al., 2012). Spi-B-deficiency in bone marrow pDCs was accompanied by altered pDC-specific genes expression such as *Klra17* (Ly49Q), *Clec4g*, and *Klk1*. E2-2 expression was not affected in the absence of Spi-*B* supporting the notion that Spi-B acts downstream of E2-2 (Cisse et al., 2008). Spi-B seems therefore involved in the acquisition and/or the maintenance of the functional properties of pDCs rather than their early development in mice (Fig. 7.1).

4.3. The CD8α^{-} lineage

4.3.1 RelB

RelB was the first transcription factor described to affect a particular DC subset (Wu et al., 1998). RelB is a NF-κB family member, most highly expressed in the CD8α$^-$ and CD11b$^+$ DC subsets and loss of *Relb* results in a cell-autonomous reduction of these populations (Fig. 7.1; Burkly et al., 1995; Wu et al., 1998). The NF-κB family of transcription factors consists of p50, p52, RelA (also called p65), c-Rel, and RelB. These family members are characterized by the presence of an N-terminal Rel homology domain responsible for homo- and heterodimerization as well as for targeting specific DNA-binding sequences. Unlike RelA and c-Rel that predominantly heterodimerize with p50, RelB preferentially heterodimerizes with p52 or its precursor form, p100 (Vallabhapurapu & Karin, 2009).

Despite the important role of RelB in DC differentiation, the mechanism by which this occurs has not been investigated. RelB has the peculiarity of possessing a LZ domain (Hayden & Ghosh, 2008). Such LZ domains have recently been described in the Batf to allow interaction with Irf family members to mediate cooperative gene activation (Tussiwand et al., 2012). Given the importance of Irf4 in CD8α$^-$ DC development, it seems plausible that it could be a target or a partner of the RelB pathway. Whether the LZ domain confers additional functional specificity to RelB, including its heterodimerization with other partners, remains to be determined.

4.3.2 Interferon regulatory factor 4

Interferon regulatory factor 4 (Irf4) is one of nine Irf family members. All Irf proteins share similar structure containing an N-terminal DBD and, expect Irf1 and Irf2, carry a C-terminal Irf-associated domain (IAD) that is responsible interactions with other family members or other transcription factors including ETS factors and AP1 (activator protein 1) family members. Irf4 is a critical regulator of many aspects of B- and T-cell differentiation and cell metabolism (Biswas et al., 2012; De Silva, Simonetti, Heise, & Klein, 2012; Eguchi et al., 2011). In DCs, Irf4 is highly expressed in the CD4$^+$ subset and in a fraction pDCs (Tamura et al., 2005). In line with this expression pattern, tissue-resident CD4$^+$ DCs and nearly half the pDC population are absent from the spleen of *Irf4*$^{-/-}$ mice (Suzuki et al., 2004; Tamura et al., 2005). Irf4 is intrinsically required for the development of CD11b$^+$ DCs and this can be mimicked *in in vitro* culture systems supplemented with the growth factors GM-CSF or Flt3-ligand (Tamura et al., 2005). Most of our understanding of the role of Irf4 comes from analyses of spleen and LNs, and the role of Irf4 in nonlymphoid tissue DC subsets has only been explored in skin-derived DCs to date (Bajana, Roach, Turner, Paul, & Kovats, 2012). One report suggests that Irf4-deficient DCs have altered migration from the dermis although *Irf4*$^{-/-}$ mice have normal numbers of LCs and increased numbers of dermal CD11b$^+$ and CD103$^+$ DCs, suggesting development of skin-resident DC subsets does not depend Irf4 (Bajana et al., 2012).

Irf4 does not appear to be required for the development of the earliest DC progenitors but precisely when Irf4 first acts and the mechanisms by which it directs DC development are currently undescribed. The estrogen receptor (ER)-α (encoded by nuclear receptor subfamily 3, groups A, member 1, NR3A1) is a ligand-inducible transcription factor that promotes Irf4 expression in DCs and regulates cDC and pDC development and function (Carreras et al., 2008; Douin-Echinard et al., 2008; Seillet et al., 2012). DCs that develop under GM-CSF conditions rely mainly on Irf4 (Tamura et al., 2005). ERα signaling is required for the induction of Irf4 in the DC precursors to promote this GM-CSF-mediated DC differentiation (Carreras et al., 2008). Conserved consensus estrogen response elements are present in the promoter region of the Irf4 locus, but whether ERα directly controls Irf4 induction, or alternately cooperates with other partners such as RelB, is not yet known.

4.3.3 Notch

The Notch family provides an evolutionarily conserved signaling network that plays a key role in the development of a variety of immune cells. Its role in DC differentiation has been controversial but more recent data is beginning to clarify how Notch promotes DC development and function. Notch signaling is initiated through the binding of Notch ligands: Jagged and Delta. Proteolytic cleavage of the transmembrane subunit of Notch receptor results in the release and translocation of the intracellular domain to the nucleus where it can interact with the transcriptional repressor CSL (C-promoter binding factor, suppressor of hairless, and Lag1; also designated CSL or RBP-Jκ, recombination signal binding protein for immunoglobulin kappa J region). This results in the displacement of corepressor complexes and activation of transcription by promoters that possess CSL binding domains (Allman, Punt, Izon, Aster, & Pear, 2002; Osborne & Minter, 2007).

Notch 1 was initially implicated in *in vitro* differentiation of DCs (Cheng, Nefedova, Miele, Osborne, & Gabrilovich, 2003; Zhou, Cheng, Youn, Cotter, & Gabrilovich, 2009). However, a number of studies described a different role Notch as conditional deletion of Notch1 showed that the number of thymic DCs and cDCs and LCs was normal (Radtke et al., 2000). Inhibition of Notch signaling with the inhibitor γ-secretase, or conditional deletion of Notch in T-cell progenitors, switched fate towards DCs (Feyerabend et al., 2009). Although deletion of Notch-1 does not appear to affect pDC differentiation, loss of RBP-J resulted in enhanced pDC numbers and was shown to be an important regulatory of non-CD8 DCs in spleen (Caton, Smith-Raska, & Reizis, 2007). Deletion of Notch2 resulted in loss of splenic $CD8^{-}CD11b^{+}$ DCs and these were a specific subset marked by expression of the adhesion molecule ESAM (endothelial cell-specific adhesion molecule) (Fig. 7.1; Lewis et al., 2011). Notch2/RBP-J blockade was also accompanied by reduced priming of $CD4^{+}$ T cells. In addition, intestinal lamina propria $CD11b^{+}CD103^{+}$ DCs thought to be responsible for trafficking antigen to the lymph node were ablated resulting in a loss of priming of Th17 helper T-cell immune responses. Notch2 appears to initiate and maintain differentiation and is required at the pre-DC stage. In the nonlymphoid tissues such as the intestine, the impact of Notch may occur after this progenitor stage. Dissecting out specifically where Notch family members act has demonstrated that Notch can have DC subset-specific effects in DC fate specification rather than its proposed a generalized role in DC differentiation (Cheng et al., 2003; Lewis et al., 2011; Zhou et al., 2009).

4.4. The pathway to the CD8 DC lineage

$CD8\alpha^{+}$ DCs and migratory $CD103^{+}$ DCs are typically grouped in the same family owing to their shared dependence on the transcription factors Irf8, Id2, Nfil3, and Batf3 (Table 7.1) and highly similar functional attributes (Ginhoux et al., 2009; Hildner et al., 2008; Jackson et al., 2011). It seems highly likely that these two subsets represent lymphoid tissue-resident and peripheral tissue DC counterparts although it is not clear how each population is homeostatically regulated nor how transitions between the two different phenotypes might be mediated. Nevertheless, the development of different fluorescent reporter mice for lineage tracing (e.g., $Zbtb46^{GFP/+}$ (Satpathy et al., 2012), $Id2^{GFP/GFP}$ (Jackson et al., 2011) strains) and combination of such lines with various knockout strains has identified these four transcription factors as core to the development of the $CD8\alpha^{+}$ and $CD103^{+}$ DCs. In addition, it has raised some surprising findings that have been critical to the development of the field.

4.4.1 *Interferon regulatory factor 8*

Interferon regulatory factor 8 (Irf8), also known as interferon consensus sequence-binding protein, is a component of the Irf transcription factor family. Irf8 is differentially expressed in DCs and is particularly highly expressed in CDPs, pDCs, and CD8α DCs (Becker et al., 2012; Tamura et al., 2005; Tsujimura, Tamura, & Ozato, 2003). $Irf8^{-/-}$ mice lack pDCs, CD8α DCs,

Table 7.1 Requirement for transcription factors by different DC subsets at steady-state and during immune responses

	Transcription factor					
	Irf8	**Id2**	**Nfil3**	**Batf3**	**Batf**	**Batf2**
Steady-state DCs						
$CD8\alpha^+$ DCs	✓	✓	✓	✓/–	✓/–	–
CD103 DCs (spleen)	✓	✓	✓	✓	–	–
Immune response DCs						
Inflammatory DCs	✓	–	–	–	?	?
Emergency $CD8\alpha^+$ DCs	✓	–	–	–	?	?
Cytokine-driven DCs (IL-12, IFN-γ)	✓	–	–	–	–	✓
$CD103^+$ DC (intestine)	✓	–	–	–	?	?

and $CD103^+$ DCs and have a reduction of LCs frequency (Aliberti et al., 2003; Edelson et al., 2010; Schiavoni et al., 2002, 2004; Tsujimura, Tamura, Gongora, et al., 2003; Tsujimura, Tamura, & Ozato, 2003). In addition, they can develop a spontaneous myeloproliferative syndrome characterized by hyperproliferation of granulocytes (Holtschke et al., 1996), implying an important role for Irf8 in regulation of proliferation and differentiation of hematopoietic progenitor cells. Indeed, Irf8 was recently found to promote common dendritic cell precursor (CDP) development and the initial commitment to the DC lineage by inhibiting granulopoiesis. Thus, Irf8 appears to regulate the GMP (granulocyte–macrophage progenitor) versus CDP fate decision downstream of the common myeloid progenitor (CMP) (Fig. 7.1; Becker et al., 2012).

The function of Irf8 in DC development appears to be conserved across humans and mice. Molecular mechanisms regulated by Irf8 that drive the generation and control of DC functions remain largely unknown. The identification of mutations within Irf8 in both man and mouse has facilitated teasing out some of these details. Irf8 mutations in the DNA-binding domain (i.e., K108E and T80A) in man are associated with an inhibition of monocyte and/or DC production myeloproliferation of granulocyte precursors (Hambleton et al., 2011). More precisely, the autosomal recessive mutation (K108E) was accompanied by a complete lack of all DC and circulating monocytes. The T80A variant was associated with a selective loss of $CD11c^+CD1c^+$ circulating DCs (Hambleton et al., 2011).

Irf8 can interact with partner proteins of the Ets family, such as Pu.1 and Spi-B, to cooperatively assemble on composite Ets-Irf DNA (EICE) elements. BXH2 mice carry a spontaneous point mutation in Irf8 (Irf8^{R294C}), which also causes a form of myeloproliferative disease. Intriguingly, this specifically affects CD8α^+ DC and migratory CD103$^+$ DC generation but does not affect the pDC population (Ginhoux et al., 2009; Tailor, Tamura, Morse, & Ozato, 2008; Turcotte et al., 2004). pDCs and CD8α DCs are the major producer of type I IFN and IL-12, respectively, and help to establish antiviral and antimicrobial responses. These functions are also impaired in *Irf8*$^{-/-}$ mice, which are more susceptible to viral infection, a phenotype shared by the human patients bearing Irf8 mutations (Hambleton et al., 2011; Schiavoni et al., 2002; Tsujimura, Tamura, & Ozato, 2003). In mice, Irf8^{R294C} mutation is located within the IAD, which is important for the interaction of Irf8 with partner proteins. This suggests that Irf8 may interact with a distinct partner to regulate target genes in pDCs and cDCs or that pDC development exclusively relies on Irf8 independent of cofactor association. The identity of Irf8 partner proteins is of great interest for further understanding the molecular regulation of the pDCs and resident spleen CD8α^+ DC developmental programs.

4.4.2 Inhibitor of DNA-binding 2

Inhibitor of DNA-binding 2 (Id2) is a helix-loop-helix (HLH) transcriptional regulator that is known to antagonize E protein activity. It lacks the basic domain that is important for binding to E-box sequences on the DNA of target genes (Murre, McCaw, Vaessin, et al., 1989). The HLH domain of Id proteins interacts with the bHLH domain of E proteins to form heterodimers. This heterodimerization then renders E proteins unable to bind DNA. Id2 is required for the development of NK cells and lymphoid tissue-inducer cells thus mice that lack Id2 fail to develop lymph nodes, Peyer's patch, and other secondary lymphoid (reviewed in Rankin, Groom, Mielke, Seillet, & Belz, 2013). In addition, *Id2*$^{-/-}$ mice display a selective lack of LCs and Langerin-expressing dermal DCs and a severe reduction of CD8α^+ and CD103$^+$ DCs (Ginhoux et al., 2009; Hacker et al., 2003; Kusunoki et al., 2003). Unlike Irf8, Id2 is not expressed in DC precursors such as CDP and pre-DC (Jackson et al., 2011), suggesting that it is involved in the diversification and the terminal differentiation of DC subsets rather than influencing early lineage-commitment decisions. Nevertheless, all cDC subsets express Id2, but this expression is highest in LCs, CD8α^+, and CD103$^+$ DCs, while pDCs express very low levels of

Id2, supporting its role in antagonizing the expression of E2-2 in the cDC differentiation pathway (Jackson et al., 2011). The requirement for Id2 for LC development is restricted to steady-state conditions as short-term reconstitution of LCs from Gr-1^{high} monocytes under inflammatory conditions can occur independent of this transcription factor (Sere et al., 2012). The cytokines GM-CSF and Flt3L have been shown to induce the expression of Id2 and E2-2 through the signal transducer and activator of transcription (STAT) pathway. Overexpression of STAT3 in multipotent bone marrow progenitors induces expression of Pu.1 and enhances the differentiation of both pDCs and cDCs (Onai, Obata-Onai, Tussiwand, Lanzavecchia, & Manz, 2006). Induction of STAT5 appears to drive Id2 expression and enhance cDC development, while in contrast, pDC development relies on STAT3 expression (Li, Yang, et al., 2012). Thus, DC fate determination appears to depend at least in part on cytokine-driven STAT regulation of Id and E protein transcriptional regulators.

4.4.3 Nuclear factor interleukin-3 regulated

Nuclear factor interleukin-3 regulated (Nfil3 or E4BP4) is a basic LZ transcription factor originally identified as a transcriptional repressor of an adenovirus E4 promoter and therefore named E4BP4 (Cowell, Skinner, & Hurst, 1992). It is also known as Nfil3 as it was independently identified as a transactivator of the IL-3 promoter in human T cells (Zhang et al., 1995). Nfil3 has recently emerged as a key factor for NK-cell development, and Nfil3$^{-/-}$ mice display a pronounced NK-cell-specific developmental defect (Gascoyne et al., 2009; Kamizono et al., 2009). More recently, Nfil3 has been found to also affect CD4^{+} T-cell development and was shown to be required for the development of DCs (Kashiwada et al., 2011; Seillet et al., 2013). Indeed, Nfil3 appears to be expressed in all cDC subsets to some extent but *Nfil3*$^{-/-}$ mice have specific reduction of CD8α (Kashiwada et al., 2011) and CD103^{+} DCs (Seillet et al., 2013) while maintaining relatively normal numbers of CD8α^{-} DCs and pDCs. In NK cells, Nfil3 appears to be involved in the development of an early precursor stage, while in bone marrow, the DC precursors, namely, the CDPs and pre-DCs, appear not to be affected by loss of *Nfil3*. Deficiency in the immediate splenic precursors of CD8α DCs is observed *Nfil3*$^{-/-}$ mice; thus, a developmental blockade occurs between the pre-cDC and CD8α-committed precursor stage and thus participates to the terminal differentiation of this subset. The expression of the transcription factor Batf3 was reduced in *Nfil3*$^{-/-}$ pre-DCs compared to wild-type, suggesting that Batf3 could be downstream of Nfil3 (Fig. 7.1).

Enforced expression of Batf3 in *Nfil3*$^{-/-}$ bone marrow progenitors was able to partially rescue CD8α DC development supporting this connection (Kashiwada et al., 2011).

4.4.4 Batf3

Batf3 is part of the Batf family, which includes Batf, Batf2, and Batf3. Batf family members belong to the AP-1 superfamily of basic LZ transcription factors that includes Fos, Jun, and Atf proteins (Dorsey et al., 1995). AP-1 proteins usually contain a transcriptional activation domain in C-terminal position, but Batf proteins only contain a basic region and LZ domain. All three Batf proteins compete with Fos for the available pool of Jun and generate heterodimers unable to induce transcription of AP-1 genes. Thus, they are known as potent inhibitors of AP-1-mediated gene expression (Dorsey et al., 1995; Echlin, Tae, Mitin, & Taparowsky, 2000). However, recent studies highlighted the fact that Batf proteins also possess transcriptional activity, allowing them to interact with Irf protein through their LZ domain and bind AP1-ISRE composite element (Glasmacher et al., 2012; Li, Spolski, et al., 2012; Tussiwand et al., 2012). These cooperative interactions between AP-1 and Irf family members increase the possibility of interaction with responsive element on DNA and extend the repertoire recognized by each transcription factor family.

Batf3 has gained considerable attention as it was the first transcription factor identified that selectively perturbed homeostatic development of the CD8α^{+} DC subset (Hildner et al., 2008). Unlike Irf8, Id2, and Nfil3 that are required for the development of other immune cells, mice that lacked *Batf3* mice were reported to exhibit a selective loss of splenic CD8α^{+} DCs (Hildner et al., 2008). Later it was discovered that these mice also lacked peripheral CD103^{+} DC subsets but other lymphoid lineages were unaffected (Edelson et al., 2010). Initial studies showed that *Batf3*$^{-/-}$ mice on the 129SvEv background completely lacked CD8α^{+} DCs, which provided an elegant explanation for the inability of *Batf3*$^{-/-}$ mice to cross present cell-associated or viral antigens (Hildner et al., 2008). In contrast, precursor of CD8α^{+} DCs could be recovered from tissues derived from *Batf3*$^{-/-}$ mice crossed to the reporter line *Id2*$^{GFP/GFP}$ in which all DC precursor and intermediate and mature DC stages are differentially tagged with fluorescent protein, allowing their differentiation to be traced (Jackson et al., 2011). The capacity for CD8α^{+} DC precursors recovered from *Batf3*$^{-/-}$ *Id2*$^{GFP/GFP}$ mice to differentiate *in vitro* and *in vivo* suggested that Batf3 was not always essential for CD8α^{+} DCs differentiation but may instead be involved in maturation and/or maintenance (Jackson et al., 2011). It was later found that much of the antigen presenting capacity of *Batf3*$^{-/-}$ DCs appeared not to be significantly disrupted as reported earlier (Seillet et al., 2013). These discrepancies between studies led to more detailed analyses of the *Batf3*$^{-/-}$ mice. Indeed, it was found that mice generated on a C57BL/6 background retained a population of CD8α^+ DCs in spleen (3–7%) and had a normal CD8α^+ DCs in skin-draining lymph nodes (Edelson et al., 2011). This suggested that Batf3 was not essential for DCs that expressed the classical CD8α marker but that either Batf3 could be compensated by other transcription factors and/or CD8α^+ DC development could occur independent of the classical transcription factors known to affect their differentiation. The strong homology between Batf and Batf3 lead the group of Ken Murphy to investigate whether Batf could replace Batf3 in DC development (Tussiwand et al., 2012). Ectopic expression of Batf in *Batf3*$^{-/-}$ bone marrow cells fully restored differentiation and function of CD103$^+$ DC *in vitro*. Moreover, they could show that the remaining population of CD8α^+ DC observed in C57BL/6 *Batf3*$^{-/-}$ mice was lacking in C57BL/6 *Batf*$^{-/-}$*Batf3*$^{-/-}$, demonstrating that Batf was responsible for the persistence of CD8α^+ DCs in C57BL/6 *Batf3*$^{-/-}$ (Tussiwand et al., 2012). In addition, Batf2 expression could be induced by cytokines and could compensate for Batf3-deficiency during infection, leading to the rescue of CD8α^+ DC in these settings. Thus, an alternative cytokine-driven pathway can occur following inflammation to allow DCs to bypass the requirement for some transcription factors previously thought to be crucial for DC development.

5. ALTERNATIVE DC GENERATION: EMERGENCY HEMATOPOIESIS

Rapid recruitment of antigen presenting cells is essential under conditions of stress such as emergency hematopoiesis. Following inflammation, monocytes rapidly differentiate and acquire substantial antigen-presenting capacity necessary to ward off pathogen infections (Cheong et al., 2010). These inflammatory DCs express a transcriptional signature that includes *Irf8*, *Batf3*, *Irf4*, *Flt3*, *CSF1R*, and *Zbtb46* and appear to be essential to promote and maintain Th17 CD4$^+$ T-cell differentiation (Segura et al., 2013). These inflammatory DCs appear not to rely on transcription factors such as Id2. A similar situation appears to emerge in response to a nonpathogen-driven emergency requirement for hematopoietic cells. In this case, a DC subtype emerges that closely resembles the classical CD8α^+ DCs (see Table 7.1; Seillet et al., 2013). These so-called "induced" DCs can readily present self and pathogen-derived antigens, and they express a number of markers that are hallmarks of the $CD8\alpha^+$ subset including $CD8\alpha$ itself, in addition to CD24, Clec9A, Xcr1, Id2, and TLR3. Despite the similarities, these DCs did not require Id2, Nfil3, or Batf3 for their development although these signaling molecules are likely to be important for the long-term maintenance of the DCs. It is not yet clear whether these DCs depend on either Batf or Batf2 to drive this developmental pathway. This transcriptional profile is in a number of ways akin to the lack of requirement for these transcription factors for the development of intestinal $CD103^+$ DCs that are not altered in the absence of either Id2 or Batf3 (Ginhoux et al., 2009; Jackson et al., 2011). Collectively, these studies appear to have uncovered an alternate pathway for development of DCs that is independent of many of the known transcription factors. Further dissection of this pathway will be essential in understanding how DCs utilize this pathway under different physiological conditions compared with the more fully described pathway of DC differentiation that gives rise to the classical DC subsets.

6. PERSPECTIVES

Over the last two decades, surface markers defining the different DC subsets have been an extremely useful starting point to understand the heterogeneity of the DC family. They have allowed us to begin to dissect in great detail the locational and functional differences between the various DC populations and to develop a broad map of the cellular regulation of these cells. It is now appreciated that many surrogate markers used for identification of subsets are not solely restricted to the cell type of interest and interpretation of results may be confounded by this feature. Resolution of this problem is not straightforward. The use of fluorescent reporter mice has greatly expanded our ability to refine our understanding of DC subset specification, but like surface markers, the endogenous genes driving fluorescent protein expression may be dynamically regulated. Thus, the integration of each of these approaches together with a deep understanding of genome wide data and an appreciation of the capacity for signaling pathways to contribute in a combinatorial manner is likely be a powerful way forward in understanding the mechanisms controlling DC lineage specification.

Recent work has greatly illuminated the transcriptional network that gives rise to the phenotypically and functionally distinct subsets found in steady-state conditions. It is now becoming evident that differentiation of

DCs into unique subsets reflects a set of terminal, rather than early, differentiation events guided by a specific set of transcription factors. Establishing when each of these different transcription factors is switched on and how they are modulated will be important to further understanding of the homeostatic regulation of DC subsets. It has also become clearer that a second alternative pathway of DC differentiation is used during emergency hematopoiesis. This pathway may be akin to that used by intestinal DCs and monocytes under inflammatory conditions. It will be critical to examine how the requirements of DCs change in response to pathogen infections and how the balance between steady-state DCs and inflammatory DCs is achieved. Thus, a logical next step will be to endeavor to understand how steady-state DCs are affected by infection and adopt phenotypic changes in response to micro- and macroenvironmental changes. Finally, it will be essential to elucidate the transcription factors that are important for the "alternate" pathway of DC differentiation and determine whether this pathway represents a common pathway of replacement of DCs under conditions of stress.

ACKNOWLEDGMENTS

We thank S. Nutt and M. Chopin for helpful discussions and critical reading of the manuscript. This work is supported by the National Health and Medical Research Council (NHMRC) of Australia. G.T.B is a recipient of an Australian Research Council Future Fellowship, and this work was made possible through Victorian State Government Operational Infrastructure Support and Australian Government NHMRC IRIIS.

REFERENCES

Aliberti, J., Schulz, O., Pennington, D. J., Tsujimura, H., Reis e Sousa, C., Ozato, K., et al. (2003). Essential role for ICSBP in the in vivo development of murine CD8alpha+ dendritic cells. *Blood, 101*, 305.

Allman, D., Dalod, M., Asselin-Paturel, C., Delale, T., Robbins, S. H., Trinchieri, G., et al. (2006). Ikaros is required for plasmacytoid dendritic cell differentiation. *Blood, 108*, 4025.

Allman, D., Punt, J. A., Izon, D. J., Aster, J. C., & Pear, W. S. (2002). An invitation to T and more: Notch signaling in lymphopoiesis. *Cell, 109*(Suppl.), S1.

Anderson, K. L., Perkin, H., Surh, C. D., Venturini, S., Maki, R. A., & Torbett, B. E. (2000). Transcription factor PU.1 is necessary for development of thymic and myeloid progenitor-derived dendritic cells. *Journal of Immunology, 164*, 1855.

Asselin-Paturel, C., Brizard, G., Pin, J. J., Briere, F., & Trinchieri, G. (2003). Mouse strain differences in plasmacytoid dendritic cell frequency and function revealed by a novel monoclonal antibody. *Journal of Immunology, 171*, 6466.

Auffray, C., Fogg, D. K., Narni-Mancinelli, E., Senechal, B., Trouillet, C., Saederup, N., et al. (2009). CX3CR1+ CD115+ CD135+ common macrophage/DC precursors and the role of CX3CR1 in their response to inflammation. *The Journal of Experimental Medicine, 206*, 595.

Back, J., Allman, D., Chan, S., & Kastner, P. (2005). Visualizing PU.1 activity during hematopoiesis. *Experimental Hematology, 33*, 395.

Bajana, S., Roach, K., Turner, S., Paul, J., & Kovats, S. (2012). IRF4 promotes cutaneous dendritic cell migration to lymph nodes during homeostasis and inflammation. *Journal of Immunology, 189*, 3368.

Bakri, Y., Sarrazin, S., Mayer, U. P., Tillmanns, S., Nerlov, C., Boned, A., et al. (2005). Balance of MafB and PU.1 specifies alternative macrophage or dendritic cell fate. *Blood, 105*, 2707.

Bar-On, L., Birnberg, T., Lewis, K. L., Edelson, B. T., Bruder, D., Hildner, K., et al. (2010). CX3CR1+ CD8alpha+ dendritic cells are a steady-state population related to plasmacytoid dendritic cells. *Proceedings of the National Academy of Sciences of the United States of America, 107*, 14745.

Becker, A. M., Michael, D. G., Satpathy, A. T., Sciammas, R., Singh, H., & Bhattacharya, D. (2012). IRF-8 extinguishes neutrophil production and promotes dendritic cell lineage commitment in both myeloid and lymphoid mouse progenitors. *Blood, 119*, 2003.

Bedoui, S., Whitney, P. G., Waithman, J., Eidsmo, L., Wakim, L., Caminschi, I., et al. (2009). Cross-presentation of viral and self antigens by skin-derived CD103+ dendritic cells. *Nature Immunology, 10*, 488.

Belz, G. T., & Nutt, S. L. (2012). Transcriptional programming of the dendritic cell network. *Nature Reviews Immunology, 12*, 101.

Biswas, P. S., Gupta, S., Stirzaker, R. A., Kumar, V., Jessberger, R., Lu, T. T., et al. (2012). Dual regulation of IRF4 function in T and B cells is required for the coordination of T-B cell interactions and the prevention of autoimmunity. *The Journal of Experimental Medicine, 209*, 581.

Bogunovic, M., Ginhoux, F., Helft, J., Shang, L., Hashimoto, D., Greter, M., et al. (2009). Origin of the lamina propria dendritic cell network. *Immunity, 31*, 513.

Burkly, L., Hession, C., Ogata, L., Reilly, C., Marconi, L. A., Olson, D., et al. (1995). Expression of relB is required for the development of thymic medulla and dendritic cells. *Nature, 373*, 531.

Carotta, S., Dakic, A., D'Amico, A., Pang, S. H., Greig, K. T., Nutt, S. L., et al. (2010). The transcription factor PU.1 controls dendritic cell development and Flt3 cytokine receptor expression in a dose-dependent manner. *Immunity, 32*, 628.

Carreras, E., Turner, S., Paharkova-Vatchkova, V., Mao, A., Dascher, C., & Kovats, S. (2008). Estradiol acts directly on bone marrow myeloid progenitors to differentially regulate GM-CSF or Flt3 ligand-mediated dendritic cell differentiation. *Journal of Immunology, 180*, 727.

Caton, M. L., Smith-Raska, M. R., & Reizis, B. (2007). Notch-RBP-J signaling controls the homeostasis of CD8− dendritic cells in the spleen. *The Journal of Experimental Medicine, 204*, 1653.

Chen, H. M., Zhang, P., Voso, M. T., Hohaus, S., Gonzalez, D. A., Glass, C. K., et al. (1995). Neutrophils and monocytes express high levels of PU.1 (Spi-1) but not Spi-B. *Blood, 85*, 2918.

Cheng, P., Nefedova, Y., Miele, L., Osborne, B. A., & Gabrilovich, D. (2003). Notch signaling is necessary but not sufficient for differentiation of dendritic cells. *Blood, 102*, 3980.

Cheong, C., Matos, I., Choi, J. H., Dandamudi, D. B., Shrestha, E., Longhi, M. P., et al. (2010). Microbial stimulation fully differentiates monocytes to DC-SIGN/CD209(+) dendritic cells for immune T cell areas. *Cell, 143*, 416.

Cisse, B., Caton, M. L., Lehner, M., Maeda, T., Scheu, S., Locksley, R., et al. (2008). Transcription factor E2-2 is an essential and specific regulator of plasmacytoid dendritic cell development. *Cell, 135*, 37.

Cowell, I. G., Skinner, A., & Hurst, H. C. (1992). Transcriptional repression by a novel member of the bZIP family of transcription factors. *Molecular and Cellular Biology*, *12*, 3070.

D'Amico, A., & Wu, L. (2003). The early progenitors of mouse dendritic cells and plasmacytoid predendritic cells are within the bone marrow hemopoietic precursors expressing Flt3. *The Journal of Experimental Medicine*, *198*, 293.

De Silva, N. S., Simonetti, G., Heise, N., & Klein, U. (2012). The diverse roles of IRF4 in late germinal center B-cell differentiation. *Immunological Reviews*, *247*, 73.

den Haan, J. M., Lehar, S. M., & Bevan, M. J. (2000). CD8+ but not CD8− dendritic cells cross-prime cytotoxic T cells in vivo. *The Journal of Experimental Medicine*, *192*, 1685.

Dorsey, M. J., Tae, H. J., Sollenberger, K. G., Mascarenhas, N. T., Johansen, L. M., & Taparowsky, E. J. (1995). B-ATF: A novel human bZIP protein that associates with members of the AP-1 transcription factor family. *Oncogene*, *11*, 2255.

Douin-Echinard, V., Laffont, S., Seillet, C., Delpy, L., Krust, A., Chambon, P., et al. (2008). Estrogen receptor alpha, but not beta, is required for optimal dendritic cell differentiation and CD40-induced cytokine production. *Journal of Immunology*, *180*, 3661.

Dzionek, A., Fuchs, A., Schmidt, P., Cremer, S., Zysk, M., Miltenyi, S., et al. (2000). BDCA-2, BDCA-3, and BDCA-4: Three markers for distinct subsets of dendritic cells in human peripheral blood. *Journal of Immunology*, *165*, 6037.

Echlin, D. R., Tae, H. J., Mitin, N., & Taparowsky, E. J. (2000). B-ATF functions as a negative regulator of AP-1 mediated transcription and blocks cellular transformation by Ras and Fos. *Oncogene*, *19*, 1752.

Edelson, B. T., Bradstreet, T. R., KC, W., Hildner, K., Herzog, J. W., Sim, J., et al. (2011). Batf3-dependent CD11b low/− peripheral dendritic cells are GM-CSF-independent and are not required for Th cell priming after subcutaneous immunization. *PloS One*, *6*, e25660.

Edelson, B. T., Kc, W., Juang, R., Kohyama, M., Benoit, L. A., Klekotka, P. A., et al. (2010). Peripheral CD103+ dendritic cells form a unified subset developmentally related to CD8alpha+ conventional dendritic cells. *The Journal of Experimental Medicine*, *207*, 823.

Eguchi, J., Wang, X., Yu, S., Kershaw, E. E., Chiu, P. C., Dushay, J., et al. (2011). Transcriptional control of adipose lipid handling by IRF4. *Cell Metabolism*, *13*, 249.

Esashi, E., Wang, Y. H., Perng, O., Qin, X. F., Liu, Y. J., & Watowich, S. S. (2008). The signal transducer STAT5 inhibits plasmacytoid dendritic cell development by suppressing transcription factor IRF8. *Immunity*, *28*, 509.

Feyerabend, T. B., Terszowski, G., Tietz, A., Blum, C., Luche, H., Gossler, A., et al. (2009). Deletion of Notch1 converts pro-T cells to dendritic cells and promotes thymic B cells by cell-extrinsic and cell-intrinsic mechanisms. *Immunity*, *30*, 67.

Fogg, D. K., Sibon, C., Miled, C., Jung, S., Aucouturier, P., Littman, D. R., et al. (2006). A clonogenic bone marrow progenitor specific for macrophages and dendritic cells. *Science*, *311*, 83.

Gascoyne, D. M., Long, E., Veiga-Fernandes, H., de Boer, J., Williams, O., Seddon, B., et al. (2009). The basic leucine zipper transcription factor E4BP4 is essential for natural killer cell development. *Nature Immunology*, *10*, 1118.

Geissmann, F., Manz, M. G., Jung, S., Sieweke, M. H., Merad, M., & Ley, K. (2010). Development of monocytes, macrophages, and dendritic cells. *Science*, *327*, 656.

Georgopoulos, K., Bigby, M., Wang, J. H., Molnar, A., Wu, P., Winandy, S., et al. (1994). The Ikaros gene is required for the development of all lymphoid lineages. *Cell*, *79*, 143.

Ghosh, H. S., Cisse, B., Bunin, A., Lewis, K. L., & Reizis, B. (2010). Continuous expression of the transcription factor e2-2 maintains the cell fate of mature plasmacytoid dendritic cells. *Immunity*, *33*, 905.

Ginhoux, F., Liu, K., Helft, J., Bogunovic, M., Greter, M., Hashimoto, D., et al. (2009). The origin and development of nonlymphoid tissue CD103+ DCs. *The Journal of Experimental Medicine*, *206*, 3115.

Ginhoux, F., Tacke, F., Angeli, V., Bogunovic, M., Loubeau, M., Dai, X. M., et al. (2006). Langerhans cells arise from monocytes in vivo. *Nature Immunology, 7*, 265.

Glasmacher, E., Agrawal, S., Chang, A. B., Murphy, T. L., Zeng, W., Vander Lugt, B., et al. (2012). A genomic regulatory element that directs assembly and function of immune-specific AP-1-IRF complexes. *Science, 338*, 975.

Grouard, G., Rissoan, M. C., Filgueira, L., Durand, I., Banchereau, J., & Liu, Y. J. (1997). The enigmatic plasmacytoid T cells develop into dendritic cells with interleukin (IL)-3 and CD40-ligand. *The Journal of Experimental Medicine, 185*, 1101.

Guerriero, A., Langmuir, P. B., Spain, L. M., & Scott, E. W. (2000). PU.1 is required for myeloid-derived but not lymphoid-derived dendritic cells. *Blood, 95*, 879.

Hacker, C., Kirsch, R. D., Ju, X. S., Hieronymus, T., Gust, T. C., Kuhl, C., et al. (2003). Transcriptional profiling identifies Id2 function in dendritic cell development. *Nature Immunology, 4*, 380.

Hambleton, S., Salem, S., Bustamante, J., Bigley, V., Boisson-Dupuis, S., Azevedo, J., et al. (2011). IRF8 mutations and human dendritic-cell immunodeficiency. *The New England Journal of Medicine, 365*, 127.

Hayden, M. S., & Ghosh, S. (2008). Shared principles in NF-kappaB signaling. *Cell, 132*, 344.

Henri, S., Vremec, D., Kamath, A., Waithman, J., Williams, S., Benoist, C., et al. (2001). The dendritic cell populations of mouse lymph nodes. *Journal of Immunology, 167*, 741.

Hildner, K., Edelson, B. T., Purtha, W. E., Diamond, M., Matsushita, H., Kohyama, M., et al. (2008). Batf3 deficiency reveals a critical role for CD8alpha+ dendritic cells in cytotoxic T cell immunity. *Science, 322*, 1097.

Hohaus, S., Petrovick, M. S., Voso, M. T., Sun, Z., Zhang, D. E., & Tenen, D. G. (1995). PU.1 (Spi-1) and C/EBP alpha regulate expression of the granulocyte-macrophage colony-stimulating factor receptor alpha gene. *Molecular and Cellular Biology, 15*, 5830.

Holtschke, T., Lohler, J., Kanno, Y., Fehr, T., Giese, N., Rosenbauer, F., et al. (1996). Immunodeficiency and chronic myelogenous leukemia-like syndrome in mice with a targeted mutation of the ICSBP gene. *Cell, 87*, 307.

Hume, D. A. (2011). Applications of myeloid-specific promoters in transgenic mice support in vivo imaging and functional genomics but do not support the concept of distinct macrophage and dendritic cell lineages or roles in immunity. *Journal of Leukocyte Biology, 89*, 525.

Jackson, J. T., Hu, Y., Liu, R., Masson, F., D'Amico, A., Carotta, S., et al. (2011). Id2 expression delineates differential checkpoints in the genetic program of CD8alpha(+) and CD103(+) dendritic cell lineages. *EMBO Journal, 30*, 2690.

Kamizono, S., Duncan, G. S., Seidel, M. G., Morimoto, A., Hamada, K., Grosveld, G., et al. (2009). Nfil3/E4bp4 is required for the development and maturation of NK cells in vivo. *The Journal of Experimental Medicine, 206*, 2977.

Kashiwada, M., Pham, N. L., Pewe, L. L., Harty, J. T., & Rothman, P. B. (2011). NFIL3/E4BP4 is a key transcription factor for CD8{alpha}+ dendritic cell development. *Blood, 117*, 6193.

Kingston, D., Schmid, M. A., Onai, N., Obata-Onai, A., Baumjohann, D., & Manz, M. G. (2009). The concerted action of GM-CSF and Flt3-ligand on in vivo dendritic cell homeostasis. *Blood, 114*, 835.

Kusunoki, T., Sugai, M., Katakai, T., Omatsu, Y., Iyoda, T., Inaba, K., et al. (2003). TH2 dominance and defective development of a CD8+ dendritic cell subset in Id2-deficient mice. *The Journal of Allergy and Clinical Immunology, 111*, 136.

Laouar, Y., Welte, T., Fu, X. Y., & Flavell, R. A. (2003). STAT3 is required for Flt3L-dependent dendritic cell differentiation. *Immunity, 19*, 903.

Leon, B., Lopez-Bravo, M., & Ardavin, C. (2007). Monocyte-derived dendritic cells formed at the infection site control the induction of protective T helper 1 responses against Leishmania. *Immunity, 26*, 519.

Lewis, K. L., Caton, M. L., Bogunovic, M., Greter, M., Grajkowska, L. T., Ng, D., et al. (2011). Notch2 receptor signaling controls functional differentiation of dendritic cells in the spleen and intestine. *Immunity*, *35*, 780.

Li, P., Spolski, R., Liao, W., Wang, L., Murphy, T. L., Murphy, K. M., et al. (2012). BATF-JUN is critical for IRF4-mediated transcription in T cells. *Nature*, *490*(7421), 543–546.

Li, H. S., Yang, C. Y., Nallaparaju, K. C., Zhang, H., Liu, Y. J., Goldrath, A. W., et al. (2012). The signal transducers STAT5 and STAT3 control expression of Id2 and E2-2 during dendritic cell development. *Blood*, *120*, 4363.

Meredith, M. M., Liu, K., Darrasse-Jeze, G., Kamphorst, A. O., Schreiber, H. A., Guermonprez, P., et al. (2012). Expression of the zinc finger transcription factor zDC (Zbtb46, Btbd4) defines the classical dendritic cell lineage. *The Journal of Experimental Medicine*, *209*, 1153.

Miller, J. C., Brown, B. D., Shay, T., Gautier, E. L., Jojic, V., Cohain, A., et al. (2012). Deciphering the transcriptional network of the dendritic cell lineage. *Nature Immunology*, *13*, 888.

Murre, C., McCaw, P. S., & Baltimore, D. (1989). A new DNA binding and dimerization motif in immunoglobulin enhancer binding, daughterless, MyoD and Myc proteins. *Cell*, *56*, 777.

Murre, C., McCaw, P. S., Vaessin, H., Caudy, M., Jan, L. Y., Jan, Y. N., et al. (1989). Interactions between heterologous helix-loop-helix proteins generate complexes that bind specifically to a common DNA sequence. *Cell*, *58*, 537.

Nagasawa, M., Schmidlin, H., Hazekamp, M. G., Schotte, R., & Blom, B. (2008). Development of human plasmacytoid dendritic cells depends on the combined action of the basic helix-loop-helix factor E2-2 and the Ets factor Spi-B. *European Journal of Immunology*, *38*, 2389.

Naik, S. H., Metcalf, D., van Nieuwenhuijze, A., Wicks, I., Wu, L., O'Keeffe, M., et al. (2006). Intrasplenic steady-state dendritic cell precursors that are distinct from monocytes. *Nature Immunology*, 7, 663.

Naik, S. H., Sathe, P., Park, H. Y., Metcalf, D., Proietto, A. I., Dakic, A., et al. (2007). Development of plasmacytoid and conventional dendritic cell subtypes from single precursor cells derived in vitro and in vivo. *Nature Immunology*, *8*, 1217.

Nichogiannopoulou, A., Trevisan, M., Neben, S., Friedrich, C., & Georgopoulos, K. (1999). Defects in hemopoietic stem cell activity in Ikaros mutant mice. *The Journal of Experimental Medicine*, *190*, 1201.

Nutt, S. L., Metcalf, D., D'Amico, A., Polli, M., & Wu, L. (2005). Dynamic regulation of PU.1 expression in multipotent hematopoietic progenitors. *The Journal of Experimental Medicine*, *201*, 221.

Omatsu, Y., Iyoda, T., Kimura, Y., Maki, A., Ishimori, M., Toyama-Sorimachi, N., et al. (2005). Development of murine plasmacytoid dendritic cells defined by increased expression of an inhibitory NK receptor, Ly49Q. *Journal of Immunology*, *174*, 6657.

Onai, N., Obata-Onai, A., Schmid, M. A., Ohteki, T., Jarrossay, D., & Manz, M. G. (2007). Identification of clonogenic common Flt3+M-CSFR+ plasmacytoid and conventional dendritic cell progenitors in mouse bone marrow. *Nature Immunology*, *8*, 1207.

Onai, N., Obata-Onai, A., Tussiwand, R., Lanzavecchia, A., & Manz, M. G. (2006). Activation of the Flt3 signal transduction cascade rescues and enhances type I interferon-producing and dendritic cell development. *The Journal of Experimental Medicine*, *203*, 227.

Osborne, B. A., & Minter, L. M. (2007). Notch signalling during peripheral T-cell activation and differentiation. *Nature Reviews Immunology*, 7, 64.

Radtke, F., Ferrero, I., Wilson, A., Lees, R., Aguet, M., & MacDonald, H. R. (2000). Notch1 deficiency dissociates the intrathymic development of dendritic cells and T cells. *The Journal of Experimental Medicine*, *191*, 1085.

Rankin, L., Groom, J., Mielke, L., Seillet, C., & Belz, G. T. (2013). Diversity, function and transcriptional regulation of gut innate lymphocytes. *Frontiers in Immunology*, *4*, 22. http://dx.doi.org/10.3389/fimmu.2013.00022.

Rathinam, C., Geffers, R., Yucel, R., Buer, J., Welte, K., Moroy, T., et al. (2005). The transcriptional repressor Gfi1 controls STAT3-dependent dendritic cell development and function. *Immunity*, *22*, 717.

Ray-Gallet, D., Mao, C., Tavitian, A., & Moreau-Gachelin, F. (1995). DNA binding specificities of Spi-1/PU.1 and Spi-B transcription factors and identification of a Spi-1/Spi-B binding site in the c-fes/c-fps promoter. *Oncogene*, *11*, 303.

Sasaki, I., Hoshino, K., Sugiyama, T., Yamazaki, C., Yano, T., Iizuka, A., et al. (2012). Spi-B is critical for plasmacytoid dendritic cell function and development. *Blood*, *120*, 4733.

Satpathy, A. T., Kc, W., Albring, J. C., Edelson, B. T., Kretzer, N. M., Bhattacharya, D., et al. (2012). Zbtb46 expression distinguishes classical dendritic cells and their committed progenitors from other immune lineages. *The Journal of Experimental Medicine*, *209*, 1135.

Schiavoni, G., Mattei, F., Borghi, P., Sestili, P., Venditti, M., Morse, H. C., 3rd., et al. (2004). ICSBP is critically involved in the normal development and trafficking of Langerhans cells and dermal dendritic cells. *Blood*, *103*, 2221.

Schiavoni, G., Mattei, F., Sestili, P., Borghi, P., Venditti, M., Morse, H. C., 3rd., et al. (2002). ICSBP is essential for the development of mouse type I interferon-producing cells and for the generation and activation of CD8alpha(+) dendritic cells. *The Journal of Experimental Medicine*, *196*, 1415.

Schotte, R., Nagasawa, M., Weijer, K., Spits, H., & Blom, B. (2004). The ETS transcription factor Spi-B is required for human plasmacytoid dendritic cell development. *The Journal of Experimental Medicine*, *200*, 1503.

Schotte, R., Rissoan, M. C., Bendriss-Vermare, N., Bridon, J. M., Duhen, T., Weijer, K., et al. (2003). The transcription factor Spi-B is expressed in plasmacytoid DC precursors and inhibits T-, B-, and NK-cell development. *Blood*, *101*, 1015.

Segura, E., Touzot, M., Bohineust, A., Cappuccio, A., Chiocchia, G., Hosmalin, A., et al. (2013). Human inflammatory dendritic cells induce Th17 cell differentiation. *Immunity*, *38*, 336.

Seillet, C., Jackson, J. T., Markey, K. A., Hill, G. R., Macdonald, K. P., Nutt, S. L., et al. (2013). CD8alpha+ DCs can be induced in the absence of transcription factors Id2, Nfil3 and Batf3. *Blood*, *121*, 1574.

Seillet, C., Laffont, S., Tremollieres, F., Rouquie, N., Ribot, C., Arnal, J. F., et al. (2012). The TLR-mediated response of plasmacytoid dendritic cells is positively regulated by estradiol in vivo through cell-intrinsic estrogen receptor alpha signaling. *Blood*, *119*, 454.

Sere, K., Baek, J. H., Ober-Blobaum, J., Muller-Newen, G., Tacke, F., Yokota, Y., et al. (2012). Two distinct types of Langerhans cells populate the skin during steady state and inflammation. *Immunity*, *37*, 905.

Siegal, F. P., Kadowaki, N., Shodell, M., Fitzgerald-Bocarsly, P. A., Shah, K., Ho, S., et al. (1999). The nature of the principal type 1 interferon-producing cells in human blood. *Science*, *284*, 1835.

Spits, H., Couwenberg, F., Bakker, A. Q., Weijer, K., & Uittenbogaart, C. H. (2000). Id2 and Id3 inhibit development of CD34(+) stem cells into predendritic cell (pre-DC)2 but not into pre-DC1. Evidence for a lymphoid origin of pre-DC2. *The Journal of Experimental Medicine*, *192*, 1775.

Spooner, C. J., Cheng, J. X., Pujadas, E., Laslo, P., & Singh, H. (2009). A recurrent network involving the transcription factors PU.1 and Gfi1 orchestrates innate and adaptive immune cell fates. *Immunity*, *31*, 576.

Su, G. H., Chen, H. M., Muthusamy, N., Garrett-Sinha, L. A., Baunoch, D., Tenen, D. G., et al. (1997). Defective B cell receptor-mediated responses in mice lacking the Ets protein, Spi-B. *EMBO Journal*, *16*, 7118.

Sung, S. S., Fu, S. M., Rose, C. E., Jr., Gaskin, F., Ju, S. T., & Beaty, S. R. (2006). A major lung CD103 ({alpha}E)-beta7 integrin-positive epithelial dendritic cell population expressing langerin and tight junction proteins. *Journal of Immunology*, *176*, 2161.

Suzuki, S., Honma, K., Matsuyama, T., Suzuki, K., Toriyama, K., Akitoyo, I., et al. (2004). Critical roles of interferon regulatory factor 4 in CD11bhighCD8alpha− dendritic cell development. *Proceedings of the National Academy of Sciences of the United States of America*, *101*, 8981.

Tailor, P., Tamura, T., Morse, H. C., 3rd., & Ozato, K. (2008). The BXH2 mutation in IRF8 differentially impairs dendritic cell subset development in the mouse. *Blood*, *111*, 1942.

Tamura, T., Tailor, P., Yamaoka, K., Kong, H. J., Tsujimura, H., O'Shea, J. J., et al. (2005). IFN regulatory factor-4 and -8 govern dendritic cell subset development and their functional diversity. *Journal of Immunology*, *174*, 2573.

Tsujimura, H., Tamura, T., Gongora, C., Aliberti, J., Reis e Sousa, C., Sher, A., et al. (2003). ICSBP/IRF-8 retrovirus transduction rescues dendritic cell development in vitro. *Blood*, *101*, 961.

Tsujimura, H., Tamura, T., & Ozato, K. (2003). Cutting edge: IFN consensus sequence binding protein/IFN regulatory factor 8 drives the development of type I IFN-producing plasmacytoid dendritic cells. *Journal of Immunology*, *170*, 1131.

Turcotte, K., Gauthier, S., Mitsos, L. M., Shustik, C., Copeland, N. G., Jenkins, N. A., et al. (2004). Genetic control of myeloproliferation in BXH-2 mice. *Blood*, *103*, 2343.

Tussiwand, R., Lee, W. L., Murphy, T. L., Mashayekhi, M., Wumesh, K. C., Albring, J. C., et al. (2012). Compensatory dendritic cell development mediated by BATF-IRF interactions. *Nature*, *490*, 502.

Vallabhapurapu, S., & Karin, M. (2009). Regulation and function of NF-kappaB transcription factors in the immune system. *Annual Reviews in Immunology*, *27*, 693.

Vremec, D., Pooley, J., Hochrein, H., Wu, L., & Shortman, K. (2000). CD4 and CD8 expression by dendritic cell subtypes in mouse thymus and spleen. *Journal of Immunology*, *164*, 2978.

Wang, J. H., Nichogiannopoulou, A., Wu, L., Sun, L., Sharpe, A. H., Bigby, M., et al. (1996). Selective defects in the development of the fetal and adult lymphoid system in mice with an Ikaros null mutation. *Immunity*, *5*, 537.

Wu, L., D'Amico, A., Winkel, K. D., Suter, M., Lo, D., & Shortman, K. (1998). RelB is essential for the development of myeloid-related CD8alpha− dendritic cells but not of lymphoid-related CD8alpha+ dendritic cells. *Immunity*, *9*, 839.

Wu, L., Nichogiannopoulou, A., Shortman, K., & Georgopoulos, K. (1997). Cell-autonomous defects in dendritic cell populations of Ikaros mutant mice point to a developmental relationship with the lymphoid lineage. *Immunity*, *7*, 483.

Zhang, D. E., Hetherington, C. J., Chen, H. M., & Tenen, D. G. (1994). The macrophage transcription factor PU.1 directs tissue-specific expression of the macrophage colony-stimulating factor receptor. *Molecular and Cellular Biology*, *14*, 373.

Zhang, J., Raper, A., Sugita, N., Hingorani, R., Salio, M., Palmowski, M. J., et al. (2006). Characterization of Siglec-H as a novel endocytic receptor expressed on murine plasmacytoid dendritic cell precursors. *Blood*, *107*, 3600.

Zhang, W., Zhang, J., Kornuc, M., Kwan, K., Frank, R., & Nimer, S. D. (1995). Molecular cloning and characterization of NF-IL3A, a transcriptional activator of the human interleukin-3 promoter. *Molecular and Cellular Biology*, *15*, 6055.

Zhou, J., Cheng, P., Youn, J. I., Cotter, M. J., & Gabrilovich, D. I. (2009). Notch and wingless signaling cooperate in regulation of dendritic cell differentiation. *Immunity*, *30*, 845.

CHAPTER EIGHT

Diversity of Pathogen Sensors in Dendritic Cells

Silvia Cerboni[*,†], **Matteo Gentili**[*,†], **Nicolas Manel**[*,†,1]
[*]Institut Curie, 12 rue Lhomond, Paris, France
[†]INSERM U932, 12 rue Lhomond, Paris, France
[1]Corresponding author: e-mail address: nicolas.manel@curie.fr

Contents

Abstract

Dendritic cells (DCs) associate the capacity to sense pathogens with the initiation of adaptive immunity. Pathogens can be sensed through pathogen-associated molecular patterns by pathogen-recognition receptors expressed on host cells. Pathogen-encoded activities can also be sensed when they modify normal host cellular processes. The diversity of pathogen sensors has been highlighted by the identification of several cytosolic sensors involved in the recognition of nucleic acids from pathogens. The number of these pathogen cytosolic sensors has dramatically increased recently. Different DC populations appear to be equipped with distinct sensors but the precise expression pattern and the regulation of these sensors remain to be established, especially in humans. The engagement of sensors in DCs by pathogens leads to antipathogen effects

Advances in Immunology, Volume 120
ISSN 0065-2776
http://dx.doi.org/10.1016/B978-0-12-417028-5.00008-9

through multiple mechanisms including interferon responses and promotes effector pathways that can shape the adaptive immune response. How the diversity of cytosolic pathogen sensors impacts these processes is incompletely understood. Investigating the expression, regulation, and crosstalk of the sensors should shed light on how pathogen sensing impacts pathogen replication and host immune responses.

1. INTRODUCTION

1.1. Definitions

In general terms, a sensor is defined as a device that converts a physical property into a response. In the context of pathogen recognition, a pathogen sensor is a molecule (or a complex) that recognizes physical properties of the pathogen and converts such property into a modification of the cell state. In dendritic cells (DCs), the modification of the cellular state potentially impacts immune responses.

DCs can be considered as a heterogeneous population of hematopoietic cells endowed with a capacity to associate pathogen sensing with initiation of an immune response. DCs efficiently prime naïve $CD4^+$ and $CD8^+$ T cells (Banchereau & Steinman, 1998). This capacity is linked to the MHC-II expression on these cells and the expression of costimulatory molecules. These molecules are less expressed in nonactivated DCs, which are less capable of T-cell priming. Upon pathogen encounter, pathogen sensors are triggered, and they convert pathogen recognition into a signaling pathway that activates DCs (a process also referred to as maturation). Activated DCs express more costimulatory molecules and MHC-II at their surface. Activation of DCs is also accompanied by vast phenotypic changes such as in cell migration, cellular morphology, vesicular trafficking, and cytokine profile. These changes also contribute to efficient priming of T cells. In addition, within the general process of activation, different pathogens can trigger distinct pathogen sensors with unique signaling properties leading to distinct DC functional responses. Thus, the diversity of sensors in DCs allows both to recognize a large spectrum of pathogens and to initiate immune responses that are qualitatively specific to the encountered pathogen.

1.2. Function of pathogen sensors

A molecule or complex can be considered as a sensor strictly on the basis of its ability to signal at the molecular level. In the case of pathogen sensing, it is implied that the sensor also has a functional consequence on the immune response against the pathogen. Thus, pathogen sensors should not be viewed solely as signal converters, but should be considered in the context of cellular and host responses. These responses include at least the ability to modify the replication of the pathogen (resistance), such as by inducing antiviral effectors through type I interferon (IFN), and the susceptibility of the host to the pathogenic effectors (tolerance) (Read, Graham, & Raberg, 2008). Clearance of acute viral infections can be seen as a resistance mechanism (e.g., influenza virus), while resistance to the pathogenic effects of chronic viral replication can be seen as a tolerance mechanism (e.g., HIV-1 and HIV-2 nonprogressors).

In both cases, pathogen sensing is viewed as a mechanism to generate antipathogenic effects matched to the burden of pathogens. However, since pathogens have often coevolved with their hosts, it is also likely that pathogens have usurped sensor engagement into propathogenic host factors (Towers, 2007).

1.3. Models of pathogen sensing

1.3.1 The pathogen-associated molecular patterns and danger-associated molecular patterns models

In vertebrates, the best-characterized pathogen sensors are pathogen-recognition receptors (PRRs) (Medzhitov, Preston-Hurlburt, & Janeway, 1997; Fig. 8.1). Sensors of this class bind directly to molecules of the pathogen. Recognition (sensing) is based on the physical binding property of the pathogen molecules to the sensor. Pathogen diversity is sensed on the basis of chemically defined molecular patterns, absent in the host and present in the pathogen. The concept of pathogen sensing has now evolved to encompass more general aspects of host–pathogen interactions. The self/nonself criteria of the PRRs model has been modulated by the danger model in which the presence of pathogens at the host level is detected by integrating host danger signals or danger-associated molecular patterns (DAMPs) (Matzinger, 2002). This may be particularly relevant at mucosal surface, where microorganisms are abundant and PRRs are constantly ligated by pathogen-associated molecular patterns (PAMPs). The abundance of PAMPs from a very large number of microbes present at mucosal surfaces does not lead to an immune response against all of these microbes. Presumably only microbes that are damaging to the host integrity and that induce the production of DAMPs should elicit an immune response. However, the presence of DAMPs is not necessarily sufficient either to initiate an immune response in the absence of PAMPs (Matzinger, 2002).

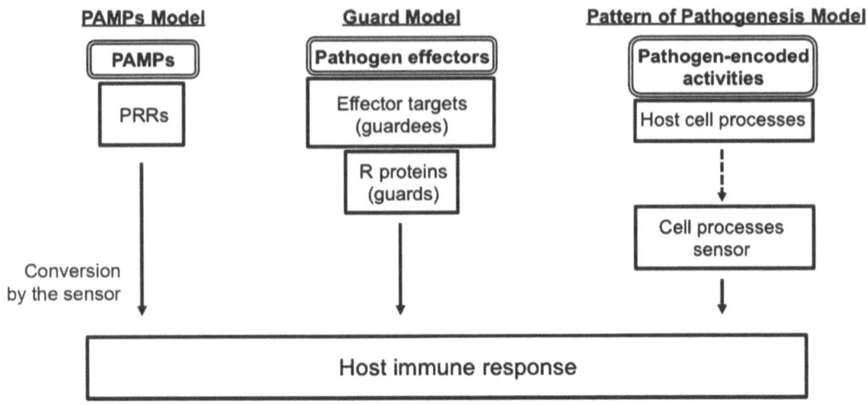

Figure 8.1 Three models of pathogen sensing. In the PAMPs Model, pathogen-associated molecular patterns directly associate with host pattern recognition receptors, leading to activation of an immune response. In the Guard Model, pathogen effectors associate with host targets of the effectors. The targets are associated with guard factors, and modifications of the targets by the pathogen effectors activate the guards, leading to activation of an immune response. In the Pattern of Pathogenesis Model, pathogen-encoded activities alter cellular host processes. This leads to indirect modification of downstream cellular factors, which are normally dependent on these processes. Such indirect modifications are detected by cellular sensors for these factors, leading to activation of an immune response.

The PAMPs Model has also been complexified with the notion of spatiotemporal regulation. PRRs binding to PAMPs do not always occur in the same subcellular location where PRRs signal occurs (reviewed in Kagan, 2012). Based on these results, it was predicted that microbe-induced trafficking factors are present to induce relocalization of the PRRs following pathogen recognition (Kagan, 2012). In addition, subcellular location of PRRs can also be regulated upstream of PAMPs recognition (Garcia-Cattaneo et al., 2012), pointing to a central role of subcellular partitioning of PRRs in their regulation.

1.3.2 The Guard Model

In plants, clonal (adaptive) selection of circulating cells and somatic DNA rearrangements does not occur. Thus, individual immunity relies on non-clonal, germ-line-encoded (innate) pathogen-sensing pathways. A key principle to the understanding of plant immunity has been the necessity to explain how plants manage to elicit immunity against diverse pathogens in the absence of somatic recombination. Genetic evidences identified a limited number of resistance (R) genes, and experimental evidences indicated that the protein products of these genes often do not interact directly with pathogen factors. To explain these observations, the Guard Model (and its more recent variation, the Decoy Model) has been proposed (reviewed in Schwessinger & Ronald, 2012; Spoel & Dong, 2012; van der Hoorn & Kamoun, 2008; Fig. 8.1). In this model, host pathogen sensors are encoded by R (resistance) genes (i.e., genes required for antipathogen functions and resistance to the pathogen) whose function is to guard a host target of the pathogen effector (or guardee). R proteins do not directly interact with PAMPs but instead, R proteins sense state modifications of guardee factor. The guardee factor may be a restriction or a virulence factor in the absence of R (Guard Model) or may have no effect on the pathogen fitness in the absence of R (Decoy Model). In both models, R proteins sense the state of the guardee factor. A central feature of the R model is that a limited number of R proteins are sufficient to monitor a great diversity of pathogens, provided that the different pathogens converge at targeting a restricted guardee (but such targeting can occur through different molecular mechanism according to the pathogen). This model thus provides an explanation as to how plants manage eliciting immunity against diverse pathogens in the absence of somatic recombination.

It should be noted that despite the lack of clonal selection based on somatic DNA rearrangements in an individual plant, a form of immune memory is transmitted to next generations, possibly through epigenetics modifications (Spoel & Dong, 2012). Interestingly, a form of epigenetic memory in immune cells has recently been described in vertebrates (Ostuni et al., 2013). It will be important to determine if such epigenetic memory in vertebrates is transmitted through cell division in the host.

1.3.3 The Pattern of Pathogenesis Model

The R model implies that the host response to pathogens depends not only on a response to PAMP but also to modifications in the state of the host. In vertebrates, evidences indeed suggest that innate immune activation can occur in response to a modification of the cellular state, in the absence of apparent PAMPs. For instance, cells exposed to DNA damaging agents were shown to activate IFN regulatory factor (IRF) 3 (Karpova, Trost, Murray, Cantley, & Howley, 2002; Kim et al., 1999). Direct stressing of the ER by molecular compounds can also lead to activation of the transcription factor IRF3 (Liu et al., 2012). Interestingly, this direct effect of ER stress on initiation of innate immunity may intersect with ER stress pathways that are known to modulate innate immunity (Todd, Lee, & Glimcher, 2008).

Inhibition of protein translation and amino acid starvation by pathogen factors were also found to induce host innate immune response pathway (Chakrabarti, Liehl, Buchon, & Lemaitre, 2012; Fontana et al., 2011; Tattoli et al., 2012), though the signaling pathways involved are not completely defined.

Altogether, these results indicate that innate immune responses in vertebrates can be induced in the absence of PAMPs in a manner reminiscent of the Guard Model in plants. This mode of pathogen sensing has been termed the Pattern of Pathogenesis Model (Vance, Isberg, & Portnoy, 2009; Fig. 8.1). In this model, pathogen sensing relies on sensors of pathogen-encoded activities in addition to PAMPs. Nonetheless, the Guard Model and Pattern of Pathogenesis Model differ. The Guard Model describes effector-triggered immunity in plants and assumes that pathogen effectors directly interact with the guardees. In contrary, the Pattern of Pathogenesis Model does not assume a direct physical interaction between the pathogen effector and the guardee. This is exemplified in the case of pathogen effectors that inhibit protein translation, leading to induction of an immune response (Fontana et al., 2011; Losick & Isberg, 2006). It was suggested that short-lived negative regulators of host signaling pathways such as IκB function as "guards" (Fontana et al., 2011). Another interpretation possibly more consistent with the Guard Model is that the guard is NF-κB and the guardee is IκK. IκK, because of its short half-life, reflects the state of protein translation, which is the actual process targeted by pathogen effectors. In other words, NF-κB guards IκK, and modifications in IκK state, such as its degradation, lead to activation of NF-κB. The pathogen effectors that affect protein translation do not need to physically interact with IκK to elicit an immune response.

However, activation of NF-κB has pleiotropic effects on transcription and is not a strict inducer of immune responses. The transcriptional activity of factors such as NF-κB depends on the cell type in which it is activated and its intracellular context. Inhibition of protein translation, such as during physiological ER stress, does not systematically elicit an innate immune response either. Along this line, host cell processes such as cell migration can also induce an immune activation of DCs, but this does not normally lead to autoimmune activation (Jiang et al., 2007). This suggests that pathogen sensing has unique attributes compared to general stress and that it is not equivalent to every modifications of the cell state. A subset of host cell state modifications can lead to a host immune response comparable to PAMPs-elicited immune response, and only these can be considered as pathogen sensing. The molecular mechanisms that restrict pathogen sensing to a subset of the host cell processes remain unclear. One hypothesis is that pathogen sensing corresponds to nonphysiological damages to the host cell (Vance et al., 2009) but the unique features of such damages compared to generic damages are still unclear.

1.3.4 Pathogen sensing: an amplified process

Another hypothesis could potentially explain how pathogen-elicited damages may differ from generic cellular stress or damage so that an immune response is elicited in the former but not in the later, without involving PAMPs. At the cellular level, normal individual cells recover from limited stress or damage, or they inevitably initiate a death process in case of irreversible stress or damage. In contrast, pathogen-induced cellular damages, which induce an immune response, may be interpreted as an irreversible damage to the infected cells that does not immediately kill the host cell. Evidently, extensive intracellular pathogen replication may eventually kill the host cell, but this would occur after pathogen sensing has been triggered by damages preceding cell death. At the signaling level, this indicates that management of generic stress or damage is subject to a negative feedback regulation (Fig. 8.2A), that is, the cell can recover and shut down the repair pathways, while pathogen sensing is under a positive feedback regulation (Fig. 8.2B), that is, infected cells respond increasingly to the pathogen. In this regard, it is interesting to note that a number of IFN-stimulated genes (ISGs) are pathogen sensors (Schoggins et al., 2011). This has been linked to the alerting function of type I IFN in *trans*, such that neighboring uninfected cells raise levels of pathogen-sensing machinery. It may also be important in *cis*, in the infected cells. In fact, a number of ISG are induced during the primary transcription response induced by IRF transcription factors, in the absence of autocrine type I IFN (Hasan et al., 2013; Honda et al., 2003; Nakaya et al., 2001). Thus, by increasing the expression of pathogen sensors, if a cell is truly infected by a pathogen, this will lead to a feedforward reinforcement of innate-activating signaling pathways. Unlike sterile damage, the pathogen will also replicate, increasing its burden over time. On the contrary, in the absence of pathogen replication, cellular damage would not lead to reinforcement of the signaling response and would thus terminate by constitutive negative feedback mechanisms. In other words, a specific property of pathogen sensing is driven by amplification, while response to sterile damage is self-attenuating. Interestingly, noninfected hosts are under steady-state regulation by tonic type I IFN signaling (Gough, Messina, Clarke, Johnstone, & Levy, 2012), and this may set or prime these pathways.

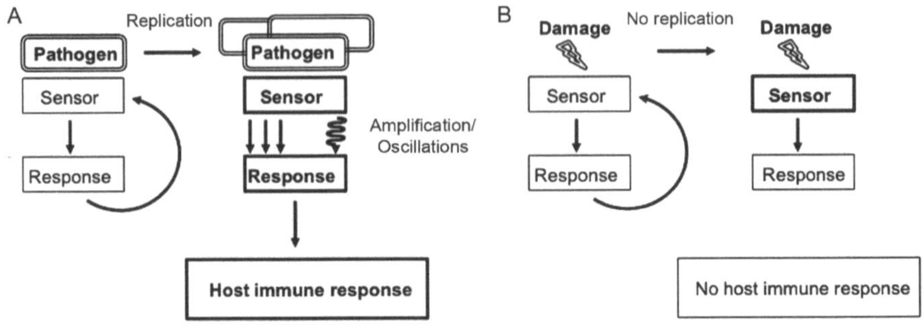

Figure 8.2 Pathogen sensing is an amplified process. (A) The presence of a pathogen activates a sensor, which induces a cellular response. The cellular response includes increasing the expression of the sensors. In addition, the pathogen replicates. Over time, more sensors are activated by a positive feedback mechanism, allowing modifications in the qualities of the signaling (amplification, instability, oscillations) that activates a host immune response. (B) In the absence of pathogen replication, such as during stress, physical damage, sterile PAMPs, or dead pathogens, the cell responds to the stimuli as in (A) and increases the level of sensor. However, there is no increase in stimuli burden over time in absence of replication. The burden can also decrease due to effector activity of the initial cell response. Consequently, the signal attenuates and resolves. No host immune response is induced.

Importantly, negative feedback is self-regulating and leads to stability, while positive feedback leads to instability, exponential responses, and oscillations. Strikingly, oscillation of a stress response has recently been reported following RNA virus replication (Ruggieri et al., 2012). Hence, the specificities of pathogen sensing in terms of initiating an immune response may reflect signal dynamic requirements emanating from sensors.

In the following parts, we will first describe the diversity of pathogen sensing in DCs, by focusing on cytosolic DNA and RNA sensors. Next, we will describe one example of how pathogen-sensing pathways may interact with other cellular pathways. Finally, we will analyze effectors of pathogen sensing and describe few examples where pathogen sensing impacts immune responses. This will not provide an exhaustive review of the literature nor a consensus viewpoint, but rather present some aspects of our perspective on the field.

2. DIVERSITY OF PATHOGEN SENSORS IN DCs

2.1. Specialization of pathogen sensing within DC subsets

DCs represent a family of heterogeneous cells that can be differentiated by surface markers. In mouse spleen, three different DC populations can be found at steady state: $CD8\alpha^+$ DCs, $CD11b^+$ (comprising $CD4^+$ and $CD8\alpha^-CD4^-$) DCs, and plasmacytoid pre-DC (pDC). DC heterogeneity is also found in humans. In the adult peripheral blood, the BDCA-1^+ DC, BDCA-3^+ DC, and pDC subsets have been identified. These populations have different functions within the organism. Such difference in function between these DC subsets can be inferred from differences in cellular protein expression, particularly that of PRRs.

In particular, proteomic approaches revealed that TLR12, TLR2, and other proteins of the Siglecs and of the C-type lectin receptor family are differentially expressed by the $CD8\alpha^+$ and $CD11b^+$ subsets (Segura et al., 2010). In this study, the analysis focused on cell surface membrane toll like receptors (TLRs) and other PRRs. These differences and membrane "specialization" likely contribute to the functional specialization of the DC network.

Specialization can also be found within the cytosol of DC subsets. Indeed in the defense against pathogens, in particular against viruses, cytosolic RNA and DNA sensors are present. Viral infections may also trigger directly or indirectly other cytosolic sensors such as the NOD-like receptors (NLRs) (Allen et al., 2009). A number of these sensors have been identified in the recent years, but much less is known about their regulation and expression in distinct DC subsets and how they may associate a given sensing mechanism with specialized DC functions.

2.2. Cytosolic RNA sensors

RLH, or RIG-like helicases, represents a family of RNA sensors composed by three members: retinoic acid-inducible gene-I (RIG-I), melanoma differentiation antigen 5 (MDA5), and laboratory of genetics and physiology 2 (LGP2 or RLH3) (Gitlin et al., 2006; Rothenfusser et al., 2005; Yoneyama et al., 2004). More recently, the helicases DDX1, DDX21, and DHX36 have been also suggested to play a role in RNA sensing (Zhang, Kim, et al., 2011).

RIG-I and MDA5 are cytosolic RNA helicases that upon RNA unwinding are capable of interacting with adaptor molecules through their CARD domains. LGP2 does not contain a CARD domain and is thought to participate in the regulation of RIG-I activity (Saito et al., 2007). DDX1, DDX21, and DHX36 do not contain apparent signaling domains. It will be important to determine how they convert RNA binding to a signaling event, an essential criteria for a sensor. Distinctly to TLRs, RLH signal through adaptor proteins such as mitochondrial antiviral-signaling protein

(MAVS, also known as VISA, Cardiff, or IPS-1) (Meylan et al., 2005), but similarly to several TLRs, their triggering converges on the activation of type I IFN (Navarro & David, 1999) and NF-κB (Medzhitov et al., 1997) responses with the consequent production of inflammatory cytokines.

The abundance of viral sensing molecules and the antiviral response in mouse DC subsets has been first characterized using a proteomic approach (Luber et al., 2010). Using a label-free quantitation, the relative protein expression in murine pDCs, $CD8\alpha^+$, and $CD11b^+$, was established, focusing on the expression of PRRs. A differential expression of TLRs between the populations was observed, confirming previous studies, but a different expression of RLHs was also detected. A much higher expression of RIG-I and MDA5 in $CD11b^+$ DCs was found. An increased quantity of the protein NLRX1, a regulator of MAVS, was also identified in this subset. pDCs were found to express TLRs, particularly TLR7 and TLR9, RIG-I-like receptors (RLRs), and the IRF4, 7, and 8, which is in accordance with the ability of this subset to respond to viral infections with a massive IFN response. These results are consistent with the differential response of the mouse DC subsets to Sendai virus, an ssRNA virus, known to activate a RIG-I-mediated IFN response (Kato et al., 2005). Even though all cellular subsets were infected by the virus, only $CD11b^+$ DCs showed an upregulation of CD86 expression and production of IFN-α. Accordingly, in Myd88-deficient mice, only $CD11b^+$ DCs maintained the ability to become activated in response to Sendai virus presumably through cytosolic sensing, whereas in MAVS-deficient mice, only pDCs mounted an IFN-α response, confirming TLRs key role in promoting virus response in this latter subset. Altogether, these results picture a differential role of DCs regarding viral infections at the level of cytosolic viral sensing. Similar to pDCs that are capable of rapidly detecting pathogens in endosomes through TLRs, $CD11b^+$ DCs, which constitutively express high levels of RIG-I, can be seen as professional cytoplasmic virus sensing cells. Thanks to the constitutive expression of cytosolic sensing machinery, these cells are capable of rapidly sensing a viral infection and efficiently mounting an IFN response, which may be particularly relevant against pathogens that escape TLR sensing.

In humans, data available for primary DC subsets remains scarce. Whole transcriptome analysis has shown that blood BDCA-3^+ DCs are closely related to splenic $CD8\alpha^+$ murine cells, whereas mouse splenic $CD11b^+$ DCs share similarity in their transcriptome with human blood BDCA-1^+ DCs (Robbins et al., 2008). The analogy between human blood BDCA-3^+ DCs and mouse splenic $CD8\alpha^+$ DCs was further confirmed by cell surface phenotyping and functional analysis (Bachem et al., 2010; Crozat et al., 2010; Jongbloed et al., 2010; Poulin et al., 2010). Regarding sensing, it was found that human BDCA-3$^+$ DCs purified from peripheral blood mononuclear cells respond to transfection of dsRNA, poly(I:C) treatment, or HCV particles derived from Huh7.5 cells by producing type III IFN (IFN-λ or IL-28a, IL-28b, and IL-29), while this class of IFN was not induced by pDCs or BDCA-1$^+$ DCs in similar conditions (Yoshio et al., 2012). Whether BDCA-3$^+$ cells superior ability to produce type III IFN reflects a difference at the level of sensor diversity or at the level of downstream signaling pathways, compared to BDCA-1$^+$ DCs and pDCs remains to be determined. Results have also been generated in monocyte-derived DCs (MDDCs), which clearly differ from primary DCs (McCurley & Mellman, 2010; Robbins et al., 2008) but can be a potentially relevant model. In subpopulations based on the expression of the marker CD1a from bulk cultures of MDDCs differentiated *in vitro*, a distinct profile of RLR expression was detected (Szabo et al., 2012). However, to what extent these differences in RLR expression based on CD1a after *in vitro* culture reflect differentiated DC subsets is not known. Overall, these results suggest that human DC subsets are functionally specialized of at the level of cytosolic viral RNA sensing.

2.3. DNA sensors

Several studies suggested the presence of cytosolic sensors of DNA. Transfected DNA was found to be toxic in macrophages, suggesting that cells can respond to DNA (Stacey, Ross, & Hume, 1993). More recent studies demonstrated the existence of a cytosolic, TLR9-independent, response to DNA. This response was described in DCs generated *in vitro* from bone marrow in the presence of GM-CSF or FLT3L (Ishii et al., 2006; Stetson & Medzhitov, 2006). This response was found to be independent of Myd88, TRIF, RIG-I, and MDA5 but dependent on TBK1 and IRF3, but the entities responsible for such innate immune responses were not known. A wide range of cytosolic DNA sensors responding to various form of DNA have now been characterized and the number is still growing (Table 8.1).

The first sensor identified was DNA-dependent activator of IFN-regulatory factors (DAI) (Takaoka et al., 2007), known also as ZBP1 because of its previous known capacity to bind to Z-form of dsDNA. Its mRNA has been shown to be upregulated upon B-form dsDNA challenge in mouse

Table 8.1 Cytosolic DNA sensors

DNA sensor	Cells of identification	Response to pathogens/stimuli	Response activated
DAI	L929 (Takaoka et al., 2007)	hCMV (DeFilippis, Alvarado, Sali, Rothenburg, & Fruh, 2010)	TBK1/IRF3-dependent type I IFN
LRRFIP	Murine macrophages (Yang et al., 2010)	Listeria monocytogenes, VSV (Yang et al., 2010)	β-catenin interaction and IRF3 activation
DHX36 and DHX9	Human primary pDCs (Kim et al., 2010)	CpG dsDNA (Kim et al., 2010)	Myd88 interaction with IRF7 and p50 activation
AIM2	THP1 cell line (Burckstummer et al., 2009)	VACV (Hornung et al., 2009)	ASC interaction and IL1β production
IFI16	THP1 cell line (Unterholzner et al., 2010)	HSV (Unterholzner et al., 2010), CMV (Gariano et al., 2012)	Interaction with STING, TBK1/IRF3-mediated type I IFN response
DDX41	D2SC cell line, murine GM-CSF-derived DCs, THP1 cell line (Zhang, Yuan, et al., 2011)	HSV, adenoviruses (Zhang, Yuan, et al., 2011)	Interaction with STING, TBK1/IRF3-mediated type I IFN response
Ku70	Murine monocyte-derived macrophages 21398614	HSV (Zhang, Brann, et al., 2011)	IRF1 and IRF7 activation
DNA-PK	MEFs (Ferguson, Mansur, Peters, Ren, & Smith, 2012)	VACV, HSV (Ferguson et al., 2012)	STING mediated, TBK1/IRF3-mediated type I IFN response
LSm14A	MEFs (Li et al., 2012)	SeV, HSV (Li et al., 2012)	VISA mediated for RNA, STING mediated for DNA, type I IFN response
cGAS	L929 cell line, THP1 cell line (Sun, Wu, Du, Chen, & Chen, 2012)	HSV, VACV (Sun et al., 2012)	Activation of STING through cGAMP synthesis, TBK1/IRF3-mediated type I IFN response

embryonic fibroblasts (MEFs) and L929 cell line, and it is capable of eliciting an IRF3/TBK1-dependent type I IFN response after dsDNA binding, placing it in a positive feedback loop. This protein presents two domains capable of binding Z-form of DNA and one domain responsible for the binding to the B-form of DNA, and its C-terminal domain is responsible for the recruitment of TBK1 and IRF3. Its implication in viral DNA sensing has been demonstrated for hCMV in human fibroblasts (DeFilippis et al., 2010). However, DAI deficiency did not impair the production of type I IFN in MEFs, DCs generated from bone marrow with GM-CSF or FLT3L, and macrophages, suggesting that other DNA sensors were present (Ishii et al., 2008).

Another sensor, LRRFIP1, was identified in macrophages of mice challenged with *L. monocytogenes* and VSV. This protein contains a leucine-rich repeat (LRR) domain through which it binds DNA and through its interaction with β-catenin induces an IRF-3 dependent IFN-β response (Yang et al., 2010).

In addition to RNA sensing, DHX36 and DHX9 have been identified as DNA sensors through a biochemical approach in human primary pDCs. These proteins are capable of binding synthetic CpG dsDNA via the DEAH box domain, for DHX36, and via the DUF domain, for DHX9. Upon sensing, these proteins interact with the TIR domain of Myd88 and lead to the activation of IRF7 and p50 responses (Kim et al., 2010).

Another important family of proteins that acts as DNA sensors is the family of IFN-inducible-HIN200 or AIM2-like receptors (ALRs). This family comprises 13 genes in mouse and 4 genes in human (Brunette et al., 2012). This family is characterized by two types of domains: HIN domains that are capable of binding DNA and pyrin domains required to interact with other proteins. To date, only AIM2 and IFI16 have been identified as playing a role in DNA sensing in the innate immune system.

Absent in melanoma 2, AIM2, is the only member of this family to induce a response against cytosolic DNA through the inflammasome (Burckstummer et al., 2009). This sensor binds DNA and subsequently interacts with ASC through its pyrin domain. Its activation leads to the development of a caspase-mediated cell death response and to the production of IL-1β.

IFI16 is the second DNA sensor of the family of ALRs. This sensor is the only member of the family that encodes two DNA-binding HIN domains. It interacts with STING through its pyrin domain, leading to activation of a type I IFN responses. Its activity has been characterized in response to HSV (Unterholzner et al., 2010) and to human CMV (Gariano et al., 2012).

DDX41 is another cytosolic DNA sensor whose activity has been characterized in various cell lines (D2SC, murine GM-CSF-derived DCs, and THP-1) (Zhang, Yuan, et al., 2011). It has been shown that DDX41 is capable of inducing a type I IFN response after challenging of these cells with DNA viruses such as HSV and adenovirus. In order to elicit such response, the Walker A and Walker B domains of the sensor are required to bind DNA, whereas the DEADc domain is required for its interaction with STING.

A component of the heterodimeric Ku complex, required for a variety of nuclear DNA processes, has been identified as capable of eliciting a type III IFN response rather than a type I IFN response. Ku70 has been identified by a biochemical immunoprecipitation approach and its activity as a DNA sensor has been described in murine monocyte-derived macrophages challenged with HSV and ssDNA. This response seems to be dependent on IRF-1 and IRF-7 whose presence at the type III IFN promoter is increased upon Ku70 activation (Zhang, Brann, et al., 2011). Ku70 has been also proposed to play a stabilizing role, enhancing the DNA-binding capabilities of a newly identified sensor, DNA-PKcs (Ferguson et al., 2012). DNA-PK has been proposed to act as a heterotrimeric complex composed by Ku70/Ku80 and DNA-PKcs. Its activity as a type I IFN response inducer has been demonstrated in MEFs infected with VACV and HSV. The response to VACV challenging was impaired in MEFs derived from DNA-PKcs knockout mice, while type I IFN response was not strongly affected in MEFs derived from KO mice for Ku70 or Ku80. For this reason, it was proposed that even though Ku is capable of binding to DNA in the absence of DNA-PKcs, it functions in enhancing DNA-PKcs signaling process by boosting the affinity of the protein complex for DNA. Upon DNA-PK activation, TBK1 and STING are required to elicit a type I IFN response (Ferguson et al., 2012).

Crossing the line between RNA and DNA sensing, LSm14A has been recently identified as capable of responding to infection by RNA and DNA viruses. Its activity has been demonstrated in MEFs in response to SeV and HSV infection. It binds to both synthetic RNAs and DNAs through its FDF_TFG box and it is capable of activating a type I IFN response at early steps of viral infection. When activated by SeV infection, VISA and RIG-I were also required in order to elicit the antiviral response, whereas activation of the IFN response by HSV infection required STING (Li et al., 2012). It remains unclear if LSm14A satisfy the defining requirements for being classified as a sensor.

Finally, the most recently discovered is a DNA sensor with a catalytic activity that is linked to STING activation, cGAS. Identified by a biochemical approach, cGAS is a cytosolic cyclic GMP–AMP synthase that binds DNA through its N-terminal domain. DNA binding activates the ability of cGAS to synthetize cyclic GMP–AMP (cGAMP), a STING ligand (Wu et al., 2012), which in turns activates STING and elicits a type I IFN response. This mechanism has been demonstrated to occur upon HSV infection in murine L929 cell line and human THP-1 cell line (Sun et al., 2012).

Identification of this plethora of DNA sensors may indicate a highly redundant innate protective barrier against viruses at the cellular level. A unifying theme for most if not of all these molecules is the downstream signaling pathway that requires STING to induce IRF-3 dimerization. STING is a transmembrane protein located in the ER (Ishikawa & Barber, 2008). STING-deficient mice demonstrated that this adaptor plays a fundamental role in type I IFN response against DNA viruses. In STING knockout mice, MEFs, macrophages, cDCs, and pDCs were shown to be incapable of producing type I IFN after being challenged with various DNA viruses. Moreover HSV-infected STING-deficient mice showed a significant increase in mortality compared to wild-type mice challenged with the same virus (Ishikawa, Ma, & Barber, 2009).

Overall, great efforts have been put in identifying novel DNA sensors. Given that proteins containing a DNA-binding domain are abundant in the genome, more may be discovered. However, DNA sensors have been predominantly identified in cell lines and in *in vitro* models, and to date, little is known about the physiological role covered by these sensors in various in DC subsets, particularly in humans. In mouse, DAI was found to be expressed in a higher amount in $CD11b^{+}$ DCs (Luber et al., 2010). In humans, the expression and functions of the different DNA sensors in the distinct DC subset is not yet known.

The redundancy in the DNA sensor machinery may reflect the high risk posed by the presence of any cytosolic DNA in terms of host survival, whether this DNA originates from pathogens or from the host. DNA sensors may indeed also play an important in preventing abnormal pathways of DNA metabolism, which could lead for instance to cellular transformation and cancer or autoimmunity. The diversity in DNA sensors may also reflect the diversity of pathogens and their immune escape mechanisms. Alternatively, the diversity in DNA sensors also suggests that different sensors could be differently localized within a cell. Compartmentalization of sensors could allow a more efficient response to various pathogens in a complex environment such as the cell cytoplasm. Upon activation and in the case of type I IFN-inducing sensors, DNA sensors could potentially translocate from the pathogen-recognition site to interact and signal through a common adaptor such as STING (Kagan, 2012). It is therefore intriguing that all these different DNA sensors would signal through STING only, providing a non-redundant target for intracellular pathogens to counteract. It is possible that STING-independent DNA-dependent cytosolic sensing pathways that also induce type I IFN expression remain to be discovered.

3. INTERACTIONS AND EFFECTORS

3.1. Interactions between pathogen sensors and other receptors: SIGLEC-1 is a new player in cell surface capture of HIV by DCs

Sensing may be subject to regulation by interactions of the pathogens with other receptors. Conversely, such interactions may be modified as a consequence of sensing. A recent example of these concepts has been provided by the recent discovery that SIGLEC-1 is implicated in the cell surface capture of HIV-1 by mature human MDDCs and blood BDCA-1^+ DCs (Izquierdo-Useros et al., 2012; Puryear et al., 2013).

Human DCs have the remarkable property of enhancing in *trans* the susceptibility of $CD4^+$ T cells to infection by HIV-1 (Cameron et al., 1992). The mechanism underlying this property and its relevance to HIV-1 infection *in vivo* remains an open question. *Trans*-enhancement of HIV-1 infection has been associated with the ability of DCs to capture and internalize virus. The internalized virus can have different fates in the DCs including low level of direct infection, degradation, and storage. *Trans*-enhancement of T-cell infection is thought to contribute to the latter pool of virus stored in an infectious state. Because the initial virus inoculate is stored, it indicates that its capture by DCs is either non-receptor mediated (such as by micropinocytosis) or mediated by a receptor that does not lead to entry of the virus into the cytosol of the DCs.

In light of these properties, efforts have been made toward the identification of cell surface proteins specifically expressed by MDDCs that could interact with HIV-1. Such receptor, that must recognize physical properties of the pathogen, could thus also act as a sensor or regulate other sensors. The C-type lectin DC-SIGN was first identified as a cell-specific HIV-1-binding protein that binds the HIV-1 envelope glycoprotein gp120 (Geijtenbeek et al., 2000) and considered a putative receptor implicated in the *trans*-enhancement of T-cell infection by MDDCs. However, as reviewed elsewhere (Silvin & Manel, 2013), the role of DC-SIGN in this process appeared to be more complex than initially considered. In particular, MDDCs can capture virus independently of gp120. By comparing the ability of mature (activated) MDDCs to capture HIV-1 virus-like particles (VLPs) produced from cells to their ability to capture artificial large unilamellar vesicles, it became apparent that the presence of gangliosides, and in particular sialic acids in the viral envelope glycoprotein, was required for the capture of HIV-1 VLPs by mature MDDCs (Izquierdo-Useros et al., 2012). By exploring the differential expression of genes that code for proteins of the SIGLEC family, which bind sialylated ligands, SIGLEC1 was identified as a potential candidate (Izquierdo-Useros et al., 2012; Puryear et al., 2013). Strikingly, blocking antibodies against SIGLEC1 but not against SIGLEC7, SIGLEC5/14, or CD83 completely prevented capture of VLPs by LPS-matured DCs and virus transfer to an HIV-1-infection reporter cell line, TZM-bl (Izquierdo-Useros et al., 2012).

It remains to be determined whether and how truly, pure, immature DCs may transfer virus to $CD4^+$ T cells. This is particularly relevant as it is usually assumed that this mechanism could play a role in capture of virus at mucosal surfaces, where DCs are generally inactivated at steady state (Inaba et al., 1994; Larsen, Ritchie, Pearson, Linsley, & Lowry, 1992).

Because SIGLEC1 is unusual in the family since it possesses a short cytoplasmic tail of 47 amino acids that is not conserved between human and mouse (Hartnell et al., 2001), this does not favor the hypothesis that SIGLEC1 could signal in response to HIV-1 binding but should nonetheless be explored. In particular, SIGLEC-1 and DC-SIGN may be simultaneously engaged at the cell surface of DCs and this may modulate the previously reported signaling properties of DC-SIGN (Hodges et al., 2007). Overall, SIGLEC-1 emerges as an important player in the capture and transfer of HIV-1 by DCs whose interplay with innate sensors is now to be examined.

3.2. Diversity of antiviral effectors

The process of sensor activation in DCs can lead to a large variety of responses. In terms of viral replication, the best-characterized response is the induction of the type I IFN response. Type I IFN responses are induced by binding of soluble IFN-beta (one isoform in humans) or IFN-alpha (multiple isoforms) (Pestka, Krause, & Walter, 2004) to the type I IFN receptor, IFNAR (composed of two chains, IFN-αR1 and IFN-αR2c). Type I IFN can act in an autocrine manner on DCs and in a paracrine manner on neighboring cells. The interest in the downstream products of IFN signaling is generally confined into a restricted group of ISGs (Der, Zhou, Williams, & Silverman, 1998; Rusinova et al., 2013). Recent progresses have been made in the understanding of the function of individual ISGs (Schoggins et al., 2011). Intriguingly, a significant fraction of the ISGs validated as effectors in this study were previously identified as viral sensors. It remains to be clarified whether these effector activities may due to signaling and induction of endogenous ISG in the cells used in the study or whether these sensors possess intrinsic effector activity. Nevertheless, this suggests that the processes of viral sensing and effector responses are interdependent. Triggering of a sensor will lead to activation of the IFN signaling pathway and coexpression of different ISGs that can inhibit the viral cycle at different levels and also concomitantly participate to the sensing process as positive or negative regulators. In DCs, it will be important to examine how interactions between sensors and effector ISG impact the functions of these cells, beyond the regulation of type I IFN secretion.

3.3. Antiviral mechanisms

Novel insights into how type I IFN inhibits HIV-1 replication particularly in primary human cells have emerged in the recent years. In monocyte-derived macrophages and $CD4^+$ T cells pretreated with IFN-α, the level of viral inhibition ranges from 80% to more than 95% among a broad range of HIV-1 pseudotypes (Goujon & Malim, 2010). Interestingly, the effect of IFN-α on HIV-1 cDNA accumulation appears more potent in macrophages than in $CD4^+$ T cells. Monocyte-derived macrophages such as those used in this study may correspond to a subset of inflammatory macrophages found at mucosal sites (Bain et al., 2013). This suggests that HIV-1 replication at these sites may be particularly susceptible to the amount of type I IFN present in the tissue environment.

Effector antiviral mechanisms have also been described in $CD4^+$ T cells from elite controllers (ECs). Isolated cells from these patients are less susceptible to HIV-1 infection *in vitro* compared to HIV-1 negative individuals and HIV-1 progressors, suggesting that these cells may have intrinsic resistant mechanisms to HIV-1 replication (Bergamaschi et al., 2009; Buzon et al., 2011; Chen et al., 2011). In particular, the expression of p21 was selectively detected in $CD4^+$ T cells from ECs. RNAi experiments showed that p21 expression is required to inhibit HIV-1 replication in *ex vivo* HIV-1 infection assay (Chen et al., 2011). This was further validated using a chemical inhibitor of p21. Interestingly, p21 has not been characterized as an ISG. It will be important to determine the contribution of type I IFN signaling in the induction of p21. These results raise the possibility that effector antiviral mechanisms may be regulated after pathogen sensing by processes independent of type I IFN. Because DCs couple pathogen sensing and induction of IFN responses to shaping of the adaptive immune system, they appear as attractive cellular inducers of these effectors mechanisms.

3.4. Shaping the adaptive immune response

In DCs, triggering of pathogen sensors has a dual role. While sensing of the virus by DCs induces the production of type I IFN to prevent the viral replication in neighboring cells, DCs also become effective antigen-presenting cells and activate T cells, a process during which IFN has a non-antiviral effect on responding T cells.

3.4.1 $CD8^+$ T-cell responses

The mechanisms by which type I IFN affects the generation of $CD8^+$ T-cell responses and the survival of memory $CD8^+$ T cells are still elusive. Lymphocytic choriomeningitis virus (LCMV) is a mouse experimental model that has been studied to investigate $CD8^+$ T-cell responses against acute and chronic infection (Wang et al., 2012). In this model, the Armstrong (ARM) strain elicits an acute infection that is cleared by a strong $CD8^+$ T-cell response, while the Clone13 (CL13) strain has a higher replication capacity, targets a wider group of cells than ARM, and leads to chronic infection. An important question was to determine the source of type I IFN potentially implicated in shaping these different $CD8^+$ T-cell responses.

pDCs were thought to play a major role in type I IFN responses due to their fast and robust production of IFN following TLR7 or TLR9 stimulation, but whether this response or other sources of type I IFN were responsible for the modulation of the $CD8^+$ T-cell responses was not known.

Conditional pDC depletion in mice infected with LCMV resulted in the reduction of IFN-α production within 16 h of infection but without affecting IFN-α production at later time points (Wang et al., 2012). pDC depletion in mice infected with CL13 did not affect the generation of antiviral $CD8^+$ T cells in the spleen, even when pDC depletion was extended for 30 days after infection, suggesting that these cells are unlikely to play a major role in the control of the LCMV infection. Thus, pDCs contribute with early and transient type I IFN production upon infection but they exert a limited effect on $CD8^+$ T-cell responses.

In double TRIF-deficient MyD88-deficient mice that lack TLR responses, serum IFN-α levels were reduced within 24 h of infection with the ARM strain but reached wild-type levels at later time points, which is consistent with the role of pDCs in the production of type I IFN at early time points. In contrast, in mice deficient for the cytosolic sensor MDA5, IFN-α production was significantly impaired at all time points. This suggested that other cellular sources of type I IFN than pDCs were involved. In addition, in MDA5-deficient animals, the $CD8^+$ T-cell responses were delayed and infection was cleared less efficiently. Thus, cytosolic MDA5, but not TLR7 or TLR9 on pDCs, is a central sensor required for shaping antiviral $CD8^+$ T-cell response in this model. Since MDA5 is a cytosolic sensor, LCMV-infected cells are presumably the main source of type I IFN implicated in $CD8^+$ T-cell responses. This implies that the cellular tropism of LCMV is a determinant of the quality and quantities of the type I IFN response and, consequently, of the $CD8^+$ T-cell responses. Interestingly, the ARM and CL13 strains have different tropism, since ARM targets preferentially macrophages, while CL13 infects macrophages, DCs, hematopoietic progenitors, and fibroblast (Wang et al., 2012). Altogether, these results show that the type I IFN response induced by cytosolic sensing after LCMV infection is a major determinant of the $CD8^+$ T-cell responses and of the resolution of the infection.

3.4.2 $CD4^+$ T-cell responses

Pathogen sensing also affects the magnitude and qualities of the $CD4^+$ T-cell responses. Type I IFN modifies the proliferation of $CD4^+$ memory T cells (Gallagher, Lauder, Rees, Gallimore, & Godkin, 2009). Cooperation and interaction between pathogen sensors also influences the cytokine profile of polarized T helper subsets (Schwarz et al., 2012; van Beelen et al., 2007). It is likely that the recent advances in the regulation of type I IFN responses will also contribute to a better understanding of how type I IFN might impact $CD4^+$ T-cell responses.

4. PERSPECTIVES

Although a large number of PAMP-based pathogen sensors have been described, new sensors of pathogen-encoded activities have recently emerged as important players in the recognition and response to infection. DCs are equipped with a large number of pathogen sensors. Further insight into the specific expression and function of pathogen sensors, particularly the cytosolic sensors, in the different DC subsets, should further our understanding of how pathogen sensors impact the replication of pathogens and the induction of host immune responses.

ACKNOWLEDGMENTS

We apologize to authors and colleagues whose work was not cited. We thank the Manel lab for discussion and Philippe Benaroch and Vassili Soumélis for critical reading of the manuscript. SC is supported by Institut Curie International PhD Program. MG is supported by Leonardo Unipharma program. This work was supported by Institut Curie, Institut National de la Santé et de la Recherche Médicale (INSERM), ATIP-Avenir program, Agence Nationale de Recherche sur le SIDA (ANRS), Ville de Paris Emergence program, European FP7 Marie Curie Actions, European Research Council, LABEX VRI, and LABEX DCBIOL.

REFERENCES

Allen, I. C., Scull, M. A., Moore, C. B., Holl, E. K., McElvania-TeKippe, E., Taxman, D. J., et al. (2009). The NLRP3 inflammasome mediates in vivo innate immunity to influenza A virus through recognition of viral RNA. *Immunity*, *30*(4), 556–565. http://dx.doi.org/10.1016/j.immuni.2009.02.005.

Bachem, A., Guttler, S., Hartung, E., Ebstein, F., Schaefer, M., Tannert, A., et al. (2010). Superior antigen cross-presentation and XCR1 expression define human CD11c+ CD141+ cells as homologues of mouse CD8+ dendritic cells. *The Journal of Experimental Medicine*, *207*(6), 1273–1281. http://dx.doi.org/10.1084/jem.20100348.

Bain, C. C., Scott, C. L., Uronen-Hansson, H., Gudjonsson, S., Jansson, O., Grip, O., et al. (2013). Resident and pro-inflammatory macrophages in the colon represent alternative context-dependent fates of the same Ly6Chi monocyte precursors. *Mucosal Immunology*, *6*(3), 498–510. http://dx.doi.org/10.1038/mi.2012.89.

Banchereau, J., & Steinman, R. M. (1998). Dendritic cells and the control of immunity. *Nature*, *392*(6673), 245–252. http://dx.doi.org/10.1038/32588.

Bergamaschi, A., David, A., Le Rouzic, E., Nisole, S., Barre-Sinoussi, F., & Pancino, G. (2009). The CDK inhibitor p21Cip1/WAF1 is induced by FcgammaR activation and restricts the replication of human immunodeficiency virus type 1 and related primate lentiviruses in human macrophages. *Journal of Virology*, *83*(23), 12253–12265. http://dx.doi.org/10.1128/JVI.01395-09.

Brunette, R. L., Young, J. M., Whitley, D. G., Brodsky, I. E., Malik, H. S., & Stetson, D. B. (2012). Extensive evolutionary and functional diversity among mammalian AIM2-like receptors. *The Journal of Experimental Medicine*, *209*(11), 1969–1983. http://dx.doi.org/10.1084/jem.20121960.

Burckstummer, T., Baumann, C., Bluml, S., Dixit, E., Durnberger, G., Jahn, H., et al. (2009). An orthogonal proteomic-genomic screen identifies AIM2 as a cytoplasmic DNA sensor for the inflammasome. *Nature Immunology*, *10*(3), 266–272. http://dx.doi.org/10.1038/ni.1702.

Buzon, M. J., Seiss, K., Weiss, R., Brass, A. L., Rosenberg, E. S., Pereyra, F., et al. (2011). Inhibition of HIV-1 integration in ex vivo-infected CD4 T cells from elite controllers. *Journal of Virology*, *85*(18), 9646–9650. http://dx.doi.org/10.1128/JVI.05327-11.

Cameron, P. U., Freudenthal, P. S., Barker, J. M., Gezelter, S., Inaba, K., & Steinman, R. M. (1992). Dendritic cells exposed to human immunodeficiency virus type-1 transmit a vigorous cytopathic infection to CD4+ T cells. *Science*, *257*(5068), 383–387.

Chakrabarti, S., Liehl, P., Buchon, N., & Lemaitre, B. (2012). Infection-induced host translational blockage inhibits immune responses and epithelial renewal in the Drosophila gut. *Cell Host & Microbe*, *12*(1), 60–70. http://dx.doi.org/10.1016/j.chom.2012.06.001.

Chen, H., Li, C., Huang, J., Cung, T., Seiss, K., Beamon, J., et al. (2011). CD4+ T cells from elite controllers resist HIV-1 infection by selective upregulation of p21. *The Journal of Clinical Investigation*, *121*(4), 1549–1560. http://dx.doi.org/10.1172/JCI44539.

Crozat, K., Guiton, R., Contreras, V., Feuillet, V., Dutertre, C. A., Ventre, E., et al. (2010). The XC chemokine receptor 1 is a conserved selective marker of mammalian cells homologous to mouse CD8alpha+ dendritic cells. *The Journal of Experimental Medicine*, *207*(6), 1283–1292. http://dx.doi.org/10.1084/jem.20100223.

DeFilippis, V. R., Alvarado, D., Sali, T., Rothenburg, S., & Fruh, K. (2010). Human cytomegalovirus induces the interferon response via the DNA sensor ZBP1. *Journal of Virology*, *84*(1), 585–598. http://dx.doi.org/10.1128/JVI.01748-09.

Der, S. D., Zhou, A., Williams, B. R., & Silverman, R. H. (1998). Identification of genes differentially regulated by interferon alpha, beta, or gamma using oligonucleotide arrays. *Proceedings of the National Academy of Sciences of the United States of America*, *95*(26), 15623–15628.

Ferguson, B. J., Mansur, D. S., Peters, N. E., Ren, H., & Smith, G. L. (2012). DNA-PK is a DNA sensor for IRF-3-dependent innate immunity. *Elife*, *1*, e00047. http://dx.doi.org/10.7554/eLife.00047.

Fontana, M. F., Banga, S., Barry, K. C., Shen, X., Tan, Y., Luo, Z. Q., et al. (2011). Secreted bacterial effectors that inhibit host protein synthesis are critical for induction of the innate immune response to virulent *Legionella pneumophila*. *PLoS Pathogens*, 7(2), e1001289. http://dx.doi.org/10.1371/journal.ppat.1001289.

Gallagher, K. M., Lauder, S., Rees, I. W., Gallimore, A. M., & Godkin, A. J. (2009). Type I interferon (IFN alpha) acts directly on human memory CD4+ T cells altering their response to antigen. *The Journal of Immunology*, *183*(5), 2915–2920. http://dx.doi.org/10.4049/jimmunol.0801607.

Garcia-Cattaneo, A., Gobert, F. X., Muller, M., Toscano, F., Flores, M., Lescure, A., et al. (2012). Cleavage of Toll-like receptor 3 by cathepsins B and H is essential for signaling. *Proceedings of the National Academy of Sciences of the United States of America*, *109*(23), 9053–9058. http://dx.doi.org/10.1073/pnas.1115091109.

Gariano, G. R., Dell'Oste, V., Bronzini, M., Gatti, D., Luganini, A., De Andrea, M., et al. (2012). The intracellular DNA sensor IFI16 gene acts as restriction factor for human cytomegalovirus replication. *PLoS Pathogens*, *8*(1), e1002498. http://dx.doi.org/10.1371/journal.ppat.1002498.

Geijtenbeek, T. B., Kwon, D. S., Torensma, R., van Vliet, S. J., van Duijnhoven, G. C., Middel, J., et al. (2000). DC-SIGN, a dendritic cell-specific HIV-1-binding protein that enhances trans-infection of T cells. *Cell*, *100*(5), 587–597.

Gitlin, L., Barchet, W., Gilfillan, S., Cella, M., Beutler, B., Flavell, R. A., et al. (2006). Essential role of mda-5 in type I IFN responses to polyriboinosinic:polyribocytidylic acid and encephalomyocarditis picornavirus. *Proceedings of the National Academy of Sciences of the United States of America*, *103*(22), 8459–8464. http://dx.doi.org/10.1073/pnas.0603082103.

Gough, D. J., Messina, N. L., Clarke, C. J., Johnstone, R. W., & Levy, D. E. (2012). Constitutive type I interferon modulates homeostatic balance through tonic signaling. *Immunity*, *36*(2), 166–174. http://dx.doi.org/10.1016/j.immuni.2012.01.011.

Goujon, C., & Malim, M. H. (2010). Characterization of the alpha interferon-induced postentry block to HIV-1 infection in primary human macrophages and T cells. *Journal of Virology*, *84*(18), 9254–9266. http://dx.doi.org/10.1128/JVI.00854-10.

Hartnell, A., Steel, J., Turley, H., Jones, M., Jackson, D. G., & Crocker, P. R. (2001). Characterization of human sialoadhesin, a sialic acid binding receptor expressed by resident and inflammatory macrophage populations. *Blood*, *97*(1), 288–296.

Hasan, M., Koch, J., Rakheja, D., Pattnaik, A. K., Brugarolas, J., Dozmorov, I., et al. (2013). Trex1 regulates lysosomal biogenesis and interferon-independent activation of antiviral genes. *Nature Immunology*, *14*(1), 61–71. http://dx.doi.org/10.1038/ni.2475.

Hodges, A., Sharrocks, K., Edelmann, M., Baban, D., Moris, A., Schwartz, O., et al. (2007). Activation of the lectin DC-SIGN induces an immature dendritic cell phenotype triggering Rho-GTPase activity required for HIV-1 replication. *Nature Immunology*, *8*(6), 569–577. http://dx.doi.org/10.1038/ni1470.

Honda, K., Sakaguchi, S., Nakajima, C., Watanabe, A., Yanai, H., Matsumoto, M., et al. (2003). Selective contribution of IFN-alpha/beta signaling to the maturation of dendritic cells induced by double-stranded RNA or viral infection. *Proceedings of the National Academy of Sciences of the United States of America*, *100*(19), 10872–10877. http://dx.doi.org/10.1073/pnas.1934678100.

Hornung, V., Ablasser, A., Charrel-Dennis, M., Bauernfeind, F., Horvath, G., Caffrey, D. R., et al. (2009). AIM2 recognizes cytosolic dsDNA and forms a caspase-1-activating inflammasome with ASC. *Nature*, *458*(7237), 514–518. http://dx.doi.org/10.1038/nature07725.

Inaba, K., Witmer-Pack, M., Inaba, M., Hathcock, K. S., Sakuta, H., Azuma, M., et al. (1994). The tissue distribution of the B7-2 costimulator in mice: Abundant expression on dendritic cells in situ and during maturation in vitro. *The Journal of Experimental Medicine*, *180*(5), 1849–1860.

Ishii, K. J., Coban, C., Kato, H., Takahashi, K., Torii, Y., Takeshita, F., et al. (2006). A Toll-like receptor-independent antiviral response induced by double-stranded B-form DNA. *Nature Immunology*, 7(1), 40–48. http://dx.doi.org/10.1038/ni1282.

Ishii, K. J., Kawagoe, T., Koyama, S., Matsui, K., Kumar, H., Kawai, T., et al. (2008). TANK-binding kinase-1 delineates innate and adaptive immune responses to DNA vaccines. *Nature*, *451*(7179), 725–729. http://dx.doi.org/10.1038/nature06537.

Ishikawa, H., & Barber, G. N. (2008). STING is an endoplasmic reticulum adaptor that facilitates innate immune signalling. *Nature*, *455*(7213), 674–678. http://dx.doi.org/10.1038/nature07317.

Ishikawa, H., Ma, Z., & Barber, G. N. (2009). STING regulates intracellular DNA-mediated, type I interferon-dependent innate immunity. *Nature*, *461*(7265), 788–792. http://dx.doi.org/10.1038/nature08476.

Izquierdo-Useros, N., Lorizate, M., Contreras, F. X., Rodriguez-Plata, M. T., Glass, B., Erkizia, I., et al. (2012). Sialyllactose in viral membrane gangliosides is a novel molecular recognition pattern for mature dendritic cell capture of HIV-1. *PLoS Biology*, *10*(4), e1001315. http://dx.doi.org/10.1371/journal.pbio.1001315.

Jiang, A., Bloom, O., Ono, S., Cui, W., Unternaehrer, J., Jiang, S., et al. (2007). Disruption of E-cadherin-mediated adhesion induces a functionally distinct pathway of dendritic cell maturation. *Immunity*, *27*(4), 610–624. http://dx.doi.org/10.1016/j.immuni.2007.08.015.

Jongbloed, S. L., Kassianos, A. J., McDonald, K. J., Clark, G. J., Ju, X., Angel, C. E., et al. (2010). Human CD141 + (BDCA-3)+ dendritic cells (DCs) represent a unique myeloid DC subset that cross-presents necrotic cell antigens. *The Journal of Experimental Medicine*, *207*(6), 1247–1260. http://dx.doi.org/10.1084/jem.20092140.

Kagan, J. C. (2012). Signaling organelles of the innate immune system. *Cell*, *151*(6), 1168–1178. http://dx.doi.org/10.1016/j.cell.2012.11.011.

Karpova, A. Y., Trost, M., Murray, J. M., Cantley, L. C., & Howley, P. M. (2002). Interferon regulatory factor-3 is an in vivo target of DNA-PK. *Proceedings of the National Academy of Sciences of the United States of America*, *99*(5), 2818–2823. http://dx.doi.org/10.1073/pnas.052713899.

Kato, H., Sato, S., Yoneyama, M., Yamamoto, M., Uematsu, S., Matsui, K., et al. (2005). Cell type-specific involvement of RIG-I in antiviral response. *Immunity, 23*(1), 19–28. http://dx.doi.org/10.1016/j.immuni.2005.04.010.

Kim, T., Kim, T. Y., Song, Y. H., Min, I. M., Yim, J., & Kim, T. K. (1999). Activation of interferon regulatory factor 3 in response to DNA-damaging agents. *The Journal of Biological Chemistry, 274*(43), 30686–30689.

Kim, T., Pazhoor, S., Bao, M., Zhang, Z., Hanabuchi, S., Facchinetti, V., et al. (2010). Aspartate-glutamate-alanine-histidine box motif (DEAH)/RNA helicase A helicases sense microbial DNA in human plasmacytoid dendritic cells. *Proceedings of the National Academy of Sciences of the United States of America, 107*(34), 15181–15186. http://dx.doi.org/10.1073/pnas.1006539107.

Larsen, C. P., Ritchie, S. C., Pearson, T. C., Linsley, P. S., & Lowry, R. P. (1992). Functional expression of the costimulatory molecule, B7/BB1, on murine dendritic cell populations. *The Journal of Experimental Medicine, 176*(4), 1215–1220.

Li, Y., Chen, R., Zhou, Q., Xu, Z., Li, C., Wang, S., et al. (2012). LSm14A is a processing body-associated sensor of viral nucleic acids that initiates cellular antiviral response in the early phase of viral infection. *Proceedings of the National Academy of Sciences of the United States of America, 109*(29), 11770–11775. http://dx.doi.org/10.1073/pnas.1203405109.

Liu, Y. P., Zeng, L., Tian, A., Bomkamp, A., Rivera, D., Gutman, D., et al. (2012). Endoplasmic reticulum stress regulates the innate immunity critical transcription factor IRF3. *The Journal of Immunology, 189*(9), 4630–4639. http://dx.doi.org/10.4049/jimmunol.1102737.

Losick, V. P., & Isberg, R. R. (2006). NF-kappaB translocation prevents host cell death after low-dose challenge by Legionella pneumophila. *The Journal of Experimental Medicine, 203*(9), 2177–2189. http://dx.doi.org/10.1084/jem.20060766.

Luber, C. A., Cox, J., Lauterbach, H., Fancke, B., Selbach, M., Tschopp, J., et al. (2010). Quantitative proteomics reveals subset-specific viral recognition in dendritic cells. *Immunity, 32*(2), 279–289. http://dx.doi.org/10.1016/j.immuni.2010.01.013.

Matzinger, P. (2002). The danger model: A renewed sense of self. *Science, 296*(5566), 301–305. http://dx.doi.org/10.1126/science.1071059.

McCurley, N., & Mellman, I. (2010). Monocyte-derived dendritic cells exhibit increased levels of lysosomal proteolysis as compared to other human dendritic cell populations. *PLoS One, 5*(8), e11949. http://dx.doi.org/10.1371/journal.pone.0011949.

Medzhitov, R., Preston-Hurlburt, P., & Janeway, C. A., Jr. (1997). A human homologue of the Drosophila Toll protein signals activation of adaptive immunity. *Nature, 388*(6640), 394–397. http://dx.doi.org/10.1038/41131.

Meylan, E., Curran, J., Hofmann, K., Moradpour, D., Binder, M., Bartenschlager, R., et al. (2005). Cardif is an adaptor protein in the RIG-I antiviral pathway and is targeted by hepatitis C virus. *Nature, 437*(7062), 1167–1172. http://dx.doi.org/10.1038/nature04193.

Nakaya, T., Sato, M., Hata, N., Asagiri, M., Suemori, H., Noguchi, S., et al. (2001). Gene induction pathways mediated by distinct IRFs during viral infection. *Biochemical and Biophysical Research Communications, 283*(5), 1150–1156. http://dx.doi.org/10.1006/bbrc.2001.4913.

Navarro, L., & David, M. (1999). p38-dependent activation of interferon regulatory factor 3 by lipopolysaccharide. *The Journal of Biological Chemistry, 274*(50), 35535–35538.

Ostuni, R., Piccolo, V., Barozzi, I., Polletti, S., Termanini, A., Bonifacio, S., et al. (2013). Latent enhancers activated by stimulation in differentiated cells. *Cell, 152*(1–2), 157–171. http://dx.doi.org/10.1016/j.cell.2012.12.018.

Pestka, S., Krause, C. D., & Walter, M. R. (2004). Interferons, interferon-like cytokines, and their receptors. *Immunological Reviews, 202*, 8–32. http://dx.doi.org/10.1111/j.0105-2896.2004.00204.x.

Poulin, L. F., Salio, M., Griessinger, E., Anjos-Afonso, F., Craciun, L., Chen, J. L., et al. (2010). Characterization of human DNGR-1+ BDCA3+ leukocytes as putative

equivalents of mouse CD8alpha+ dendritic cells. *The Journal of Experimental Medicine*, *207*(6), 1261–1271. http://dx.doi.org/10.1084/jem.20092618.
Puryear, W. B., Akiyama, H., Geer, S. D., Ramirez, N. P., Yu, X., Reinhard, B. M., et al. (2013). Interferon-inducible mechanism of dendritic cell-mediated HIV-1 dissemination is dependent on Siglec-1/CD169. *PLoS Pathogens*, *9*(4), e1003291. http://dx.doi.org/10.1371/journal.ppat.1003291.
Read, A. F., Graham, A. L., & Raberg, L. (2008). Animal defenses against infectious agents: Is damage control more important than pathogen control. *PLoS Biology*, *6*(12), e4. http://dx.doi.org/10.1371/journal.pbio.1000004.
Robbins, S. H., Walzer, T., Dembele, D., Thibault, C., Defays, A., Bessou, G., et al. (2008). Novel insights into the relationships between dendritic cell subsets in human and mouse revealed by genome-wide expression profiling. *Genome Biology*, *9*(1), R17. http://dx.doi.org/10.1186/gb-2008-9-1-r17.
Rothenfusser, S., Goutagny, N., DiPerna, G., Gong, M., Monks, B. G., Schoenemeyer, A., et al. (2005). The RNA helicase Lgp2 inhibits TLR-independent sensing of viral replication by retinoic acid-inducible gene-I. *The Journal of Immunology*, *175*(8), 5260–5268.
Ruggieri, A., Dazert, E., Metz, P., Hofmann, S., Bergeest, J. P., Mazur, J., et al. (2012). Dynamic oscillation of translation and stress granule formation mark the cellular response to virus infection. *Cell Host & Microbe*, *12*(1), 71–85. http://dx.doi.org/10.1016/j.chom.2012.05.013.
Rusinova, I., Forster, S., Yu, S., Kannan, A., Masse, M., Cumming, H., et al. (2013). INTERFEROME v2.0: An updated database of annotated interferon-regulated genes. *Nucleic Acids Research*, *41*(D1), D1040–D1046. http://dx.doi.org/10.1093/nar/gks1215.
Saito, T., Hirai, R., Loo, Y. M., Owen, D., Johnson, C. L., Sinha, S. C., et al. (2007). Regulation of innate antiviral defenses through a shared repressor domain in RIG-I and LGP2. *Proceedings of the National Academy of Sciences of the United States of America*, *104*(2), 582–587. http://dx.doi.org/10.1073/pnas.0606699104.
Schoggins, J. W., Wilson, S. J., Panis, M., Murphy, M. Y., Jones, C. T., Bieniasz, P., et al. (2011). A diverse range of gene products are effectors of the type I interferon antiviral response. *Nature*, *472*(7344), 481–485. http://dx.doi.org/10.1038/nature09907.
Schwarz, H., Posselt, G., Wurm, P., Ulbing, M., Duschl, A., & Horejs-Hoeck, J. (2012). TLR8 and NOD signaling synergistically induce the production of IL-1beta and IL-23 in monocyte-derived DCs and enhance the expression of the feedback inhibitor SOCS2. *Immunobiology*, http://dx.doi.org/10.1016/j.imbio.2012.06.007.
Schwessinger, B., & Ronald, P. C. (2012). Plant innate immunity: Perception of conserved microbial signatures. *Annual Review of Plant Biology*, *63*, 451–482. http://dx.doi.org/10.1146/annurev-arplant-042811-105518.
Segura, E., Kapp, E., Gupta, N., Wong, J., Lim, J., Ji, H., et al. (2010). Differential expression of pathogen-recognition molecules between dendritic cell subsets revealed by plasma membrane proteomic analysis. *Molecular Immunology*, *47*(9), 1765–1773. http://dx.doi.org/10.1016/j.molimm.2010.02.028.
Silvin, A., & Manel, N. (2013). Interactions between HIV-1 and innate immunity in dendritic cells. *Advances in Experimental Medicine and Biology*, *762*, 183–200. http://dx.doi.org/10.1007/978-1-4614-4433-6_7.
Spoel, S. H., & Dong, X. (2012). How do plants achieve immunity? Defence without specialized immune cells. *Nature Reviews Immunology*, *12*(2), 89–100. http://dx.doi.org/10.1038/nri3141.
Stacey, K. J., Ross, I. L., & Hume, D. A. (1993). Electroporation and DNA-dependent cell death in murine macrophages. *Immunology & Cell Biology*, *71*(Part 2), 75–85. http://dx.doi.org/10.1038/icb.1993.8.

Stetson, D. B., & Medzhitov, R. (2006). Recognition of cytosolic DNA activates an IRF3-dependent innate immune response. *Immunity*, *24*(1), 93–103. http://dx.doi.org/10.1016/j.immuni.2005.12.003.
Sun, L., Wu, J., Du, F., Chen, X., & Chen, Z. J. (2012). Cyclic GMP-AMP synthase is a cytosolic DNA sensor that activates the type I interferon pathway. *Science*, http://dx.doi.org/10.1126/science.1232458.
Szabo, A., Bene, K., Gogolak, P., Rethi, B., Lanyi, A., Jankovich, I., et al. (2012). RLR-mediated production of interferon-beta by a human dendritic cell subset and its role in virus-specific immunity. *Journal of Leukocyte Biology*, *92*(1), 159–169. http://dx.doi.org/10.1189/jlb.0711360.
Takaoka, A., Wang, Z., Choi, M. K., Yanai, H., Negishi, H., Ban, T., et al. (2007). DAI (DLM-1/ZBP1) is a cytosolic DNA sensor and an activator of innate immune response. *Nature*, *448*(7152), 501–505. http://dx.doi.org/10.1038/nature06013.
Tattoli, I., Sorbara, M. T., Vuckovic, D., Ling, A., Soares, F., Carneiro, L. A., et al. (2012). Amino acid starvation induced by invasive bacterial pathogens triggers an innate host defense program. *Cell Host & Microbe*, *11*(6), 563–575. http://dx.doi.org/10.1016/j.chom.2012.04.012.
Todd, D. J., Lee, A. H., & Glimcher, L. H. (2008). The endoplasmic reticulum stress response in immunity and autoimmunity. *Nature Reviews Immunology*, *8*(9), 663–674. http://dx.doi.org/10.1038/nri2359.
Towers, G. J. (2007). The control of viral infection by tripartite motif proteins and cyclophilin A. *Retrovirology*, *4*, 40. http://dx.doi.org/10.1186/1742-4690-4-40.
Unterholzner, L., Keating, S. E., Baran, M., Horan, K. A., Jensen, S. B., Sharma, S., et al. (2010). IFI16 is an innate immune sensor for intracellular DNA. *Nature Immunology*, *11*(11), 997–1004. http://dx.doi.org/10.1038/ni.1932.
van Beelen, A. J., Zelinkova, Z., Taanman-Kueter, E. W., Muller, F. J., Hommes, D. W., Zaat, S. A., et al. (2007). Stimulation of the intracellular bacterial sensor NOD2 programs dendritic cells to promote interleukin-17 production in human memory T cells. *Immunity*, *27*(4), 660–669. http://dx.doi.org/10.1016/j.immuni.2007.08.013.
van der Hoorn, R. A., & Kamoun, S. (2008). From Guard to Decoy: A new model for perception of plant pathogen effectors. *The Plant Cell*, *20*(8), 2009–2017. http://dx.doi.org/10.1105/tpc.108.060194.
Vance, R. E., Isberg, R. R., & Portnoy, D. A. (2009). Patterns of pathogenesis: Discrimination of pathogenic and nonpathogenic microbes by the innate immune system. *Cell Host & Microbe*, *6*(1), 10–21. http://dx.doi.org/10.1016/j.chom.2009.06.007.
Wang, Y., Swiecki, M., Cella, M., Alber, G., Schreiber, R. D., Gilfillan, S., et al. (2012). Timing and magnitude of type I interferon responses by distinct sensors impact CD8 T cell exhaustion and chronic viral infection. *Cell Host & Microbe*, *11*(6), 631–642. http://dx.doi.org/10.1016/j.chom.2012.05.003.
Wu, J., Sun, L., Chen, X., Du, F., Shi, H., Chen, C., et al. (2012). Cyclic GMP-AMP is an endogenous second messenger in innate immune signaling by cytosolic DNA. *Science*, http://dx.doi.org/10.1126/science.1229963.
Yang, P., An, H., Liu, X., Wen, M., Zheng, Y., Rui, Y., et al. (2010). The cytosolic nucleic acid sensor LRRFIP1 mediates the production of type I interferon via a beta-catenin-dependent pathway. *Nature Immunology*, *11*(6), 487–494. http://dx.doi.org/10.1038/ni.1876.
Yoneyama, M., Kikuchi, M., Natsukawa, T., Shinobu, N., Imaizumi, T., Miyagishi, M., et al. (2004). The RNA helicase RIG-I has an essential function in double-stranded RNA-induced innate antiviral responses. *Nature Immunology*, *5*(7), 730–737. http://dx.doi.org/10.1038/ni1087.

Yoshio, S., Kanto, T., Kuroda, S., Matsubara, T., Higashitani, K., Kakita, N., et al. (2012). Human BDCA3(+) dendritic cells are a potent producer of IFN-lambda in response to hepatitis C virus. *Hepatology,* http://dx.doi.org/10.1002/hep.26182.

Zhang, X., Brann, T. W., Zhou, M., Yang, J., Oguariri, R. M., Lidie, K. B., et al. (2011). Cutting edge: Ku70 is a novel cytosolic DNA sensor that induces type III rather than type I IFN. *The Journal of Immunology, 186*(8), 4541–4545. http://dx.doi.org/10.4049/jimmunol.1003389.

Zhang, Z., Kim, T., Bao, M., Facchinetti, V., Jung, S. Y., Ghaffari, A. A., et al. (2011). DDX1, DDX21, and DHX36 helicases form a complex with the adaptor molecule TRIF to sense dsRNA in dendritic cells. *Immunity, 34*(6), 866–878. http://dx.doi.org/10.1016/j.immuni.2011.03.027.

Zhang, Z., Yuan, B., Bao, M., Lu, N., Kim, T., & Liu, Y. J. (2011). The helicase DDX41 senses intracellular DNA mediated by the adaptor STING in dendritic cells. *Nature Immunology, 12*(10), 959–965. http://dx.doi.org/10.1038/ni.2091.

CHAPTER NINE

Transcriptional Control of Dendritic Cell Development

Kenneth M. Murphy[*,†,1]
[*]School of Medicine, Department of Pathology and Immunology, Washington University, St. Louis, Missouri, USA
[†]School of Medicine, Howard Hughes Medical Institute, Washington University, St. Louis, Missouri, USA
[1]Corresponding author: e-mail address: kmurphy@wustl.edu

Contents

Abstract

Dendritic cells (DCs) drive both adaptive and innate immunity. Recent findings support the notion that distinct subsets of classical DCs favor alternative modules of immunity, acting on innate lymphoid-like cells (ILCs) and T cells similarly to promote either ILC1/Th1/CTL- or ILC3/Th17-type responses. Coordination between DC subsets and their favored immune module might imply that the genetic programs for DC diversification preceded the emergence of recombination-activating gene-dependent adaptive

Advances in Immunology, Volume 120
ISSN 0065-2776
http://dx.doi.org/10.1016/B978-0-12-417028-5.00009-0

immunity and operate initially in coordinating ILC repertoires for appropriate responses against pathogens. Consequently, understanding the molecular basis of DC developmental and diversification is important for an underlying appreciation of immune regulation. Currently, the basis for DC development into the recognized subsets/lineages is only partially understood, based on the requirements for several transcription factors including PU.1, Bcl11a, Irf8, E2-2, Id2, Irf4, Irf8, Batf3, and other BATF family members. This chapter will briefly review recent transcriptional aspects of DC development and function and then highlight some currently unresolved questions.

1. DENDRITIC CELLS COMPRISE FUNCTIONALLY HETEROGENEOUS SUBSETS

1.1. Initial classification of murine dendritic cells

Dendritic cells (DCs) were initially identified by their potent activation of naïve T cells (Banchereau & Steinman, 1998; Nussenzweig, Steinman, Gutchinov, & Cohn, 1980; Steinman & Witmer, 1978), and several cell types have been described with phenotypic and functional attributes overlapping with Steinman's classical DCs (cDCs) (Hashimoto, Miller, & Merad, 2011). It has been difficult to determine the relationships between these various cells based only on cell surface markers and functional responses because of their variability among different myeloid cells on cellular activation state and location (Geissmann, Gordon, Hume, Mowat, & Randolph, 2010). But at present, four major cell types are still considered generally to fall within the category of DCs: cDCs, plasmacytoid DCs (pDCs), Langerhans cells (LCs), and monocyte-derived DCs.

cDCs are short-lived phagocytic antigen-processing cells that are dependent on FMS-related tyrosine kinase 3 ligand and are continuously replaced in the periphery from bone marrow (BM) precursors (Liu et al., 2007; Maraskovsky et al., 1997; McKenna et al., 2000; Waskow et al., 2008). cDCs are migratory, and when they encounter and capture antigens in peripheral tissues, they move through afferent lymphatics to the T-cell zones of secondary lymphoid organs and initiate adaptive responses (Villadangos & Schnorrer, 2007). Newly differentiated cDCs exist in an immature state where they exhibit high endocytic activity but low surface MHC class I and II proteins, but on encountering microbial or inflammatory stimuli, transport peptide–MHC complexes to their cell surface, and induce costimulatory molecules and chemokine receptors directing their migration to lymphoid tissues (Inaba et al., 2000; Mellman & Steinman, 2001; Pierre et al., 1997).

1.2. Heterogeneity of murine DCs

Originally considered homogeneous, studies from Steinman (Crowley, Inaba, Witmer-Pack, & Steinman, 1989) and Shortman (Ardavin & Shortman, 1992; Vremec et al., 1992) identified subsets of cDCs based on differential CD8-α expression. Later, a $CD4^+$ cDC subset was identified in lymphoid organs (Shortman & Liu, 2002; Vremec, Pooley, Hochrein, Wu, & Shortman, 2000). Cross presentation of antigen to $CD8^+$ T cells was found to be carried out more efficiently by CD8-α^+ cDCs than $CD4^+$ cDCs, which were considered to function in $CD4^+$ T-cell activation (den Haan, Lehar, & Bevan, 2000; Dudziak et al., 2007; Kamphorst, Guermonprez, Dudziak, & Nussenzweig, 2010; Pooley, Heath, & Shortman, 2001). cDC in peripheral nonlymphoid organs is divided into two related groups, with CD103 ($\alpha_E\beta7$ integrin) expression, and low CD11b corresponds to the lymphoid-resident CD8-α^+ cDCs, whereas high CD11b (but absent CD4) corresponds to the lymphoid-resident $CD4^+$ cDCs (Bedoui et al., 2009; Bursch et al., 2007; Crozat, Guiton, Guilliams, et al., 2010; del Rio, Rodriguez-Barbosa, Kremmer, & Forster, 2007; Edelson et al., 2010; Ginhoux et al., 2007, 2009; Heath & Carbone, 2009; Poulin et al., 2007). Additional heterogeneity within $CD11b^+$ cDCs is possible (Lewis et al., 2011; Plantinga et al., 2013) but not worked out yet.

1.3. Heterogeneity of human DCs and murine counterparts

Human counterparts or "equivalents" of murine CD8-α^+ and $CD11b^+$ cDC subsets have been identified in lymphoid and nonlymphoid organs that express XCR1, BDCA3, and CLEC9A and cross present antigens (Bachem et al., 2010; Crozat, Guiton, Contreras, et al., 2010; Crozat, Guiton, Guilliams, et al., 2010; Jongbloed et al., 2010; Lindstedt, Lundberg, & Borrebaeck, 2005; Poulin et al., 2010; Robbins et al., 2008; Segura et al., 2012). Human $CD11b^+$ equivalents express $BDCA1^+$ and resemble their murine counterpart in their transcriptional profile (Crozat, Guiton, Guilliams, et al., 2010; Robbins et al., 2008).

pDCs are distinct from cDCs in morphology and function (high interferon production, poor phagocytic, and antigen-presenting capacity) and markers (expressing B220, Siglec-H, and Bst2) (Blasius et al., 2006; Cella et al., 1999; Colonna, Trinchieri, & Liu, 2004; Grouard et al., 1997; Reizis, Colonna, Trinchieri, Barrat, & Gilliet, 2011; Reizis et al., 2011; Siegal et al., 1999; Villadangos & Schnorrer, 2007; Zhang et al., 2006) but are developmentally related to cDCs in arising from a common and Flt3L-dependent progenitor (Naik et al., 2010, 2007; Onai et al., 2007).

Cross presentation has been analyzed in human DC subsets. Both LCs and CD1a+ DCs, but not CD14+ DCs, are able to efficiently cross present antigens (Klechevsky et al., 2008). pDCs from blood reportedly cross present soluble and particulate antigens (Di Pucchio et al., 2008; Hoeffel et al., 2007). Blood BDCA3+ DCs, the proposed CD8-α^+ equivalent (Bachem et al., 2010; Crozat, Guiton, Contreras, et al., 2010; Jongbloed et al., 2010; Poulin et al., 2010), are superior in cross presentation than BDCA1+ DCs from blood. A difference between DC subsets in cross presentation may involve predetermined states of vesicular trafficking, since experimental deliver of exogenous antigens to early endosomes can minimize experimental differences between DC subsets (Cohn et al., 2013). This may indicate that one of the specific functional distinctions between different DC subsets for their *in vivo* ability to cross present antigens resides in preset differences in vesicular machinery, in addition to different receptors.

2. DC DEVELOPMENT

2.1. DC subsets develop from hematopoietic progenitors in BM

DCs arise *in vivo* predominantly from the common myeloid progenitor (CMP) (Onai et al., 2007; Schlenner et al., 2010; Traver et al., 2000). A CMP-derived macrophage–DC precursor (MDP) retaining DC potential (Auffray et al., 2009; Fogg et al., 2006) may generate pDCs, cDCs, and macrophages but not neutrophils or other myeloid lineages. A common dendritic cell progenitor (CDP) with exclusive potential for pDC and cDCs expresses the macrophage colony-stimulating factor receptor (M-CSFR) and Flt3, like the MDP, but expressed stem cell factor receptor (c-Kit) at levels lower than the MDP (Naik et al., 2007; Onai et al., 2007).

The CDP may represent the immediate precursor of the pre-cDC, which is an immature precursor to cDC lineages that exits the BM and seeds lymphoid and nonlymphoid tissues (Liu et al., 2009; Naik et al., 2006). pDCs mature in the BM and travel to secondary lymphoid organs. A residual capacity for pDC potential in the currently defined pre-cDC populations, being reduced about twofold relative to whole BM (Fig. S3 in Ref. Liu et al., 2009), might indicate that the steps of commitment by CDPs and pre-cDCs need to be examined in greater detail. In addition, a population of CCR9$^-$ immature pDCs can differentiate reportedly and can generate cDC subsets *in vitro* and *in vivo* (Schlitzer et al., 2012, 2011), again suggesting early pDC development can be diverted toward the cDC lineage.

2.2. Regulation of DC development by transcription factors

As DC development and function were reviewed recently (Satpathy, Wu, Albring, & Murphy, 2012), we will briefly discuss DC transcription factors but focus on inconsistencies and uncertainties in current models (Fig. 9.1). Ikaros (Allman et al., 2006; Wu, Nichogiannopoulou, Shortman, & Georgopoulos, 1997), PU.1 (Anderson et al., 2000; Carotta et al., 2010; Guerriero, Langmuir, Spain, & Scott, 2000), and Gfi1 (Rathinam et al.,

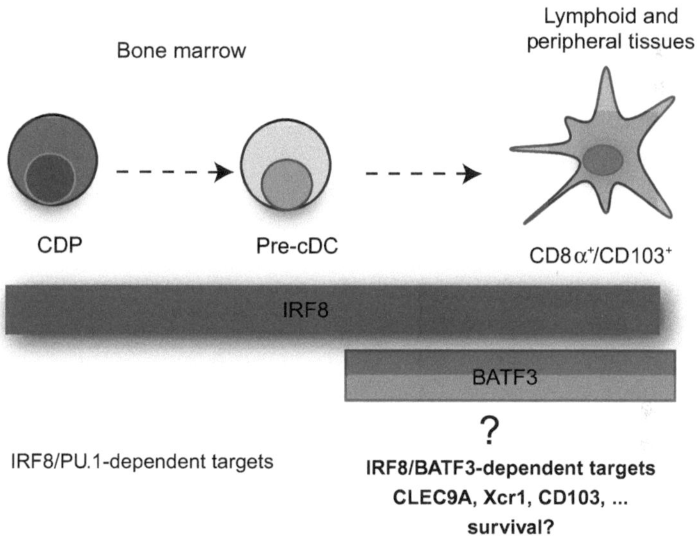

Figure 9.1 Role of Batf3 in CD8-α^+ cDC development. The requirement for Batf3 in the development of CD8-α^+ and CD103 peripheral tissue-resident cDCs is clear, but the molecular basis for this is not. Batf3 can act cooperatively with IRF4 and IRF8 proteins in transcription of genes in T cells, B cells, and DCs, but the basis for the differential actions of IRF4 and IRF8 with BATF factors is still under investigation. Further, although Batf3 and IRF8 could potentially cooperatively regulate a number of the target genes that together cluster to define the identity of the CD8-α^+, such as XCR1, DEC205, and CLEC9A, it also seems that the survival of CD8-α^+ cDCs may be influenced by Batf3. It is not clear that all of IRF8's actions in its role in CD8-α^+ cDC development are all mediated through interactions with Batf3. More likely, IRF8 acts to control both PU.1-dependent and Batf3-dependent target genes. Since Batf3 itself is expressed rather late in the development, first appearing at the pre-cDC stage, this stratification of PU.1 and Batf3 dependence would seem to be a sequential process. (See color plate.)

2005) are all required for all DC lineages, perhaps through control of Flt3 expression. Likewise, Bcl11a and the core-binding factor subunit beta, which is required for the action of the RUNX factors, are required for development of all DC lineages, as well as other hematopoietic branches (unpublished). RelB was the first transcription factor found that regulated the development of a specific DC subset (Burkly et al., 1995; Wu et al., 1998). RelB becomes expressed at the pre-cDC stage and is preferentially maintained in the $CD11b^+$ DC subset. Loss of RelB causes a marked decrease in $CD11b^+$ DC numbers. Similarly, Irf4 is preferentially expressed in $CD11b^+$ DCs (Suzuki et al., 2004). Irf4 can interact with PU.1, and Ets family factor, and can either activate or repress gene expression (Brass, Kehrli, Eisenbeis, Storb, & Singh, 1996; Eisenbeis, Singh, & Storb, 1995). As we will see, our understanding of Irf4 in regulating DC development and function is currently in a state of change. Irf4 was first thought to be required for $CD4^+$ $CD11b^+$ DC development (Tamura et al., 2005), but recent findings indicate that it is the migratory function rather than overall development that is Irf4 dependent (Bajana, Roach, Turner, Paul, & Kovats, 2012).

Irf8, by contrast with Irf4, is required for CD8-α^+ cDCs and pDCs (Schiavoni et al., 2002; Tamura et al., 2005). However, loss of Irf8 also impairs $CD11b^+$ cDC development in the setting of competitive chimerism with wild-type progenitors and reduces the numbers of CDPs (Becker et al., 2012). But in a noncompetitive setting, $CD11b^+$ cDCs do develop in the absence of Irf8, although their function has not been examined in depth (Aliberti et al., 2003). *Irf8*-deficient DC progenitors show reduced expression of several important transcription factors, *Id2*, *Bach2*, *Klf4*, and *Bcl* (Becker et al., 2012). Id2 is induced *in vitro* by granulocyte-macrophage colony-stimulating-factor (GM-CSF) and is required *in vivo* for development of CD8-α^+ DCs and for LCs, but not other DC subsets (Hacker et al., 2003). *Bcl6* is required for $CD11b^+$ and CD8-α^+ DC development (Ohtsuka et al., 2011), and Klf4 and Bach2 are expressed in DC progenitors and mature DCs, but their role in development has not been reported (Heng & Painter, 2008). Thus, Irf8 controls several factors regulating, or potentially regulating, DC development.

2.3. pDC development, transcription factors and specialized functions

E2-2 is a class I basic helix–loop–helix (bHLH) transcription factor that is required for development of pDCs in mice and humans (Cisse et al., 2008). E2-2 and the related bHLH factors E12, E47, and HEB form homodimers or heterodimers that bind a conserved E-box DNA motif (Kee, 2009). E2-2 controls the transcription include *Spi-B*, *Irf8*, and *Bcl11a*, as well as genes acting in pDC function such as *Tlr7*, *Tlr9*, and *Bdca2* (Cisse et al., 2008; Ghosh, Cisse, Bunin, Lewis, & Reizis, 2010). Both *Bcl11a* and *Spi-B* are now known to function in pDC development (Ghosh et al., 2010; Nagasawa, Schmidlin, Hazekamp, Schotte, & Blom, 2008).

Inhibitor of differentiation (Id) HLH family proteins, including Id2, can associate with E proteins, but because they lack a DNA binding domain, the heterodimer does not bind DNA (Hacker et al., 2003; Jackson et al., 2011; Kusunoki et al., 2003; Laiosa, Stadtfeld, & Graf, 2006; Spits, Couwenberg, Bakker, Weijer, & Uittenbogaart, 2000). Id2 overexpression inhibits *in vitro* pDC development (Spits et al., 2000), and $Id2^{-/-}$ mice have increased pDC numbers (Hacker et al., 2003). Conditional deletion of *E2-2* in mature pDCs led to increased expression of Id2 and other genes not associated with pDC identity (Ghosh et al., 2010). *Id2* expression in pre-cDCs could prevent E2-2 activity and stabilize cDC commitment.

The deletion of E2-2 by CD11c-Cre reduced T-cell responses to viral infections due to reduced interferon production (Cervantes-Barragan et al., 2012). The ablation of pDCs caused increased viral burden and reduced T-cell priming (Reizis et al., 2011). MHC class II-deficient pDCs however were able to support normal T-cell responses. pDC-derived type I interferon supported $CD8^+$ T-cell survival, suggesting that pDC supports immune responses by cytokine production rather than by direct antigen presentation. A system allowing pDC ablation through expression of diphtheria toxin receptor (DTR) under the control of the human *Bdca2* gene promoter (Swiecki, Gilfillan, Vermi, Wang, & Colonna, 2010) confirmed this role in type I interferon production during viral infection. In contrast to these studies, a third system was used to argue for a direct role of pDC in cross presentation of viral antigens (Takagi et al., 2011). In this study, DTR was expressed under control of the Siglec-H locus and DT treatment used to deplete pDCs. The more broad actions attributed to pDCs by this study may be due to inadvertent reduction in other lineages, since Siglec-H has been now recognized to be expressed on progenitors of cDCs (Satpathy, KC, et al., 2012). However, this issue awaits more formal resolution, since the status of cDC subsets was not evaluated (Takagi et al., 2011).

2.4. Irf8 and Batf3 in cDC development and function

Although $Irf8^{-/-}$ mice previously indicated that CD8-α^+ DCs were a source of IL-12 during infection by *Toxoplasma gondii* (Scharton-Kersten,

Contursi, Masumi, Sher, & Ozato, 1997), *Irf8*$^{-/-}$ mice also harbor additional defects in other myeloid lineages, B-cell development, and expression of IFN-γ-inducible genes that could have contributed to altered responses to *T. gondii* infection (Aliberti et al., 2003; Tsujimura, Tamura, Gongora, et al., 2003). *Batf3*$^{-/-}$ mice exhibit a more selective defect, restricted to a loss of CD8-α^{+} DCs and their CD103+ peripheral counterpart (Hildner et al., 2008). Studies with *Batf3*$^{-/-}$ mice showed that CD8-α^{+} or peripheral CD103^{+} cDCs are a crucial source of IL-12 for early defense against *T. gondii* infection (Mashayekhi et al., 2011). CD8-α^{+} cDCs express Tlr11 (Koblansky et al., 2013; Yarovinsky et al., 2005) and highly express Irf8 (Wu, Maeda, Contursi, Ozato, & Seder, 1999), which may enable these responses. A population of monocyte-derived DCs also produces IL-12 that is important for defense at sites of infection (Goldszmid et al., 2012), although their dependence on Irf8 and Batf3 is unclear at present.

Analysis of *Batf3*$^{-/-}$ mice showed that splenic CD8-α^{+} DCs were an obligate point of entry for establishing infection by *Listeria monocytogenes* in an intravenous infection model (Edelson, Bradstreet, Hildner, et al., 2011), in agreement with earlier studies (Alaniz, Sandall, Thomas, & Wilson, 2004; Neuenhahn et al., 2006). It appears that CD8-α^{+} DCs act as a Trojan horse to carrying Listeria from its point of blood clearance, the marginal zone, into lymphoid follicles, where B and T cells are killed by the pathogen (Merrick, Edelson, Bhardwaj, Swanson, & Unanue, 1997). Why CD8-α^{+} cDCs are unique among immune lineages in acting as this Trojan horse is unclear. They might be inherently more susceptible to infection compared to other myeloid cells, or alternately, only these cells migrate from the marginal zone (MZ) into lymphoid areas during early infection. This latter possibility seems unlikely, but it is also known that other cell types can become infected. It is possible that some connection between cross presentation by CD8-α^{+} cDCs and their apparently greater infectivity by Listeria exists, although even the relative inherent capacity for cross presentation by these cells is not undisputed (Dudziak et al., 2007).

Combined analysis of *Batf3*$^{-/-}$ mice and conditional deletion of the type I interferon receptor implies that CD8-α^{+} DCs require signaling by type I interferon receptors for supporting antitumor responses (Diamond et al., 2011; Fuertes et al., 2011). Other studies indicate that cross presentation by CD8-α^{+} DCs also requires maturational signals such as GM-CSF or Toll-like receptor (TLR) ligands (de Brito et al., 2011; Sathe et al., 2011; Zhan et al., 2011). Migratory Batf3-dependent CD1103^{+} DCs capture apoptotic cell-associated antigens in the lung and traffic to draining lymph nodes to present antigen to $CD8^+$ T cells (Desch et al., 2011).

Batf3$^{-/-}$ mice appear to exclude some proposed actions of CD8-α^+ DCs, such as a role in Treg development (Hildner et al., 2008; Proietto et al., 2008; Yamazaki et al., 2008) and a role for $CD103^+$ DCs in experimental autoimmune encephalomyelitis (EAE) (King, Kroenke, & Segal, 2010), since *Batf3*$^{-/-}$ mice develop EAE without these subsets (Edelson, Bradstreet, KC, et al., 2011). Also, CD8-α^+ and $CD103^+$ DCs are not required for dextran sodium sulfate (DSS)-induced colitis or contact hypersensitivity (Edelson et al., 2010), which had been controversial based on differing results from earlier studies (Bursch et al., 2007; Wang et al., 2008). While responses to West Nile virus (Hildner et al., 2008; Pinto et al., 2011), herpes simplex virus (Zelenay et al., 2012), and mouse cytomegalovirus (MCMV) (Torti, Walton, Murphy, & Oxenius, 2011) require CD8-α^+ and $CD103^+$ DCs, the inflation of immunodominant T-cell specificities in latent MCMV infection does not (Torti et al., 2011).

Human $CLEC9A^+$ $BDCA3^+$ DCs, thought to be the equivalent of the murine CD8-α^+ DCs (Bachem et al., 2010; Crozat, Guiton, Guilliams, et al., 2010; Jongbloed et al., 2010; Poulin et al., 2010; Segura et al., 2012), were recently found to depend on IRF8 and BATF3 for development (Hambleton et al., 2011; Poulin et al., 2012). Mutation in human IRF8 (K108E) is associated with defects in DC and monocyte development and severe opportunistic infections (Hambleton et al., 2011). The *in vitro* development of human CD8-α^+ DC equivalent, the $CLEC9A^+BDCA3^+$ DC, was sensitive to loss of BATF3 (Poulin et al., 2012).

2.5. Notch and lymphotoxin signaling in functional maturation of $CD11b^+$ cDCs

Recently, studies have advanced the understanding of the $CD11b^+$ subset of cDCs (Caton, Smith-Raska, & Reizis, 2007; Lewis et al., 2011). Deletion of Rbp-J, a mediator of the Notch signaling, using a CD11c-Cre deleter strain in mice led to a 50% reduction in the $CD8^-$ $CDCD11b^+$ subset of splenic DCs (Caton et al., 2007). Subsequently, the splenic $CD11b^+$ DCs were recognized to comprise two subpopulations distinguished by CX3CR1 and ESAM expression. Notch2, but not other Notch receptors, was found to be required for the $CX3CR1^{lo}$ $ESAM^{hi}$ subset (Lewis et al., 2011). Also reduced IL-17 production by intestinal $CD4^+$ T cells was reported in these mice (Lewis et al., 2011), consistent with reported role of $CD11b^+$ cDCs in priming of Th17 cells *in vitro* (Denning, Wang, Patel, Williams, &

Pulendran, 2007). A role for CD11b$^+$ cDCs in IL-23 production after TLR5 signaling (Kinnebrew et al., 2012) and in inducing innate lymphocyte cells to produce IL-22 (Ota et al., 2011; Zheng et al., 2008) suggested that DC subsets might have specialized activities in driving CD4$^+$ T cells toward distinct effector subsets. However, currently, it is not known at what level such specificity exerted by DC subsets would be enforced, which could involve differences between Irf4 and Irf8 targets, as either PU.1- or Batf3-dependent transcriptional effects, and reside at either inherently different capacity for IL-12 (p35) or IL-23 (p19) production or alternately in the expression of distinct TLR or other sensors.

Both ESAM$^+$ and ESAM$^-$ subsets of CD11b$^+$ cDCs are dependent on Flt3 signaling, but only ESAM$^+$ Notch2-dependent cDCs appear selectively dependent on signaling from the lymphotoxin (LT) β receptor. Previously, LTβR was shown to be required for homeostasis of splenic cDCs (Kabashima et al., 2005). These findings suggest that Notch2 and LTβR may act in series, perhaps with Notch2 promoting DC interactions with cells in the MZ that produce LTαβ. Notch2 deficiency did not affect tissue-resident DCs in sites other than the intestine, where the CD11b$^+$CD103$^+$ DCs were severely decreased. This finding also suggests that the CD11b$^+$CD103$^+$ cDCs are not the tissue-resident homolog of *Batf3*-dependent CD103$^+$ cDC present in other peripheral tissues, but rather are an intestinal homolog of lymphoid-resident CD11b$^+$ DCs.

3. ZBTB46 AND CDCS

3.1. Zbtb46 identifies committed cDCs

Zbtb46 (BTBD4) is a member of the broad complex, tramtrack, bric-a-brac, and zinc finger (BTB-ZF) family (Kelly & Daniel, 2006) that is expressed selectively in cDCs among immune lineages (Meredith, Liu, Darrasse-Jeze, et al., 2012; Satpathy, KC, et al., 2012). In peripheral organs, *Zbtb46* was expressed not only by both CD103$^+$CD11b$^-$ cDCs and CD103$^+$CD11b$^+$ cDCs but also in some CD103$^-$CD11b$^+$ cells that may indicate remaining heterogeneity among presumptive macrophage populations that still require deeper examination. The lack of *Zbtb46* expression by Tip-DCs and LCs suggests they may be more closely related to monocytes and macrophages rather than DC (Satpathy, KC, et al., 2012). A subset of the CD169$^+$ subcapsular sinus macrophages (SSMs) also appeared to be positive for *Zbtb46* based on green fluorescent protein (GFP) expression (Satpathy,

KC, et al., 2012), but proof that this does not involve transfer from other cells, such the described membrane transfer between SSMs and innate lymphocytes (Gray, Friend, Suzuki, Phan, & Cyster, 2012), has not been reported.

3.2. Zbtb46 reveals heterogeneity in DC progenitor populations

The analysis of *Zbtb46*-GFP mice has revealed heterogeneity within the currently defined DC progenitor populations (Satpathy, KC, et al., 2012). Pre-cDCs (Liu et al., 2007) could be separated into four populations based on Siglec-H and Zbtb46-GFP expression. An unresolved point is that pre-cDCs as defined (Liu et al., 2007) did retain some potential for pDC development, although reduced quantitatively from unfractionated BM. Zbtb46-GFP$^+$ cells with the pre-cDC fraction, including those expressing Siglec-H, were limited to development into cDCs and did not generate pDCs. Siglec-H$^+$ Zbtb46-GFP-negative pre-cDCs were able to turn on expression of *Zbtb46* (Satpathy, KC, et al., 2012). This finding is consistent with cDC development from progenitors in the pre-cDC gate with potential for both pDCs and cDCs. This observation is consistent with a recent report that a CCR9- immediate precursor to pDCs in BM retained developmental plasticity for generation of cDC-like cells (Schlitzer et al., 2011). The function of Zbtb46 in cDCs has been partially addressed (Meredith, Liu, Kamphorst, et al., 2012; Satpathy, KC, et al., 2012), but there may be more to learn. First, forcing *Zbtb46* expression by retrovirus into BM progenitors showed that it exerts a developmental bias toward sDCs at the expense of other myeloid lineages such as neutrophils in cultures where growth of both lineages is supported (Satpathy, KC, et al., 2012). However, the germ line deletion of *Zbtb46* did not lead to a perceptible distortion of neutrophil/DC ratios. Indeed, another study showed that loss of *Zbtb46* led to an increased level of class II MHC expression and indicated that this gene acts as a repressor of MHCII in immature cDCs, which repression is lifted when cDCs become activated and by degradation of Zbtb46 protein (Meredith, Liu, Kamphorst, et al., 2012). This effect was not observed in *Zbtb46*$^{gfp/gfp}$ (Satpathy, KC, et al., 2012), however, in which both alleles have been targeted and disrupt normal Zbtb46 transcription leading to loss of Zbtb46 expression. Instead, that study found only minor increases in the expression of *Csf3r* (G-CSF receptor) and *LifR* (leukemia inhibitory factor receptor). What this might do functionally has not yet been examined. Thus, it would seem that there may be additional functions to be discovered for the role of Zbtb46. Conceivably, a phenotype may require analysis of specific induced responses, a situation often encountered in genes involved in immunity.

4. ONGOING ISSUES IN DC DEVELOPMENT

4.1. The role of Batf3 in CD8α$^+$ DC development

While we know that Batf3 acts in the terminal stages of sDC development, probably only after the divergence of the Irf4- and Irf8-expressing lineages, the essential basis of its requirement in CD8-α$^+$ DC development is still obscure (Fig. 9.1). Examination of an Id2-GFP reporter line showed sequential actions of Irf8, Id2, and Batf3 in CD8-α$^+$ DC development (Jackson et al., 2011). Irf8 was required for the development for all *Id2*-expressing progenitors.

We recently reported that *Batf* and *Batf2* can compensate for the loss of *Batf3* in CD8-α$^+$ DC development (Tussiwand et al., 2012). Specifically, *Batf* and *Batf2* expression provides a compensatory "bypass" pathway in place of *Batf3* that is responsible for the reappearance of CD8-α$^+$ DCs in *Batf3*$^{-/-}$ mice that are infected with intracellular pathogens such as mycobacterium tuberculosis, or treated with IL-12, and requires the generation of IFN-γ *in vivo* (Tussiwand et al., 2012). The ability of *Batf* and *Batf2* to carry out this activity is based on the ability of all BATF leucine zipper regions to mediate interactions with Irf8, which is required for the normal function of Batf3 in CD8-α$^+$ DC development. So it is likely that Batf3 interacts directly with Irf8 in driving expression of genes required for CD8-α$^+$ DC development.

The transcription factor *Nfil3* is also required for CD8-α$^+$ DC development, and *Batf3* expression was reduced in *Nfil3*$^{-/-}$ DC progenitors (Kashiwada, Pham, Pewe, Harty, & Rothman, 2011), implying Nfil3 acts upstream of Batf. It seems likely that Batf3, along with Irf8, might directly control the transcription of many genes that together represent the defining characteristics of the CD8-α$^+$ DC, such as CD103 (and CD8a in lymphoid tissues), Xcr1, DEC205, and CLEC9A$^+$. However, our own unpublished evidence also points to an important role in promoting survival of committed Irf8-expressing progenitors of these cells. Still, mechanism for Batf3's requirement in CD8-α$^+$ DC development is unexplained.

4.2. Compensation by Batf and Batf2 for Batf3 in CD8-α$^+$ DC Development

The cytokines IL-12 and IFN-γ induced during infections with intracellular pathogens can drive the development of CD8-α$^+$ DCs in *Batf3*$^{-/-}$ mice by compensation involving *Batf* and/or *Batf2* as described in the preceding text

(Tussiwand et al., 2012; Fig. 9.2). A phenomenon of Batf3-independent development of CD8-α^+ DCs that seems likely to be another example of this same compensatory pathway was reported recently in the setting of BM transplantation (Seillet et al., 2013). When *Batf3*$^{-/-}$ BM cells are adoptively grafted into lethally irradiated recipient mice, a transient generation of CD8-α^+ DCs is observed, which gradually subsides over time. The setting of the posttransplant period may mimic the production of cytokines capable of inducing compensatory bypass of Batf3, although the study did not examine the role of Batf of Batf2 in the phenomenon

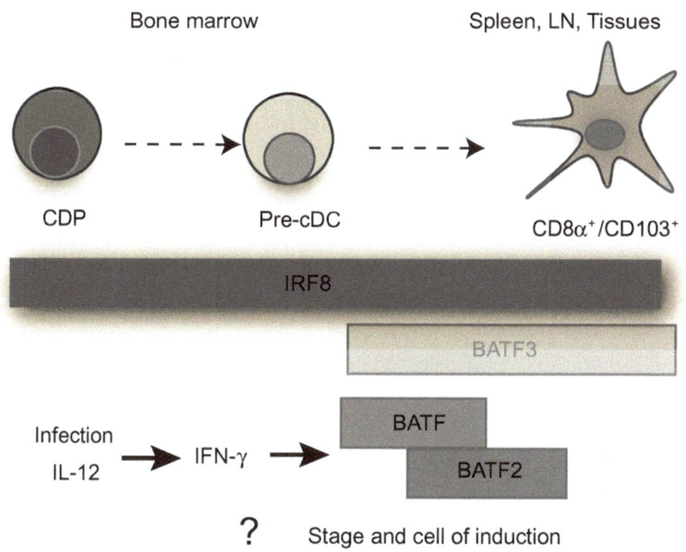

Figure 9.2 Compensation between Batf, Batf2, and Batf3 in CD8-α^+ cDC development. The surprising reappearance of CD8-α^+ and CD103 peripheral tissue-resident cDCs in Batf3$^{-/-}$ mice that were infected with intracellular pathogens or treated with IL-12 led to the recognition that Batf and Batf2 can both be induced and compensate for the loss of Batf3. The molecular basis for the unique actions of Batf3, and for the ability of Batf and Batf2 to functionally compensate, resides in the unique leucine zipper region of the BATFs. The BATF LZ is able to mediate the interaction of IRF factors with the BATF/JUN heterodimer, thus acting on distinct DNA elements called AICE, present in target genes. The issues needing resolution currently are when Batf or Batf2 are each used in compensation under physiologic conditions, as it is clear that Batf, for example, can and is used in some murine strains to drive CD8-α^+ and CD103 peripheral tissue-resident cDC development. Needed is an answer to when one or the other factor is induced, at what stage of cellular development the factor acts, and is it being induced in bone marrow progenitors or in tissue-resident pre-cDCs or immature cDCs. (See color plate.)

(Seillet et al., 2013), since it was carried out before the reporting of the BATF "bypass" pathway in DCs (Tussiwand et al., 2012). However, the study showed that defective development of CD8-α^+ DCs was restored in the transplant setting using donor BM from *Batf3*$^{-/-}$, *Nfil3*$^{-/-}$, and Id2$^{-/-}$ mice. Indirectly, this might suggest that the loss of all three factors, which each individually causes loss of CD8-α^+ DCs, can be "compensated" by Batf or Batf2. If *Nfil3* normally drives expression of *Batf3*, then the transient rescue of CD8-α^+ DCs would be as expected. Consistent with this idea is the fact that forced retroviral expression of *Batf3* into *Nfil3*$^{-/-}$ progenitors rescues development of Sirpα^- DEC205$^+$ DCs *in vitro* (Kashiwada et al., 2011). It is possible that unanticipated compensatory bypass of the Batf3 requirement may have been at work in another setting as well (Poulin et al., 2012). Knockdown of human *Batf3* prevented development of human CLEC9A$^+$ DCs *in vitro*, but when the cells were transplanted into sublethally irradiated humanized mice, Batf3 knockdown did not prevent their development (Poulin et al., 2012). Conceivably, as with BM transplantation (Seillet et al., 2013), unrecognized compensatory bypass of the *Batf3* requirement is induced by the inflammatory response to irradiation. Finally, how *Id2* exerts its selective effect on CD8-α^+ DC development is also presently unknown but is sensitive to compensation in BMT similar to *Nfil3*. Settling these issues will require an understanding of the relationships and mechanisms of all these transcription factors in CD8-α^+ DC development.

4.3. The role of GM-CSF in development of CD8-α^+ cDCs

An unresolved issue is whether GM-CSF is required for development of CD8-α^+ cDCs (Fig. 9.3). Using CD103 to identify the *Batf3*-dependent DCs in tissues is complicated by CD103 regulation by GM-CSF, IL-3, and TGF-β (Edelson, Bradstreet, KC, et al., 2011; Jackson et al., 2011; Sathe et al., 2011; Zhan et al., 2011). This issue has led to differing conclusions, as to whether GM-CSF signaling is required for development of *Batf3*-dependent DCs or, alternately, is simply required for CD103 expression on DCs (Bogunovic et al., 2009; Edelson, Bradstreet, KC, et al., 2011; Greter et al., 2012; King et al., 2010). One study found that in *GM-CSFR*$^{-/-}$ mice, CD103$^+$CD11b$^-$ cDCs did develop in all organs, identified by being CD24$^+$CD11b$^-$ and EPCAM^{lo}, as the Batf3-dependent cDCs in WT mice, but they expressed lower levels of CD103 than WT mice (Edelson, Bradstreet, KC, et al., 2011). The addition of GM-CSF to

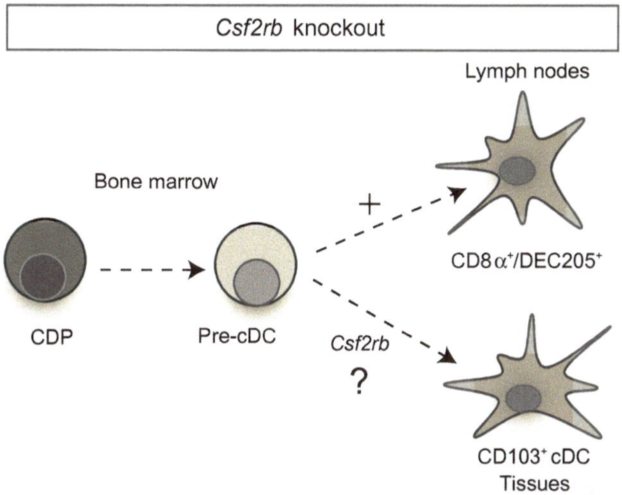

Figure 9.3 Role of *Csfr2b* in CD103$^+$ cDC development. Mice lacking the receptor for GM-CSF (*Csfr2b*) have a defect in the development of the peripheral tissue-resident CD103$^+$ cDC subset but clearly have the normal population of CD8-α^+ cDCs in lymph nodes and spleen. The defect has been represented differently by the two studies that have examined it. Either the subset is present and simply expressed less CD103 at normal homeostasis in the absence of GM-CSF, or it is missing. Why one branch of the Batf3-dependent cDC would behave differently is unclear. (See color plate.)

in vitro Flt3L-DC cultures induced CD103 expression in the CD24$^+$Sirpα^- cDCs (CD8-α^+ equivalent) *in vitro*.

In contrast, a second study reported that CD103$^+$ cDCs were absent in peripheral tissues in *GM-CSFR*$^{-/-}$ mice (Greter et al., 2012). Mixed chimera analysis indicated that DC progenitors were unaffected in *GM-CSFR*$^{-/-}$ mice but that CD103$^+$ cDCs did develop but had shorter survival compared to WT cDCs. This issue probably needs clarification based on analysis of markers of the Batf3-dependent cDC subset that are not directly GM-CSF inducible.

4.4. The divergence of Irf4-dependent and Irf8-dependent DCs

It is remarkable that there is essentially no information regarding what controls developmental divergence of cDCs into Irf8- and Irf4-expressing subsets (Fig. 9.4). Irf8 was associated first with development of pDCs and CD8-α^+ cDCs (Aliberti et al., 2003; Schiavoni et al., 2002; Tsujimura, Tamura, Gongora, et al., 2003; Tsujimura, Tamura, & Ozato, 2003) and, later, Irf4 with CD11b$^+$ cDC development (Suzuki et al., 2004; Tamura

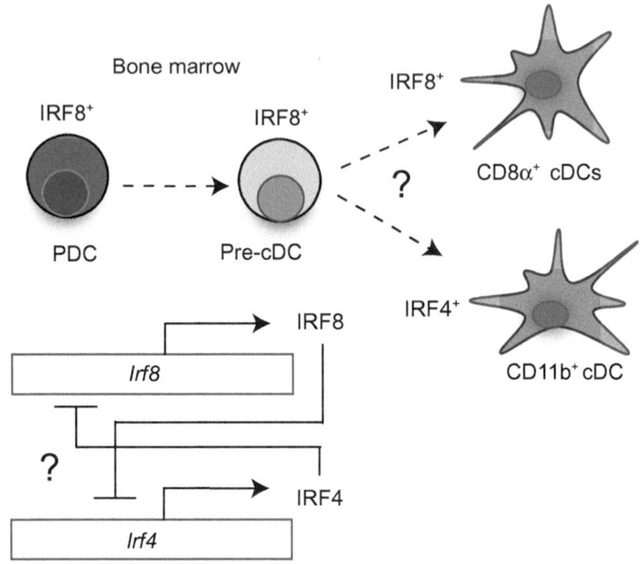

Figure 9.4 Molecular basis of cDC divergence. The major division in classical DCs is between the IRF8-expressing and the IRF4-expressing subsets. The IRF8-expressing cDCs include the CD8-α^+ cDCs of the lymph nodes and spleen and the $CD103^+$ peripheral tissue-resident cDCs. The IRF4-expressing cDCs include several subsets best characterized by the high expression of CD11b. The recognized CDP progenitor of the cDCs expresses IRF8, but it is entirely unknown what regulates the switch from high IRF8 expression in the progenitor to either maintain this expression in one cDC subset or turn it off and replace it with IRF4 in the other. (See color plate.)

et al., 2005). The notions of an exclusive and symmetric requirements gained rapid acceptance, and several reviews repeated and reinforced this notion that *Irf-4* was required for $CD8\alpha^-$ $CD11b^+$ DCs (Belz & Nutt, 2012; Merad & Manz, 2009). However, in reexamination of the original reports of *Irf4*$^{-/-}$ and *Irf4*$^{-/-}$ *Irf8*$^{-/-}$ double-deficient mice (Suzuki et al., 2004; Tamura et al., 2005), it is clear that $CD4^-$CD8-α^- cDCs were increased, although no analysis of their CD24 or Sirp-α status was shown. Recently, CD8-$\alpha^-$$CD11b^+$ cDCs were shown to develop in peripheral tissues of *Irf4*$^{-/-}$ mice, but failed to migrate to draining lymph nodes due to defective induction of CCR7 (Bajana et al., 2012). Further, $CD103^+CD11b^+$ cDCs are present in lamina propria of *Irf4*$^{-/-}$ mice that can resist *Citrobacter rodentium*, unlike mice with CD11c-Cre-driven Notch2 deficiency (Satpathy et al., 2013), indicating that local IL-23 production can occur without Irf4.

Thus, the symmetry for development of these subsets may not be so clear cut, with Irf8 deficiency causing an apparent complete loss of CD8-α^+ cDCs but Irf4 deficiency causing a mixed picture of altered surface marker expression and functional deficits. However, currently, there is no explanation at the molecular level for how the divergence in Irf4/Irf8 expression occurs. The persistence of CD1b$^+$ cDCs in *Irf4*$^{-/-}$ mice would argue against a symmetric model of Irf4–Irf8 antagonism in which only one factor can maintain expression and determine a CD11b$^+$ (Irf4) or CD11b$^-$ (Irf8) phenotype. The precise stage at which this event begins has not been addressed.

4.5. Divergence between pDCs and cDCs

In addition, there is little mechanistic understanding as to the precise circuit that regulates the divergence between pDCs and cDCs (Fig. 9.5). The potential for Id2 to heterodimerize with E2-2 and inhibit its transcriptional activity has been discussed as a possible bistable circuit in pDC and cDC development (Ghosh et al., 2010). A drawback to this notion is that Id2 deficiency leads to loss LCs and CD8-α^+ cDCs, but not to a loss of CD11b$^+$ cDCs (Hacker et al., 2003). Thus, a direct symmetric antagonism between E2-2 and Id2 would not explain the selective persistence of CD11b$^+$ cDCs in Id2 deficiency. Further, recent expression data indicates that E2-2 is expressed early in the CDP, where Id2 expression is low and Id2 expression is not increased until the later pre-cDC stage (Satpathy, Murphy, & KC, 2011). Given the current uncertainly regarding the precise progenitor stages at which specification and commitment occur (Reizis, 2012), it is probably too early to know whether Id2 directly interacts with E2-2 for titrating E2-2 activity required for pDC development. Current definitions of CDP and pre-cDP may be subdivided with higher granularity by markers such as Siglec-H and the *Zbtb46*^{gfp} allele (Satpathy, KC, et al., 2012) in a way that might allow additional factors involved in specification and commitment to be identified. However, at present, the basis for E2-2 induction or maintenance in DC progenitors versus the loss of E2-2 in developing cDCs is not fully understood.

4.6. Roles of DCs in innate versus adaptive immunity

DCs were discovered on the basis of their potency activation of T cells and recognized as a critical link in driving the adaptive immune response. And although DCs can influence innate immune responses, for example, by production of cytokines, it is only recently that experimental evidence has

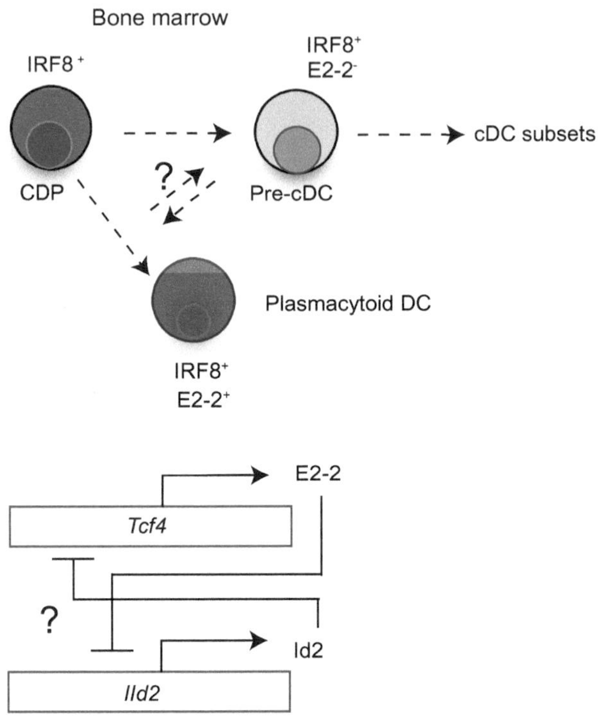

Figure 9.5 Divergence of pDCs and cDCs. The separation of the pDC and cDC lineages is accompanied by acquisition of high levels of expression of the genes Tfc4 or Id2, respectively, but the basis of this divergence is not understood. It has been suggested that the Id2 protein could conceivably bind with and neutralize the transcriptional activity of the *Tcf4* gene product, E2-2. However, it is not clear that it is Id2 itself that carries out this function or is simply induced as a result of some other factor acting to inhibit E2-2 expression. Lack of information about the single-cell pattern of expression of these factors makes it unclear whether Id2 is expressed early enough to be responsible for the divergence of pDCs at the CDP progenitor stage. Id2 is expressed first clearly at the pre-cDC stage, when commitment to cDCs has presumably already occurred. Further, evidence for flexibility even at relatively later stages of pDC development calls into question whether we even have sufficient granularity in defining the stages of DC development for meaningful attribution of stages of commitment. (See color plate.)

supported a *necessary* role of DCs in innate defenses against pathogens. In one case, elimination of Batf3-dependent cDC subsets dramatically increased susceptibility to *T. gondii* (Mashayekhi et al., 2011). The probable mechanism at work is loss in early IL-12 production in response to infection, thus allowing early expansion of the pathogen. The Irf8-expressing Batf3-dependent CD8-α^+ cDC lineage appears to be the superior source of

IL-12 relative to IRF4-expressing cDCs, but the molecular basis for is not worked out. It is known that IRF8 is required for expression of the p40 subunit of IL-12 (Schiavoni et al., 2002), but this alone cannot completely explain better IL-12 production, since the IRF4-expression cDCs can produce (Kinnebrew et al., 2012; Satpathy et al., 2013) and so must also express the IRF8-dependent p40 gene. The basis for p40 expression by IRF4-dependent cDCs needs to be examined in greater detail. Part of the difference in cytokine production by cDC subsets might reside at the level of differential TLR expression or expression of other receptors involved in pathogen detection. Alternately, the difference may reside in the capacity of the DC subsets to express the p35 and p19 subunits of IL-12 and IL-23, respectively. Whatever the molecular basis, it seems that the Batf3-dependent cDC subset is necessary and mediates protection by activating IFN-γ production by cells of the innate immune system (Satpathy et al., submitted). In this case, the IFN-γ-producing cells include NK cells but probably also innate lymphoid-like cells (ILCs) of the ILC1 subtype (Spits & Di Santo, 2011).

A symmetric requirement has been observed for the CD11b$^+$ cDC subset in the lamina propria for the protection of mice against the attaching and effacing pathogen *C. rodentium* (Satpathy et al., submitted). Here, the Notch2-dependent subset of CD11b$^+$ cDCs has a role in protection, again by activating innate defenses through production of IL-23 and activation of the ILC3 subtype to produce the cytokine IL-22 that drives protective responses in the intestinal epithelium (Zheng et al., 2007, 2008). Thus, at least two different cDC subsets can act in a necessary manner for protection against pathogens but mediate protection first by activating innate, rather than adaptive, immunity. The two cDC subsets in these examples are also associated with driving different types of adaptive immune responses. The Batf3-dependent cDC subset, being a better IL-12 producer and cross presenter, favors T helper type 1 (T_H1) and CD8$^+$ T-cell activation, while the Notch2-dependent CD11b$^+$ cDC subset is associated with IL-23 production and T_H17 development (Lewis et al., 2011).

Thus, the two currently recognized functional subtypes of cDCs divide their functions without respect to the innate or adaptive system, but rather by which immune module they promote. CD8-α^+ cDCs promote the type 1 module, both for innate and adaptive immunity. Likewise, Notch2-dependent CD11b$^+$ cDCs promote the type 3, for ILC3 (for IL-22 production in *C. rodentium* infection) and T_H17 development (Lewis et al., 2011). It seems likely that a cDC subset will be found that selectively participates in

ILC2/T_H2 immunity (Plantinga et al., 2013), although its requirement in infection and molecular characteristics remain for future studies.

The divided function of DC subsets along distinct immune modules could suggest that DC diversification preceded adaptive immunity. Conceivably, DCs, and their subsets, could predate the emergence of recombination-activating gene (RAG) acquisition and development of the adaptive immune system in invertebrates. The diversity in DCs at this early stage of evolution might have initially functioned in providing for selective activation of appropriate ILCs, which act in different innate immune modules. This would act in defense from different types of pathogen infections. In this model, the DC would provide the intelligence in the system that appropriately selects the type of defense brought to bear against an infection. Diversified DC subsets could intelligently carry out this function by coordinating their expression of distinct pathogen sensors with their production of appropriate cytokines that would activate particular types of ILCs. Thus, the intelligence of choice would reside in the evolutionary coordination of different detection systems and responses in a few types of DC subsets. During the emergence of RAG-dependent adaptive immunity, DCs could have retained their subset-based diversification schemes while acquiring their capacity for antigen presentation, at the same time that T cells co-opted the preexisting transcriptional circuitry to copy the patterns of cytokine production from the ILC lineages. Since adaptive immune systems other than RAG-dependent T- and B-cell systems of the vertebrates have now been recognized (Bajoghli et al., 2011; Boehm et al., 2012; Cooper & Alder, 2006), it may be possible to test this idea by examining hagfish for the presence of diversified DC.

ACKNOWLEDGMENTS

This work was supported by the Howard Hughes Medical Institute and a grant from the Alvin J. Siteman Cancer Center, which is supported in part by National Cancer Institute Cancer Center Support Grant #P30 CA91842. The author has no conflicting financial interests.

REFERENCES

Alaniz, R. C., Sandall, S., Thomas, E. K., & Wilson, C. B. (2004). Increased dendritic cell numbers impair protective immunity to intracellular bacteria despite augmenting antigen-specific CD8+ T lymphocyte responses. *The Journal of Immunology*, *172*, 3725–3735.

Aliberti, J., Schulz, O., Pennington, D. J., Tsujimura, H., Reis E Sousa, C., Ozato, K., et al. (2003). Essential role for ICSBP in the in vivo development of murine CD8alpha+ dendritic cells. *Blood*, *101*, 305–310.

Allman, D., Dalod, M., Asselin-Paturel, C., Delale, T., Robbins, S. H., Trinchieri, G., et al. (2006). Ikaros is required for plasmacytoid dendritic cell differentiation. *Blood*, *108*, 4025–4034.

Anderson, K. L., Perkin, H., Surh, C. D., Venturini, S., Maki, R. A., & Torbett, B. E. (2000). Transcription factor PU.1 is necessary for development of thymic and myeloid progenitor-derived dendritic cells. *The Journal of Immunology*, *164*, 1855–1861.

Ardavin, C., & Shortman, K. (1992). Cell surface marker analysis of mouse thymic dendritic cells. *European Journal of Immunology*, *22*, 859–862.

Auffray, C., Fogg, D. K., Narni-Mancinelli, E., Senechal, B., Trouillet, C., Saederup, N., et al. (2009). CX3CR1+ CD115+ CD135+ common macrophage/DC precursors and the role of CX3CR1 in their response to inflammation. *The Journal of Experimental Medicine*, *206*, 595–606.

Bachem, A., Guttler, S., Hartung, E., Ebstein, F., Schaefer, M., Tannert, A., et al. (2010). Superior antigen cross-presentation and XCR1 expression define human CD11c+ CD141+ cells as homologues of mouse CD8+ dendritic cells. *The Journal of Experimental Medicine*, *207*, 1273–1281.

Bajana, S., Roach, K., Turner, S., Paul, J., & Kovats, S. (2012). IRF4 promotes cutaneous dendritic cell migration to lymph nodes during homeostasis and inflammation. *The Journal of Immunology*, *189*, 3368–3377.

Bajoghli, B., Guo, P., Aghaallaei, N., Hirano, M., Strohmeier, C., McCurley, N., et al. (2011). A thymus candidate in lampreys. *Nature*, *470*, 90–94.

Banchereau, J., & Steinman, R. M. (1998). Dendritic cells and the control of immunity. *Nature*, *392*, 245–252.

Becker, A. M., Michael, D. G., Satpathy, A. T., Sciammas, R., Singh, H., & Bhattacharya, D. (2012). IRF-8 extinguishes neutrophil production and promotes dendritic cell lineage commitment in both myeloid and lymphoid mouse progenitors. *Blood*, *119*, 2003–2012.

Bedoui, S., Whitney, P. G., Waithman, J., Eidsmo, L., Wakim, L., Caminschi, I., et al. (2009). Cross-presentation of viral and self antigens by skin-derived CD103(+) dendritic cells. *Nature Immunology*, *10*, 488–495.

Belz, G. T., & Nutt, S. L. (2012). Transcriptional programming of the dendritic cell network. *Nature Reviews Immunology*, *12*, 101–113.

Blasius, A. L., Giurisato, E., Cella, M., Schreiber, R. D., Shaw, A. S., & Colonna, M. (2006). Bone marrow stromal cell antigen 2 is a specific marker of type I IFN-producing cells in the naive mouse, but a promiscuous cell surface antigen following IFN stimulation. *The Journal of Immunology*, *177*, 3260–3265.

Boehm, T., McCurley, N., Sutoh, Y., Schorpp, M., Kasahara, M., & Cooper, M. D. (2012). VLR-based adaptive immunity. *Annual Review of Immunology*, *30*, 203–220.

Bogunovic, M., Ginhoux, F., Helft, J., Shang, L., Hashimoto, D., Greter, M., et al. (2009). Origin of the lamina propria dendritic cell network. *Immunity*, *31*, 513–525.

Brass, A. L., Kehrli, E., Eisenbeis, C. F., Storb, U., & Singh, H. (1996). Pip, a lymphoid-restricted IRF, contains a regulatory domain that is important for autoinhibition and ternary complex formation with the Ets factor PU.1. *Genes & Development*, *10*, 2335–2347.

Burkly, L., Hession, C., Ogata, L., Reilly, C., Marconi, L. A., Olson, D., et al. (1995). Expression of relB is required for the development of thymic medulla and dendritic cells. *Nature*, *373*, 531–536.

Bursch, L. S., Wang, L., Igyarto, B., Kissenpfennig, A., Malissen, B., Kaplan, D. H., et al. (2007). Identification of a novel population of Langerin+ dendritic cells. *The Journal of Experimental Medicine*, *204*, 3147–3156.

Carotta, S., Dakic, A., D'Amico, A., Pang, S. H., Greig, K. T., Nutt, S. L., et al. (2010). The transcription factor PU.1 controls dendritic cell development and Flt3 cytokine receptor expression in a dose-dependent manner. *Immunity*, *32*, 628–641.

Caton, M. L., Smith-Raska, M. R., & Reizis, B. (2007). Notch-RBP-J signaling controls the homeostasis of CD8− dendritic cells in the spleen. *The Journal of Experimental Medicine, 204*, 1653–1664.

Cella, M., Jarrossay, D., Facchetti, F., Alebardi, O., Nakajima, H., Lanzavecchia, A., et al. (1999). Plasmacytoid monocytes migrate to inflamed lymph nodes and produce large amounts of type I interferon [see comments]. *Nature Medicine, 5*, 919–923.

Cervantes-Barragan, L., Lewis, K. L., Firner, S., Thiel, V., Hugues, S., Reith, W., et al. (2012). Plasmacytoid dendritic cells control T-cell response to chronic viral infection. *Proceedings of the National Academy of Sciences of the United States of America, 109*, 3012–3017.

Cisse, B., Caton, M. L., Lehner, M., Maeda, T., Scheu, S., Locksley, R., et al. (2008). Transcription factor E2-2 is an essential and specific regulator of plasmacytoid dendritic cell development. *Cell, 135*, 37–48.

Cohn, L., Chatterjee, B., Esselborn, F., Smed-Sorensen, A., Nakamura, N., Chalouni, C., et al. (2013). Antigen delivery to early endosomes eliminates the superiority of human blood BDCA3+ dendritic cells at cross presentation. *Journal of Experimental Medicine, 210*, 1049–1063.

Colonna, M., Trinchieri, G., & Liu, Y. J. (2004). Plasmacytoid dendritic cells in immunity. *Nature Immunology, 5*, 1219–1226.

Cooper, M. D., & Alder, M. N. (2006). The evolution of adaptive immune systems. *Cell, 124*, 815–822.

Crowley, M., Inaba, K., Witmer-Pack, M., & Steinman, R. M. (1989). The cell surface of mouse dendritic cells: FACS analyses of dendritic cells from different tissues including thymus. *Cellular Immunology, 118*, 108–125.

Crozat, K., Guiton, R., Contreras, V., Feuillet, V., Dutertre, C. A., Ventre, E., et al. (2010). The XC chemokine receptor 1 is a conserved selective marker of mammalian cells homologous to mouse CD8alpha+ dendritic cells. *Journal of Experimental Medicine, 207*, 1283–1292.

Crozat, K., Guiton, R., Guilliams, M., Henri, S., Baranek, T., Schwartz-Cornil, I., et al. (2010). Comparative genomics as a tool to reveal functional equivalences between human and mouse dendritic cell subsets. *Immunological Reviews, 234*, 177–198.

de Brito, C., Tomkowiak, M., Ghittoni, R., Caux, C., Leverrier, Y., & Marvel, J. (2011). CpG promotes cross-presentation of dead cell-associated antigens by pre-CD8alpha+ dendritic dells. *The Journal of Immunology, 186*, 1503–1511.

del Rio, M. L., Rodriguez-Barbosa, J. I., Kremmer, E., & Forster, R. (2007). CD103(−) and CD103(+) bronchial lymph node dendritic cells are specialized in presenting and cross-presenting innocuous antigen to CD4(+) and CD8(+) T cells. *The Journal of Immunology, 178*, 6861–6866.

den Haan, J. M., Lehar, S. M., & Bevan, M. J. (2000). CD8(+) but not CD8(−) dendritic cells cross-prime cytotoxic T cells in vivo. *The Journal of Experimental Medicine, 192*, 1685–1696.

Denning, T. L., Wang, Y. C., Patel, S. R., Williams, I. R., & Pulendran, B. (2007). Lamina propria macrophages and dendritic cells differentially induce regulatory and interleukin 17-producing T cell responses. *Nature Immunology, 8*, 1086–1094.

Desch, A. N., Randolph, G. J., Murphy, K., Gautier, E. L., Kedl, R. M., Lahoud, M. H., et al. (2011). CD103+ pulmonary dendritic cells preferentially acquire and present apoptotic cell-associated antigen. *The Journal of Experimental Medicine, 208*, 1789–1797.

Di Pucchio, T., Chatterjee, B., Smed-Sorensen, A., Clayton, S., Palazzo, A., Montes, M., et al. (2008). Direct proteasome-independent cross-presentation of viral antigen by plasmacytoid dendritic cells on major histocompatibility complex class I. *Nature Immunology, 9*, 551–557.

Diamond, M. S., Kinder, M., Matsushita, H., Mashayekhi, M., Dunn, G. P., Archambault, J. M., et al. (2011). Type I interferon is selectively required by dendritic cells for immune rejection of tumors. *The Journal of Experimental Medicine, 208*, 1989–2003.

Dudziak, D., Kamphorst, A. O., Heidkamp, G. F., Buchholz, V. R., Trumpfheller, C., Yamazaki, S., et al. (2007). Differential antigen processing by dendritic cell subsets in vivo. *Science, 315*, 107–111.

Edelson, B. T., Bradstreet, T. R., Hildner, K., Carrero, J. A., Frederick, K. E., KC, W., et al. (2011). CD8a+ dendritic cells are an obligate cellular entry point for productive infection by *Listeria monocytogenes*. *Immunity, 35*, 236–248.

Edelson, B. T., Bradstreet, T. R., KC, W., Hildner, K., Herzog, J. W., Sim, J., et al. (2011). Batf3-dependent CD11b(low/−) peripheral dendritic cells are GM-CSF-independent and are not required for Th cell priming after subcutaneous immunization. *PLoS One, 6*, e25660.

Edelson, B. T., KC, W., Juang, R., Kohyama, M., Benoit, L. A., Klekotka, P. A., et al. (2010). Peripheral CD103+ dendritic cells form a unified subset developmentally related to CD8alpha+ conventional dendritic cells. *Journal of Experimental Medicine, 207*, 823–836.

Eisenbeis, C. F., Singh, H., & Storb, U. (1995). Pip, a novel IRF family member, is a lymphoid-specific, PU.1-dependent transcriptional activator. *Genes & Development, 9*, 1377–1387.

Fogg, D. K., Sibon, C., Miled, C., Jung, S., Aucouturier, P., Littman, D. R., et al. (2006). A clonogenic bone marrow progenitor specific for macrophages and dendritic cells. *Science, 311*, 83–87.

Fuertes, M. B., Kacha, A. K., Kline, J., Woo, S. R., Kranz, D. M., Murphy, K. M., et al. (2011). Host type I IFN signals are required for antitumor CD8+ T cell responses through CD8{alpha}+ dendritic cells. *The Journal of Experimental Medicine, 208*, 2005–2016.

Geissmann, F., Gordon, S., Hume, D. A., Mowat, A. M., & Randolph, G. J. (2010). Unravelling mononuclear phagocyte heterogeneity. *Nature Reviews Immunology, 10*, 453–460.

Ghosh, H. S., Cisse, B., Bunin, A., Lewis, K. L., & Reizis, B. (2010). Continuous expression of the transcription factor e2-2 maintains the cell fate of mature plasmacytoid dendritic cells. *Immunity, 33*, 905–916.

Ginhoux, F., Collin, M. P., Bogunovic, M., Abel, M., Leboeuf, M., Helft, J., et al. (2007). Blood-derived dermal langerin+ dendritic cells survey the skin in the steady state. *The Journal of Experimental Medicine, 204*, 3133–3146.

Ginhoux, F., Liu, K., Helft, J., Bogunovic, M., Greter, M., Hashimoto, D., et al. (2009). The origin and development of nonlymphoid tissue CD103+ DCs. *The Journal of Experimental Medicine, 206*, 3115–3130.

Goldszmid, R. S., Caspar, P., Rivollier, A., White, S., Dzutsev, A., Hieny, S., et al. (2012). NK cell-derived interferon-gamma orchestrates cellular dynamics and the differentiation of monocytes into dendritic cells at the site of infection. *Immunity, 36*, 1047–1059.

Gray, E. E., Friend, S., Suzuki, K., Phan, T. G., & Cyster, J. G. (2012). Subcapsular sinus macrophage fragmentation and CD169(+) Bleb acquisition by closely associated IL-17-committed innate-like lymphocytes. *PLoS One*, 7, e38258.

Greter, M., Helft, J., Chow, A., Hashimoto, D., Mortha, A., Agudo-Cantero, J., et al. (2012). GM-CSF controls nonlymphoid tissue dendritic cell homeostasis but is dispensable for the differentiation of inflammatory dendritic cells. *Immunity, 36*, 1031–1046.

Grouard, G., Rissoan, M. C., Filgueira, L., Durand, I., Banchereau, J., & Liu, Y. J. (1997). The enigmatic plasmacytoid T cells develop into dendritic cells with interleukin (IL)-3 and CD40-ligand. *The Journal of Experimental Medicine, 185*, 1101–1111.

Guerriero, A., Langmuir, P. B., Spain, L. M., & Scott, E. W. (2000). PU.1 is required for myeloid-derived but not lymphoid-derived dendritic cells. *Blood*, *95*, 879–885.

Hacker, C., Kirsch, R. D., Ju, X. S., Hieronymus, T., Gust, T. C., Kuhl, C., et al. (2003). Transcriptional profiling identifies Id2 function in dendritic cell development. *Nature Immunology*, *4*, 380–386.

Hambleton, S., Salem, S., Bustamante, J., Bigley, V., Boisson-Dupuis, S., Azevedo, J., et al. (2011). IRF8 mutations and human dendritic-cell immunodeficiency. *The New England Journal of Medicine*, *365*, 127–138.

Hashimoto, D., Miller, J., & Merad, M. (2011). Dendritic cell and macrophage heterogeneity in vivo. *Immunity*, *35*, 323–335.

Heath, W. R., & Carbone, F. R. (2009). Dendritic cell subsets in primary and secondary T cell responses at body surfaces. *Nature Immunology*, *10*, 1237–1244.

Heng, T. S., & Painter, M. W. (2008). The Immunological Genome Project: Networks of gene expression in immune cells. *Nature Immunology*, *9*, 1091–1094.

Hildner, K., Edelson, B. T., Purtha, W. E., Diamond, M., Matsushita, H., Kohyama, M., et al. (2008). Batf3 deficiency reveals a critical role for CD8alpha+ dendritic cells in cytotoxic T cell immunity. *Science*, *322*, 1097–1100.

Hoeffel, G., Ripoche, A. C., Matheoud, D., Nascimbeni, M., Escriou, N., Lebon, P., et al. (2007). Antigen cross-presentation by human plasmacytoid dendritic cells. *Immunity*, *27*, 481–492.

Inaba, K., Turley, S., Iyoda, T., Yamaide, F., Shimoyama, S., Sousa, C. E., et al. (2000). The formation of immunogenic major histocompatibility complex class II-peptide ligands in lysosomal compartments of dendritic cells is regulated by inflammatory stimuli. *The Journal of Experimental Medicine*, *191*, 927–936.

Jackson, J. T., Hu, Y., Liu, R., Masson, F., D'Amico, A., Carotta, S., et al. (2011). Id2 expression delineates differential checkpoints in the genetic program of CD8alpha(+) and CD103(+) dendritic cell lineages. *The EMBO Journal*, *30*, 2690–2704.

Jongbloed, S. L., Kassianos, A. J., McDonald, K. J., Clark, G. J., Ju, X. S., Angel, C. E., et al. (2010). Human CD141(+) (BDCA-3)(+) dendritic cells (DCs) represent a unique myeloid DC subset that cross-presents necrotic cell antigens. *The Journal of Experimental Medicine*, *207*, 1247–1260.

Kabashima, K., Banks, T. A., Ansel, K. M., Lu, T. T., Ware, C. F., & Cyster, J. G. (2005). Intrinsic lymphotoxin-beta receptor requirement for homeostasis of lymphoid tissue dendritic cells. *Immunity*, *22*, 439–450.

Kamphorst, A. O., Guermonprez, P., Dudziak, D., & Nussenzweig, M. C. (2010). Route of antigen uptake differentially impacts presentation by dendritic cells and activated monocytes. *The Journal of Immunology*, *185*, 3426–3435.

Kashiwada, M., Pham, N. L., Pewe, L. L., Harty, J. T., & Rothman, P. B. (2011). NFIL3/E4BP4 is a key transcription factor for CD8{alpha}+ dendritic cell development. *Blood*, *117*, 6193–6197.

Kee, B. L. (2009). E and ID proteins branch out. *Nature Reviews Immunology*, *9*, 175–184.

Kelly, K. F., & Daniel, J. M. (2006). POZ for effect—POZ-ZF transcription factors in cancer and development. *Trends in Cell Biology*, *16*, 578–587.

King, I. L., Kroenke, M. A., & Segal, B. M. (2010). GM-CSF-dependent, CD103+ dermal dendritic cells play a critical role in Th effector cell differentiation after subcutaneous immunization. *The Journal of Experimental Medicine*, *207*, 953–961.

Kinnebrew, M. A., Buffie, C. G., Diehl, G. E., Zenewicz, L. A., Leiner, I., Hohl, T. M., et al. (2012). Interleukin 23 production by intestinal CD103(+)CD11b(+) dendritic cells in response to bacterial flagellin enhances mucosal innate immune defense. *Immunity*, *36*, 276–287.

Klechevsky, E., Morita, R., Liu, M., Cao, Y., Coquery, S., Thompson-Snipes, L., et al. (2008). Functional specializations of human epidermal Langerhans cells and CD14+ dermal dendritic cells. *Immunity*, *29*, 497–510.

Koblansky, A. A., Jankovic, D., Oh, H., Hieny, S., Sungnak, W., Mathur, R., et al. (2013). Recognition of profilin by Toll-like receptor 12 is critical for host resistance to Toxoplasma gondii. *Immunity*, *38*, 119–130.

Kusunoki, T., Sugai, M., Katakai, T., Omatsu, Y., Iyoda, T., Inaba, K., et al. (2003). TH2 dominance and defective development of a CD8+ dendritic cell subset in Id2-deficient mice. *The Journal of Allergy and Clinical Immunology*, *111*, 136–142.

Laiosa, C. V., Stadtfeld, M., & Graf, T. (2006). Determinants of lymphoid-myeloid lineage diversification. *Annual Review of Immunology*, *24*, 705–738.

Lewis, K. L., Caton, M. L., Bogunovic, M., Greter, M., Grajkowska, L. T., Ng, D., et al. (2011). Notch2 receptor signaling controls functional differentiation of dendritic cells in the spleen and intestine. *Immunity*, *35*, 780–791.

Lindstedt, M., Lundberg, K., & Borrebaeck, C. A. (2005). Gene family clustering identifies functionally associated subsets of human in vivo blood and tonsillar dendritic cells. *The Journal of Immunology*, *175*, 4839–4846.

Liu, K., Victora, G. D., Schwickert, T. A., Guermonprez, P., Meredith, M. M., Yao, K., et al. (2009). In vivo analysis of dendritic cell development and homeostasis. *Science*, *324*, 392–397.

Liu, K., Waskow, C., Liu, X., Yao, K., Hoh, J., & Nussenzweig, M. (2007). Origin of dendritic cells in peripheral lymphoid organs of mice. *Nature Immunology*, *8*, 578–583.

Maraskovsky, E., Pulendran, B., Brasel, K., Teepe, M., Roux, E. R., Shortman, K., et al. (1997). Dramatic numerical increase of functionally mature dendritic cells in FLT3 ligand-treated mice. *Advances in Experimental Medicine and Biology*, *417*, 33–40.

Mashayekhi, M., Sandau, M. M., Dunay, I. R., Frickel, E. M., Khan, A., Goldszmid, R. S., et al. (2011). CD8a+ dendritic cells are the critical source of interleukin-12 that controls acute infection by Toxoplasma gondii tachyzoites. *Immunity*, *35*, 249–259.

McKenna, H. J., Stocking, K. L., Miller, R. E., Brasel, K., De Smedt, T., Maraskovsky, E., et al. (2000). Mice lacking flt3 ligand have deficient hematopoiesis affecting hematopoietic progenitor cells, dendritic cells, and natural killer cells. *Blood*, *95*, 3489–3497.

Mellman, I., & Steinman, R. M. (2001). Dendritic cells: Specialized and regulated antigen processing machines. *Cell*, *106*, 255–258.

Merad, M., & Manz, M. G. (2009). Dendritic cell homeostasis. *Blood*, *113*, 3418–3427.

Meredith, M. M., Liu, K., Darrasse-Jeze, G., Kamphorst, A. O., Schreiber, H. A., Guermonprez, P., et al. (2012). Expression of the zinc finger transcription factor zDC (Zbtb46, Btbd4) defines the classical dendritic cell lineage. *The Journal of Experimental Medicine*, *209*, 1153–1165.

Meredith, M. M., Liu, K., Kamphorst, A. O., Idoyaga, J., Yamane, A., Guermonprez, P., et al. (2012). Zinc finger transcription factor zDC is a negative regulator required to prevent activation of classical dendritic cells in the steady state. *The Journal of Experimental Medicine*, *209*, 1583–1593.

Merrick, J. C., Edelson, B. T., Bhardwaj, V., Swanson, P. E., & Unanue, E. R. (1997). Lymphocyte apoptosis during early phase of Listeria infection in mice. *American Journal of Pathology*, *151*, 785–792.

Nagasawa, M., Schmidlin, H., Hazekamp, M. G., Schotte, R., & Blom, B. (2008). Development of human plasmacytoid dendritic cells depends on the combined action of the basic helix-loop-helix factor E2-2 and the Ets factor Spi-B. *European Journal of Immunology*, *38*, 2389–2400.

Naik, S. H., Metcalf, D., van Nieuwenhuijze, A., Wicks, I., Wu, L., O'Keeffe, M., et al. (2006). Intrasplenic steady-state dendritic cell precursors that are distinct from monocytes. *Nature Immunology*, 7, 663–671.

Naik, S. H., O'Keeffe, M., Proietto, A., Hochrein, H., Shortman, K., & Wu, L. (2010). CD8+, CD8−, and plasmacytoid dendritic cell generation in vitro using flt3 ligand. *Methods in Molecular Biology*, *595*, 167–176.

Naik, S. H., Sathe, P., Park, H. Y., Metcalf, D., Proietto, A. I., Dakic, A., et al. (2007). Development of plasmacytoid and conventional dendritic cell subtypes from single precursor cells derived in vitro and in vivo. *Nature Immunology, 8*, 1217–1226.

Neuenhahn, M., Kerksiek, K. M., Nauerth, M., Suhre, M. H., Schiemann, M., Gebhardt, F. E., et al. (2006). CD8alpha+ dendritic cells are required for efficient entry of Listeria *monocytogenes* into the spleen. *Immunity, 25*, 619–630.

Nussenzweig, M. C., Steinman, R. M., Gutchinov, B., & Cohn, Z. A. (1980). Dendritic cells are accessory cells for the development of anti-trinitrophenyl cytotoxic T lymphocytes. *The Journal of Experimental Medicine, 152*, 1070–1084.

Ohtsuka, H., Sakamoto, A., Pan, J., Inage, S., Horigome, S., Ichii, H., et al. (2011). Bcl6 is required for the development of mouse CD4+ and CD8alpha+ dendritic cells. *The Journal of Immunology, 186*, 255–263.

Onai, N., Obata-Onai, A., Schmid, M. A., Ohteki, T., Jarrossay, D., & Manz, M. G. (2007). Identification of clonogenic common Flt3(+) M-CSFR+ plasmacytoid and conventional dendritic cell progenitors in mouse bone marrow. *Nature Immunology, 8*, 1207–1216.

Ota, N., Wong, K., Valdez, P. A., Zheng, Y., Crellin, N. K., Diehl, L., et al. (2011). IL-22 bridges the lymphotoxin pathway with the maintenance of colonic lymphoid structures during infection with *Citrobacter rodentium*. *Nature Immunology, 12*, 941–948.

Pierre, P., Turley, S. J., Gatti, E., Hull, M., Meltzer, J., Mirza, A., et al. (1997). Developmental regulation of MHC class II transport in mouse dendritic cells. *Nature, 388*, 787–792.

Pinto, A. K., Daffis, S., Brien, J. D., Gainey, M. D., Yokoyama, W. M., Sheehan, K. C., et al. (2011). A temporal role of type I interferon signaling in CD8+ T cell maturation during acute West Nile virus infection. *PLoS Pathogens*, 7, e1002407.

Plantinga, M., Guilliams, M., Vanheerswynghels, M., Deswarte, K., Branco-Madeira, F., Toussaint, W., et al. (2013). Conventional and monocyte-derived CD11b(+) dendritic cells initiate and maintain T helper 2 cell-mediated immunity to house dust mite allergen. *Immunity, 38*, 322–335.

Pooley, J. L., Heath, W. R., & Shortman, K. (2001). Cutting edge: Intravenous soluble antigen is presented to CD4 T cells by CD8− dendritic cells, but cross-presented to CD8 T cells by CD8+ dendritic cells. *The Journal of Immunology, 166*, 5327–5330.

Poulin, L. F., Henri, S., de Bovis, B., Devilard, E., Kissenpfennig, A., & Malissen, B. (2007). The dermis contains langerin+ dendritic cells that develop and function independently of epidermal Langerhans cells. *The Journal of Experimental Medicine, 204*, 3119–3131.

Poulin, L. F., Reyal, Y., Uronen-Hansson, H., Schraml, B., Sancho, D., Murphy, K. M., et al. (2012). DNGR-1 is a specific and universal marker of mouse and human Batf3-dependent dendritic cells in lymphoid and non-lymphoid tissues. *Blood, 119*, 6052–6062.

Poulin, L. F., Salio, M., Griessinger, E., Anjos-Afonso, F., Craciun, L., Chen, J. L., et al. (2010). Characterization of human DNGR-1+ BDCA3+ leukocytes as putative equivalents of mouse CD8alpha+ dendritic cells. *Journal of Experimental Medicine, 207*, 1261–1271.

Proietto, A. I., van Dommelen, S., Zhou, P., Rizzitelli, A., D'Amico, A., Steptoe, R. J., et al. (2008). Dendritic cells in the thymus contribute to T-regulatory cell induction. *Proceedings of the National Academy of Sciences of the United States of America, 105*, 19869–19874.

Rathinam, C., Geffers, R., Yucel, R., Buer, J., Welte, K., Moroy, T., et al. (2005). The transcriptional repressor Gfi1 controls STAT3-dependent dendritic cell development and function. *Immunity, 22*, 717–728.

Reizis, B. (2012). Classical dendritic cells as a unique immune cell lineage. *The Journal of Experimental Medicine, 209*, 1053–1056.

Reizis, B., Colonna, M., Trinchieri, G., Barrat, F., & Gilliet, M. (2011). Plasmacytoid dendritic cells: One-trick ponies or workhorses of the immune system? *Nature Reviews Immunology, 11*, 558–565.

Robbins, S. H., Walzer, T., Dembele, D., Thibault, C., Defays, A., Bessou, G., et al. (2008). Novel insights into the relationships between dendritic cell subsets in human and mouse revealed by genome-wide expression profiling. *Genome Biology, 9*, R17.

Sathe, P., Pooley, J., Vremec, D., Mintern, J., Jin, J. O., Wu, L., et al. (2011). The acquisition of antigen cross-presentation function by newly formed dendritic cells. *The Journal of Immunology, 186*, 5184–5192.

Satpathy, A. T., KC, W., Albring, J. C., Edelson, B. T., Kretzer, N. M., Bhattacharya, D., et al. (2012). Zbtb46 expression distinguishes classical dendritic cells and their committed progenitors from other immune lineages. *Journal of Experimental Medicine, 209*, 1135–1152.

Satpathy, A. T., Murphy, K. M., & KC, W. (2011). Transcription factor networks in dendritic cell development. *Seminars in Immunology, 23*, 388–397.

Satpathy, A. T., Wu, X., Albring, J. C., & Murphy, K. M. (2012). Re(de)fining the dendritic cell lineage. *Nature Immunology, 13*, 1145–1154.

Satpathy, A. T., Briseño, C. G., Lee, J. S., Ng, D., Manieri, N. A., Kc, W., et al. (2013). Notch2-dependent classical dendritic cells orchestrate intestinal immunity to attaching-and-effacing bacterial pathogens. *Nature Immunology, 14*, 937–948.

Scharton-Kersten, T., Contursi, C., Masumi, A., Sher, A., & Ozato, K. (1997). Interferon consensus sequence binding protein-deficient mice display impaired resistance to intracellular infection due to a primary defect in interleukin 12 p40 induction. *The Journal of Experimental Medicine, 186*, 1523–1534.

Schiavoni, G., Mattei, F., Sestili, P., Borghi, P., Venditti, M., Morse, H. C., III., et al. (2002). ICSBP is essential for the development of mouse type I interferon-producing cells and for the generation and activation of CD8alpha(+) dendritic cells. *The Journal of Experimental Medicine, 196*, 1415–1425.

Schlenner, S. M., Madan, V., Busch, K., Tietz, A., Laufle, C., Costa, C., et al. (2010). Fate mapping reveals separate origins of T cells and myeloid lineages in the thymus. *Immunity, 32*, 426–436.

Schlitzer, A., Heiseke, A. F., Einwachter, H., Reindl, W., Schiemann, M., Manta, C. P., et al. (2012). Tissue-specific differentiation of a circulating CCR9 – pDC-like common dendritic cell precursor. *Blood, 119*, 6063–6071.

Schlitzer, A., Loschko, J., Mair, K., Vogelmann, R., Henkel, L., Einwachter, H., et al. (2011). Identification of CCR9 – murine plasmacytoid DC precursors with plasticity to differentiate into conventional DCs. *Blood, 117*, 6562–6570.

Segura, E., Valladeau-Guilemond, J., Donnadieu, M. H., Sastre-Garau, X., Soumelis, V., & Amigorena, S. (2012). Characterization of resident and migratory dendritic cells in human lymph nodes. *The Journal of Experimental Medicine, 209*, 653–660.

Seillet, C., Jackson, J. T., Markey, K. A., Hill, G. R., Macdonald, K. P., Nutt, S. L., et al. (2013). CD8alpha + DCs can be induced in the absence of transcription factors Id2, Nfil3 and Batf3. *Blood, 121*, 1574–1583.

Shortman, K., & Liu, Y. J. (2002). Mouse and human dendritic cell subtypes. *Nature Reviews Immunology, 2*, 151–161.

Siegal, F. P., Kadowaki, N., Shodell, M., Fitzgerald-Bocarsly, P. A., Shah, K., Ho, S., et al. (1999). The nature of the principal type 1 interferon-producing cells in human blood. *Science, 284*, 1835–1837.

Spits, H., Couwenberg, F., Bakker, A. Q., Weijer, K., & Uittenbogaart, C. H. (2000). Id2 and Id3 inhibit development of CD34(+) stem cells into predendritic cell (pre-DC)2 but not into pre-DC1. Evidence for a lymphoid origin of pre-DC2. *The Journal of Experimental Medicine, 192*, 1775–1784.

Spits, H., & Di Santo, J. P. (2011). The expanding family of innate lymphoid cells: Regulators and effectors of immunity and tissue remodeling. *Nature Immunology*, *12*, 21–27.
Steinman, R. M., & Witmer, M. D. (1978). Lymphoid dendritic cells are potent stimulators of the primary mixed leukocyte reaction in mice. *Proceedings of the National Academy of Sciences of the United States of America*, *75*, 5132–5136.
Suzuki, S., Honma, K., Matsuyama, T., Suzuki, K., Toriyama, K., Akitoyo, I., et al. (2004). Critical roles of interferon regulatory factor 4 in CD11bhighCD8alpha− dendritic cell development. *Proceedings of the National Academy of Sciences of the United States of America*, *101*, 8981–8986.
Swiecki, M., Gilfillan, S., Vermi, W., Wang, Y., & Colonna, M. (2010). Plasmacytoid dendritic cell ablation impacts early interferon responses and antiviral NK and CD8(+) T cell accrual. *Immunity*, *33*, 955–966.
Takagi, H., Fukaya, T., Eizumi, K., Sato, Y., Sato, K., Shibazaki, A., et al. (2011). Plasmacytoid dendritic cells are crucial for the initiation of inflammation and T cell immunity in vivo. *Immunity*, *35*, 958–971.
Tamura, T., Tailor, P., Yamaoka, K., Kong, H. J., Tsujimura, H., O'Shea, J. J., et al. (2005). IFN regulatory factor-4 and -8 govern dendritic cell subset development and their functional diversity. *The Journal of Immunology*, *174*, 2573–2581.
Torti, N., Walton, S. M., Murphy, K. M., & Oxenius, A. (2011). Batf3 transcription factor-dependent DC subsets in murine CMV infection: Differential impact on T-cell priming and memory inflation. *European Journal of Immunology*, *41*, 2612–2618.
Traver, D., Akashi, K., Manz, M., Merad, M., Miyamoto, T., Engleman, E. G., et al. (2000). Development of CD8alpha-positive dendritic cells from a common myeloid progenitor. *Science*, *290*, 2152–2154.
Tsujimura, H., Tamura, T., Gongora, C., Aliberti, J., Sousa, C. R. E., Sher, A., et al. (2003). ICSBP/IRF-8 retrovirus transduction rescues dendritic cell development in vitro. *Blood*, *101*, 961–969.
Tsujimura, H., Tamura, T., & Ozato, K. (2003). Cutting edge: IFN consensus sequence binding protein/IFN regulatory factor 8 drives the development of type I IFN-producing plasmacytoid dendritic cells. *The Journal of Immunology*, *170*, 1131–1135.
Tussiwand, R., Lee, W. L., Murphy, T. L., Mashayekhi, M., Wumesh, K. C., Albring, J. C., et al. (2012). Compensatory dendritic cell development mediated by BATF-IRF interactions. *Nature*, *490*, 502–507.
Villadangos, J. A., & Schnorrer, P. (2007). Intrinsic and cooperative antigen-presenting functions of dendritic-cell subsets in vivo. *Nature Reviews Immunology*, *7*, 543–555.
Vremec, D., Pooley, J., Hochrein, H., Wu, L., & Shortman, K. (2000). CD4 and CD8 expression by dendritic cell subtypes in mouse thymus and spleen. *The Journal of Immunology*, *164*, 2978–2986.
Vremec, D., Zorbas, M., Scollay, R., Saunders, D. J., Ardavin, C. F., Wu, L., et al. (1992). The surface phenotype of dendritic cells purified from mouse thymus and spleen: Investigation of the CD8 expression by a subpopulation of dendritic cells. *The Journal of Experimental Medicine*, *176*, 47–58.
Wang, L., Bursch, L. S., Kissenpfennig, A., Malissen, B., Jameson, S. C., & Hogquist, K. A. (2008). Langerin expressing cells promote skin immune responses under defined conditions. *The Journal of Immunology*, *180*, 4722–4727.
Waskow, C., Liu, K., Darrasse-Jeze, G., Guermonprez, P., Ginhoux, F., Merad, M., et al. (2008). The receptor tyrosine kinase Flt3 is required for dendritic cell development in peripheral lymphoid tissues. *Nature Immunology*, *9*, 676–683.
Wu, L., D'Amico, A., Winkel, K. D., Suter, M., Lo, D., & Shortman, K. (1998). RelB is essential for the development of myeloid-related CD8alpha− dendritic cells but not of lymphoid-related CD8alpha+ dendritic cells. *Immunity*, *9*, 839–847.

Wu, C. Y., Maeda, H., Contursi, C., Ozato, K., & Seder, R. A. (1999). Differential requirement of IFN consensus sequence binding protein for the production of IL-12 and induction of Th1-type cells in response to IFN-gamma. *The Journal of Immunology, 162*, 807–812.

Wu, L., Nichogiannopoulou, A., Shortman, K., & Georgopoulos, K. (1997). Cell-autonomous defects in dendritic cell populations of Ikaros mutant mice point to a developmental relationship with the lymphoid lineage. *Immunity*, 7, 483–492.

Yamazaki, S., Dudziak, D., Heidkamp, G. F., Fiorese, C., Bonito, A. J., Inaba, K., et al. (2008). CD8+ CD205+ splenic dendritic cells are specialized to induce Foxp3+ regulatory T cells. *The Journal of Immunology, 181*, 6923–6933.

Yarovinsky, F., Zhang, D., Andersen, J. F., Bannenberg, G. L., Serhan, C. N., Hayden, M. S., et al. (2005). TLR11 activation of dendritic cells by a protozoan profilin-like protein. *Science, 308*, 1626–1629.

Zelenay, S., Keller, A. M., Whitney, P. G., Schraml, B. U., Deddouche, S., Rogers, N. C., et al. (2012). The dendritic cell receptor DNGR-1 controls endocytic handling of necrotic cell antigens to favor cross-priming of CTLs in virus-infected mice. *Journal of Clinical Investigation, 122*, 1615–1627.

Zhan, Y., Carrington, E. M., van Nieuwenhuijze, A., Bedoui, S., Seah, S., Xu, Y., et al. (2011). GM-CSF increases cross presentation and CD103 expression by mouse CD8 (+) spleen dendritic cells. *European Journal of Immunology, 41*, 2585–2595.

Zhang, J., Raper, A., Sugita, N., Hingorani, R., Salio, M., Palmowski, M. J., et al. (2006). Characterization of Siglec-H as a novel endocytic receptor expressed on murine plasmacytoid dendritic cell precursors. *Blood, 107*, 3600–3608.

Zheng, Y., Danilenko, D. M., Valdez, P., Kasman, I., Eastham-Anderson, J., Wu, J., et al. (2007). Interleukin-22, a T(H)17 cytokine, mediates IL-23-induced dermal inflammation and acanthosis. *Nature, 445*, 648–651.

Zheng, Y., Valdez, P. A., Danilenko, D. M., Hu, Y., Sa, S. M., Gong, Q., et al. (2008). Interleukin-22 mediates early host defense against attaching and effacing bacterial pathogens. *Nature Medicine, 14*, 282–289.

CHAPTER TEN

Transcriptional Control of Macrophage Identity, Self-Renewal, and Function

Kaaweh Molawi[*,†,‡,§], Michael H. Sieweke[*,†,‡,§,1]

[*]Centre d'Immunologie de Marseille-Luminy, UM2 Aix-Marseille Université, Marseille cedex 9
[†]INSERM, Marseille, France
[‡]CNRS, Marseille, France
[§]Max-Delbrück-Centrum für Molekulare Medizin, Berlin, Germany
[1]Corresponding author: e-mail address: sieweke@ciml.univ-mrs.fr

Contents

Abstract

Macrophages not only are prominent effector cells of the immune system that are critical in inflammation and innate immune responses but also fulfill important functions in tissue homeostasis. Transcription factors can define macrophage identity and control their numbers and functions through the induction and maintenance of specific transcriptional programs. Here, we review the mechanisms employed by lineage-specific transcription factors to shape macrophage identity during the development from hematopoietic stem and progenitor cells. We also present current insight into how specific transcription factors control macrophage numbers, by regulating coordinated proliferation and differentiation of myeloid progenitor cells and self-renewal of mature macrophages. We finally discuss how functional specialization of mature macrophages

Advances in Immunology, Volume 120
ISSN 0065-2776
http://dx.doi.org/10.1016/B978-0-12-417028-5.00010-7

in response to environmental stimuli can be induced through synergistic activity of lineage- and stimulus-specific transcription factors that plug into preexisting transcriptional programs. Understanding the mechanisms that define macrophage identity, numbers, and functions will provide important insights into the differential properties of macrophage populations under various physiological and pathological conditions.

Macrophages are fully differentiated cells of the myeloid lineage and represent a major component of the mononuclear phagocyte system (MPS), which is composed of circulating monocytes, macrophages, and dendritic cells (DCs) (Geissmann et al., 2010). The MPS and macrophages, in particular, not only serve essential roles in maintaining tissue homeostasis under steady-state conditions but also can activate functional programs critically involved in pathological disturbances such as infections, autoimmunity, inflammation, cancer, or injury.

Macrophages can be derived from different stem or progenitors cells in the yolk sac, fetal liver, and bone marrow. Their final numbers depend to a large extent on the proliferative rate of their progenitor cells as monocytes and macrophages, like most differentiated cells, typically withdraw from the cell cycle upon maturation. It has become clear recently, however, that mature macrophages also have the ability to reenter cell cycle under specific conditions. Mature macrophages can fulfill various functions depending on the challenges they face. In this chapter, we aim to highlight the concepts of how transcription factors create macrophage identity during myelopoiesis, how they control macrophage cell numbers, and how they induce macrophage specialization and functional activation.

1. CREATING MACROPHAGE IDENTITY

Although simple at first sight, the question what constitutes macrophage identity can be complex. As their name suggests, macrophages were originally defined based on their phagocytic activity by their discoverer Elie Metchnikoff in the nineteenth century (Metchnikoff, 1891). While phagocytosis remains a key defining function of macrophages, they were also found to have important immunomodulatory and antigen-presenting functions and serve critical trophic roles for nonimmune cells in cancer, development, tissue homeostasis, and repair. Besides such functional criteria, macrophages in general and specific subtypes in particular have been defined by their location, surface marker expression, gene expression profile and epigenetic enhancer repertoire, their dependence on the cytokine macrophage colony-stimulating factor (M-CSF, also known as CSF-1), as well as by their ontogeny. Macrophages can develop from early yolk sac progenitors and hematopoietic stem cells (HSCs) of the fetal liver in the embryo or the bone marrow in the adult (Ginhoux et al., 2010; Iwasaki & Akashi, 2007; Schulz et al., 2012). Whereas until recently, macrophages were thought to mainly develop from bone marrow-derived monocytes, new evidence indicates that this is only one pathway of macrophage generation, possibly restricted to certain tissues, embryonic and neonatal development, inflammation, and macrophage reconstitution after myeloablation. It has become apparent that major proportions of tissue macrophages are rather derived from early yolk sac progenitors (Ginhoux et al., 2010; Hoeffel et al., 2012; Schulz et al., 2012; Yona et al., 2013). The exact contribution of these different sources to tissue macrophages is not finally resolved but appears to depend on the tissue context during homeostasis and the particular insult during a challenge situation, such as inflammation, infection, or injury that can induce macrophage replacement or amplification. While the transcription factors orchestrating embryonic macrophage development remain poorly defined, transcriptional control of monocyte and macrophage development from HSC has been studied in detail. HSC-derived monocytes develop through defined steps of differentiation, which are governed by transcription factor expression and competition, and can differentiate into macrophages under inflammatory and steady-state conditions. This process can also be recapitulated by *in vitro* differentiation protocols that have been useful for genome-wide transcription factor-binding studies. In this chapter, we will therefore mainly focus on these cells, when discussing the role of transcription factors in shaping macrophage identity.

1.1. Macrophage development from HSCs

Blood monocytes can leave the circulation and enter the tissue to differentiate into macrophages, particularly under inflammatory conditions. Monocytes are generated from HSCs via several commitment steps that involve successive cell fate decisions (Fig. 10.1A), which are governed by defined combinatorial expression of transcription factor and their synergistic or competitive interactions. In the bone marrow, HSCs give rise to the common myeloid progenitors (CMPs), the granulocyte/macrophage progenitor (GMP), and the macrophage/DC progenitor (MDP) (Fogg et al., 2006). MDPs can further develop into DCs via the common dendritic cell progenitor (CDP) that has lost monocyte/macrophage potential. The *in vivo*

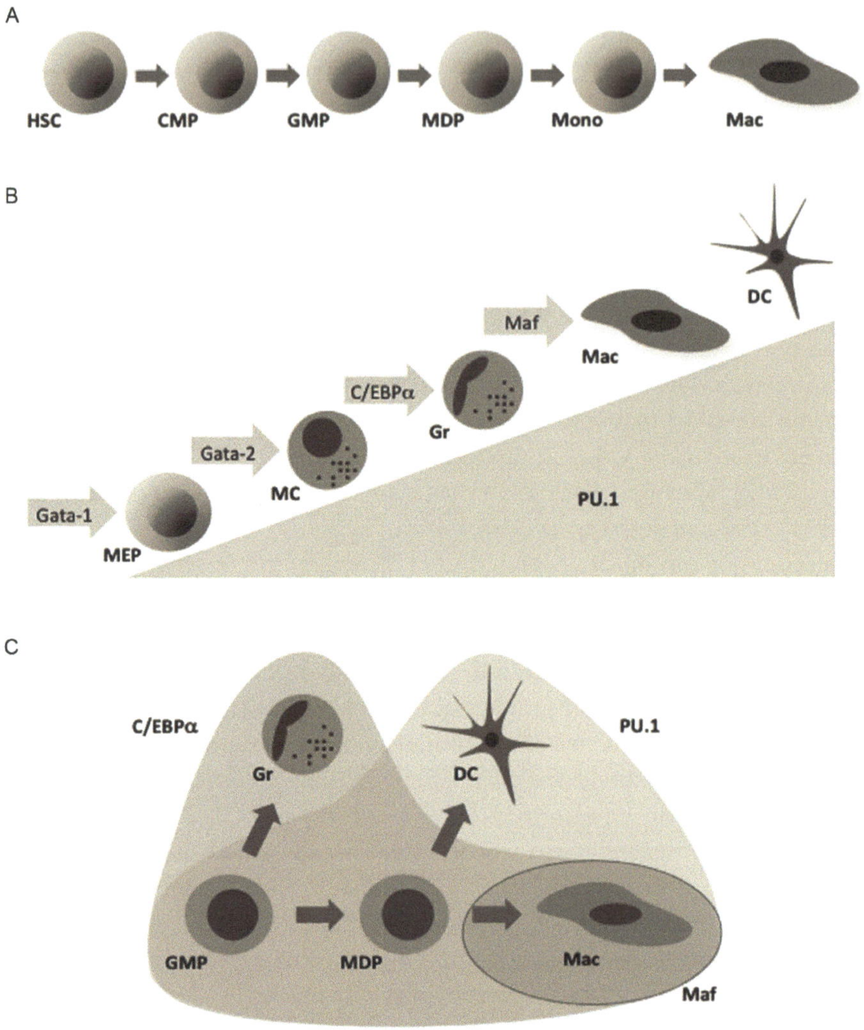

Figure 10.1 (A) Blood monocytes (Mono) that can give rise to macrophages (Mac) under certain conditions develop from hematopoietic stem cells (HSC) through defined myeloid progenitor stages, involving the common myeloid progenitor (CMP), the granulocyte/macrophage progenitor (GMP) and the macrophage/dendritic cell progenitor (MDP). The developmental pathway of HSC-independent macrophages from yolk sac-derived progenitors is currently under investigation. (B) The master transcription factor PU.1 is successively competing with other lineage-specific transcription factors at different branch points of myelopoiesis. The lineage choices are strongly influenced by the balance of the competing factors and increasing PU.1 levels over the course of macrophage and DC differentiation. Importantly, the antagonism of competing transcription factors is not absolute, they may cooperate at low levels but compete at high levels (see text). (C) Cell fate decisions are governed by combinatorial action of transcription factors, where the presence, absence and the relative expression levels of particular transcription factors provide a code for cell identity. This principle is illustrated in a highly simplified scheme showing expression domains of C/EBPα, PU.1, and Maf transcription factors in myeloid and macrophage differentiation. (For color version of this figure, the reader is referred to the online version of this chapter.)

existence of a proliferative, monocyte-restricted progenitor downstream of the MDP that may correspond to the monoblast described in culture has been proposed since the 1970s (Goud, Schotte, & van Furth, 1975; Saha & Geissmann, 2011) but remains to be demonstrated. Each of the described commitment steps can be seen as a successive restriction of developmental potential of the respective progenitor cell. For example, CMPs have lost lymphoid potential, GMPs cannot give rise to megakaryocytic–erythroid lineages (Iwasaki & Akashi, 2007), MDPs lack granulocyte potential, and the CDPs and postulated monocyte progenitor have lost monocyte or DC potential, respectively. These successive branch points along the differentiation pathway are controlled by several lineage-specific transcription factors. By focusing on the best-understood examples, we will highlight the mechanistic principles of how transcription factors can govern these decisions from the stem cell to the mature macrophage to shape macrophage identity.

1.2. Principal transcription factors of macrophage differentiation

The Ets family transcription factor PU.1 is central for directing macrophage development and identity, as indicated by both gain- and loss-of-function experiments and genome-wide DNA-binding studies (see Section 1.4). Although PU.1 deletion also affects other lineages, in particular lymphoid development, PU.1-deficient mice reveal an absolute requirement of PU.1 for macrophage development (McKercher et al., 1996; Scott, Simon, Anastasi, & Singh, 1994). Importantly, PU.1 is necessary both for the development of yolk sac-derived tissue macrophages that are absent in PU.1-deficient embryos (Schulz et al., 2012) and for monocyte development in the adult (Dakic et al., 2005; Iwasaki & Akashi, 2007). It is already critical for the initial steps of lineage commitment along the myeloid differentiation pathway that leads towards macrophages. PU.1 is expressed in the earliest myeloid committed progenitors (Arinobu et al., 2007) and it is required for the generation of CMPs from HSCs (Dakic et al., 2005; Iwasaki & Akashi, 2007). PU.1 induction in HSCs by high levels of M-CSF (Mossadegh-Keller et al., 2013) or in HSCs sensitized to the cytokine (Sarrazin et al., 2009) results in increased production of myeloid progeny. Consistent with this, ectopic expression of PU.1 in multipotent progenitors also promotes myeloid differentiation (Nerlov & Graf, 1998). PU.1 is also critical for lineage decisions at later branch points of the macrophage differentiation pathway, which will be discussed in Section 1.3.3.

Similar to PU.1, the transcription factor CCAAT/enhancer-binding protein-α (C/EBP-α) is necessary to establish myelopoiesis early in the differentiation pathway. Its expression is upregulated from HSC to CMP and GMP stages (Akashi, Traver, Miyamoto, & Weissman, 2000) and is essential for GMP generation (Zhang et al., 2004). C/EBP-α-deficient mice are therefore defective for downstream myeloid development, including monocytes (Zhang et al., 2004).

The central role of PU.1 and C/EBP-α in establishing macrophage identity is most dramatically indicated by the fact that other cell types such as B cells (Xie, Ye, Feng, & Graf, 2004), T cells (Laiosa, Stadtfeld, Xie, de Andres-Aguayo, & Graf, 2006), and fibroblasts (Feng et al., 2008) can be reprogrammed into macrophages by forced expression of PU.1 and C/EBP-α. This is reflected in the macrophage-specific epigenetic enhancer repertoire established by these factors, as discussed in more detail in Section 1.4.

Given the central role of PU.1 in the establishment of a macrophage identity, the regulation of PU.1 expression itself during macrophage differentiation is of significant interest. PU.1 expression can be induced by M-CSF at the earliest stage of myeloid commitment in HSCs (Mossadegh-Keller et al., 2013), likely by signaling to transcription factors that can activate the PU.1 gene. Indeed, several control elements in the enhancer and promoter regions of the PU.1 gene can be regulated by transcription factors expressed in early stem and progenitor cells (Lichtinger et al., 2012), in particular C/EBP-α (Yeamans et al., 2007) and Runx1 (Hoogenkamp et al., 2009; Huang et al., 2008; Zhang et al., 1996). Runx1 appears to be important for the initiation of PU.1 expression but is not required for its maintenance (Hoogenkamp et al., 2007; Lichtinger et al., 2012). This may be explained by the fact that PU.1 regulates control elements of its own gene (Okuno et al., 2005; Staber et al., 2013) and could thus sustain its own expression by an autoregulatory positive feedback loop, once it has been sufficiently activated (Chen et al., 1995; Leddin et al., 2011; Okuno et al., 2005). Consistent with this, Runx1 is essential for development of HSCs from the hemogenic endothelium (Chen, Yokomizo, Zeigler, Dzierzak, & Speck, 2009;Lancrin et al., 2009) at the onset of definitive hematopoiesis in the embryo (Okuda, van Deursen, Hiebert, Grosveld, & Downing, 1996; Wang et al., 1996) but is not required for adult hematopoiesis (Chen et al., 2009; Growney et al., 2005; Lancrin et al., 2009; Lichtinger et al., 2012; Putz, Rosner, Nuesslein, Schmitz, & Buchholz, 2006). As Runx1 is also expressed in primitive myeloid yolk sac progenitors (Ginhoux et al., 2010;

Samokhvalov, Samokhvalova, & Nishikawa, 2007), which give rise to PU.1-dependent tissue macrophages (Schulz et al., 2012), it is likely that Runx1 can also initiate PU.1 expression in these cells and might therefore be important for the development of both macrophage lineages. Although Runx1 does not appear to be required for the later steps of macrophage differentiation (Chen et al., 2009; Lancrin et al., 2009; Lichtinger et al., 2012), it is expressed in mature monocytes and macrophages (North, Stacy, Matheny, Speck, & de Bruijn, 2004). Runx1 is also important for the regulation of M-CSF receptor-enhancer elements (Himes, Cronau, Mulford, & Hume, 2005; Krysinska et al., 2007), and therefore is likely involved in regulating M-CSF-dependent proliferation in the macrophage lineage. Indeed, ectopic expression (Himes et al., 2005) or conditional deletion (Growney et al., 2005; Putz et al., 2006) of Runx1 leads to perturbations of proliferation in the myeloid lineage.

Other myeloid-specific transcription factors play critical roles at later branching points of macrophage differentiation. Interferon regulatory factor 8 (IRF8) is expressed in CMP and GMP progenitors as well as macrophages (Yamamoto et al., 2011), and IRF8-deficient mice show decreased numbers of macrophages (Scheller et al., 1999; Yamamoto et al., 2011) and M-CSF-dependent colony formation (Scheller et al., 1999), whereas numbers of myeloid progenitors, granulocytes, and osteoclast are increased (Holtschke et al., 1996; Scheller et al., 1999; Yamamoto et al., 2011; Zhao et al., 2009). Accordingly, expression of IRF8 in myeloid progenitors induces macrophage but inhibits granulocyte differentiation (Tamura, Nagamura-Inoue, Shmeltzer, Kuwata, & Ozato, 2000; Yamamoto et al., 2011). Together, these results indicate a role of IRF8 in driving M-CSF-dependent macrophage development at the branch point of granulocytes and monocytes, possibly the GMP stage. As IRF8 deficiency affects not only monocytes but also certain DC populations (Geissmann et al., 2010; Tamura et al., 2000), IRF8 may become essential at the further downstream MDP stage. Interestingly, the role of IRF8 in mononuclear phagocyte development appears to be conserved in humans, as patients with autosomal recessive IRF8 mutations lack monocytes and certain DC populations (Hambleton et al., 2011). Finally, IRF8 may also be important for yolk sac-derived macrophages, as Langerhans cell development is impaired in IRF8-deficient mice (Schiavoni et al., 2004) and development of microglia from yolk sac progenitors is IRF8 dependent (Kierdorf et al., 2013).

Egr proteins (Egr-1 and Egr-2) and Nab2 are induced by high levels of PU.1 in GMPs and are contributing to monopoiesis while repressing granulopoiesis (Laslo et al., 2006; Nguyen, Hoffman-Liebermann, & Liebermann, 1993). Similarly, the Kruppel-like factor 4 (Klf4) is induced by PU.1 (Feinberg et al., 2007) and IRF8 (Kurotaki et al., 2013) during monocyte differentiation in a stage-specific pattern. It is promoting monocyte differentiation of progenitor cells (Feinberg et al., 2007) and can partially rescue monocyte/macrophage differentiation of IRF8 deficient progenitors (Kurotaki et al., 2013). It is also involved in the control of macrophage proliferation and polarization as discussed in Sections 2 and 3. AP-1 transcription factors as well as the transcription factors MafB and c-Maf are upregulated in monocytes and macrophages and indirectly drive differentiation by promoting macrophage specialization and cells cycle arrest, respectively, as we will discuss in Sections 2 and 3 (Hegde, Zhao, Ashmun, & Shapiro, 1999; Kelly, Englmeier, Lafon, Sieweke, & Graf, 2000; Lord, Abdollahi, Hoffman-Liebermann, & Liebermann, 1993; Sieweke, Tekotte, Frampton, & Graf, 1996).

1.3. Principles of transcription factor induced macrophage specification

Several general principles of transcription factor action are important for macrophage differentiation and will be outlined using well-studied examples.

1.3.1 Cooperative interactions

Lineage-specific transcription factors are not acting isolated but in an orchestrated fashion. Synergistic complex formation and direct protein–protein interactions can therefore play an important role in macrophage differentiation. As outlined in the preceding text, PU.1 and C/EBP-α functionally cooperate in macrophage specification, which is also reflected in the joint activation of specific myeloid genes. One of the best-described examples of this is the M-CSF receptor-encoding gene *c-fms,* where Runx1, PU.1, and C/EBP-α synergistically drive gene activity (DeKoter, Walsh, & Singh, 1998; Himes et al., 2005; Zhang, Hetherington, Chen, & Tenen, 1994). Transcription factor complex formation has been demonstrated at *c-fms* promoter and enhancer sites in early myeloid progenitors (Krysinska et al., 2007; Tagoh et al., 2002; Tenen, Hromas, Licht, & Zhang, 1997). As we suggested previously in the "cocktail party" model of differentiation (Sieweke & Graf, 1998), transcription factor complex formation is dynamic and differentiation stage specific. Runx1 thus forms complexes and cooperates with PU.1 during the initiation of *c-fms* expression but is dispensable at later stages of differentiation (Hoogenkamp et al., 2009), where Egr-2 cooperates with PU.1 (Krysinska et al., 2007). Similarly, at later stages of differentiation, the transcription factor IRF8 can cooperatively interact with DNA-bound PU.1 without binding to DNA itself and thereby enhances macrophage differentiation through targeted gene induction (Sharf et al., 1997; Tamura, Thotakura, Tanaka, Ko, & Ozato, 2005). Finally, AP-1 transcription factors such as Jun and Fos function as heterodimeric leucine zipper complexes on DNA, but Fos can also form heterodimers with bZIP transcription factors MafB and c-Maf. They thus represent another example for alternative heterotypic cooperative interaction between macrophage-specific transcription factors that may have complex-specific activity in different differentiation or activation states (Kataoka, Fujiwara, Noda, & Nishizawa, 1994; Kataoka, Noda, & Nishizawa, 1994; Lord et al., 1993; Sieweke & Graf, 1998).

1.3.2 Competitive interactions

In contrast to the synergistic transcription factor interactions described in the preceding text, there are also antagonistic protein–protein interactions between transcription factors involved in controlling lineage commitment during hematopoiesis. PU.1 is governing many cells fate decisions along the myeloid/macrophage differentiation pathway together with antagonistic partners through such inhibitory interactions. For example, through mutual cross inhibition, PU.1 and Gata-1 control the lineage choice between myeloid and erythroid differentiation at the HSC and CMP stages (Nerlov, Querfurth, Kulessa, & Graf, 2000; Rekhtman, Radparvar, Evans, & Skoultchi, 1999; Zhang et al., 2000), whereas PU.1 and Gata-2 antagonism controls myeloid versus mast cell commitment at the CMP stage (Walsh et al., 2002). This involves direct interactions of the antagonistic partners and high levels of PU.1 determine myeloid differentiation (Nerlov et al., 2000; Rekhtman et al., 1999; Stopka, Amanatullah, Papetti, & Skoultchi, 2005; Walsh et al., 2002; Zhang et al., 2000). At the bipotent GMP stage, high levels of PU.1 are driving macrophage differentiation by antagonizing the progranulocytic activity of C/EBP-α (Dahl et al., 2003). Similarly, at the branch point between macrophage and DC development, high levels of PU.1 antagonize the macrophage-specific transcription factor MafB and direct DC development, whereas moderate PU.1 levels are permissive for MafB-dependent macrophage differentiation (Bakri et al., 2005; Carotta et al., 2010). Thus, it appears that PU.1 is successively competing with antagonizing transcription factors to direct lineage decisions at the branch points of myeloid differentiation towards macrophages (Fig. 10.1B).

As the example of PU.1 and MafB is illustrating, this antagonism is not absolute but critically dependent on relative expression levels and the balance between the involved transcription factors. Where high expression levels of PU.1 overrule the cell fate implied by an antagonistic partner, low or equal levels act synergistically with the respective transcription factor (Bakri et al., 2005; Dahl et al., 2003; Walsh et al., 2002). This shows the combinatorial control of cell fate decisions by several transcription factors, where the presence, absence, and expression levels of several factors are important to determine cell fate. Whereas macrophages require cell type-specific levels of MafB and c-Maf, C/EBP and PU.1, DCs express PU.1 at higher levels but lack C/EBP and Mafs (Fig. 10.1C).

1.3.3 Expression levels

Transcription factors can be involved in the development of several hematopoietic lineages and adjustment of the correct cellular levels is critical for cell fate decisions. This is particularly important for the cooperation (Section 1.3.1) or competition (Section 1.3.2) with other transcription factors, as only certain levels may be sufficient to initiate a cooperative interaction or to outcompete an inhibitory factor. For example, PU.1 is driving myeloid development of hematopoietic progenitors when it is expressed at high levels, whereas low concentration induces B-cell development (DeKoter & Singh, 2000). The levels of PU.1 are also important for the choice between macrophage and DC differentiation (Bakri et al., 2005). Expression levels of PU.1 are controlled not only through *cis*-regulatory elements of the gene, which are critical for PU.1-induced lineage decisions (Okuno et al., 2005; Rosenbauer et al., 2006), but also on the message level via miRNA-155 (Xiao & Rajewsky, 2009). Besides regulation at the transcriptional and mRNA level, posttranslational control of transcription factor activity through dominant-negative isoforms generated by alternative translational start sites (Calkhoven, Muller, & Leutz, 2002), phosphorylation (Ross et al., 2004) and sumoylation (Tillmanns et al., 2007) have also been described and offer additional regulatory options to control transcription factor levels. This should also serve as a cautionary note for global gene expression analysis on the mRNA level. Whereas such studies yield useful general gene expression profiles (Gautier et al., 2012), they may miss key regulators. For example, macrophages and DC show little difference of PU.1 on the message but a strong difference on the protein level

(Bakri et al., 2005). Proteome analysis of macrophages, their subtypes, and progenitors may therefore yield new insights in the future.

1.3.4 Feedforward loops

The M-CSF receptor gene is expressed all along the differentiation pathway from HSCs to mature monocytes and macrophages including all intermediate myeloid progenitors (Miyamoto et al., 2002; Pixley & Stanley, 2004; Sarrazin et al., 2009; Sasmono et al., 2003). As a defining characteristic of the lineage, macrophage development is strongly dependent on the M-CSF receptor and its ligands M-CSF and IL-34 (Dai et al., 2002; Kawasaki et al., 1985; Lin et al., 2008). We observed recently that already in long-term HSCs, M-CSF signaling induces PU.1 expression, one of the key factors of macrophage identity, and directly instructs myeloid cell fate change (Mossadegh-Keller et al., 2013). Such an initial signal can be further amplified and stabilized by two positive feedforward loops. First, PU.1 binds control elements of its own gene (Okuno et al., 2005; Staber et al., 2013) and can stimulate its own expression by an autoregulatory positive feedback loop (Chen et al., 1995; Leddin et al., 2011; Okuno et al., 2005). Second, as described in detail in Section 1.3.1, PU.1 activates *c-fms*, the M-CSF receptor gene, which leads to higher receptor expression and sensitivity to its ligands, which in turn will induce more PU.1. As we proposed before, an initially weak stimulus of lineage choice can thus be consolidated and stabilized in maturing cells by positive feedback loops between pairs of cytokine receptors and transcription factors such as the M-CSF receptor and PU.1 (Sarrazin et al., 2009; Sarrazin & Sieweke, 2011).

1.3.5 Integrated networks

To induce differentiation pathways and lineage-specific transcriptional programs, key transcription factors govern complex gene regulatory networks that can involve several downstream transcription factors. This is especially well studied for PU.1 and C/EBP-α at the branch point of neutrophil and macrophage development in GMPs. High PU.1 expression leads to upregulation of Egr-1/Egr-2 and Nab2, which act as secondary macrophage cell fate determinants at this stage (Laslo et al., 2006). In contrast, G-CSF stimulates neutrophil development through increased expression of C/EBP-α and successively Gfi-1 (Dahl et al., 2003; Laslo et al., 2006). Primary and secondary cell fate determinants synergistically regulate expression of macrophage- or neutrophil-specific genes, and negative feedback loops between Egr/Nab2 and Gfi-1 (Laslo et al., 2006) as well as between Gfi-1 and PU.1 (Hock et al., 2003; Laslo et al., 2006) are stabilizing the selected respective genetic programs. However, genome-wide expression data indicate that these transcriptional networks are likely much more complex and that so far unidentified factors remain to be integrated into the proposed models (Laslo et al., 2006).

Taken together, lineage choices during macrophage differentiation are governed by fine-tuned expression levels (Section 1.3.3) of transcription factors and their synergistic (Section 1.3.1) and antagonistic (Section 1.3.2) interactions within complex regulatory networks (Sections 1.3.4 and 1.3.5). Importantly, the same transcription factor can influence various lineage decisions depending on the developmental stage and the cooperative or antagonistic interaction partners in a given context (Sieweke & Graf, 1998).

1.4. Enhancer landscape defined macrophage identity

In recent years, chromatin immunoprecipitation-sequencing (Chip-seq) technology has made it possible to analyze transcription factor binding and histone modifications on a genome-wide scale (Farnham, 2009). This has shown that transcription factor binding to cell type-specific enhancer regions represents the majority of binding sites in the genome and appears to be important to induce and maintain a cell type-specific chromatin organization and gene expression (Heintzman et al., 2009; Natoli, 2010).

This advancement has been aided by the discovery that enhancers are associated with specific chromatin signatures (Heintzman et al., 2007), mainly mono- and bimethylation of Lys4 of histone H3 (H3K4me1 and H3K4me2) and low levels of H3K4 trimethylation (H3K4me3). This definition has allowed cell type-specific enhancer identification that correlated well with cell type-specific gene expression (Heintzman et al., 2009).

Genome-wide DNA-binding studies of PU.1 in macrophages by Chip-seq analysis revealed that the vast majority of binding sites in the genome are associated with enhancers (Ghisletti et al., 2010; Heinz et al., 2010). Moreover, it appears that PU.1 actively contributes to the creation of this enhancer repertoire, as it is required for the deposition of H3K4me1 marks, and can induce macrophage-specific enhancer formation *de novo* in fibroblast (Ghisletti et al., 2010). The comparison of genome-wide PU.1 binding in macrophages and in B cells revealed that the binding profile is cell type specific (Heinz et al., 2010). Consistent with the importance of enhancer distribution for cell identity, the differential binding sites are mainly located at enhancer regions, whereas promoter regions near the transcriptional start sites are relatively conserved among cell types (Heinz et al., 2010). In line with the functional cooperation of PU.1 with other myeloid transcription factors, significant proportions of macrophage-specific PU.1 enhancer sites also show overlapping binding for C/EBP and IRF8 in Chip-seq analysis (Heinz et al., 2010; Kurotaki et al., 2013). Interestingly, only few DNA-binding motifs of macrophage transcription factors, such as PU.1, C/EBP, AP-1, and Runx, are enriched in H3K4me1-marked enhancer regions of macrophages (Ghisletti et al., 2010; Heinz et al., 2010) indicating that in addition to PU.1, only few other lineage-specific factors contribute to the cell type-specific enhancer landscape that defines macrophage identity. Therefore, PU.1 function may go beyond the activation of specific target genes comprising selection and maintenance of a macrophage-specific enhancer repertoire that may not only control promoter activation but also induce a cell type-specific three-dimensional organization of the genome (Natoli, 2010; Spilianakis, Lalioti, Town, Lee, & Flavell, 2005).

The deposition of H3K4me1 marks and nucleosome dislocation initiated by lineage-specific transcription factor complexes may render these sites accessible to signal-dependent transcription factors, by either direct DNA binding or indirect protein–protein interactions, and therefore allow enhancer-controlled responses to environmental stimuli (Ghisletti et al., 2010; Heinz et al., 2010), which will be discussed in Section 3.2. The selection of a macrophage-specific enhancer repertoire by PU.1 and cooperating transcription factors may therefore be critical for shaping robust macrophage identity while maintaining responsiveness to different stimuli and enabling different activation states.

2. CONTROLLING MACROPHAGE NUMBERS AND PROLIFERATION

As discussed in the preceding text, myelopoiesis involves several successive progenitor stages. These successive progenitor cells do differ not only in their increasingly restricted differentiation options but also in their proliferation rates and capacity to self-renew. Under steady-state conditions, the majority of HSCs are mostly quiescent and cycling cells have a low proliferation rate, whereas certain transient-amplifying progenitor cells display high proliferation rates and are mainly responsible for generating the required high numbers of mature monocytes and macrophages, which exit the cell cycle under steady-state conditions (Auffray, Sieweke, & Geissmann, 2009). However, recent data indicate that some mature macrophages retain

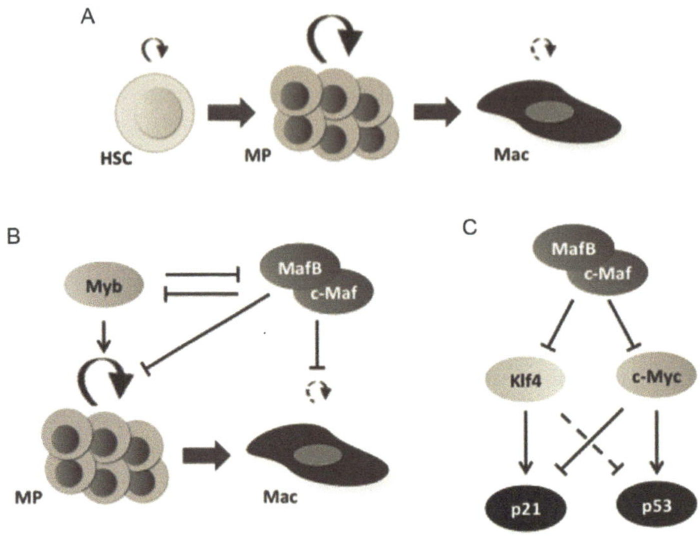

Figure 10.2 (A) Macrophages and their progenitor cells have different capacities to proliferate and self-renew. HSCs have a low proliferation rate but give rise to highly proliferative myeloid progenitors (MP). Mature macrophages retain the capacity to proliferate and self-renew under specific conditions as indicated by the dashed arrow. (B) The transcription factor Myb induces MP proliferation and prolonged Myb activity prevents macrophage maturation. In contrast, MafB and c-Maf antagonize Myb activity and indirectly induce macrophage maturation through suppression of proliferation. In mature macrophages they prevent cell cycle entry. (C) Macrophage self-renewal is controlled through a regulatory network downstream of MafB and c-Maf. Deficiency for these two factors leads to increased activity of Klf4 and c-Myc and balanced changes in cell cycle regulators. (For color version of this figure, the reader is referred to the online version of this chapter.)

the ability to proliferate in response to certain challenges and can maintain tissue populations through local self-renewal (Fig. 10.2A; Ginhoux et al., 2010; Jenkins et al., 2011; Schulz et al., 2012; Tagliani et al., 2011). Here, we will discuss the current view of how transcription factors control proliferation in myeloid progenitors and mature macrophages.

2.1. Transcriptional control of myeloid progenitor expansion during macrophage differentiation

Myeloid progenitor cells can undergo rapid proliferation before differentiating into mature monocytes and macrophages. This balance between proliferation and differentiation is tightly controlled through the expression kinetics of stage-specific transcription factors that drive differentiation and/or cell cycle arrest.

Importantly, the cytokine M-CSF induces macrophage differentiation and proliferation in progenitor cells, whereas mature macrophages normally do not proliferate in response to M-CSF (Klappacher et al., 2002).

The proliferative effect of M-CSF on myeloid progenitor cells is in part mediated through induction of Ets- and AP-1-mediated transcriptional programs (Klappacher et al., 2002). As part of this, the transient upregulation of Ets-1 and Ets-2 transcription factors leads to the transactivation of the pro-proliferative genes *c-Myc* and *c-Myb* (Roussel, Davis, Cleveland, Ghysdael, & Hiebert, 1994; Sullivan, Feeley, Guerra, & Boxer, 1997). Expression of c-Myb and c-Myc in myeloid progenitor cells and forced expression in mature macrophages induce cell cycle entry and proliferation (Graf, 1992; Roussel, 1997). C-Myb-deficient mice show a complete lack of definitive hematopoieses in the fetal liver, suggesting a role in HSCs or early progenitors. However, gain of function and tissue-specific or transient gene inactivation studies also indicate a role in later myeloid progenitors. Treatment of human bone marrow cells with c-Myb antisense oligonucleotides results in a decrease in both size and number of granulocyte-macrophage colony-forming units (CFU-GM) (Gewirtz & Calabretta, 1988) and conditional c-Myb knockout mice have functionally impaired CMP and GMP progenitors (Lieu & Reddy, 2012). Constitutive expression of c-Myb inhibits macrophage maturation and constitutively active Myb alleles drive myeloid progenitor proliferation (Gonda, Buckmaster, & Ramsay, 1989; Gonda, Ramsay, & Johnson, 1989; Sumner, Crawford, Mucenski, & Frampton, 2000; Yanagisawa et al., 1991). However, primitive hematopoiesis in the yolk sac functions independently of c-Myb and yolk sac progenitor-derived tissue macrophages do not require c-Myb, demonstrating differential transcription factor involvement in different macrophage lineages (Mucenski et al., 1991; Schulz et al., 2012), possibly because yolk sac-derived macrophages may not go through a c-Myb-dependent transient-amplifying progenitor stage in their differentiation pathway.

Several transcription factors are involved in inducing cell cycle arrest in mature macrophages. For example, C/EBP-α is an important regulator of progenitor cell proliferation during myelopoiesis through negative regulation of c-Myc expression. Furthermore, C/EBP-α also suppresses activity of cell cycle promoting E2F transcription factors and therefore inhibits the proliferative potential of myeloid progenitor cells via this pathway (Johansen et al., 2001; Porse et al., 2005; Slomiany, D'Arigo, Kelly, & Kurtz, 2000).

Similarly, MafB is driving terminal macrophage differentiation and promotes cell cycle arrest in myeloid progenitor cells (Kelly et al., 2000;

Tillmanns et al., 2007). This antiproliferative capacity of MafB is mediated through a cross inhibitory interaction with c-Myb, which is balancing the transition from proliferating progenitor cells to nonproliferative differentiated cells (Tillmanns et al., 2007). At the same time, MafB is also able to repress Ets-1 (Sieweke et al., 1996) and might therefore indirectly decrease Myb levels and promote cell cycle exit through this mechanism (Roussel et al., 1994; Sullivan et al., 1997). Ets activity in maturing macrophages is also inhibited by replacement of Ets-1 and Ets-2 on pro-proliferative genes with the Ets repressor METS (mitogen Ets transcriptional suppressor, also called PE1 or ETV3) (Klappacher et al., 2002). Additionally, c-Maf also interacts with c-Myb to form complexes that inhibit Myb-mediated gene expression and therefore drives differentiation at the expense of proliferation (Hedge, Kumar, Kurschner, & Shapiro, 1998; Hegde et al., 1999). Taken together with the observation that MafB deficiency leads to compensatory upregulation of c-Maf in macrophages (Aziz et al., 2006), this indicates that MafB and c-Maf cooperatively antagonize the proliferative activity of progenitor cells, leading to macrophage maturation as a secondary consequence of cell cycle arrest (Fig. 10.2B; Aziz et al., 2006).

2.2. Uncoupling terminal differentiation and cell cycle arrest in macrophages

MafB and c-Maf show paralleled expression patterns during macrophage development and can functionally compensate for each other when driving macrophage maturation and cell cycle arrest. Surprisingly, double deficiency for MafB and c-Maf does not cause defective macrophage maturation or myeloproliferative defects in reconstituted mice, but results in normal numbers of functional monocytes and macrophages (Aziz, Soucie, Sarrazin, & Sieweke, 2009). However, MafB/c-Maf double-deficient macrophages are proliferating *in vitro* when exposed to M-CSF and can be maintained without affecting or reversing their differentiation state, demonstrating that the parallel processes of differentiation and cell cycle arrest are not intrinsically linked but can be dissociated.

The proliferative effect of M-CSF on MafB/c-Maf double-deficient macrophages is in part mediated through M-CSF-dependent upregulation of c-Myc and Klf4 (Aziz et al., 2009). Both factors are required for self-renewal of MafB/c-Maf double-deficient macrophages as knockdown of either factor ablates the self-renewal capacities of the cells (Aziz et al., 2009). Importantly, MafB/c-Maf double-deficient macrophages are not tumorigenic, demonstrating that they are still capable to respect homeostatic control mechanisms and that there are additional, yet unknown mechanisms limiting proliferation *in vivo* (Aziz et al., 2009). Notably, besides their described role in macrophage differentiation and myeloid progenitor proliferation, these two factors are involved in the control of the self-renewal capacity of embryonic stem cells (Cartwright et al., 2005; Jiang et al., 2008). Klf4 has been shown to act as a tumor suppressor by inducing cell cycle arrest through p21. Conversely, Klf4 inhibits transcription of the tumor suppressor p53 in the absence of p21, highlighting its ambivalent properties in cell cycle control (Rowland & Peeper, 2006). In contrast, c-Myc induces proliferation through suppression of p21 but can induce p53-mediated apoptosis (Yamanaka, 2007). Therefore, the balanced expression of c-Myc and Klf4 seems to be critical for inducing proliferation and self-renewal of macrophages in the absence of transformation (Fig. 10.2C).

The physiological relevance of these control mechanisms of macrophage proliferation is becoming increasingly evident in recent years. Several reports have demonstrated cytokine-dependent local macrophage proliferation *in vivo* in response to specific stimuli such as helminth infection or pregnancy-associated tissue growth (Jenkins et al., 2011; Tagliani et al., 2011). Intriguingly, c-Myc and Klf4 are not only critical for controlling macrophage proliferation but are also involved in IL-4-induced alternative activation of macrophages (Liao et al., 2011; Pello et al., 2012). During parasite infection, IL-4 not only mediates alternative activation of macrophages but also induces macrophage proliferation (Jenkins et al., 2011), indicating that these two processes might be controlled by similar or overlapping genetic programs. Also, recent reports indicate that yolk sac progenitor-derived tissue macrophages such as microglia and Langerhans cells are self-renewing throughout life without contribution of HSC-derived cells to the populations in steady state (Ginhoux et al., 2010; Hoeffel et al., 2012; Schulz et al., 2012; Yona et al., 2013). HSC-independent tissue macrophage populations develop independently from the pro-proliferative factor c-Myb, which is required for macrophage differentiation form HSCs, indicating that proliferation control of yolk sac-derived macrophages during development and in the adult tissue employs different mechanisms than the Myb-dependent progenitor proliferation described in the preceding text.

3. TRANSCRIPTIONAL CONTROL OF MACROPHAGE SPECIALIZATION AND FUNCTIONAL ACTIVATION STATES

Differentiated macrophages can acquire a continuum of many functionally distinct phenotypes, depending on their tissue microenvironment and the external stimuli they are exposed to during infection and inflammation, tissue injury, or tumorigenesis.

The influence of the microenvironment on macrophage phenotypes is illustrated by the significant diversity of the gene expression profiles in different tissue macrophages, which have been analyzed for microglia, peritoneal, lung, and spleen red pulp macrophages (Gautier et al., 2012) and may reflect organ specific homeostatic functions in the steady state. As several transcription factors are exclusively expressed in only one of the examined populations, it appears evident that transcription factors may also be involved in this specialization of specific tissue macrophages. For example, the PU.1-related transcription factor Spi-C is exclusively expressed at high levels in spleen red pulp macrophages and is required for their development and organ specific function, the clearance of trapped red blood cells (Kohyama et al., 2009).

Macrophages can also assume diverse activation states in response to different stimuli under nonhomeostatic conditions. Two extreme poles of this activation spectrum are usually referred to as classically activated M1 macrophages and alternatively activated M2 macrophages (Mosser & Edwards, 2008; Sica & Mantovani, 2012). The M1-polarized phenotype of macrophages develops in response to IFN-γ, the prevalent cytokine of T helper 1 (T_H1)-driven immune responses, and is characterized by the activation of several characteristic marker genes, such as *Nos2*, *Ciita*, *Il12b*, and inflammatory cytokines including *Tnf-α*, *Il1*, and *Il6*. Alternatively activated M2 macrophages develop upon exposure to IL-4 and/or IL-13, the principal cytokines of T_H2-driven immune responses, as found, for example, in parasite infections. They also upregulate a characteristic set of markers including arginase-1 (*Arg1*), Ym1(*Chi3l3*), mannose receptor (*Mrc1*), and Fizz1 (*Retnla*) and the Il-4 receptor (Il4ra) itself. However, the M1 and M2 nomenclature is only loosely defined and stimulation with GM-CSF or lipopolysaccharide (LPS) results in a similar M1 activation state as IFN-γ, whereas M-CSF and parasite pathogen associated molecular patterns (PAMPs) such as chitin also lead to M2 type polarizations. Importantly, although different M1- or M2-type stimuli result in similar marker activation and feed into connected regulatory networks, the induced gene expression profiles and activated transcription factors are not identical. For example, although the receptors for IL-4 and IL-13 share the IL-4R-alpha chain, the two cytokines have distinct functions and induce different phenotypes of alternatively activated macrophages due to signal specific modulators of the cellular response (Gordon & Martinez, 2010). Finally, there is a plethora of macrophage phenotypes in addition to these extreme states of macrophage polarization, and we are only beginning to understand the molecular and transcriptional mechanisms directing macrophage activation in response to diverse stimuli in a changing microenvironment (Mosser & Edwards, 2008; Ostuni et al., 2013; Sica & Mantovani, 2012). Therefore, it is probably most prudent to initially investigate the transcription factors involved in mediating the response to individual stimuli and in a second step analyze their possible connection in regulatory loops after combined or consecutive stimulation, as it might be occurring *in vivo*. The role of transcription factors in macrophage M1 and M2 polarization has been treated in an excellent recent review (Lawrence & Natoli, 2011). Here, we will highlight some examples of prominent transcription factors of functionally distinct activation states. We will discuss the most recent developments and general principles of transcriptional control of macrophage activation, especially with respect to the chromatin modifications involved.

3.1. Transcriptional control of macrophage activation

Binding of the classical M1 stimulus IFN-γ to its receptor leads to activation of the Janus kinase-signal transducer and activator of transcription (JAK-STAT) pathway, leading to phosphorylation and dimerization of STAT1, which enables subsequent binding and transactivation of *cis*-regulatory elements of genes associated with classical macrophage activation (Darnell, Kerr, & Stark, 1994). STAT1 also mediates the response to type I interferons through heterodimerization with STAT2. STAT1 and STAT2 can also form a complex with IRF9 that induces upregulation of M1 genes through binding to interferon-stimulated response elements (Park, Li, Cha, & Schindler, 2000). In contrast, alternative stimulation of macrophages with IL-4 or IL-13 leads to activation of the JAK-STAT6 pathway mediating M2-specific gene expression through active STAT6, which is required for alternative activation of macrophages during parasite infection (Goenka & Kaplan, 2011; Herbert et al., 2004; Takeda et al., 1996).

IRFs represent another family of transcription factors playing important roles during functional specialization of macrophages in either direction of the M1–M2 spectrum. A recent report demonstrates that IRF5 is critically involved in directing proinflammatory polarization of human macrophages. IRF5 is upregulated in response to inflammatory stimuli and directly activates transcription of IL-12 and IL-23, while actively repressing IL-10. Genome-wide expression data revealed that IRF5 reciprocally regulated M1 and M2 genes by upregulating proinflammatory genes and dampening expression of M2 markers (Krausgruber et al., 2011), which is a common functional principle of transcription factors governing macrophage polarization.

On the other hand, the IRF family member IRF4 is critical for alternative macrophage activation *in vivo* and *in vitro* response to chitin, a mimetic of helminth or fungal infection (Satoh et al., 2010). This IRF4-mediated alternative activation requires epigenetic modifications by Jumonji domain containing-3 (Jmjd3) histone H3K27 demethylase. Importantly, Jmjd3 does not influence alternative activation of macrophages in response to IL-4 demonstrating the stimulus specificity of the mechanisms directing polarization (Satoh et al., 2010).

The nuclear receptors peroxisome proliferator-activated receptor-γ (PPAR-γ) is a regulator of lipid metabolism in macrophages and is strongly induced upon IL-4 stimulation in a STAT6-dependent manner (Glass & Saijo, 2010; Szanto et al., 2010). Besides positively regulating gene expression involved in lipid metabolism, PPAR-γ is a repressor of NF-κB- and AP-1-mediated proinflammatory gene expression and has been shown to be required for alternative activation of macrophages (Odegaard et al., 2007; Ricote, Li, Willson, Kelly, & Glass, 1998).

It has been demonstrated recently that Nur77, an orphan nuclear receptor also called NR4A1, is highly expressed in Ly6C-negative monocytes and is required for differentiation and survival of these specialized monocytes (Hanna et al., 2011). Deficiency for Nur77 induces a bias towards proinflammatory macrophage activation, which is associated with increased toll-like receptor 4 expression and NF-κB activation (Hamers et al., 2012; Hanna et al., 2012).

The bZIP family transcription factors cAMP-responsive element-binding protein (CREB) and C/EBP-β play an important role during alternative activation of macrophages in the context of tissue repair after injury, toll-like receptor (TLR) signaling, and tumor formation (Ananieva et al., 2008; Marigo et al., 2010; Ruffell et al., 2009). On the other hand, C/EBP-β is also involved in LPS-/IFN-γ-mediated upregulation of proinflammatory molecules through a CREB-independent mechanism (Gorgoni, Maritano, Marthyn, Righi, & Poli, 2002), demonstrating the context dependence of regulatory networks directing development of diverse macrophage phenotypes upon differential stimulation.

As discussed in the preceding text, the transcription factor c-Myc has important functions in the control of macrophage numbers and proliferation during differentiation, but c-Myc expression is also upregulated in macrophages in response to IL-4 stimulated M2 macrophage polarization. Almost half of the genes induced by IL-4 are affected by c-Myc inhibition due to both direct and indirect mechanisms (Pello et al., 2012). It is therefore tempting to speculate that upregulation of c-Myc may also contribute to IL-4 induced proliferation of alternatively activated macrophages during helminth infection *in vivo* (Jenkins et al., 2011). Interestingly, IL-4 stimulation also leads to upregulation of Klf4, which collaborates with STAT6 to activate M2-associated genetic programs, inhibits NF-κB, and induces a proregenerative phenotype in the context of wound healing (Liao et al., 2011). As Klf4 and c-Myc are important both for alternative activation and for proliferation of macrophages (Aziz et al., 2009), it appears possible that regulated macrophage proliferation might be a functionally important aspect of M2 polarization during parasite infection or tissue regeneration.

3.2. Chromatin modifications of macrophage activation

External stimuli of macrophages lead to dynamic changes of gene expression. For example, LPS-induced changes in gene expression can be classified into different classes of genes according to their kinetic response pattern (Bhatt et al., 2012), which include direct transcriptional responses (primary response genes) and responses that require protein synthesis (secondary response genes) (Ramirez-Carrozzi et al., 2009). Furthermore, an initial stimulation changes the responsiveness of macrophages to secondary stimuli, which has been termed LPS tolerance for genes that cannot be reactivated (Foster, Hargreaves, & Medzhitov, 2007). However, some genes also become hyperinducible by prior priming (Foster et al., 2007), which can include increased responsiveness to stimuli other than the initial one (Ostuni et al., 2013). As described in the preceding text, transient stimuli like IFN-γ or IL-4 can also lead to the development of stable phenotypes of macrophage subtypes. The transcriptional changes associated with these phenomena are mediated by stimulus-induced transcription factors and altered chromatin organization both on promoter and enhancer regulatory elements. For example, promoters of primary response genes contain nucleosome-depleted CpG islands and are constitutively bound by RNA polymerase II, which upon stimulation allows rapid recruitment of transcription factors such as NF-kB or AP-1 and activation of transcription (Hargreaves, Horng, & Medzhitov, 2009; Ramirez-Carrozzi et al., 2009; Valouev et al., 2011). In contrast, promoters of secondary response genes have a high nucleosome density, are not immediately accessible to inducible transcription factors, and require SWI-/SNF-dependent chromatin remodeling. This can be mediated by some LPS-induced transcription factors like IRF3 that can bind to closed chromatin and interact with the remodeling complex (Ramirez-Carrozzi et al., 2009; Ramirez-Carrozzi et al., 2006). Stimuli such as IL-1-β and TNF-α that are unable to activate IRF3 are unable to induce secondary response genes, illustrating how functionally related inflammatory stimuli lead to different gene expression profiles and macrophage phenotypes. These differences may be exploited for pharmacological intervention. For example, the small compound I-BET specifically inhibits secondary LPS response genes in macrophages (Nicodeme et al., 2010) by competing with acetylated histones for binding to the chromatin-modifying bromodomain and extra terminal domain (BET) proteins (Hargreaves et al., 2009). Due to the suppression of specific inflammatory genes, I-BET could protect against experimentally induced sepsis, which highlights the therapeutic potential of pharmacologically modifying macrophage phenotypes.

External stimuli also lead to major changes on distal gene regulatory elements and modify the enhancer landscape of macrophages. As outlined in Section 1.4, the lineage-specific factor PU.1 can act as a pioneering factor to promote histone displacement and deposition of H3K4me1 enhancer marks during macrophage differentiation to shape a macrophage-specific enhancer repertoire. It has been shown that stimulus-induced transcription factors such as NF-κB, IRFs, or LXR factors land on this preexisting enhancer platform to induce an appropriate response in activated macrophages (Barish et al., 2010; Escoubet-Lozach et al., 2011; Natoli, Ghisletti, & Barozzi, 2011). Furthermore, LPS stimulation leads to recruitment of the acetyltransferase p300 and an increase of H3K27 acetylation, a modification mediated by this enzyme, to a subset of preexisting enhancers associated with inflammatory genes (Ghisletti et al., 2010; Ostuni et al., 2013). The enhancers showing these markers of activation can be classified into several categories: previously active enhancers that increased activity or poised enhancers that only became active upon stimulation (Ghisletti et al., 2010; Ostuni et al., 2013). Although the large majority of activated enhancers fell into these categories, stimulation also led to the activation of a smaller group of latent enhancers that were not preoccupied by lineage-specific transcription factors or showed H3k4me1 enhancer marks. The analysis of latent enhancers activated in response to a variety of TLR, inflammatory or immune-modulatory stimuli revealed not only stimulus-specific enhancers but also overlaps that reflected the functional similarity of the stimuli. For example, IL-4 and IFN-γ stimulation resulted in little overlap of activated latent enhancers, consistent with the distinct M1 and M2 polarizations at the extreme ends of macrophage activation induced by these cytokines. Interestingly, the establishment of these enhancers depended on Stat1 and Stat6, respectively. This enabled recruitment of PU.1 to low-affinity sites and deposition of enhancer marks indicating that stimulus-activated transcription factors can cooperate with lineage-specific factors to establish new enhancers. Importantly, a first stimulation of naïve macrophages establishes an epigenetic memory that renders latent enhancer sites more responsive to secondary activation with the same or a different secondary stimulus (Ostuni et al., 2013). This may provide a molecular explanation for the extraordinary macrophage plasticity and the observation that transient environmental stimuli can lead to the establishment of stable macrophage subtypes.

4. CONCLUDING REMARKS

In the last few years, significant progress has been made to unravel how transcription factors define macrophage identity and control macrophage self-renewal during homeostasis or in challenge situations. At the same time, our understanding of the transcriptional programs that govern macrophage specialization in particular tissue environments and induce distinct activation states in response to diverse stimuli is growing rapidly. With the discovery of new developmental pathways, the advent of new technology, and the increasing availability of genome-wide information, future studies will doubtlessly identify new players and mechanisms that determine phenotypical and functional differences and similarities of different macrophage populations. Given the importance and multifaceted contribution of macrophages in many physiological and pathological conditions, ranging from infection, immunity, inflammation, regeneration, to cancer, a deeper understanding of these mechanisms is of high interest, as it will allow the development of novel therapeutic strategies to orient macrophage activity in desired directions.

ACKNOWLEDGMENTS

We gratefully acknowledge grants from the "Association pour la recherche sur le Cancer" (3422) and the "Agence nationale de la Recherche" (BLAN07-1_205752). M. S. is a "Fondation pour la Recherche Médicale" (DEQ20071210559; DEQ20110421320) and INSERM-Helmholtz group leader. K. M. is supported by a HFSP long-term fellowship.

REFERENCES

Akashi, K., Traver, D., Miyamoto, T., & Weissman, I. L. (2000). A clonogenic common myeloid progenitor that gives rise to all myeloid lineages. *Nature*, *404*(6774), 193–197.

Ananieva, O., Darragh, J., Johansen, C., Carr, J. M., McIlrath, J., Park, J. M., et al. (2008). The kinases MSK1 and MSK2 act as negative regulators of Toll-like receptor signaling. *Nature Immunology*, *9*(9), 1028–1036.

Arinobu, Y., Mizuno, S., Chong, Y., Shigematsu, H., Iino, T., Iwasaki, H., et al. (2007). Reciprocal activation of GATA-1 and PU.1 marks initial specification of hematopoietic stem cells into myeloerythroid and myelolymphoid lineages. *Cell Stem Cell*, *1*(4), 416–427.

Auffray, C., Sieweke, M. H., & Geissmann, F. (2009). Blood monocytes: Development, heterogeneity, and relationship with dendritic cells. *Annual Review of Immunology*, *27*, 669–692.

Aziz, A., Soucie, E., Sarrazin, S., & Sieweke, M. H. (2009). MafB/c-Maf deficiency enables self-renewal of differentiated functional macrophages. *Science*, *326*(5954), 867–871.

Aziz, A., Vanhille, L., Mohideen, P., Kelly, L. M., Otto, C., Bakri, Y., et al. (2006). Development of macrophages with altered actin organization in the absence of MafB. *Molecular and Cellular Biology*, *26*(18), 6808–6818.

Bakri, Y., Sarrazin, S., Mayer, U. P., Tillmanns, S., Nerlov, C., Boned, A., et al. (2005). Balance of MafB and PU.1 specifies alternative macrophage or dendritic cell fate. *Blood*, *105*(7), 2707–2716.

Barish, G. D., Yu, R. T., Karunasiri, M., Ocampo, C. B., Dixon, J., Benner, C., et al. (2010). Bcl-6 and NF-kappaB cistromes mediate opposing regulation of the innate immune response. *Genes & Development*, *24*(24), 2760–2765.

Bhatt, D. M., Pandya-Jones, A., Tong, A. J., Barozzi, I., Lissner, M. M., Natoli, G., et al. (2012). Transcript dynamics of proinflammatory genes revealed by sequence analysis of subcellular RNA fractions. *Cell*, *150*(2), 279–290.

Calkhoven, C. F., Muller, C., & Leutz, A. (2002). Translational control of gene expression and disease. *Trends in Molecular Medicine*, *8*(12), 577–583.

Carotta, S., Dakic, A., D'Amico, A., Pang, S. H., Greig, K. T., Nutt, S. L., et al. (2010). The transcription factor PU.1 controls dendritic cell development and Flt3 cytokine receptor expression in a dose-dependent manner. *Immunity*, *32*(5), 628–641.

Cartwright, P., McLean, C., Sheppard, A., Rivett, D., Jones, K., & Dalton, S. (2005). LIF/STAT3 controls ES cell self-renewal and pluripotency by a Myc-dependent mechanism. *Development*, *132*(5), 885–896.

Chen, H., Ray-Gallet, D., Zhang, P., Hetherington, C. J., Gonzalez, D. A., Zhang, D. E., et al. (1995). PU.1 (Spi-1) autoregulates its expression in myeloid cells. *Oncogene*, *11*(8), 1549–1560.

Chen, M. J., Yokomizo, T., Zeigler, B. M., Dzierzak, E., & Speck, N. A. (2009). Runx1 is required for the endothelial to haematopoietic cell transition but not thereafter. *Nature*, *457*(7231), 887–891.

Dahl, R., Walsh, J. C., Lancki, D., Laslo, P., Iyer, S. R., Singh, H., et al. (2003). Regulation of macrophage and neutrophil cell fates by the PU.1:C/EBPalpha ratio and granulocyte colony-stimulating factor. *Nature Immunology*, *4*(10), 1029–1036.

Dai, X. M., Ryan, G. R., Hapel, A. J., Dominguez, M. G., Russell, R. G., Kapp, S., et al. (2002). Targeted disruption of the mouse colony-stimulating factor 1 receptor gene results in osteopetrosis, mononuclear phagocyte deficiency, increased primitive progenitor cell frequencies, and reproductive defects. *Blood*, *99*(1), 111–120.

Dakic, A., Metcalf, D., Di Rago, L., Mifsud, S., Wu, L., & Nutt, S. L. (2005). PU.1 regulates the commitment of adult hematopoietic progenitors and restricts granulopoiesis. *The Journal of Experimental Medicine*, *201*(9), 1487–1502.

Darnell, J. E., Jr., Kerr, I. M., & Stark, G. R. (1994). Jak-STAT pathways and transcriptional activation in response to IFNs and other extracellular signaling proteins. *Science*, *264*(5164), 1415–1421.
DeKoter, R. P., & Singh, H. (2000). Regulation of B lymphocyte and macrophage development by graded expression of PU.1. *Science*, *288*(5470), 1439–1441.
DeKoter, R. P., Walsh, J. C., & Singh, H. (1998). PU.1 regulates both cytokine-dependent proliferation and differentiation of granulocyte/macrophage progenitors. *The EMBO Journal*, *17*(15), 4456–4468.
Escoubet-Lozach, L., Benner, C., Kaikkonen, M. U., Lozach, J., Heinz, S., Spann, N. J., et al. (2011). Mechanisms establishing TLR4-responsive activation states of inflammatory response genes. *PLoS Genetics*, 7(12), e1002401.
Farnham, P. J. (2009). Insights from genomic profiling of transcription factors. *Nature Reviews. Genetics*, *10*(9), 605–616.
Feinberg, M. W., Wara, A. K., Cao, Z., Lebedeva, M. A., Rosenbauer, F., Iwasaki, H., et al. (2007). The Kruppel-like factor KLF4 is a critical regulator of monocyte differentiation. *The EMBO Journal*, *26*(18), 4138–4148.
Feng, R., Desbordes, S. C., Xie, H., Tillo, E. S., Pixley, F., Stanley, E. R., et al. (2008). PU.1 and C/EBPalpha/beta convert fibroblasts into macrophage-like cells. *Proceedings of the National Academy of Sciences of the United States of America*, *105*(16), 6057–6062.
Fogg, D. K., Sibon, C., Miled, C., Jung, S., Aucouturier, P., Littman, D. R., et al. (2006). A clonogenic bone marrow progenitor specific for macrophages and dendritic cells. *Science*, *311*(5757), 83–87.
Foster, S. L., Hargreaves, D. C., & Medzhitov, R. (2007). Gene-specific control of inflammation by TLR-induced chromatin modifications. *Nature*, *447*(7147), 972–978.
Gautier, E. L., Shay, T., Miller, J., Greter, M., Jakubzick, C., Ivanov, S., et al. (2012). Gene-expression profiles and transcriptional regulatory pathways that underlie the identity and diversity of mouse tissue macrophages. *Nature Immunology*, *13*(11), 1118–1128.
Geissmann, F., Manz, M. G., Jung, S., Sieweke, M. H., Merad, M., & Ley, K. (2010). Development of monocytes, macrophages, and dendritic cells. *Science*, *327*(5966), 656–661.
Gewirtz, A. M., & Calabretta, B. (1988). A c-myb antisense oligodeoxynucleotide inhibits normal human hematopoiesis in vitro. *Science*, *242*(4883), 1303–1306.
Ghisletti, S., Barozzi, I., Mietton, F., Polletti, S., De Santa, F., Venturini, E., et al. (2010). Identification and characterization of enhancers controlling the inflammatory gene expression program in macrophages. *Immunity*, *32*(3), 317–328.
Ginhoux, F., Greter, M., Leboeuf, M., Nandi, S., See, P., Gokhan, S., et al. (2010). Fate mapping analysis reveals that adult microglia derive from primitive macrophages. *Science*, *330*(6005), 841–845.
Glass, C. K., & Saijo, K. (2010). Nuclear receptor transrepression pathways that regulate inflammation in macrophages and T cells. *Nature Reviews. Immunology*, *10*(5), 365–376.
Goenka, S., & Kaplan, M. H. (2011). Transcriptional regulation by STAT6. *Immunologic Research*, *50*(1), 87–96.
Gonda, T. J., Buckmaster, C., & Ramsay, R. G. (1989). Activation of c-myb by carboxy-terminal truncation: Relationship to transformation of murine haemopoietic cells in vitro. *The EMBO Journal*, *8*(6), 1777–1783.
Gonda, T. J., Ramsay, R. G., & Johnson, G. R. (1989). Murine myeloid cell lines derived by in vitro infection with recombinant c-myb retroviruses express myb from rearranged vector proviruses. *The EMBO Journal*, *8*(6), 1767–1775.
Gordon, S., & Martinez, F. O. (2010). Alternative activation of macrophages: Mechanism and functions. *Immunity*, *32*(5), 593–604.
Gorgoni, B., Maritano, D., Marthyn, P., Righi, M., & Poli, V. (2002). C/EBP beta gene inactivation causes both impaired and enhanced gene expression and inverse regulation

of IL-12 p40 and p35 mRNAs in macrophages. *Journal of Immunology, 168*(8), 4055–4062.
Goud, T. J., Schotte, C., & van Furth, R. (1975). Identification and characterization of the monoblast in mononuclear phagocyte colonies grown in vitro. *The Journal of Experimental Medicine, 142*(5), 1180–1199.
Graf, T. (1992). Myb: A transcriptional activator linking proliferation and differentiation in hematopoietic cells (Review). *Current Opinion in Genetics & Development, 2*(2), 249–255.
Growney, J. D., Shigematsu, H., Li, Z., Lee, B. H., Adelsperger, J., Rowan, R., et al. (2005). Loss of Runx1 perturbs adult hematopoiesis and is associated with a myeloproliferative phenotype. *Blood, 106*(2), 494–504.
Hambleton, S., Salem, S., Bustamante, J., Bigley, V., Boisson-Dupuis, S., Azevedo, J., et al. (2011). IRF8 mutations and human dendritic-cell immunodeficiency. *The New England Journal of Medicine, 365*(2), 127–138.
Hamers, A. A., Vos, M., Rassam, F., Marinkovic, G., Kurakula, K., van Gorp, P. J., et al. (2012). Bone marrow-specific deficiency of nuclear receptor Nur77 enhances atherosclerosis. *Circulation Research, 110*(3), 428–438.
Hanna, R. N., Carlin, L. M., Hubbeling, H. G., Nackiewicz, D., Green, A. M., Punt, J. A., et al. (2011). The transcription factor NR4A1 (Nur77) controls bone marrow differentiation and the survival of Ly6C− monocytes. *Nature Immunology, 12*(8), 778–785.
Hanna, R. N., Shaked, I., Hubbeling, H. G., Punt, J. A., Wu, R., Herrley, E., et al. (2012). NR4A1 (Nur77) deletion polarizes macrophages toward an inflammatory phenotype and increases atherosclerosis. *Circulation Research, 110*(3), 416–427.
Hargreaves, D. C., Horng, T., & Medzhitov, R. (2009). Control of inducible gene expression by signal-dependent transcriptional elongation. *Cell, 138*(1), 129–145.
Hedge, S. P., Kumar, A., Kurschner, C., & Shapiro, L. H. (1998). c-Maf interacts with c-Myb to regulate transcription of an early myeloid gene during differentiation. *Molecular and Cellular Biology, 18*(5), 2729–2737.
Hegde, S. P., Zhao, J., Ashmun, R. A., & Shapiro, L. H. (1999). c-Maf induces monocytic differentiation and apoptosis in bipotent myeloid progenitors. *Blood, 94*(5), 1578–1589.
Heintzman, N. D., Hon, G. C., Hawkins, R. D., Kheradpour, P., Stark, A., Harp, L. F., et al. (2009). Histone modifications at human enhancers reflect global cell-type-specific gene expression. *Nature, 459*(7243), 108–112.
Heintzman, N. D., Stuart, R. K., Hon, G., Fu, Y., Ching, C. W., Hawkins, R. D., et al. (2007). Distinct and predictive chromatin signatures of transcriptional promoters and enhancers in the human genome. *Nature Genetics, 39*(3), 311–318.
Heinz, S., Benner, C., Spann, N., Bertolino, E., Lin, Y. C., Laslo, P., et al. (2010). Simple combinations of lineage-determining transcription factors prime cis-regulatory elements required for macrophage and B cell identities. *Molecular Cell, 38*(4), 576–589.
Herbert, D. R., Holscher, C., Mohrs, M., Arendse, B., Schwegmann, A., Radwanska, M., et al. (2004). Alternative macrophage activation is essential for survival during schistosomiasis and downmodulates T helper 1 responses and immunopathology. *Immunity, 20*(5), 623–635.
Himes, S. R., Cronau, S., Mulford, C., & Hume, D. A. (2005). The Runx1 transcription factor controls CSF-1-dependent and -independent growth and survival of macrophages. *Oncogene, 24*(34), 5278–5286.
Hock, H., Hamblen, M. J., Rooke, H. M., Traver, D., Bronson, R. T., Cameron, S., et al. (2003). Intrinsic requirement for zinc finger transcription factor Gfi-1 in neutrophil differentiation. *Immunity, 18*(1), 109–120.
Hoeffel, G., Wang, Y., Greter, M., See, P., Teo, P., Malleret, B., et al. (2012). Adult Langerhans cells derive predominantly from embryonic fetal liver monocytes with a minor contribution of yolk sac-derived macrophages. *The Journal of Experimental Medicine, 209*(6), 1167–1181.

Holtschke, T., Lohler, J., Kanno, Y., Fehr, T., Giese, N., Rosenbauer, F., et al. (1996). Immunodeficiency and chronic myelogenous leukemia-like syndrome in mice with a targeted mutation of the ICSBP gene. *Cell*, *87*(2), 307–317.

Hoogenkamp, M., Krysinska, H., Ingram, R., Huang, G., Barlow, R., Clarke, D., et al. (2007). The Pu.1 locus is differentially regulated at the level of chromatin structure and noncoding transcription by alternate mechanisms at distinct developmental stages of hematopoiesis. *Molecular and Cellular Biology*, *27*(21), 7425–7438.

Hoogenkamp, M., Lichtinger, M., Krysinska, H., Lancrin, C., Clarke, D., Williamson, A., et al. (2009). Early chromatin unfolding by RUNX1: A molecular explanation for differential requirements during specification versus maintenance of the hematopoietic gene expression program. *Blood*, *114*(2), 299–309.

Huang, G., Zhang, P., Hirai, H., Elf, S., Yan, X., Chen, Z., et al. (2008). PU.1 is a major downstream target of AML1 (RUNX1) in adult mouse hematopoiesis. *Nature Genetics*, *40*(1), 51–60.

Iwasaki, H., & Akashi, K. (2007). Myeloid lineage commitment from the hematopoietic stem cell. *Immunity*, *26*(6), 726–740.

Jenkins, S. J., Ruckerl, D., Cook, P. C., Jones, L. H., Finkelman, F. D., van Rooijen, N., et al. (2011). Local macrophage proliferation, rather than recruitment from the blood, is a signature of TH2 inflammation. *Science*, *332*(6035), 1284–1288.

Jiang, J., Chan, Y. S., Loh, Y. H., Cai, J., Tong, G. Q., Lim, C. A., et al. (2008). A core Klf circuitry regulates self-renewal of embryonic stem cells. *Nature Cell Biology*, *10*(3), 353–360.

Johansen, L. M., Iwama, A., Lodie, T. A., Sasaki, K., Felsher, D. W., Golub, T. R., et al. (2001). c-Myc is a critical target for c/EBPalpha in granulopoiesis. *Molecular and Cellular Biology*, *21*(11), 3789–3806.

Kataoka, K., Fujiwara, K. T., Noda, M., & Nishizawa, M. (1994). MafB, a new Maf family transcription activator that can associate with Maf and Fos but not with Jun. *Molecular and Cellular Biology*, *14*(11), 7581–7591.

Kataoka, K., Noda, M., & Nishizawa, M. (1994). Maf nuclear oncoprotein recognizes sequences related to an AP-1 site and forms heterodimers with both Fos and Jun. *Molecular and Cellular Biology*, *14*(1), 700–712.

Kawasaki, E. S., Ladner, M. B., Wang, A. M., Van Arsdell, J., Warren, M. K., Coyne, M. Y., et al. (1985). Molecular cloning of a complementary DNA encoding human macrophage-specific colony-stimulating factor (CSF-1). *Science*, *230*(4723), 291–296.

Kelly, L. M., Englmeier, U., Lafon, I., Sieweke, M. H., & Graf, T. (2000). MafB is an inducer of monocytic differentiation. *The EMBO Journal*, *19*(9), 1987–1997.

Kierdorf, K., Erny, D., Goldmann, T., Sander, V., Schulz, C., Perdiguero, E. G., et al. (2013). Microglia emerge from erythromyeloid precursors via Pu.1- and Irf8-dependent pathways. *Nature Neuroscience*, *16*(3), 273–280.

Klappacher, G. W., Lunyak, V. V., Sykes, D. B., Sawka-Verhelle, D., Sage, J., Brard, G., et al. (2002). An induced Ets repressor complex regulates growth arrest during terminal macrophage differentiation. *Cell*, *109*(2), 169–180.

Kohyama, M., Ise, W., Edelson, B. T., Wilker, P. R., Hildner, K., Mejia, C., et al. (2009). Role for Spi-C in the development of red pulp macrophages and splenic iron homeostasis. *Nature*, *457*(7227), 318–321.

Krausgruber, T., Blazek, K., Smallie, T., Alzabin, S., Lockstone, H., Sahgal, N., et al. (2011). IRF5 promotes inflammatory macrophage polarization and TH1-TH17 responses. *Nature Immunology*, *12*(3), 231–238.

Krysinska, H., Hoogenkamp, M., Ingram, R., Wilson, N., Tagoh, H., Laslo, P., et al. (2007). A two-step, PU.1-dependent mechanism for developmentally regulated chromatin remodeling and transcription of the c-fms gene. *Molecular and Cellular Biology*, *27*(3), 878–887.

Kurotaki, D., Osato, N., Nishiyama, A., Yamamoto, M., Ban, T., Sato, H., et al. (2013). Essential role of the IRF8-KLF4 transcription factor cascade in murine monocyte differentiation. *Blood*, *121*(10), 1839–1849.

Laiosa, C. V., Stadtfeld, M., Xie, H., de Andres-Aguayo, L., & Graf, T. (2006). Reprogramming of committed T cell progenitors to macrophages and dendritic cells by C/EBP alpha and PU.1 transcription factors. *Immunity*, *25*(5), 731–744.

Lancrin, C., Sroczynska, P., Stephenson, C., Allen, T., Kouskoff, V., & Lacaud, G. (2009). The haemangioblast generates haematopoietic cells through a haemogenic endothelium stage. *Nature*, *457*(7231), 892–895.

Laslo, P., Spooner, C. J., Warmflash, A., Lancki, D. W., Lee, H. J., Sciammas, R., et al. (2006). Multilineage transcriptional priming and determination of alternate hematopoietic cell fates. *Cell*, *126*(4), 755–766.

Lawrence, T., & Natoli, G. (2011). Transcriptional regulation of macrophage polarization: Enabling diversity with identity. *Nature Reviews. Immunology*, *11*(11), 750–761.

Leddin, M., Perrod, C., Hoogenkamp, M., Ghani, S., Assi, S., Heinz, S., et al. (2011). Two distinct auto-regulatory loops operate at the PU.1 locus in B cells and myeloid cells. *Blood*, *117*(10), 2827–2838.

Liao, X., Sharma, N., Kapadia, F., Zhou, G., Lu, Y., Hong, H., et al. (2011). Kruppel-like factor 4 regulates macrophage polarization. *The Journal of Clinical Investigation*, *121*(7), 2736–2749.

Lichtinger, M., Ingram, R., Hannah, R., Muller, D., Clarke, D., Assi, S. A., et al. (2012). RUNX1 reshapes the epigenetic landscape at the onset of haematopoiesis. *The EMBO Journal*, *31*(22), 4318–4333.

Lieu, Y. K., & Reddy, E. P. (2012). Impaired adult myeloid progenitor CMP and GMP cell function in conditional c-myb-knockout mice. *Cell Cycle*, *11*(18), 3504–3512.

Lin, H., Lee, E., Hestir, K., Leo, C., Huang, M., Bosch, E., et al. (2008). Discovery of a cytokine and its receptor by functional screening of the extracellular proteome. *Science*, *320*(5877), 807–811.

Lord, K. A., Abdollahi, A., Hoffman-Liebermann, B., & Liebermann, D. A. (1993). Proto-oncogenes of the fos/jun family of transcription factors are positive regulators of myeloid differentiation. *Molecular and Cellular Biology*, *13*(2), 841–851.

Marigo, I., Bosio, E., Solito, S., Mesa, C., Fernandez, A., Dolcetti, L., et al. (2010). Tumor-induced tolerance and immune suppression depend on the C/EBPbeta transcription factor. *Immunity*, *32*(6), 790–802.

McKercher, S. R., Torbett, B. E., Anderson, K. L., Henkel, G. W., Vestal, D. J., Baribault, H., et al. (1996). Targeted disruption of the PU.1 gene results in multiple hematopoietic abnormalities. *The EMBO Journal*, *15*(20), 5647–5658.

Metchnikoff, E. (1891). Lecture on phagocytosis and immunity. *British Medical Journal*, *1*(1570), 213–217.

Miyamoto, T., Iwasaki, H., Reizis, B., Ye, M., Graf, T., Weissman, I. L., et al. (2002). Myeloid or lymphoid promiscuity as a critical step in hematopoietic lineage commitment. *Developmental Cell*, *3*(1), 137–147.

Mossadegh-Keller, N., Sarrazin, S., Kandall, P. K., Espinosa, L., Standley, R. E., Nutt, S. L., et al. (2013). M-CSF instructs myeloid lineage fate in single haematopoietic stem cells. *Nature*, *497*(7448), 239–243.

Mosser, D. M., & Edwards, J. P. (2008). Exploring the full spectrum of macrophage activation. *Nature Reviews. Immunology*, *8*(12), 958–969.

Mucenski, M. L., McLain, K., Kier, A. B., Swerdlow, S. H., Schreiner, C. M., Miller, T. A., et al. (1991). A functional c-myb gene is required for normal murine fetal hepatic hematopoiesis. *Cell*, *65*(4), 677–689.

Natoli, G. (2010). Maintaining cell identity through global control of genomic organization. *Immunity*, *33*(1), 12–24.

Natoli, G., Ghisletti, S., & Barozzi, I. (2011). The genomic landscapes of inflammation. *Genes & Development*, *25*(2), 101–106.
Nerlov, C., & Graf, T. (1998). PU.1 induces myeloid lineage commitment in multipotent hematopoietic progenitors. *Genes & Development*, *12*(15), 2403–2412.
Nerlov, C., Querfurth, E., Kulessa, H., & Graf, T. (2000). GATA-1 interacts with the myeloid PU.1 transcription factor and represses PU.1-dependent transcription. *Blood*, *95*(8), 2543–2551.
Nguyen, H. Q., Hoffman-Liebermann, B., & Liebermann, D. A. (1993). The zinc finger transcription factor Egr-1 is essential for and restricts differentiation along the macrophage lineage. *Cell*, *72*(2), 197–209.
Nicodeme, E., Jeffrey, K. L., Schaefer, U., Beinke, S., Dewell, S., Chung, C. W., et al. (2010). Suppression of inflammation by a synthetic histone mimic. *Nature*, *468*(7327), 1119–1123.
North, T. E., Stacy, T., Matheny, C. J., Speck, N. A., & de Bruijn, M. F. (2004). Runx1 is expressed in adult mouse hematopoietic stem cells and differentiating myeloid and lymphoid cells, but not in maturing erythroid cells. *Stem Cells*, *22*(2), 158–168.
Odegaard, J. I., Ricardo-Gonzalez, R. R., Goforth, M. H., Morel, C. R., Subramanian, V., Mukundan, L., et al. (2007). Macrophage-specific PPARgamma controls alternative activation and improves insulin resistance. *Nature*, *447*(7148), 1116–1120.
Okuda, T., van Deursen, J., Hiebert, S. W., Grosveld, G., & Downing, J. R. (1996). AML1, the target of multiple chromosomal translocations in human leukemia, is essential for normal fetal liver hematopoiesis. *Cell*, *84*(2), 321–330.
Okuno, Y., Huang, G., Rosenbauer, F., Evans, E. K., Radomska, H. S., Iwasaki, H., et al. (2005). Potential autoregulation of transcription factor PU.1 by an upstream regulatory element. *Molecular and Cellular Biology*, *25*(7), 2832–2845.
Ostuni, R., Piccolo, V., Barozzi, I., Polletti, S., Termanini, A., Bonifacio, S., et al. (2013). Latent enhancers activated by stimulation in differentiated cells. *Cell*, *152*(1–2), 157–171.
Park, C., Li, S., Cha, E., & Schindler, C. (2000). Immune response in Stat2 knockout mice. *Immunity*, *13*(6), 795–804.
Pello, O. M., De Pizzol, M., Mirolo, M., Soucek, L., Zammataro, L., Amabile, A., et al. (2012). Role of c-MYC in alternative activation of human macrophages and tumor-associated macrophage biology. *Blood*, *119*(2), 411–421.
Pixley, F. J., & Stanley, E. R. (2004). CSF-1 regulation of the wandering macrophage: Complexity in action. *Trends in Cell Biology*, *14*(11), 628–638.
Porse, B. T., Bryder, D., Theilgaard-Monch, K., Hasemann, M. S., Anderson, K., Damgaard, I., et al. (2005). Loss of C/EBP alpha cell cycle control increases myeloid progenitor proliferation and transforms the neutrophil granulocyte lineage. *The Journal of Experimental Medicine*, *202*(1), 85–96.
Putz, G., Rosner, A., Nuesslein, I., Schmitz, N., & Buchholz, F. (2006). AML1 deletion in adult mice causes splenomegaly and lymphomas. *Oncogene*, *25*(6), 929–939.
Ramirez-Carrozzi, V. R., Braas, D., Bhatt, D. M., Cheng, C. S., Hong, C., Doty, K. R., et al. (2009). A unifying model for the selective regulation of inducible transcription by CpG islands and nucleosome remodeling. *Cell*, *138*(1), 114–128.
Ramirez-Carrozzi, V. R., Nazarian, A. A., Li, C. C., Gore, S. L., Sridharan, R., Imbalzano, A. N., et al. (2006). Selective and antagonistic functions of SWI/SNF and Mi-2beta nucleosome remodeling complexes during an inflammatory response. *Genes & Development*, *20*(3), 282–296.
Rekhtman, N., Radparvar, F., Evans, T., & Skoultchi, A. I. (1999). Direct interaction of hematopoietic transcription factors PU.1 and GATA-1: Functional antagonism in erythroid cells. *Genes & Development*, *13*(11), 1398–1411.
Ricote, M., Li, A. C., Willson, T. M., Kelly, C. J., & Glass, C. K. (1998). The peroxisome proliferator-activated receptor-gamma is a negative regulator of macrophage activation. *Nature*, *391*(6662), 79–82.

Rosenbauer, F., Owens, B. M., Yu, L., Tumang, J. R., Steidl, U., Kutok, J. L., et al. (2006). Lymphoid cell growth and transformation are suppressed by a key regulatory element of the gene encoding PU.1. *Nature Genetics*, *38*(1), 27–37.
Ross, S. E., Radomska, H. S., Wu, B., Zhang, P., Winnay, J. N., Bajnok, L., et al. (2004). Phosphorylation of C/EBPalpha inhibits granulopoiesis. *Molecular and Cellular Biology*, *24*(2), 675–686.
Roussel, M. F. (1997). Regulation of cell cycle entry and G1 progression by CSF-1. *Molecular Reproduction and Development*, *46*(1), 11–18.
Roussel, M. F., Davis, J. N., Cleveland, J. L., Ghysdael, J., & Hiebert, S. W. (1994). Dual control of myc expression through a single DNA binding site targeted by ets family proteins and E2F-1. *Oncogene*, *9*(2), 405–415.
Rowland, B. D., & Peeper, D. S. (2006). KLF4, p21 and context-dependent opposing forces in cancer. *Nature Reviews. Cancer*, *6*(1), 11–23.
Ruffell, D., Mourkioti, F., Gambardella, A., Kirstetter, P., Lopez, R. G., Rosenthal, N., et al. (2009). A CREB-C/EBPbeta cascade induces M2 macrophage-specific gene expression and promotes muscle injury repair. *Proceedings of the National Academy of Sciences of the United States of America*, *106*(41), 17475–17480.
Saha, P., & Geissmann, F. (2011). Toward a functional characterization of blood monocytes. *Immunology & Cell Biology*, *89*(1), 2–4.
Samokhvalov, I. M., Samokhvalova, N. I., & Nishikawa, S. (2007). Cell tracing shows the contribution of the yolk sac to adult haematopoiesis. *Nature*, *446*(7139), 1056–1061.
Sarrazin, S., Mossadegh-Keller, N., Fukao, T., Aziz, A., Mourcin, F., Vanhille, L., et al. (2009). MafB restricts M-CSF-dependent myeloid commitment divisions of hematopoietic stem cells. *Cell*, *138*(2), 300–313.
Sarrazin, S., & Sieweke, M. (2011). Integration of cytokine and transcription factor signals in hematopoietic stem cell commitment. *Seminars in Immunology*, *23*(5), 326–334.
Sasmono, R. T., Oceandy, D., Pollard, J. W., Tong, W., Pavli, P., Wainwright, B. J., et al. (2003). A macrophage colony-stimulating factor receptor-green fluorescent protein transgene is expressed throughout the mononuclear phagocyte system of the mouse. *Blood*, *101*(3), 1155–1163.
Satoh, T., Takeuchi, O., Vandenbon, A., Yasuda, K., Tanaka, Y., Kumagai, Y., et al. (2010). The Jmjd3-Irf4 axis regulates M2 macrophage polarization and host responses against helminth infection. *Nature Immunology*, *11*(10), 936–944.
Scheller, M., Foerster, J., Heyworth, C. M., Waring, J. F., Lohler, J., Gilmore, G. L., et al. (1999). Altered development and cytokine responses of myeloid progenitors in the absence of transcription factor, interferon consensus sequence binding protein. *Blood*, *94*(11), 3764–3771.
Schiavoni, G., Mattei, F., Borghi, P., Sestili, P., Venditti, M., Morse, H. C., 3rd., et al. (2004). ICSBP is critically involved in the normal development and trafficking of Langerhans cells and dermal dendritic cells. *Blood*, *103*(6), 2221–2228.
Schulz, C., Gomez Perdiguero, E., Chorro, L., Szabo-Rogers, H., Cagnard, N., Kierdorf, K., et al. (2012). A lineage of myeloid cells independent of Myb and hematopoietic stem cells. *Science*, *336*(6077), 86–90.
Scott, E. W., Simon, M. C., Anastasi, J., & Singh, H. (1994). Requirement of transcription factor PU.1 in the development of multiple hematopoietic lineages. *Science*, *265*(5178), 1573–1577.
Sharf, R., Meraro, D., Azriel, A., Thornton, A. M., Ozato, K., Petricoin, E. F., et al. (1997). Phosphorylation events modulate the ability of interferon consensus sequence binding protein to interact with interferon regulatory factors and to bind DNA. *The Journal of Biological Chemistry*, *272*(15), 9785–9792.
Sica, A., & Mantovani, A. (2012). Macrophage plasticity and polarization: In vivo veritas. *The Journal of Clinical Investigation*, *122*(3), 787–795.

Sieweke, M. H., & Graf, T. (1998). A transcription factor party during blood cell differentiation. *Current Opinion in Genetics & Development*, *8*(5), 545–551.

Sieweke, M. H., Tekotte, H., Frampton, J., & Graf, T. (1996). MafB is an interaction partner and repressor of Ets-1 that inhibits erythroid differentiation. *Cell*, *85*(1), 49–60.

Slomiany, B. A., D'Arigo, K. L., Kelly, M. M., & Kurtz, D. T. (2000). C/EBPalpha inhibits cell growth via direct repression of E2F-DP-mediated transcription. *Molecular and Cellular Biology*, *20*(16), 5986–5997.

Spilianakis, C. G., Lalioti, M. D., Town, T., Lee, G. R., & Flavell, R. A. (2005). Interchromosomal associations between alternatively expressed loci. *Nature*, *435*(7042), 637–645.

Staber, P. B., Zhang, P., Ye, M., Welner, R. S., Nombela-Arrieta, C., Bach, C., et al. (2013). Sustained PU.1 levels balance cell-cycle regulators to prevent exhaustion of adult hematopoietic stem cells. *Molecular Cell*, *49*(5), 934–946.

Stopka, T., Amanatullah, D. F., Papetti, M., & Skoultchi, A. I. (2005). PU.1 inhibits the erythroid program by binding to GATA-1 on DNA and creating a repressive chromatin structure. *The EMBO Journal*, *24*(21), 3712–3723.

Sullivan, J., Feeley, B., Guerra, J., & Boxer, L. M. (1997). Identification of the major positive regulators of c-myb expression in hematopoietic cells of different lineages. *The Journal of Biological Chemistry*, *272*(3), 1943–1949.

Sumner, R., Crawford, A., Mucenski, M., & Frampton, J. (2000). Initiation of adult myelopoiesis can occur in the absence of c-Myb whereas subsequent development is strictly dependent on the transcription factor. *Oncogene*, *19*(30), 3335–3342.

Szanto, A., Balint, B. L., Nagy, Z. S., Barta, E., Dezso, B., Pap, A., et al. (2010). STAT6 transcription factor is a facilitator of the nuclear receptor PPARgamma-regulated gene expression in macrophages and dendritic cells. *Immunity*, *33*(5), 699–712.

Tagliani, E., Shi, C., Nancy, P., Tay, C. S., Pamer, E. G., & Erlebacher, A. (2011). Coordinate regulation of tissue macrophage and dendritic cell population dynamics by CSF-1. *The Journal of Experimental Medicine*, *208*(9), 1901–1916.

Tagoh, H., Himes, R., Clarke, D., Leenen, P. J., Riggs, A. D., Hume, D., et al. (2002). Transcription factor complex formation and chromatin fine structure alterations at the murine c-fms (CSF-1 receptor) locus during maturation of myeloid precursor cells. *Genes & Development*, *16*(13), 1721–1737.

Takeda, K., Tanaka, T., Shi, W., Matsumoto, M., Minami, M., Kashiwamura, S., et al. (1996). Essential role of Stat6 in IL-4 signalling. *Nature*, *380*(6575), 627–630.

Tamura, T., Nagamura-Inoue, T., Shmeltzer, Z., Kuwata, T., & Ozato, K. (2000). ICSBP directs bipotential myeloid progenitor cells to differentiate into mature macrophages. *Immunity*, *13*(2), 155–165.

Tamura, T., Thotakura, P., Tanaka, T. S., Ko, M. S., & Ozato, K. (2005). Identification of target genes and a unique cis element regulated by IRF-8 in developing macrophages. *Blood*, *106*(6), 1938–1947.

Tenen, D. G., Hromas, R., Licht, J. D., & Zhang, D. E. (1997). Transcription factors, normal myeloid development, and leukemia. *Blood*, *90*(2), 489–519.

Tillmanns, S., Otto, C., Jaffray, E., Du Roure, C., Bakri, Y., Vanhille, L., et al. (2007). SUMO modification regulates MafB-driven macrophage differentiation by enabling Myb-dependent transcriptional repression. *Molecular and Cellular Biology*, *27*(15), 5554–5564.

Valouev, A., Johnson, S. M., Boyd, S. D., Smith, C. L., Fire, A. Z., & Sidow, A. (2011). Determinants of nucleosome organization in primary human cells. *Nature*, *474*(7352), 516–520.

Walsh, J. C., DeKoter, R. P., Lee, H. J., Smith, E. D., Lancki, D. W., Gurish, M. F., et al. (2002). Cooperative and antagonistic interplay between PU.1 and GATA-2 in the specification of myeloid cell fates. *Immunity*, *17*(5), 665–676.

Wang, Q., Stacy, T., Binder, M., Marin-Padilla, M., Sharpe, A. H., & Speck, N. A. (1996). Disruption of the Cbfa2 gene causes necrosis and hemorrhaging in the central nervous system and blocks definitive hematopoiesis. *Proceedings of the National Academy of Sciences of the United States of America*, *93*(8), 3444–3449.

Xiao, C., & Rajewsky, K. (2009). MicroRNA control in the immune system: Basic principles. *Cell*, *136*(1), 26–36.

Xie, H., Ye, M., Feng, R., & Graf, T. (2004). Stepwise reprogramming of B cells into macrophages. *Cell*, *117*(5), 663–676.

Yamamoto, M., Kato, T., Hotta, C., Nishiyama, A., Kurotaki, D., Yoshinari, M., et al. (2011). Shared and distinct functions of the transcription factors IRF4 and IRF8 in myeloid cell development. *PLoS One*, *6*(10), e25812.

Yamanaka, S. (2007). Strategies and new developments in the generation of patient-specific pluripotent stem cells. *Cell Stem Cell*, *1*(1), 39–49.

Yanagisawa, H., Nagasawa, T., Kuramochi, S., Abe, T., Ikawa, Y., & Todokoro, K. (1991). Constitutive expression of exogenous c-myb gene causes maturation block in monocyte-macrophage differentiation. *Biochimica et Biophysica Acta*, *1088*(3), 380–384.

Yeamans, C., Wang, D., Paz-Priel, I., Torbett, B. E., Tenen, D. G., & Friedman, A. D. (2007). C/EBPalpha binds and activates the PU.1 distal enhancer to induce monocyte lineage commitment. *Blood*, *110*(9), 3136–3142.

Yona, S., Kim, K. W., Wolf, Y., Mildner, A., Varol, D., Breker, M., et al. (2013). Fate mapping reveals origins and dynamics of monocytes and tissue macrophages under homeostasis. *Immunity*, *38*(1), 79–91.

Zhang, D. E., Hetherington, C. J., Chen, H. M., & Tenen, D. G. (1994). The macrophage transcription factor PU.1 directs tissue-specific expression of the macrophage colony-stimulating factor receptor. *Molecular and Cellular Biology*, *14*(1), 373–381.

Zhang, D. E., Hetherington, C. J., Meyers, S., Rhoades, K. L., Larson, C. J., Chen, H. M., et al. (1996). CCAAT enhancer-binding protein (C/EBP) and AML1 (CBF alpha2) synergistically activate the macrophage colony-stimulating factor receptor promoter. *Molecular and Cellular Biology*, *16*(3), 1231–1240.

Zhang, P., Iwasaki-Arai, J., Iwasaki, H., Fenyus, M. L., Dayaram, T., Owens, B. M., et al. (2004). Enhancement of hematopoietic stem cell repopulating capacity and self-renewal in the absence of the transcription factor C/EBP alpha. *Immunity*, *21*(6), 853–863.

Zhang, P., Zhang, X., Iwama, A., Yu, C., Smith, K. A., Mueller, B. U., et al. (2000). PU.1 inhibits GATA-1 function and erythroid differentiation by blocking GATA-1 DNA binding. *Blood*, *96*(8), 2641–2648.

Zhao, B., Takami, M., Yamada, A., Wang, X., Koga, T., Hu, X., et al. (2009). Interferon regulatory factor-8 regulates bone metabolism by suppressing osteoclastogenesis. *Nature Medicine*, *15*(9), 1066–1071.

INDEX

Note: Page numbers followed by "*f*" indicate figures, and "*t*" indicate tables.

CONTENTS OF RECENT VOLUMES

Volume 88

Volume 89

Volume 90

Volume 91

Volume 92

Volume 93

Volume 94

Volume 95

Volume 96

Volume 97

Volume 98

Volume 99

Volume 100

Volume 101

Volume 102

Volume 103

Volume 104

Volume 105

Volume 106

Volume 107

Volume 108

Volume 109

Volume 110

Volume 111

Volume 112

Volume 113

Volume 114

Volume 115

Volume 116

Volume 117

Volume 118

Volume 119

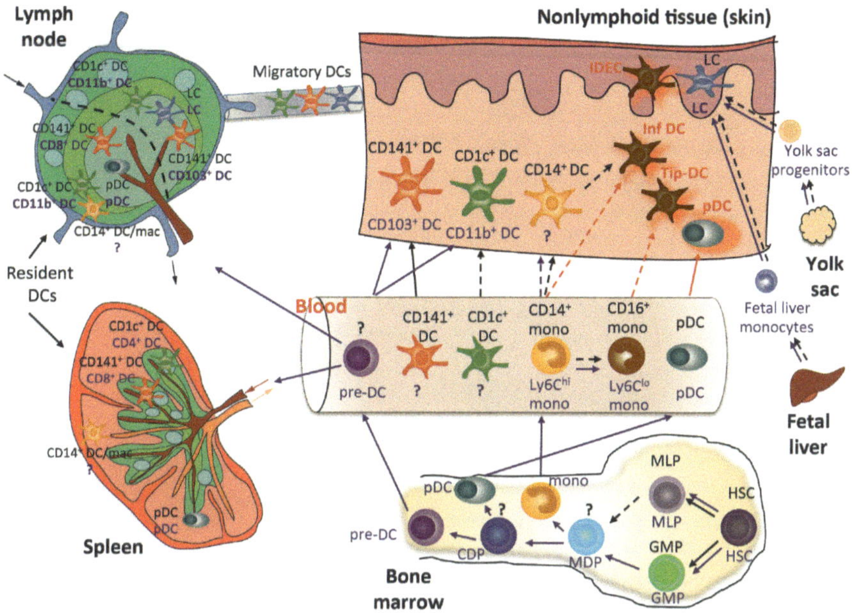

Chapter 1, Figure 1.1 (See page 10 of this volume.)

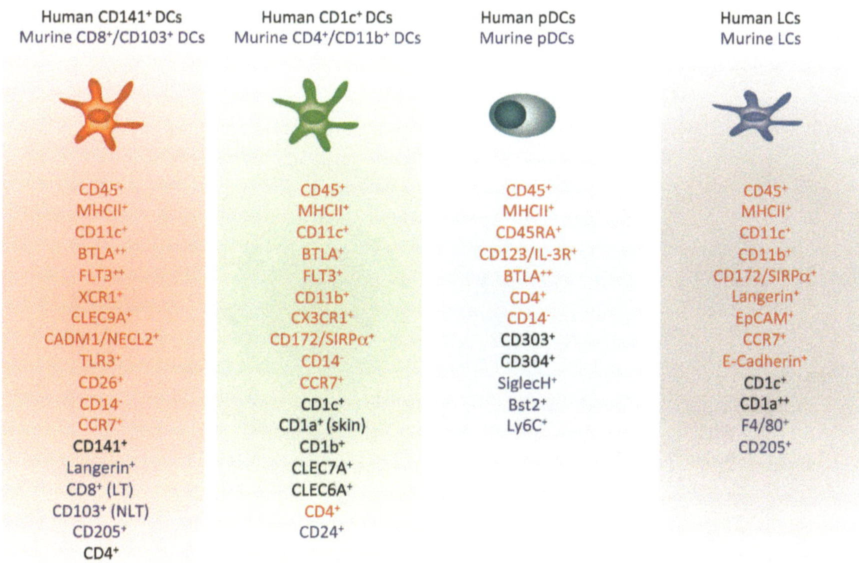

Chapter 1, Figure 1.2 (See page 31 of this volume.)

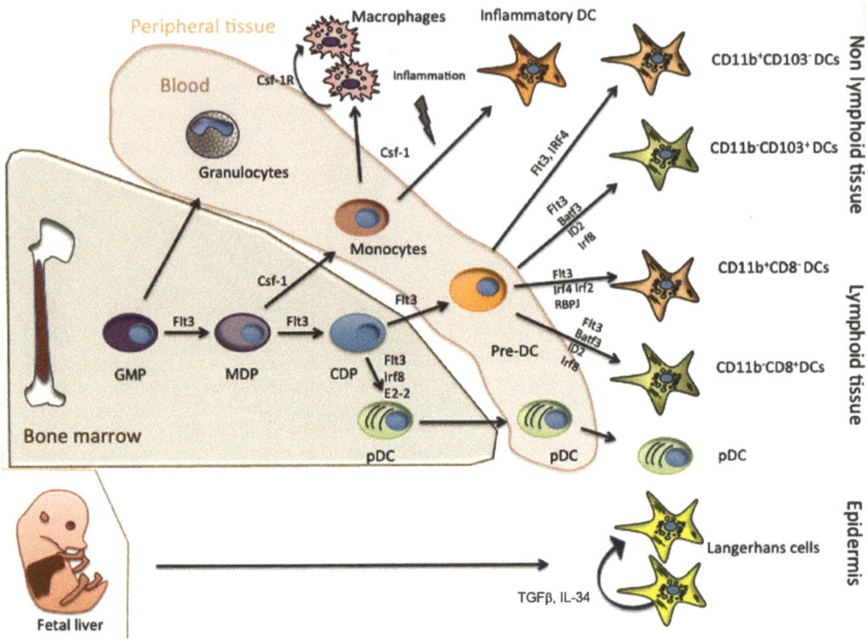

Chapter 5, Figure 5.1 (See page 131 of this volume.)

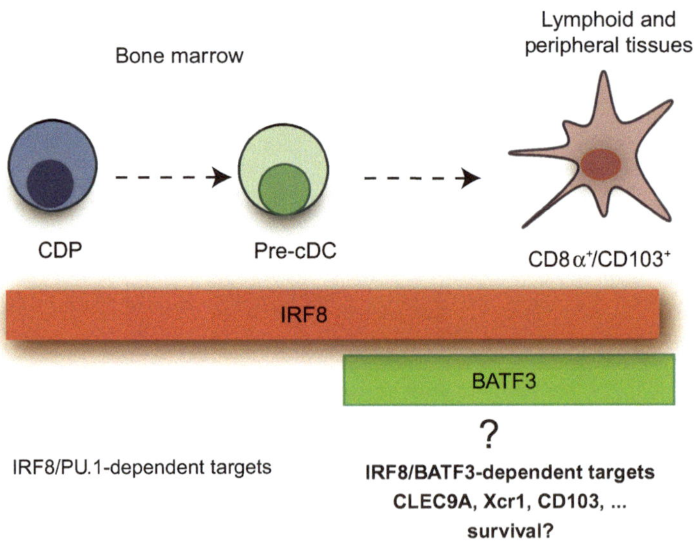

Chapter 9, Figure 9.1 (See page 243 of this volume.)

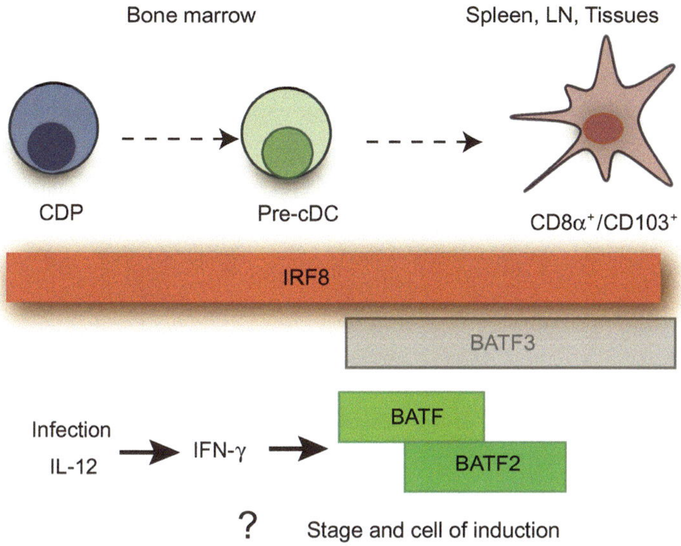

Chapter 9, Figure 9.2 (See page 251 of this volume.)

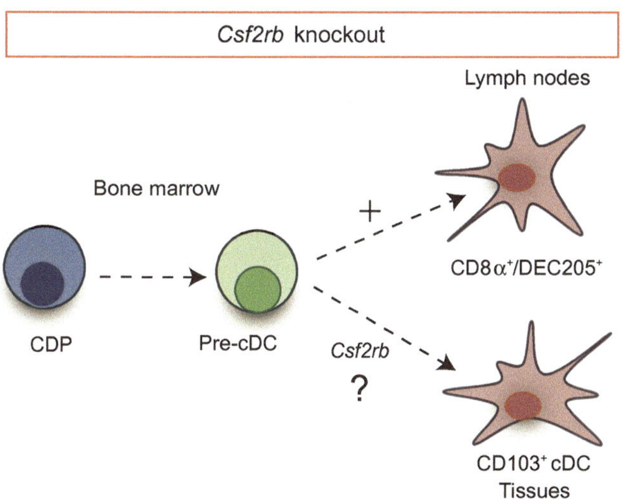

Chapter 9, Figure 9.3 (See page 253 of this volume.)

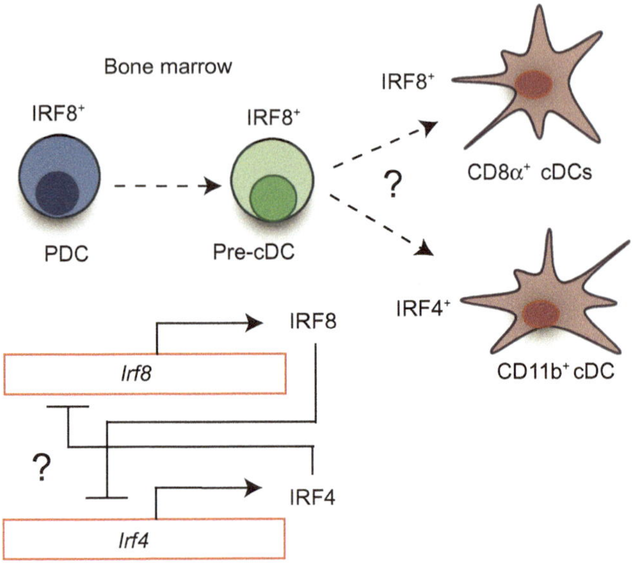

Chapter 9, Figure 9.4 (See page 254 of this volume.)

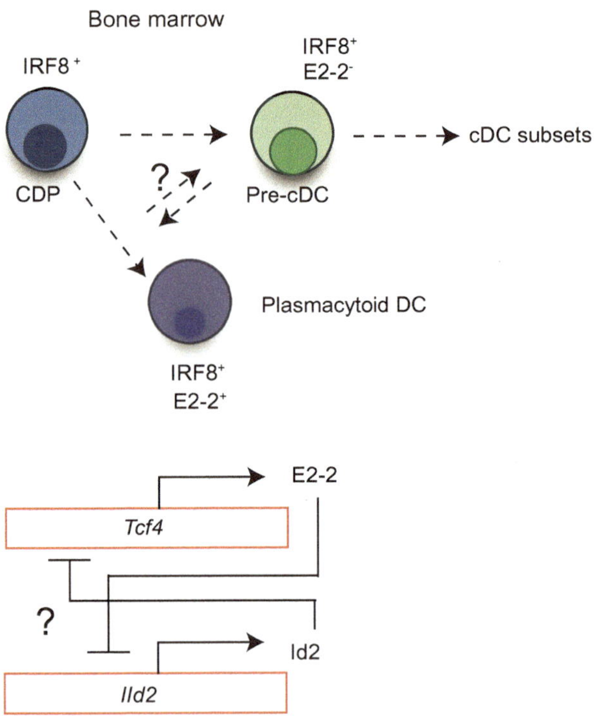

Chapter 9, Figure 9.5 (See page 256 of this volume.)

Kolibri 360 GmbH
Ferdinand-Jühlke-Straße 7
99095 Erfurt, Deutschland
produktsicherheit@kolibri360.de